Dina y Daniel Carro

Aug. 86

THE WORD
OF TRUTH

THE WORD OF TRUTH

A SUMMARY OF CHRISTIAN DOCTRINE BASED ON BIBLICAL REVELATION

DALE MOODY

GRAND RAPIDS
WILLIAM B. EERDMANS PUBLISHING COMPANY

Library of Congress Cataloging in Publication Data

Moody, Dale.
The word of truth.
Includes index.
1. Theology, Doctrinal. I. Title.
BT75.2.M59   230   80-19103
ISBN 0-8028-3533-3

To Southern Baptist Theological Seminary
My theological home since 1937
My teaching post since 1945

CONTENTS

PREFACE

The publication of *The Word of Truth* is meant to issue a clarion call to the reformation and revival of theology on the basis of the historical exegesis which is so prominent a feature of recent biblical scholarship.

This book thus represents a conscious effort to bring together the insights of several disciplines in a constructive harmony which is both biblical and systematic. Biblical theology, modern science, various types of biblical criticism (textual, source, form, redaction), historical theology, and the history of doctrine — all these have a significant part to play in the development of a systematic theology. As in my earlier books, I have emphasized the importance of worship in the formation of a biblical theology.* Numerous references to the best source materials offer the user guidance for further study.

My use of the resources of these disciplines and my high degree of appreciation for the insights of the non-Christian religions of the world as well as the ideas set forth by philosophers of religion are all in the context of a higher view of the inspiration and authority of Scripture. Those who fear that using the findings of modern science and the critical-historical method of Bible study is inevitably uncongenial to a strong view of biblical authority will, I hope, find the explorations of this book a pleasant surprise.

Because of this subservience to Scripture, I have not hesitated, on the basis of retranslations and newer interpretations of biblical passages, to explore errors and weaknesses in traditional Catholic and Protestant theologies — including my own Baptist tradition. In this connection, it is interesting to note that the biblical scholars from various traditions often find themselves agreeing across the traditional lines of demarcation.

Generally speaking, I have organized the book according to fairly traditional patterns, departing from them when it seemed to me that important

---

*A new study which uses worship as the frame of reference for articulating a systematic theology is Geoffrey Wainwright's *Doxology* (Oxford Univ. Press, New York, 1980); unfortunately, the present manuscript went to press before the publication of Wainwright's book.

theological presuppositions called for some variation. I trust that this will enhance the value of the book as a summary of Christian doctrine for all who wish to probe more deeply into the truth of Christian theology as it is unfolded in biblical revelation — just as its anchorage in Scripture will open it to Christians of all denominations and faith groups.

* * * * *

Several typists in Office Services at Southern Baptist Theological Seminary, under the direction of Alicia Gardner, have labored over my difficult handwriting. To all of them I offer my gratitude. Under the supervision of Danny Stiver, my Fellow in Christian Theology, Paula Jackson, Beth Stiver, Dwight A. Moody, and Ralph Dowell have made the final corrections on the proofs and compiled the indexes. Rachel Tedards went beyond the call of duty to keep the indexes on schedule. To these thoughtful and helpful friends I will ever be grateful.

Louisville, Kentucky   DALE MOODY

I. INTRODUCTION

A. SOURCES FOR A CHRISTIAN THEOLOGY

A Christian theology is an effort to think coherently about the basic beliefs that create a community of faith around the person of Jesus Christ. Other theologies have been formulated with other centers of reference. Judaism is focused on Moses and the Torah, and Islam around the Qur'an of Mohammed. Hinduism is a polymorphic devotional theism that springs from the social system of India, and Buddhism is based on the doctrines taught by Gautama the Buddha. The center of reference gives coherence to each system of thought.

In Christian theology as in any theology the starting point is of crucial importance. With Christ as the center one may adopt the method and principle of some philosophical system that offers avenues of approach for the understanding of the Christian faith at a special juncture in history. For centuries Platonism was the handmaiden of theological reflection, but the greatest system of Roman Catholic theology was that of St. Thomas Aquinas in the thirteenth century, and it was based on Aristotle's philosophy.

Protestant theologies made their appeal to the Scriptures, but the voices of Plato and Aristotle can still be heard in the classical systems of Protestantism. The nearest thing to a Protestant philosophy was the system of ethical idealism formulated by Immanuel Kant at the end of the eighteenth century, and this was developed in the new theologies that followed in the nineteenth century.

The philosophy of existentialism with its concern with questions about human existence has been the major philosophical system that has stimulated theological reflection in the twentieth century. Karl Barth, the major Protestant theologian, and Karl Rahner, the most creative Roman Catholic of the last generation, are incomprehensible without some knowledge of the existential movement. Perhaps the most consistent effort to construct a systematic theology with the use of existential ideas is that by John Macquarrie in his *Principles of Christian Theology* (1966). He is able to relate most of the orthodox theological beliefs to his profound under-

1

standing of the philosophy of Martin Heidegger, the most original of the existential philosophers.

A complete system of theology based on process theology has not yet appeared, but the many writings of Norman Pittenger have covered most Christian doctrines. The impact of this philosophy on the study of theology will be sketched in Part I.5 and Part II.16.

Accommodations to philosophical systems have always been resisted by confessional theological systems. With some denominational position as the point of appeal, philosophical and biblical ideas have been brought into the system to bolster those tenets that distinguish a given communion. The centuries of separate groups within Christianity have produced massive systems of Eastern Orthodoxy, Roman Catholicism, Lutheranism, Calvinism, Anglicanism, and the various Free Church modifications of such groups as Congregationalists, Baptists, Methodists, Quakers and Pentecostals.

The need for common ground has become a major concern, with the polemical and exclusive theologies turning toward the method of dialogue among the many traditions. It is hardly to be expected that some philosophical system will be honored as "the Christian philosophy," although helpful insights may be gained from many. It is not likely that any one confessional tradition will win the allegiance of all Christians. The whole Christian world will hardly rush to embrace any "historic position" even for the sake of Christian unity.

It is possible, in an atmosphere of respect and understanding, to learn from all confessional traditions. A good example of this is the admirable work by Wilhelm Niesel, *The Gospel and the Churches* (second German edition, 1960). May the irenic spirit of a Macquarrie or a Niesel be an example for all. Philosophical systems and confessional positions need to be heard.

Where then should a Christian theology begin in search for common ground? It is increasingly recognized that the only common ground possible is that of the canonical Scriptures already accepted by most Christians. This grows out of the most sustained revival of biblical study in the history of Christianity. There are those who fear that belief in the authority and inspiration of the Scriptures will be undermined if biblical theology is interpreted in the framework of modern science and biblical criticism. Brevard Childs is no doubt correct in his *Biblical Theology in Crisis* (1970) when he calls for us to take the canonical Scriptures of the Christian church more seriously. It is hoped that the pages that follow will illustrate how the historical-critical study of the Scriptures is the best way to relate the Scriptures to modern science and society.

1. The Source of Scripture

The ultimate source for a Christian theology has always been the Scriptures of the Old and New Testaments. Even the most philosophical theologies presuppose that philosophy must in some way and to some degree support biblical faith. It should also be said that those who appeal to Scripture often distort Scripture by the use of philosophical and confessional presuppositions. Nevertheless, in both cases the Scriptures are ostensibly supreme.

How then is it possible to hold a balance between extremes? A first step in the use of Scripture should be a search for the center. A so-called flat Bible approach is a distortion of historical revelation. No one really believes 1, 2 Chronicles stand on the level with 1, 2 Corinthians. Esther hardly holds the place of Ephesians in Christian faith. Not even the Old Testament as a whole can be put on the level with the New. To do so would lead to Judaism rather than Christianity. Here practice is usually sounder than theory.

It is reassuring to note how the simple and devout who read Scripture without critical training will discern the heart even of the Old Testament. Exodus, Deuteronomy, Isaiah, and Psalms often form the pillars of their faith. That is what a glance at New Testament usage will indicate also. All know that the death and resurrection of Jesus in the Passion Narratives are central even if they have never heard of *Formgeschichte!* Some of the best introductions have brought this into focus.[1]

Christian theology cannot afford to forget its supreme source, even as it dare not ignore the influence of tradition and the impact of philosophy. It may be compared to a vast river system. At some ultimate point is "the source," but many tributaries flow in, some to enrich and some to pollute. Some systems may deviate so far from the main stream as to become different faiths altogether, but usually the process of development flows on with the central core of a biblical faith. That is why it is so important to maintain a posture of *critical conservatism* and to listen attentively to what both critical and conservative scholars have to say. Perhaps a *dialogical* method in which biblical theology is interpreted and applied in the setting of modern science and society is a better way to describe the method needed.

Recent research into the biblical history of the Old Testament sustains the first impression of a simple reading of the New Testament. At the heart of the complicated traditions in the Hebrew Torah, the Pentateuch, are certain major themes, and the "Guidance out of Egypt" occupies first place.[2] The introduction to the Decalogue begins with a fixed formula of Israel's earliest faith: "I am the Lord your God, who brought you out of the land of Egypt, out of the house of bondage" (Ex. 20:2).

In the words of Martin Noth: "In the case of the 'guidance out of Egypt' we are dealing with a *primary confession* [*Urbekenntnis*] of Israel, one that

1. G. Ernest Wright and R. H. Fuller, *The Book of the Acts of God* (Garden City, N.Y.: Doubleday & Co., 1957); Arnold B. Rhodes, *The Mighty Acts of God* (Richmond, Va.: The CLC Press, 1964).
2. Martin Noth, *A History of Pentateuchal Traditions*, tr. Bernhard W. Anderson (Englewood Cliffs, N.J.: Prentice-Hall, Inc., 1972), pp. 46-50.

is expressed rather strictly in hymnic form, and at the same time with the *kernel of the whole subsequent Pentateuchal tradition*. Although we know very little about the inner life of ancient Israel, we have here — unless we are completely mistaken — a *common* confession of *all* Israel."[3] Yet Noth and his school of thought often speak as if this was not historically true. It is the contradiction between radical criticism and valid insight that has led to the German pun on "Die Nothschule," meaning the distressed school, over against the school of Albrecht Alt, *Die Altschule*, meaning the old school!

After the Decalogue in Deuteronomy is a list of things the Hebrews are to teach their children. In answer to questions about the meaning of testimonies, statutes and ordinances the Hebrew father says to his son: "We were Pharaoh's slaves in Egypt; and the Lord brought us out of Egypt with a mighty hand; and the Lord showed signs and wonders, great and grievous, against Egypt and against Pharaoh and all his household before our eyes; and brought us out from there, that he might bring us in and give us the land he swore to give to our fathers" (6:21–23).

An expanded confession in Deut. 26:5–10 begins with Jacob's semi-nomadic life, but the Exodus from Egypt remains the event on which the faith of Israel is focused. Gerhard von Rad regarded this as the oldest *credo* of all (*Old Testament Theology*, I, 166).

The narratives in the Former Prophets, the so-called Deuteronomic historians from Joshua through 2 Kings, presuppose this bedrock of "*historical occurrence*" (Noth). Joshua reminds the people of these mighty acts of God (Josh. 24:6f.). At his call Gideon remembers that the Lord brought his people out of Egypt (Judg. 6:13), and David in his response to Nathan's prophecy marvels at these deeds of redemption (2 Sam. 7:23).

Classical prophecy in the the Latter Prophets is introduced and penetrated by this perspective. By the "election love" of the Lord, Israel became his child (Hos. 11:1):

> *When Israel was a child, I loved him,*
> *and out of Egypt I called my son.*

These words introduce a theme that thunders on to fall in torrents of theological refreshing in Isaiah 40–55.

In the five scrolls of the Pentateuch, the four of the Former Prophets, and the four of the Later Prophets, the throbbing heart of Israel's faith is frequently felt. The praise in the Writings, the last collection of the Hebrew Scriptures, has summed up what Old Testament study has discovered anew (Ps. 103:7):

3. *Ibid.*, p. 49. Cf. Gerhard von Rad, *Old Testament Theology*, tr. D. M. G. Stalker (Philadelphia: The Westminster Press, 1962), I, 175-187.

He made known his ways to Moses,
  his acts to the people of Israel.

Christian theology gladly embraces this Hebrew heritage, and on its foundation the cathedral of a true theology for our time may be constructed.

As the mighty acts of God associated with the Exodus from Egypt became the central core of the Old Testament, so the Easter event, the death and resurrection of Jesus Christ, became the heart of the New Testament. This became the Christian Passover, rooted in the Jewish Passover. The Apostle Paul could say: "For Christ, our paschal lamb, has been sacrificed for us" (1 Cor. 5:7).

The primary letters of Paul presuppose this apostolic preaching. On this presupposition Christian theology stands or falls: "For since we believe that Jesus died and rose again . . ." (1 Thess. 4:14; cf. 1:10). For Paul this was a premise, not a problem. It was his fulcrum for faith.

This faith does not fade into the background in later writings. The so-called pillar letters (1, 2 Corinthians, Galatians, Romans) leave no doubt as to the meaning of the gospel. Jesus preached the good news about the approaching kingdom of God, already dawning in his person and works, but the apostles proclaimed good news about Jesus, about his death and resurrection.

The earliest Easter faith was clear. Paul declared the gospel to be (1 Cor. 15:3f.):

> *Christ died for our sins*
>   *in accordance with the scriptures,*
> *he was buried,*
> *he was raised on the third day*
>   *in accordance with the scriptures.*

It is true that this is often more of a problem than a proclamation in our time, but modern skepticism should not blur the very basis for apostolic faith. A new appraisal of the nature and significance of the Easter events is indeed a pressing problem, but a beginning has been made.[4] It is not a question that can be put aside, not if theology is to remain Christian in any New Testament sense.

Paul's letter to the Roman Christians is no doubt the most influential New Testament document in the whole history of Christian theology.[5] The importance of the Easter event penetrates this document. At the end of Paul's classic discussion of justification he summarizes (4:25): "It will be reckoned to us who believe in him that raised . . . Jesus our Lord,

---

4. Reginald H. Fuller, *The Formation of the Resurrection Narratives* (New York: The Macmillan Company, 1971).
5. For my detailed views see *Broadman Bible Commentary*, Vol. 10 (Nashville: Broadman Press, 1970).

who was delivered up for our trespasses
and raised for our justification.

There are no less than seven more appeals to this pillar principle in 1:2–5; 5:10; 6:4f.; 7:4; 8:31–34; 10:8f.; 14:9.

In the Acts of the Apostles at least seven sermons expand this apostolic preaching (2:14–39; 3:13–26; 4:8–12; 5:10–32; 7:1–53; 10:36–43; 13:17–41). Five of these are attributed to Peter, one to Stephen, and one to Paul, but there is basic agreement with the confessions in the letters of Paul. A battle rages about the historical nature of these sermons, but there is little question about their theological value. This seems almost obvious now, but a generation back it was a sensational New Testament discovery.[6]

The documents called the Gospels are really expansions of this apostolic preaching. It is the Easter event that brings unity into the variety that characterizes the Four Gospels. Here again is the story of thrilling discovery. A flood of new light has been shed on the theology and structure of the Gospels since the publication of the monumental work by B. H. Streeter.[7] There have been so many other great contributions that have advanced our understanding of the theological nature of the Gospels that the beginner is almost bewildered without a guide.[8]

Behind all the details the essential elements of the New Testament *kerygma* can be discovered. It has been said that apostolic preaching fed the flock with a three-pronged fork! Each sermon had three points: (1) the Old Testament promise was fulfilled; (2) the story of the life, death, resurrection, and exaltation of Jesus was the *fulfillment*; and (3) the call was repent and believe this good news, the gospel about Jesus Christ.

2. The Tributaries of Tradition

In some theological traditions the very idea of tradition is repugnant. It may even be claimed that they follow Scripture only (*sola scriptura*), but those who protest the loudest are often most laden with traditions, oral or written, difficult to support from Scripture. Traditions are the oral and written interpretations that have developed out of the original source in Scripture, and out of various historical interpretations of Scripture. It is impossible to escape from this situation, so it is best to understand the meaning and value of tradition.

Tradition is used in both a good and a bad sense in the New Testament. It is true that Jesus denounced "the traditions of the elders" that made void

---

6. C. H. Dodd, *The Apostolic Preaching and Its Developments* (London: Hodder and Stoughton, 1936); A. M. Hunter, *The Message of the New Testament* (Philadelphia: The Westminster Press, 1944).
7. *The Four Gospels* (New York: Macmillan and Company, 1924).
8. A good guide is R. C. Briggs, *Interpreting the Gospels* (Nashville: Abingdon Press, 1969).

the word of God (Mark 7:3–13; Matt. 15:2–6), but Paul instructed the Thessalonians to avoid those who departed from the apostolic traditions (2 Thess. 2:15; 3:6). Tradition may be the original deposit of faith or a foreign element that destroys that which was the true source.[9]

It is necessary to distinguish between the apostolic tradition of the New Testament and ecclesiastical traditions that may either develop or distort the original deposit. The apostolic tradition was even prior to the New Testament Scriptures. The two major forms of ecclesiastical tradition are the creeds that developed in the days of undivided Christianity and the confessions that attempt to justify the separate denominations. Confessions tend to focus on the issues that caused divisions.

Creeds

The most universal creed is the Nicene Creed. A shorter form of this creed was issued at the Council of Nicaea in 325 (hence the name), but the longer form of the creed developed later.[10] Since the Council of Chalcedon (451) the long form has been regarded as the Creed of the Council of Constantinople (381), so it is also known as the Niceno-Constantinopolitan Creed.

A careful reading of the final form reveals how much even the most non-creedal Christians owe to this historic formulation of Christian faith.

> We believe in one God the Father all sovereign, maker of heaven and earth, and of all things visible and invisible:
>
> And in one Lord Jesus Christ, the only-begotten Son of God, begotten of the Father before the ages, Light of Light, true God of true God, begotten not made, of one substance with the Father, through whom all things were made; who for us men and our salvation came down from the heavens, and was made flesh of the Holy Spirit and the Virgin Mary, and became man, and was crucified for us under Pontius Pilate, and suffered and was buried, and rose again on the third day according to the Scriptures, and ascended into the heavens, and sitteth on the right hand of the Father, and cometh again with glory to judge living and dead, of whose kingdom there shall be no end:
>
> And in the Holy Spirit, the Lord and Life-giver, that proceedeth from the Father, who with the Father and Son is worshipped together and glorified together, who spake through the prophets:
>
> In one holy Catholic and Apostolic Church:

9. A useful survey of tradition is F. F. Bruce, *Tradition: Old and New* (Grand Rapids: Zondervan Publishing House, 1970).
10. J. N. D. Kelly, *Early Christian Creeds* (New York: Longmans, Green and Co., 1950), pp. 231-262.

We acknowledge one baptism unto remission of sins. We look
for a resurrection of the dead, and the life of the age to come.[11]

In the West a similar creed came to be known as the Apostles' Creed.
It is possible that the earliest form developed in Rome much as the early
roots of the Nicene Creed reached back to Jerusalem.[12] Both follow the
pattern of the long form of the Great Commission in Matthew 28:19-20
which speaks of baptism "in the name of the Father and of the Son and of
the Holy Spirit." The short form speaks of making disciples "in my name,"
but the emphasis on the Trinity led to the longer form and three immersions
rather than the original one immersion in the name of Jesus Christ or the
Lord Jesus, as in the Acts of the Apostles.

Abundant evidence indicates that the three parts of both creeds were
intended as a baptismal confession as the early church struggled against
the threats of heresy. Both of these have been widely used in the worship
of the West, and their influence on the development of Christian theology
has been enormous. The sixth-century Gallican form of the Apostles' Creed
found in a sermon by Caesarius, Bishop of Arles (503-543), says:

> I believe in God the Father almighty.
> I also believe in Jesus Christ his only Son, our Lord,
> conceived of the Holy Spirit, born of the Virgin Mary,
> suffered under Pontius Pilate, crucified, dead and buried; he
>   descended into hell,
> rose again the third day,
> ascended into heaven,
> sat down at the right hand of the Father,
> thence he is to come to judge the living and the dead.
> I believe in the Holy Ghost,
> the Holy Catholic Church, the communion of saints,
> the remission of sins,
> the resurrection of the flesh and life eternal.[13]

The so-called Athanasian Creed has also been widely used in the West.
The Creed was not composed by Athanasius, the great defender of orthodoxy in the fourth century, but it does give strong support to the doctrines
of the Trinity and the Incarnation that Athanasius frequently advocated. It
is possible that Caesarius of Arles was also responsible for it, if not the
actual composer.[14] Lutherans, Calvinists, Anglicans, Baptists and most
other Protestant denominations embraced all of these three Creeds. The

11. Henry Bettenson, *Documents of the Christian Church*, Second Edition (London: Oxford
University Press, 1963), pp. 36f.
12. J. N. D. Kelly, *op. cit.*, pp. 100-166.
13. Henry Bettenson, *op. cit.*, p. 34.
14. J. N. D. Kelly, *The Athanasian Creed* (New York: Harper & Row, 1964), is a standard
study of this third and least known of the three ecumenical creeds.

most thorough and in many ways the most original and satisfactory statement of faith from Baptists, was the Orthodox Creed of 1679. Article
XXXVIII accepts and quotes the three creeds.[15]

Confessions

The Protestant Reformation of the sixteenth century resulted in schism. In
response to the Protestant challenge, the Roman Catholics agreed to the
Council of Trent (1543-63) and the pronouncements of that council on such
subjects as Scripture and tradition, original sin, justification and the sacraments formed a wall of separation that did not begin to crumble until
Vatican Council II, 1963-65, reviewed the ecumenical situation. It remains
to be seen what new directions will develop from the *Documents of Vatican II*, but they are of first importance for understanding the form of Christian theology now in process in the Roman Catholic Church.[16]

The Anglican tradition remained nearest to Rome, but a separate communion developed out of this conflict. The most important confessional
statement in Anglicanism is the Thirty-Nine Articles of 1563, but these
articles must be read in the context of *The Book of Common Prayer* of
1662. The articles are not a full statement of doctrine, but they do define
the Anglican response to the controversies of the sixteenth century.

Lutheranism responded with a more authoritative document in The
Confession of Augsburg in 1530, but this is better understood in the
context of the *Book of Concord* of 1580.[17] The first half of the Augsburg
Confession states in 21 articles the Lutheran view on doctrine, the most
elaborate of which is the 20th, on faith and good works, and this became
the basis for a review of abuses in the practice of the Roman Catholic
Church.

The Calvinism of the Reformed Churches is a living tradition also, but
the Westminster Confession of 1643-47 is no doubt the basic bridge between continental and English-speaking Calvinism. In beautiful prose, the
Christian faith is expounded from creation to the final judgment in 33
articles. The doctrine of election was modified to make room for free will
and secondary causes, and the statements on the two covenants, the relationship between the visible and the invisible church, and the identification
of the Jewish Sabbath with the Christian Sunday became definitive.

The Book of Confessions adopted by the United Presbyterian Church
in 1967 includes the Westminster Confession and adds only a supplement

15. W. L. Lumpkin, *Baptist Confessions of Faith*, Revised Edition (Valley Forge: The Judson Press, 1969), pp. 326f.
16. A convenient edition is Walter Abbott, ed., and Joseph Gallagher, tr. (New York: The
American Press, 1966).
17. Theodore G. Tappert, tr. and ed., *The Book of Concord* (Philadelphia: Fortress
Press, 1959).

on the relevance of reconciliation to the ecumenical and social situation today.[18]

The Second London Confession of Faith published by Baptists in 1677 was no more than an adaptation of the Westminster Confession on such topics as baptism and congregational polity. In 1833 the New Hampshire Confession of Faith modified Baptist theology in the direction of Congregationalism, and *The Baptist Faith and Message* adopted in Memphis in 1925 and restated in Kansas City in 1963 combined the two traditions in the light of controversies precipitated by modern science (1925) and biblical criticism (1963). Many would elevate *The Baptist Faith and Message* to the status of a creed, without using the word, but the basic loyalty of Baptists is still to the supreme authority of the New Testament, in which light all creeds and confessions are to be judged.[19]

The principle of the sole authority of Scripture led to the restoration movement, a call for reformation in the present and a union of all Christians on this basis, but this movement produced other denominations.[20] Much can be learned from Methodism apart from Anglicanism with which it has been so vitally related. A reading of the works of John Wesley is not without profit for those of other denominations, especially when this is combined with the current editions of the *Methodist Book of Discipline*.[21]

Small as the Society of Friends (Quakers) have been in number, Robert Barclay's *Apology for the Quakers* of 1676, which exalts the inner light above all external authority, should be read as a corrective for those who would confine the light of God to canon, creed and clergy combined with excessive institutionalism and sacramentalism.[22]

The smaller sects of recent origin often recover insights long neglected that need to be brought back to the center of attention. The source of Christian faith is one, but springs burst forth in many places and through many persons.[23]

Theological confessions have left groups of code words in which certain terms are associated with certain denominations: sacrament — Roman Catholic, episcopacy — Episcopalian, justification — Lutheran, predestination — Calvinist, baptism — Baptist, holiness (sanctification) — Methodist, Holy

---

18. *The Book of Confessions* (Philadelphia: The General Assembly of the United Presbyterian Church in the U.S.A., 1966, 67).
19. W. L. Lumpkin, *op. cit.*; Herschel H. Hobbs, *The Baptist Faith and Message* (Nashville: Broadman Press, 1971).
20. The basic system of theology was by Alexander Campbell, *The Christian System*, 1835 (Nashville: Gospel Advocate Company, 1970).
21. *John Wesley*, edited by Albert C. Outler (New York: Oxford University Press, 1964).
22. Edited by Dean Freiday in modern English (Philadelphia: Friends Book Store, 1967).
23. Elmer T. Clark, *The Small Sects of America*, Revised Edition (New York: Abingdon–Cokesbury Press, 1949).

Spirit — Pentecostal. The time has come to reflect on the theological signif-icance of such terms rather than to react in an irrational manner.

Impatience with the past often makes us prisoners of the present. Awareness of our historical developments and unhappy divisions may be painful, but a restatement of faith for the present requires recognition of our roots in the past that condition our perceptions of truth. Indifference to this process often leads to a generation of rootless wonders.

B. THE HISTORICAL FUNCTIONS OF CHRISTIAN THEOLOGY

3. The Roots of Christian Theology

Popular prejudice against a systematic theology often finds expression in such statements as: "Why don't we just go back to the Bible?" or "We must defend our historic position." Historical study soon exposes how impossible it was to maintain such simple solutions. The needs of the church soon made further statement necessary. Out of this need the roots and branches of Christian theology developed.

Emil Brunner has made the brilliant statement that Christian theology developed out of three roots: the polemical, the exegetical, and the cate-chetical.[24] The first was to refute false teachings, the second to systematize Bible doctrine, and the third to instruct young Christians before and after baptism.

The polemical root is well illustrated by the teachings of Irenaeus (130?-202?). He was probably reared in ancient Smyrna, studied in Rome and became bishop in Lyon in Gaul c. 178. As the first great theologian of the church he at first requested toleration for the Montanism of Asia Minor with its emphasis on the Holy Spirit and the millennium, but as bishop he became a strong opponent of the Gnostic dualism between spirit and matter. His treatise *Against Heresies* had the full title *Five Books of Unmasking and Overthrow of the Falsely Named Gnosis*, and this indicates the need for such a writing. In his polemics against Gnosticism at least three fun-damental doctrines were developed.[25] After Irenaeus named certain Gnos-tics in two books, these basic Orthodox beliefs appear in a series of excursuses.

A second work, *Proof of the Apostolic Preaching,* expounds these

---

24. *Truth as Encounter*, tr. Amandus W. Loos and David Cairns (Philadelphia: The West-minster Press, 1964), pp. 66-68; *Dogmatics*, tr. Olive Wyon (Philadelphia: The Westminster Press, 1950), Vol. I, pp. 9-13.
25. Anders Nygren, *Agape and Eros*, tr. Philip S. Watson (Philadelphia: Westminster Press, 1953), pp. 393-412. For guidance on "Gnosticism" see E. H. Pagels in the Supplementary Volume of *The Interpreter's Dictionary of the Bible*.

doctrines in a more systematic way (3-42) and finds proof of them in the Old Testament (43-97). These doctrines were creation, incarnation and the resurrection of the dead, and the unity of these three works was demonstrated with a defense of the Trinity (98-100). This follows the pattern of the Apostles' Creed, which has influenced systematic theology to this day.[26]

The logic of Irenaeus was very clear. If a good God did not create all things good before the corruption of the Fall, then the Son of God, the Logos, could not become flesh without becoming a sinful man. Further, if the body of Jesus was not human, then the human body would not be redeemed by the resurrection of the dead. The Gnostics consistently denied all three fundamentals, but Irenaeus in his biblical theology defended all three.

The exegetical root for a systematic theology grew out of an encounter with philosophy. As the polemical approach came from the school of Asia Minor, so the exegetical came from Alexandria. The greatest of the Alexandrian theologians was Origen (c. 185-c. 254). After a controversy with Demetrius, his bishop, he moved to Caesarea in 231.

His most important theological work was *On First Principles* (*De principiis*) in four books. Book I gathers the biblical teachings on God and the heavenly beings, both divine and demonic. God is described as complete transcendence, but he becomes immanent in his Son, the subordinate Image of the Invisible God. God has dominion over all creation, the Son over all rational creatures, and the Spirit is confined to the church both in this world and the next. In the beginning all was a unity, and in the end all will be restored to this primitive state, even Satan himself.

Book II, on man and the world, speaks of a plurality of worlds that eternally succeed one another, of the incarnation and the consummation of all things as they were at the beginning. Man's soul is interpreted as pure spirit and by nature immortal. The soul of Jesus differed from that of other men because of the plenitude or fulness of the indwelling *Logos* (Word).

Book III, on the freedom of the will and its consequences, describes the struggle of human action under Divine Providence until there is a final and complete conformity with God in a state in which God will become "all in all" (1 Cor. 15:28). Each of the first three books ends with universalism, a doctrine still accepted in Eastern Orthodoxy but condemned as heresy by most Roman Catholics and Protestants.

Book IV, concerned with the exegesis of Scripture, seeks to support his theology of universalism by a threefold sense of Scripture. Most of the Old Testament, especially Gen. 1–3, is interpreted in a figurative sense. His

---

26. Cf. Gustaf Wingren, *Man and the Incarnation*, tr. Ross MacKenzie (Edinburgh: Oliver and Boyd, 1959).

exegesis of the Temptation of Jesus indicates how he departed from literalism even in the New Testament. A summary of his whole system may be found at the end.[27]

The catechetical root for a systematic Christian theology came from the pastoral need of instruction for the immature. A good example of this may be found in the writings of Augustine of Hippo (354-430), the most important of the early Latin theologians. In many ways he illustrates all three roots, and his influence on both Catholic and Protestant theology has been enormous.

The oldest Christian catechism for beginners that has survived is his book *On Instructing the Unlearned* (*De catechizandus rudibus*), written about 400 and dedicated to the good deacon Deogratias of Carthage. As he explains how instruction is to be given in two hours or a half hour, the pattern is one of salvation history, from the creation in Genesis to the consummation in Revelation. Seven ages are discerned (ch. 22), much as in the covenant theology of Johannes Cocceius (1603-69) and in modern dispensationalism!

A survey of Bible history is required for an understanding of the revelation of the love of God, disclosed in prophecy and fulfillment, typology and theology, with the love of God in Christ at the center (John 3:16). Narration and exhortation are mingled especially as the final judgment comes into focus. It is interesting indeed to note how one who knew most of the systems of ancient philosophy turns to the Bible for the beginning of Christian instruction.[28] What a lesson for modern philosophical theologies void of biblical content!

A second system of Christian doctrine, designed for laymen and dedicated to Laurentius, indicates the type of instruction needed to mature faith after baptism. Written about 420, this so-called *Handbook* (*Enchiridion*) is a treatise on faith, hope, and love.[29] Most of the book is an exposition of the Apostles' Creed, the content of faith, but he finally gets around to the Lord's Prayer as a summary of hope (30) and a collection of texts on love for God and man. He still sees clearly that "God is love" (1 John 4:16), but faith has now become more important for him than hope and love. It was not until the twentieth century that theologies of hope and love would be popular![30]

27. G. W. Butterworth, *Origen on First Principles* (London: S.P.C.K., 1936), pp. 313-328.
28. J. P. Christopher, *St. Augustine: The First Catechetical Instruction* (Westminster, Md.: The Newman Press, 1962).
29. Ernest Evans, *St. Augustine's Enchiridion* (London: S.P.C.K., 1953).
30. Jürgen Moltmann, *Theology of Hope*, tr. James W. Leitch (New York: Harper and Row, 1967); Daniel Day Williams, *The Spirit and the Forms of Love* (New York: Harper and Row, 1968). Anders Nygren has called the romantic love of Peter Abelard and other forms of medieval thought a *charitas* synthesis.

4. The Branches of Christian Theology

Eastern Orthodoxy

The first major branch of Christian theology is that found in Eastern Orthodoxy.

A few years ago it would have been logical to go on from Augustine to the Roman Catholic branch of Christian theology, but this is too narrow for today. These words are being written near Bethlehem, a few hours after an unforgettable visit to the Greek Orthodox monastery at Mar Saba in the wilderness of Judea. St. Sabas (439-532) was from Cappadocia in Asia Minor, the second major center of Orthodox theology after Alexandria. Ecumenical encounter across the ages reminds rational Westerners that *The Mystical Theology of the Eastern Church* (1944), to use the title of Vladimir Lossky's useful book, has a contribution to make.[31]

Out of the system of catechetical instruction in early Christianity, Gregory of Nyssa (c. 330-c. 395), one of the Cappadocian Fathers, composed his famous "Catechetical Orations" or "The Great Cathechism" in which he expounded the fundamental doctrines included in the Nicene Creed. The influence of Origen is evident in his allegorical interpretation of Scripture and the eschatology of universalism. In his interpretation of the atonement as a ransom paid to the Devil, he introduced the illustration of Jesus as the bait on a fishhook that deceived Satan the deceiver.

Much of the Cappadocian theology influenced both Catholic and Protestant theology through John of Damascus (c. 675-c. 749), a "Doctor of the Church," also from Mar Saba, who summarized theology for Eastern Orthodoxy much as Thomas Aquinas did for Catholicism and John Calvin did for Protestantism. His most important work, the *Fountain of Wisdom*, was in three parts: philosophies, heresies, and the Orthodox faith. It was the third part that was destined to be the beginning of the theological cathedral of the Eastern Church.

To the basic doctrines of the Nicene Creed and the Cappadocian Fathers he added discussions on Mariology and Images. His most important ideas pertained to the Holy Trinity and the Incarnation. The conception of *perichōrēsis* (circumincession) expressed the inner relations of the Trinity as the interpenetration of three infinite persons, a concept that avoids the popular notion of three finite persons limiting one another. His defense of the two natures of Christ drove him to adopt the Enhypostasia theory of Leontius of Byzantium (6th century), who saw the deity and humanity of Jesus as interpenetrating. This retained the full humanity of Jesus, the Anhypostasia, taught by the followers of Cyril of Alexandria (d. 444).

If John of Damascus sounds irrelevant, it is because one does not listen attentively to much popular thought that gives the distinct impression that

31. Tr. Fellowship of St. Alban and St. Sergius (London: James Clarke, 1957).

belief in the Holy Trinity is belief in "three gods in a pod," i.e., tritheism, and that belief in the deity of Christ is belief in Jesus as "God in a human body," "God in a bod" in superficial jargon. The Holy Trinity can be interpreted as three persons only when it is clear that the three persons are infinite, not finite, and belief in the Incarnation is the New Testament faith only when Jesus is seen as a complete man in whom God fully dwelt, not God walking around in a human body without a human mind.

The theological cathedral begun by John of Damascus was expanded and beautified in later centuries. John's favorite among the Cappadocian Fathers was Gregory Nazianzus (329-389), who wrote a treatise "On the Holy Spirit" as his "Fifth Theological Oration." Basil the Great (c. 330-379), the brother of Gregory of Nyssa and the third of the Great Cappadocians, also wrote a treatise "On the Holy Spirit," which today is often recommended by Orthodox theologians as the best introduction to Eastern Spirituality.

The real blossoming of Orthodox spirituality came in Hesychasm, a mysticism propagated by the monks of Mt. Athos, Greece, in the fourteenth century. A few years ago this Eastern quietism was hardly known in the West and few knew much about Gregory Palamas (c. 1296-1359), the greatest theologian in this movement of mystical contemplation. Hesychasm means beginning in silent meditation and proceeding with praise in increasing awareness of God until one sees a vision of the Uncreated Light of the Godhead, "seeing the light of Tabor" as it is called. Acquaintance with a modern Orthodox theologian of the calibre of Jean Meyendorf reminds one how much the rational West can learn from the mystical East. It also helps in understanding what Jewish mysticism means by the Shekinah glory.

Roman Catholicism

The second major branch of Christian theology is Roman Catholicism. As one moves from Eastern Orthodoxy to Roman Catholicism there is a distinct shift from the spiritual to the sacramental. These are not exclusive, but there is a change in emphasis. The so-called seven sacraments of Roman Catholicism were first formulated in the *Four Books of Sentences* by Peter Lombard (c. 1100-1160), the most widely used text in the medieval schools.

The greatest theological cathedral was constructed later in the monumental *Summa Theologica* by Thomas Aquinas (c. 1221-1274). Even today one reads a work of this type with awe and admiration at the learning and clarity with which the great Dominican monk expressed his theological conclusions. With the philosophy of Aristotle recently recovered he used it as the basis for his theology.

Aquinas did not claim that all theological knowledge came through sense-perception interpreted by reason, for there is a revealed theology from above, but he did not begin with mystical meditation and the direct communion of human spirit with Holy Spirit as in Eastern Hesychasm.

He thought the ontological argument of Anselm, which began with necessary being, was for the angels. Corporeal human beings had to start with sense-perception. Therefore, his arguments for the existence of God are all cosmological, moving from the created cosmos to God. Yet, he argued that God as Holy Trinity and the creation of the world in time could be known only by revelation.

Part II of the *Summa* speaks of God as the end of man and of man's return to God in much the same way that Part I treats God and creation, but Part III, on the sacraments and eschatology, distinguishes Roman Catholic theology from later Protestantism. It is hardly correct for Anton C. Pegis to edit *The Basic Writings of St. Thomas Aquinas* with none of Part III of the *Summa Theologica* included.[32]

Of course Pegis was more concerned with Aquinas' philosophical method than sacramental theology, but sacramental worship is distinctive in Roman Catholic theology. For Aquinas the Eucharist was the sacrament of all sacraments and the priesthood was the highest of all orders. Transubstantiation, defined by the Fourth Lateran Council in 1215, he interpreted in terms of the Aristotelian distinction between substances and accidents. The substance of the bread and wine changes, he taught, but the accidents remain.

Protestantism

The third major branch of Christian theology came to be known as Protestantism, an unfortunate name for a movement seeking to restore the supremacy of Scripture in Christian theology. It is too often forgotten that Martin Luther (1483-1546), the leader of the German Reformation, was professor of Scripture in Wittenberg from 1511 to the day of his death.

The first systematic statement of Reformation theology, *The Loci Communes* (1521) by Philip Melanchthon (1497-1560), was nothing less than a topical study of Bible doctrines arranged in the order of Lutheran logic and expounded in the light of pressing needs. Lutheran logic then and now begins with man and his sin in need of justification by faith alone, an insight that came to Luther in the form of a sudden revelation in his famous "Tower experience" (*Turmerlebnis*) between 1511 and 1515. *Sola scriptura – sola fides* (Scripture alone—faith alone) have remained slogans in Lutheran theology.

The roots of the Reformed wing of the Reformation are to be found in Ulrich Zwingli's *Commentary on True and False Religion* (1525), in which the symbolic presence of Christ in the Lord's Supper was taught. He had developed the polemical root of Protestantism as Philip Melanchthon had developed the exegetical. A conflict between Zwingli and Melanchthon took place in Marburg in 1529, and the presence of Christ in the Lord's Supper

32. (New York: Random House, 1945), 2 vols.

was the heart of the debate. Calvin is the finest example of the catechetical root.

The Reformed wing of the Reformation found the Scriptural orientation of Luther and the humanism of Melanchthon combined in one man, John Calvin (1509-64). His *Institutes of the Christian Religion*, passing through five editions between 1536 and 1559, did for Protestantism what the *Fountain of Wisdom* by John of Damascus did for Eastern Orthodoxy and what the *Summa Theologica* by Thomas Aquinas did for Roman Catholicism. If it is proper to continue the figure of speech in this case, it remains the first great theological cathedral of Protestantism. He who knows these three writings and the branches built on them understands much about Christian theology before the impact of modern science.

The first edition of Calvin's *Institutes* put the Decalogue before the Apostles' Creed and the Lord's Prayer, the sacraments and church government, as the basis for Christian theology, and this emphasis on the Old Testament has been a distinctive of Calvinism. The final edition had four parts: God the Creator, God the Redeemer, the Holy Spirit, the means of grace and the Church. This God-centered approach, along with the Old Testament emphasis, is a sure sign of Reformed theology.

Until the beginning of the nineteenth century most of the growing edges of theology were found on one of the three branches outlined above. It was not until the impact of modern science that new systems were introduced, like new trees planted in new soil. In the two centuries between the Protestant Reformation and the reconstruction of theology in modern times, a Protestant scholasticism developed much as a Catholic scholasticism characterized the later Middle Ages. A thaw was bound to come. Even in the time of the Reformation the Anabaptists called for a more complete restoration of New Testament faith, but no system of theology was perpetuated.

C. MAIN CURRENTS OF MODERN THEOLOGY

5. Philosophical Liberalism

In the modern landscape of Christian theology, as a theological astronaut would see it, five movements in theology appear: (1) the philosophical liberalism that reached its crest in the nineteenth century and has fanned out into a broad delta in the twentieth; (2) the reaction of Protestant fundamentalism at the end of the nineteenth century and the beginning of the twentieth; (3) the resurgence of a biblical theology in neo-orthodoxy between World Wars I and II, which has returned to its channel in the second generation; (4) the revolt of many forms of radical theology in recent times with no clear vision for the future; and (5) reconstruction in several forms of recent theology.

The philosophical liberalism first formulated since around 1800 was well nigh the length and shadow of Immanuel Kant (1724-1804). Kant's critical philosophy offered a theory of knowledge for those unable to accept the papal authority of Roman Catholicism or the biblical authority of Protestant conservatism. Needless to say, the present tensions between conservatives and liberals in both camps are replays of old tunes.

Among the three critiques (*The Critique of Pure Reason*, 1781, 1787, *The Critique of Practical Reason*, 1788, and *The Critique of Judgment*, 1790), the first produced only a philosophy of religion that became for many a substitute for a systematic Christian theology. It is interesting to remember that Kant was professor of Logic from 1770 until his death, and his one solution to the problems proposed by the deadlock between English empiricism and Continental rationalism was in understanding (*Verstand*). For him the understanding prescribed the nature of its law. It was "all in the mind," not in the objective world of empirical data.

Speculative Rationalism

The towering figure who explored these limits of speculative rationalism was Georg Wilhelm Friedrich Hegel (1770-1831), whose first teaching post was also in Logic and Metaphysics. From the very beginning he was obsessed with the relationship between the finite and the infinite. This relation he believed could be found only in the concrete facts of history. He intended to be a philosopher of the Word which became flesh (John 1:14), but Lutheran orthodoxy did not see him in this light!

His philosophy of religion at first subordinated all philosophy to religion. His massive system was first formulated in *The Phenomenology of Mind* (*Geistes*) in 1806. Ten years later he became professor of philosophy in Berlin where he also applied his logic to subjects other than religion, but his system seemed never to change. For him "the real is rational and the rational is real." A new Aristotle was on the scene.

The dialectical process by which he pursued truth always involved a thesis succeeded by an antithesis brought together by a synthesis of the whole. The truth was always in the whole (*Die Wahrheit ist das Ganze*). Applied to Christian doctrine this evolutionary process could be made to sound very orthodox. God and man found a synthesis first in the Incarnation of deity and humanity in Christ (the Word made flesh) and then in the consummation when God would be "all in all" (1 Cor. 15:28). Theology needed only to be stripped of mythology. Even the Holy Trinity was made acceptable again through the Father and the Son finding unity in the Spirit, the synthesis. It is not surprising that there is now a new interest in Hegel's thought.

Christian Experience

A colleague of Hegel in the University of Berlin took up the theme of Kant's third critique, *The Critique of Judgment*, but Hegel held him in contempt.

He was Friedrich Daniel Ernst Schleiermacher (1768-1834), at times called "the father of modern theology." Schleiermacher found the key to theology in feeling, not reason. His was "a heart-felt religion" but far more sophisticated than that term connotes.

This son of a Reformed army chaplain was greatly influenced by Herrnhuter Brethren. Schleiermacher found real meaning in the pietistic conversion experience. In fact he was willing to advocate his beliefs to the representatives of the Romantic Movement, which also put great emphasis on feeling. As early as 1799 he outlined his theology in his *Speeches on Religion*, intended for the educated of Berlin society. The book was translated into English in 1893, when Schleiermacher's influence was at a peak. This volume had the well-chosen title *On Religion, Speeches to its Cultured Despisers*.

If there is a theological cathedral in nineteenth-century theology, it is perhaps Schleiermacher's *The Christian Faith* (1821-22). On the basis of intuition and feeling, the personal experience of union with the infinite, he constructed a consistent system that made room for the most conservative Christian beliefs. He is truly fascinating to read, and his immense influence on Protestant theology is not difficult to understand.

He too had three prongs on his theological fork or philosophical dialectic: (1) the feeling of absolute dependence on God, (2) the consciousness of sin and guilt, and (3) the experience of grace. Around these three empirical feelings he constructed his whole system of Christian theology. The purest expression of all this he found in the monotheism of the Christian faith and the experience of the Christian fellowship, much as he had first experienced God among the Brethren. He was certainly no cultured despiser of his childhood religion.

He constructed an appealing synthesis between the man-centered theology of classic Lutheranism and the God-centered theology of Calvinism, but he did not unite the two camps! Between the two World Wars Schleiermacher took a pounding from both the orthodox and the neo-orthodox, but there are indications that his theological method is making a comeback, and that in the most unexpected quarters. Richard Reinhold Niebuhr, son of Helmut Richard and nephew of Reinhold Niebuhr, two of the leaders of American neo-orthodoxy, has recently taken the role of the Pied Piper to lead a new generation of bewildered theologians back to Schleiermacher.[33]

Moral Values

A third movement more properly known as liberalism finds its founder in Albrecht Ritschl (1822-89), at times looked upon as just another follower

---

33. See Richard Reinhold Niebuhr's Torchbook Introduction to *The Christian Faith* (New York: Harper and Row, 1963), Vol. I, pp. ix-xx; *Experiential Religion* (New York: Harper and Row, 1972).

of Schleiermacher. If Hegel can be viewed as an extension of Kant's *Critique of Pure Reason* and Schleiermacher of *The Critique of Judgment*, it is not farfetched to see Ritschl as a by-product of Kant's second critique, *The Critique of Practical Reason*. At least Ritschl understood Christian faith as the solution to practical problems and his followers magnified Kant's basic religious affirmations (God, freedom and immortality) as "the essence of Christianity."[34]

Ritschl, the so-called giant of Göttingen University, very early left the Hegelian rationalism of the Tübingen University school, but he did not "go over" to the school of Schleiermacher. He constructed his own system of Christian theology, especially in his great book that had a real Lutheran ring even in the title, *The Christian Doctrine of Justification and Reconciliation* (1870-74).

Ritschl believed Christian theology had a foundation all its own. It does not rest upon a series of facts interpreted by the reason of philosophical idealism. It rests upon value-judgments or faith-affirmations made independent of reason. For example, one does not say "Jesus is God," as in pious conservatism, but one says Jesus has the revelational-value (*Offenbarungswert*) of God for those who trust in him and worship God in a believing community gathered around the figure of the historical Jesus. This sounds very much like "faith in faith," as in much recent Lutheran theology, but it seems fair to Ritschlian liberalism.

At least two doctrines stand out in Ritschl: the forgiveness of sin and the kingdom of God. Justification is the forgiveness of sins achieved in the priesthood of believers in which Jesus is the great high priest. The kingdom of God is a kingdom of moral values intended for the integration of all humanity. This kingdom, interpreted by a mistranslation of Luke 17:21, is "within you" (cf. RSV), not a future reign of God that began to dawn at the first coming of Jesus. These views too are often heard from some of the most conservative Christians, and Ritschl himself still has appeal.[35]

After World War I, there was indeed an Indian summer of liberalism, especially in the United States where the devastations of war were not fully felt.[36] Most of the new growth was due to a new graft on the process philosophy of A. N. Whitehead. Whitehead's *Process and Reality* (1929) became the virtual Bible used by a group of young religious philosophers centered around Charles Hartshorne of the University of Chicago. This new growth developed the idea of a growing God whose primordial nature, prior

---

34. *Das Wesen des Christentums* was the title of a book by Adolf Harnack, 1900, that attracted wide attention; E. T. *What Is Christianity?* (1901), tr. Thomas Bailey Saunders (Magnolia, Mass.: Peter Smith, 1958).

35. David L. Mueller, *Introduction to the Theology of Albrecht Ritschl* (Philadelphia: Westminster Press, 1969).

36. William H. Hordern, *A Layman's Guide to Protestant Theology*, Revised Edition (New York: The Macmillan Co., 1968), pp. 73-110. *An Outline of Christian Theology* (1894) by William Newton Clarke is a good example from before the War.

to all creativity (the principle of concretion), is so enriched by the cosmic process that we may think of his consequent nature also. Norman Pittenger, formerly of General Theological Seminary in New York and Cambridge University, used Whitehead in most of his theological reconstruction, but the best theological expression of the movement in one volume is perhaps John Cobb's *A Christian Natural Theology* (1965). The school of process theology has many other advocates and many angles.[37]

6. Protestant Fundamentalism

In 1909, two symbolic publications began. Two brothers, Lyman and Milton Stewart, made a generous gift of money for the distribution of a series of booklets called *The Fundamentals*, and C. I. Scofield published the first edition of his *Scofield Reference Bible*. The points made by the two publications are not always the same, but they were perhaps the most influential documents in the rapid spread of fundamentalism.

It should not be assumed that 1909 was the "birthday" of fundamentalism. A detailed history begins with the year 1875, but no special reason is given for that date.[38] In general the whole movement should be seen as a reaction against liberalism, and the broad outlines may be expressed as: (1) the conservation of the Protestant orthodoxy formulated before modern science and biblical criticism, (2) the assimilation in part of the dispensational deviations of the nineteenth and twentieth centuries, and (3) a consolidation of many groups in opposition to liberalism under the general nomenclature of conservative evangelicalism. The terms conservatives, dispensationalists, and evangelicals are used with these meanings.

Conservatism

The most influential systematic theology adopted by conservatives was that of Charles Hodge (1797-1878). His *Systematic Theology* (1871-73) defended the traditional Calvinism of the so-called Princeton School. According to Francis L. Patton: "He was fond of saying that Princeton had never originated a new idea; but this meant no more than that Princeton was the advocate of historical Calvinism in opposition to the modified and provincial Calvinism of a later day."[39]

A centennial comment on Hodge's celebrated theology points out the strange silence his *Systematic Theology* had on the doctrine of the Church,

---

37. *Process Theology*, ed. Ewert H. Cousins (New York: Newman Press, 1971); Robert B. Mellert, *What Is Process Theology?* (New York: Paulist Press, 1975); John B. Cobb, Jr., and David Ray Griffin, *Process Theology* (Philadelphia: Westminster Press, 1976).

38. George W. Dollar, *A History of Fundamentalism* (Greenville, S.C.: Bob Jones University Press, 1973).

39. *The New Schaff-Herzog Encyclopedia of Religious Knowledge*, edited by Samuel Macauley Jackson (Grand Rapids, Michigan: Baker Book House, 1950), Vol. V, p. 306.

destined to be a major concern of the twentieth century.[40] On the doctrine of the Church and on many other topics *Systematic Theology* (1907) by the Baptist theologian A. H. Strong is more adequate, but Strong finally capitulated to the theory of evolution, a view suspect by even the most ecumenical evangelicals. Few fundamentalists are able to digest the confident confession of Strong when he says: "Neither evolution nor the higher criticism has any terrors to the one who regards them as parts of Christ's creating and educating process."[41] Hodge's last writing, *What is Darwinism?* (1874), took a more defensive view.

Fundamentalism

Five points very soon became the hard core of fundamentalism. They were: (1) the verbal inerrancy of Scripture, (2) the virgin birth of Jesus Christ, (3) the substitutionary atonement, (4) the bodily resurrection of Christ, and (5) the imminent return of Christ in a personal, visible and bodily form.[42]

Dispensationalism

The dispensationalists accepted all the five points of fundamentalism, but many fundamentalists did not embrace dispensationalism with its insistence on seven dispensations, eight covenants, and the dubious theory of a pre-tribulation Rapture that has not been traced beyond 1830. Many fundamentalists repudiate all the pre-millennialism which is so much a part of dispensationalism.

The most representative dispensational theologian is no doubt L. S. Chafer, founder and first President of Dallas Theological Seminary. His massive *Systematic Theology* (1947-48) in eight volumes deviates very little from the notes in the *Scofield Reference Bible*, but he leans heavily on earlier Protestant conservatism, especially that in the modified Calvinist tradition.

Evangelicalism

The evangelicals have been called, perhaps unfairly, fundamentalists who have Ph.D. degrees. However, their more reasonable approach in debate is a great improvement over the old feuding, fighting fundamentalism that was so rampant after World War I.

Evangelicals differ from the old conservatives in their stance, to use one of their favorite words, toward modern science and social issues. The

40. David Wells, "The Stout and Persistent Theology of Charles Hodge," *Christianity Today*, Vol. XVIII, No. 23 (August 30, 1974), p. 15.
41. *Systematic Theology* (Philadelphia: The Judson Press, 1907), p. vii. See Part II, ch. 17 for the impact of biblical criticism and modern science.
42. *The Fundamentals for Today*, edited with revisions by Charles L. Feinberg (Grand Rapids, Michigan: Kregel Publications, 1958).

old conservatism was formulated in a pre-critical and pre-scientific age and found no need to wrestle with the questions raised by the possibility that the earth is as old as four and a half billion years and that human life has been on earth for at least two million years. These are questions that trouble evangelicals, but they are more courageous in facing social issues about which the old conservatives had little conscience.

It is not so easy to select a representative evangelical theologian. No Hodge or Chafer stands out, at least not in America. The learned G. C. Berkouwer of Holland belongs more to the old conservative camp than to the new evangelical trend. The best brief statement that is representative of many evangelicals is perhaps *Basic Christian Doctrines* (1962), a collection of essays edited by Carl F. H. Henry.[42a]

The essays are of uneven value. The opening chapters on revelation are brief but of very high quality and clear perception. Yet a tension may often be detected in other essays between the authority of Scripture and ecclesiastical tradition.

The chapter on "Original Sin, Imputation and Inability" by Cornelius Van Til, a Presbyterian, still clings to the old Augustinian idea that "All men have sinned in Adam," a theory that both Protestant and Catholic scholars recognize as based on an inaccurate translation of Rom. 5:12.[43]

A scholar with the reputation of Otto Michel, a Lutheran, writes a chapter on "Regeneration," yet it has been put before "Repentance and Conversion," as if God regenerates people before they repent and believe. Furthermore, Michel perpetuated the old Alexandrian idea that the Father begets the Son, apparently at his baptism (?), an idea that Jerome read into the Latin Vulgate with another incorrect translation.[44]

A growing group of "new evangelicals" are bold to debate the issues posed by modern science and society, and this seems a step in the right direction, but these "conservative evangelicals," to use another self-designation, need to go on to a critical conservatism before I would be able to be confident and comfortable in their evangelical Zion. There are some signs, especially in England, that they are going in that direction.[45] Evangelicals should know by now there is no going back to a pre-critical and pre-scientific posture in Christian theology.

42a. Reprint by Baker Book House, 1971.
43. P. 111. See also *The Common Catechism*, edited by Johannes Feiner and Lukas Vischer (New York: The Seabury Press, 1975), p. 378.
44. P. 190. See Part VI.44.
45. Kenneth G. Howkins, *The Challenge of Religious Studies* (Downers Grove, Illinois: Inter-Varsity Press, 1973). For further study see Richard J. Coleman, *Issues of Theological Warfare: Evangelicals and Liberals* (Grand Rapids, Michigan: Wm. B. Eerdmans Publishing Co., 1972); Richard Quebedeaux, *The Young Evangelicals* (New York: Harper and Row, 1974); David F. Wells and John D. Woodbridge, ed., *The Evangelicals* (New York: Abingdon, 1975).

7. Neo-Orthodoxy

At the end of World War I a so-called "theology of crisis" or "dialectical theology" began to blow down from the Swiss Alps. In America it came to be known as biblical realism (in Reinhold Niebuhr) or Neo-Orthodoxy (in Edwin Lewis).

Karl Barth

Neo-Orthodoxy really began with Karl Barth, a pastor of the Reformed Church in Switzerland, who published his *Commentary on Romans* in 1919, and it immediately became a watershed in Protestant theology. Karl Adam, a Roman Catholic theologian in Tübingen, said "it fell like a bombshell on the playground of the theologians."[46] Very soon (1921) he became professor at Göttingen, Ritschl's playground, then in Münster (1925), later in Bonn (1930).

While in Bonn, although a Swiss citizen, he joined in the struggle against Hitler's National Socialism. The Barmen Declaration of 1934, largely Barth's work, declared: "We repudiate the false teaching that the church can turn over the form of her message and ordinances at will or according to some dominant ideological and political conviction." The Nazis considered him a traitor. When he refused to take an oath of unconditional allegiance to Hitler, he was fired (1935) and went to the University of Basel, Switzerland, where he was a professor for the rest of his life. In 1948 a favorite story still was how the University of Münster deprived him of his doctorate in 1939 because of his opposition to Hitler, and restored it, after the death of Hitler, in 1945.

If ever the Reformed tradition of Calvinism built a theological cathedral, Karl Barth was the builder, in a mammoth work entitled *Church Dogmatics*. Since the work was bound in white in German, Barth himself, out of his love for *Moby Dick*, humorously called the growing volumes "the white whale." Many of Barth's opponents would agree with that figure of speech, which is supposed to symbolize the problem of evil!

He planned his *Church Dogmatics* to be five volumes, but only the first three and most of Volume IV were ever published. Volume, however, does not mean binding. Volume I alone is two huge bindings of 1,480 pages in English translation. It is concerned with the problem of revelation and is called "The Doctrine of the Word of God." The Word of God, according to Barth, comes to us in a threefold form: preached, written, and revealed. It reveals God in another threefold unity: the Father as creator, the Son as reconciler, and the Holy Spirit as redeemer.

In the history of revelation it would seem that the Word of God came in reverse order, but Barth is thinking like a preacher! His scheme of the

---

46. According to R. Birch Hoyle, in *The Protestant Dictionary*, edited by Charles Sydney Carter and G. E. Allison Weeks (London: The Harrison Trust, 1933), p. 78.

Holy Trinity seems to violate the unity of God and sounds at first like a swing-shift Trinity in which the Father, Son and Holy Spirit work on three different shifts. Barth's disciple, Heinrich Vogel, in his *Gott in Christo* (1951) made this appear even more so. But Barth insisted that all three are eternal and that there is a unity to the Holy Trinity in all his work.

Volume II, 1,505 pages in two bindings, is called "The Doctrine of God." He has hastened to expound the Holy Trinity in Volume I, perhaps in revolt against nineteenth-century liberalism, which brought the doctrine of the Trinity into almost total eclipse. He also drove home the point that the *only* revelation of God was the special revelation in Jesus Christ. He made little room for a general revelation of God in creation and man. Out of that soil he saw the source of Nazism.

What more does he have to say? The knowledge of God and the reality of God come up for consideration in the first half volume of 697 pages! In my judgment his discussion of God in action is one of the richest parts of his *Church Dogmatics*. Pastors pushed by a program and a TV generation are not likely to read his detailed discussion, but he who reads it will be rewarded.

Barth's views on election and a section on his ethics are included in the second half of Volume II. The most Christ-centered view of election yet formulated, as far as I know, is developed in the discussion of the pattern of grace, Jesus Christ, the community, and the individual. As Jesus Christ is the only revelation of God, so he is the only elect one. The community and the individual are elected in Christ. Yet at the end he ruins a good idea by coming to the very brink of universalism. His old friend Emil Brunner, breaking away from his theology, did not hesitate to point this out.[47]

As Schleiermacher stated his doctrine of God at three different places, with no doctrine of the Trinity, so Barth hit upon the idea of putting a section on ethics in each volume. There was no connection with Schleiermacher in his mind. In that way, the teacher of ethics who reads him will get exposed to theology! His liberal critics could hardly say he had no ethics, as he expounds the love commandment with great power and passion.

His liberal critics did say Barth needed a doctrine of creation, but he put an end to that in Volume III, 2,337 pages in four bindings entitled "The Doctrine of Creation"!

In the crucial year 1934 Schleiermacher and Barth had a fierce debate on that issue. Barth maintained that there was no general revelation in creation and that the image of God in man was obliterated by the Fall and could be recreated only in Christ. I have never been sure what Barth meant by the Fall. These words are being written a few days before the Jewish New Year of 5,734 since creation. Barth never believed in such a Fall after

47. *The Christian Doctrine of God*, tr. Olive Wyon (Philadelphia: Westminster Press, 1949), pp. 346-353.

that date, but he talked much about a Fall. It is one of those points on which many other theologians are not always clear, but more on that later.

Volume IV, *The Doctrine of Reconciliation*, is unfinished, but it has 2,632 pages in four bindings plus a fragment on baptism with 226 pages and an index with 676 pages. *The Doctrine of Reconciliation* contains, as would be expected, the most pronounced "Christomonism" in all of Barth's writings. His Christology is always "from above," with none of the search for the historical Jesus "from below" which was so characteristic of liberalism and is now becoming a "new quest." Under this heading he discusses sin and salvation, the Church, and the Christian life. That is why the "fragment" on baptism was included.

The fragment on baptism does not make his Calvinistic colleagues happy. Here, more than any other place, Barth sounds like a Baptist. As far back as 1947, in his booklet *The Teaching of the Church Regarding Baptism*, Barth questioned the sacramental theology of infant baptism. His son, Markus Barth, wrote a large volume against baptism as a sacrament in 1951, but this "bomb fragment" on baptism by Karl Barth is the clearest statement of all.

For this time of "the theology of hope" it is a great disappointment that Barth did not live to state his eschatology. At the time of Barth's death, Thomas Merton, the famous Trappist monk, was accidentally electrocuted in another part of the world. At St. Agnes Church in Louisville there was a joint Protestant-Catholic memorial service for both. I was asked to read some selections and prayers from Barth, and a monk from Gethsemane Monastery, near Louisville, read from Merton. The day following, a Roman Catholic nun of great ecumenical spirit and strong belief in personal immortality, exclaimed in conversation: "Don't you know Karl Barth and Thomas Merton are happy together in Paradise now." I smiled in pleasant surprise to hear she believed they were in the same place!

Emil Brunner

Emil Brunner was no "Little Sir Echo" of Karl Barth, as some superficial writers seem to think. Brunner was far nearer to the philosophical liberalism of the nineteenth century. In fact, his major writings until 1937 were greatly influenced by the philosophy of Kant. It is true that his first major book, *Mysticism and the Word* (1924), was a slashing attack on Schleiermacher and all other forms of mysticism, but he never went as far as Barth in his blasts at liberalism.

The reader of Brunner's *The Mediator* (1927) will soon see how Kant's apparent distinction between the phenomenal that can be experienced through sense data and the noumenal that is ultimate reality and beyond experience has influenced Brunner's view of the historical Jesus and the eternal Word of God that became flesh in Jesus. At times one really wonders why Brunner needed the historical Jesus at all, with all his emphasis on the Word. His distinction between the Jesus of history and the Christ of faith, as taught by Martin Kähler, increased this radical dualism.

Brunner's ethic in *The Divine Imperative* (1932) was deeply indebted to Kant's concept of the categorical imperative. It is a big jump from the content of Kant's categorical imperative in the human conscience to Brunner's divine imperative of love that comes through revelation, but the parallels after that jump are striking. Brunner was influenced by his knowledge of Kant.

In *Man in Revolt* (1937), which Brunner considered his most important book up to 1937, the concept of man's contradiction in sin recalls Kant's concept of radical evil explored in *Religion Within the Limits of Reason Alone* (1793), Kant's other major book after the three critiques. Again the content is different, but the form provokes reflection on parallels and possible debt.

In 1937, in his Olaus Petri Lectures in Sweden on *Truth as Meeting*, Brunner made his breakthrough into a new formulation of theology. The I–Thou philosophy associated with the Jew Martin Buber (*I and Thou*, 1923) and the Lutheran Karl Heim (*God Transcendent*, 1931) was applied to the whole of Christian theology with striking results. For example, the Church as a fellowship (*Gemeinde*) was put over against the church as an institution (*Kirche*), and Brunner was so pleased with his conclusions and their relevance to the present predicament that he later wrote *The Misunderstanding of the Church* (1951) as an expansion of this idea.

Revelation and Reason (1941) was his first big book after this breakthrough, and there he developed the idea of I–Thou even more as he expounded knowledge of God in the most personal way. The very title of this book, his most important after 1937, is a radical reversal of the long tradition, especially since Aquinas, in which theology moved from reason to revelation rather than from revelation to reason. There are really two different conceptions of truth, as Brunner emphasized in a summary chapter.[48] The former starts with the impersonal conception of truth in the I–It world and runs the danger of reducing even God to a thing, an idol at man's disposal; but the second approach so characteristic of biblical revelation begins with the personal disclosure of God, in an I–Thou meeting in which man comes to know God as Person, not just some ideas *about* God. The influence of Karl Heim's classic statement is evident here and throughout the volume.

This survey of Brunner's personal pilgrimage from idealism to personalism should suggest how Brunner was a bridge theologian between nineteenth-century liberal theology dominated by Lutheranism and the biblical realism of the twentieth century in which the reaffirmation of the radical transcendence of a personal God resounds from the Reformed tradition of

48. Pp. 362-374.

Calvinism. It must ever be said that Barth was the peak of the range, but Brunner was the theologian who helped a generation to get over the mountain through the Brunner Pass!

Brunner's three-volume *Dogmatics* (1946-1960) very soon became familiar to students as *Dog.* I, etc. No other system has as yet replaced it as a theological text among professors who give priority to a biblical theology. The discussion on "The Nature of God and His Attributes," Section One of Vol. I, betrays a debt to Barth's classic discussion on the "perfections" of the divine loving and the divine freedom, but Section Two is well nigh a bombardment of Barth's "double predestination" and universalism.

Dog. II, *The Christian Doctrine of Creation and Redemption*, is mostly a restatement of views expressed in his previous books. However, at one point there is a rather radical revision of his views. The Christology of *The Mediator* started with the Word and had little room for the historical Jesus, but *Dog.* II makes much of how important it is to begin with the Work of Christ, as Melanchthon did at the Reformation, rather than with the Person, as soon became traditional through Brunner's *The Mediator*.[49] After reading *God Was in Christ* by D. M. Baillie, Brunner reversed his approach. This was long before Pannenberg and his friends started talking about doing Christology "from below."

Dog. III, *The Christian Doctrine of the Church, Faith and the Consummation*, is also, in the main, a restatement of his published theology. Here it is especially important to read his preface. In 1947 my unpublished dissertation on Brunner discerned what he said about Christoph Blumhardt at the end of the preface: "I regard my theological work as the harvest of his sowing." In the part on the church he follows the radical personalism of *The Misunderstanding of the Church* (1951). He is notably more restrained in his criticism of infant baptism, but there is still enough refreshing honesty, as in Barth, to create anxiety in all advocates of a state church into which one enters by procreation rather than by regeneration. Brunner is emphatic in saying one enters the true *ekklēsia*, the people of God, not "by being born but by being born again."[50]

This is followed by a statement of "the New Life in Christ." If anyone doubts Brunner's debt to Martin Buber and Karl Heim on the personal nature of faith, he should read Brunner's final admission of this fact, yet Brunner gives credit for this insight to the lesser known Ferdinand Ebner. However, it becomes clear that Brunner would never have moved from liberalism to personalism without the work of Karl Heim. Brunner will later say that it was Heim who first appreciated the I–Thou personalism of Buber as a "Copernican Revolution" in theology.[51]

49. *Dogmatics*, II, 271.
50. P. 56.
51. P. 159.

Barth did not live to state his eschatology, but Brunner's views on last things were published in 1953 in his book *Eternal Hope*. These views were assimilated into the last part of his *Dogmatics* after Brunner had a slight stroke and realized that he was drawing near to the time when faith would become sight. In many ways Brunner's personalism supplies a missing note to Moltmann's *Theology of Hope* (1964), which was to get greater attention later. The German title of Brunner's *Eternal Hope* is more exactly *The Eternal as Future and Present*. It is the present that is such a vacuum in Moltmann's book, but the influence of the Blumhardts, father and son, gave a charismatic emphasis on the present experience of the Holy Spirit to much of Brunner's thought. Moltmann has finally sounded a charismatic note in *The Church in the Power of the Spirit* (1975).

The Spread of Neo-Reformation Theology

Barth and Brunner got their best reception in Scotland. T. F. Torrance of Edinburgh is often more Barthian than Barth. In jest Barth once remarked that there was more rejoicing about his theology in Edinburgh than in heaven! John Baillie, the older colleague of Torrance, was more critical of Barth, having written two major books to refute the narrow view of revelation advocated by Barth.[52]

Brunner was widely accepted in Scotland, but there were some major revisions. D. M. Baillie of St. Andrews, brother of John, wrote a little classic in protest against the skimpy treatment of the historical Jesus in Barth, Brunner and Bultmann, and Brunner accepted these criticisms in gratitude.[53] However, a strong defense of Brunner's views on the image of God in man was made in another little gem by David Cairns of Aberdeen.[54]

Mention should be made of two other ancillary theological movements often associated with the neo-Reformation theology of Barth and Brunner. In the United States the Social Gospel that went back to the prophetic utterances of Walter Rauschenbusch (1861-1918) received new life from the Christian realism of Reinhold Niebuhr (1892-1971).

The major contribution on man and sin in the social situation was Niebuhr's *The Nature and Destiny of Man* (1941-43). Edwin Lewis, a Methodist representative of this movement, called it neo-orthodoxy, but very few identified themselves by that term. It was used mostly by conservatives who lamented when young theologians went "neo."

A second movement came to be known as neo-Lutheran or Lundensian theology, because the chief spokesmen came from the Lutheran theological faculty at the University of Lund, Sweden. *Christus Victor* (1931) by Gustaf

---

52. *Our Knowledge of God* (New York: Charles Scribner's Sons, 1939); *The Idea of Revelation in Recent Thought* (New York: Columbia University Press, 1956).
53. *God Was in Christ* (New York: Charles Scribner's Sons, 1948, 2nd ed. 1955).
54. *The Image of God in Man* (London: SCM, 1953). There is a second edition in the Fontana Library (London: Collins, 1973).

Aulén revived the Patristic ransom theory of the atonement and claimed this as Luther's distinctive view. Luther's view of *agapē* was developed by Aulén into a systematic theology called *The Faith of the Christian Church* (1932).

Anders Nygren, Aulén's colleague, wrote a classic called *Agape and Eros* (tr. 1932-39) in which he made radical distinctions between *erōs* in Plato, *charitas* in Augustine, and *agapē* in Luther. His *Commentary on Romans* (1944) used Luther's idea of two ages as the central concept in the theology of Paul.

A recent systematic theology in the general Scandinavian school of neo-Lutheranism is Regin Prenter, *Creation and Redemption* (E.T. 1967), which undertakes to give creation a central place in modern theology. This concern with *ktisiology* (the doctrine of creation) is a special emphasis in much Scandinavian theology, and Prenter has brought most of it together in his book.

D. CURRENT TRENDS IN CHRISTIAN THEOLOGY

8. Radical Theology

A central figure in the rise of radical theology was Paul Tillich.[55] This is not intended as a slur. It is a statement of fact. It may be added that I served as Tillich's assistant in 1944-45. His students loved him very much as a person, but often in jest he was called "that magnificent old heretic!" His whole system of thought was gathered up in his *Systematic Theology* (1951-1963), which is really a philosophical ontology worked out in the order and with some of the vocabulary of systematic theology.

The preface to his first volume says:

> Furthermore, it has been impossible to make extensive references to the Bible or the classical theologians. The elaboration of the line of thought has consumed all effort and space. The biblical and ecclesiastical character of the solutions to theological problems presented in this volume will not be difficult to recognize, although it is more implicit than explicit.

This quotation was copied from a personal copy once owned by the New Testament scholar Paul Minear of Yale, and on the margin two question marks appear!

Tillich is described in *The Oxford Dictionary of the Christian Church* as influenced by Karl Barth and existentialism; but Barth in his first volume

---

55. John Charles Cooper, *The Roots of the Radical Theology* (Philadelphia: The West-minster Press, 1967), pp. 125-230.

speaks of Tillich as a "bloodless and abstract thinker" (I, 1, 82), and there is but one critical reference to Tillich (II, 1, 635) in all the rest of Barth's *Church Dogmatics*. It is hard to find two theologies farther apart than the biblical realism of Barth and the speculative rationalism of Tillich.

In brief, by the method of correlation, Tillich undertakes to explain "the contents of the Christian faith through existential questions and theological answers in mutual interdependence" (I, 68). In many ways, Tillich, with the whole system of existentialism, is the logical outcome of the man-centered approach of Lutheran theology. It is significant that Kierkegaard, the father of existential philosophy, sprang from Lutheranism, not Calvinism. The same is true of Rudolf Bultmann, who has applied existential philosophy to the New Testament.

With all the dangers of existentialism it is still difficult to conclude that theology should anchor *solely* to the Christonomy of Karl Barth which rules out all philosophical speculation in theory and brings much of it in the back door in actual practice. A balanced theology needs to listen to both the man-centered theology so central in Lutheranism and the God-centered or Christ-centered theology of Calvinism. The truth often lies in between the two.

Despite the sparsity of Scripture in Tillich's system, he does try to escape from the supernaturalism of fundamentalism and the naturalism of liberalism. The first part of his theology retains the traditional approach of "Reason and Revelation," but it is not the two-storied theology of dualism between the natural and the supernatural seen in Thomas Aquinas. By the use of a "kerygmatic" theology, Tillich tries to emphasize "the unchangeable truth of the message (*kerygma*) over against the changing demands of the situation" (I, 4). This sounds much like Rudolf Bultmann's program of demythologization.

At its core Tillich's system follows a Trinitarian pattern that recalls the use of reason in Hegel's philosophy, but the terminology is often that of Martin Heidegger. Part II on "Being and God," based on his fundamental belief that there is an essential unity between man and everything, finds the answer to human finitude in the infinity of God. On one occasion in private conversation, Tillich pointed to a picture on the wall of his study in which the "finite shore" was meeting the "infinite sea" and said: "My whole system is in that picture." The idea of God as Being Itself has attracted much attention, but there is very little of the emphasis on the moral attributes of being so powerfully stated in both Barth and Brunner.

Part III, "Existence and the Christ," was given as his first Gifford Lectures at the University of Aberdeen, Scotland. Here he finds in the symbol of Jesus as the Christ the answer to the question of man's existential self-estrangement and all other self-destructive tendencies. It should be noted that Jesus as the Christ is primarily a symbol for Tillich. As long ago as 1911, he said — and this was later affirmed in his *Interpretation of His-*

tory — that his system would not be undermined if it could be shown that the historical Jesus never lived. In an unforgettable private discussion in 1945, he maintained this position (cf. *Systematic Theology,* II, 118). It was then that I realized how far we were apart and how Hegelian Tillich really was. In the years that followed, the jest was often made that when Tillich heard that an archaeologist claimed he had found the bones of Jesus, he exclaimed: "He really did live!"

Part IV, "Life and the Spirit," has distinct echoes of Hegel's synthesis of all things in the Spirit (mind), but Tillich has done more than rehash Hegel in this second year of Gifford Lectures. Life for Tillich, as for Hegel, was the concrete actuality in historical process. As such it is characterized by ambiguities and contradictions that can be overcome only in the unity of the Spirit. If another little anecdote may be used, it will serve to illustrate Tillich's distinction between spirit and Spirit. On one occasion it was pointed out that in English, unlike German, we usually spell spirit with a little "s" when we have reference to man and with a big "S" when we have reference to God. Later, when he was asked to summarize this part of his theology, he said in broken English: "It is zie relation of zie spirit with zie little s with zie Spirit with zie big S."

The last part of Tillich's theology, V, "History and the Kingdom of God," serves as the conclusion to his Trinitarian system. He thinks the ambiguities of history as a whole find unity in the biblical symbol of the kingdom of God. This ultimate unity is so pronounced that Tillich's statements often sounded like the pantheism which he steadfastly denied. Discerning once, as I still think, that a unity like Hegel's synthesis was the thing he had in mind, I suggested that he use the term pan-en-theism, coined by K. C. F. Krause (1781-1832) for his own system. This means God's Being penetrates the whole universe, but God's Being is not exhausted by the universe. This he did but only at the one place (III, 421)! Tillich still stuck to his favorite idea of essentialization, which indeed does sound pantheistic.

If Paul Tillich may be called the "father" of radical theology, four highly publicized debates may be described as its forms. A starting point for understanding the results of radical theology is the Honest to God debate stirred up by the publication of John A. T. Robinson's book by that title in 1962. He gathered together insights from three German theologians: Rudolf Bultmann, Dietrich Bonhoeffer, and Paul Tillich.

Rudolf Bultmann undertook to demythologize the New Testament, i.e. separate theological ideas from the mythological language in which they have been expressed. Robinson refused to reduce the resurrection of Jesus to a myth, but he did think much New Testament language was a hindrance to the modern mind.

Dietrich Bonhoeffer, a victim of Nazism, made certain criticisms of the conforming church during the last years of his life. Despairing of the institutional church, he called for a secular Christianity, i.e. a Christian witness outside established ecclesiasticism. Robinson, as an Anglican Bishop, saw some relevance for a secular Christianity outside his own rigid traditionalism in the Church of England. He saw in Bonhoeffer's *Prisoner of God* some signs of hope outside the organized church which had been under the heel of Hitler.

The third and most important influence on the English Bishop was Paul Tillich's idea of God as the ground of being or as Being Itself. Many pious people felt that his criticisms of "the God up there" shot God right out of the sky and amounted to atheism. Karl Barth summed up the situation with the quaint remark that Robinson "put three German beers together and got a lot of froth." The debate produced an enormous reaction and sold many books![56]

At the time the Honest to God debate was raging, the Death of God debate began. An article in the *London Observer* spread the first debate. *Time* magazine, Oct. 22, 1965, shook the devout world. The issue included a survey of some Death of God writers including Thomas J. J. Altizer, who promised a forthcoming book, *The Gospel of Christian Atheism* (1966). This produced another flood of writings and more sales.[57]

Altizer used the motif of the dying and rising God in primitive religion to argue that the transcendent God became Jesus; thus when Jesus died, God died. Rejecting the historicity of Jesus' resurrection, he concluded that God is dead and only humanity is left. These ideas were repeated in endless verbiage, but the shallowness of the debate was soon discerned. The logical outcome of this type of thinking is Buddhism, implicit from the beginning, and this has been frankly stated by Altizer in another book.[58]

A milder debate was the Secular City debate stimulated by a book with that title by Harvey Cox.[59] Those acquainted with the positivism of Auguste Comte (1798-1857) soon discerned that Cox was using current ideas to take his readers through Comte's three stages by which humanity moved from the theological through the metaphysical to the positive or scientific stage in which the secularity of this age made man of age. Cox himself has moved more toward an authentic Christian theology since his secularity gained him fame.

Another debate that brought fame to an author was the Situation Ethics debate that followed the publication of Joseph Fletcher's *Situation Ethics*

56. David L. Edwards, ed., *The Honest to God Debate* (London: SCM Press, 1963).
57. Jackson Lee Ice and John J. Carey, ed., *The Death of God Debate* (Philadelphia: The Westminster Press, 1967); Thomas J. Ogletree, *The Death of God Controversy* (Nashville: Abingdon Press, 1966).
58. *The Descent into Hell* (Philadelphia: J. B. Lippincott, 1970). See also *The Self-Embodiment of God* (New York: Harper and Row, 1977).
59. Daniel J. Callahan, ed., *The Secular City Debate* (New York: The Macmillan Co., 1966).

(1966).[60] Adopting the idea that love alone without ethical norms was the Christian ethic, Fletcher gave sensational illustrations of how fornication could be a true expression of love (agapē) under such situations as a concentration camp where a girl gained freedom for her family by giving her body to a guard. The idea was not really new, for such questions were discussed earlier by Reinhold Niebuhr, but it took Fletcher's book to sell the notion in the marketplace.

9. Recent Theological Reorientation

After radical theology had reached a peak in the secular sixties, a search for reorientation in theological reconstruction began. None has been developed to the point of a complete theological system as yet, but this is very likely.

A Christological reorientation has been made by Wolfhart Pannenberg and his "circle" of friends. A Christocentric theology is nothing new, for Karl Barth worked most of his life on that theological cathedral. However, Pannenberg does Christology "from below" beginning with the resurrection of Jesus, not "from above" with the eternal Word of God as in Barth.

He also tries to take account of revelation before the Christ event by adopting the promissory theology of Gerhard von Rad, a leading German Old Testament theologian who was one of Pannenberg's mentors. The distinction between manifestations of God before the "self-revelation" of God in the resurrection of Jesus Christ is not as clear as the old distinction between promise and fulfillment in the special revelation of Scripture, which is further distinguished from a general revelation of God in all history and creation.[61] The dialectical philosophy of Georg Hegel also has been blended with biblical theology, but this is not as evident as in the theology of Jürgen Moltmann. Moltmann, of course, got his Hegelianism through *The Principle of Hope* (1959) and other works by Ernst Bloch.

An eschatological reorientation began with the publication of the *Theology of Hope* by Jürgen Moltmann in 1964, the very year Pannenberg published the German edition of his book *Jesus, God and Man*. Many years ago the grand old Methodist theologian Edwin Lewis said to me that the theologian who wrote theology with an eschatological reorientation would ride the wave of the future. In the same year, 1964, my book *The Hope of Glory* outlined such an approach, but most who read it said it was too "biblical" and did not "dialogue" with society as much as it did with science.

Moltmann's *Theology of Hope* was certainly not too biblical, and he wrote in dialogue with and greatly dependent on the Hegelian Marxism in

60. Harvey Cox, ed., *The Situation Ethics Debate* (Philadelphia: The Westminster Press, 1968).
61. An effort to systematize Pannenberg may be found in E. Frank Tupper, *The Theology of Wolfhart Pannenberg* (Philadelphia: The Westminster Press, 1973).

the philosophy of Ernst Bloch, particularly Bloch's book on *The Principle of Hope* (1959). This was not the only influence on Moltmann, but the ghost of Georg Hegel magnified in the political philosophy of Karl Marx and Ernst Bloch can be seen behind all that Moltmann has written.[62] This is blended with the Pauline polarity between the resurrection of Jesus in the past and the resurrection of the dead in the future (cf. 1 Cor. 15), but these are often little more than concepts without content, *Gestalt ohne Gehalt* in German. However, it is possible to give more content to these concepts, and Moltmann has made a beginning in his book *The Crucified God* (1972), which anchors theology to a Jew crucified by Pontius Pilate on political charges and explores a new approach to the doctrine of the Trinity.[63] Moltmann completed his trilogy with *The Church in the Power of the Spirit* (1975), a note all but missing in his earlier books. It is reported that he is now working on the Trinity. The beginner who finds Moltmann's books difficult reading should consult some of the lucid books by the American Lutheran theologian Carl E. Braaten, the best guide to this debate.[64] Moltmann himself has published a book of sermons on the theme.[65]

This dialogue between Christian eschatology and Marxist philosophy has had offshoots in many types of liberation theology. A moderate approach was made when the Dutch theologian J. Verkuyl interpreted salvation in terms of liberation.[66] Ernst Käsemann, Moltmann's colleague, has called for the liberation of theologians from ecclesiastical oppression that quenches new ideas.[67] Gustavo Gutiérrez of South America has called for the liberation of the poor in tones that question American foreign policy and arouse anxiety among the rich in church and state.[68] A black theology of liberation by James H. Cone borders on racism in reverse, but it is part of the dialogue on freedom and bondage.[69] The liberation of women has not gone wanting for a theological voice (I dare not say spokesman!).[70] There are many other facets to this movement.[71]

Moltmann has also been used by those who advocate a theology of

---

62. M. Douglas Meeks, *Origins of the Theology of Hope* (Philadelphia: Fortress Press, 1974).
63. *The Crucified God*, tr. R. A. Wilson and John Bowden (London: SCM, 1974).
64. *The Future of God* (New York: Harper and Row, 1969); *Eschatology and Ethics* (Minneapolis, Minnesota: Augsburg Publishing House, 1974).
65. *The Gospel of Liberation*, tr. Wayne Pipkin (Waco, Texas: Word Books, 1973).
66. *The Message of Liberation in Our Age*, tr. Dale Cooper (Grand Rapids: Wm. B. Eerdmans Publishing Company, 1972). See also Frederick Herzog, *Liberation Theology* (New York: The Seabury Press, 1972).
67. *Jesus Means Freedom*, tr. Frank Clarke (Philadelphia: Fortress Press, 1970).
68. *A Theology of Liberation* (London: SCM, 1973). Cf. Orlando E. Costas, *The Church and Its Mission* (Wheaton, Illinois: Tyndale, 1974).
69. *A Black Theology of Liberation* (Philadelphia: J. B. Lippincott, 1970).
70. Georgia Harkness, *Woman in Church and Society* (Nashville: Abingdon Press, 1971). Phyllis Trible, *God and The Rhetoric of Sexuality* (Philadelphia: The Westminster Press, 1978).
71. N. Piediscalzi and R. G. Thobaben, *From Hope to Liberation* (Philadelphia: Fortress Press, 1974); *Interpretation*, XXVIII. 4 (October, 1974).

celebration. A theology of play was the subject of a dialogue between Moltmann and three American theologians, but Moltmann's response was in the
tone of battle, not play. There is too much suffering in the world to dance
with Sam Keen and to feast with Harvey Cox.[72] The Americans have missed
the big game altogether. They should know, remarks Moltmann, that: "Play
should liberate, not tranquilize, awaken, and not anesthetize."[73]

There is another movement about which the theologians of liberation
and celebration know little. The theme is hardly mentioned in the early
theology of Moltmann. Perhaps they think it is too conservative to deserve
attention, but many people are finding new hope in this movement, and
theologians are doomed if they do not dialogue with such phenomena. This
is the charismatic movement, but only a few theologians have made an
effort to make pneumatology the point of reorientation for theological reconstruction.[74] The theology of hope is so concerned with social action that
it has looked askance at this "pietistic" concern about personal relation with
God here and hereafter. Could it not be used more as a basis for hope in
society as well as for personal immortality?

On the level of life and work more attention, both pro and con, is given
to the charismatic movement. As the older Pentecostalism magnified the
Day of Pentecost in Acts 2, so the charismatic movement dwells much on
1 Cor. 12-14 where Paul uses the Greek term *charismata* (gifts, 12:4, 31) —
hence the name. Whereas the older Pentecostalism was restricted to certain
sects, the charismatic movement has since 1960 gained the attention and
respect of Christian leaders of many types.

In 1960 Dennis J. Bennett, at that time rector of St. Mark's Episcopal
Church in Van Nuys, California, received what he called "the baptism in
the Holy Spirit." It is interesting indeed to see a book on the phenomenon
edited by the Canon of Washington Cathedral.[75] When contributions by
Krister Stendahl, the scholarly dean of Harvard Divinity School, and Jo-
sephine Massyngberde Ford, the charismatic biblical scholar of Notre Dame,
appear in the same volume with a selection by Dennis Bennett, it is time

72. Cf. Sam Keen, *To a Dancing God* (New York: Harper & Row, 1970); Harvey Cox,
Feast of Fools (Cambridge: Harvard University Press, 1969).
73. *The Theology of Play*, tr. Reinhard Ulrich (New York: Harper & Row, 1971), p. 113.
74. My book *Spirit of the Living God* (Philadelphia: The Westminster Press, 1968) has
made a beginning in biblical exegesis and recent literature. Dale Bruner, *A Theology of the
Holy Spirit* (Grand Rapids: Wm. B. Eerdmans Publishing Company, 1970), has advanced
the dialogue with the charismatics, but he has not worked out a theological system from
this perspective. There is a useful classic by H. Wheeler Robinson, *The Christian Experience
of the Holy Spirit* (New York: Harper & Brothers, 1928), and the *Pneumatologia* (1674) by
the Puritan theologian John Owen should not be forgotten. Owen has been simplified and
updated by Edwin H. Palmer, *The Person and Ministry of the Holy Spirit* (Grand Rapids:
Baker Book House, 1974), but his rigid framework of five-point Calvinism hinders more
than it helps.
75. Michael P. Hamilton, ed., *The Charismatic Movement* (Grand Rapids: Wm. B. Eerdmans Publishing Company, 1975). A flood of other books could be listed. See also John
Koenig, *Charismata: God's Gifts for God's People* (Philadelphia: Westminster Press, 1978).

that the *avant-garde* that rambles on about relevance awake from dogmatic slumber.

The great tradition grows, and new light and life continually change the direction of the theological stream. He who thinks he has already penetrated the "depths of the riches of the wisdom and knowledge of God" is revealing his own nearsightedness. The discussions that follow are intended as a sharing of what light God has given thus far.

II. REVELATION

A. SPECIAL REVELATION

10. The Meaning of Special Revelation

Special revelation is an event in which God discloses himself to those who are ready to receive him. This revelation implies a special place, a special people, and a special history. It may be that there is some knowledge of God in all places, by all peoples and in all history. That general revelation is the subject of Section B. In this first half the focus of concern is this "scandal of particularity" that is implied in all historical revelation.

The Definition of Special Revelation

The first implication of special revelation is that of a Holy Land. This includes many holy places in which God has disclosed himself in space and time. People feel a little closer to God when they think of places associated with patriarchs and prophets, Jesus and the apostles. A Christian may enjoy a visit to the Yucatan, but he becomes a pilgrim as he sets his face toward the Holy Land of the Bible. There is something special about that land.[1]

The heart of the Old Testament concept is set on Jerusalem, a Holy City to the three monotheistic religions of the world. To Jews and Christians it is *the* Holy City, but even Moslems rank it along with Mecca and Medina. The struggles and conflicts of this city are like no other in all human history.[2]

It was Jerusalem, according to Deuteronomy 12, that the Lord chose as the special place to put his Name and in which the worship of Israel was to be centered. The fall of Jerusalem in 587-86 B.C. was a blow to this Deuteronomic belief, but it arose from the ruins in the apocalyptic visions of Ezekiel who saw that the Shekinah Glory of the Lord would descend there. "And the name of the city henceforth shall be, The Lord is there"

1. Michael Avi-Yonah, *The Holy Land* (London: Thames and Hudson, 1972); Yohanan Aharoni and Michael Avi-Yonah, *The Macmillan Bible Atlas* (1968).
2. Teddy Kollek and Moshe Pearlmann, *Jerusalem* (New York: Random House, 1968).

38

(Ezek. 48:35). Jesus predicted that after the destruction of Jerusalem in his generation, Jerusalem would again be central. This is a special theme in the Gospel of Luke (9:51; 13:22; 17:11; 18:31; 19:28, 41–44; 21:20–24; 23:28–31).

The second implication of special revelation is that of a Holy Nation. The land and the people are inseparable. God's revelation in a special place is always to a special people. In this place and to this people, not in some other place and to some other people, is this revelation made known. Some of the most emotional disputes can be had on this point, not just between Israeli and Arab, but even among Christians. It is indeed "the scandal of particularity."

The Lord's theophany at Sinai, one of the most holy places, proclaims to Israel: "You shall be to me a kingdom of priests and a holy nation" (Exodus 19:6). This priesthood of Israel reaches back to the beginning of the Bible (Gen. 3:15) and becomes the promise to the patriarchs (Gen. 12:3). It is, however, in the prophets, in their passionate pleas for Israel to repent, that this role is the clearest.

In a time of national crisis, the concept of Israel as a special people makes "the Valley of Achor a door of hope" (Hosea 2:15) and reveals to Hosea that the Lord will restore Israel as his faithful wife as he restored unfaithful Gomer to Hosea (2:14–3:5). Both Hosea 2:23 and Exodus 19:6 are applied to believers in 1 Peter 2:9–10. This particularity is not partiality. A central teaching in the Gospels, especially in Matthew, is that because of the rejection of the message and mission of Jesus, the kingdom of God will be taken away from Israel and "given to a nation producing the fruit of it" (21:44).

In Luke–Acts there is no way to tone down the apostolic preaching that says: "Repent therefore, and turn again, that your sins may be blotted out, that times of refreshing may come from the presence of the Lord, and that he may send the Christ appointed, Jesus, whom heaven must receive until the time for establishing all that God spoke by the mouth of his holy prophets from of old" (Acts 3:19–21). The idea that God will fulfill his promise to Israel without Israel's repentance of her rejection of Jesus finds cold comfort in this passage.

This does not mean there is no future purpose of God for Israel. Many appeal to such passages as Galatians 6:16 to support the belief that now "the Israel of God" is the church and that there is no future purpose of God for Israel. This can be done only by ignoring the plain teaching of Paul a little later when he expanded on this theme for three chapters (Rom. 9–11).[3]

The third implication of special revelation is Holy Scripture. To the

3. See my commentary on Romans in *Broadman Bible Commentary* (Nashville: Broadman Press, 1970), Vol. 10.

Holy Land and Holy Nation must be added the Holy Book, the Bible, the record of the historical revelation and the story of the land and the people to whom the original revelation was made known and who made the first response. If God's supreme revelation was made in history, as all biblical faith proclaims, then no writings may ever supplant the primacy of those records judged by the first witnesses as inspired of God for his people. The inspiration of the Scripture will be discussed in the next section, but here those documents are mentioned as an inseparable part of God's word to man and as the supreme source of Christian theology.

We are not saying that Scripture is the sole source of Christian faith. It is the supreme source, not only because of its proximity to the events of God's special disclosures but because of the testimony through the centuries of those who read them as "the oracles of God" (Rom. 3:2). It is necessary to become Christian agnostics, suspicious of all other religions, of philosophies and sciences as media of a general knowledge of God, to say God's voice is heard here and in no other source.

This point needs to be put forcefully, for there are those who feel bound to blast all other sources of revelation in order to exalt the authority and value of Holy Scripture. Scripture is supreme and developing apostolic tradition is secondary, but it surely is right to give attention to experience and revelation, culture and reason also.[4]

The Dialogue of Special Revelation

Revelation always implies reception. God's revelation is, in biblical language, God's word, and the reception is man's faith. It is a dialogue, not a monologue of either God or man. Neither God nor man speaks to himself in historical revelation. Historical revelation is that stream of salvation history in which there is this correspondence or meeting between the I and the Thou, to put it in terms of theological personalism. Despite the modern derogatory meaning of the phrase "the I and the Thou," that was once the New Testament meaning in the Authorized Version of an oracle (Acts 7:38; Rom. 3:2; Heb. 5:12; 1 Pet. 4:11) based upon the Old Testament usage for the inner sanctuary (2 Sam. 16:23; 1 Kings 6:16; 8:6; 2 Chron. 4:20; Ps. 28:2).

God's word is used in Holy Scripture with a threefold meaning, but the three are a unity. The most basic meaning is the prophetic word of God summed up in 2 Peter 1:19 in the apostolic declaration that "we have the prophetic word made more sure." This Old Testament meaning of the Word of God is profound.[5] Older beliefs about God communicating through dreams, the casting of lots and consulting the dead become secondary in

4. John Macquarrie, *Principles of Christian Theology* (New York: Charles Scribner's Sons, 1966), pp. 4-17.
5. Walther Eichrodt, *Theology of the Old Testament*, tr. J. A. Baker (Philadelphia: The Westminster Press, 1967), Vol. II, pp. 69-80.

the light of the prophetic word (cf. 1 Sam. 28:6f.). God's word is God's revelation of himself. It is the instrument of God's action in history, and God's action is to create. When God utters his word, thought becomes action. In fact, "the Hebrew mind did not distinguish between thought and action."[6]

God's word in historical action is the clue for understanding Deuteronomy and the Deuteronomic history from Joshua through 2 Kings. From the prophet Moses to the second Moses, Jesus, the prophet like Moses, God's word is heard in the succession of prophets (Deut. 18:15–18). God's word in the heart makes nothing too hard (Deut. 30:11–14; cf. Ps. 119:9–16). God's word in creative action has the same efficacy (Isa. 40:6–8). When it goes forth it does not return empty and void (Isa. 55:10f.). Yes!

> By the word of the Lord the heavens were made,
>   and all their host by the breath of his mouth. (Ps. 33:6)

The proclaimed word is the New Testament counterpart to the Old Testament prophetic word. The prophetic word is promise, but the proclaimed word is fulfillment. One is prophecy, the other is preaching. Karl Barth puts the proclaimed word first, but he does not make sufficient distinction between the two covenants.

The proclaimed word may take the form of preaching or teaching. In preaching the fulfillment, the new age in Jesus Christ is announced. In salvation history, Jesus goes forth to sow the word of God (Luke 8:11), and the growth of the word is seen in the increase of the disciples (Acts 6:7; 9:31; 12:24; 16:5; 19:20; 18:30f.). As the prophetic word was summarized in Deuteronomic history, so apostolic history is summarized in its first thirty years in six "books" of five years each. That is the significance of the six references in Acts last made.

As teaching, God's word becomes sound doctrine or healthy teaching. Unsound doctrine is the wind that tosses the immature to and fro (Eph. 4:14), a disease that will destroy the faith (2 Tim. 2:17; 2 Tim. 4:3f.). Sound doctrine confutes heresy and puts the opponent to shame (Titus 1:9; 2:7, 10). It exposes pagan morals, nourishes faith, and saves the teacher and his hearers (1 Tim. 1:10; 4:6, 13, 16). A good teacher as well as the apostle is rewarded for his faithful teaching (1 Tim. 5:17; 6:1; 2 Tim. 3:10, 16; 4:3). This emphasis on *didascalia* or doctrine is often deplored as a degeneration of the apostolic preaching, but they are the two forms by which mature disciples are molded in evangelism and education. The two supplement, first by making disciples, then by maturing them. Doctrine is dead only when it is not lived (Jas. 1:22).

God's personal Word is the third and final form of his disclosure. This

---

6. Edmond Jacob, *Theology of the Old Testament*, tr. Arthur W. Heathcote and Philip J. Allcock (London: Hodder and Stoughton, 1958), p. 128.

is a special emphasis in the incarnational Christology of the New Testament. "In many and various ways God spoke of old to our fathers by the prophets, but in the latter days he has spoken to us by a Son" (Heb. 1:1f.). This is the Word of God that is "living and active" and "before him no creature is hidden" (Heb. 4:12f.). The Word here is plainly a Person, the great high priest and living Lord Jesus.

The nearest to a systematized concept of God's word as a Person is to be found in the Johannine writings. The first of the twelve great hymns that make up 1 John is a personification of the Word of God (1:1–4).[7] A hymn to the Word or Logos has long been recognized in the prologue of the Gospel of John (1:1–5, 9f., 14, 18). The Word is none other than the eternal Son of God who became flesh in Jesus Christ.

Man's faith is the other side of the dialogue in special revelation. It is the human response to the divine revelation. Hearing the word in the Old Testament prophets is compared to hearing a lion roar (Amos 1:2; 3:8). "Hear this word" (Amos 3:1; 5:1) means heed the word of the Lord. It is a characteristic formula of the eighth-century prophets (Hosea 4:1; 5:1; Micah 1:2; 3:1; 6:1). It is formalized in the *Shema* as the central creed of Judaism (Deut. 6:4).

The subjective side of this objective event is described as a fire in the bones of Jeremiah (20:9; cf. 23:9). Even though Job's friend Eliphaz is not called a prophet, Gerhard von Rad quotes his testimony as the best description of the subjective experience of an oracle (Job 4:12–17).[8] This is what it means to hear a word from the Lord.

Believing the word is the New Testament idiom for hearing the word, for hearing is believing in the action of God through his word. The Old Testament and New Testament idioms are united in a creed with a comment applied to the Deuteronomic concept of the word. The word that enables in Deuteronomy 30:14 is interpreted as the word that saves in the creed of Romans 10:9 which says:

> If you will confess with your lips that Jesus is Lord
> and believe in your heart God raised him from the dead,
> you will be saved.

Believing in the heart and the act of confession are one in the parallel as thought and action are one in Hebrew.

11. Revelation and Inspiration

It is well that the question of inspiration be discussed at this point, for some basic agreement on this issue is necessary to establish common ground

---

7. See my book *The Letters of John* (Waco, Texas: Word, Inc., 1970).
8. *Old Testament Theology*, tr. D. M. G. Stalker (Philadelphia: The Westminster Press, 1965), II, 68.

between conservative and liberal Christians. The broad biblical basis for belief in the inspiration of Scripture will be surveyed before going into the thicket of historical theories.

Any statement about the biblical teachings on inspiration must be based upon examples, for no creedal passages are to be found. However, two summaries may serve as helpful points for the organization of the materials available. One speaks of the inspiration of holy men and the other of Holy Scripture.

Biblical Teachings

The inspiration of holy men is prior to Holy Scripture, for there were inspired prophets in the time of oral transmission. Both are included in 2 Peter 1:20f.: "First of all you must understand this, that no prophecy of scripture is a matter of one's own interpretation, because no prophecy ever came by the impulse of man, but men moved by the Holy Spirit spoke from God."

This movement of the Holy Spirit from God is the exact impression received from the Deuteronomic historians. As the transition is made from the ecstatic power of the judges, the *shopetim*, to the ecstatic prophecy of the cultic prophets, the *nebiim*, the picture is one of possession of the prophet by the Spirit of the Lord (1 Sam. 10:1–13). Saul was "turned into another man" as "God gave him another heart" (10:6, 9). Saul uttered ecstatic prophecy when the Spirit came upon him (10:6, 13). Those who followed Saul were a combination of the two, "men of valor whose hearts God had touched" (10:26). Ecstatic power was manifested when "the Spirit of the Lord took possession of Gideon" (Judg. 6:34). This experience of appearing "touched" is the meaning of possession. Ecstatic utterances are first mentioned in the Balaam oracles (Num. 24:3f.).

This phenomenon of possession among the so-called cultic prophets is raised to the higher level of inspiration in the classical prophets. Micaiah has been called "the first of the classical prophets" because of his break with the older cultic prophets (1 Kings 22:1–28).[9] His prophetic inspiration takes on the form of visions and voices that are more rational than ecstatic possession. He reports what he heard and saw with the same formula as the eighth-century prophets: "Therefore, hear the word of the Lord" (22:19, 28).[10]

New Testament prophetism reflects the same distinction in ranking inspired prophecy above ecstatic utterances in tongues (1 Cor. 14). The boundary again is the rational content of the utterance. Praying and singing with the human mind and the human spirit, the *nous* and the *pneuma*, are

---

9. Cf. Theodore Robinson, *Prophecy and the Prophets in Ancient Israel* (London: Gerald Duckworth, 1953), p. 39.
10. For details on Old Testament prophetism see Johannes Lindblom, *Prophecy in Ancient Israel*, Second Edition (Philadelphia: Muhlenberg Press, 1962).

higher forms of inspiration than praying and singing in ecstatic tongues in which only the human spirit, the *pneuma*, is active.[11]

When this is applied to the inspiration of Holy Scripture it requires a view broad enough to include the historical writings of the Old Testament and Luke–Acts of the New Testament, as well as the almost dictation view of inspiration found in such apocalyptic writings as Daniel and Revelation. *The inspiration of Holy Scripture* became a theological question when oral tradition became a written record. A complex process of composition leads from the first documents to the central summary of Old Testament Scripture. Speaking of the Septuagint, the Greek translation of the Old Testament containing the Apocrypha, 2 Timothy 3:16f. says: "All scripture is inspired by God and profitable for teaching, for reproof, for correction and for training in righteousness, that the man of God may be complete, equipped for every good work." After general agreement on the New Testament canon was achieved, this was usually applied to all Greek and Latin Bibles until the Protestant Reformation.

The formation of the Old Testament has been a matter of controversy over the last two centuries. It is impossible even to sketch this history, but the present situation may be stated by reference to two types of Bibles that are available. The views of many Christians who resist the historical reconstruction of biblical criticism are fairly stated in *The New Scofield Reference Bible* of 1967. The views of those who believe the inspiration and authority of the Scriptures are not undermined by biblical criticism are presented in *The Jerusalem Bible* of 1966 sponsored by Roman Catholics and *The New Oxford Annotated Bible* of 1973 endorsed by both Protestant and Roman Catholic scholarship. Protestants, Catholics, and Jews have collaborated on *The Interpreter's Dictionary of the Bible* of 1962, and this will introduce one to most of the current issues and much of the literature.

The canonization of Holy Scripture is not as complex as the composition, but there are also theological issues that shape the doctrines of the revelation and inspiration of the Holy Scriptures.

The Old Testament canon has three parts. The Torah or Law of Moses has five scrolls, began with Moses and reached its present form by 400 B.C. The Prophets, including the four scrolls of the Former Prophets (Joshua, Judges, 1–2 Samuel, 1–2 Kings) and the four scrolls of the Later Prophets (Isaiah, Jeremiah, Ezekiel, the Twelve Minor Prophets), reached their present form before 200 B.C. The rest of the Hebrew Old Testament has not been changed since the Council of Jamnia in A.D. 90. The Hebrew Old Testament is the same for both Judaism and Protestantism. The most debated issue in the Christian use of the Old Testament canon arose when

11. On New Testament prophetism see Harold A. Guy, *New Testament Prophecy* (London: The Epworth Press, 1947).

The Apocrypha, included in the Greek and Latin Bibles from their beginnings, was segregated by Luther in his German translation and eliminated in the Geneva Bible of 1560.

The New Testament canon was not always the same in the ancient church. Around A.D. 150, Marcion appeared in Rome with a canon that included only a short version of the Gospel of Luke and Paul's letters without the Pastorals, as is evident from Books IV and V, of Tertullian's polemical work *Against Marcion*. It is possible that Phoebe took not only Romans to Rome, but 1, 2 Thessalonians, written in Corinth also, and 1, 2 Corinthians, written to Corinth. Marcion's canon perhaps began in the Lycus Valley when Tychicus arrived with a letter for Colossae, with Philemon, and a letter for Laodicea (perhaps Ephesians) that were to be read and exchanged (Col. 4:16). At some later time, before the Pastorals were available, the rest of Paul's letters were collected, perhaps by Onesimus in Ephesus, and this, combined with proto-Luke, became the New Testament canon for Asia that Marcion used when he went from Asia to Rome.

The New Testament canon of twenty-seven books had gained general acceptance by the time Athanasius of Alexandria wrote his Paschal Letter of 367, and this was accepted by Jerome in 391 and confirmed at the Synod of Carthage in 397. Luther raised serious questions about five of these writings (James, Hebrews, 2 Peter, Jude, Revelation) and Calvin had little use for Revelation. Many would raise questions today about a closed canon. Would it be possible to add, say, the letter of Paul mentioned in 1 Cor. 5:9, 11, if it should be found? The very question has implications for biblical revelation and inspiration. Perhaps, since it would have no influence on years of tradition, such a writing should be added as an appendix.

Historical Theories

A doctrine of inspiration was not fully formulated until the Protestant Reformation when biblical authority became the supreme appeal over ecclesiastical tradition. A doctrine of biblical authority produced theories of inspiration. The Roman Catholic reaction to the Reformation declared that both Scripture and tradition were dictated by the Holy Spirit. On April 8, 1546, the Council of Trent declared that the whole of Scripture, as well as the body of unwritten tradition, was given *Spiritu sancto dictante*, at the dictation of the Holy Spirit. Vatican Council I, 1869-70 and *Providentissimus Deus*, an encyclical by Pope Leo XIII in 1893, reaffirmed this dictation view. Later pronouncements, especially *Spiritus Paraclitus* by Benedict XV in 1920 and *Afflante Spiritu* by Pius XII in 1943, dealt with the issue, but a dramatic debate took place in 1962. When the conservative constitution *Dei Verbum* was presented to Vatican II, Pope John XXIII intervened and appointed a special commission to rewrite it. The new draft, enacted on Nov. 18, 1965 by a vote of 2,344 to 6, subordinated tradition to Scripture and confined inerrancy to matters pertaining to salvation. The modern historical approach to the study of the Scriptures was approved, and the two-source view of revelation was left an open issue.[12]

The Reformers resisted the unwritten tradition, but they too adopted the dictation theory of biblical inspiration. Lutheranism hardened into a mold of biblical rigidity that still resists the historical reconstruction of biblical history and any effort to adapt the early chapters of Genesis to the modern scientific view of the world and man. A current example of this is the conflict at Concordia Theological Seminary in which the Missouri Synod of the Lutheran Church is called back to the pre-scientific and pre-critical views of the Reformation.[13]

Historic Calvinism taught the dictation view of inspiration for Holy Scripture. When Louis Cappel of the French academy of Saumur denied the verbal inspiration of the Hebrew text of the Old Testament, the Helvetic Consensus *(Formula consensus ecclesiarum Helveticarum)* of 1675 declared even the Hebrew vowel points, added centuries after the close of the canon, to be inspired. Even after the Helvetic Consensus was no longer required by most adherents of the Second Swiss Confession of 1566, this belief was widely held. The classic defense of the plenary verbal inspiration of the Holy Scriptures was no doubt Louis Gaussen's *Theopneustia* (1840), and this is the usual basis for most later defenders of the theory.

By the end of the nineteenth century A. H. Strong, in his *Systematic Theology* (1886), could delineate four theories of inspiration: (1) the intuition theory that is but the higher development of natural insight into truth, (2) the illumination theory that adds the belief in the inspiration of the writer but not of the writing, (3) the dictation theory that regards the writers as passive, and (4) the dynamic theory that holds to both a human and a divine element in inspiration. This last theory he regarded as the true view, so he was able to accept much of modern science, including evolution and higher criticism.[14] Other modified Calvinists among Baptists found Strong's view acceptable. A conservative as staunch as J. McKee Adams seemed to hold the dynamic view.[15]

The dictation view is, however, very much alive. Most who speak of the Bible as "God's inspired, infallible, and inerrant word" stop short of Strong's dynamic view. A storm of protest went up among Southern Baptists when Clifton J. Allen, in the introductory article to the *Broadman Bible*

12. *Documents of Vatican II*, pp. 107-132.
13. Robert Preus, *The Inspiration of the Scripture* (Mankato, Minnesota: Lutheran Synod Book Co., 1955); *The Theology of Post-Reformation Lutheranism* (St. Louis: Concordia Publishing House, 1970), pp. 254-378.
14. Edition of 1906, pp. vii, 202-212.
15. *Our Bible* (Nashville, Tennessee: Sunday School Board of the Southern Baptist Convention, 1937), p. 35.

Commentary (1969), advocated the dynamic view.[16] It is not sufficient to repeat Strong's exclusive approach. Even the intuition and illumination views have value when stated positively. Bible writers did have great natural insight as well as illumination by the Holy Spirit. Some passages in the Bible do approach passive reception, even though this is not the usual impression.

A biblical view of inspiration must be broad enough to include the truth in all the historical theories and adequate for a constructive theology in dialogue with the sacred writings of other world religions, the contributions of great systems of philosophy, and the discoveries of modern science. The biblical view is broad enough to include both the view in the late priestly tradition which says the two tables of stone were "written by the finger of God" (Ex. 31:18, cf. 8:19), and the older history by the Yahwist in the Hexateuch who competes with the author of the Early Source in 1–2 Samuel (who may be the same!) for the name "father of history," a title usually given to the Greek historian Herodotus who lived at least five hundred years later. The description of the apocalyptic inspiration of Ezekiel in the Later Prophets comes near to the dictation theory. Luke 1:1–2 describes a historical method evident in the composition of Luke–Acts, but it is no less inspired than Revelation and other apocalyptic writings that describe the writer in a more passive role (Rev. 1:2, 10f.; 4:2; 17:3; 21:10).

This more constructive and comprehensive view, which avoids the excessive defensiveness so often evident, becomes more acceptable where there is dialogue. It is possible to profit much from both the "evangelical" views of Clark Pinnock in his book *Biblical Revelation* (1971) and the "ecumenical" Roman Catholic statement by Bruce Vawter in his *Biblical Inspiration* (1972). What really makes the difference is the fidelity with which the authority of Scripture is elevated above ecclesiastical traditions.

12. Revelation and Authority

Authority is the corollary to inspiration in historical revelation. If one values the inspiration of holy men, he is more likely to exalt the authority of the Holy Spirit; but those who are preoccupied with the inspiration of Holy Scripture presuppose the authority of Scripture. Reliance on the authority of a Holy Church is an attempt to escape from the subjectivity of both personal inspiration and private interpretation. Christian history has often been shaped by the search for some form of authority and by the effort to fix the primary seat for the same.

16. This has now become a controversial issue in American Christianity. See Harold Lindsell, *The Battle for the Bible* (Grand Rapids: Zondervan, 1976) vs. Jack Rogers, ed., *Biblical Authority* (Waco, Texas: Word Books, 1977). Jack Rogers and Donald K. McKim, *The Authority and Interpretation of the Bible* (New York: Harper and Row, 1979) is a rare type of scholarly study on this controversial subject.

The Search for Authority

Through the search for authority the three tendencies have become three traditions. All of these have roots in the New Testament writings and, when the church was still part of Jewish institutionalism, the appeal was directly to God who spoke to the disciples through the Holy Spirit. Boldness (*parrēsia*, freedom to speak) was typical of their witness, as one of the oldest New Testament sources says (Acts 4:13, 29, 31). They thought it better to obey God rather than men and believed God gave the Holy Spirit to those who obeyed him (Acts 3:19; 5:32). Both Jewish and Gentile Hellenistic Christianity continued to sound the charismatic note (Heb. 2:1–4; 1 Cor. 2:10, 12, 14).

The later Johannine writings developed this belief into a doctrine. Subjectivity was checked by appeal to the historical objectivity of the incarnation. Indeed the criterion by which believers were to distinguish the Spirit of truth from the spirit of error was the incarnation (1 John 4:1–6). Testing the spirits continued as a canon into later Christian life. The *Didache*, an early Christian manual, elaborated a number of other tests (11–13).

A hymn to the Paraclete, the Holy Spirit, that can be discerned in the Gospel of John, is the crowning expression of belief in the Spirit of truth who continues the teaching of Jesus after the days of his flesh. There is almost a systematic teaching of the Paraclete as companion (14:15–17), teacher (14:25f.), witness (15:26f.), judge (16:7–11), and guide (16:12–15).

All through the history of the church the Paraclete tradition has sprung forth, often as a spring in the desert. From Montanism in the early church, through mysticism in the Middle Ages, to Pietism in Protestantism and the ecumenical outburst of Pentecostalism in the present the Paraclete tendency has come to the surface.[17] Quakerism does not hesitate to put the Spirit above both Scripture and Church as supreme authority in faith.[18] Some ecumenical leaders who have been nurtured by Protestant liberalism have been so impressed that they have called the Pentecostal tradition "the third force" in Christianity along with the Catholic call to order and the Protestant preaching of doctrine.[19]

---

17. Hans von Campenhausen, *Ecclesiastical Authority and Spiritual Power in the Church of the First Three Centuries*, tr. J. A. Baker (Stanford, Calif.: Stanford University Press, 1969); Ronald Knox, *Enthusiasm* (New York: Oxford University Press, 1950); Rufus Jones, *The Flowering of Mysticism* (New York: Macmillan and Company, 1939); Walter J. Hollenweger, *The Pentecostals* (London: SCM, 1972).
18. Dean Freiday, ed., *Barclay's Apology* (Philadelphia: Friends Book Store, 1967).
19. Lesslie Newbigin, *The Household of God* (New York: Friendship Press, 1954); Henry P. Van Dusen, *Spirit, Son and Father* (New York: Scribner's Sons, 1958). Ecumenical relations are certainly more than a question of *Holy Writ or Holy Church*, to use the title of a book by George Tavard (London: Burns and Oates, 1959).

The authority of the Church becomes a check against subjective spirituality. The most persistent appeal of this tradition is to the teachings of the New Testament on the primacy of Peter. It is obvious on examination that this rests on a more fragile foundation in the New Testament than does the authority of the Spirit.

The tacit assumption that Matthew 16:18 declares Peter to be the rock on which the church is founded is rocky indeed. It is well known that the Greek text says the church is built on a *petra*, feminine meaning bedrock, and that Peter is called *petros*, masculine meaning boulder rock. Appeal to a Palestinian Aramaic original in which *kepa*, rock, is used both as a proper name and a common noun does not explain the distinction in the Greek translation, if there be an original Aramaic! It is possible that the feminine *autēs* (it) in Matthew 16:19 refers to the feminine *petra*. In this case the *ekklēsia*, church, is built upon the *petra* and the gates of Hades will not prevail against the *petra*.

What then is the meaning of *petra*? 1 Peter 2:8 uses the word for Christ, not Peter or Peter's faith, as is so often said. Paul says that the *petra* from which the Israelites drank as it followed them in the wilderness was Christ (1 Cor. 10:4). Peter is called *Cephas* in the New Testament (1 Cor. 1:12; 3:22; 9:5; 15:5; Gal. 1:18; 2:9; John 1:42), but the references in Paul hardly support the primacy of Peter outside Jewish Christianity.[20] The primacy of Paul in Gentile Christianity may safely be argued from Galatians 1:18–2:10. Paul most certainly thought Peter fallible "when Cephas came to Antioch" and Paul "opposed him to his face, because he stood condemned" (2:11).

The primacy of the Pope is a claim more fragile than the primacy of Peter. Historical circumstances have given the Roman See a unique place that need never be envied. That does not mean the theories of apostolic succession and Papal infallibility are well grounded. Apostolic succession for the Roman clergy from Peter and Paul, Roman martyrs, is a claim difficult to dispute. This was claimed by Clement about A.D. 95 (1 Clem. 5:44), but the claim that a valid ministry rests upon continuity with this succession has been questioned by most Protestants and asserted with qualifications by some Catholics.[21]

The claim for Papal infallibility makes relevant the distinction between the doctrinal succession of Irenaeus and the sacramental succession of Augustine. Protestantism was an appeal to apostolic doctrine over the sacramental traditions of a hierarchy. The claim for Papal authority has a long

20. For a Catholic-Lutheran dialogue on this issue see Raymond Brown, et al., *Peter in the New Testament* (Minneapolis: Augsburg, 1973); yet the interpretation mentioned here gets no attention.
21. *A Catholic Dictionary of Theology* (New York: Thomas Nelson and Sons, 1962), I, 131-133; *Sacramentum Mundi* (New York: Herder and Herder, 1968), I, 86-90.

history that is most instructive for understanding the reasons for the Reformation.[22]

After the Reformation, sacramental succession reached a tragic stage under Pope Pius IX, who reversed the theology of Thomas Aquinas by his definition of the Immaculate Conception of Mary in 1854 and declared himself infallible in 1870. It is true that only Pius XII has used such authority, when he in 1950 defined a second dogma about the Virgin Mary that has no New Testament support, the dogma of the Assumption. Eager ecumenists avoid this problem as much as possible, but the most courageous challenge to the dogma of Papal infallibility has come from a Roman Catholic who celebrated the centennial of the dogma with a constructive critique that offers hope to Protestants devoted to the apostolic faith of the New Testament.[23]

The authority of Scripture above all claims of subjective inspiration by the Holy Spirit and objective appeal to the sacramental authority of the church was formulated as a standard because of this devotion to the apostolic faith to be found in the New Testament. The New Testament writers themselves appealed to the Old Testament for authority (1 Pet. 1:10–12; 2 Pet. 1:19f.; 2 Tim. 3:14–17). Scripture in the New Testament has reference to the Old Testament, but at one place Paul's letters are classified as Scripture also (2 Pet. 3:16). There is no doubt that the Gospel of John assigned authority not only to the Old Testament (5:39) but to the Gospel itself (20:31). With the formation of a New Testament canon of the apostolic teachings this was logically applied to all the other New Testament writings. It has already been noted that the composition of the Scriptures has become a critical problem because of biblical criticism, as canonization was a problem at the Reformation.

The Seat of Authority

This long search for authority makes the problem of the *"seat" of authority* very complex. This concept of a "seat" for authority comes from the seat or cathedra in which the Bishop sits to define dogmas and morals, but it may also be used for a restatement of authority in the light of the present situation.

A safe starting point is with the authority of Christ himself. The short form of the Great Commission of Christ has formulated this (Matt. 28:19f.):

> All authority in heaven and on earth has been given to me. Go therefore and make disciples of all nations in my name, teaching them to observe all that I have commanded you, and, lo, I am with you always, to the close of the age.

22. E. Giles, *Documents Illustrating Papal Authority* (London: S.P.C.K., 1952).
23. Hans Küng, *Infallible?*, tr. Edward Quinn (Garden City, N.Y.: Doubleday & Company, 1971).

The crucial question is how the authority of the risen Lord is expressed in the historical situation of the present.

The authority of Christ is present where the Spirit of Christ is present. That is the meaning of Pentecost, even after the institutionalism of Luke–Acts is taken into full consideration. From the time Jesus began his ministry at the age of thirty (Luke 3:23), after the devil left him, "until an opportune time" (4:13) and he "returned in the power of the Spirit into Galilee" (4:14) and until the return of Satan when he "entered into Judas called Iscariot" (22:3), there is a Jubilee year, "the acceptable year of the Lord" (4:19), A.D. 29-30. That is the meaning of the synagogue preaching of Jesus, after John was put in prison (3:20; 4:16-30).

At Pentecost the ministry of the Spirit begun in Jesus continues in the disciples. The power that came upon the Virgin Mary (Lk. 1:35) came upon disciples (24:49; Acts 1:1-8; 2:1-4). From the baptism of the Church with the Spirit to the end of Acts there was another thirty years of salvation history, A.D. 30-59.

This theological chronology creates a historical problem when compared with the longer ministry of Jesus in the Gospel of John (2:23; 6:4; 13:1), but it is not insurmountable. It is the concept of the Spirit's authority that is so important. The authority of the Father was given to the Son (5:27), but at the Feast of Tabernacles in Jerusalem Jesus proclaimed the promise of the Spirit to the disciples (7:37-39). That is the meaning of the Paraclete Hymn mentioned above and the insufflation of the Spirit on the first Easter evening (20:19-23). Both the breathing of the Spirit in John in the Upper Room on the first day after the resurrection and the baptism with the Spirit in the Temple fifty days after the death of Jesus have great significance in the witness of the Spirit to the authority of Christ.

The authority of the church as the body of Christ is a special concern for Paul. In 1 Corinthians a confession (12:1-3), a hymn about the Holy Trinity (4-6), a catalogue of spiritual gifts (7-11), a second hymn about the body of Christ and the baptism with the Spirit (12-13), followed by a second lesson (14-21), a third hymn on love (13:1-13), and by a third lesson on order (14:1-39) illustrate the authority of the Spirit in an early worship service.

The Pentecost liturgy that has come to be known as Ephesians is the consummation of this teaching about the Church as the earthly body of Christ today (1:23; 2:16; 4:4, 12, 16; 5:23, 28, 30).[24] This lofty view of the Church as the one body of Christ on earth today is rooted in belief that finds creedal formulation as "one body and one Spirit" (4:4; cf. 1:13f., 17; 2:18, 22; 3:5, 16; 4:3, 23; 5:18; 6:17f.). That is why God intends to unite

---

24. John C. Kirby, *Ephesians: Baptism and Pentecost* (Montreal: McGill University Press, 1968). Cf. the mammoth commentary by Markus Barth, *Ephesians* (Garden City, N.Y.: Doubleday and Co., 1974).

all mankind in the body of Christ (1:9f.) and make known his manifold wisdom "through the church" (3:10). A high view of the baptism in the Spirit leads to a high view of the church as the body of Christ when both are related to the Lordship of Christ, the head of the body, the church (Col. 1:18).

The authority of the Scriptures points also to the authority of Christ. It is possible to read the Scriptures in the bondage of legalism. A Pentecost *midrash* by Paul based on Exodus 34:34 strips this masquerade of Judaism from the mind and heart by a call to repentance: when "a man turns to the Lord," as Moses did on Sinai (2 Cor. 3:12–18), the mask must be taken away. There is always the danger that in searching the Scriptures one may miss the Christ about which they testify (John 5:39f.). The legalism of Judaism has been a constant threat where the authority of Christ has been subordinate to any one of the three traditions of authority outlined above.

13. Revelation and History

The Pentecost *midrash* of Paul in 2 Corinthians 3 contains two of the most important concepts of historical revelation: the two covenants and the two ages. They will be used as the two divisions of this section.

The Two Covenants

The two covenants may be observed even in covenant theology. John Calvin, in his commentary on Hebrews 9:16, makes a distinction between a covenant, as in Hebrew, and a covenant which included a testament, as in Greek. Hebrews 9:16, according to Calvin, "refers to this second meaning and argues that that promise could only be ratified and valid if they had been sealed by the death of Christ." This line of argument put Hebrews 9:22 at the very heart of Calvinism. Calvin passes over the qualification "under the law," but he hesitates at the words "almost everything is purified with blood," for "he seems to indicate that some things were cleansed differently." Nevertheless, he concludes "that even water derived its power of cleansing from the sacrifice so that the apostle is right when he says at the end that there is no remission without blood."[25]

This distinction between covenant and testament and the argument for the necessity of the shedding of blood were worked into a complete system of covenant theology in a classic work called *On the Covenant and Testament of God* (*De federe et testamento Dei*) by Johannes Cocceius of Holland in 1648, and this became known as Federal theology. Cocceius found Jesus Christ everywhere in the Old Testament, but he maintained the pattern of

25. For details on Calvin see Wilhelm Niesel, *The Theology of Calvin*, tr. Harold Knight (Philadelphia: The Westminster Press, 1956), pp. 104-109. The most extreme development of one covenant is J. Barton Payne, *The Theology of the Older Testament* (Grand Rapids, Michigan: Zondervan Publishing Co., 1962).

promise and fulfillment. Others, however, were not so wise, and their proof-text method led to a "flat Bible" that made little distinction between Leviticus and Hebrews as well as the old and new covenants.

Dispensational theology, which has developed into a dogmatic system in the twentieth century, adopted many of the typological teachings of Federal theology, but it went in another direction in its development of the idea of the covenants. Out of the nineteenth-century roots of John Nelson Darby's teachings on eschatology, C. I. Scofield gave this movement great impetus with his *Scofield Reference Bible* (1909, 1917) in which he argued not for one covenant but for eight! On the very page where Hebrews speaks of a "first covenant" and "a second" (8:7), a "new" and an "old" (8:13), there is a note that insists on eight. That is strange arithmetic!

The two covenants are so clearly taught in the New Testament that it is difficult to see how a professed biblical theology can miss it. Paul's allegory of the two women says plainly: "these women are two covenants" (Gal. 4:24). His Pentecost *midrash* on Exodus 34:34, already mentioned, speaks of the Old Testament as the Old Covenant (2 Cor. 3:14). One of the major Old Testament theologies of our time has made the covenant the first principle of Old Testament theology.[26] The uniqueness of the old covenant is found in its promise of the new. This brings to fruition the seeds sown by Calvin and Cocceius.

The new covenant is first applied to the cup at the Last Supper in one of the central sayings on the death of Christ: "This cup which is poured out for you is the new covenant in my blood" (Luke 22:20). Even if some manuscripts omit these words in Luke, it is found in essentially the same form in 1 Corinthians 11:25 where the context is that of the Lord's Supper. In time this was applied to all the New Testament writings.

When interpreted in salvation history, the concept of the new covenant brings these beliefs into focus. The first is that of the finality of the revelation and redemption in the new covenant ratified by the death of Jesus Christ (Heb. 1:1-4). This redemptive revelation is once for all, never to be repeated, as the *ephapax* in Hebrews makes so emphatic (Heb. 7:27; 9:12, 26; 10:10). The new covenant predicted by the prophet Jeremiah has come to pass (Heb. 8:8-12). Promise has reached fulfillment, as Calvin and Cocceius say so clearly. "In many and various ways God spoke of all to our fathers by the prophets, but in these days he has spoken to us by a Son" (Heb. 1:1-2).

As the finality of the new covenant points from promise to fulfillment, so the freedom of the new covenant leads from slavery to sonship. This is the theme of Paul's great Galatian letter that moved Martin Luther to write his most important commentary as Hebrews did the same for Calvin. Here is the heart of Reformation theology that intended to rebuild the theological

26. Walther Eichrodt, *op. cit.*, Vol. 1.

cathedral on a biblical foundation. After the allegory of the two women, who represent the two covenants, is the proclamation of liberation from all legalism and ceremonialism: "For freedom Christ has set us free; stand fast therefore, and do not submit again to a yoke of slavery" (Gal. 5:1; cf. 1:6–3:3; 4:8–11).

Paul's Pentecost *midrash* on Exodus 34:34 is again the classic statement. There are two sets of tablets, the tablets of stone on which Moses wrote the Decalogue that enslaves and the tablets of human hearts on which living letters are written by the Spirit of the living God (2 Cor. 3:1–3). There are two covenants, the old which is the written code that kills and the new in which the Spirit gives eternal life (4–6). There are two dispensations, that of death and condemnation and that of the Spirit and righteousness (7–11). Finally, there are two faces, that of Moses and the law that fades away in the light of the brightness of the glory revealed in the face of Jesus Christ (12–18). The Lord in Exodus 34:34 means the Spirit, "and where the Spirit of the Lord is, there is freedom" (2 Cor. 3:17). That is the message of the ministers of the new covenant.

The Two Ages

The two dispensations of 2 Corinthians 3:7–11 are a great embarrassment to the dispensational theology of the advocates of the *Scofield Reference Bible* who teach that there are seven dispensations and eight covenants. Neither is to be found in the New Testament, but the belief in two ages, along with two covenants, is the very hinge of salvation history. The teachings of Jesus about the blasphemy of the Spirit speak of sin that "will not be forgiven in this age or in the age to come" (Matt. 12:32). Those who suffer loss in "this time" for the sake of Jesus will receive "in the age to come eternal life" (Mark 10:30). In the present world it is possible to taste of "the powers of the age to come" (Heb. 6:5). There is a revelation of God in this present age, but the final and full revelation of God is in the age to come.

God's revelation comes as redemption from sin "in this present evil age" (Gal. 1:4). As a subjective experience it is an enigma (1 Cor. 13:12). The Greek word *ainigma* means a riddle,[27] and it is this riddle that the Gnostics ignored. Their claim of a direct and complete knowledge of God in the present age could only puff one up in an inflated form of egotism (8:1). Paul is very careful to check himself when he speaks of believers as those who "have come to know God" by adding "rather to be known by God" (Gal. 4:9). Only God has direct and complete knowledge in this present age. "Now I know in part; then shall I understand fully, even as I have been fully understood" (1 Cor. 13:12).

There is a progressive understanding of the riddle of revelation through

27. See *Theological Dictionary of the New Testament*, I, 178-180.

the liberation and illumination by the Holy Spirit when one, like Moses, "turns to the Lord" (2 Cor. 3:15), but this comes by reflecting God's glory seen in the face of Jesus Christ in the process of transformation by the Spirit that leads to the perfection at the end (2 Cor. 3:18f.). Perfect knowledge of God in this present age can be ours only in the relative sense of Christian maturity, but absolute perfection in which the riddle of revelation is completely clarified comes only at the resurrection of the dead (Phil. 3:12-16).

The form of revelation is also indirect in this present age. The Christ who became Jesus by the incarnation is the supreme form of all revelation (Phil. 2:6-8):

> Who, in the form of God subsisting,
> did not count equality with God a thing to be grasped for,
> but he emptied himself,
> the form of a slave taking,
> in the likeness of men becoming
> and in fashion being found as a man,
> he humbled himself,
> becoming obedient unto death
> (even death on a cross).

This rather literal translation using four parallels clarifies earlier statements by Paul. The Poor Jesus is the model for giving in the section on the Great Collection by which the Macedonians became a model to all other churches (2 Cor. 8:9). It does not support the claim of the Irvingites, a view strangely adopted by Karl Barth, that Christ became a sinner.[28] This claim, based on Romans 8:3, contradicts 2 Cor. 5:21 despite the incredible exegesis of this passage in the writings of Nels Ferré.[29] The objective form and the subjective enigma form the poles of our human dialogue with God by the Holy Spirit.

God has already pitched his tent among men in the incarnation, but this knowledge comes through the mediation of Jesus Christ, not through direct vision of God. The fifth stanza in the Hymn to the Logos in John 1:1-18 says:

> No one has ever seen God;
> the only Son [or God in some manuscripts]
> who is in the bosom of the Father,
> he has made him known.

This meaning is expanded in another Johannine hymn (1 John 2:28-3:3). A part of this Hymn Against Sin says:

28. D. M. Baillie, *God Was in Christ* (New York: Charles Scribner's Sons, 1948), pp. 16f.
29. *Evil and the Christian Faith* (New York: Harper & Brothers, 1947), pp. 34f.

And now, little children, abide in him,
*   so that when he is manifested we may have confidence*
*   (parrēsia) and not shrink from him in shame at his coming*
*   (parousia). . . .*
Beloved, now are we God's children;
*   and it is not yet manifested what we shall be,*
but we know that if it is manifested we shall be like him,
*   for we shall see him as he is.*
And everyone who has this hope set on him
*   purifies himself as that One is pure.*

It is necessary to translate this passage anew because most translations make the false assumption that it speaks of the *parousia* and manifestation of Christ, as in Paul, rather than the future apocalypse of God. The only reference to Jesus Christ in the passage is "that One" (*ekeinos*), always used of Jesus in 1 John.[30]

God has pitched his tent among us in the past. That is the meaning of the discourses at the Feast of Tabernacles in the Gospel of John (7–9), but there is a future and final dwelling of God with his people when the new Jerusalem descends out of heaven and all things are made new (Rev. 21:1–4). At that time knowledge of God will be direct. "There shall no more be anything accursed, but the throne of God and of the Lamb shall be in it, and his servants shall worship him; they shall see his face, and his name shall be on their foreheads" (22:3f.).

The glory of God that is the disclosure of God's presence in salvation history is a major teaching in biblical theology (Acts 7:2, 55).[31] It is perhaps the most important symbol in biblical apocalypticism. The Day of the Son of Man is the future disclosure of God in all his glory (Matt. 24:30; 25:31). The Day of the Son of Man is what Paul called the Day of Jesus Christ or the *parousia* (2 Thess. 2:1–12).

The great apocalypse of God, which was a belief in eclipse, has now come to the very center of theological discussion. This change was stimulated by the publication of *Theology of Hope* (1964) by Jürgen Moltmann. His polemic against the existentialism of Rudolf Bultmann has unfortunately driven him into strange contradictions. No room is allowed for present theophanies of God, yet it was in a theophany that Abraham received the promise for the future about which Moltmann talks so much (Gen. 12:7).

It is not necessary to rule out all epiphanies of God, past and present, in order to affirm the Great Apocalypse of God in the future. Without some

30. For further justification of this interpretation see my study *The Letters of John* (Waco, Texas: Word, Inc., 1970), pp. 57-60.
31. Emil Brunner, *Revelation and Reason*, tr. Olive Wyon (Philadelphia: The Westminster Press, 1946), pp. 185-193; A. M. Ramsey, *The Glory of God and the Transfiguration of Christ* (London: Longmans, Green and Co., 1949); R. E. Hough, *The Ministry of the Glory Cloud* (New York: Philosophical Library, 1955).

paradigm furnished by epiphanies, visions of the future are without much content. Epiphanies are indeed incomplete and indirect manifestations of God, but they furnish glimpses of the complete and direct revelation of God in the future. This excessive fear of epiphany religion in Moltmann accounts for the lack of emphasis on the baptism in the Holy Spirit into the body of Christ in Moltmann's theology. The present experience of the Holy Spirit is a primary reason for belief in future glory.

The word of God as event includes the inspiration of Scripture as the supreme authority in historical revelation, but this does not mean that reason is excluded in the study of Scripture.

B. GENERAL REVELATION

14. The Meaning of General Revelation

Now a hotly debated question arises. It is the question whether there is genuine revelation of God outside the special revelation of the Scriptures. The function of such revelation, if any, in the condemnation or salvation of man will be discussed at the end of this chapter. Since those who reject the claim for a general revelation of God appeal to the Scriptures, the best procedure will be to examine the biblical witness first, then to discuss the solutions proposed in church history.

The Biblical Witness

At the beginning of the Bible, before the covenant with Abraham, the Melchizedek model appears (Gen. 14:17–24). If, as already proposed, the covenant relation is the very spine of special revelation, then this story about Abram paying tithes to a Canaanite king-priest is most significant. The story not only exalts Melchizedek above Abram, but it clearly identifies the God Most High (*El Elyon*) with the Lord (*Yahweh*) of Israel (cf. Num. 24:16). If his relation to God was not genuine, it is strange indeed that both the Old Testament and the New make him a model of the Messiah (Ps. 110; Heb. 7:1–17).

After the covenant was made with Abram, now the Abraham of the Promise, a Midianite priest is made equal to if not superior to Moses. At least he counsels Moses in an amazing manner (Ex. 18:1–27). It is possible, indeed probable, that Jethro was already a worshiper of the Lord when Moses met him (Ex. 3:1). It is significant that the theophany of the Lord to Moses in the bush took place while Moses was in the service of Jethro (cf. Deut. 33:16).

Jürgen Moltmann is clearly unsatisfactory when he dismisses all epiphany religion in favor of promissory history.[32] Even to Abram the promise was made in a vision (Gen. 15:1; cf. 12:7). The direct self-revelation of God

32. *Theology of Hope*, tr. James W. Leitch (New York: Harper & Row, 1967), pp. 95-102.

in the future at the Great Apocalypse does not rule out an indirect self-revelation of God in theophanies and epiphanies, visions and dreams and auditions, as well. Moltmann rightly regards "history" as an indirect self-revelation of God, but he excludes "epiphany religions," as he calls them, with a vengeance.

Indirect self-revelation of God in the history of the promise in the covenant relation, as both Walther Eichrodt and Gerhard von Rad have pointed out with such penetration, is second only to the self-revelation of God in Jesus Christ at both his first and second coming. The history of the promise itself speaks of a general revelation of God in the cycles of the created order along with the special revelations in historical events.

Psalm 19 has what pious people have often called the Two Books of God in creation and the covenant. The two are joined together in praise. In the great Hymn to God the Creator in Psalm 104 there are many parallels to the Egyptian "Hymn to Aton" which dates from the time of Akhenaton (1380-1362 B.C.).[33] The Psalmist seems to accept this monotheism as a revelation of *Yahweh* under the name of *Aton,* just as *Yahweh* was identified with *El Elyon,* a Canaanite concept, in the story of Melchizedek.

He clearly sees the God of creation and the God of history as one in revelation when he puts Psalm 104 before the revelation of God in the mighty deeds of history of Psalms 105-106. It is possible to confine this recognition of the God of history in the order of creation to the covenant relation, as I understand Karl Barth doing, but this seems to be strained interpretation. The most obvious conclusion is that the true God revealed himself indirectly in the monotheism of Akhenaton. Why not, if his mighty deeds were done outside Israel in Cyrus the Great (Isa. 44:28; 45:1-25)?

In these days when the problem of evil and suffering has become a popular argument against belief in God, it is well that the testimony of Job be heard again. There are few testimonies equal to the voice out of the whirlwind (Job 38:1-42:6) that calls for Job to listen to the mysterious depths of the order of creation. Indirect revelation of God becomes direct in the ringing response at the end which says (42:5f.):

> *I have heard of thee by the hearing of the ear,*
> > *but now my eye sees thee;*
> *therefore I despise myself,*
> > *and repent in dust and ashes.*

The Idea of the Holy by Rudolf Otto has many other testimonies of this type.

In the New Testament the witness to a general revelation of God in creation and conscience outside the covenant and prior to Christ is implied in many places, but the *locus classicus* is Romans 1:18-4:25. A general revelation of God is possible in creation at any time, in any place, and to

33. *The Interpreter's Bible*, Vol. 4, pp. 550-556.

any person. That is the meaning we attach to the term general revelation. Special revelation is a historical event at a particular time, in a particular place and to a particular person. Those who reject a general revelation of God in creation have difficulty with Romans 1:20:

> Ever since the creation of the world his invisible nature,
> namely, his eternal power and deity,
> has been clearly perceived in the things that have been made.

It is possible to say that this general revelation of God has only a negative function that leaves man without excuse, as I understand Emil Brunner to say. But what kind of God is he who gives man enough knowledge to damn him but not enough to save him? The perception of God in creation has both negative and positive possibilities.

These possibilities, both negative and positive, are certainly present in Paul's statement about a general revelation of God in the human conscience. Romans 2:14–16 says:

> When the Gentiles who have not the law do by nature what the
>   law requires,
> they are a law to themselves,
> even though they do not have the law.
> They show that what the law requires is written on their hearts,
> while their conscience also bears witness
> and their conflicting thoughts accuse or perhaps excuse them
> (on that Day when,
> according to my gospel,
> God judges the secrets of men by Jesus Christ).

The witness of conscience, when followed, may lead to acquittal at the final judgment. Of course, it is possible for conscience to be corrupted, as it is possible for the gospel to be corrupted, but it does not follow that it will always be corrupted (cf. Romans 2:15; Acts 17:27).

Historical Views

As historical theology developed, a variety of responses were made. The view outlined above is very similar to that of the Church Fathers in the Patristic period, but appeal was made more to the Johannine writings than to Paul.

A theologian as conservative as Justin Martyr did not hesitate to call those persons Christians whose human reason came to know the pre-existent Logos long before the Logos became flesh in Jesus Christ. Around 150 A.D., he wrote in his *Apology* (66:4) that "those who live according to reason are Christians, even though they are accounted atheists. Such were Socrates and Heraclitus among the Greeks, and those like them. . . ."[34] The

---

34. Henry Bettenson, *Documents of the Christian Church*, Second Edition (London: Oxford University Press, 1963), p. 6.

Second Apology adds: "Whatever has been uttered aright by any men in any place belongs to Christians" (II.13).[35]

Liberals like Clement of Alexandria went beyond Justin by claiming that Greek "philosophy was necessary to the Greeks for righteousness, until the coming of the Lord—For philosophy was a 'schoolmaster to bring the Greek mind to Christ, as the Law brought the Hebrews.' Thus philosophy was a preparation, paving the way towards perfection in Christ" (*Stromateis* I. v. 28).[36] That is why Plato had such a great influence on Greek theology, especially after Origen of Alexandria. The influence of Greek philosophy was not altogether a mistake, and in a practical way it was necessary in the witness of the church.

The Schoolmen of the Middle Ages continued to make much use of Plato and Plotinus, the neo-Platonist of the third century, but Aristotle became dominant after St. Thomas Aquinas adopted many of his views in the thirteenth century. It has already been noted how St. Thomas built his two-story theological cathedral with natural theology on the first level and revealed theology on the second. In Europe, even today, that is why the Th.D. degree is higher than the Ph.D. (*pace* Association of Theological Schools). However, reason took the believer a long way before a special revelation of God was needed to complete theology. The natural theology of St. Thomas is in a general way what we are calling general revelation, but more properly it is a philosophy of religion.

At the time of the Protestant Reformers this favorable view toward general revelation and natural theology appeared among the Christian humanists. Huldreich Zwingli, in his *Exposition of Faith* (addressed to Francis I), enumerated those who would enter eternal life, and among them were Heracles, Theseus, Socrates, Aristides, Numan, Camillus, the two Catos, and the Scipios. Why so? "There has been no good man, there will be no saintly spirit and there is no faithful soul, from the beginning of the world till its end, whom you will not see there with God."[37] This agrees with an extraordinary New Testament statement: "He who does good is of God" (3 John 11). However, all this infuriated Martin Luther, who made little room for reason, and the more humanistic Calvin was unwilling to assign more than a negative function to reason and general revelation.

This view of Calvin was revived by Emil Brunner, but this infuriated Karl Barth.[38] Their famous debate on this issue is most instructive as Barth defends special revelation as Jesus Christ only and Brunner tries to find a place for what seems to be the view of the Apostle Paul. Barth's extremism

---

35. *Ibid.*, p. 7.
36. *Ibid.*, pp. 8f.
37. Quoted from Hendrik Kraemer, *Religion and the Christian Faith* (London: Lutterworth Press, 1956), p. 176.
38. Emil Brunner and Karl Barth, *Natural Theology*, tr. Peter Fraenkel (London: G. Bles, 1946).

may be understood sympathetically in the light of his struggle against a Nazism that claimed a revelation of God in the German blood and soil (*Blut und Boden*), but it is too narrow for biblical support and the missionary task of the church.

A doctrine of revelation that includes a general revelation of God in all creation and in every human conscience, plus the special revelation of God in the historical events of the Old Testament as promise, with the supreme revelation of God in Jesus Christ, including both his first coming and the Great Apocalypse of God in the future at his second appearing, is required for our time. This will be defended in the positive acceptance of the light of religion, philosophy, and science that follows.

John Baillie, with whom I agree so often, is surely on the right trail when he advocates the old idea of "a Noahic covenant" with all mankind. However, this covenant needs to be restated in the context of modern thought, as Baillie does.[39]

The chief objection to the belief that before the covenant with Abraham and outside the Scriptures and Christian tradition there is the possibility of a personal relation with God is an appeal to certain Scriptures that are thought to rule such encounter out.

The first appeal is usually to Acts 4:12, but that must be harmonized with Acts 14:17 and 17:27. It is the Name, the personal reality of God known in personal relation, that saves, not knowledge *about* the historical Jesus. When the great missionary chapter Romans 10 is used as an objection, the appeal to Psalm 19 along with Moses and the prophets in verses 18–21 should not be overlooked.[40]

A last-ditch stand against a personal revelation of God outside the covenant with Abraham is usually made by using John 14:6: "No one comes to the Father but by me." However, this must be understood in the light of the pre-existence of the Son of God. Abraham was indeed saved by believing the promise. Jesus said: "Your father Abraham rejoiced to see my day; he saw it and was glad" (John 8:56). The one who spoke through the historical Jesus also said: "Before Abraham was, I am" (John 8:58). Could not the pre-existent one make himself known to people before Abraham and to those today who never heard of Abraham, much less Jesus? The post-existent Jesus can make himself known also to those who do not know about the historical Jesus.

Those who perish, according to the Gospel of John, are those who are confronted by the Light of the world shining through Jesus and who reject this light, not those who have only the starlight of general revelation. Ponder these pronouncements in John also. "And this is the judgment, that the light

39. *The Idea of Revelation in Recent Thought* (New York: Columbia University Press, 1956), pp. 125-133.
40. For details see my exposition in the *Broadman Bible Commentary*, Vol. 10.

has come into the world, and men loved darkness rather than light, because their deeds were evil" (3:19). "If you were blind, you would have no guilt; but now that you say, 'We see,' your guilt remains" (John 9:41). "If I had not come and spoken to them, they would not have sin; but now they have no excuse for their sin" (John 15:22). Sin for John is unbelief (16:9). Guilt before God is gauged by the light people have, and those who follow the light they have will surely be accepted by God. A high view of the pre-existent and post-existent Son of God avoids the problems of a low missionary theology that confines all the revelation of the Son of God to the days of his flesh. The *supreme* revelation was in the days of his flesh, but it is not the sole revelation of the Son of God.

15. Revelation and Religion

The "positive" philosophy of Auguste Comte (1798-1857) traced the "Religion of Humanity" through three stages: the theological, the metaphysical and the scientific. The first two seek causes behind nature and history and develop into systems of religion and philosophy. The third relies on natural law and altruism toward humanity. When Comte saw that this required a system of devotion to humanity on a religious basis, he founded his own religion in which his wife took the place of the Virgin Mary in the religion he renounced.

In our own time this evolutionary philosophy that leads to secularity has been popularized in *The Secular City* by Harvey Cox (1966), but there are many signs that this too has led to a revival of religious concern and metaphysical philosophy, not only in Cox but in the social situation that only a few years ago boasted about "a brave new world" that no longer required "the God hypothesis" and the great systems of metaphysical thinking.

There is no doubt that society seems to move through these three stages, but there seems also to be "a law of the eternal return" to religion. That brings into focus the question of relations between the claims of special revelation and all systems of religion, philosophy and science. This will be discussed in the order of Comte's stages, beginning with biblical revelation and then building a basis for understanding by examining alternative ways of thinking.

Clues in Biblical Revelation

Against the background of tribal religion before the Exodus from Egypt, the religion of Israel passed through two main periods. These may be called the exclusive view in the period of monolatry before the Babylonian Exile and the period of monotheism that became pronounced during the Exile and was proclaimed by the great prophets until the time of Jesus.

Monolatry means the worship of one God, even though the reality of other gods is not yet denied. This is at times called henotheism, but the term monolatry puts more emphasis on the system of religious observance. A good illustration is found in the Decalogue where the Lord commanded: "You shall have no other gods before me" (Ex. 20:3). The Lord will tolerate no rivals: "You shall worship no other god, for the Lord, whose name is Jealous, is a jealous God" (Ex. 34:14). This is basic in covenant religion.

This view is dominant in all of the Deuteronomic writings of the Old Testament. A classic statement is in the Song of Moses (Deut. 32:8f.):

> When the Most High gave to the nations their inheritance,
>   when he separated the sons of men,
> he fixed the bounds of the peoples
>   according to the number of the sons of God.
> For the Lord's portion is his people,
>   Jacob his allotted heritage.

A dramatic presentation of this point of view may be seen in the Mt. Carmel contest between Elijah and the prophets of Baal (1 Kings 18).

Monolatry was followed by a monotheism that denied the very existence of other gods. This view is found repeatedly in Isaiah 40–55, the section called Deutero-Isaiah by literary critics. It is a great step forward when the Lord, the Holy One, proclaims through the prophet (Isa. 44:6):

> I am the first and the last;
>   besides me there is no god.

That is why the Lord can work through Cyrus the Great, the founder of the Persian Empire, as well as through Moses, the founder of the nation of Israel (Isa. 45:4–6).

Monotheism leads to a universal purpose and a universal purpose to missions, for those who claim to know the One True God are duty bound to share this knowledge with other nations and peoples who have not come to this light. This is a shift from the exclusive view of monolatry to the inclusive view of monotheism. It may lead to the time when the pure offerings of Gentiles are more acceptable to the Lord than the corrupt offerings of Israel (Malachi 1:11).

This inclusive view of monotheism blossoms in the missionary theology of Gentile Christianity. There is no recognition of a distinctive value in polytheism, but there are suggestions that the true God has made himself known to individuals who follow the light they have even in that social setting. God has indeed made Jesus both Lord and Christ (Acts 2:36), but the name given to him by God is by no means confined to the historical Jesus (Acts 4:12). The Name has been made known hundreds of times in the Old Testament alone, and there is no reason to reject the evidence that this personal reality of God has been made known outside the Old Testament. Other statements in Acts would support this inclusive view.

Two models of Christian monotheism seem relevant to the missionary theology of the church. The first is Paul's preaching in Lycaonia. After the healing in Lystra he said: "In past generations he allowed all the nations to walk in their own ways; yet he did not leave himself without a witness, for he did good and gave you from heaven rains and fruitful seasons" (Acts 14:16f.). They are called away from the system of nature worship and polytheism, but God's goodness has been manifested in the cycle of the seasons. God "has not left himself without a witness."

The same claim is made when Paul confronted the philosophical religion in Athens (Acts 17:22–34). God is described as the creator and sustainer of the world and as the Lord of all history and judge of all mankind. In the midst of all this all nations "should seek God, in hope that they might feel after him and find him" (17:27). The Greek tense, the second aorist optative, indicates that this is a possibility. How was it possible for them to find him? "Yet he is not far from each of us." A Greek prophet from Crete is quoted favorably (cf. Titus 1:12). He was Epimenides who said of God: "In him we live and move and have our existence."[41] The poet Aratus of Soli is also quoted, for he said of God: "For we are indeed his offspring."

These utterances became the text for Paul's famous climax that made the distinction between a time of ignorance that is excusable and the call to repentance in the preaching of the gospel. "The times of ignorance God overlooked, but now he commands all men everywhere to repent, because he has fixed a day on which he will judge the world in righteousness by a man whom he has appointed, and of this he has given assurance to all men by raising him from the dead" (Acts 17:30f.). There are still people who live in their "times of ignorance" because the gospel call to repentance has not been heard through an acceptable messenger.

The general revelation of God may be compared to the light of the stars when the moon and sun are unseen. This light is often obscured by clouds of superstition and tradition, but there are those who perceive it. The special revelation of promise in the Old Testament may be compared to the moon which often turns attention from the stars, but the fulfillment of all revelation in the New Testament is the Sun of Righteousness rising "with healing in his wings" (Malachi 4:2). The light "shines in darkness" until the Logos becomes flesh, but the incarnation does not extinguish this general revelation of God. It fulfills it.

Encounter with Other Religions

It is no easy task to translate the few suggestions in biblical revelation into the context of comparative religions. Those who have wrestled with this

---

41. Ernst Haenchen, *The Acts of the Apostles*, tr. R. McL. Wilson (Philadelphia: The Westminster Press, 1971), p. 524, n. 3, assigns this to Plato, but this is not convincing.

problem have divided into both exclusive and inclusive camps. Calvinism has tended toward an exclusive view that sees no value in other world religions, but Catholicism has seldom closed the door of possibility that a personal encounter with God may take place outside the special revelation of the Scriptures and Church tradition. Here is a place where dialogue with brotherly love is needed. There is enough heat already, but there is not enough light.

The exclusive Calvinistic view has been presented in great detail by Hendrik Kraemer, the first Director of the Ecumenical Institute of the World Council of Churches. Building on the foundations laid down by Karl Barth, Kraemer wrote his book *The Christian Message in a Non-Christian World* at the request of the International Missionary Council for use in connection with the world missionary conference held at Tambaram, Madras, India, in 1938. His view excludes all valid revelations of God and genuine encounters with God other than with the Word of God made flesh in the concrete historical revelation of Jesus Christ.

It is seldom that a writer lives to restate his views with the thoroughness to be found in Kraemer's second book of monumental importance, *Religion and the Christian Faith* (1956). Despite the learned studies of theologians such as Justin Martyr, Clement of Alexandria, and Huldreich Zwingli, he modifies his former views at only one point. His words are of great importance:

> In one respect I have tried to improve upon an attitude taken in my previous book. Acknowledging, in *The Christian Message in a Non-Christian World*, that God certainly works amongst the peoples and in the religions outside the Biblical realm of revelation, I added that it was not feasible to try to point out where spots of this divine activity are, and so I stressed mainly the point that the non-Christian religions are great human achievements.
>
> By my endeavour in this present book to point out the religious consciousness as the place of dialectic encounter with God, and of giving a negative, or partly positive but often distortedly positive, answer to this encounter, I have made more room to express definite opinions (though necessarily always open to revision) on this encounter.
>
> This means that I do not any longer maintain the unfeasibility of such attempts. It does not mean, however, that I reject my former thesis that there is a great amount of human achievement in all religions. It only means that I take now a more dialectical view of this thesis than in my previous book.[42]

We have taken this long quotation from his preface because many

42. (London: Lutterworth Press, 1956), pp. 7f.

readers of his previous book seem never to have read this great improvement. The great man was a guest on our campus soon after these words were published, and he defended this "dialectical view" before a student forum and later in my home as I probed his position. I find it a good statement, but I think it goes much further beyond his previous statement than these words indicate. However, he has gotten out of the strait-jacket of early Barthianism, and that is what is significant.

The missionary theology of Catholicism may be contrasted with that of Calvinism. This inclusive view, finally and painfully presented by Kraemer, is not far from the official pronouncements of Vatican Council II in *Lumen Gentium* (Light of the Nations), November 21, 1964. After an introduction by the eminent biblical scholar Cardinal Augustin Bea, Pope Paul VI pronounced that remarkable document on the Constitution of the Church which has these words toward the end of Chapter II:

> Those also can attain to everlasting salvation who through no fault of their own do not know the gospel of Christ or His Church, yet sincerely seek God and, moved by grace strive by their deeds to do His will as it is known to them through the dictates of conscience. Nor does divine Providence deny the help necessary for salvation to those who, without blame on their part, have not yet arrived at an explicit knowledge of God, but strive to live a good life, thanks to his grace.[43]

Things like this were being said by W. O. Carver of Southern Baptist Theological Seminary at the beginning of the twentieth century.[44]

Roman Catholic scholars seem never to have rejected a general revelation of God with positive value. Against the background of St. Thomas Aquinas this is understandable, but the most advanced statements seem to come out of the Jesuit order rather than from St. Thomas' Dominican disciples.

Future discussions will need to take account of the views elaborated in Bombay, India, November 25-28, 1964, by a group of Roman Catholic theologians concerned with the missionary task of the church.[45] The growing contacts with other religions will require consideration of this relationship. At present the old pyramid arguments that saw the Christian faith, both Law and Gospel, as the fulfillment of both the religions of law in the Near East and the religions of redemption in the Far East are not without value. Indeed, they seem required as more and more "parallels" to biblical

43. *Documents of Vatican II* (New York: Guild Press, 1966), p. 35.
44. W. O. Carver, *Missions and Modern Thought* (New York: The Macmillan Company, 1910), pp. 119-145.
45. Joseph Neuner, ed., *Christian Revelation and World Religions* (London: Burns & Oates, 1967).

faith come to light in the study of other religions. It is surely time for all Christians to do such study and when possible to know those of other religions on a personal basis.[46] This does not require a denial of the uniqueness of Jesus Christ and eliminate missionary effort and zeal. Indeed, such encounter deepens Christian faith.

16. Revelation and Philosophy

Those who believe that the supreme revelation of God is to be found in the special revelation of God in Jesus Christ may also take an exclusive or an inclusive attitude toward philosophy. An exclusive attitude assumes the polemical posture and looks upon all philosophy as a threat to faith.

Greek Philosophy

Tertullian of Carthage (c. 160-240) was a defender of the faith against Greek philosophy, yet the discerning reader detects a stream of Stoicism running through much of his theology. He seems unaware of this influence in his famous rhetorical questions (*Prescriptions Against Heretics*, VII):

> *What is there in common between Athens and Jerusalem?*
> *What between the Academy and the Church?*
> *What between heretics and Christians?*

It seems much safer to look upon philosophy with the appreciation of Clement of Alexandria who, with some exaggeration, said:

> For Philosophy was a "schoolmaster" to bring the Greeks to Christ, as the Law brought the Jews to Christ. Thus philosophy was a preparation, paving the way toward perfection in Christ (*Stromateis*, I. v. 28).

There are systems of naturalistic and humanistic philosophies that contribute little and may even collide with Christian faith, but the major systems of metaphysics have often been more of a handmaiden than a hindrance.

This appreciation for philosophy has characterized most major theologians in the history of the church. The classical philosophies were helpful in Catholic theology. The philosophy of Plato (427-347 B.C.) raised ethical, metaphysical, and theological questions that could not be avoided by a thoughtful theologian. No ethical theory could afford to ignore Plato's insights into goodness, truth, and beauty. What theologian would reject the idea that life should be concerned about "goodness of soul"?

It is true that an exaggerated dualism between body and soul opened

---

46. A good start may be made in Ninian Smart, *A Dialogue of Religions* (London: SCM, 1960); *The Religious Experience of Mankind* (New York: Charles Scribner's Sons, 1969); Hans Küng, *On Being a Christian*, tr. Edward Quinn (Garden City, N.Y.: Doubleday and Co., 1976), pp. 89-174.

the door to an unbiblical teaching on the pre-existence and transmigration of the soul, but rebels against Plato have gone too far in their denial that the human spirit can survive the death of the body and the possibility that there is an invisible world of forms or ideas beyond matter (for example, process philosophy).

Plato's theology has fascinated and influenced many theologians. His dialogue called the *Timaeus* had a doctrine of creation in which a Demiurge works as a craftsman to bring the world into existence. The whole process is guided by a cosmic Mind *(Nous)* or Soul *(Psyche)* which makes the visible world conform to the image of an eternal archetype. It is tempting to identify this Absolute Idea with God and the Demiurge with his Son, and many have fallen for the suggestion. Book X of his *Laws* advances a cosmological argument that traces all motion and goodness to a source which he called a "perfectly good soul." A second world-soul, the source of evil, is called *ananke* (necessity). *The Creator and the Adversary* (1958) by Edwin Lewis sounds much like this argument, and the Augustinian tradition in theology never allowed it to be forgotten.

Aristotle (384-322 B.C.), the tutor of Alexander the Great, did not have a major influence on Christian theology until the thirteenth century, but it is not difficult to see why St. Thomas Aquinas used him. Aristotle worked all things into a hierarchy in which the *Idea of the Good* alone is real. All things go back to this First Cause which he called the Prime Mover *(Prōton Kinoun)*. A cause could be formal, material, final or efficient, and Aristotle, in his account of the whole of reality, located all but the material cause in God. His view of the human soul united form and matter more closely than did Plato's.

At the time of the Protestant Reformation there was a resurgence of the exclusive attitude toward philosophy. Martin Luther was at first appointed to teach the philosophy of Aristotle in the newly-established University of Wittenberg, but he was delighted when he became professor of theology. All the rest of his life he found his first love in the Scriptures which he thought got to the kernel in the nut.

Luther left a place for philosophy, but he always put Scripture not only above Aristotle but also above the early Church Fathers and the medieval Schoolmen who made much of Greek philosophy.[47] One of the comments attributed to him may sum up his view: "Let philosophy remain within her bounds, as God has appointed, and let us make use of her as of a character in comedy. . . ."[48]

Neither Luther nor Lutheranism was able to avoid philosophical presuppositions. Luther himself got his Platonism second-hand in his prefer-

---

47. Jaroslav Pelikan, *Companion Volume to Luther's Works* (Saint Louis: Concordia Publishing House, 1959), pp. 77f.
48. *The Table-Talk*, tr. William Hazlitt (Philadelphia: The United Lutheran Publishing House, n.d.), p. 27.

ence for Augustine. Lutheranism today has many ambiguities. Paul Tillich was so inclusive in his attitude toward philosophy that, as has been noted, his *Systematic Theology* is really a philosophical ontology that has great appreciation for Parmenides of Elea (c. 500 B.C.) who said: "It is necessary both to say and to think that being is; for it is possible that being is, and it is impossible that non-being is; this is what I bid thee ponder."[49]

On the other hand, Jürgen Moltmann, in his focus upon the future, declares that the contemplation of the god of Parmenides "does not make a meaningful experience of history possible, but only the meaningful negation of history."[50] Yet Moltmann depends much on the philosophy of Georg Hegel mediated through the Marxist Ernst Bloch! Philosophy has a way of coming in the back door after it is ushered out the front. This happens also with the most rigid biblicists among the Lutherans (and others).

Calvinism continued the exclusive attitude toward philosophy. One of the most widely used summaries on Calvin's theology says: "Must we once again recall that the first sentence of the *Institutes* itself speaks about the 'sum of all our wisdom' which is nothing else but the sum of sacred doctrines and of Holy Scripture itself? Whoever overlooks or evades these programmatic statements of Calvin and discovers in his writings a *theologia naturalis* can hardly be regarded seriously as a scholar."[51]

Smarting under the sting of these words, one turns to read the opening words of the *Institutes* again and finds that the first reference to Holy Scripture is Acts 17:28, which explains the knowledge of self and God with the words: "In him we live and move and have our existence." Let it be said again that the words are attributed to the Cretan poet and philosopher Epimenides, who lived in the seventh century B.C. This was the poet Paul called a prophet (Titus 1:12).

Modern Philosophy

Modern philosophy and theology have been in constant dialogue and debate. It has already been seen how the Protestant theology of the nineteenth century was heavily in debt to the critical philosophy of Immanuel Kant in particular and modern philosophy in general. The revolt of biblical theology against philosophy under the leadership of Karl Barth most certainly did not escape the influence of philosophy.

At least three currents of contemporary philosophy have contributed to the reconstruction of theology since the theological typhoon of Barthianism. David H. Kelsey has described the decline of biblical authority as

---

49. *Selections from Early Greek Philosophy*, Second Edition, ed. Milton C. Nahm (New York: F. S. Crofts, 1944), p. 115.
50. *Theology of Hope*, tr. James W. Leitch (New York: Harper and Row, 1967), p. 29.
51. Wilhelm Niesel, *The Theology of Calvin*, tr. Harold Knight (Philadelphia: The Westminster Press, 1956), p. 40.

a failure to agree on a concept of scriptural authority.[52] This is due in part to the philosophical presuppositions brought to the Bible.

The most influential philosophy in recent theology has been existentialism. Existentialism understands man in terms of his actual human existence rather than in terms of essence. As a free and responsible self his anxiety drives him toward God or nothing, so existentialism may be either religious or atheistic.

The religious roots of existentialism may be found in such biblical passages as Psalm 139 in which God's searching presence and power are so central; or Romans 7 which portrays man's divided self; or the *Confessions* of Augustine which begin with the confession that man is restless until he finds rest in God; or the *Pensées* of Pascal which declare that the "heart has its reasons of which reason knows not."

Just as Socrates with his challenge for man to know himself *(gnōthi sauton)* could be called the ancient father of existentialism, so the great Dane Søren Kierkegaard (1813-1855) is the modern father of Protestant existentialism. There are also devout Catholic existentialists such as Gabriel Marcel whose Gifford Lectures on *The Mystery of Being* (1950, 1951) develops into a Christian personalism with a note of hope.

Some have seen secular existentialism in *The Will to Power* (1901) by Nietzsche, but the profoundest expression of philosophical personalism is no doubt *Being and Time* (1927) by Martin Heidegger. His analysis of man in history and time later deepens in concern for metaphysical mystery that makes it possible to identify God and being, a view distinctly congenial with Christian theology. In 1935 Martin Heidegger concluded a lecture with what he considered the first question of philosophy: "Why is there being at all rather than nothingness?" He thought that human thought and existence are dominated by the answer to this question. *An Introduction to Metaphysics* (1953) was his later answer to that question. Language becomes a metaphysical game for him when man finds his orientation by asking this question anew. This, however, has not happened in J. P. Sartre whose *Being and Nothingness* (1943) is a view of man for himself in an absurd world that leads only to anguish and disgust.

Heidegger's existentialism became the foundation for Rudolf Bultmann's interpretation of New Testament theology in which profound insights into man's sin and his justification by faith may be found. His effort to demythologize Jesus Christ and God are not so satisfactory.

It has already been noted how Paul Tillich and John Macquarrie have used Heidegger's existentialism in the restatement of a Christian theology for those who falter before fundamentalist literalism. Existentialism may be either a hindrance or a handmaid to faith depending on the point of

52. *The Uses of Scripture in Recent Theology* (Philadelphia: Fortress Press, 1975).

pilgrimage in which one finds himself. In the pages that follow it is more often a help to faith and hope than a hindrance.

A second philosophical system that has been used for the reconstruction of a Christian theology for our time is process philosophy. It is a mistake to assume that it is something entirely new. It is a precise statement in the context of modern science, but it is no exaggeration to say that one of the first process philosophers was Heraclitus of Ephesus (c. 500 B.C.) who saw all things as an ever-flowing river into which one can step only once! When a second step is taken all has changed. His vision was one of constant flux. However, the classic statement of process philosophy thus far is *Process and Reality* (1929), the Gifford Lectures by A. N. Whitehead (1928-29). There is now a corrected edition (1978).

It is necessary first to clarify some of the concepts of process philosophy. The basic concept is that of *actual occasions*. These are moments of experience, not bits of matter, dynamic becomings, not static beings. Process *is* reality, and outside process there is nothing at all.

A second concept of great importance is that of *eternal objects*. Again this is a dynamic concept far removed from the eternal forms of Plato and the abstract universals of Aristotle that are supposed to have reality beyond process. Eternal objects are pure potentials within the process itself.

A third concept sharpens the difference from Greek metaphysics. The idea of apprehension has been displaced by the term *prehension*. Prehensions are the concrete facts of relatedness, not reflections about objective or subjective realities. They are objective and subjective at once, as each relation has both a physical and conceptual aspect. A prehension is a feel for what is real. Newness increases as prehensions move away from physical repetition to the conceptual, much as in emergent evolution.

A fourth concept describes the group relations in reality. It is called the *nexus*, the group of connections in a society of actual occasions. The stream of reality in process is ever changing in endless relation, much as Heraclitus observed.

When this view of reality is applied to the concept of God, static being is discarded. God is viewed as that di-polar reality being enriched by a process that has both a primordial aspect of pure potentials and a consequent aspect in which God conserves all creative advance in himself. The subjective aim of God is satisfied in this act of concretion.

In christology the concept of two static natures is replaced by a disclosure of the divine in the act of the human. The Johannine teaching about Jesus abiding in God and God abiding in Jesus is no more an anomaly. It is a picture of reality in process. Immortality is interpreted in objective terms that have little positive to say about the subjective immortality of each person, but it does not exclude the eternal life of those who abide in God. In some ways it is more congenial with Johannine eschatology than the static and substantial concepts of Plato.

Most of the basic doctrines of Christian theology have been reviewed and revised in the light of process philosophy, but this does not mean that Christian theology is threatened by the increased use of this point of view. In some ways continuous creation, the living soul, the church as a fellowship, dynamic sacramentalism and religion in general are more meaningful in the context of process philosophy than in terms of the static categories of Greek philosophy. At several points this will be elaborated, but there is much to be done in the future.[53]

A third philosophical movement that has been used by theology has helped clarify religious language and magnify mystery in religion. At first this is not obvious to the traditionalist, but some Christian responses to the movement are most rewarding.

Against the background of logical positivism this renewed concern with the problem of language came to be known as analytical philosophy. To say it is a renewed concern is to recall how such thinkers as Plato and René Descartes were also concerned about the clarity and limitation of language. An Austrian from Vienna who did most of his teaching at Cambridge University in England has become almost a cultic figure for his followers. His writings have become almost canonical for the cult. These are the *Tractatus Logico-philosophicus* (1918), the dictated *Blue Books* (1933-34) and *Brown Books* (1934-35), and the posthumous *Philosophical Investigations* (completed in 1949) by Ludwig Josef Johann Wittgenstein (1889-1951).[54]

The wisdom of Wittgenstein, as it has been called, was primarily concerned with logic and language, but there are cryptic references to the inexpressible and mystical. Speaking of his *Tractatus*, Wittgenstein said: "Its whole meaning could be summed up somewhat as follows: what can be said at all can be said clearly: and where one cannot speak, thereon one must be silent."[55] Of this silence he later said: "There is indeed the inexpressible. This *shows* itself: it is the mystical."[56]

It is true that Wittgenstein did not develop a system of knowledge by which the mystical is related to scientific objectivity and philosophical clarity. Had he done so he would not have been the first. How many times do I remember Paul Tillich speaking of *logos* and *mythos* in Plato?

It is really unnecessary panic to use emotive language against analytical philosophy. It is far better to respond in the profound insights of John Baillie in his Gifford Lectures on *The Sense of the Presence of God* (1962). There is a "language-game" of mystery that *"shows"* itself in the mystical as well

53. A helpful introduction is Robert B. Mellert, *What Is Process Philosophy?* (New York: Paulist Press, 1975). A critical symposium with responses is John Cobb's *Theology in Process*, edited by David Ray Griffin and Thomas J. J. Altizer (Philadelphia: The Westminster Press, 1977).
54. William Donald Hudson, *Ludwig Wittgenstein* (Richmond, Va.: John Knox Press, 1968).
55. *Tractatus Logico-philosophicus*, tr. C. K. Ogden (London: Kegan Paul, 1922), p. 27.
56. *Ibid.*, p. 187.

as the precise language-game of scientific objectivity. It was none other than Wittgenstein who said: "Not *how* the world is, is the mystical, but *that* it is."[57] After some attention is given to revelation and scientific objectivity, an attempt will be made to make sense out of this "nonsense" that "shows" itself in mystery.[58]

17. Revelation and Science

If science is interpreted in terms of nature alone, as in most process philosophy and theology, then the more personal and historical dimensions of human experience are distorted. Nature and history can be reduced to one process only when nature is expanded from the normal meaning. It still seems necessary to relate special and general revelation to both historical and natural sciences.

Revelation and Historical Science

Biblical criticism is the English term used to represent the application of historical science to the study of the Bible. At least four types have been used. First, textual criticism that undertakes to get as near to the autographs as possible is used by many conservatives. A second type of criticism becomes more controversial. This search for authorship and date became known as higher criticism. The Pentateuch, Isaiah and Daniel become major storm centers. A third method came to be known as form criticism because it tries to trace the development of the tradition between the historical facts and the literary record. A fourth method is called redaction criticism because it is concerned with changes in literal accounts when used by later writers (e.g. the use of Deuteronomic history by the Chronicler in the Old Testament or the use of Mark by Matthew in the New Testament). All of these are used in a constructive way in the following pages.

Those who appeal to pre-critical creeds and confessions as "guidelines" for interpreting Scripture put themselves in the position in which most historical study of the Bible is excluded. It is really impossible to relate the Bible to the natural sciences until the Bible itself is seen as a historical document conditioned by the times in which various parts were composed. It is not only impossible to take a pre-critical, pre-scientific stance. It is a disaster to try.

Historical science has rescued the Old Testament from irrelevance. Who really believes all the legal and ceremonial regulations of the Old Testament are binding today? Even sectarianism picks and chooses such

57. *Ibid.,* p. 187.
58. Milton Munitz, *The Mystery of Existence,* and the discussion by John Macquarrie in *Thinking About God* (New York: Harper & Row, 1975), pp. 28-42.

distinctives as the Sabbath. Not even the most orthodox Jew keeps or can keep all the Old Testament ritual.

Conservatives adapt to historical science in different ways. Dispensationalism makes much of the seven ages and allegorical exegesis found in the Patristic period of church history. Others also go to extremes and reject most of the conclusions of modern methodology. For example, the vehement Calvinism of J. Barton Payne contends for only one covenant over against the eight in Dispensationalism. Using phrases from Hebrews 9, he writes a *Theology of the Older Testament* (1962), despite the plain teaching on two covenants in Hebrews 8.

The whipping boy of Old Testament biblical criticism is usually Julius Wellhausen (1844-1918) whose *History of Israel* (1878) became a symbol that threatened traditional views of biblical revelation. A good example of the more radical approach to Old Testament criticism is Martin Noth (1902-1968). His books *A History of Pentateuchal Criticism* (1948) and *A History of Israel* (1950) see Old Testament history more in the light of the period in which the documents were composed than as reliable records of ancient traditions. He thought no reliable knowledge was possible about the history of Israel before the tribes were organized into an amphictyony after the invasion of Canaan by the "house of Joseph."

Old Testament criticism has come a long way from Wellhausen to W. F. Albright and his students such as G. Ernest Wright and John Bright. It is difficult to understand why there is such ranting against "the critics" after *A History of Israel* (2nd ed., 1972) by John Bright has been digested, yet one hears sarcastic remarks, from both left and right, about the Albright-Wright-Bright method.

Historical science shapes the understanding of historical revelation. Two Old Testament theologies may be used as examples, much as Noth and Bright represent different views of history.[59] Historical science is clearly conditioned by the historical understanding of the writers when one compares the *Theology of the Old Testament* (1933, 1935, 1939) by Walther Eichrodt with the *Theology of the Old Testament* (1957, 1960) by Gerhard von Rad. Eichrodt's covenant theology is Calvinistic and perpendicular while von Rad's is Lutheran and horizontal. Both affirm historical revelation in strong terms, but both use the methods of historical science to take the reader closer to the historical events in which they believe God has disclosed himself.

If the historical transmission of tradition were static and mechanical, historical science would not be useful. The Bible would just drop down out of heaven, much as a Muslim views the Koran or a Mormon views the golden plates of Joseph Smith. But if God has revealed himself in human

---

59. See the very useful book by D. G. Spriggs, *Two Old Testament Theologies* (London: SCM, 1974).

history, including human thought and experience, then one would expect the dynamic, kerygmatic approach that has not and will never cease growing. Historical revelation requires historical science because it is a living tradition and not dead dogma.[60]

In New Testament theology there are differences in historical methods also. The more radical revision of traditional approaches to New Testament history and revelation is associated with the name of Rudolf Bultmann (1884-1976). His *History of the Synoptic Tradition* (1921) was a landmark in the effort to demythologize the first three Gospels. His *Theology of the New Testament* (1948-1953) represents the results for understanding the apostolic faith. One has little difficulty in seeing through his Lutheranism and existentialism as the shadows of both Martin Luther and Martin Heidegger stand in the wings.

Conservative evangelicals too often treat Bultmann as only a word for blaspheming, yet one would be foolish to ignore the careful studies by George Eldon Ladd of Fuller Theological Seminary. In full awareness of more radical research, he uses biblical criticism and constructs a theology on the basis of historical revelation. His book *The New Testament and Criticism* (1967) represents restrained use of biblical criticism, and *A Theology of the New Testament* (1974) reconstructs the teachings of the apostolic age. A wise student will read both Bultmann and Ladd to his profit.

The main point is that historical revelation is subject to historical study. Historical method may be derived from an *a posteriori* study of the documents, but dedicated concentration on the text is not able to escape the historical context in which the interpretation is done. That is why awareness of our own historical relativity is a restraint to dogmatism. German idealism has unfortunately shaped biblical studies more than British empiricism, but both are major conditioning factors.

Historical relativity has reduced some theologians to skepticism and despair. Since the time of Ernst Troeltsch (1865-1923) the rock of revelation has wrecked the faith of those who, following Albrecht Ritschl, built on the shifting sands of history without metaphysical pilings. Troeltsch gave up theology for the history of philosophy in the last years of his life (1915-23). His struggle with this problem from *The Absoluteness of Christianity and the History of Religions* (1901) to *Historicism and Its Problems* (1922) foreshadows the anguish of faith in his followers, as may be seen in H. Richard Niebuhr's *The Meaning of Revelation* (1941) and Van Harvey's *The Historian and the Believer* (1966). A comparison of Troeltsch's individualism and rationalism with catholicity and mysticism may be seen in

60. Walter Brueggemann and Hans Walter Wolff, *The Vitality of Old Testament Traditions* (Atlanta: John Knox Press, 1975).

the gentle criticism of Baron von Hügel written as an introduction to Troeltsch's last thoughts.[61]

Revelation and Natural Science

The great divide between pre-critical and critical thinking includes modern science as well as modern historical methods. If one can be pre-critical and pre-scientific he can be happy with a medieval Catholic or some forms of Reformation scholastic theology. Those who prescribe ancient creeds and confessions as "guidelines" seem to think this possible. It serves only to make the Bible irrelevant to the educated person. The history of conflict between science and theology has taught little to some, but it is hard to ignore. At this point the insistence on logic and objectivity in analytic philosophy has been an enrichment as well as an embarrassment!

The first major crisis between revelation and natural science arose when the scientific view of space became a threat to tradition. With little difficulty biblical revelation was translated from the big bowl view of ancient Babylon into the context of the Ptolemaic big ball view of ancient Egypt, but the geocentric view groaned in agony under the impact of modern astronomy.

The publication of *The Revolution of the Heavenly Bodies* (1543) by Copernicus was in itself a revolution. Copernicus (1473-1543), Galileo (1564-1641), Kepler (1571-1630) and Newton (1642-1727) used the scientific methods of objectivity and concluded that the earth turned on its axis, but tradition taught otherwise. The shameful treatment of Galileo as he was tried for heresy in Rome should serve as a lesson to those who reject scientific objectivity, but it does not. It was the Roman Church that forced Galileo to recant that should repent. Even Luther railed against those who were unable to see from the long day of Joshua that it is the sun, not the earth, that moves! Calvin took the same view, and the whole story is not a happy one.[62]

Knowledge of astronomy comes from scientific investigation, not divine revelation, but the revelation of God in the heavenly bodies is increased rather than diminished by discoveries down to the big bang theory that is now the center of attention. It is thought the big bang took place about ten billion years ago. Science belongs to discovery in a subject-object relation, but God is known in a subject-Subject relation that comes through disclosure.

Resistance to discoveries in geology resulted also in ridiculous statements.[63] The publication of *The Principles of Geology* (3 vols., 1830-1833)

61. *Christian Thought: Its History and Application* (New York: Living Age Books, 1957), pp. 13-32.
62. Andrew D. White, *A History of the Warfare of Science with Theology* (London: Macmillan and Co., 1896), pp. 114-208.
63. *Ibid.*, pp. 209-248; C. C. Gillespie, *Genesis and Geology* (Cambridge, Mass.: Harvard University Press, 1951).

by Charles Lyell (1797-1875) required a revision in the ancient view of time as astronomy forced a change in the concept of space. Before Lyell the usual explanations required catastrophes to explain geological formations. Afterward, the acceptance of uniform laws of nature were sufficient explanation, but catastrophism still has advocates. More will be said on these problems when the doctrine of creation is discussed.

In geology as in astronomy, British Christianity was more adaptable to science than in Latin countries on the continent. Many of the pioneers in geology were clergymen with a special interest in the natural theology that looked for design in nature as evidence for belief in God. Henry Drummond (1851-97), a layman and professor of natural science, was a well-known geologist and explorer in North America and Central America, yet he was an outstanding evangelist among university groups. D. L. Moody called him the best soul-winner he ever met.

A third crisis relating to revelation and natural science concerned the antiquity of man. Charles Darwin (1809-1882), who published *The Origin of Species* in 1859 and *The Descent of Man* in 1871, at one time considered being a clergyman too, but his theory of natural selection that found an explanation for different species in the survival of the fittest widened the gap between religion and science. The great Drummond used such evidence to support purpose in creation by writing his own book *The Ascent of Man* (1894), and used the theory of the survival of the fittest to support his belief in conditional immortality. This problem will be discussed in a constructive way with the Christian understanding of man.

In summary now, it seems clear that biblical revelation does not require the rejection of the historical method in biblical criticism nor resistance to the scientific method of natural science. A pre-critical and pre-scientific fundamentalism is not required in defense of a Christian theology based on biblical revelation. However, when creation and man come up for discussion, the resurgence of reactionary thought will be noted.

III. GOD

A. THE MYSTERY OF GOD'S BEING

18. The God of the Philosophers

It is difficult to decide on the starting point for approaching the mystery of God's being. If one begins with biblical revelation he has at least two handicaps. First, even the pious are bewildered by a biblical illiteracy that all too often goes to the Bible for little more than proof texts to bolster bias and support "the historic position" of the cult to which they are committed. On the other hand there is the problem of atheistic dogmatism that has so intimidated theology that quick compromises are made with a rigid positivism that pronounces all metaphysics nonsense. In the light of the positive view toward philosophy in the previous section, the God of general revelation will be considered before the same God in special revelation. However, special revelation will be considered before any speculation on the ontological Trinity.

Both the proof-text approach and rigid positivism are rejected as a reconsideration of the classical arguments for belief in God is ventured. Long have nervous theologians panicked at the very suggestion that these arguments need to be revived. Note that these are called "arguments for belief in God," not "proofs for the existence of God." Proofs prejudice the discussion from the beginning by assuming that God is an object in space and time whose so-called existence can be demonstrated by logical propositions. This approach concedes the debate with logical positivism at the start.

It was Paul Tillich who shocked the pious and irritated the impious by declaring that God does not "exist," stand out, as an object among other objects. Boldly he declared that God is Being Itself. I would prefer to say that God is Be-ing Himself, because he is not static essence but transcendent person in which God and being are One dynamic Be-ing. This almost obvious truth upset the pious when John A. T. Robinson published his sensational best-seller *Honest to God* (1963). This has already been recounted.

78

In reviewing recent discussions on God, John Macquarrie takes up the "belief in being" again as the Archimedean point for stating how belief in God can be stated in terms of philosophy. With his general approach no objections need to be made at this point, but it must be said most emphatically that his discussion on "The Problem of God Today" is very much in terms of the classical arguments for belief in God.[1] He is more guarded in terminology, and rightly so, but he hardly supports the sarcasm that says the old arguments are "as dead as Queen Ann." It is intellectual timidity to concede that reason and logic support atheism.

Most of the great philosophers have stated their views on God, and many of these have made a distinct impact on the biblical revelation.[2] These classical arguments for belief in God have had an interesting revival that requires consideration.[3] In general they fall into two groups: those that begin with the world in general and those that begin with man in particular. The logical structure is basically the same whether they begin with *kosmos* (world) or *anthrōpos* (man).

Arguments that begin with the world. All of the classical arguments that begin with the world have roots in Greek philosophy. The so-called ontological argument was a question for Parmenides and Plato, the cosmological was explained by Plato and Aristotle, and the teleological by Plato and the Stoics.

The ontological argument was stated in classical form for Christian theology by Anselm of Canterbury (1033-1109), who tried to get behind the *kosmos* to the question of being itself. His *Monologium* tried to establish belief in God from the consideration of truth and goodness as intellectual notions without appeal to Scripture and other authorities, but he was not satisfied until he wrote his *Proslogion* (2-4) with the formulation of the ontological argument. His identification of God with being declared that God is "that than which nothing greater can be conceived." God by definition is the self-existent one. He alone is *a se*, from himself, from which the word aseity is derived. No one has clearly refuted this definition, and many have come to his defense.

Before the revival of the debate the most famous defenders were none other than René Descartes and G. W. F. Hegel. Descartes argued that awareness of God precedes awareness of self, that the idea of the infinite substance is prior to the idea of finite substance, but realism rightly argues that the two are known together (*Meditations*, III). Hegel has subject before

1. *Thinking About God* (New York: Harper and Row, 1975), pp. 91-93.
2. Charles Hartshorne and William L. Reese, *Philosophers Speak of God* (University of Chicago Press, 1953).
3. John Hick, *Arguments for the Existence of God* (New York: Herder and Herder, 1971). Hick concedes too much to logical positivism.

object, while realism would put subject and object together. Recent defenders include both the biblical theology of Karl Barth and the philosophical theology of Charles Hartshorne.[4]

Karl Barth argued that Anselm began with the God of revelation. It is clear that the identification of God with being goes beyond the God of Parmenides, for conceptuality and actuality become one in Jesus Christ, so one is unable to argue that Anselm made an irrational leap from conception to existence. He began with faith and sought understanding (*fides quaerens intellectum*).[5] This rules out a natural theology, according to Barth. God cannot be known without God. Barth is able to escape from his subjective prison by appeal to the objective word and the subjective Spirit together.[6]

The philosophical theology of Charles Hartshorne makes a very sharp distinction between the argument for the existence of God in Anselm's *Proslogion* II and the *necessary* existence of God in *Proslogion* III. If God is the self-existent one, then existence is indeed a necessary attribute by definition. Whatever or whoever is self-existent is God, but is logical necessity actuality?

For Barth the concept and the act are one in the Word made flesh. He begins "from above," with no continuity "from below." Revelation is an inverted pyramid in which all rests on the special revelation of God in Christ. For Hartshorne God is immanent in the process and there is a continuity from "within the process" to the transcendent reality of God "beyond the process." The crux of the whole matter is the concept of God.[7]

At the end of his detailed study of Barth and Hartshorne, Robert D. Shofner sums up the question that tilts things in favor of Hartshorne against Barth on the one hand and against critics like John Hick on the other. He says:

Who, then, is the true and living God?

He is the one who is *both* Absolute *and* Relative; who is *both* independent *and* dependent; who is *both* immutable *and* mutable, who is *both* being *and* becoming: This is not paradox because God has two definite and distinct aspects: an abstract aspect as well as a concrete one. The former is to be equated with the divine essence, and the latter with the manifestation of the essence in

4. Robert D. Shofner, *Anselm Revisited* (Leiden: E. J. Brill, 1974). A very full bibliography on the problem is found in this volume.
5. Karl Barth, *Fides Quaerens Intellectum*, tr. Ian W. Robertson (Cleveland: World Publishing Co., 1962).
6. Cf. Helmut Thielicke, *The Evangelical Faith*, tr. G. W. Bromiley (Grand Rapids: Wm. B. Eerdmans, 1974), pp. 115-218.
7. The major works of Hartshorne on this problem are: *Man's Vision of God and the Logic of Theism* (1941), *The Divine Relativity* (1948), *The Logic of Perfection* (1962), *Anselm's Discovery* (1965), and *A Natural Theology for Our Time* (1967).

creation. To realize this is to know that God is the one who remains who he is even while he regards men. This is the God who is perfect, but whose divine life is continually being enriched by human activity.[8]

This dipolarity of God in both his primordial and consequent aspects is in harmony with the biblical revelation which is both general and special. God indeed cannot be known without God, but he is present in his immanence.

This is why the biblical teaching of the Creator Spirit must not be explained away, as even some conservative evangelicals tend to do.[9] Creativity, which is the unity between the primordial and consequent aspects of God, may be used to round out the doctrine of the Holy Trinity, provided the primordial nature is interpreted as being that is prior to becoming. This, however, is not the usual view in process theology.

The cosmological argument has been presented in two major forms. Thomas Aquinas argued for the "existence of God" on the basis of his famous Five Ways: (1) change or motion, (2) causation, (3) contingency, (4) gradedness, (5) purpose (*Summa Theologica*, I.2.3). The older form focused on causation as God was described as the First Cause in the chain of causation. David Hume (1711-76), using the presuppositions of empiricism, argued that causality is a habit of association, not a concept of logic. This argument has been repeated down to analytic philosophy today.

A second form of the argument shifts to contingency. A classic statement of this view may be found in the writings of Bernard J. F. Lonergan. He says:

> First, the universe of proportionate being is shot through with contingence. Second, mere contingence is apart from being, and so there must be an ultimate ground for the universe, and that ground cannot be contingent. Thirdly, the necessary ultimate ground cannot be necessitated in grounding a contingent universe, and it cannot be arbitrary in grounding an intelligible and good universe. It cannot be necessitated, for what follows necessarily from the necessary is equally necessary. It cannot be arbitrary, for what follows arbitrarily from the necessary results as a mere matter of fact without any possible explanation. But what is neither necessary nor arbitrary, yet intelligible and a value, is what proceeds freely from the reasonable choice of a rational consciousness.[10]

It is obvious that the presuppositions of Aristotle as interpreted by Thomism are behind such reasoning.

8. *Op. cit.*, p. 229. Italics in original.
9. Michael Green, *I Believe in the Holy Spirit* (Grand Rapids: Wm. B. Eerdmans, 1975), pp. 28f.
10. *Insight: A Study of Human Understanding* (London: Longmans Green, 1957), pp. 656ff.

A very important shift of emphasis comes with the contingency argument. E. L. Mascall, an ardent admirer of Lonergan, makes it very clear that this element of contingency is not only present in every object of perception, but that the ground of all contingency is personal. In the most realistic way the contingent world manifests the presence of the non-contingent God who creates and sustains all things. He does not start with the world and end up with God. God and the world are perceived together in reality.[11]

As I ponder this "contuition" of God in all finite aspects, it is difficult to see much difference between this argument and the existential approach that perceives existence and being together or the process approach that speaks of God's primordial and consequent aspects together. Mascall, however, resists the growth of God in the process. It sounds also much like the mysticism of Wittgenstein by which the whole is perceived. All turn out to be rational arguments for being, and the Be-ing is God.

Mascall's view is the epistemology of Tennyson's baby in the classic *In Memoriam* (XLV):

> *The baby new to earth and sky,*
> *What time his tender palm is pressed*
> *Against the circle of the breast,*
> *Has never thought that "this is I";*
>
> *But as he grows he gathers much,*
> *And learns the use of "I" and "me,"*
> *And finds "I am not what I see,*
> *And other than the things I touch."*

The teleological argument for belief in God calls attention to the evidence for purpose in the world. The most popular statement of this view was *Natural Theology* (1802) by William Paley, the Archdeacon of Carlisle Cathedral in England. In the atmosphere in which mathematics and astronomy were studied, it was not difficult to picture the world as a great machine behind which there is a cosmic mind. If Tennyson's baby who discovered himself in relation to the world may be used as a picture of the cosmological argument, then Paley's watch that gave evidence for a Watchmaker — mentioned at the beginning of his book — may best describe the early design argument.

The teleological argument is very much alive now, but it is based upon the model of organism rather than machine. As the scientific emphasis shifted to biology and evolution, F. R. Tennant argued, in the context of such scientific theories, that the only adequate explanation for the organic

11. *The Openness of Being* (Philadelphia: The Westminster Press, 1971), especially pp. 91-123, 141-157. I would speak also of the openness of human existence to God's being, but the general thrust seems true.

whole is a creative Spirit with purpose.[12] This cosmic teleology is developed with clarity in five different fields. John Hick argues that the design argument does not take one beyond the *possibility* of God, but the mysteriousness of the organic whole is more of an interobang than question at tea! It really gets back to the wonder of *all existence* that is so much like Mascall's theory of contuition. All three classical arguments confront the mystery of being.

Arguments that begin with man. Immanuel Kant, in his *Critique of Pure Reason* (1787), argued rightly that the teleological and cosmological arguments depended on the ontological argument, but he failed to grasp the meaning of the ontological argument.

His *Critique of Practical Reason* (1788) attempted to argue from the sense of moral obligation to God, freedom, and immortality, but this is an argument from man to God in the same way the classical arguments moved from the world to God. This sense of a categorical imperative that posits a God of command and grace is perhaps true, but it is based upon presuppositions that are more realistic than idealistic.

The moral argument has lived on in such impressive works as A. E. Taylor's *The Faith of a Moralist* (1930). It has received renewed emphasis in H. P. Owen's book *The Moral Argument for Christian Theism* (1965). Owen, building on Taylor, argues that moral claims can be perceived even by the non-religious, but they cannot be explained without appeal to the holiness of God. The implication of moral obligation is Christian theism.

A second argument for belief in God that begins with man shifts from morality to mind. William Temple's Gifford Lectures entitled *Nature, Man and God* (1934) argued that an evolutionary process that moved through levels from matter through life to human minds suggested a cosmic transcendent Mind more than a machine of blind chance. By beginning with the possession of a human mind, which all would no doubt profess to have, it is difficult to explain this presence of mind as the product of the lower levels. Minds are at the top of the process because Mind is behind the process. In the context of creative emergent evolution, which Temple accepted, this is a cogent argument.

A third argument for belief in God that begins with man broadens the discussion to include the total self. A good example of this is in the book *Finite and Infinite* (1943, 1959) by Austin M. Farrer. Farrer does not claim that the human soul or self is the only place where the creative activity of God can be recognized, but he does think it is the easiest place to meet God. Freedom increases as newer levels emerge, and the highest level thus far is human freedom. A book by Farrer, *The Freedom of the Will* (1958),

12. *Philosophical Theology* (Cambridge: University of Cambridge Press, 1930), Vol. II, pp. 78-120.

extends this argument on finite freedom as evidence for infinite freedom, the Infinite God. The fact that this reminds one of Descartes' Third Meditation on the Infinite and the finite does not discount its value.

A fourth argument for belief in God revives the structure of thought in F. D. E. Schleiermacher, who built all theology on Christian experience. A classic expression of this was *The Idea of the Holy* (1917) by Rudolf Otto. Otto believed that a numinous experience of awe and self-abasement is present in all religious consciousness. The numinous belongs to the non-rational and amoral experience of man. I would call it pre-rational and pre-moral awareness of God. A supreme example of this *mysterium tremendum* was described in his book on Jesus, *The Kingdom of God and the Son of Man* (1938), which outlines the charismatic type of which Jesus was the model, but he did not deny that this type could be found in other world religions. If this is stated in the context of realism rather than idealism, it is even more impressive. *The Natural and the Supernatural* (1931) by John Oman has elaborated this immediate, self-authenticating awareness of God.

It will perhaps produce convulsions of laughter in any logical positivist who would condescend to read this brief survey of seven arguments for belief in God, three that begin with the world and four with man, but all of them seem to have some validity. All lines of evidence lead more to theism than to atheism.

19. The God of the Patriarchs

The passionate prayer found sewn into the coat of Blaise Pascal after his death was addressed to the "God of Abraham, Isaac and Jacob, not the God of savants and philosophers." On Nov. 23, 1653, Pascal had experienced an ecstatic conversion, a remarkable experience of the presence of God, not unlike those of Paul on the Damascus road and Augustine in the garden of Milan, and, although he had little knowledge of Protestantism, like Martin Luther in his Tower Experience and the later experiences of John Wesley at Aldersgate Street and D. L. Moody on a street of Brooklyn, N. Y.

This type of theology has received classic expression in such writings as *The Varieties of Religious Experience* by William James (1902) and *The Idea of the Holy* (1917) by Rudolf Otto, and they are not to be derided. However, it must be remembered that Pascal was speaking as a mathematician and mystic in his polemics against the rationalism of the Jesuits. The problem was much like that of Dostoyevsky as he, in *The Brothers Karamazov* (chs. 3-5), wrestled with the skepticism of the Euclidean mind. It is not necessary to set the God of the patriarchs in such a radical distinction to the God of the philosophers, but there are modern examples of that *mysterium tremendum et fascinans* about which Otto talked with great insight. The exclusive attitude of Pascal has therefore been rejected in favor of an inclusive attitude for which biblical revelation makes a place (Exodus 3:14; Hosea 1:9; Isa. 41:4; 43:10; 44:6; 48:12).

The designation of God as the God of some person's father is found a dozen times in Genesis and Exodus (Genesis 26:24; 31:5, 42, 53; 43:23; 46:1, 3; 49:25; 50:17; Exodus 3:6; 15:2; 18:4). The Elohist regarded this deity as the same as "the God of Abraham, the God of Isaac, and the God of Jacob" (Exodus 3:6, 15, 16; 4:5). The God of the patriarchs is not known in the general and abstract terms used to describe the God of the philosophers. He is known in concrete and historical ways, in relation to particular persons and clans. The view that the patriarchs are no more than eponyms for wandering clans has been advocated, but that theory is here rejected. The basic history by John Bright concludes: "We may assent with full confidence that Abraham, Isaac, and Jacob were actual historical individuals."[13]

The general semitic name for God is *El*.[14] It apparently is derived from a root meaning "power." "Basically the word designates the numinous divine power that fills men with awe and dread."[15] The fact that this power is worshipped indicates how the giving of a name is the recognition of an I–Thou relation. The name is known by a personal disclosure in which the numinous reality and the revelation are inseparable. The name by itself in the Old Testament is found mostly in poetic passages such as Exodus 15:2:

> *The Lord is my strength and my song,*
> *and he has become my salvation;*
> *this is my God (El), and I will praise him,*
> *my father's God (El), and I will exalt him.*

The oldest combination with El in Genesis seems to be *El Shaddai* (God Almighty). Before the patriarchs left Upper Mesopotamia, they apparently worshipped God using this name, and the Priestly Writer (P) should be taken seriously when he reports the Lord as saying: "I am the Lord. I appeared to Abraham, and to Isaac, and to Jacob, as God Almighty, but by my name the Lord I did not make myself known to them" (Exodus 6:3; cf. Gen. 17:1; 28:3; 35:11; 43:14; 48:3; 49:25). It may be that the name was originally attached to a place, for it means "God, the One of the Mountain," but it very early became detached, as *El Shaddai* became the God of the Arameans (cf. Deut. 26:5).[16]

As the patriarchs wandered from place to place they did not leave their God behind. The God of Abraham was the Shield of Abraham who pro-

---

13. *A History of Israel*, Second Edition (Philadelphia: The Westminster Press, 1972), p. 91. See p. 95 n. 58 for references to the classic writing by Albrecht Alt (1929) and later modifications of his views.
14. Marvin H. Pope, *El in the Ugaritic Texts* (Leiden: E. J. Brill, 1955).
15. *The Interpreter's Bible*, Vol. 2, p. 411.
16. For evidence that the name and the patriarchs come from Upper not Lower Mesopotamia, see John Bright, *A History of Israel*, pp. 88-91.

tected him wherever he went and promised him the reward of numerous posterity and the land of Palestine. In the Yahwist's account of a vision the Lord said: "Fear not, Abram, I am your shield; your reward shall be very great" (Gen. 15:1). As Abram fell into a deep sleep he received a revelation that illustrates the *mysterium tremendum et fascinans*. "As the sun was going down, a deep sleep fell on Abram; and lo, a dread and a great darkness fell upon him" (15:12). It is superficial to dismiss this basic form of revelation through vision and dream as a primitive form of "spooky religion."

In later references to "the God of Abraham," the Elohist, after Abram's name was changed to Abraham, incorporated it in the covenant faith and promise of land and people. Its use in Genesis hardly justifies the conclusion that it was confined to Mamre-Hebron. A significant formula for the God of the patriarchs is used: "I am the Lord, the God of Abraham your father and the God of Isaac" (28:13). As this formula was expanded, the God of Isaac becomes "the Fear of Isaac" or perhaps "the Kinsman of Isaac" (31:42). The relation between the person and God is further illuminated when, according to the Elohist, Laban and Jacob call God as witness to their covenant at Mizpah, the Watchpost. After the "Mizpah benediction" (31:49), Laban said to Jacob: "The God of Abraham and the God of Nahor, the God of their father, judge between us" (31:53). These two gods of Abraham and Nahor are identified with the Fear or Kinsman of Isaac as if they are one.

The Shield of Abram and the Fear of Isaac are titles that are united with the concept of the Champion or Mighty One of Jacob. In the Blessing of Jacob, dating from the time of David and so important for the dream of modern Israel, the blessing for Joseph is a picture of the partial fulfillment of the promise of prosperity in the land and numerous posterity. His enemies are defeated (Gen. 49:24-25)

> by the hands of the Mighty One of Jacob
>   (by the name of the Shepherd, the Rock of Israel),
> by the God of your father who will help you,
>   by God Almighty who will bless you
>   with blessings of heaven above,
> blessings of the deep that couches beneath,
>   blessings of the breasts and of the womb.

The Mighty One of Jacob is a title of "the God of the Patriarchs" (cf. Isa. 1:24; 49:26).

The other combinations with the word *El* are at times related to persons and at still other times to places. These are both important for understanding "the God of the patriarchs" in relation to the general semitic views, but the detachment of God from a place and his special attachment to a person is a great moment in the development toward a universal monotheism.

As the God of persons becomes attached to places, it is almost certain that the proper place to begin is the ancient tree sanctuary to the east of

Shechem, a place of major importance in both the Abraham and Jacob traditions (Gen. 12:6-8; 33:18-20; 35:1-5). In the development of the Pentateuchal traditions, it seems that the Jacob tradition was formulated first, then the Abraham tradition was added.[17]

Even before the Israelites worshipped *El Berith*, the God of the Covenant, the Canaanites worshipped Berith at Shechem (Josh. 24; Judg. 8:33; 9:4, 46). The fact that this sacred place of the Canaanites and the concept of the covenant can be utilized by later Israelites indicates a vital connection between God's general revelation of himself to all peoples and the special covenant he made with Israel from the time of the patriarchs and Moses.

The sacred tree of Israel was called the "oracle giver," the oak or terebinth of Moreh, because it was there that God revealed himself to Israel. The *massebah*, now shown by archaeologists, was called *El-Elohe Israel*, "God, the God of Israel" (Gen. 33:20).

The story of a pilgrimage from Shechem to the sanctuary of Bethel marks the transfer to a second holy place and reflects the practice of pilgrimages at the time the tradition was formed.[18] By ritual acts of renunciation and purification, two of the basic cultic observances of Covenant faith, the people are exhorted to "rise and go up to Bethel" (Gen. 35:3), a theme that has rightly been used for fervent sermons on "Back to Bethel"! As the people made their pilgrimage "a terror from God fell upon the cities round about them" (35:5). A "terror from God" was an expression used to describe the mysterious and numinous panic that paralyzed the enemy in times of holy war (Ex. 23:27: Josh. 10:10).

As Jacob erected his *massebah* he called the place *El-Bethel*, "the God of Bethel." It was at this place that he had previously experienced the holiness of God in a memorable way when he left for Paddan-Aram. A double dream is reported. He saw a vision of angels ascending and descending a ladder to heaven and heard a voice speaking from God. Jacob's response was: "Surely the Lord is in this place; and I did not know it — How awesome is this place! This is none other than the house of God, and this is the gate of heaven" (Gen. 28:16f.).

In the Abraham tradition of the south the Song of Melchizedek in ancient Salem becomes as significant in the faith of Israel as the *El Berith* in Shechem (Gen. 14:19f.). He said:

> *Blessed be Abram by God Most High,*
> *maker of heaven and earth;*
> *and blessed be God Most High,*
> *who has delivered your enemies into your hand!*

17. Martin Noth, *A History of Pentateuchal Traditions*, tr. Bernhard W. Anderson (Englewood Cliffs, N. J.: Prentice-Hall, Inc., 1972), pp. 79-87.
18. Albrecht Alt, *Essays on Old Testament History and Religion*, tr. R. A. Wilson (Oxford: Basil Blackwell, 1966).

The importance of Melchizedek for both the Davidic monarchy and belief in a future Messiah in the Old Testament and for the New Testament Christology in Hebrews has often been noted (Ps. 110; Heb. 1:13; 7:1–22). However, it is also another major step toward monotheism and the belief in God as creator. Belief in God Most High (*El Elyon*), a "Baal of heaven" as monarch over all earthly baals, may be abundantly illustrated by the Ras Shamra tablets (*ANET*, 129-142), and the oath of Abraham identifies this with the Lord, the one God of Israel, "Lord God Most High" (Gen. 14:22). This identification and the homage of Abraham to a Canaanite priest-king is a shock to theological zealots who suppress such tolerance, but there it is, in the Bible they profess to believe. It is interesting to note that the LXX omitted this, and other texts say only God (*ha-elohim*).[19] God Most High, first associated with Salem, i.e. Jerusalem, is a bridge between belief in the one God of Israel and belief in some type of god among the Gentiles (cf. Num. 24:16; 2 Sam. 22:14; Pss. 21:7; 46:4–7; 47:2; 50:14; 57:2 and especially Deut. 32:8f. with the hymns of Luke 1–2, especially at 1:32 and 76).

There are two other combinations with the word *El* in the Abraham stories. One is associated with the sacred place of Beer-lahai-roi. At the birth of Ishmael, which means "God heard," his mother Hagar was sent into the desert where the Lord himself, manifested by an angel or messenger, appeared to her as the Seeing God (*El Roi*), or the God of seeing (cf. Ex. 4:11). The identification of the Lord, the covenant God of Israel, with the angel of the Lord and the Seeing God is beyond doubt in the text (Gen. 16:7–14, especially v. 13). This was a numinous experience so associated with time and space that Hagar called the place Beer-lahai-roi, the well of one who sees and hears. It is possible that the old word for prophet, the Seer (*Roeh*), has some relation to this term (cf. 1 Sam. 9:9).

A third story in the Abraham cycle relates the Everlasting God (*El Olam*) to Beer-sheba. Abraham's stable relation with Abimelech, which had been disturbed by conflict over a well of water, was sealed by a covenant of loyalty (*chesed*). A note about the place says: "Abraham planted a tamarisk tree in Beer-sheba, and called on the name of the Lord, the Everlasting God" (Gen. 21:33). After this identification, the "Everlasting God" became an epithet for the Lord (Pss. 90; 102:25–28). All else begins and ends, but the Lord extends forward and backward, in salvation history, without end.

As *El Shaddai* formed the theological bridge between the general semitic view of El and the combinations with El, so Elohim, the plural of *Eloah*, became the central concept for both the Elohist (E) and the Priestly Writer (P) until the time of Moses. After Moses all terms became synonyms

19. Gerhard von Rad, *Genesis*, tr. John H. Marks (Philadelphia: The Westminster Press, 1961), pp. 174-176.

for Yahweh, the Lord of the Covenant. *Eloah* is found forty-two times in Job and fifteen times elsewhere. It seems to be used as a more general concept for God than the special word *Yahweh*. Echoes of polytheism are found in the plural *Elohim*, as in Ex. 18:11 where Jethro declares Yahweh greater than the other *Elohim*; but it is used mostly in the singular sense as a "plural of majesty" and as a synonym for Yahweh (cf. Gen. 1:26; 1 Kings 18:21). It is therefore possible to say Yahweh Elohim (Gen. 2:4, 5, 7).

B. THE MAJESTY OF GOD'S BEING

20. The Majesty of God's Name

Majesty is the most comprehensive word for God's manifestation of himself in biblical revelation. This monarchical view may seem offensive to a democratic culture. It would indeed be unfortunate to confine God to the concept of a Thutmose III or a Louis XIV in the sky, but this starting point for the sole deity of God is never discarded in biblical revelation.

As God's revelation of himself increases, "in many and various ways" (Heb. 1:1), the mystery of God's being becomes the greatness of his majesty (Ex. 15:7). This majesty of God has a special association with the name Yahweh, the Lord. As *El Shaddai*, God Almighty, formed the bridge from the general semitic names of deity to the special revelations of "the God of the Patriarchs," so the majestic revelation of Yahweh as the God of the covenant with all the people of Israel prepared the way for the modes of God's being made manifest by the revelation of "the God and Father of our Lord Jesus Christ" (2 Cor. 1:3).

The origin of the name Yahweh has stimulated fascinating studies. At the present time two theories compete most for acceptance among Old Testament scholars. The so-called Midianite-Kenite theory has long been accepted and supported by considerable logic and evidence.[20] In brief the theory holds that Yahweh was the name of the tribal deity of Jethro, the father-in-law of Moses, and that Moses learned of this name while he was in the land of Midian. It is further argued that Yahweh was worshipped by the Kenites, going back to Cain as their eponymous ancestor, and that the name Yahweh was the mark placed upon Cain (Gen. 4:15).

More recent research has raised some important objections to the Midianite-Kenite theory.[21] It is pointed out that Exodus 3:1 and 18:1, the key passages in the Midianite-Kenite theory, call Jethro "the priest of Midian," not "the priest of Yahweh" and that it is not likely that the Hebrews in Egypt would have followed a foreign name. Further appeal is made to several personal names among the Amorites, of which the Hebrews were

---

20. H. H. Rowley, *From Joseph to Joshua* (London: The British Academy, 1950), pp. 149-160.
21. J. Philip Hyatt, *Exodus* (London: Oliphants, 1971), pp. 78-81.

a part. These were combinations with Yahweh, the most notable of which is Jochebed, the mother of Moses (Ex. 6:20; Num. 6:59). The fact that Yahweh is also called the God of the patriarchs may indicate that the name was used for a patron deity of one of Moses' ancestors before he became, through the mediation of Moses himself, the God of the Covenant with the whole people of Israel (cf. Ex. 3:6; 15:2; 18:4).

God's revelation of his mystery by the majesty of his name has elements of what was later called in Latin both *deus absconditus* and *deus revelatus*, God hidden and God revealed.[22] God's hiddenness is a teaching that finds classic expression in the JE account of the Call of Moses at the Burning Bush (Exodus 3:1–4:17).[23] The question of the relation of this theophany to the myth of Horus at Edfu is impossible to answer.[24] It is possible, however, to see how God, out of his hiddenness, makes his majestic name known.

The theophany of the Lord was indeed a majestic manifestation of the mysterious. "And the angel of the Lord appeared to him in a flame of fire out of the midst of a bush, and he looked, and lo, the bush was burning, yet it was not consumed" (Ex. 3:2). The angel of the Lord was a manifestation of the Lord himself (3:4), a temporary embodiment of deity (cf. Gen. 21:15–19; Judg. 6:11, 14). The flame, imitated in the halo of the saints, represents the personal presence of the Lord (Ex. 19:18; Ezek. 1:27; Ps. 104:4; 1 Tim. 6:16).

The response of Moses to this manifestation of deity is a good example of the *mysterium tremendum et fascinans*. He first "hid his face, for he was afraid to look at God" (3:6). The call of the Lord to Moses is followed by the command: "Do not come near; put off your shoes from your feet, for the place on which you are standing is holy ground" (Ex. 3:5). This distance between the high and holy God and humble and lowly man is symbolized by the Moslem practice of removing the shoes on entering any sanctuary even today. The experience is so awesome that Moses four times pleads his inadequacy to be used of God to deliver his people (3:11; 4:1, 10, 13). By the majestic name of the Lord, now identified with the God of the patriarchs, the great I AM is "to be remembered throughout all generations" (3:15). The Lord is indeed "him who dwelt in the bush" (Deut. 33:16; cf. Acts 7:30).

The revelation of the hidden God is even more central in the so-called Second Exodus theology of Second Isaiah (40–55). Second Isaiah contains a song on The Conversion of the Nations in six strophes (45:14–15, 16–17, 18–19, 20–21, 22–23, 24–25).[25] The monolatry of Moses that com-

---

22. John Dillenberger, *God Hidden and Revealed* (Philadelphia: Muhlenberg Press, 1953).
23. J. Philip Hyatt, *op. cit.*, p. 70.
24. George E. Mendenhall, *The Tenth Generation* (Baltimore: The Johns Hopkins University Press, 1973), pp. 54, 59.
25. James Muilenburg, in *The Interpreter's Bible*, V, 528-534.

manded the worship of only one God has flowered into the monotheism of Second Isaiah that says there is only one God to be worshipped.[26] All others are idols that do not act in history. It is not enough for one nation to confess that the Lord has acted in her particular history and leave the other nations to other gods. There is only one God for all nations, and he acts in all history and in all nations in a hidden and mysterious way. It is not enough to see God acting through Moses in Israel's history, for the Lord acts also in a hidden way in Cyrus the Great and universal history (Isa. 44:28; 45:1).

The first three strophes are a declaration, and the last three are a debate. The nations rightly confess (Isa. 45:15):

> Truly, thou art a God who hidest thyself,
> O God of Israel, the Savior.

The hidden God has come forth to reveal himself in Cyrus the Great, the liberator of Israel. God acted in hiddenness in the history of Israel also (8:17; 40:27; Deut. 29:29; Jer. 14:7–9), but it is his actions in other nations that call forth the confession of the nations.

When God speaks out of his mysterious hiddenness, what he says is clear. As he brings order out of chaos in creation, so in history he says (Isa. 45:19):

> I did not speak in secret,
>   in a land of darkness;
> I did not say to the offspring of Jacob,
>   "Seek me in chaos."
> I the Lord speak the truth,
>   I declare what is right.

His word is never esoteric nonsense that can be understood only by the initiated. He speaks through his mighty acts of historical revelation (Deut. 30:11–14). All this the prophet wants to debate in the assembly of the nations with a universal invitation to salvation (Isa. 45:20–25).

God's revelation of himself in history includes all salvation history, both the temporary embodiment of himself in theophanies and the permanent embodiment of himself in Christ, the perfect incarnation, and the Church, the incomplete process by which the incarnation is continued. By this process the deus absconditus becomes deus revelatus.

The theophanies of Exodus are from a cloud of thick darkness, the cloud symbolized so often in Israel as golden sunlight hidden behind the dark clouds of the rainy season. This has well been called "The Mask of Yahweh."[27] When it is understood that this is symbolic language to express

---

26. See John Bright, A History of Israel, Second Edition (Philadelphia: The Westminster Press, 1972), pp. 153f. for a summary of the modern discussion on Moses and monotheism. On monolatry see Exodus 20:3; Deuteronomy 32:8f.; Psalms 82:1; 86:8; 95:3; 96:4; 97:7, 9; 135:5; 136:2; 138:1 and notes in The New Oxford Annotated Bible.
27. George E. Mendenhall, op. cit., pp. 56-66.

the Presence of God in both his hiddenness and his revealedness, the Exodus pattern of salvation and revelation becomes relevant today.

It is possible to argue that the cloud phenomenon is derived from the Book of Jashar, apparently an ancient national song book that contained such poetry as Joshua's Song to the Sun and the Moon and David's Lament for Saul and Jonathan (Josh. 10:12–13; 2 Sam. 1:17–27). It may be that this was an epic poem. Some think the Book of the Wars of the Lord is another name for the same epic (Num. 21:14; cf. Ex. 15:21; Judg. 5). The LXX version calls it the Book of Song and attributes the Prologue to Solomon's Prayer at the dedication of the temple to the same source; and there, after "a cloud filled the house of the Lord," it is remembered that the Lord "has said that he would dwell in thick darkness" (1 Kings 8:11–13). The thick darkness of the temple had reference to the inner sanctuary which had no windows, but it is an echo of the *hanan* (cloud) of the traditions of the Exodus and Sinai.

It is far more likely that the cloud phenomenon, mentioned in all of the literary sources of the Pentateuch, was the original form by which the Lord manifested himself to Moses.[28] The cloud theophany was a way to reveal the Lord's presence as he guided them out of Egypt (Exodus 13:20–22J). The two pillars, the cloud by day and the fire by night, are identified as only one as the Lord exercised his sovereignty by protecting the Israelites and by attacking the armed forces of Egypt as they pursued them (Ex. 14:19b–20, 24–25J). In the end the fear that Israel had for the Egyptians was transformed into fear for the Lord who did a great work among them (Ex. 14:10–14, 30–31J). In salvation history, the appearances at the Exodus are second only to the appearances after the resurrection of Jesus. The *mal'ak* (messenger) and the *panim* (face) are other ways to express the visible manifestation of the Lord's presence (Ex. 14:19aE; 33:1–6Rd, 7–11E, 12–23J).

The Sinai theophany in Exodus 19 is also a composite from the major literary sources of the Pentateuch. The Priestly Writer (P) associates the event with the Feast of Weeks (Pentecost) and locates it in the wilderness of Sinai (1–2a). The Deuteronomic redactor (Dr) summarizes the covenant theology in a manner resembling a cultic ceremony that may reflect later pilgrimages to Sinai to celebrate the revelation (3b–8). The climax and core of the theophany is the Yahwist's (J) description of the Lord's coming down in the *hanan* (cloud) to Mt. Sinai to meet Moses (9a–16a, 18). The Yahwist supplement is a commentary on the theophany (20–24). It is obvious again that the revelation of the Lord in the cloud phenomenon goes back to Moses and belongs to the very heart of the Hebrew understanding of God.

The majesty of the name of the Lord in his revelation was the first step

28. *Ibid.*, p. 57.

toward belief in his unity and the explicit teaching of monotheism. The meaning of monotheism gets involved in a quibble over words. It is used here to describe the worship of one God because the very existence of other gods is explicitly denied. The worship of one God without this explicit denial of the existence of other gods should be called monolatry, from *mono* (single) and *latreia* (worship). It is in this light that the arguments for monotheism in the time of Moses, as stated by W. F. Albright and his followers, are rejected.[29]

The supreme deity of the Lord over all other gods is emphasized by the Elohist. This has cultic expression in the covenant blessing of Jethro the father-in-law of Moses, when he met Moses to make a covenant between the Midianites and Israelites.[30] The cultic celebration confessed these words (Ex. 18:10–11E):

> *"Blessed be the Lord,*
> *who has delivered you out of the hands of the Egyptians*
> *and out of the hand of Pharaoh.*
> *Now I know that the Lord is greater than the gods,*
> *because he delivered the people from under the hand of the*
> *Egyptians,*
> *when he dealt arrogantly with them."*

The first commandment in the ancient Decalogue included by the Elohist in Exodus 20:3 ("You shall have no other gods before me") makes this clear.

The supreme deity of the Lord is central in the Deuteronomic theology that has its classic summary in the *Shema* of Deuteronomy 6:4 ("Hear, O Israel: The Lord our God is one Lord; and you shall love the Lord your God with all your heart, and with all your soul, and with all your might"). The cultic confession of the Deuteronomic covenant at Shechem (Josh. 24:2–13) and the call of Joshua to serve the Lord alone have the same force (16–23). Then Joshua wrote these words in a book and erected the *massebah* (great stone) that can be seen to this day (25–28). This same Deuteronomic monolatry underlies the theology of the Elijah story, especially the contest on Mount Carmel that has the cultic confession (1 Kings 18:39):

> *"The Lord, he is God;*
> *The Lord, he is God."*

The sole deity of the Lord had its heyday in the explicit monotheism of Deutero–Isaiah at the close of the Babylonian Exile. Implicit monotheism may be found in the universalism of Amos (1:2–2:16; 9:7–10), but specific statements on the non-existence of other gods do not appear until we reach

---

29. John Bright, *op. cit.*, pp. 153f.
30. J. Philip Hyatt, *op. cit.*, p. 187.

the mountain of monotheism in Isaiah (40–55). It is there that his absolute sovereignty bursts forth with such declarations as (44:6–8; cf. 43:8–13):

> *Thus says the Lord, the King of Israel,*
>   *and the Redeemer, the Lord of hosts:*
> *"I am the first and the last;*
>   *besides me there is no god.*
> *Who is like me? Let him proclaim it,*
>   *let him declare and set it forth before me.*
> *Who has announced from of old the things to come?*
>   *Let him tell us what is yet to be.*
> *Fear not, nor be afraid;*
>   *have not I told you from of old and declared it?*
>   *And you are my witnesses!*
> *Is there a God besides me?*
>   *There is no Rock; I know not any.*

Cyrus the Great was unaware that the Lord commissioned him, but the Lord says to him (45:5–6):

> *I am the Lord, and there is no other,*
>   *besides me there is no God;*
> *I gird you, though you do not know me,*
>   *that men may know, from the rising sun*
>   *and from the west, that there is none besides me;*
> *I am the Lord, and there is no other.*

This is the majesty of monotheism that brings to a climax the majesty of Mosaic monolatry.

It is not always easy to distinguish the language about the name of God from the nature of God. In places like Psalms 8 and 29 the majesty of his name and the majesty of his nature are blended together. It is possible to separate the two more in thought than in life.

21. The Majesty of God's Nature: His Holiness

The concept of holiness is the ground on which all religions meet. Gustaf Aulén has well said that holiness is the "background of the conception of God."[31] Rudolf Otto (1869-1937), with his wide knowledge of comparative religion, was so impressed with this basic sense of religious consciousness that he coined the term "numinous" to designate this religious *a priori* that

---

31. *The Faith of the Christian Church*, tr. Eric H. Wahlstrom and Everett Arden (Philadelphia: The Muhlenberg Press, 1948), pp. 120-124.

is beyond all rational and ethical categories. It is closely akin to Schleier-macher's concept of feeling (*Gefühl*), but the emphasis upon the twofold feeling of religious awe and fascination has made it a major contribution to theological understanding. The polemic against this concept was a fatal flaw in the neo-orthodoxy of Karl Barth. It is time to restore it to theological respectability.

Religious thought requires the distinction between the sacred and the profane.[32] Those who regard all things as sacred usually end up treating all things as profane. That was the fate of the fad for secularity that had its delirious decade that was so disastrous for vital faith.[33] Holy Scripture stands on the idea of the Holy. What belongs to Yahweh (the Lord) is holy (*qodesh*), and what belongs to another god must be destroyed (*cherem*). That belief was illustrated by the concept of a holy war (1 Sam. 15). Norman H. Snaith has well said: "One god's *qodesh* was another god's *cherem*."[34] Companion ideas involved the distinction between the clean and the common or unclean. What belongs to God is clean; what belongs to man is common (1 Sam. 21:1-6). This can hardly be discarded as an outmoded primitive Old Testament idea, since it is the basis for the distinction between a communion meal and a common meal in the New Testament (1 Cor. 10). Even Christian marriage is based upon it (1 Cor. 7:14). When applied to the biblical understanding of God the idea is the starting point, the *terminus a quo*.

The Perfection of God's Holiness[35]

It must first be said of God that his majesty is his holiness. He is indeed "majestic in holiness" (Ex. 15:11). But what does that mean? A distinction may be made between metaphysical and moral holiness, but biblical revelation does not separate them. Of all the great proclamations by the holy God in the Old Testament, Hosea 11:8f. is a balanced summary:

> *How can I give you up, O Ephraim!*
> *How can I hand you over, O Israel!*
> *How can I make you like Admah!*
> *How can I treat you like Zeboiim!*
> *My heart recoils within me,*
> *my compassion grows warm and tender.*

32. Mircea Eliade, *The Sacred and the Profane* (New York: Harcourt, Brace and Co., 1959).
33. John Macquarrie, *God and Secularity* (Philadelphia: The Westminster Press, 1967).
34. *The Distinctive Ideas of the Old Testament* (Philadelphia: The Westminster Press, 1946), p. 40.
35. Karl Barth, *Church Dogmatics*, II/1, 358-368; Emil Brunner, *Dogmatics*, I, 157-174; Walther Eichrodt, *Theology of the Old Testament*, I, 270-282; Edmond Jacob, *Theology of the Old Testament*, pp. 86-93.

> *I will not execute my fierce anger,*
> *I will not again destroy Ephraim;*
> *for I am God and not man,*
> *the Holy One in your midst,*
> *and I will not come to destroy.*

The destruction of the enemy belonged to the very heart of the concept of Holy War, a concept beyond which many Jews and Arabs have never been willing to go, otherwise the constant conflict in the Middle East would cease. Holiness without love is the fanaticism of *jihad*, the holy war of Moslems against their enemies. The God of the covenant refuses to destroy his people, and the new covenant in Jesus Christ extends this love even to the enemy who persecutes and seeks to destroy (Matt. 5:43–48).

The call of Isaiah provides a model experience of the holiness of God (Isa. 6:1–9). In his vision of the sovereign and transcendent Lord, "high and lifted up," Isaiah heard the heavenly cherubim calling back and forth in antiphonal words (6:3):

> *Holy, holy, holy is the Lord of hosts;*
> *the whole earth is full of his glory.*

His response to the vision and voices is graphically described in the words "woe," "lo," "go"!

He first expressed his conviction that he was a sinful man over against a holy God. Norman H. Snaith has well said that holiness is "the positive activity of the Personal Other" against our sin.[36] This is an awareness of both a metaphysical transcendence that is beyond all creation and creatures and of a moral purity that convicts man of his sin.

The second word, "lo" in the AV, "behold" in the RSV, expresses the experience of cleansing or purification when sin is confessed and forgiveness is received. This confession of sin and belief in the readiness of God to forgive is essential to vital personal religious experience, and its absence leads to a chalky ceremonialism so characteristic of all priestly worship. Isaiah was a priest who became a prophet by the call and commission of God.

This commission which was added to conviction and cleansing is summed up in the word "go." God comes to the prophet that the prophet may go to the people. The coming of God and the going of man is the purpose of all revelation and redemption.

Out of this prophetic call of Isaiah came the conception of God as the Holy One, a term used no less than twenty-eight times in the Book of Isaiah. It indicates not God's remoteness from sinful man but otherness, the Wholly Other of Rudolf Otto. Among the many pronouncements of God's holiness in Isaiah is this one (57:15):

---

36. *Op. cit.*, p. 60.

> *For thus says the high and lofty One*
> *Who inhabits eternity, whose name is Holy:*
> *"I dwell in the high and holy place,*
> *   and also with him who is of a contrite and humble spirit."*

The Properties of God's Holiness

The perfection of the Holy One may be illustrated by the sevenfold menorah, the lampstand so symbolic of the Old Testament revelation of God. God's holiness is revealed in at least seven ways.

The first is the revelation of the wrath of God, a teaching so essential in the Old Testament understanding of God, yet so offensive to the Protestant liberal who thinks of a God with a frozen smile. Perhaps that is why there are so many modern Marcionites. To speak of "the Lord, whose name is Jealous," as in Ex. 34:14, is to provoke the wrath (*sic*) of the old-fashioned liberal who finds no place for wrath in God's reaction to man's sin. The affirmation of the wrath of God is one of the strong points in Emil Brunner's doctrine of God.[37]

The best-known argument against the wrath of God in any personal sense may be found in C. H. Dodd's creative and stimulating commentary on Romans. He argued that the wrath of God is an impersonal process of retribution that can never be personalized and rationalized as an attribute of God. "In the long run," he said, "we cannot think with full consistency of God in terms of the highest human ideals of personality and yet attribute to Him the irrational passion of anger."[38] His most persistent opponent has been Leon Morris, equally stimulating and equally one-sided as he becomes impatient with the idea of reconciliation in his defense of the dubious concept of propitiation.[39]

For both Dodd and Morris religious experience must be personalized and rationalized by human standards, but this would relegate the *mysterium tremendum et fascinans* to primitive man alone and leave modern man with no sense of the numinous. That may be his predicament, and it accounts for the upsurge of so much cultic irrationalism among those disillusioned with traditional Christianity. The establishment is notorious for intolerance toward the ecstatic and the charismatic too!

The wrath of God is observed and experienced in the historical process of the present much as Paul saw it when he said: "God's wrath is revealed coming down from heaven upon all the sin and evil of men, whose evil ways prevent the truth from being known" (Rom. 1:18 TEV). God's wrath is exhausted neither by human reason nor by the historical process, for it belongs also to the unknown and eschatological future "on the Day when

37. *Dogmatics*, I, 161-174.
38. *The Epistle of Paul to the Romans* (New York: Harper, 1932), p. 24.
39. *The Cross in the New Testament* (Grand Rapids: Wm. B. Eerdmans, 1965), pp. 189-192.

God's wrath and right judgments will be revealed" (Rom. 2:5 TEV). Only then will reason and the right be the same. At the very point where greatest emphasis is given to the love of God it can be said of the disobedient that "the wrath of God rests upon him" (John 3:36).

A second property of God's holiness is his righteousness.[40] In the midst of woes against the wicked it is said (Isa. 5:16):

> But the Lord of hosts is exalted in justice,
>   and the Holy One shows himself holy in righteousness.

God's righteousness is at times described as social activity by which injustice is rectified. The words of Amos of Tekoa have been heard anew in our own time, as social prophets have echoed (Amos 5:24):

> But let justice roll down like waters,
>   and righteousness like an ever-flowing stream.

Justice is the right decision rendered according to the righteous standard which God restores in times of injustice.

God's righteousness is also his saving activity as he delivers his people from oppression and sin. At times the deliverance is from a foreign foe as when Israel came back from Babylonian Exile (Isa. 51:5f.):

> My deliverance draws near speedily,
>   my salvation has gone forth,
>   and my arms will rule the peoples;
> the coastlands wait for me,
>   and for my arm they hope.
> Lift up your eyes to the heavens,
>   and look at the earth beneath;
> for the heavens will vanish like smoke,
>   they will wear out like a garment,
>   and they who dwell in it will die like gnats;
> but my salvation will be forever,
>   and my deliverance will never be ended.

It will be noted how deliverance, which translates the Hebrew word for righteousness, is used as a synonym for salvation and how the prediction reaches far beyond return from Babylonian Exile.

It is this saving activity of God, repeated by the prophet Habakkuk (2:4), that is, in a far more personal sense, the theme of the Letter of Paul to the Romans (1:17), a point discerned with great insight in the work by C. H. Dodd mentioned above. It is not necessary to split the Gospel asunder by the false antithesis between God in social action and God in saving

40. Karl Barth, *Church Dogmatics*, II/1, 375-406; Emil Brunner, *Dogmatics*, I, 275-281.

action, a superficial distinction often made between the "social gospel" and the "simple gospel," for Romans holds the two together in perfect balance.

A third property of God's holiness is his power.[41] Ezekiel believed that the power of God would vindicate his "holy name" by delivering Israel from Babylon (Ezek. 36:20–24). It was noted how the Song of the Sea saw this in the deliverance of Israel from Egypt (Ex. 15:6):

> Thy right hand, O Lord, glorious in power,
> thy right hand, O Lord, shatters the enemy.

This concept of the power of the Lord's "right hand" was also expressed by Paul in "the power of God for salvation to every one who has faith" (Romans 1:16).

This power of God in personal salvation does not exclude many philosophical implications of God's omnipotence, even though these speculations do at times get far beyond the average need for pious assurance. The renowned Jewish philosopher Abraham Heschel was no doubt correct in seeing God as "the power to be."[42] Paul Tillich pondered God not only as "the power to be" himself but as the power of all being or, better expressed, as the power of all existence.[43] John Macquarrie expresses much the same in a way that sounds too negative or passive for the living God of historical revelation. Macquarrie says God or Being "is nothing apart from its appearance in and through and with particular beings" and that "Being cannot itself be a person."[44] His conclusion is only partly true when he says: "But we must be careful not to let this word 'Being' betray us into a static notion of God. We have seen that Being always includes becoming, and that the essence of Being is the dynamic art of letting-be."[45] Such language sounds as if God just steps aside and lets it happen! This is clearly not satisfactory.

A fourth property of God's holiness is his constancy through all change.[46] This embraces both Being and becoming, but it does not require that God must become in order to be. God does not happen as if he were no more than a creative event; he creates the event and is prior to the event. He has the power to be without becoming, yet he has the power to become in his sovereign freedom and grace. God is neither static immutability nor dynamic event when viewed alone. He is the Eternal Being who acts in freedom and is constant through all change.

The living God of the Bible does change in his activity for man and in his attitude toward man, but he remains the same in the constancy of his

---

41. Karl Barth, *Church Dogmatics*, II/1, 522-607; Emil Brunner, *Dogmatics*, I, 248-255; Stephen Charnock, *The Attributes of God* (1681), pp. 357-445; Helmer Ringgren, *The Prophetical Conception of Holiness* (Uppsala, 1948).
42. *Who Is Man?* (Stanford U. P., 1965).
43. *Systematic Theology*, I, 163-289.
44. *Op. cit.*, p. 104.
45. *Ibid.*, p. 110.
46. Karl Barth, *Church Dogmatics*, II/1, 490-522; Emil Brunner, *Dogmatics*, I, 268-271.

character and the counsel of his will. It is possible for biblical writers to speak of the repentance of God in one sense and to deny it in another (Gen. 6:6; 1 Sam. 15:29, 35; Amos 7:3, 6). *The Oracles of Balaam* holds the two ideas in balance (Num. 23:19):

> God is not man, that he should lie,
>   or a son of man, that he should repent.
> Has he said, and will he not do it?
>   Or has he spoken, and will he not fulfill it?

A second idea used to express God's constancy through all change is the face of God. This may express God's favor and peace as in the Aaronic benediction (Num. 6:24–26):

> The Lord bless you and keep you:
> The Lord make his face to shine upon you,
>   and be gracious to you:
> The Lord lift up his countenance upon you,
>   and give you peace.

The parallel concepts of face and countenance are used often in the covenant relation (Pss. 31:16; 80:3, 7, 19; 4:6; 44:3; 89:15).

When the people of God fail to keep the covenant the Lord may withdraw his favor by turning away his face in wrath (Isa. 54:8; cf. 64:7):

> In overflowing wrath for a moment
>   I hid my face from you,
> but with everlasting love I will have compassion on you,
>   says the Lord, your Redeemer.

The process theology that builds on the philosophy of A. N. Whitehead has made a contribution by speaking of the enrichment of God in the creative process, but this emphasis on God's immanent and dynamic involvement in the process is often done at the expense of God's transcendence over process.

This constancy through all change retains belief in "the unchangeable character of his purpose" (Heb. 6:17).

A fifth property of God's holiness is his eternity.[47] The eternity of God is power to persist. The Holy One is the Eternal One, but not in the sense of static being. It is also not necessary to adopt some rigid rationalism of God's eternal decrees and double predestination to say that God is pretemporal, i.e. before all time. God's eternity does not depend on particular things. It stands over and against the transitoriness of man. As the Psalmist said (Ps. 90:2):

47. Karl Barth, *Church Dogmatics*, II/1, 608-640; Emil Brunner, *Dogmatics*, I, 266-268; Stephen Charnock, *op. cit.*, pp. 69-97.

Before the mountains were brought forth,
or ever thou hadst formed the earth and the world,
from everlasting to everlasting thou art God.

This is far more than Macquarrie's statement that Being "is nothing apart from its appearance in and through and with particular beings."

God is also supra-temporal, above time. As the Reformation emphasis on God's eternal decrees put the wrong emphasis on the pretemporal, so the reaction of nineteenth-century idealism turned to the supra-temporal. It is not wrong to speak of God as above, for he inhabits eternity (Isa. 57:15). The Most High God is the true God, and "Glory to God in the highest" is always appropriate. Error creeps in only when the past and the future are neglected.

God is also post-temporal. That is the valid point in Jürgen Moltmann's *Theology of Hope* (1964) that has been such a jolt to idealistic liberalism. Yet Moltmann is so intent on the future that he neglects the past and the present. God is "the God of steadfastness and encouragement" (Rom. 15:5) who keeps his promises of the past before he is "the God of hope" (Rom. 15:13). One of the weakest points in Moltmann's theology is his neglect of the work of the Holy Spirit in the present. He proclaims only a phrase out of his favorite scripture (Rom. 15:13):

May the God of hope fill you with all joy and peace in believing,
so that by the power of the Spirit you may abound in hope!

In this way "the God of steadfastness and encouragement" and "the God of hope" becomes "the God of peace" in the present (Rom. 15:33).

The eternity of God includes the present, always the starting point for personal knowledge of God, then the past and the future. The coming God of Isaiah (40:3–11) is the Creator God of the past (40:12–26) and the Everlasting God of the present (40:27–31). The God of all history answers the questions as to who did the great deeds of the past (41:4; cf. 43:10; 44:6; 48:12):

I, the Lord, the first,
and with the last; I am He.

A Pauline hymn concludes with the affirmation (Rom. 11:36):

For from him and through him and to him are all things.
To him be glory for ever. Amen.

The Johannine Apocalypse identifies the Christian God with the God of Israel in the declaration (1:8):

"I am the Alpha and the Omega," says the Lord God,
who is and who was and who is to come, the Almighty.

The sixth property of God's holiness is his glory.[48] The glory of God is the manifested Presence of God. It is his naked holiness. It symbolizes his omnipresence, but the static statements on omnipresence in scholastic theology, both Catholic and Protestant, fall far short of the potentiality of God's dynamic presence in every moment of actuality.

The universal glory was manifested in a special way in the Exodus and in the Temple. The Song of the Sea marvels at the manifestation of this potentiality in the actual presence of the Lord at the deliverance of Israel from Egypt (Ex. 15:11):

> *Who is like thee, O Lord, among the gods?*
> *Who is like thee, majestic in holiness,*
>   *terrible in glorious deeds, doing wonders?*

His majestic holiness is seen in his "glorious deeds."

The psalm of Habakkuk extols the holiness and the glory of the Lord as he marches forth to deliver his people (3:3; cf. 2:14):

> *God came from Teman,*
>   *and the Holy One from Mount Paran.*
> *His glory covered the heavens,*
>   *and the earth was full of his praise.*

It has already been noted how Isaiah saw a vision and heard the cherubim chant the holiness of the Lord and his universal glory at the time of his call (6:1-3; cf. 40:5; 58:8; 59:19; 60:1). This prophetic conception of God's holiness uncovered by the manifestation of glory becomes highly developed in the prophet Ezekiel. "It was Ezekiel who saw the vision of glory" (*Ben Sirach* 49:8). In Ezekiel the manifestation of glory *is* the manifestation of the Lord himself. The two are not to be separated, and the two are used as interchangeable terms (9:3, 4). In the consummation the presence of the glory in the Temple is the presence of the Lord (43:1-12; 48:35).

The priestly conception of the connection between the Lord's presence and the manifestation of glory is of special interest to the Priestly Writer (P) in the Pentateuch. The Deuteronomic history has a similar interest (1 Kings 8:10, 27). The glory of Sinai is seen in creation, especially in man, the image of God (Genesis 1). In the Exodus and in the Tent in the Wilderness the Lord is present (Exodus 14:4-17; 16:10; 24:17; 29:43; 33:7f., 18ff.; 40:34-38; Lev. 9:23f.; Num. 14:21; 17:7).

The Psalms, the song book of the Second Temple, are rich in references to the glory of the Lord as his manifested presence in the past, the present and the future (19:1-4; 29:1; 49:17; 57:6-12; 72:19; 73:24).

The universal glory of God became incarnate in Jesus Christ. James

---

48. Karl Barth, *Church Dogmatics*, II/1, 640-677; Emil Brunner, *Dogmatics*, I, 285-289; Stephen Charnock, *op. cit.*, pp. 144-180; Edmond Jacob, *op. cit.*, pp. 79-82.

calls Jesus "the Lord of Glory" (2:1). The Petrine writings look forward to the future revelation of the glory of God at the *parousia*, the Second Coming of Jesus, but this glory has already been manifested in the Transfiguration (1 Pet. 1:11; 5:1; 2 Pet. 1:17).

The Pauline writings also declare the Crucified One to be "the Lord of glory" (1 Cor. 2:8) and build belief in the resurrection of the dead (15:43) and the present process of transformation (2 Cor. 3:18) on the Priestly portrait of man as the image of God. Even creation will participate in the uncovering of God's glory when both God's creation and God's children are set free (Rom. 8:18–25).

The seventh property of God's holiness is God's wisdom.[49] As the glory of God is a biblical way to express God's dynamic omnipresence, so the wisdom of God expresses his omniscience, his universal knowledge of all things, persons and events. At this point it is especially important to steer clear of abstract speculations about questions that are unanswerable by human wisdom and to concentrate on the concrete meaning of the wisdom of God manifested in his universal ordering toward the future revelation of his mysterious and majestic ways.

The wisdom of God belongs to a very old tradition that has produced a wisdom literature in the Bible itself.[50] Most of it is in the Old Testament, and most of the teachings are concerned with the art by which right thought issues in appropriate action. This practical expression of wisdom makes the wise man, but there is a metaphysical wisdom which belongs to God alone. One of the profoundest questions ever asked was put by Job in the Hymn on Wisdom (28:12):

> *But where shall wisdom be found?*
> *And where is the place of understanding?*

One answer to this question is creation. The prophet Jeremiah saw that (10:12). The Discourses of the Lord in Job 38–41 suggest that answer, but the Speech of the Prophetess Wisdom in Proverbs 8 describes wisdom, *chokmah*, as the agent of creation. This personification of wisdom approaches a doctrine of pre-existence that was later perverted into the creature Christology of Arius of Alexandria, but the concept of God's ordering of creation is extremely important in the present scientific age. It was also important in the worship of the Second Temple (Psalm 104).

The most crucial manifestation of wisdom for the Christian faith was

---

49. Karl Barth, *Church Dogmatics*, II/1, 422-439; Emil Brunner, *Dogmatics*, I, 282-285; Stephen Charnock, *op. cit.*, pp. 261-439; Edmond Jacob, *op. cit.*, pp. 118f.
50. Martin Noth and D. Winton Thomas, ed., *Wisdom in Israel and in the Ancient Near East* (Leiden: E. J. Brill, 1955); Coert Rylaarsdam, *Revelation in Jewish Wisdom Literature* (University of Chicago Press, 1946); R. N. Whybray, *Wisdom in Proverbs* (London: SCM, 1965); William McKane, *Prophets and Wise Men* (London: SCM, 1965); *Proverbs* (Philadelphia: The Westminster Press, 1970).

the cross of Christ (1 Cor. 1:24; 2:6–3:3). This is continued in the mission of the church (Eph. 3:10f.), and will be completed and clarified in the consummation (Rom. 11:33).

22. The Majesty of God's Nature: His Love

A cultic confession about the Lord in Ex. 34:6 is very near to the heart of the Old Covenant.

> *The Lord, the Lord,*
> *a God merciful and gracious,*
> *slow to anger,*
> *abounding in steadfast love and faithfulness. . . .*

This belief may well be called "the five points of Yahwism." It is repeated with variations and abbreviations in many other passages (Ex. 20:5–6; Num. 14:18; Deut. 5:9–10; Neh. 9:17, 31; Pss. 86:15; 103:8; 145:8; Jer. 32:18; Nahum 1:3; Joel 2:13; Jonah 4:2).

The Holy One is Holy Love, even in the Old Testament. Holiness is central in the Old Testament, but love is not neglected. Holiness and love do not contradict, as Marcion, a second-century Christian heretic, thought when he rejected the Old Testament Scriptures in favor of the canon confined to the Gospel of Luke and the first ten letters of Paul. The Creator God and the Redeemer God are one God, as the monotheism of Isaiah 40–55 says with such great power (41:14; 44:6; 47:4). A biblical synthesis of Holy Love is a bulwark against the *Antitheses* of Marcion and so much sentimental and superficial theology today.

The Properties of God's Love

The properties of God's love will be considered before its perfection much as they appear in historical revelation. As holiness is the starting point, so love is the high point in the biblical unfolding of the nature of God. One is the outer court and the other is the inner sanctuary in the theological temple of God. As the properties of holiness are the branches in the menorah of monotheism, so the properties of love are the beams that give light and warmth to what could be a barren theology of being. Being itself becomes moral being. The anemic ontology of Paul Tillich gets a transfusion from the red-blooded theology of Karl Barth. In this way the truth of a statement by Abraham Heschel can be seen when he says that "the Bible is not the theology of man, but the anthropology of God."[51]

The first property of God's love that is found in the cultic confession of Exodus 34:6 is mercy, and this is often a corollary of God's wrath. To the God of the covenant one may in confidence pray: "in the midst of wrath

---

51. *Man is Not Alone* (New York: Farrar, Straus & Young, 1951), p. 129.

remember mercy" (Hab. 3:2). Wrath is so modified by mercy that it is never possible to say that God is wrath, as one may say that "God is love." The mercy of God is always a picture of the condition of man on the one hand and of the compassion of God on the other. Here concrete examples are more important than precepts.

A prophet of Israel married a temple prostitute, and to them three children were born before she ran away to live with other lovers. It is doubtful that the prophet was the father of the three children (Hos. 2:4f.). Years after Gomer the prostitute left Hosea the prophet, she was sold as a slave in the market place, and Hosea bought her back, disciplined her, and reaffirmed his devotion to her (3:1-5).

The story has too much pathos for many people to believe that the Lord of the covenant actually said: "Go, take to yourself a wife of harlotry and have children of harlotry, for the land commits great harlotry by forsaking the Lord" (Hos. 1:2). One writer who led a crusade against a young scholar for having difficulty with God's command to Abraham to sacrifice his only son Isaac goes into great detail to explain away the clear command of the Lord to Hosea.[52] He could believe that the Lord commanded a patriarch to kill his son, but he was unable to believe God told a prophet to marry a prostitute.

The example of Hosea and the problem made for legalistic religion reveals much of how one thinks of God. The command to Hosea is obviously intended to be taken as historical fact, but the theological truth probes the great pathos in the heart of the living God. God will do for Israel what he commanded Hosea to do for Gomer. He made a covenant with her when she came out of Egypt, but now she has gone off after the strange gods of Baalism. Still God will redeem her, discipline her, and renew his devotion to her. "And I will betroth you to me forever; I will betroth you to me in righteousness and in justice, in steadfast love, and in mercy. I will betroth you to me in faithfulness, and you shall know the Lord" (Hos. 2:19f.). The property of mercy is paramount in this prophet.[53]

The stories of God's mercy on Israel in Babylonian Exile (Isa. 54:7-10), of Jesus' response to the pitiful condition of blind Bartimaeus (Mark 10:45-52), the baptismal songs of the apostolic church (Eph. 2:4-10; Titus 3:4-7), and numerous other passages in the Bible magnify the mercy of God.[54]

A second property of God's love is grace, and it is often closely linked with mercy (Exodus 33:19). The main words for the concept are *chen* in Hebrew and *charis* in Greek, but these are closely related to the other words

52. K. O. White, *Studies in Hosea* (Nashville, Tennessee: Convention Press, 1957), pp. 17-19.
53. Norman H. Snaith, *Mercy and Sacrifice* (London: SCM, 1953). See also H. Wheeler Robinson, *The Cross of Hosea*, ed. Ernest A. Payne (Philadelphia: The Westminster Press, 1949); Roy L. Honeycutt, *Hosea and His Message* (Nashville: Broadman Press, 1975), p. 5.
54. Karl Barth, *Church Dogmatics*, II/1, 368-375, is at his best on the mercy of God.

in the "five points of Yahwism." As the mercy of God modifies the wrath of God, so the grace of God gives saving power to the righteousness of God. God's grace is far more than his unmerited favor. It is God giving himself in many ways, especially in the humiliation of Jesus Christ. A central confession on the grace of God in Jesus Christ is included in an exposition of the grace of giving for the great collection Paul took to Jerusalem in A.D. 55. The Corinthians are challenged with the words (2 Cor. 8:9):

> For you know the grace of our Lord Jesus Christ,
>   that though he was rich,
> yet for your sake he became poor,
>   so that by his poverty you might become rich.

God's grace is then God revealing himself in his self-communication to his own. A Hymn on Righteousness relates the central theme in the Letter of Paul to the Romans (1:17) to the grace of God revealed in the expiation of sin by Jesus Christ, God's Mercy Seat (Rom. 3:21–26).[55]

God's revelation of his grace in the death of Christ will continue in the power of his resurrection in the coming ages. A Hymn on Resurrection, both his in the past and ours in the present, attributes the whole process of salvation to the revelation of God's grace (Eph. 2:4–10).

God's grace is also God reigning over the powers of sin and death through the death and resurrection of Christ. A Hymn on Adam and Christ proclaims Adam as the type and Christ as the antitype as God's grace comes to reign (Rom. 5:12–21).[56]

These pillar passages became the basis for both development and distortion of the doctrine of grace. Roman Catholic theology has tended to think of grace as an infused substance, an imparting of powers and virtues by which man merits the beatific vision of God and the immortality of his soul. In the words of Ignatius of Antioch, grace is "the medicine of immortality" (Ep. xx. 2). This *donum superadditum*, supernatural gift, was lost by the Fall of Adam and Eve, but it is restored by the sacrifice of Christ through the sacraments of the Church. This doctrine of grace is defended by subtle theological distinctions.[57]

The Protestant Reformers supplanted the infusion of grace with the irresistible grace of a sovereign will that denied the freedom of the human will. For Martin Luther (1483-1546) God is grace acting out his very being in freedom and faith that have their source in God alone. The Roman

---

55. See my commentary on Romans in *Broadman Bible Commentary*, Vol. 10, pp. 181-185.
56. *Ibid.*, pp. 195-198.
57. Karl Rahner and Herbert Vorgrimler, *Concise Theological Dictionary*, edited by Cornelius Ernst and translated by Richard Strachan (New York: Herder and Herder, 1965), pp. 192-198; Karl Rahner, et al., ed., *Sacramentum Mundi* (New York: Herder and Herder), Vol. 2, pp. 409-424; *A Catholic Dictionary of Theology* (London: Thomas Nelson and Sons, 1967), II, 340-348.

Catholic distinction between the *similitudo dei*, the likeness of God lost by the Fall, and the *imago dei*, the image of God retained after the Fall, was rejected as false exegesis of the parallelism in Genesis 1:26. John Calvin (1509-64) was more moderate in his views than was Luther in his book *The Bondage of the Will* (1525), but the neo-Calvinism of Karl Barth still teaches, in the setting of modern biblical criticism, the essential views of the sixteenth-century Reformers.[58]

The third property of God's love is his patience. This must always be considered as a restraint to his power. Power without patience is destruction. In the cultic confession of Ex. 34:6 and the later restatements this patience is expressed in the negative phrase "slow to anger." In a more positive manner it is called God's longsuffering. "The Lord is not slack concerning his promise, as some men count slackness; but is longsuffering toward you, not willing that any should perish but that all should come to repentance" (2 Pet. 3:9).

God's slowness to anger and longsuffering may also be called his passivity, his refusal to act at times when he is acted upon. This seems to be a better way to express this quality of patience than to speak of God's nonresistance, as Gordon D. Kaufman does.[59] Kaufman also has a confused Christology that makes no distinction between the Father and his Son when he assigns what is said of the servant of the Lord in Isaiah 53 to the Lord himself. As Tertullian said of Praxeas: "he crucified the Father" (*Against Praxeas*, I).

God's passivity gives time to man. These are the "times of ignorance" which God overlooked before the resurrection of Jesus (Acts 17:30; cf. 14:16). They are also a time for repentance before both the first coming of Christ (Acts 14:15) and the second coming at the *parousia* (2 Pet. 3:9).

God's passivity also gives time to God. This is a time for revelation. "This was to show God's righteousness, because in his divine forbearance he had passed over former sins; it was to prove at the present time that he himself is righteous and that he justifies him who has faith in Jesus" (Rom. 3:25b-26). This is also a time before retribution. God is rich in kindness and forbearance and patience as he seeks to lead men to repentance, but those who are impenitent and harden their hearts are storing up wrath "on the day of wrath when God's righteous judgment will be revealed" (Rom. 2:5). In order "to show his wrath and to make his power known," God "endured with much patience the vessels of wrath" who, by their resistance to God, "fit themselves for destruction" (Rom. 9:22 with the middle participle translation). There is hardly a statement in the Bible more important for our understanding of the balance between the power and patience of God than this.

58. *Church Dogmatics*, II/1, 351-358.
59. *Systematic Theology* (New York: Charles Scribner's Sons, 1968), pp. 219-222.

God's patience is also the "passibility" of God, the positive suffering of God in his involvement with his creation and his creatures. There is much truth in what was once condemned as patripassianism, the belief that the Father suffers in his Son and in himself because of the evil and sin in the world.

G. A. Studdert-Kennedy wrote some moving and eloquent poetry on "the sorrows of God" when he said:

> The sorrors o' God must be 'ard to bear
>   If 'E really 'as Love in 'Is 'eart,
> And the 'ardest part i' the world to play
>   Must surely be God's part. . . .
>
> Not just that 'E suffered once for all
>   To save us from our sins,
> And then went up to 'Is throne on 'igh
>   To wait till 'Is 'eaven begins.
>
> But what if 'E came to the earth to show,
>   By the paths o' pain that 'E trod
> The blistering flame of eternal shame
>   That burns in the heart o' God?
>
> O God, if that's 'ow it really is,
>   Why, bless ye, I understands,
> And I feels for you wi' your thorn-crowned 'ead
>   And your ever-piercèd 'ands. [60]

There is much to be learned from Kazoh Kitamori when he says that God's pain "could not have existed had not the Redeemer, the personification of God's pain, been a historical figure."[61]

But the death of God theology that assumed that God became a man in Jesus Christ and that God died when Jesus died goes too far. In protest against a God of radical transcendence the death of God theology ended up with a God of radical immanence that is no God at all, as *The Gospel of Christian Atheism* by Thomas J. J. Altizer so blatantly proclaimed.

The kindness of God is the fourth point in the five points of the cultic confession in Exodus 34:6. The Hebrew word *chesed* is often translated lovingkindness, as in the ASV, and steadfast love, as in the RSV, but all of these are efforts to express loyalty to the covenant relation with God. It is "the power which guarantees a covenant and makes it strong and durable."[62]

In covenant relation with God the moral attributes are manifested in

---

60. Walter Marshall Horton, *Contemporary English Theology* (New York: Harper and Brothers, Publishers, 1936), p. 51.
61. *The Theology of the Pain of God* (Richmond, Va.: John Knox Press, 1965), p. 35.
62. Edmond Jacob, *op. cit.*, p. 104. See pp. 103-107 for a summary of research and Old Testament usage.

a manner impossible outside the covenant. Human covenants required loyalty (*chesed*), as in the covenants between Abimelech and Abraham, Abimelech and Isaac, and Laban and Jacob (Gen. 21:23; 26:29; 31:32). Loyalty to the covenant is maintained even between the deceptive Gibeonites and Israelites (Judg. 9:26; 10:16f.). As the Israelites made an attack on the Amalekites, the Midianites were called out from the Amalekites because the Midianites "showed *chesed* to all the people of Israel when they came out of Egypt" (1 Sam. 15:6).

In covenant relation with God *chesed* is the typical relationship of prayer. The Prayer of Abraham's Servant, as he arrived at the well in Mesopotamia, was (Gen. 24:12):

> O Lord, God of my master Abraham,
>   grant me success today, I pray thee,
>   and show steadfast love to my master Abraham.

Steadfast love is *chesed* in Hebrew. As the servant, perhaps Eliezer, met Rebekah, the future wife of Isaac, he blessed the Lord with these words (24:27):

> Blessed be the Lord, the God of my master Abraham,
>   who has not forsaken his steadfast love
>   and his faithfulness toward my master.

The Prayer of Jacob, when he met Esau on his return from Paddanaram, was based on this same belief in the *chesed* of the Lord (39:9f.).

The Song of the Sea in Exodus 15:2-18 begins by saying the Lord is "glorious in power" (v. 6) and "majestic in holiness" (v. 11), but the climax is reached when "steadfast love" (v. 13) is ascribed to the Lord.

The Hebrew *chesed* has rightly been called covenant love.[63] The breach of this relationship is the burden of the prophet and of the Lord in the book of Hosea. The portrait of Hosea is one of *chesed*. The representation of God as compassionate father who is so deeply grieved that he must chastise his disobedient and wayward son in Hosea 11 comes very near to the heart of God revealed in the cross of Christ.[64]

It is God's constancy with compassion. A good example of the theology of *chesed* is the Thanksgiving in Psalm 136, in which there is a review of God's work in creation (vv. 4-9) and in the history of Israel (vv. 10-22) and in which the congregation responds at the end of each of the twenty-six verses with the words: "for his steadfast love endures forever." Steadfast love is *chesed*. This durability of the Lord, like that of a loyal friend, wears well with the years.

63. Norman H. Snaith, *The Distinctive Ideas of the Old Testament* (Philadelphia: The Westminster Press, 1946), pp. 118-166.
64. H. Wheeler Robinson, *op. cit.*

The Greek word *chrēstos*, kindness, is the nearest New Testament word to the Hebrew *chesed*. Jesus taught that the Most High God is "kind to the ungrateful and the selfish" (Luke 6:35). A newborn babe in the Christian life is one who has "tasted the kindness of the Lord" (1 Peter 2:3). The wicked should not presume upon God's kindness. The hard of heart are asked: "Or do you presume upon the riches of his kindness and forbearance and kindness? Do you not know that God's kindness is meant to lead you to repentance?" (Rom. 2:4).

God's kindness is eternal. He has raised us up with Christ "that in the coming ages he might show the immeasurable riches of his grace in kindness toward us in Christ" (Eph. 2:7). The Hymn of Resurrection in Ephesians 2:4–7 is a blend of God's mercy, grace, and kindness experienced in the spiritual realm, "the heavenly places."

God's kindness is historical. The Hymn of Epiphany in Titus 3:4–7 celebrates that historical appearance in the coming of Christ and at one's baptism into the Christian life. There again mercy, grace, and kindness are blended with God's love toward man (*philanthrōpia*).

The fifth property of God's love in the cultic confession of Exodus 34:6 is his faithfulness, *emunah* in Hebrew, *pistos* in Greek.

Hosea saw in his faithfulness to Gomer even in her time of unfaithfulness the covenant love of God. In the restoration of Israel as the faithful wife of the Lord the words of betrothal are: "I will betroth you to me in faithfulness; and you shall know the Lord" (2:20). Faithfulness between the Lord and his people is compared to the intimate knowledge between a faithful husband and a faithful wife.

The Pauline writings seem to be quoting a confession which says: "God is faithful" (1 Cor. 1:9; 10:13; 2 Cor. 1:18; cf. 1 Thess. 5:24; 2 Thess. 3:3). Among the "faithful" sayings of the Pastoral Letters (Titus 3:8; 1 Tim. 1:5; 3:1; 4:9; 2 Tim. 2:11) is an early Christian hymn which says (2 Tim. 2:11–13):

> *If we have died with him, we shall also live with him;*
> *if we endure, we shall also reign with him;*
> *if we deny him, he also will deny us;*
> *if we are faithless, he remains faithful —*

for he cannot deny himself." This last comment explains why the Lord's denial of the faithless is not due to his faithlessness. When the covenant is broken it is always broken from man's side, never from God's side.

The Johannine writings never speak about the faithfulness of man, but the faithfulness of God is the very basis for belief in the confession of sin (1 John 1:9): "If we confess our sins, he is faithful and just to forgive our sins and cleanse us from all unrighteousness."

A sixth property of God's love is goodness. This goes beyond the "five points" of Exodus 34:6, but it has a large place in both biblical and philosophical theology. "We understand by goodness the sum of all that is right and friendly and wholesome: the three taken together."[65] The radiant majesty of God's glory may become a manifestation of God's goodness. When Moses asked the Lord to show his glory, it was the Lord's goodness that passed by (Ex. 33:18f.). This goodness manifested in glory may be experienced in worship (Ps. 34:8). At times the goodness and compassion of God are substituted for his faithfulness (Ps. 145:9).

God's goodness is the source of all good things. The supreme good for Israel was the *Torah* (Deut. 30:1ff.), but there were many other good things as well. "Every good endowment and every perfect gift is from above, coming down from the Father of lights with whom there is no variation or shadow due to change" (Jas. 1:17).

Absolute goodness may be applied to God alone. Not even Jesus may be called good without a recognition of his ultimate relation to God (Mark 10:17f.). However, there is a relative goodness that may be attributed to godly people (Rom. 5:7). Barnabas was "a good man, full of the Holy Spirit and of faith" (Acts 11:24). His goodness was his fullness in God.

Analytical philosophy would hesitate to apply goodness to any other than man. It is argued that infinite goodness is nonsense. If infinite goodness is put at the end of a series it is nonsense, but if infinite goodness is manifested in all good things and good persons as a quality then it becomes a synonym for God.[66]

Process philosophy has less difficulty with God as the source of human goodness. Henry N. Wieman argued that human good arises out of creative events in which man is rightly related to others and to his environment. These relations call forth a growing awareness of beauty, truth and knowledge that is agreeable to human value.[67]

I would want to add that there is both a natural and a supernatural environment much in the way John Oman put it in his book *The Natural and the Supernatural*, but that which is agreeable to man in all of his relationships is very near the meaning of the goodness of God.

The seventh property of God's love is knowledge. God's knowing is God's loving. In biblical thought the sexual relation between man and woman is the basic metaphor for knowing another person. When Cain knew his wife, he had sexual relations with her (Gen. 4:17). When the Virgin Mary said she knew no man, she meant that she had never had sexual relations (Luke 1:34).

The prophet Amos used the analogy of man knowing woman in sexual

65. Karl Barth, *Church Dogmatics*, II/2, p. 708.
66. Ian T. Ramsey, *Religious Language* (London: SCM Press, 1957), pp. 66-71.
67. *The Source of Human Good* (Chicago: University of Chicago Press, 1946).

love and loyalty to declare the covenant relation between the Lord and Israel. The Lord says (Amos 3:2):

> *You only have I known*
> *of all the families of the earth;*
> *therefore I will punish you*
> *for all your iniquities.*

The Lord, of course, was not ignorant of other families in the sense of omniscience, but knowledge is a covenant relation of love and loyalty.

Psalm 139, the so-called *locus classicus* on omnipresence, describes knowledge (vv. 1-6), presence (vv. 7-12), and power (vv. 13-18) in terms of intimate personal love. This intimate knowledge extends to the whole creation with which the Lord is concerned (Ps. 104:19; Job 37:16; 38:33).

This intimate knowledge of personal concern includes the individual as well as the covenant community and the whole creation. The Father in heaven knows our needs before we ask, and the birds and flowers are not beyond his loving concern and intimate knowledge (Matt. 6:8; 7:25-29). If God is concerned with daily needs, he surely knows those who belong to him as trusting children (2 Tim. 2:19). Even the loving relations of heaven are expressed in terms of knowledge (Matt. 25:12; Rev. 22:4).

Under the influence of Greek philosophy this dynamic and intimate personalism of biblical faith was weakened, but not even Augustine excluded freedom from the knowledge of God. God's foreknowledge included knowledge of human freedom (*City of God*, V. 10). When this dropped into the background a fatal doctrine of predestination in the form of determinism took over. Neither Martin Luther nor John Calvin escaped this debacle, and this has colored Protestant theology through most of its history.[68]

Even the experiential theology of F. D. E. Schleiermacher did not escape this deterministic idea that knowledge and willing are the same (*The Christian Faith*, 55, 1). A debt is owed to Emil Brunner for his protest, in the name of dynamic personalism, against such theology. His argument is simple but significant:

> As we know the *present* not only as something that is necessary, but also as something that is accidental, contingent, so also God knows the *future* as something contingent. The future stands equally directly before Him as the present stands before us. God knows that which takes place in freedom in the future as something which happens in freedom.[69]

His present knowledge of us is one of freedom in love and love in freedom, an I-Thou relation, not an It-It relation. "But if one loves God, one is

---

68. Stephen Charnock, *op. cit.*, pp. 181-260.
69. *Dogmatics*, I, 262. Italics in original.

known by him" (1 Cor. 8:3). Not even things are related with such logical determinism as some theologians have done with the sovereign God and predestined man. Man is more a deciding person than a thinking thing.

The Perfection of God's Love

As the perfection of holiness is the point of departure for understanding God's moral attribute or nature, so the perfection of God's love is the peak of all special revelation. In the promissory revelation of the Old Testament, it is the love of the covenant relation; in the time of fulfillment in the New Testament, it is the love manifested in the cross of Christ; and in the continuation of revelation in the church, it is the love of the community of faith and hope.

This love of the covenant is first of all election love.[70] It is prior to the covenant relation of *chesed* (steadfast love), for it answers the question as to why there was a covenant in the first place. The great Hebrew word that points to this election love is *ahabah*.

The blossoming of the concept is associated with the reformation theology of the seventh century B.C. It seems that the Deuteronomic view of God introduced a new element to explain the Lord's election of Israel. It was not something in Israel but something in God that explained this special relation. "And because he loved your fathers and chose their descendants after them, and brought you out of Egypt with his own presence, by his great power, driving out before you nations greater and mightier than yourselves, to bring you in, to give you their land for an inheritance, as at this day; know therefore this day, and lay it to your heart, that the Lord is God in heaven above and on earth beneath; there is no other" (Deut. 4:37-39).

The *ahabah* of the Lord should motivate the worship and obedience of Israel. The *Shema*, from the Hebrew for "hear," became, therefore, the most important statement in the faith of Israel. "Hear, O Israel: the Lord our God is one Lord; and you shall love the Lord your God with all your heart, and with all your soul, and with all your might" (Deut. 6:4f.).

The prophet Jeremiah proclaimed this covenant love as the eternal nature of the Lord, who says (31:2f.):

> *The people who survived the sword*
> *found grace in the wilderness;*
> *when Israel sought for rest,*
> *the Lord appeared to him from afar.*
> *I have loved you with an everlasting love;*
> *therefore I have continued my faithfulness to you.*

The failure of Israel did not frustrate the purpose of the Lord, for he made a new covenant with a new relation of love.

70. Norman Snaith, *The Distinctive Ideas of the Old Testament*, pp. 167-182; Edmond Jacob, *op. cit.*, pp. 108-112.

The love of the cross is the particular emphasis of Paul's Letter to the Romans. This was and is the supreme revelation of love. A hymn of vicarious love shows how the love of the cross is the answer to the human condition (Rom. 5:6–11). The first human condition from which God's love delivers us is that of weakness (Rom. 5:6). Plato's idea of *erōs* (sexual love) measured love by the worth of the object, but the Pauline idea of *agapē* (sacrificial love) declares that "Christ died for the ungodly." The death of the godly for the ungodly reveals the source of love in the subject rather than the object. God loves us not because of what we are but because of what he is.

A second human condition for which *agapē* is the remedy is that of sinfulness (Rom. 5:8). Even if one should on occasion die for a good person, it would be difficult to comprehend love for those who are bad, but "God shows his love for us in that while we were yet sinners Christ died for us." Again love is determined by the nature of the lover rather than the beloved.

A third human condition reveals for the third time the nature of God's love toward the unlovely. God loves even those who are his enemies (Rom. 5:10). This does not mean that God was the enemy of man until Christ died. If enmity is ascribed to God, then consistent exegesis would require God to be involved in weakness and sinfulness — which is absurd. The "we" has reference to us in each case (Rom. 5:6, 8, 10). God is the reconciler but never the reconciled, so the idea of the propitiation and reconciliation of God must be rejected.

A hymn on the victorious love of God takes the *agapē* of the cross a step farther (Rom. 8:31–39). By the power of God's love there is neither condemnation (vv. 31–34) nor separation (vv. 35–39) from God for those "in Christ Jesus our Lord." When the victorious love of God is applied to those not in Christ it leads either to the idea of universal salvation or to the false notion that one remains secure even in the repudiation of Christ. There is indeed "the security of the believer" who abides in Christ, but there is no security for the unbeliever who repudiates Christ (Rom. 14:13–23). Belief is the response of the beloved to the lover, but this love becomes wrath when resisted. God's love must not be spurned and repudiated.

A major contribution to modern theology recovered this *agapē* of the cross.[71] Some have argued that the so-called Lundensian theology, out of the University of Lund in Sweden, made too radical a distinction between New Testament *agapē* and the *erōs* of Plato, especially when the so-called *charitas* synthesis in Roman Catholic theology was declared illegitimate, but this is hard to prove. It is strange that no appeal is made to the election love of *ahabah* in the Old Testament as background for New Testament *agapē*, but Lundensian theology is no doubt correct in the claim that the supreme manifestation of love in history was the *agapē* of the cross.

71. Anders Nygren, *Agape and Eros*, tr. Philip S. Watson (Philadelphia: The Westminster Press, 1953), pp. 105-145.

The *agapē* of the community (*koinōnia*, fellowship) goes beyond the historical manifestation at the cross. This identification of God with *agapē* is indeed "the coping-stone, so to speak, on the edifice of the primitive Christian concept of Agape."[72] Nothing greater can be said of God. It proclaims a metaphysical love in which God himself is said to be *agapē* (1 John 4:8, 16). This metaphysical *agapē* is behind all historical manifestations. The eternal relationship between the Father and the Son is based upon the belief that God is *agapē*. The Father loved the Son "before the foundation of the world" (John 17:24; cf. 3:35; 5:20; 15:9).

The manifestation of this metaphysical love is twofold: love for God and love for one another. These are corollaries that can never be separated. It is a lie to say that we love God whom we do not see when we do not love our brother whom we see (1 John 4:19–21). The love that is eternal *koinōnia* between the Father and the Son and that creates *koinōnia* between the disciples excludes love for the *kosmos* (world) that is passing away (1 John 2:15–17). *Koinōnia* is participation in light, life, and love that abide forever.

C. THE MODES OF GOD'S BEING: HOLY TRINITY

23. The Holy Trinity as Manifestation: The Economic Trinity

The language used to describe the Holy Trinity makes a distinction between the economic Trinity and the ontological Trinity. The economic Trinity designates the historical manifestations of God in a trinitarian pattern of some combination of Father, Son, and Spirit. Belief in the ontological Trinity grew out of the theological conviction that the God of eternal being corresponds to his historical manifestations. In other words, God has revealed his reality.

The point at which Christianity differs from the monotheism of both Judaism and Islam is hardly mentioned in much Protestant theology.[72a] The point of difference is belief in God as a Holy Trinity. It is therefore a surprise to read a defense of the doctrine of the belief by a leading Old Testament theologian.[73] This then is the crucial question: Is the doctrine of the Holy Trinity a deviation or is it a logical development of biblical monotheism?

The historical preparation of the Old Testament must first be examined. It is not necessary to resort to unhistorical and allegorical exegesis to see how belief in "the God of the Hebrews" went beyond the ethical monotheism already surveyed. "The God of the Hebrews," as he is called in

---

72. *Ibid.*, p. 148.
72a. E.g., Hans Schwarz, *The Search for God* (Minneapolis: Augsburg Publishing House, 1975).
73. G. A. F. Knight, *A Biblical Approach to the Doctrine of the Trinity* (Edinburgh: Oliver and Boyd, 1953).

Exodus (3:18; 5:3; 7:16; 9:1, 13), was first identified with the Lord (Yahweh, 3:15; 6:3); the idea of a first-born son of the Lord follows immediately. Belief in a God who has a Son is no barren monotheism.

At first the son of God (the Lord) is Israel (4:22f.). This means that the Lord is so involved in the history of the Hebrews that Israel becomes his peculiar possession (cf. Deut. 32:9). The prophet Hosea recalled how the Lord brought his son out of the land of Egypt in the Exodus (Hos. 11:1). A second step declares the dynasty of David to be God's son (2 Sam. 7:14), and a coronation Psalm declares the king the Lord's begotten son (Psalm 2:7).

If Israel as a nation and the king as the Lord's representative before the people can be called the son of God, then those who accept the Old Testament as Holy Scripture should not think it absurd to speak of Jesus as the Son of God as the Gospel of Mark does on at least seven occasions (1:11, 24; 5:7; 9:7; 12:6; 13:32; 15:39).

There is one great difference between the Old Testament teaching on sonship and the New Testament teaching. In the Old Testament Israel and the king were adopted as God's son, but there is no adoptionism in the New Testament. Some have argued that there is adoptionism in the New Testament.[74]

As the teaching of the first-born son of the Lord became the seed for binitarianism, the belief in a unique relation between God and his Son, so the teaching about the Spirit of the Lord furnished the seed for trinitarianism, the belief that God's relation to both his Son and his Spirit is unique.

The Spirit of the Lord was a cardinal concept in the Deuteronomic history. In Judges the deeds of ecstatic leaders are described in terms of possession by the Spirit of the Lord (3:10; 6:34; 11:29; 13:25; 14:6, 19; 15:14). Spiritual possession is elevated to spiritual inspiration in the words of the prophets (1 Sam. 10:6, 10; 11:6; 16:13; 1 Kings 18:12; 2 Kings 2:15f.), but the distinction between possession and inspiration can be pushed too far.

The Spirit of the Lord will rest upon all the people in the future (Ezekiel 37), especially upon the leader who will deliver the Lord's people in a greater deliverance than that seen in the times of the Judges. As branch, servant, and prophet this representative of the people will do the deeds of the Lord by the Spirit of the Lord (Isa. 11:2, 4; 42:1; 61:1). It is no wonder that Matthew 12:15–22 sees Jesus as the servant and Luke 4:18–21 sees him as the prophet.

The unique relation between the Lord and his Spirit leads to the idea of "the holy Spirit" (Isaiah 63:10f.; Psalm 51:11) as a synonym for the

---

74. John Knox, *Jesus: Lord and Christ* (New York: Harper & Brothers, 1958), pp. 45f., 141f., 145ff., 151; *The Humanity and Divinity of Christ* (Cambridge: Cambridge University Press, 1967).

Spirit of the Lord (Isaiah 63:14). The Spirit of the Lord is the holy Spirit because the Spirit is the unique possession of the Lord as the human spirit is the unique possession of each human soul. Indeed it may be that the idea of the human spirit is derived from the idea of the holy Spirit.

After the Lord is described as Father all the terms for the doctrine of the Holy Trinity have been developed into a richer view of God. When even Abraham and Israel no longer acknowledge the people, the Lord as Father does (Isa. 63:16). The Lord shapes his people as a potter does the clay, because he is Father (Isa. 64:8).

If a unique relation exists between the Lord and his Son and his Spirit, it is clear why the three are so frequently mentioned together in the New Testament teachings. At the baptism of Jesus the Son of God, the Spirit of God comes upon him, and the voice of God the Father speaks from heaven (Mark 1:10f.). The teachings on blasphemy manifest a unity between the Father, the Son, and the Holy Spirit; but the distinction between the Son and the Spirit is unmistakable (Matthew 12:30–32). The teachings on the coming of the Son of Man in glory make a distinction between the Father and the Son and the angels that is just as obvious (13:41–43). These elementary things need to be said again and again as long as this oneness in threeness and threeness in oneness is not observed in theology.

The most natural way for the early Christians to describe their experience of God was to follow a trinitarian pattern. The Letter of Jude has the exhortation (20f.):

> Pray in the Holy Spirit;
> keep yourselves in the love of God;
> wait for the mercy of our Lord Jesus Christ.

Belief in God as Holy Trinity developed out of the worship of God. The order of persons may begin with Father, Son or Spirit, and the order is not rigid. For example, the trinitarian formula at the beginning of 1 Peter is Father–Spirit–Son. The people of God had been (1 Pet. 1:2):

> Chosen and destined by God the Father
> and sanctified by the Spirit
> for obedience to Jesus Christ.

Immediately afterward, a Christian berakah speaks of God the Father (1 Pet. 1:3–5), of Jesus Christ his Son (1 Pet. 1:6–9) and of the Spirit of Christ at work before and after the sufferings of Christ (1 Pet. 1:10–12).

The Letter to the Hebrews warns the drifter in the Lord–God–Holy Spirit pattern (Heb. 2:3f.). "Christ . . . through the eternal Spirit offered himself without blemish to God" (Heb. 9:14). God will judge one "who has spurned the Son of God and outraged the Spirit of grace" (Heb. 10:29).

The manifestation of God's multiplicity becomes a trinitarian formula in both the Pauline and Johannine writings of the New Testament. The most profitable place to trace the steps in this pattern is perhaps 1 Corinthians. A confession in 8:6 takes the first step, i.e. binitarianism:

> Yet for us there is one God, the Father,
>   from whom are all things and for whom we exist,
> and one Lord, Jesus Christ,
>   through whom are all things and through whom we exist.

There is no compromise of monotheism in the claim of one God, but the uniqueness of Jesus is retained in the confession of one Lord.

A later confession of faith is a further clarification of this binitarianism (1 Timothy 2:5):

> For there is one God,
> and there is one mediator of God and man,
> the man Christ Jesus.

A return to 1 Corinthians will show how binitarianism and trinitarianism were believed side by side, and neither was a compromise of monotheism as the so-called unitarian pattern theology has argued. A hymn in 1 Corinthians states the trinitarian pattern while confessing only one God (12:4–6):

> Now there are varieties of gifts,
>   but the same Spirit;
> and there are varieties of service,
>   but the same Lord;
> and there are varieties of working,
>   but the same God.

The sequence Spirit–Lord–God indicates the centrality of the Spirit in charismatic worship, but a benediction in 2 Corinthians 13:14 begins with neither the Father nor the Spirit but with "the grace of the Lord Jesus Christ." It is the unity of the trinitarian pattern, not the order, that is of supreme importance in Christian monotheism.

The most trinitarian writing in the Pauline tradition is the Ephesian Letter. The great doxology with which it begins is the *locus classicus* of trinitarian worship in the order Father–Son–Spirit. The "praise of his glory" marks the end of each part of the threefold blessing of God (1:6, 12, 14) — the first the Father, the second the Son, and the third the Spirit. At other places there is unity in trinity (2:18; 3:14–19; 4:4–6; 5:19).

The Johannine writings speak much of the Father, Son, and Spirit, but the hymn on the Holy Spirit as Paraclete moves always in a trinitarian direction (John 14:16f., 25f.; 15:26f.; 16:7–11). The first saying makes a distinction between two Paracletes, one being Jesus as the visible manifestation of the Father and the other being the Holy Spirit the invisible man-

ifestation known only by the disciples (14:16f.). The second saying declares
the Holy Spirit as Paraclete will be sent from the Father in the name of
Jesus (14:25f.). The third saying has precipitated controversy between Eastern Orthodoxy and Roman Catholicism by confining the procession of the
Holy Spirit to the Father, as in Eastern Orthodoxy, and saying nothing
about "and the Son," as in Roman Catholicism, but the trinitarian pattern
is obvious in either formulation. The fourth and fifth sayings make clear
that the ministry of the Holy Spirit follows the earthly ministry of Jesus
without any identification of the Son and the Spirit.

Some New Testament passages are much debated. 2 Corinthians 3:17
has been used much by those who claim that Paul taught only a pneumatic
binitarianism that identified the Holy Spirit with the risen Lord. The simple
language of TEV (*Good News for Modern Man*) is a satisfactory solution
to this problem when it says: "Now, 'the Lord' in this passage is the Spirit;
and where the Spirit of the Lord is present, there is freedom." In other
words, the Lord in Exodus 34:34 made the face of Moses glow as the Holy
Spirit now, "coming from the Lord who is the Spirit, transforms us into his
very likeness, in an even greater degree of glory" (2 Cor. 3:18).

No appeal has been made to the Great Commission in Matthew 28:18–
20, since many believe that "the longer text" of "baptizing them in the name
of the Father and of the Son and of the Holy Spirit" is a second-century
addition made when threefold immersion took the place of one immersion.[75]
Enough has been said elsewhere to indicate why the belief in an economic
Trinity led to the historical discussions about an ontological Trinity. The
Authorized King James Version has a passage that may be interpreted as
teaching the ontological Trinity in 1 John 5:7, but this is definitely not in
the better manuscripts of the New Testament. However, the economic Trinity is clearly indicated in 1 John 4:13–15 in the Spirit–Son–Father sequence.

24. The Holy Trinity as Metaphysics: The Ontological Trinity

The origin of threefold immersion in the early church is hidden in mystery.
It seems impossible to determine whether the reference to "baptizing them
in the name of the Father and of the Son and of the Holy Spirit" is the
cause or the result of the change. It is obvious in the Acts of the Apostles
that the first-century practice was one immersion in the name of Jesus
Christ or the Lord Jesus (2:38; 19:5).

By the middle of the second century the early forms of both the Nicene
Creed of the East and the Apostles' Creed of the West followed the threefold
confession that corresponded to the threefold immersion, but there was no

---

75. Details on all passages about the Holy Spirit may be found in my book *Spirit of the
Living God* (Philadelphia: The Westminster Press, 1968).

teaching about three gods. As in the Great Commission there was only one "name" for God the Holy Trinity. Historical discussions were soon to follow with emphasis either on the threeness or the oneness, but always there was the effort to retain the oneness in the threeness and the threeness in the oneness.[76]

The Greek Triad

Metaphysical speculation on the threefold mode of eternal being is very clear in Theophilus of Antioch in the late second century. He distinguished between the intelligence of the Father, *logos endiathetos*, and the going forth of the Word to create, *logos prophorikos* (*Ad Autolycum*, XXII). He seems to be the first Greek writer to use the Triad (*trias*) to describe the eternal being of God.

The distinction between Son and Spirit within the being of God was made more vivid when Irenaeus of Lyons, whose background was in Smyrna and Rome, spoke of the Son and the Spirit as the two hands of God (*Against Heresies*, IV, preface). He goes on to say that the Father is the invisibility of the Son and the Son is the visibility of the Father (IV, 6, 6). Although the deity of the Holy Spirit is not developed as was that of the Son, Irenaeus makes it very clear that it was the Spirit, not the Son, who descended upon Jesus at his baptism (III, 17, 4).

A more developed ontology was introduced by Origen of Alexandria and Caesarea (c. 185-c. 254). The neo-Platonic philosopher Plotinus (c. 205-270) spoke of eternal being as One, Nous (mind), and World-Soul, and this speculation reveals the roots of much that Origen said about God. Origen studied under Ammonius Saccas, the teacher of Plotinus. Origen introduced into Christian theology the concepts of *ousia* and *hypostasis* that were to be so important in the full formulation of the Greek doctrine of the Holy Triad or Trinity. However, the terms were synonymous for him. Although the Son is eternally generated by the Father and there was never a time when the Son was not, Origen lacked the later precision.[77]

It was not until the great Cappadocians that a clear distinction between *ousia* (being or essence) and *hypostasis* was made. Basil, his brother Gregory of Nyssa, and Gregory of Nazianzus (the so-called "three lights of Cappadocia") developed the formula "one being in three *hypostases*" (*mia ousia kai treis hypostaseis* in Greek), and this became defined as Orthodoxy at the Council of Constantinople of 382 which says: "As regards the tome of

76. Space forbids more than a select survey of the historical figures who contributed to the Western doctrine of the Holy Trinity, but more details may be found in Robert S. Franks, *The Doctrine of the Trinity* (London: Gerald Duckworth, 1958) and Edmund J. Fortman, *The Triune God* (Philadelphia: The Westminster Press, 1972).
77. G. W. Butterworth, *Origen on First Principles* (London: S. P. C. K., 1936), pp. xxxi-xxxiii.

the Western bishops, we have also received those in Antioch who confess the one Divinity of the Father, Son, and Holy Ghost."[78]

Justification for this formulation may be found in the *Five Theological Orations* of Gregory Nazianzus. Gregory argued that *ousia* belongs to God's unity and *hypostasis* to the threefold distinction in the unity. God is not one person (*prosopon*) but three, so that the Monad of the Monarchia moves toward a Dyad and comes to rest in a Triad of Father, Son, and Holy Spirit (III, 2). He speaks of the Father as the Unbegotten (*agennēton*), of the Son as the Begotten (*gennēton*), and of the Holy Spirit as Proceeding. The three are one in the Godhead.

When Gregory Nazianzus uses Adam, Eve, and Seth as examples (V, 11), tritheism threatens, but Gregory of Nyssa stoutly denied that the orthodox doctrine of the Holy Triad was the worship of three gods. In his writing *On "Not Three Gods"* he argues that God is not only one in nature but in the operation of the Godhead, and there are not three gods. One may speak of Peter, James, and John as three men, although they have one nature, but they are not always one in action. In the case of the Holy Trinity, the Godhead — Father, Son, and Holy Spirit — always act together. In creation and redemption the action of the Holy Trinity is one operation. No swing-shift Trinity that separates the works of God and assigns them to different persons of the Godhead is allowed.

A further stage in the unity of the Greek Triad was reached when John of Damascus (c. 675-c. 749) introduced the term *perichōrēsis* (circumincession in Latin) to describe the interpenetration of the Three Persons in the Holy Trinity. Just as the Three Persons have "the same substance and dwell in one another, and have the same will and operation and power and authority and movement, so to speak, we recognize the indivisibility and unity of God. For verily there is one God, and His Word, and Spirit" (*The Orthodox Faith*, I. 8).

The Father begets, the Son is begotten, and the Holy Spirit proceeds from the Father *through* the Son, according to the Second Council of Nicaea in A.D. 787. At this point Eastern Orthodoxy has retained the doctrine of the Holy Triad. Adoration of God as Father, Son, and Holy Spirit has become the center of all their worship.

The Latin Trinity

The doctrine of the Latin Trinity has followed along these same lines in general, but there have been some significant differences. The East seemed always threatened by tritheism with its emphasis on the three subordinate *hypostases*, but the West produced forms of unitarianism, at times by emphasizing the unity of God.

---

78. J. Stevenson, ed., *Creeds, Councils, and Controversies* (London: S. P. C. K., 1972), p. 149.

At the very beginning of Latin theology stands the great Tertullian of Carthage (c. 160-c. 225). One of his major contributions came out of his attack upon a form of unitarianism in Rome called Monarchianism, because of its emphasis on the sovereignty of the one God. A certain Praxeas became the object of Tertullian's trinitarian thrust. Tertullian said: "Thus Praxeas at Rome managed two pieces of the devil's business: he drove out prophecy and introduced heresy; he put to flight the Paraclete and crucified the Father" (*Against Praxeas*, 1).[79] When Tertullian wrote these words he had embraced the new prophecy of Montanism, a charismatic movement, and his strong trinitarianism must be understood as a polemic against the Monarchianism of Rome that made no distinction between the Father and the Son.

The trinitarianism of Tertullian anticipated the Second Council of Nicaea in A.D. 787 by teaching that the Holy Spirit "proceeds from the Father *through* the Son" (*Against Praxeas*, 4). This view was taught in the West as late as John Scotus Erigena (c. 810-c. 877), but his strong neo-Platonism has a pantheistic flavor that identifies God and Nature. There is no subordinationism of substance or nature, but Tertullian does not hesitate to say that the Holy Spirit is third, following God and his Son (*ibid.*, 8). He illustrated this threefold sequence with sun–ray–illumination, root–shoot–fruit, spring–stream–channel as he sought to establish one substance and three persons in the Holy Trinity (*ibid.*, 8).

Out of this came the formula *una substantia et tres personae* (one substance and three persons). *Persona* means a mask, and the Monarchianism of a certain Sabellius pictured the one God as wearing three successive masks, one to create the world, a second to redeem the world and a third to sanctify the world. Tertullian's emphasis was on three simultaneous *personae* of the Holy Trinity that creates, redeems and sanctifies. This takes Tertullian beyond belief in the economic Trinity of manifestation to the ontological Trinity in which manifestation and metaphysics are one. God has manifested himself as he really is in eternal reality. The two views of the Holy Trinity do not contradict.

The second major step in the development of the Latin doctrine of the Holy Trinity came with Augustine (A.D. 354-430). His major work on the Holy Trinity, *De Trinitate*, written over many years, A.D. 400-418, departed from the subordinationism of the Greek doctrine by saying the Father and the Son are equally the source of the Holy Spirit (V. 14, 15). This was taught by Cyril of Alexandria in the Greek tradition. This later led to the *filioque* (and the Son) controversy between the East and the West and remains a point of contention until this day.

Augustine's doctrine of the Holy Trinity led to two traditions in Latin

79. The standard edition is by Ernest Evans, *Tertullian's Treatise Against Praxeas* (London: S. P. C. K., 1948).

theology. A sociological analogy developed from his "trinity of love" in which subject (lover), object (beloved) and relation (love) are central (*De Trinitate*, VIII). However, his chief emphasis was on the psychological analogy that became a "Trinity of mind" in which the self-knowledge of mind, knowledge and love are realized in memory, understanding, and will (*ibid*., IX, X).[80]

In the fifth century, perhaps after A.D. 428, the so-called Athanasian Creed appeared with an elaborate statement on both the Holy Trinity and the Incarnation.[81] This formulation was not by Athanasius and is not a creed. It originated in South Gaul, perhaps at Lerins, and it is more like a hymn to be used in worship. The double procession of the Holy Spirit from the Father *and the Son* appears in this creed. However, a movement away from the subordinationism of the Greek *Trias* and Tertullian's *Trinitas* is already evident. This, however, is qualified with the words: "He is equal to the Father in his divinity but He is inferior to the Father in his humanity."

A more radical shift from Tertullian came with a redefinition of *persona*. Tertullian did not move much beyond the mask idea in Monarchianism, although he had three masks at the same time; but Boethius (c. 480-c. 524), the first Latin translator of Aristotle, adopted Aristotle's definition of a person as an individual substance with a rational nature (*persona est naturae rationalis individua substantia*). With this definition three persons would suggest three substances.

Richard of St. Victor (d. 1173), in his *De Trinitate*, explored the sociological analogy of Augustine and made a Holy Trinity of Absolute Love conjoined with Absolute Power and Absolute Beatitude. The Father as First Person required a Second Person worthy of his love. The Holy Spirit was proposed as a Third Person to share Absolute Beatitude. Richard thought he could demonstrate this by reason alone, and those who followed his sociological analogy moved beyond illustration to demonstration of the doctrine. This was bound to meet the same resistance as the effort to demonstrate the existence of God. In each instance God became finite, either as one or as three.

At the Fourth Lateran Council, A.D. 1215, the definition of person adopted by Boethius became official doctrine. The Council defended Peter Lombard against the charge of quaternitarianism leveled by Joachim of Flora. Peter's famous *Four Books of Sentences* was organized around the persons of the Holy Trinity in the first three books, and the fourth book was on the one God. Joachim argued that this made the one substance a different reality, so he divided all history into an economic Trinity manifested in three ages. This sounded like Tritheism to the Council, so Peter was strongly defended.

80. John Burnaby, ed., *Augustine: Later Works* (Philadelphia: The Westminster Press, 1955), pp. 26-28.
81. This standard edition is J. N. D. Kelly, *The Athanasian Creed* (New York: Harper and Row, 1964).

The real climax of the Roman Catholic doctrine came with Thomas Aquinas, who built on the psychological analogy and on the formulations of the Fourth Lateran Council. He rejected Richard of St. Victor's claim that the mystery of the Holy Trinity could be demonstrated by natural reason alone. As in the symbol on the back of a one dollar bill, the top of the pyramid belongs in the realm of revealed theology. However, later Thomists and Scotists indulged in much rational speculation about such things as the generation of the Son and the spiration of the Spirit! With zeal he rejected subordinationism, but it was with reluctance that he defined a person as a rational substance. Quaternitarianism did not appeal to him, but the suggestion of three substances does point toward the Tritheism advocated by Joachim of Flora. That led him to speak of "a distinct subsistent in an intellectual nature." This has remained the standard for Roman Catholicism.[82]

The Protestant Problem

The dilemma of Unitarianism versus Tritheism dogged Roman Catholic dogma down to the Protestant Reformation. It was no wonder that Luther and Melanchthon shifted from the long debates on the Holy Trinity to the work of Christ in redemption. "To know Christ is to know his benefits, not as the Schoolmen teach, to know His natures and the modes of His incarnation," said Philip Melanchthon in the introduction to his *Loci Theologici* (A.D. 1521).

The first edition of John Calvin's *Institutes* (A.D. 1536) gave very little attention to the doctrine of the Holy Trinity. However, the rise and threat of Anti-Trinitarianism under the leadership of people like Michael Servetus forced Calvin to defend in more detail the traditional view of the Trinity, especially as formulated by Augustine.[83] After the decline of Protestant Orthodoxy, the doctrine of the Holy Trinity became a secondary doctrine, and many times it was rejected outright.

It is no exaggeration to say that this eclipse of Trinitarianism did not pass until Barthianism came on the scene after World War I.[84] Karl Barth, with his emphasis on special revelation and the psychological analogy, began to speak of God the Father as Revealer, God the Son as the Revelation, and God the Holy Spirit as the subjective Revealedness of the objective Son. He, of course, would reject the suggestion that this is a psychological analogy!

His whole system was organized around the three modes of the Holy Trinity, with God as Creator, the Son as Reconciler, and the Holy Spirit as Redeemer. Like Aquinas' idea of the Three Persons, Boethius' definition

82. Dom Mark Pontifex, *Belief in the Trinity* (London: Longmans, 1954).
83. Roland Bainton, *Hunted Heretic: The Life and Death of Michael Servetus* (Boston: Beacon Press, 1953).
84. Claude Welch, *In This Name* (New York: Charles Scribner's Sons, 1952).

created problems. Indeed, this Trinity of Revelation has overtones of Sabellius and Joachim of Flora, but the details defend an eternal Trinity of Father, Son and Holy Spirit.[85]

If Barth is a reminder of Augustine, Leonard Hodgson's *The Doctrine of the Trinity* (1943) may be called a revival of the social analogy developed by Richard of St. Victor. On the basis of a philosophical empiricism that turns away from German idealism Hodgson argues for an organic unity of three persons that is to be distinguished from a mathematical unity. The Holy Trinity is the point of beginning, not the unity of God as in John of Damascus, but this seems rather close to the Greek idea of *perichōrēsis*. The point of departure may be from the point of view of oneness as in the East or threeness as in the West, but the central point is an organic unity of Father, Son, and Holy Spirit. It seems very important to emphasize that the three persons are three infinite persons in interpenetration, not three finite persons as separate centers of consciousness.

Restatements of belief in God as a Holy Trinity do not require empiricism. Existentialism and process philosophy may also be useful, as were Platonism and Aristotelianism in Roman Catholicism. John Macquarrie is a good example of how existentialism may be employed. Macquarrie, in his *Principles of Christian Theology* (Scribner's, 1966), identifies primordial being with the Father, expressive being with the Son and unitive being with the Holy Spirit.

It is possible in process theology to relate the primordial nature of God to the Father, the principle of concretion to the incarnate Son and the resultant nature or aspect of God to the final unity of the Holy Spirit. At least a Trinitarian pattern of reality does appear in process theology, but with the possible exception of Norman Pittenger process theologians have not developed this possibility in Whitehead's thought.[86] There is still too much resistance to inadequate statements in traditional Trinitarianism.

If being or process or history represents eternal reality, then God must be identified with that reality, for whatever or whoever is eternal is God. God is that eternal reality whose being is manifested in moral values and historical action, the greatest value being *agapē* and the greatest action being the historical disclosure of God in Jesus Christ. Any rational representation of that reality seems to require a threefold unity in God.

In the pastoral task of the church it is of first importance to follow closely the fundamental trinitarian patterns in Scripture. John Calvin did this in his resistance to the threat of Unitarianism in his time. However, the historical formulations of Greek and Latin theology have become so much a part of creedal and confessional statements that it is impossible to avoid discussion of the philosophical problems presented by this approach.

85. See his massive *Church Dogmatics*; cf. Eberhard Jüngel, *The Doctrine of the Trinity*, tr. Horton Harris (Scottish Academic Press, 1976), which is more Barthian than Barth!
86. Cf. W. Norman Pittenger, *The Divine Triunity* (Philadelphia: Pilgrim Press, 1977).

When the historical developments are ignored by those who claim to follow Scripture alone, it is almost certain that the errors of history will be repeated. One must clarify the relationship between God our Father, his Son Jesus Christ, and his Holy Spirit to the degree that translation into theological and philosophical categories does not distort the apostolic origin of trinitarian faith.

IV. CREATION

25. The God of Creation

All through the history of the Christian faith belief in God as Creator, the world as creation, and man as more than creature and crown of all creation has a way of returning after times of neglect. The Apostles' Creed, formulated in the second century of the church, begins with the affirmation "God the Father almighty, maker of heaven and earth," and this became the first of the three fundamentals of early Catholicism.

Protestantism did not depart from this belief in God and his creation. The title of book one of Calvin's *Institutes of the Christian Religion* (1559) is "The Knowledge of God the Creator." Indeed, the first three of the four books follow the structure of the Apostles' Creed, and this has shaped the theology of Calvinism down to the massive work of Karl Barth that dedicated some two thousand three hundred pages in English to this subject!

Biblical creationism was the basis for belief in the Creator-God at each stage in the history of the church. However, the impact of modern science has led some astray with the suggestion that Scripture is no longer relevant to the questions raised in a scientific age. This attitude has led to the reaction among many conservative Christians that has often rejected the major conclusions of modern science on the history of the earth and of man on the earth. In all seriousness the Creation Research Society today attempts to confine all scientific evidence to no more than ten thousand years. Much that is written by advocates of this so-called "scientific creationism" does not require a rejection of the dates inserted into the margin of the Authorized (King James) Version by Archbishop James Ussher of Armagh, Ireland.

The date 4004 B.C. as the time of the creation was included in the *Scofield Reference Bible* of 1917 (p. 3). *The New Scofield Bible* of 1967 does not begin dating until the birth of Abraham, calculated c. 1950 B.C. (p. 18, note 2). The Creation Research Society resorts to the theory of catastrophism which argues for a "young earth" and "flood geology," so both

127

the 1917 and 1967 editions of the *Scofield Reference Bible* are blasted as a compromise with uniformitarianism.

At the logical place the relevance of Genesis 1:1–2:4a in a scientific age will be discussed, but this survey of biblical creationism attempts to trace the steps by which the covenant faith of Israel moved from God's action in Israel to God's action in all nations. After the Babylonion Exile and the restoration of the people to the land under the decree of Cyrus the Great, 538 B.C., biblical creation had its heyday. It seems best to follow the historical order of the Scriptures, as best as this can be discerned, to discover the logic of creation faith. In this way science and Scripture can be related in a constructive synthesis for a biblical faith. Modern science and biblical criticism have turned out to be friends of creation faith rather than the dreaded foe imagined by conservative fundamentalism.

The God of creation is the God of the Holy Trinity. It has already been pointed out how, due to the influence of the Apostles' Creed, traditional theology has assigned the work of creation to God the Father, while reconciliation and sanctification have been assigned to the Son and the Spirit respectively. Barthian theology has revived this after the eclipse of the Holy Trinity in theological liberalism. However, this is not acceptable. This swing-shift Trinity approaches the ancient Sabellianism that was denounced as heresy by Tertullian.

On the other hand, Karl Barth contributed much, not only to the restoration of the doctrine of the Holy Trinity to a central position, but in his most extensive writing on the doctrine of creation — 2337 pages! This, however, included the doctrine of man and the ethics of creation, but he has 428 pages on "The Work of Creation" alone. I know of no discussion on the theological significance of Gen. 1:1–2:4a that equals Barth's exposition.

Conservative Baptist theologians such as E. Y. Mullins and W. T. Conner hardly touched on either creation or man. This was a safe position in days when evolution was such a controversial issue. The results of this evasion are still present in minds that imagine that one must choose between Scripture and science rather than bridge the yawning chasm into which many have fallen.

The very concept of God is greatly altered when the living God is understood as the Creator God. It is interesting to note that perhaps the oldest statement about a Creator God is ascribed to the God Most High, the El Elyon of Melchizedek (Gen. 14:19–20):

> *Blessed be Abram by God Most High,*
>> *maker of heaven and earth;*
> *and blessed be God Most High,*
>> *who has delivered your enemies into your hand!*

The God of creation is the God of history. Langdon Gilkey, one of the first American theologians to write a *ktisiology*, a doctrine of creation, has appropriately called his book *Maker of Heaven and Earth* (1959).

The recognition that the God of universal history is also the God of the whole creation bursts like thunder at the beginning of Isaiah 40–55. Indeed, Handel used some of these rousing words at the beginning of his majestic oratorio called the *Messiah*. The first chapter ascribes to the Lord, the Holy One of Israel, all power, future, past and present, in that order.

In the future the Lord is the Coming God, the God of hope, about which Jürgen Moltmann has made so much (Isa. 40:3–11). God comes to meet his people in celestial grandeur and compassion, as ruler and shepherd (Isa. 40:10–11):

> *Behold, the Lord comes with might, and his arm rules for him;*
> *behold, his reward is with him,*
> *and his recompense before him.*
> *He will feed his flock like a shepherd,*
> *he will gather the lambs in his arms,*
> *he will carry them in his bosom,*
> *and gently lead those who are with young.*

Like David, the ideal Shepherd King, he will gather God's people together.

The Coming God of future history is the Creator God of all history. Using three probing questions Isaiah sets forth his view of the Creator as infinite (Isa. 40:12–20). He measures all things, the waters and the heavens and the earth, then the dust of the earth, the mountains and the hills (Isa. 40:12). As infinite Spirit he requires no counselor or teacher (Isa. 40:13f.). Whole nations along with things and persons are mere dust and nothing before him (Isa. 40:15–17). It is hardly possible to improve on this concept of infinite Spirit over against and beyond all creation and history.

This infinite God is also incomparable (Isa. 40:18–24). With six more questions man is made aware of the utter uniqueness of God. He is indeed, as Rudolf Otto saw so clearly, the Wholly Other, the Holy One of Isaiah. In this light all idols are rejected (Isa. 40:18–20). All the inhabitants of the earth, people and rulers alike, are mere grasshoppers and nothing (Isa. 40:18–23). His judgments are on the earth (Isa. 40:24) and his wonders are in the heavens (Isa. 40:25f.). As the popular theme of the Billy Graham broadcasts has it in the hymn of Carl Boberg:

> *O Lord my God, when I in awesome wonder*
> *Consider all the worlds Thy hands have made,*
> *I see the stars, I hear the rolling thunder,*
> *Thy power throughout the universe displayed.*

> *Then sings my soul, my Savior God, to Thee;*
> *How great Thou art, how great Thou art!*
> *Then sings my soul, my Savior God, to Thee;*
> *How great Thou art, how great Thou art!*

A child, looking at the Orion and the Pleiades on a cold winter night, feels this awe. What a pity if, when a grown man is looking through a powerful telescope, he feels only the coldness of empty space. Science and the sacred belong together in the wonders of God's creation.

With two more questions the Creator God is declared the Everlasting God who is inexhaustible in strength (Isa. 40:27–31). Prayer to him is the pause that refreshes! Many a weary pilgrim has been encouraged by these words (Isa. 40:28b–31):

> *The Lord is the everlasting God,*
> *the Creator of the ends of the earth.*
> *He does not faint or grow weary,*
> *his understanding is unsearchable.*
> *He gives power to the faint,*
> *and to him who has no might he increases strength.*
> *Even the youths shall faint and be weary,*
> *and young men shall fall exhausted;*
> *but they who wait for the Lord shall renew their strength,*
> *they shall mount up with wings like eagles,*
> *they shall run and not be weary,*
> *they shall walk and not faint.*

Creation is the corollary of the God of creation. Belief in the relation between creation and God modifies our perspective on what is called nature as much as it changes our view of God. The classic expression of this relation between the creation and God is still Isaiah 40–55.

The Lord God is Creator of all things on earth and in heaven. On earth water and trees find their Source in God (Isa. 41:17–20):

> *When the poor and needy seek water,*
> *and there is none,*
> *and their tongue is parched with thirst,*
> *I the Lord will answer them,*
> *I the God of Israel will not forsake them.*
> *I will open rivers on the bare heights,*
> *and fountains in the midst of the valleys;*
> *I will make the wilderness a pool of water,*
> *and the dry land springs of water.*
> *I will put in the wilderness the cedar,*
> *the acacia, the myrtle, and the olive;*

> *I will put in the desert the cypress,*
>   *the plane and the pine together;*
> *that men may see and know,*
>   *may consider and understand together,*
> *that the hand of the Lord has done this,*
>   *the Holy One of Israel has created it.*

He who gives the water and the trees is God, the Lord of Israel who creates the heavens and the earth and all that inhabit them (Isa. 42:5-9). He is the hope of the past and the future. He says (Isa. 42:9):

> *Behold, the former things have come to pass,*
>   *and new things I now declare;*
> *before they spring forth*
>   *I tell you of them.*

The God of history is the God of all creation.

The Creator who makes nature a creation makes a nation a covenant people. This too is a form of creation in which he says (Isa. 43:6f.):

> *I will say to the north, Give up,*
>   *and to the south, Do not withhold;*
> *bring my sons from afar*
>   *and my daughters from the end of the earth,*
> *every one who is called by my name,*
>   *whom I created for my glory,*
>   *whom I formed and made.*

The Redeemer of Israel is the Creator of Israel. The Holy One who brought them out of Egypt in the First Exodus will bring them back from Babylon in the Second Exodus. The prophet speaks of the Lord as Israel's Creator (Isa. 43:1). And the Lord himself says (Isa. 43:15):

> *I am the Lord, your Holy One,*
>   *the Creator of Israel, your King.*

He is Creator of the nation and of nature.

The Creator of Israel's history is also the Creator of universal history. He can anoint Cyrus the Great, the founder of the Persian Empire, and make him his instrument for both weal and woe. He is the Lord who says (Isa. 45:7):

> *I form light and create darkness,*
> *I make weal and create woe,*
> *I am the Lord, who does all these things.*

The Lord who gives the rain gathers his people again (Isa. 45:8).

Chaos along with calamity is not beyond his control. The inhabitants

of earth and heaven are also his creation (Isa. 45:12). He is indeed the Lord
(Isa. 45:18)

> *who created the heavens*
> *(he is God!),*
> *who formed the earth and made it*
> *(he established it;*
> *he did not create it a chaos,*
> *he formed it to be inhabited!).*

Without his creative activity there would be neither the weapons of war nor
the ravage of the land (Isa. 54:16). Good and evil alike are impossible
without a Creator God. When man conforms to his order all is well, but
when there is resistance evil results in nature, the nation, and the whole
universe he has made.

In the light of this summary on God the Creator in Isaiah 40–55, it is
difficult to see why some literary critics see only Greek thought in Paul's
Areopagus address in Acts 17:24–31. There Hebrew and Hellenistic thought
meet, and on this foundation the "creation theology" of Christianity is based.

God as Lord of all history and creation is the unifying force in all
things. The biblical term that expresses this unity is Spirit (Isa. 40:13). As
Spirit the Lord is sovereign over the past, present, and the future. His
sovereignty over the past is the basis for belief in the beginning of creation.
God is the eternal and all else belongs to space-time. He is infinite and all
else is finite. His sovereignty over the present is expressed in the preservation of creation, as his sovereignty over the future constitutes the consummation of creation.

In the faith of the Old Testament creation is celebrated in the worship
of the Lord God. The time of celebration for the beginning of creation was
the weekly Sabbath (Gen. 1:1–2:4a), for the preservation of creation the
annual Feast of Tabernacles (Psalm 104) and for the consummation of
creation the Year of Jubilee (Isa. 61–66). When these celebrations are interpreted as worship without the details of modern science, a constructive
relationship between Scripture and science is possible.

26. The Consummation of Creation

The traditional approach to the doctrine of creation begins with the past.
If present and future creation are discussed at all, they are subordinated to
other topics. That is one of the many reasons why the literary history of
the Scriptures should be considered in the construction of Christian doctrine. If the generally accepted views of Old Testament literature are included as a guide to the order of topics, then future creation comes logically
after the God of creation. As Isaiah 40–55 proclaims God as Creator, so
Isaiah 56–66 develops the hope of a future creation. The Coming God
promises a future creation. These statements assume that the Book of Isaiah

includes the theology not only of eighth-century Isaiah but also that of his disciples who followed after him (cf. Isa. 8:16).

The consummation of creation includes both a penultimate restoration in this age and an ultimate renewal in the age to come when all things are renewed by the Great Apocalypse of God and Jesus Christ in glory. This recalls the discussion of the two ages (cf. II.13). It is at times difficult to know when Scripture crosses the boundary between the two, but the following framework attempts to formulate an orientation to future creation. The first shall be last and the last first! This could be called eschatological ktisiology, from the Greek words for the last things and creation.

The Consummation as Penultimate Restoration

The restoration of Third Isaiah is a vision of the future glory of God's people, reaching its highest potential in the land of promise (Isa. 65:17–25). The introduction to this oracle of future orientation is fundamental for later developments in biblical eschatology (Isa. 65:17f.):

> For behold, I create new heavens and a new earth;
> and the former things shall not be remembered
>   or come into mind.
> But be glad and rejoice for ever
>   in that which I create;
> for behold, I create Jerusalem a rejoicing,
>   and her people a joy.

The verses that follow make it clear that the prophet speaks of a historical restoration and rejuvenation that belong to this age, but the earth will be about as near to heaven as it can be before heaven and earth become one.

This future creation of the land and people together is later called a making, but making and creating seem to mean the same. The worship of the Lord will become the way of life for all in the land (Isa. 66:22f.):

> For as the new heavens and the new earth
>   which I make
> shall remain before me, says the Lord;
>   so shall your descendants and your name remain.
> From new moon to new moon,
>   and from sabbath to sabbath,
> all flesh shall come to worship me,
>   says the Lord.

The failure to distinguish between penultimate approaches to God's ultimate act in a new creation has at times led to false identifications. This was especially obvious in eighteenth-century post-millennialism which had a tendency to identify the British Empire with the kingdom of God on earth.

Daniel Whitley (1638-1726), the formulator of post-millennialism, was sure that evangelism could overthrow Roman Catholicism and bring in the kingdom of God on earth. His *Paraphrase and Commentary on the New Testament* (1703) had enormous influence.

Augustine and Calvin prepared the way for this form of "realized eschatology," but Adam Smith had a religious motif when he called his book on capitalism *The Wealth of Nations* (1776), a title taken from Isaiah 60:5, 11; 61:6; 66:12. In this setting William Carey (1761-1834) made his stirring call for missions in 1792, and he used a text from Isaiah (54:2) as he promulgated the watchword, "Expect great things from God; attempt great things for God." Who has not heard the words, "Arise, shine, for thy light is come" (Isa. 60:1)?

A few years later William Blake, in his poem *Milton* (1804-1808), made the vow:

> *I shall not cease from Mental Fight,*
> *Nor shall my Sword sleep in my hand*
> *Till we have built Jerusalem*
> *In England's green and pleasant Land.* [1]

More religious melodies such as *Beulah Land*, a hymn by Edgar Page Stites (1836-1921) based on Isa. 62:4, took pious pilgrims in their religion of individualism to "heaven's borderland." The chorus proclaimed:

> *O Beulah Land, sweet Beulah Land!*
> *As on the highest mount I stand,*
> *I look away across the sea,*
> *Where mansions are prepared for me,*
> *And view the shining glory-shore,*
> *My heav'n, my home for evermore!*

Some may find support for this type of "realized eschatology" in the New Testament. A new order of social regeneration has been seen in the *palingenesia* proclaimed in Matthew 19:28, but this seems to point toward an ultimate and cosmic order in a new creation. The same approach, on a more evangelistic note, has been made on the basis of the promise of "the times of the restitution of all things" in Peter's apostolic preaching (Acts 3:21, AV).

The Consummation as Ultimate Renewal

New Testament eschatology, with renewed emphasis on the two ages of history, goes far beyond the penultimate eschatology of historical eschatology. In at least three settings the Pauline tradition suggests cosmic renewal. The first setting is that of reconciliation. Although John Reumann confines

---

1. *The Complete Poetry of William Blake* (New York: The Modern Library, 1941), p. 838.

the teachings of Paul's Great Parenthesis in 2 Cor. 2:14–7:4 to the newness of the Christian life, some factors suggest a new creation, *kainē ktisis*, with cosmic implications.[2] A literal translation of 2 Cor. 5:17 would be: "If any one is in Christ, *kainē ktisis*; old things have passed away, behold, they have become new." The neuter for "old things" would suggest more than a "new creature," especially when the new is related to the reconciliation of the world (*kosmos*, 5:19). There is also no good reason to exclude the cosmic connotations of the new creation in Galatians 6:15.

A later reference to the redemption of creation (*ktisis*) at the time the human body is redeemed goes beyond the resurrection (Rom. 8:18–24). This setting of both cosmic and bodily redemption, which comes at the climax of the Great Parenthesis between Romans 1–4 and 9–11, looks upon the Christian life of the present as only the first-fruits of which the full harvest is the liberation of the whole of creation. The groaning of God's creation and the groaning of God's children are joined with the groaning of God's Spirit in the longing for freedom from the futility of the present age of suffering (Rom. 8:18, 26f.).

The third setting in the Pauline tradition is that of recapitulation, "to unite all things in him, things in heaven and things on earth" (Eph. 1:10). By the work of the Holy Spirit in the human mind the new man (*kainos anthrōpos*) is being renewed by the creative act of God (Eph. 4:23f.), and this is not complete until the Day of Redemption (4:30).

A special problem is confronted in the interpretation of the "new heavens and a new earth" in the Petrine tradition. The special problem concerns the authenticity of 2 Peter. 2 Peter is dated as late as A.D. 150 by some literary critics, but it is not impossible to date it around the Feast of Tabernacles in A.D. 67, shortly before the martyrdom of Peter. This is certainly the claim of the letter (1:12–15).

It is also possible that the parallels with Jude in chapter 2 indicate the use of a common source rather than the use of Jude by 2 Peter. Not even the evidence for a collection of Paul's letters as Scripture in 2 Peter 3:15 is conclusive for a late date. The reference is perhaps to 1, 2 Thessalonians, written seventeen years before A.D. 67; but some of Paul's letters were considered Scripture when they left his hand (Col. 4:16). If all of Paul's prison letters were written from Herod's Praetorium in Caesarea (cf. Acts 23:25), as is probable, there is no solid evidence against a Pauline canon of ten letters by A.D. 65, if Onesimus, with the original three letters taken by Tychicus to the Lycus Valley, A.D. 57, expressed his devotion to the Apostle by collecting Paul's letters in Ephesus, where he was destined to become Bishop by the beginning of the second century.

Critical orthodoxy does not even pause to discuss this possibility, but

2. *Creation and New Creation* (Minneapolis: Augsburg Publishing House, 1973), pp. 89-99.

a rethinking of the problem in the light of the role of the amanuensis in the composition of letters puts the problem in a new light. After all, both 1, 2 Thessalonians and 1, 2 Peter claimed to be written by Silvanus (1 Thess. 1:1; 2 Thess. 1:1; 1 Pet. 5:12; 2 Pet. 3:1). This with a comparison of the eschatology of these writings requires second thought.

In any case the concept of new heavens and a new earth has a vital relation to the *parousia*, the second coming of Jesus Christ, and to the ethical attitudes of the Christian life (2 Pet. 3:11–13). This coming *parousia* is both a catastrophe for the wicked and a cosmic consummation of creation for the righteous. The roots in Isaiah are obvious in the statement (2 Pet. 3:13): "But according to his promise we wait for new heavens and a new earth in which righteousness dwells."

The climax of the consummation in the new heavens and the new earth is found in the Johannine tradition, in the third vision of the Apocalypse of John (17:1–21:8). The penultimate picture of the new heavens and the new earth is that of a "camp of the saints and the beloved city" in Revelation 20:9.

A note in *The New Oxford Annotated Bible* says of the thousand-year reign that "nothing is said here about a reign on earth," but Revelation 20:9 says those who wage war at the battle of Gog and Magog "marched up over the broad earth and surrounded the camp of the saints and the beloved city." The scoffing at a state in which risen saints rule over those who have not even died reflects generations of prejudice. It is no more absurd than belief in the communion of living saints with the departed who once lived in bodies and angel spirits that never lived in bodies (cf. Heb. 12:22–24).

The ultimate picture is the descent of the New Jerusalem from heaven to earth in the consummation of all creation (Rev. 21:1–8). Cosmic catastrophe and cosmic consummation are finally reached when heaven and earth become one and God and man dwell together. Personal eschatology and historical eschatology are always penultimate until the ultimate arrives in the cosmic consummation of him who says: "Behold, I make all things new" (Rev. 21:5).

In summary, it may be said that the vision of a Coming God is followed by the vision of a Coming Creation. *Eschatology*, belief in things to come at the end, becomes the basis for belief in *ktisiology*, the belief in a Creator God who will make all things new in the future. The Creator God creates, makes and forms the creation in deeds that are past, present and future, but the focus in Isaiah 40–66 is upon the future.[3] However, as in salvation history the pattern is always one of promise and fulfillment, not an eternal return of the end to the beginning, as in Hermann Gunkel's *Schöpfung und*

---

3. Bernhard Anderson, *Creation Versus Chaos* (New York: Association Press, 1967), pp. 124-126.

Chaos in Urzeit und Endzeit (1895). The mythical symbols have been transformed by historical revelation.[4]

This is not an effort to reinterpret the doctrine of creation in the light of "the theology of hope," but it is not out of line with this perspective. It is the result of careful exegetical work in the Old Testament, and the chapters that follow will have the same orientation. "In the Bible creation opens toward the horizon of the future."[5]

27. The Preservation of Creation

Belief in God as creator denies self-existence to things. Things are dependent upon God not only in their origin but also in their continuation and consummation. The action of God in the continuation of creation is his work of preservation.

As belief in the future restoration of the people of Israel became the basis for belief in the future creation of a new heaven and a new earth, so belief in the creation and preservation of the nation became the basis for belief in the creation and preservation of all things. The background for this belief in preservation may be seen in the orderly rising and falling of the Nile and the monotheism that prevailed in Egypt for awhile under Akhenaton (1380-1362 B.C.).[6]

This analogy does not mean that Israel did no more than borrow monotheism and order from Egyptian thought, for historical revelation in covenant relation was the root from which Israel's distinctive belief in a Creator God sprang, but much of Old Testament theology becomes clearer when this continuous process is kept in mind.[7] Theological and Christological formulations of creation faith are found in Scripture.

Theological Formulations

Theological formulations that praise God's preservation of his creation are found often in doxological passages. At first there is the movement of faith from the creation and preservation of the nation to the creation and preservation of all things, but the fuller development of belief in God as creator and preserver of all things reverses the order from the creation and preservation of all things to the creation and preservation of the nation.

From the creation and preservation of the nation to the creation and preservation of all things. The Song of Moses in Exodus 15:18 celebrates the passage through the Red Sea in terms of the Lord's reign over chaos, a theme found in other Old Testament passages (Psalms 77:16–20; 78:12f.;

4. *Ibid.*, pp. 114, 131, 135.
5. *Ibid.*, p. 110.
6. See *The Interpreter's Bible*, IV, 550-557.
7. Bernhard W. Anderson, *op. cit.*, pp. 43-77.

106:7–11; 136:13–15; Hab. 3:8–15). Even the crossing of the Jordan, in the creation of the nation, is described in terms of the Lord's reign over the threat of chaos (Psalm 114:3–6). This reigning of God precedes his resting (cf. Gen. 2:1–4a).

The Blessing of Moses in Deut. 33:1–29, which praises the Lord as king, celebrates the conditions that prevailed in the early period of the monarchy by proclaiming God the preserver of the nation and ruler of the heavens as well. It concludes that (Deut. 33:27):

> The eternal God is your dwelling place,
> and underneath are the everlasting arms.

The origin and preservation of the nation lead to belief in the preservation of creation.

From the creation and preservation of all things to the creation and preservation of the nation. The Song in the prophet Amos puts the preservation of creation in the actual language of the rising and falling of the Nile (4:13; 5:8f.; 9:5–6).

> For lo, he who forms the mountains and creates the wind,
>   and declares to man what is his thought;
> who makes the morning darkness,
>   and treads on the heights of the earth —
> the Lord, the God of hosts, is his name!
>
> He who made the Pleiades and Orion,
>   and turns deep darkness into morning,
>   and darkens the day into night,
> who calls for the waters of the sea,
>   and pours them upon the surface of the earth,
> the Lord is his name
> (who makes destruction flash forth against the strong,
>   so that destruction comes upon the fortress).
>
> The Lord, God of hosts,
> he who touches the earth and it melts,
>   and all who dwell in it mourn,
> and all of it rises like the Nile,
>   and sinks again, like the Nile of Egypt;
> who builds up his chambers in the heavens,
>   and founds his vault upon the earth;
> who calls for the waters of the sea,
>   and pours them out upon the surface of the earth —
> the Lord is his name.

The Song of Jeremiah on creation has much the same theme as the

Song of Amos, but it adds a polemic against idols, which have no place in the worship of the Creator (10:12-16; 51:15-19). A later oracle in Jeremiah uses the fixed cycle of the created order to reverse the order from the preservation of nation to the preservation of creation to emphasize the continued existence of Israel (31:35f.).

These general doxologies that praise God's preservation had a special significance at the beginning of the Jewish New Year *(Rosh Hashanah)*. The Hymn to the Lord as Creator in Psalm 104 parallels Genesis 1:1-2:4a at many points, but the preservation of creation in God's continuous action is emphasized more strongly (cf. Pss. 145:15; 147:8f., 16f.). Eastern Christianity has preserved this praise by extensive use of Psalm 104 in worship. God's continuous creation is ascribed to the action of his Spirit (104:30):

> *When thou sendest forth thy Spirit, they are created;*
> *and thou renewest the face of the ground.*

God's control over the creation in which he is always present leads to complete victory over chaos. Praise for God's creation and preservation of all things is followed by praise for God's creation and preservation of the nation in Psalm 105.

Christological Formulations

As the creation and preservation of the nation became the basis for belief in the creation and preservation of all things, so does belief in Jesus as the Christ produce Christological formulations for belief in the preservation of creation. Great festival occasions again become occasions for such celebrations.

The Day of Atonement *(Yom Kippur)* became the occasion for the great Christological hymn at the beginning of the Letter to the Hebrews. Hebrews, which is a Christian *midrash* (explanation) on the Day of Atonement, not only exalts Jesus as the one "through whom he created the world" (1:2), but (1:3):

> *He reflects the glory of God*
> *and bears the very stamp of his nature,*
> *upholding all things by his word of power.*

The God who created and upholds all things took up his perfect abode in the man Jesus.

The Feast of Passover was the occasion for at least two great Christological formulations of preservation in the writings of Paul. Written perhaps between Passover and Pentecost in A.D. 53, his first Corinthian letter declares (8:6):

> *Yet for us there is one God, the Father,*
> *from whom are all things*
> *and for whom we exist,*

and one Lord, Jesus Christ,
through whom are all things
and through whom we exist.

This so-called binitarianism that relates the Father and the Son in an eternal way ascribes both creation and preservation to Jesus Christ.

The Passover letter to the Colossians has a long Christological hymn (1:15–20) that ascribes both creation and preservation (15–17) to the one in whom the fulness of God dwelt and who died and rose again (18–20). The beginning and coherence of creation are grounded in Jesus Christ.[8]

A final Christological formulation of God's preservation of creation is included in the Prologue to the Gospel of John (1:1–18). Creation and history are again linked together as Jesus is portrayed as the Passover Lamb who "takes away the sin of the world" (1:29). As the eternal *Logos* (1:3f.):

He was in the beginning with God;
all things were made through him,
and without him was not anything made.
That which was made in him was life,
and the life was the light of men.

The fallen world is indeed passing away, but that which abides in him will not only be preserved now, but will never perish.

On the basis of this biblical view of the preservation of creation some theologians and philosophers most exposed to modern science have made a solid synthesis of Scripture and science. In the last generation Karl Heim of Tübingen found the dynamic view of the universe most congenial to belief in a living God who creates the world continuously anew. A static view of God may find Heim's God "hyperactive," as a philosopher once said to me, but his statements are most congenial to a warm evangelical faith.[9]

The great scientist and modern father of process philosophy, A. N. Whitehead, at times startles with such statements as: "The world lives by the incarnation of God in itself."[10] On this basis one can see how the creator and preserver of the world became fully incarnate in Jesus and how this process of incarnation in the world and in the church continues until God is "all in all" (1 Corinthians 15:28). It is only a cold and rigid orthodoxy that feels threatened by such thought.

This pattern of creation and preservation avoids both the pantheism

8. This hymn has been studied in great detail by Hans Gabathuler, *Jesus Christus: Haupt der Kirche, Haupt der Welt* (Zürich: Zwingli Verlag, 1965).
9. *God Transcendent*, tr. Edgar Primrose Dickie (New York: Charles Scribner's Sons, 1936), p. 182; *Christian Faith and Natural Science*, tr. Neville Horton Smith (London: SCM, 1953), p. 65.
10. *Religion in the Making* (Cambridge: Cambridge University Press, 1930).

of the Age of Romanticism, which saw only God's immanence, and the mechanism of the Age of Deism, which saw only God's transcendence. God as creator does transcend the world, but God as preserver is immanent in all that he has created. As Epimenides said long ago in a statement accepted by Paul (Acts 17:28, TEV):

In him we live and move and exist.

This is true Christian existentialism.

28. The Beginning of Creation

In the light of the vision of a future consummation of creation, the beginning of creation was formulated at the beginning of the Bible (Gen. 1:1–2:4a, RSV). It is introduced with the proclamation of faith: "In the beginning God created the heavens and the earth." The footnote in the RSV states as the alternate translation: "When God began to create," but this is doubtful and vigorously opposed by those who believe in an original perfection. However, the "rigid evangelical" paraphrase by Kenneth Taylor, *The Living Bible*, adopts this view. The statement about "the generations of the heavens and the earth when they were created" at the end of the psalm is an effort of the editor to bring it into line with a frequent formula in the Priestly source (cf. 5:1; 6:9; 10:1, 32; 11:10, 27; 25:12f., 19; 36:1, 9; 37:22).

A Catastrophic View

Traditional literalism interpreted the psalm in terms of the belief that the universe was created about six thousand years ago in six literal days of twenty-four hours each. Questions were raised about details, and allegorical applications were made, but there was little doubt about this chronology until the impact of modern science. The exposition of Augustine was a model until modern time.[11] The Second London Confession of Faith of 1677, following the Westminster Confession of Faith, took this view (IV.1).

Even after the impact of modern science this traditional chronology has been defended, at times with great detail. This pre-scientific consistency is achieved by subordinating modern science to a pre-critical interpretation of the Bible. At times this traditional view may appear in scientific texts which claim that geological history can be explained in this short span of a few thousand years. A perfect world is posited at the beginning and Noah's flood accounts for the mighty upheaval in earth's history.[12] Creationism and catastrophism are viewed as inseparable.

11. *Confessions*, Bk. XIII.
12. Harold G. Coffin, *Creation: Accident or Design* (Washington, D.C.: Review and Herald Publishing Association, 1969).

At times there is a resurgence of this view in scientific studies. Critics of evolution are by no means confined to the clergy. Advocates of a late date for creation that makes room for a more literal interpretation of Genesis 1:1–2:4a seem to be on the increase among those trained in science. Evolutionary orthodoxy needs to confront the criticism formulated in a series of essays called *A Symposium on Creation*.[13] In science as in theology open dialogue is a necessity if uncritical dogmatism is to be avoided.

Scientific creationism, the self-style term by which this catastrophism is designated, has developed an extensive curriculum which its proponents hope can be either permitted or made mandatory in public schools. A major commentary, *The Genesis Record* (1977) by Henry M. Morris, the "founder" of the movement, is a challenge to Scripture interpretation that allows room for the generally accepted views of modern science.

However, the exposure of differences, discrepancies, and discontinuities in historical geology has not led to impressive evidence for an earth history of more than six thousand years. It is neither good science nor good theology to claim that God created the world "which had an appearance of age" that in reality does not exist.[14] Science is not infallible, but God is hardly deceptive.

At other times there is a resurgence of the traditional view in biblical exposition. A recent statement by a Missouri Synod theologian is hailed as a "treatment of both biblical and scientific evidences" which "makes the evolutionary viewpoint look pallid and irrational by contrast."[15]

A Concordistic View

Some conservatives are more impressed with the results of modern science, so they resort to a concordistic or compromise view that is less consistent than the traditional view. A first compromise is usually the gap theory that puts most geological history between verses 2 and 3 of Genesis 1. A prehistorical fall of Satan and the rebellious angels is supposed to account for millions of years in which the earth was "without form and void," but then God, a few thousand years ago, recreated the world for man's habitation. This would make two beginnings and a discontinuity between things created during the six days and things that formed the geological ages. Scientific scrutiny hardly supports such a theory.

13. Grand Rapids: Baker Book House, Vol. 1, 1968; Vol. 2, 1970; Vol. 3, 1971; Vol. 4, 1972. Those who wish to keep abreast with the debates and views of "scientific creationism" should read the regular reports of the Institute for Creation Research, 2716 Madison Avenue, San Diego, California, 92116.
14. Thomas F. Heinze, *Creation Vs. Evolution*, Second Revised Edition (Grand Rapids: Baker Book House, 1973), p. 106.
15. Alfred M. Rehwinkel, *The Wonders of Creation* (Minneapolis, Minn.: Bethany Fellowship, 1974), back cover.

A second compromise view agrees that the six days are not literal but six geological ages of indefinite length. Much is made of the meaning of *yom* (day) in Genesis 2:4, and a whole series of books has been produced on the basis of this hypothesis.[16] Such a theory runs into difficulty when a schoolboy asks how vegetation and animals survived millions of years of darkness as millions of years of light were awaited. The theory is an awkward position to take in the light of the simple rotation of the earth that accounts for day and night. Yet with both the widely used *Scofield Reference Bible* (1917) and the *New Scofield Reference Bible* (1967) taking this compromise stance, it is impossible to act as if this does not confront the critical or historical approach to Old Testament literature. Although the massive dispensational theology of L. S. Chafer, who usually follows the *Scofield Reference Bible*, offers no help on this problem, a real upsurge of such thinking is evident.[17]

However, the concordistic compromise has run into reaction among conservatives as creative evolution is considered as a possible compromise between the two warring camps that demand a decision between creation and evolution. This either/or stance hardly agrees with the present state of studies in either Scripture or science, but the pre-critical and pre-scientific school of interpretation has gone into shock at the prospect of peace in the warfare of Scripture with science. The concord proposed by the publication of *The Christian View of Science and Scripture* by Bernard Ramm in 1954 has fallen into discord.[18]

A Constructive View

A constructive view that does justice to both the historical study of Scripture and the impressive evidence from modern science is required. A pre-critical view of Scripture is forced into a pre-scientific stance on science, and the effort to adapt to the scientific view of the world without the historical-critical method of Bible study falls into contradictions.

The central theme of Genesis 1:1–2:4a is the cultic celebration of creation in the framework of the seven-day week. The oldest celebration of the Sabbath was based upon the older Exodus theology out of which the later creation theology developed. This has been preserved by the Deuteronomic

---

16. Harry Rimmer, *Monkeyshines* (Los Angeles: Research Science Bureau, 1926); *The Theory of Evolution and the Facts of Science* (Grand Rapids: Wm. B. Eerdmans Publishing Co., 1935); *The Harmony of Science and Scripture* (Grand Rapids: Wm. B. Eerdmans Publishing Co., 1936); *Modern Science and the Genesis Record* (Grand Rapids: Wm. B. Eerdmans Publishing Co., 1940).
17. Samuel J. Schultz, *The Gospel of Moses* (New York: Harper and Row, 1974), pp. 48-67.
18. Robert F. Coote, "Back to the Boiling Point in the Bible-Science Debate," *Evangelical Newsletter*, Vol. 1, Nos. 25, 26 (Oct. 11, 26, 1974); cf. Davis Young, *Creation and the Flood* (Grand Rapids: Baker Book House, 1977) and Robert C. Newman and Herman J. Eckelmann, Jr., *Genesis One and the Origin of the Earth* (Downers Grove, Illinois: Inter-Varsity Press, 1977).

writer (Deut. 5:12–15). The later Priestly writer based the observance of
the Sabbath on belief in creation (Exodus 20:8–11). Sabbatarianism refuses
to recognize this developing theology of weekly celebration.[19]

A second consideration for a constructive view requires an examination
of the sources for Genesis 1:1–2:4a. A great furor followed the publication
of *The Babylonian Account of Genesis* (1876) by George Smith.[20] Parallels
such as the use of *tiamat* for the monster of chaos in the Babylonian account
and the Hebrew use of *tehom* for the deep led to heated debate about the
dependence of Genesis 1:1–2:4a upon the *Enuma elish*, as the account is
called from the opening words.

Further study revealed the great differences between the polytheistic
version of creation in the *Enuma elish* and the lofty monotheism of Genesis
1:1–2:4a. Indeed, the differences far exceed the similarities, but it is not
necessary to deny all relations.[21]

As to the origin of creation, the Hebrew version of the beginning developed into the belief in *creatio ex nihilo* (creation out of nothing). Plato
taught that the universe was made from pre-existent matter, but creation
out of nothing was clearly stated as early as 2 Maccabees 7:28 and creation
by the word of God is even earlier (Ps. 33:6–9). "By faith we understand
that the world was created by the word of God, so that what is seen was
made out of things which do not appear" (Heb. 11:3). God "calls into
existence the things that do not exist" (Rom. 4:17).

Some Church Fathers, such as Justin Martyr (*Apol.* 1.59) and Clement
of Alexandria (*Strom.* v.14) agreed with Plato, but the views of Theophilus
of Antioch (*Ad Autolycum* ii.4), who taught creation out of nothing, came
to prevail in both Catholic and Protestant theology. There is a tendency to
return to Plato in both the existential theology of John Macquarrie, who
says that there is no Being without beings, and in some forms of process
theology; but belief in continuous creation, as advocated earlier, does not
require this conclusion.

As to the order of creation, Genesis 1:1–2:4a stands in majestic contrast to the chaotic instability of the *Enuma elish*. Latin theology often
distinguished between the *opus divisionis* (work of division) in the first
three days of Genesis 1:3–13 and the *opus ornatus* (work of ornamentation)
in the next three days of Genesis 1:14–31. These obvious parallels proclaim
belief in an orderly creation grounded in the faithfulness and steadfast
purpose of God, but there is no denial of the freedom of God and man in

19. For a detailed study of the whole history of weekly cultic celebration see Willy Rordorf,
Sunday, tr. A. A. K. Graham (Philadelphia: The Westminster Press, 1968).
20. Bernhard W. Anderson, *Creation versus Chaos* (New York: Association Press, 1967),
pp. 16-22.
21. A good summary is William G. Heidt, *The Book of Genesis, Chapters 1–11*, Old Testament Reading Guide, 9 (Collegeville, Minnesota: The Liturgical Press, 1967), pp. 7-19.

the creative process. In fact, man as the image of God in dominion over the created order is the crown and climax of the six tables.

God's sovereign freedom runs through all stages of creative action, especially in the creation of the heavens and the earth (1:1), life in the sea (1:21), and man (1:27), but God's sovereign freedom is most clearly stated in his Sabbath rest (2:1–4a). In his rest he reigns supremely over all chaos.

It is not necessary to describe all efforts to relate Scripture to archaeology and natural science as "dilettante entanglements," to use the words of Karl Barth. But he is surely correct in the belief that there is "free scope for natural science beyond what theology describes as the work of the Creator." However, he recognizes that "future workers in the field of the Christian doctrine of creation will find many problems worth pondering in defining the point and the manner of this twofold boundary."[22] Only as the boundary is recognized is it possible to have a biblical theology in the world of modern science.

29. The Goodness of Creation

According to the biblical view, creation may become corrupt, but it is not in itself evil. When it is corrupt it is a good thing spoiled. God's intention in all creation is to manifest his glory in his manifold goodness to all his creatures. Any deviation from this good intention is natural evil in creation and sin when it involves the will of man. This goodness of creation has both theological and ethical significance.

Theological Significance

The great psalm with which the Bible begins proclaims the goodness of creation seven times (Genesis 1:4, 10, 12, 18, 21, 25, 31). Six times the creative acts of God are declared good, but the climax and crown of creation in the dominion of Man as male and female makes the creation "very good" (1:31). The basic meaning of this goodness is found in conformity to the purpose of God.

The goodness of creation is found neither in its present form nor in the judgment of man. It is good for the purpose of God. There is much in the present process that does not seem good in the eyes of man, who shrinks back from suffering. One who has given profound study to this portion of Scripture says:

> A work which a worker or master craftsman prepares is, from the very start, always in a certain context; it is prepared so that it is good for some purpose or for some person. 'Good' in this context does not mean some sort of objective judgement, a judgement

22. *Church Dogmatics*, III/1, p. x.

given according to already fixed and objective standards. It is rather this: it is good or suited for the purpose for which it is being prepared; it corresponds to its goal.[23]

The creation story of Genesis 1:1–2:4a is not indifferent to man. Man is the crown of creation, even though he is only a part of this good purpose of God. Man's place is to recognize the creative process as the work of God and rejoice in it. A further comment on Genesis 1:31 says:

> The joy of Creation is thereby opened up to man. That is the meaning of the sentence that in God's eyes all was very good. Man is freed from passing judgement on the whole, he is freed from swaying from positive to negative, he is freed from deciding for an ideological optimism or pessimism. He is freed, too, to rejoice in the fact of his creation and in his Creator without anxiety and without doubt. This sentence at the end of the Creation Story, that in the eyes of God all was very good, makes possible a full, un-fettered joy in the gifts of Creation, a revelling in the limitless forces given to nature, a rejoicing with the happy, and an immer-sion in the fullness and abundance that belongs to Creation. But the sentence likewise makes possible suffering with him who suf-fers, the ability to withstand catastrophes, to persevere in the midst of questions after the why, simply because the goodness of what is created can be disturbed only by the Creator himself.[24]

The details of Genesis 1:1–2:4a are discussed in a masterful commentary by the same author.[25]

This eschatological approach transforms the Greek idea that goodness is beauty. The nearest the Old Testament comes to this aesthetic idea is in the LXX translation of the Hebrew *tōb* with the Greek *kalos* in Genesis 1:31. In this context the sense is that of successful completion or well done.[26] The humanistic judgment on "the problem of evil" in the goodness of God is not the last word. Neither the beauty of the process nor the comfort of man is sufficient for a final judgment on the process of the whole. Only in the ultimate purpose of God do ugliness and suffering have meaning. The cross of Christ is the Christian criterion for belief in the

---

23. Claus Westermann, *Creation*, tr. John J. Scullion (Philadelphia: Fortress Press, 1974), p. 61.
24. *Ibid.*, p. 62.
25. *Genesis* (Neukirchen-Vluyn: Neukirchen Verlag, 1974), pp. 104-244.
26. *TDNT*, III, 544. The effort to build on beauty may be seen in the theology of William D. Dean, *Coming To: A Theology of Beauty* (Philadelphia: The Westminster Press, 1972); *Love Before the Fall* (Philadelphia: The Westminster Press, 1976). A good analysis that turns toward a future orientation is by Lewis S. Ford, "Divine Persuasion and the Triumph of Good" in *Philosophy of Religion*, edited by Norbert O. Schedler (New York: Macmillan, 1974), pp. 479-495.

goodness of God and his creation, and this is neither aesthetic beauty nor humanistic comfort.

Belief in the goodness of God's purpose in creation belongs to the very heart of festival worship in the Old Testament. In all suffering and even in the temporary reverses in salvation history there is praise for the God of all history and all creation. The Psalms are abundant evidence for this belief (cf. Psalm 148). In the apocalyptic visions this belief is not weakened but intensified (Revelation 4f., 19f.).

Modern music and religious poetry often focus on God's goodness in creation. However, the emphasis is often more aesthetic than eschatological. Haydn's oratorio *The Creation* makes the goodness of God in the creation of man in Genesis 1:31 a point of emphasis, but the future purpose is lacking. Even the black theology of James Weldon Johnson that is so confident about prayer and immortality fails to go beyond the aesthetic in its threefold stress on the goodness of creation in the moving poem *Creation*.[27] God is not lonely as the *erōs* motif asserts, and he does not look upon creation as an end in itself.

In the world of Greek thought the order of the *kosmos* took the place of God's purpose as the standard of goodness. Beauty was the highest value, and desire for the beautiful was the major motive. The Greek word for desire, both heavenly and earthly, is *erōs*, from which the adjective erotic is derived, but it was not regarded as evil. Evil was identified with disorder and desire for the lesser good.

One of the classics of twentieth-century theology has argued that the Christian theology of the early Alexandrian school, Clement and Origen in particular, substituted the Greek *erōs* for the New Testament *agapē* (love).[28] The *erōs* theology had no place for the biblical view of the goodness of creation that put Creation, Incarnation, and the Resurrection of the flesh at the center of Christian faith.

At the other extreme was the *agapē* theology of the New Testament defended in its most classic form by Irenaeus of Lyon.[29] With "the three fundamentals" of the Apostles' Creed as his bulwark, Irenaeus fought against the suggestion that God's intention in Creation was not good, for this would undermine the Incarnation of the Son of God in human flesh and the Resurrection of the body of flesh. Flesh was really the focal term in the conflict with Gnosticism, which viewed all flesh as evil. Modern theology often hesitates at this point.

The *nomos* theology of Judaism, with emphasis on law (*nomos*), diluted the *agapē* theology of Christianity in Latin Theology. The founder of this theology was Tertullian of Carthage. With great zeal he waged theo-

27. *God's Trombones* (New York: The Viking Press, 1927), pp. 17-20.
28. Anders Nygren, *Agape and Eros*, tr. Philip S. Watson (Philadelphia: The Westminster Press, 1953), pp. 349-392.
29. *Ibid.*, pp. 393-412.

logical warfare against the Gnosticism of the heretic Marcion who thought that an evil god created the world and a good god manifested first in Jesus redeemed the world.[30]

Nygren saw a radical form of *agapē* theology in Marcion, who rejected the Old Testament altogether. Tertullian's attack on Marcion, especially his *Five Books Against Marcion*, does not adopt the *erōs* motif of Alexandria, but his Latin mentality drove him into a rigid legalism (the *nomos* motif). However, the great Carthaginian not only defended the goodness of creation; he also defended the Incarnation and the Resurrection with great insight, especially in his writings *On the Flesh of Christ* and *On the Resurrection of the Flesh*.

Out of this conflict between *erōs*, *agapē*, and *nomos* came a *charitas* synthesis in the theology of Augustine of Hippo.[31] *Charitas* is the Latin for charity. Among the three great controversies of Augustine the first was with the Gnostic dualism of Manichaeism. After nine years of adherence to the Manichaean sect, in the very year of his conversion to Christianity, 386, Augustine's *De ordine*, on the providence of God and the problem of evil, began to wrestle with the problem of evil in a faith that affirms the goodness of God the Creator of all things. His final writing against the sect, *On the Nature of Good*, 404, was an abstruse and difficult effort to trace evil to the privation of the good, all natural evil to imperfection, and all sin to free will. This last point was greatly weakened in his third controversy, the Pelagian, when he developed a rigid doctrine of human depravity that confined free will to the period before the Fall. With a future orientation in which sin is falling short of the glory of God this disaster could have been avoided.

Ethical Significance

The theological idea of the goodness of creation has decisive ethical significance also. In the conflict with Gnostic dualism and asceticism in the New Testament writings the most specific application of creation theology is in 1 Timothy 4:1–5. As early as A.D. 66-67, if Paul be the author of the Pastorals, these harsh words of condemnation appear:

> Now the Spirit expressly says that in the later times some will depart from the faith by giving heed to deceitful spirits and doctrines of demons, through the pretensions of liars whose consciences are seared, who forbid marriage and enjoin abstinence from food which God created to be received with thanksgiving by those who believe and know the truth. For everything created by God is good, and nothing is to be rejected if it is received with

30. *Ibid*., pp. 317-348.
31. *Ibid*., pp. 449-562.

thanksgiving; for then it is consecrated by the word of God and prayer.

The negation of creation is attributed to the inspiration of demonic powers that lead people into apostasy. The agents of this heresy are brainwashed liars "whose consciences are seared" to teach the twin heresies of celibacy and abstinence, doctrines that have become "baptized paganism" in much of the history of Christianity. Marriage is not required for holy living, but any prohibition of marriage on the grounds that sex as such is sinful negates God's good creation of male and female. Abstinence from foods may be required for reasons of health, but abstinence based on the belief that meat and other foods are taboo is a rejection of that good thing which a good God has created.

The affirmation of all creation is a distinctive biblical teaching. All that God has created has a good use. It may be misused as in the case of sex, alcohol, tobacco, in fact anything used to an excess; but some good purpose is possible. Scientific research usually finds some good purpose for all that comes from the good creation. Some earthly things (peanuts and soybeans, for example) have an incredible number of good uses. External use of alcohol usually serves a good purpose, while large amounts are harmful when used internally.

Even in cases where things have been used for unholy purposes it is possible for them to be dedicated to God for some holy purpose that reflects the goodness of the Creator and brings good results for people. It would be interesting to explore the possibility for the good in cases where this is not so obvious.

Historical theology reveals the process by which the door was opened for Gnostic ideas to gain entrance into theology.[32] The single life is indeed preferable to marriage in some New Testament examples and teachings. As far as evidence goes, John the Baptist and Jesus, Barnabas and Paul were never married. Jesus taught that some become eunuchs for the sake of God's kingdom (Matthew 19:12). Paul exalted the unmarried state for eschatological and devotional reasons (1 Corinthians 7:25–38). However, at no place does the New Testament either forbid marriage or demand it.

The heretic Marcion and his school were among the first Christians to demand either celibacy or continence within marriage, but this was one of the points Tertullian used to condemn the movement. After the "conversion of Constantine" and the lowering of standards for entrance into the church, there was a distinct emphasis on celibacy for the clergy over against marriage for the laity. This attitude was first institutionalized in monasticism, and some of the most extreme statements made to defend this attitude may be found in the Latin tradition of Jerome. He even recommended the study

32. A good survey is Roland Bainton, *What Christianity Says About Sex, Love and Marriage* (New York: Association Press, 1957).

of Hebrew to subordinate sexual desires! In the Greek tradition Chrysostom was less extreme and was, even though unmarried, a good marriage counselor. However, extreme views against marriage developed in Greek monasticism. For years pussycats and hens were forbidden on the Holy Mountain of Athos. Only the need for eggs was able to accomplish a slight reformation!

After Augustine the subordination of marriage for the laity and celibacy for the clergy became fixed in Catholic theology. In the reforms of Gregory VII in the eleventh century celibacy was required among the clergy as it is in most of the Catholic world to this day. However, forbidding marriage altogether was never endorsed by Catholicism. The movements that fell into the error were usually infected by Manichaeism.[33] The Albigensians of the Middle Ages, known also as the Cathari, were so opposed to marriage that they not only forbade marriage but also taught that the Virgin Mary gave birth to Jesus through her ear!

By the end of the Middle Ages the sacramental view of marriage that called for monogamy and forbade divorce was established in Roman Catholicism. Many loopholes allowed for the subterfuge of annulment that was no barrier to a new marriage, but the major exception to the sacramental theory was the romantic view of the Renaissance that thought of love as ennobling even outside the marriage vow.

Protestantism recovered the biblical view of marriage as a partnership of equals in which both male and female could realize the goodness of God's creation with no impediments to sexual union. The classic example for Protestant theology was the marriage of Martin Luther to the talented and intelligent nun Katherine von Bora. Despite slanderous suggestions to the contrary, this marriage seemed a true vocational partnership. Roland Bainton's standard biography tells this story with obvious approval and admiration and even gusto! Smuggling nuns in herring barrels was an unusual ministerial function, but Luther did it![34]

Protestant Puritanism was not without rigid extremes about sex. Sex was to be enjoyed but not discussed. It is said that the learned Jonathan Edwards, in the tradition of Calvinism, rebuked his wife Sarah for using the word "pregnant" when she learned that she was to become the mother of their first child. He required her never to use that word in his presence again, and this she did as an obedient Puritan wife even though she went through the experience many more times!

Protestantism was not without its aberrations either. A good example is the American Shaker movement that required husbands and wives to separate on joining the community.[35] The couples were allowed to see one

---

33. A survey is the article on "New Manichaeans" in *The New Schaff-Herzog Encyclopaedia*.
34. *Here I Stand* (New York: Abingdon-Cokesbury Press, 1950), pp. 286ff.
35. An introduction to the movement is in William Warren Sweet, *Religion in the Development of American Culture* (New York: Charles Scribner's Sons, 1952), pp. 295-300.

another and touch hands only in the meeting house under the watchful eyes of elders. The historic community of Pleasant Hill, Shakertown, Kentucky, is now no more than a tourist attraction. There were no little Shakers to inherit the industrious tradition of the community.

Abstinence from meat and wine was common in the New Testament church at Rome (Romans 14:1-4, 20f.). On such issues Paul taught that the strong Christian should tolerate the weak on the basis of love lest he cause those who had not developed beyond the life of conscience to fall away (14:13-23f.; cf. 1 Corinthians 8). Out of Puritanism came the Prohibition movement in America that taught total abstinence from all alcoholic beverages. 1 Timothy 5:23, which instructs Timothy to "use a little wine for the sake of your stomach and your frequent ailments," is often quoted over against Romans 14:21, but the modern problem of alcoholism has persuaded many to follow the example rather than the permission of Paul.

In this brief survey the implications of a doctrine of God's goodness in creation in such practices as marriage and abstinence have great practical value. All that God has created has a useful purpose, but usage must be guided by love. "We know that in everything God works for good with those who love him, who are called according to his purpose" (Romans 8:28). More must yet be said on this point.

30. The Purpose of Creation (Providence)

Providence is a doctrine with roots in both biblical revelation and philosophical speculation. Some have viewed the doctrine as synonymous with religion itself. H. H. Farmer, following Theodore Häring, has made the bold declaration that "To deny providence *is* to deny religion."[36] Still others have shunned all "mixed articles" and claimed this for Christian revelation alone.[37] Belief in God's providential concern for his creation is certainly an article in biblical faith, but it can hardly be denied that light has been shed by metaphysical thinking.

The Concept of Providence

Belief in providence affirms God's purpose in all creation and his special care and concern for mankind. The word means "to see ahead," implying that God is at work in the present with a view to the future outcome of his purpose. It embraces the whole process of creation (future, present and past). The question of providence is a central theme in both biblical and philosophical theology.

36. *The World and God* (London: Nisbet & Co., 1935), p. 99. Italics in original.
37. G. C. Berkouwer, *The Providence of God*, tr. Lewis Smedes (Grand Rapids: Wm. B. Eerdmans, 1952), p. 48.

Biblical. Perhaps the clearest statement in the Scriptures is that of Paul: "We know that in everything God works for good with those who love him, who are called according to his purpose" (Rom. 8:28, RSV). The AV (King James Version) falls into determinism with the translation that says "all things work together for good." It is God who co-operates with the process of creation and human history, who brings good out of adverse situations and events. God, not things, has the last word on behalf of those who are called according to his purpose.

Belief in providence grows out of belief in God's personal interest in those who have responded to his call in covenant relation. A good Old Testament example of how, in retrospect, the community of faith saw God's providential care is the story of Joseph. Even though his brothers intended to banish him into oblivion in Egypt, God worked in these circumstances to accomplish his purpose in Israel. Joseph was able to say to his brothers: "So it was not you who sent me here, but God; and he made me a father to Pharaoh, and lord of all his house and ruler over all the land of Egypt" (Gen. 45:8). Even Cyrus the Great, who was outside the covenant people, was used to accomplish God's purpose in Israel (Isaiah 44:28).

As Job wrestled with the problem of evil, he saw an answer only in his vindication by a redeemer in the future (Job 19:25f.). In the present, things do not balance on the scales of justice.

The supreme example of God's providential rule over human circumstances in all history may be seen in the death and resurrection of Jesus. The Romans and the Jews intended to destroy a disturber of the *status quo*, but God turned apparent defeat into victory. "Let all the house of Israel therefore know assuredly that God has made him both Lord and Christ, this Jesus whom you crucified" (Acts 2:36; cf. 3:13–15; 4:10f., 24–28).

In common parlance providence has been expressed in other terms. It may find an intellectual element in the "counsel" of God that is both eternal and wise. Eternal counsel expresses God's purpose before the beginning of time (Acts 15:18; Eph. 1:4; 2 Tim. 1:9). Life lived in harmony with his counsel combines practical wisdom with metaphysical meaning (Prov. 3:19; 19:21; Pss. 33:11; 104:24; Jer. 10:12; 51:15; Eph. 3:10f.).

God's "will" is the volitional element by which God's purpose guides all who hear his call (Isa. 49:8; 53:10; Ps. 51:19; Eph. 1:11). That does not mean that all that happens is the will of God. Much that happens is made possible in God's permissive will that allows room for natural law and human freedom. Those who ascribe all to the direct will of God end up with a God who may be feared but is difficult to love.

God's "good pleasure" is found only in those things which are a fulfilment of his purpose, but there are many things that do not give God "good pleasure." Creation is indeed the theatre of God's glory, as emphasized in

Calvinism, and of God's love, as in Lutheranism, but some events do not bring glory to God and do not express his love.

Philosophical. Greek philosophy looked for a purpose in the cosmos even though the biblical view of the covenant and creation was unknown. Heraclitus found unity in the cosmos through the Logos, and Anaxagoras suggested Mind. Diogenes of Apollonia expanded the ideas to include organic life. Sophocles the dramatic poet made the justice of God the central point in divine providence. Teleological metaphysics pervaded the philosophies of Plato and Aristotle, and the Stoics made providence the pillar of their pantheistic interpretation of world order. It is not difficult to see why Greek and Latin theology made use of ancient philosophy, at times in a constructive way, but not always.[38]

Out of this mixture of biblical faith and metaphysical philosophy have come systems of teleology and theodicy. In 1728 Christian Wolff coined the term teleology (from *telos*, end) to denote the system of causes he believed behind cosmic purpose. Beyond all mechanistic and organic processes Wolff believed there was a design and purpose. His disciples developed the teleological argument for belief in God already discussed; and modern science, despite modern philosophy, has renewed interest in this explanation.

The presence of evil in the cosmos and human history led others to develop theodicies that attempted to justify the ways of God in a random world under the threat of chaos and of evil. Indeed, without belief in providence there would be no "problem of evil."

The term theodicy (from *theos*, God, and *dikē*, justice) was coined by G. W. Leibnitz in 1710 to explain why there is evil in a world created and under the providential care of a God both good and omnipotent. All religions have wrestled with this problem, but it was the natural theology of the eighteenth century that argued that evil is necessary in the development of goodness, and that this is the best possible world. Superficial scoffing at this view is somewhat sobered by the defense of "this dysteleological quality" in serious wrestling with the problem.[39]

The dysteleological quality of the cosmos and of human existence does not destroy confidence in the providence of God. The relationship between the Creator and the creation makes room for both finitude and freedom, and where these are given both the disorders of natural evil and the disobedience of moral evil are possible. Responsibility and the possibility of redemption, not rationalization of the *status quo*, point toward a solution of the problem of evil. Evil is to be overcome, not explained.

---

38. The systems of creation and providence through the nineteenth century have been surveyed by Leo Scheffczyk, *Creation and Providence*, tr. Richard Strachan (New York: Herder and Herder, 1970).
39. H. H. Farmer, *op. cit.*, p. 95.

The result of this blend of optimism and pessimism is often more romantic than realistic, but belief in providence does not die out in the practical living of those who press on believing that a "higher power" will help them "muddle through" the meaningless maze of modern life. Even those who reject evolution in theory find hope in the evolutionary eschatology of Tennyson's *Locksley Hall*:

> *Yet I doubt not through the ages one*
> *increasing purpose runs,*
> *And the thoughts of men are widened*
> *with the process of the suns.*

Death was not able to destroy Tennyson's belief expressed in his *In Memoriam*:

> *That which ever lives and loves*
> *one God, one law, one element,*
> *and one far-off divine event,*
> *To which the whole creation moves.*

In this practical sense belief in providence is very near to belief in God.

Clarification of the Concept of Providence

It will perhaps be helpful to distinguish belief in God's providence from three theories often confused with the concept. They are (1) the naturalistic view of fate, (2) the deterministic interpretation of predestination, and (3) the humanistic idea of destiny.

The naturalistic view of fate has roots in Greek drama and philosophy. Prometheus, the mythological Titan who was portrayed as the pioneer of civilization, was, in *Prometheus Bound* by Aeschylus, chained naked to a rocky pillar in the Caucasus Mountains, where his liver was devoured each day by an eagle or a vulture and restored each night. Prometheus means forethought. This powerful symbol of fate is connected with providence when it is remembered that Heracles finally released him, but Zeus who bound him is hardly the God of providential care who was revealed in Jesus Christ. According to fate, good is realized only in the rational choice of human beings.[40] That is technological civilization without God.

Shakespeare's tragedies were a revival of the concept of fate, and the *Invictus* of William Ernest Henley expresses the mood of modern man caught in circumstances over which he has no control and from which he sees no escape. He said:

40. For the history of the Greek idea of fate, good, and evil as far as John Milton, see William Chase Greene, *Moira* (Cambridge, Mass.: Harvard University Press, 1944).

> *In the fell clutch of circumstance*
> *I have not winced nor cried aloud.*
> *Under the bludgeonings of chance*
> *My head is bloody but unbowed.*[41]

Predestination is a New Testament term that states God's purpose in Christ, but it has often been used to designate a theological determinism in creation. Against the background of the Augustinian tradition, it was John Calvin who formulated theological determinism for his followers. Despite denials by Calvinists, there are statements in the writings of Calvin that border on fatalism. In reference to creation Calvin declared: "It is certain that not a drop of rain falls without the express command of God" (*Institutes*, I, xvi, 5). Of human action he said, "men do nothing save at the secret instigation of God, and do not discuss and deliberate on anything but what he has previously decreed with himself, and brings to pass by his secret directions" (*Institutes*, I, xviii, 1). The doctrine of eternal decrees is hardly providential care and concern.

The humanistic interpretation of destiny rises above rationalistic fate, but it falls short of belief in God's providential care. Paul Tillich has defined destiny in this way:

> Our destiny is that out of which our decisions arise; it is the indefinitely broad basis of our centred selfhood; it is the concreteness of our being which makes all our decisions *our* decisions. . . . Destiny is not a strange power which determines what shall happen to me. It is myself as given, formed by nature, history, and myself.[42]

Anxiety and ambiguity remain until there is trust in the God who cares. Providence points to the activity of God in nature and history as God confronts the self. Tillich has placed responsibility upon the self, but he has left out God.

At several points belief in destiny falls short of belief in God's providential care and concern for his creation and human creatures. Destiny as Tillich defined it sounds too individualistic to express the covenant relation of Christian community. The lonely self seems a characteristic of much existential thinking from Kierkegaard to Sartre.[43]

A second weakness in Tillich's definition is the absence of God's action in the nature and history that shape human destiny.[44] Is God's providence no more than the impact of external forces on human decisions that shape

---

41. From Jerome Hamilton Buckley, *William Ernest Henley* (Princeton, New Jersey: Princeton University Press, 1945), p. 65.
42. *Systematic Theology* (Chicago: University of Chicago Press, 1951), I, pp. 184f.
43. Cf. Roger Hazelton, *God's Way With Man* (New York: Abingdon Press, 1956), pp. 11-33.
44. Georgia Harkness, *The Providence of God* (New York: Abingdon Press, 1960), pp. 38f.

destiny? Surely the God who cares for birds and flowers and numbers the hairs of our heads is more than mere destiny (Matt. 6:25–34; 10:29f.).

Some old "solutions" to the problem of evil have had a surprising revival in recent thought. For example, the theory of universalism advocated by Origen of Alexandria in the third century has been argued by some well-known theologians in England and America.[45]

The kenotic theory that was applied to the incarnation of God in Jesus Christ in modern Protestant theology has been applied to God. It is argued that in both creation and redemption there is a self-limitation of God that makes the possibility of evil possible.[46] This was taken to the radical extreme in the death of God theology, but others have grounded the belief in the *agapē* of God.

A less satisfactory view of the limitation of God in the process of persuasion rather than in omnipotent coercion avoids the question of the consummation, as in universalism, and the consideration of creation, as in the kenotic theory.[47] It seems, however, that any satisfactory solution must include creation and consummation as well as a present process of persuasion.

31. Prayer

At no point is belief in God's providential care and concern more pronounced than in the practice of prayer. Prayer is always in the first person, the I–Thou dimension of faith, and prayer is the basic form of faith. Believing is praying. One does not pray *about* God; he prays *to* God. In this light Karl Barth has argued that where there is no prayer there is no theology! "Theological work does not merely begin with prayer and is not merely accompanied by it; in its totality it is peculiar and characteristic of theology that it can be performed only in the act of prayer."[48]

Before continuing this perspective, it will be helpful to survey (1) the place of prayer in Scripture; (2) the forms of prayer in the life of the church, and (3) the validity of prayer in a scientific age.

The Place of Prayer in the Scriptures

Prayer is a presupposition in all biblical revelation. Events of disclosure are moments in which man draws near to God and God draws near to man.

45. John Hick, *Evil and the God of Love* (London: Macmillan, 1966); Langdon Gilkey, *Naming the Whirlwind* (Indianapolis: Bobbs-Merrill, 1969); *Reaping the Whirlwind* (New York: Seabury, 1976).
46. Geddes Macgregor, *He Who Lets Us Be* (New York: Seabury, 1975).
47. David Ray Griffin, *God, Power and Evil: A Process Theodicy* (Philadelphia: The Westminster Press, 1976).
48. *Evangelical Theology* (London: SCM, 1963), p. 160. This theological perspective has been elaborated in a little gem by Barth's successor in Basel, Heinrich Ott, *God*, tr. Iain and Ute Nichol (Edinburgh: The Saint Andrew Press, 1974).

Many Hebrew words were used for prayer, but the proper word was *tepil-lah*, meaning intercession. Prayer is always addressed to the Lord, and the petitions usually have to do with this life. Both blessings and curses are pronounced in prayer. Some major examples of prayer in the Old Testament are those by Abraham (Gen. 18:20–32), Eliezer (Gen. 24:12–14), Jacob (Gen. 32:10–13), Moses (Exodus 32:11–24; Numbers 14:13–19), Gideon (Judges 6:36–40), Samson (Judges 15:18; 16:28), Hannah (1 Samuel 1:10ff.), David (2 Samuel 7:18–29), Solomon (1 Kings 3:6–9; 8:23–53), and Elijah (1 Kings 18:36f.). Elijah was used in the early church as a model for intercessory prayer (James 5:13–19).

The prophets, like Moses, were intercessors (Jer. 7:16; 11:14; 14:11–13; Amos 7:16). Prayer is frequent in the prophets and the Psalms. In the post-exilic writings the prayers are longer and more formal (Ezra 9:6–15). It is impossible to conceive of the worship of Israel without prayers of praise and petition. In the Old Testament as in the New it is impossible to reduce prayer to meditation.

Christian prayer found in Jesus a model and in his teachings the meaning of prayer. His life was one of both public and private prayer (Mark 1:21, 35). His exorcisms are ascribed to the power of prayer (9:29), and prayer prepared him for his supreme sacrifice (14:32–42). In fact his life as a Son–Father relation with God was a life of prayer. Such is the portrait of prayer in the Gospel of Mark.

The Gospel of Matthew magnifies this portrait in the teachings of Jesus, the most important being the Model Prayer (the Our Father) with the two foci of God and man (Matt. 6:9–13). It is composed of an invocation and seven petitions.[49] What he demonstrated in his intimate I–Thou relation with God he instructs his disciples to do as the supreme act of piety in approaching God.

The most striking emphasis on prayer in the Synoptic Gospels is in the Gospel of Luke. At several crucial moments Luke underlines the role of prayer in the life and teachings of Jesus (3:21; 5:16; 6:12; 9:18, 28f.; 11:1; 22:42). This theology of prayer is portrayed also in the life of the disciples in Acts (1:14; 2:42; 3:1; 6:4; 10:4, 31; 12:5; 16:13, 16). One could well conclude that Luke believed the mission of Christ and of the church was impossible without prayer.

The high-priestly prayer in the Gospel of John (17) brings to a climax the role of prayer in the life of Jesus, the disciples, and all that would ever believe. The Epistle to the Hebrews thinks of the heavenly ministry of Jesus as High Priest in terms of intercessory prayer.

The meaning of prayer in the New Testament may be summarized with

---

49. For a detailed study of The Lord's Prayer see Joachim Jeremias, *The Prayers of Jesus* (London: SCM, 1967).

the primary words of Paul in 1 Timothy 2:1.[50] Supplication is a recognition of human need with the belief that God can supply that need. In prayer man turns to God believing that God will turn toward man in personal relation. Intercession includes others in the dialogue of devotion, and thanksgiving is the recognition of benefits God has already bestowed. The daily practice of these four steps sustains the I–Thou relation to God as no argument could ever do. The practice of prayer is the best proof that God responds to human need.

The Forms of Prayer in the Church

A secular age is surprised to discover the devotion of the Church Fathers to the theology and practice of prayer. Origen's orthodoxy was questioned, but his instruction on prayer had a major influence on Greek life and thought.[51] Tertullian withdrew from the Catholic Church and founded his own sect, but his book on the theology and practice of prayer guided Latin theology and practice for a long while.[52]

It was John of Damascus who laid the foundation for the distinction between mental and vocal prayer. He said: "Prayer is either the ascent of the mind to God or the decently beseeching of Him" (*The Orthodox Faith*, III.4). Thomas Aquinas divided vocal prayer into common and private prayer as observed in the life of Jesus (*Summa* II (2), q. 83, art. 13). This accounts for such guides as the *Book of Common Prayer* in the Church of England.

At the time of the Protestant Reformation there was a decline in mystical meditations in mental prayer. Friedrich Heiler's classical study on *Prayer* (1918) from the shouts of primitive man to the techniques of mystical contemplation in Roman Catholicism and Eastern Orthodoxy attributes meditation to the influence of neo-Platonism and a so-called prophetic type in Protestantism to the Bible! In general this is true, but meditation has become more acceptable to many modern people than the petitions of prophetic prayer.

The Validity of Prayer in a Scientific Age

Part of the iconoclasm in the book *Honest to God* (1963) by John A. T. Robinson was his attack upon the traditional practices of prayer. His chapter "Worldly Holiness" calls for engagement in the problems of the world in the place of the disengagement of routine prayer and retreats. The Thou is to be met in another person to whom we give ourselves in love. This sounds far from the words by Karl Barth written at about the same time, but the two points of view are two extremes.

50. For most of the prayers of the New Testament see Donald Coggan, *Prayers of the New Testament* (London: Hodder and Stoughton, 1967).
51. Eric George Jay, *Origen's Treatise on Prayer* (London: S.P.C.K., 1954), has a superb history of prayer up to Origen.
52. Ernest Evans, *Tertullian's Tract on Prayer* (London: S.P.C.K., 1953).

The protest of Robinson is not the mood of later reflection on prayer. Prayer in relation to God has been reviewed in the Hulsean Lectures of 1966 by Peter Baelz of Cambridge University. Baelz defends both petition and intercession. Barth's view of God's radical transcendence and freedom is modified by the recognition that communion with God is a possibility here and now.[53] Barth's ideas must be balanced by Schleiermacher's analysis of the immediate consciousness of finite man as one of absolute dependence upon the Infinite God who is immanent in the world.[54]

Baelz believes "that an interpretation of man's communion with God in personal categories will make room for both these elements and the element of co-operation."[55] Communion with God in personal categories is seen most clearly in the incarnation and interpenetration of God in the man Christ Jesus. Complete in his humanity and complete in his deity, Jesus lived a life in which no elements of true openness to God and man were violated.

Confrontation with God includes the otherness of which Karl Barth has made so much. The Wholly Other as the Holy One calls man out of his sin into salvation, and out of his darkness and death into the light and life of God. Even the eschatological emphasis on God as the one who meets us as the Coming One is included in this confrontation. The Coming One goes before us as God and not man.

Co-operation with God calls attention to the fact that the God who works in us is also alongside us. The exclusive view of Harvey Cox should be rejected in favor of the more balanced statement of Baelz that includes alongsideness with communion and confrontation. Dependence upon God does not release man from responsibility in social action.

Prayer in relation to others is well illustrated in the existential theology of John Macquarrie. The saint who lives a life in the discipline of prayer is described as one in whom communion with God modifies his relation with others. "We might describe it as an inner strength or an inner depth, at once stable and dynamic. It has also a creative character — the saint is not only good, he enables others to be good, just by the kind of person he is. The inner strength welling up in him overflows in his relations with others."[56]

Prayer passes from passionate to compassionate thinking, and compassionate thinking takes the form of intercessory prayer in the Christian faith. "Basically, it seems to me that intercessory prayer provides, as it were, openings into the dense texture of the human situation through which can come the creative and healing power of the reality we call God; and because within that human situation our lives are all bound together in a mysterious solidarity, then God's power is able to operate far beyond the

---

53. *Providence and Prayer* (London: SCM, 1968), pp. 16-19.
54. *Ibid.*, p. 52.
55. *Ibid.*, p. 105.
56. *Paths in Spirituality* (London: SCM, 1972), p. 5.

particular person who offers the prayer, though through him. Prayer, as prayer and intercession, helps to make the human reality porous to the divine reality — the whole human reality, and not only that part of it actively engaged in prayer."[57]

Prayer in relation to nature is a perspective of process theology. This study of prayer has led to the conclusion that most of the problems arise out of belief in a mechanistic world and a static view of divine sovereignty. A shift to an organic view of creation and a dynamic and changing view of reality and God removes most of the intellectual barriers. What remains is the practice of prayer by which many people of the highest intelligence and moral integrity testify that prayer does make a difference in man, God and total reality.

Support for intercessory prayer at times comes from the most unexpected sources. The practice of prayer as meditation has been a characteristic of Catholic mysticism and belief in prayer as petition has been professed much by Protestant pietism, but theological support now appears in some forms of process theology. Process philosophy, as existential philosophy, may be atheistic, but the emphasis on process as reality often opens new perspectives for belief in God and prayer. Both God and man are so involved in the creative process that it becomes logical to believe that prayer may change not only things and persons but even God himself! Objective ideas are potentialities or possibilities that God may accept or reject as concrete actualities. Skepticism, then, not science, is the greatest hindrance to prayer.

Process theology has not explored the possibilities of prayer with the same intensity manifested in Macquarrie's existential theology, but a leading process theologian has made a beginning in a brief statement of personal authenticity. He describes private prayer as the path by which one comes to know the mystical presence of God, the essence of which is recounted in his testimony about his army days. He says: "One night as I knelt beside my bed in Arlington, Virginia, I had a vivid sense of spiritual presence. It lasted hardly a minute, but in that minute I knew total acceptance and love and came to understand what is meant by the word *bliss* in distinction from ordinary happiness."[58]

The authenticity of private prayer and the presence of God may also be experienced in public worship. A joint study by Roman Catholic and Lutheran theologians in Germany has yielded many surprising results. One result is the effort to state the necessity of public prayer and the corporate worship of God. Prayer, worship, and the sacraments are logical corollaries of life before God. Verbal and visible expressions of the I–Thou relation to

57. *Ibid.*, pp. 27f.
58. John B. Cobb, Jr., *To Pray or Not To Pray: A Confession* (Nashville: The Upper Room, 1974), p. 5.

God are essential in a covenant community of faith.[59] The details of this will be discussed with the doctrine of the church.

Prayer includes human wholeness in thought, word and deed. Meditation, liturgical worship and social action are all required in reaching out for the presence of God. In God's presence many possibilities become actualities that involve change in nature, man, and God.

32. Miracles

Belief in miracles is difficult for the so-called modern man whose mind has been shaped by the presuppositions of most natural sciences. In the sciences nature has often been viewed as a closed system outside which there is nothing. Nature and natural law interpreted by reason alone is all of reality, so any appeal to the supernatural is viewed with skepticism.

At least two views have developed out of this modern mold. In the pantheism of Benedict Spinoza (1632-77) there was no room for appeal to the higher power of the supernatural which had been the belief of Christendom since Augustine (354-430). In A Theological-Political Treatise (1670), Spinoza expounded a mechanistic view of the world and rejected the idea of miracle as a violation of natural law. For him God and Nature are identical and worship is submission to the order of natural laws. G. W. F. Hegel (1770-1831) wavered between this pantheism and panentheism, but he has been used to support the determinism that rules out miracles.

The deism of John Tolland (1670-1722) and Matthew Tindal (1655-1733) defended belief in the supernatural by separating God completely from the present process of natural law with the exception of rare interventions by this remote deity. The result was the skepticism about miracles transmitted to modern thought by David Hume of Scotland (1711-1776).

Hume's "Essay on Miracles" (1748) has often been accepted as the obituary of all belief in miracles. He too followed the view of natural law advocated by deism, but he reduced miracles to no more than a probability that falls short of proof. What Hume did for theology was to demonstrate that a system which begins with the absence of God will not end with the affirmation of the presence of God.

Miracles are occasions when God's presence is disclosed in the depths of human existence.[60] Since G. E. Lessing published his book On the Proof of the Spirit and of Power (1677) there has been an effort to determine the

59. Johannes Feiner and Lukas Vischer, ed., The Common Catechism (New York: The Seabury Press, 1975), pp. 347-378.
60. Cf. John Macquarrie, Principles of Christian Theology (New York: Charles Scribner's Sons, 1966), pp. 225-232; Karl Rahner, ed., Sacramentum Mundi (New York: Herder and Herder, 1969), IV, 44-49.

meaning of miracles, but many still cling to belief in a closed universe.[61] If the presupposition of a closed universe is embraced without question the belief in the possibility of miracles is very likely to remain a problem. However, if the presupposition of a closed universe has been questioned not only by theology but within the realm of the natural sciences, new doors have been opened for the reconciliation of faith with modern science.

This idea of a closed universe is even more foreign to biblical faith. In the story of the ten miracles of Moses, the first great cycle in the Bible, a blend of the natural and the supernatural is evident. It can be said that Moses delivered the Israelites, but it is just as true that the Lord delivered them through Moses (Exodus 3:8, 10). It can be said that Pharaoh hardened his heart in resistance to God, but it is just as true that the Lord hardened Pharaoh's heart (Exodus 7:3, 14, 22; 8:15, 32; 9:7, 12, 34f.).

The Lord worked and still does work through human and natural instrumentalities, and man and nature are never identical with and never independent from God. Any effort to build a fixed barrier between the natural and the supernatural is futile. It is the closed mind in a closed universe that finds it necessary to separate the natural and the supernatural, the immanent and the transcendent.

If it is possible for modern people to divest themselves of distorted views of Spirit, the biblical view of God's relation to the world is better than the philosophical ideas of immanence and transcendence. Biblical faith thought of God as Holy Spirit, and the idea of man as human spirit was derived from that. So thinking of God as Spirit who is both within and beyond the world, as man is human spirit within and beyond the body, is the best model for miracle. As there are special events in which knowledge of God is disclosed beyond the voices of creation and conscience, so there are special historical occasions when God's *presence* is disclosed as miracle.[62]

Terms for Miracles

Miracle is a term that embraces several Hebrew ideas of the Old Testament and Greek ideas of the New Testament. In general the English words "power," "wonder," "sign," and "works" express the different dimensions of miracle (cf. Acts 2:22; Heb. 2:4). A miracle is a power or mighty work (Hebrew, *geburah*; Greek, *dynamis*) because it discloses the dynamic Be-ing, that on which all existence depends. When Jesus performed a healing miracle he felt power go out from him (Mark 5:30). This power may be used as a

---

61. Ernst and Marie-Luise Keller, *Miracles in Dispute*, tr. Margaret Kohl (Philadelphia: Fortress Press, 1969); Richard Swinburne, *The Concept of Miracle* (London: Macmillan, 1970).
62. H. H. Farmer, *The World and God* (London: Nisbet and Co., 1935), pp. 107-127, 145-179, is still a satisfactory study of miracles in the context of personal religion.

synonym for God (14:62). Luke had a special interest in miracles as power (Luke 5:17; 6:19; Acts 3:12; 8:10; 19:11).

A miracle is a wonder (Hebrew, *mopet*; Greek, *teras*) to those who witness the disclosure of God's presence. Peter's sermon at Pentecost spoke of "Jesus of Nazareth, a man attested to you by God with mighty works and wonders and signs which God did through him" (Acts 2:22; cf. Heb. 2:4). Wonders and signs or signs and wonders are frequently mentioned together in Acts (2:43; 4:30; 5:12; 6:8; 7:36; 8:13; 14:3; 15:12). At least thirty-five combinations are found in the Old Testament (e.g. Deuteronomy 6:20–24; 26:5–10).

A miracle is above all a sign (Hebrew, *ot*; Greek, *sēmeion*) of God's presence. In the New Testament signs are always mentioned with wonders. In the Gospel of John there are seven great miracles, all of which are signs of the Divine Presence (Hebrew, *Shekinah*) in the events. The idea of sign-events is deeply rooted in Old Testament history, but the supreme sign of God's presence in salvation history was his incarnation in Jesus Christ.

The language about God and revelation is the language of miracle. To believe in God who reveals himself in history is to believe in miracles, the events of God's self-manifestation.[63] That is why Jesus in the Gospel of John speaks of his miracles as the "works" (*erga*) of the Father (5:36; 9:3; 10:32), the revelatory events which are the acts of God's disclosure to the believer.

Types of Miracles

If miracles are sign-events in history then the primary type of miracle would be historical, but miracles of healing and of nature are not to be excluded. The basic miracles in the Bible are the events by which the people of God are gathered together in covenant relation with God. Historical science is more central than natural science. Analogy and correlation, as Ernst Troeltsch argued, are basic for historical method, but they must not be used to rule out the unusual and the unique.

The miracle of history on which the Old Testament faith was focused was the Exodus from Egypt. Natural and supernatural elements are included in the story, but it was the sign-event as a whole that constituted the self-disclosure of God in salvation history. Scholars still sift for sources with some success, but the Song of Miriam suggests the central truth (Exodus 15:1, 21):

> *I will sing to the Lord, for he has triumphed gloriously;*
> *the horse and the rider he has thrown into the sea.*

The Song of Moses (1–18) and later elaborations have been added to celebrate this fundamental miracle in Israel's faith.

---

63. B. W. Anderson, "Signs and Wonders," in *The Interpreter's Dictionary of the Bible*, IV, 348-351.

The miracle of history by which the new covenant fulfilled the promise of the old covenant was the death and resurrection of Jesus.[64] The oldest formulation of this faith was perhaps (cf. 1 Corinthians 15:3f.):

> *Christ died for our sins;*
> *he was buried;*
> *he was raised on the third day.*

In this fundamental fact the interpretation of Paul in 1 Corinthians 15 and the other statements in the New Testament see the central disclosure of God before the *parousia* (Second Coming).

When the historical miracles of Exodus and Easter are believed, healing miracles of both body and mind are not so hard to accept. Restorations to life and exorcism are included in the concept of healing miracles, although Matthew 4:24 may think of them as separate types. Appeal to eyewitnesses constitutes the first evidence for the resurrection of Jesus, but eschatological verification alone can furnish analogy. However, numerous analogies of healing miracles have been claimed in the history of the church (and even outside the church) as well as in the Scriptures. Such claims need to be critically examined, but it is unlikely that all of them can be explained away.[65] Healing miracles had a distinctive background in Messianic expectations (Isa. 29:18; 35:5; 61:1).

Nature miracles are most difficult for modern thought, for natural science was dominated by a mechanistic view of the world, especially in the seventeenth and eighteenth centuries, but the organic view of the world that has come to the fore in the last century has fewer problems. Belief in the miracle of the creation of the world does not dominate the Scriptures as do the historical miracles, but modern cosmology is not in mortal conflict with nature miracles.

Most of the miracles of the Old Testament are nature miracles.[66] In the New Testament the Old Testament theology of creation and the Exodus has greatly influenced the interpretation of nature miracles. In a collection of three miracles in Mark 4:35–5:43 God's control over chaos in creation is most obvious in the stilling of the storm (4:35–41).

A second collection in Mark has two nature miracles in which the typology of the Exodus under Moses forms the background (6:31–56). These are the miracles of the feeding of the five thousand and the walking

64. I. T. Ramsey, *et al.*, *The Miracles and the Resurrection* (London: S.P.C.K., 1964). Ch. 4 by M. C. Perry has special reference to the resurrection of Jesus.
65. C. F. D. Moule, ed., *Miracles* (London: A. R. Mowbray & Co., 1965); M. A. H. Melinsky, *Healing Miracles* (London: A. R. Mowbray & Co., 1968).
66. H. Wheeler Robinson, *Inspiration and Revelation in the Old Testament* (Oxford: At the Clarendon Press, 1946), pp. 34-48. For a survey of New Testament miracles see A. Richardson, *Miracles Stories of the Gospels*.

on the water. The testimony of the ten miracles in the parallel and expanded collection of Matthew 8:1–9:38 is part of the portrait of Jesus as the Second Moses, for Moses also performed ten miracles. Some have thought the ten miracles also had reference to the ten miracles in favor of the temple (*Pirke Aboth*, 5:8). Luke alone omits the walking on the water, but all four of the Gospels have the miracles of the feeding of the five thousand.

The Gospel of John adds the long discussion on the Bread of Life to the two major nature miracles (6:22–71). Some have reduced the miracles to symbolic stories with no factual and historical basis, but this is difficult to derive from the sources. It is the interpretation of the history, not the history itself, that John adds. A faith that can affirm the miracles of creation and deliverance from Egypt had no difficulty in believing the central nature miracles. Only a false idea of natural law rules them out of the realms of nature and history.[67]

The Truth in Miracles

Miracles are not to be reduced to wonder stories with no basis in nature and history. The canons of neither natural science nor historical science give grounds for their dismissal. In the very realm of the physical sciences, where a mechanistic view of the universe first ruled miracles out, the quantum theory of modern physics has pointed out the "law" of indeterminism. Sir Edmund Whittaker may have made too much of this in his argument for an open universe, but John Macquarrie goes too far in his defense of Troeltsch and his declaration that the principle of uncertainty in quantum dynamics is irrelevant.[68]

The shift from the mechanical to an organic view of the universe which speaks of new levels and new forms of life is far more congenial to belief in God's action in both nature and history. However, the personal model, of which H. H. Farmer made so much, transcends both the mechanical and the organic view of the universe and leaves miracles in the realm of possibility. Empirical evidence and personal experience are more relevant than scientific and philosophical speculation on what can or cannot happen. What if miracles did and do really happen? Evidence and experience certainly leave the door open.[69]

33. Angels

The existence of spirits that never lived in human bodies is viewed with skepticism and scorn by many. They may argue fervently for forms of hu-

---

67. Robert M. Grant, *Miracle and Natural Law* (Amsterdam: North-Holland Publishing Co., 1952), pp. 182-208.
68. *Op. cit.*, p. 227. Cf. Norbert A. Luyten, ed., *Zufall, Freiheit, Vorsehung* (München: Karl Alber, 1975).
69. Detailed study on each miracle by Jesus has been done by H. Van Der Loos, *The Miracles of Jesus* (Leiden: E. J. Brill, 1965).

man life on other planets in other solar systems on the basis of analogy and statistical average, for which there is no claim of empirical evidence, while rejecting all biblical, historical and philosophical evidence and reasoning for angels. The result is a wide diversity of views ranging from the radical mythological approach of Rudolf Bultmann to the literal anthropomorphism embraced by some conservative Catholics and evangelical Protestants.[70]

In the light of this broad problem, the present approach to the subject will be made along the lines of biblical teaching, historical tradition, and philosophical reasoning. Karl Barth based his belief in angels on biblical theology alone. Karl Rahner has found it necessary to reinterpret angelology in harmony with the teachings of the Roman Catholic Church. John Macquarrie finds belief in angels consistent with the ontology of his philosophical existentialism. Surely such support requires a consideration of the subject in a survey of creation and providence.

The biblical approach to angels in Karl Barth's "The Limits of Angelology" interprets angels as "faithful servants of God and man, . . . who victoriously ward off the opposing forms and forces of chaos."[71] With this he makes his defense against modern dismissals of the subject.

A brief survey of the biblical evidence discloses an affirmation of angels in some form and function from Genesis to Revelation. The multiplicity of ministries ascribed to angels has been surveyed in Edward Langton, *The Ministries of the Angelic Powers* (1937). The general picture presented in the Bible is often similar to parallels outside, and this should restrain those who regard the biblical revelation as exclusive. No doubt most people believed in a primitive revelation of invisible powers under the control of the Most High God.

The Scriptures affirm angels to the degree of classification and personification. The nature of angels is indicated by such terms as Elohim, Sons of Elohim, Sons of Elim, and Holy Ones. This puts them beyond the boundary of the visible world. They function as messengers from God to man. They are the heavenly hosts as well as watchers over human beings. That angels are personal is evident from their roles as mediators between God and man and from such names as Gabriel and Michael. There are even orders among the angels.

From the beginning of the Bible there is a special Angel of the Lord who manifests the Lord to people. The Angel of the Lord appeared to Hagar in her distress (Genesis 16:7-11; 21:17) and restrained Abraham when he was about to sacrifice Isaac (22:15). It becomes evident, especially in the Exodus from Egypt, that the Angel of the Lord is none other than the

---

70. Billy Graham, *Angels* (Garden City, New York: Doubleday, 1975).
71. *Church Dogmatics*, III/3, 369.

personal presence of the Lord, for the Lord's "name is in him" (Exodus 23:21).

Other special angelic figures are the cherubim and the seraphim. The cherubim guard the earthly sanctuaries of the Lord (Genesis 3:24), and the seraphim perform the same functions in heaven (Isaiah 6:6).

In the post-exilic period of the Old Testament there is both a decline and an increase of emphasis on angels. The Priestly Writer speaks only vaguely of "the host" of heaven and earth (Genesis 2:1), for he is more interested in how God acts through his invisible word than through angelic manifestations, but some post-exilic writers have much to say about angels (Zechariah, Daniel). Both the priestly and the prophetic traditions include Satan among the servants of the Lord (Zechariah 3; Job 1; 1 Chronicles 21:1).

The New Testament adds little to the Old Testament teachings on angels. They minister to both Christ and the church. A polemic against the worship of angels is evident in Paul's Letter to the Colossians (2:18). However, the nearest thing to an angelology in the Bible may be found in The Letter to the Hebrews where man is exalted above the angels in the purpose of God and the worship of angels is silenced. Angels are only servants for people who are heirs of salvation (1:14). They belong to the celestial world indeed, for they gather with "the spirits of just men made perfect" (12:23), but they may appear on earth under the guise of strangers (13:2). This highly developed angelology is now subordinated to Christology. The role of angels in the book of Revelation became paramount, but the worship of angels is forbidden.

This Christological subordination of angels is the central point in Karl Rahner's critique of excessive anthropomorphism.[72] Rahner affirms the existence of angels as "personal spiritual principalities and powers" that belong essentially to the world, i.e. to "the totality of the evolutionary spiritual and material creation." This effort to establish angels as conscious, created, finite "principles of the structure of various parts of the cosmic order" is an interesting contrast to Karl Barth's strong emphasis on "the kingdom of heaven." However, both celestial and cosmic angels seem to be included in Paul's idea of "principalities and powers in the heavenly places" (Eph. 3:10). It is not necessary to make a choice between Barth's celestial angelology and Rahner's cosmic angelology. Both are thoroughly Christological.

Perhaps the protest of Rahner is in part justified by the excessive emphasis on the celestial hierarchy in medieval Christianity by a writer who passed himself off as the Dionysius the Areopagite converted by Paul in Athens (Acts 17:34).[73] His excessive neo-Platonism, around A.D. 500,

72. *Sacramentum Mundi*, I, 27-35.
73. An introduction to his system is in C. E. Rolt, *Dionysus the Areopagite on the Divine Names and the Mystical Theology* (London: S.P.C.K., 1940), pp. 1-49.

identified angels with emanations from God and divided them into three celestial groups of three classifications each: Seraphim, Cherubim and Thrones; Dominions, Virtues and Powers; Principalities, Archangels and Angels. Only the last two have an immediate mission to men. The title of the first of his four writings was the "Celestial Hierarchy."

The Schoolmen of the Middle Ages took over the system of Pseudo-Dionysius and developed the elaborate angelology that brought the belief into disrepute. After the publication of the *Four Books of Sentences* by Peter Lombard (c. 1100-60) there were frequent debates on the fine points of angelology. The Dominican Thomas Aquinas developed angelology in the direction of pure spirituality, but the Franciscan Duns Scotus thought of angels as nearer to men in individuality and freedom. In general the Spanish Jesuit Francisco de Suarez (1548-1617) tried to form a synthesis between the two schools. In recent times Erik Peterson's *Das Buch von den Engeln* (Leipzig, 1935; Eng. tr. 1964) has gathered most of the angel lore for further study.[74]

Protestant theologians tend to avoid any detailed discussion of angels, but the former Presbyterian and now Anglican theologian John Macquarrie is an interesting exception. His section "The Holy Angels" uses the philosophical categories of Being and existence to make the existence of angels a reasonable belief.[75]

By the method of extrapolation Macquarrie views creation as a hierarchy of beings that participate in Being (God). Man indeed heads the visible series, but there is no reason to conclude that the series must terminate with man. As there are levels below man in the visible world, so there may be levels beyond man in the invisible world. As a cat does not understand all human experience, so we may not understand the life of angels.

As Karl Barth spoke of the limits of angelology, so Macquarrie speaks of the limits of anthropology. With different orders of spirits that have never lived in bodies the sin of man may be better understood. Sin is a possibility without a human body, if there be sinning and falling among angels, and spiritual sin as pride is graver than sensuality. Perhaps that is why the Bible does not mention the redemption of angels.

The positive side of belief in angels, according to Macquarrie, is that it makes room not only for other races on other planets but for other orders of spiritual beings that accompany man in the cosmic process.

It is this belief that is encouragement to the pilgrims and priests who read about "the great cloud of witnesses" who have gone before and joined the celestial choir. The visible world may fail. "But you have come to Mount Zion and to the city of the living God, the heavenly Jerusalem, and to

74. A modern example in the setting of astrophysics is D. E. Harding, *The Hierarchy of Heaven and Earth* (London: Faber and Faber, 1952).
75. *Op. cit.*, pp. 215-218.

innumerable angels in festal gathering, and to the assembly of the first-born who are enrolled in heaven, and to a judge who is God of all, and to the spirits of just men made perfect, and to Jesus, the mediator of a new covenant, and to the sprinkled blood that speaks more graciously than the blood of Abel" (Hebrews 12:22-24).

Perhaps the most popular belief among devout believers is the New Testament belief in guardian angels that look after both children and the godly (Matthew 18:10; Acts 12:15). This function includes the presentation of their prayers to God (Revelation 8:3f.). The angels also take the disembodied spirits of the righteous to Paradise at the moment of death (Luke 16:22). Thus, belief in angels is related to the other teachings on providence and prayer.

V. MAN

34. The Soul: Man and Life

Modern man has often turned away from the mystery of God only to find himself a mystery almost as great, for he is unable to understand himself apart from his relation to God. The living God and the living soul are corollaries in the great dialogues of life, and the God-man dialogue is the greatest of all. After that come the dialogues of man with his neighbor and himself.

An understanding of man in all his relations, in both biblical theology and modern psychology, may most profitably begin with the concept of the living soul. We will make an almost complete circle in our discussion, from the living soul of the Bible, through the immortal soul of Plato's philosophy, to the concrete soul of modern process philosophy and theology. This brings biblical theology and modern psychology to much common ground in their understanding of man in his historical existence.

The Living Soul in Scripture

The *locus classicus* on the soul in the Bible is Genesis 2:7 where it is said that "the Lord God formed man of the dust from the ground and breathed into his nostrils the breath of life; and man became a living soul."[1] Almost every phrase in this statement is loaded with special meaning. The whole setting of Genesis 2:7 is that of a theology in striking contrast to that of Genesis 1:1–2:4a. The source of water is an *êd* ("flood," "mist," "spring"), and the first step in the making of man is the union of water and dust (*āphār*). The second step is the imparting of life to this dust man. This model of the potter molding his clay may also be applied to all God's people (Jer. 18:1–12; cf. Rom. 9:20–24).

The source itself stands out as the only place in the Pentateuch, other than Exodus 9:30, where God is designated as Lord God, and that twenty times in Genesis 2:4b–3:21. Of the other twenty-three times in the Old

---

1. All Scripture translations unless otherwise indicated are either the Revised Standard Version or mine.

170

Testament where the term Lord God is used, thirteen are in Chronicles and
Nehemiah, both postexilic writings. Of the other ten only three are beyond
doubt.[2] If Genesis 2:4b–3:21 be a new preface to the Pentateuch added in
postexilic times before the preface of the psalm in Genesis 1:1–2:4a, then
it belongs to the very climax of Old Testament history and theology.

The concept of the man (*ādām*) made from the dust of the ground
(*adāmāh*) will be discussed in detail later, but here it should be noted that
ādām came from *adāmāh*, and it is the *adāmāh* that *ādām* tills until the
toils of life are over and he returns to the *adāmāh* again (2:5; 3:19). Man
is indeed a "frail creature of dust and feeble as frail" even though he trusts
in God who does not fail (Robert Grant). Shakespeare left off the last
statement and saw man at the end as "dead and turned to clay," useful only
"to stop a hole to keep the wind away" (*Hamlet*, v, i).

The formation of man from "the dust of the ground" applies to every
man, not just to the first man. Job complains that the God who made him
from clay, curdled him like cheese, and clothed him with skin, flesh, bones,
and sinews is about to destroy him. He says to God (10:9–11):

> *Remember that thou hast made me of clay;*
> *and wilt thou turn me to dust again?*
> *Didst thou pour me out like milk*
> *and curdle me like cheese?*
> *Thou didst clothe me with skin and flesh,*
> *and knit me together with bones and sinews.*

Clay, cheese, clothing—what picturesque language about the formation of
Job and every other person who has existed and exists!

The fact that God makes every person does not rule out the biological
process. The biblical writers had little knowledge of the process of procreation and none of the theory of evolution, but the author of Psalm 139:13–
16 would have adjusted more easily to modern science than those who hold
to a literal interpretation of Genesis 2:4b–7 as if scientific theories are a
mortal threat to the biblical view of each person's origin.

Psalm 139:13 is noted for its biological realism:

> *For thou didst form my inward parts,*
> *thou didst knit me together in my mother's womb.*

There is no stork story here, but there is an I–Thou dimension missing in
too much modern science. The biological and the theological are in perfect
balance and harmony, but the I–Thou relation between man and God is
most pronounced. The Psalm goes on to say (139:14–18):

2. Henricus Renckens, *Israel's Concept of the Beginning*, tr. Charles Napier (New York:
Herder and Herder, 1964), p. 130.

I praise thee, for thou art fearful and wonderful.
　Wonderful are thy works!
Thou knowest me right well;
　my frame was not hidden from thee,
when I was being made in secret,
　intricately wrought in the depths of the earth.
Thy eyes beheld my unformed substance;
　in thy book were written, every one of them,
the days that were formed for me,
　when as yet there was none of them.
How precious to me are thy thoughts, O God!
　How vast is the sum of them!
If I count them, they are more than sand.
　When I wake, I am still with thee.

What a rebuke to the theory of an absentee God in classical and contemporary Deism!

The assumption that once upon a time God made the world and man and then became emeritus to work no more is so foreign to this way of thinking. The belief that God was, and is, and will ever be at work in his creation is reassured in this and other biblical passages (Jeremiah 1:5; Job 31:15; Isaiah 64:8; Acts 17:24–26). It may be that all men have descended from a primal pair, but it matters not if that was 20,000,000 years ago or more recently. The unity of mankind is found in the I–Thou dimension, not I–It. The I–Thou and allegorical interpretation of Genesis 1–3 in Augustine's *Confessions* has unfortunately been emphasized less than the literal interpretation found in *The City of God.*

The breath of life mentioned in Genesis 2:7 is another idea of great importance for understanding the biblical view of the living soul. There is again a wordplay on the sound of Hebrew words. When the *neshāmāh* (breath) of God is breathed into man's nostrils man becomes a living soul (*nephesh*). This again is true not just in the case of the first man, but in the case of each man. Each man depends upon God for his very existence. Elihu rightly said to Job (34:14f.):

If he should take back his spirit to himself,
　and gather to himself his breath,
all flesh would perish together,
　and man would return to dust.

Note here that spirit (*ruach*) and breath (*neshāmāh*) are used as synonyms for the action of God in the creative process.

The great passage on continuous creation in Psalm 104:29f. says:

> When thou hidest thy face, they are dismayed;
> when thou takest way their breath, they die
> and return to their dust.
> When thou sendest forth thy Spirit, they are created;
> and thou renewest the face of the ground.

Here all life depends upon the presence of the Lord. God is the Person in the process, not just a God of the gaps. In his absence there is only chaos and dismay.

As *ruach* (spirit) becomes a synonym for *neshāmāh* (breath), the unity of flesh and spirit as a living soul becomes clear. Flesh comes from the side of man and spirit comes from God. These two sides are well expressed in another *locus classicus* (Isaiah 31:3):

> The Egyptians are men and not God;
> and their horses are flesh, and not spirit.

Of course there are four kinds of flesh (1 Corinthians 15:39). The unity of the two elements in the human soul was a mystery to the Preacher (*Qoheleth*) in Ecclesiastes 11:5 where he declares: "As you do not know how the spirit comes to the bones in the womb of a woman with child, so you do not know the work of God who makes everything." Man must die like the beast, since they have the same breath (3:19), but the spirit of man returns to God (3:20f.; 12:7; cf. Psalm 104:29).

The living soul is the most important term of Genesis 2:7. The Hebrew *nephesh* means the principle of life, but the *nephesh* may be alive or dead (Leviticus 19:28; Numbers 6:6). Man does not *have* a soul, because he *is* a soul. All animate life may be described as a living soul. This is obscured in English translations that do not render the phrase the same in Genesis 2:7 where it is used of man, and Genesis 2:19 where the same phrase is used of animals. In the P story of creation the phrase is not used of man, who is said to be in the image of God, but it is used of life in the sea (Genesis 1:20f.), on the earth (1:24) and in the air (1:30). All that has breath is *nephesh* (soul). This agrees with the possible origin of the word from the Akkadian *napâsi* (expand) and the derivation *napishtu* (throat, neck) with the resultant meaning "breath–soul."

The above definition of the soul in the Old Testament is further illuminated by descriptions of the soul in dialogue. At no place is this more impressive than in Psalms 42–43 — one psalm in Hebrew — where the depressions of the soul are portrayed in the language of the desert (42:1–5). The taunt of others turns the soul toward God. Three times the soul says to itself (42:5, 11; 43:5):

Why are you cast down, O my soul,
and why are you disquieted within me?
Hope in God; for I shall again praise him,
my help and my God.

Many of the other psalms of the Old Testament present facets of this dialogue of the soul with itself, others and God.

Hebrew psychology as distinguished from Greek psychology has brought the biblical understanding of man's soul as self to the center of relevant discussion. In many ways the leader of this movement was the Baptist scholar H. Wheeler Robinson whose essay "Hebrew Psychology" was epoch-making.[3] His point of view is well summarized in his oft-quoted statement: "The Hebrew conceived man as an animated body and not as an incarnate soul."[4]

Further details on Hebrew psychology were elaborated in the important work by another Baptist scholar, A. R. Johnson.[5] Johnson points out the polarity of meaning in the Hebrew *nephesh* by which it can describe almost anything from the principle of conscious life to a dead corpse, but this does not violate the meaning of soul as self.

The New Testament unites many of the Old Testament ideas with the ancient Greek teaching on the soul (*psychē*) as the principle of life.[6] At times body and soul are distinguished, and both may be destroyed in *Gehenna*, the place of final punishment (Matthew 10:28). The soul and the spirit may be divided, and spirits may live on after death (Hebrews 4:12; 12:9, 23). Body, soul and spirit may be used together to describe personal wholeness (1 Thessalonians 5:23). Cf. Plato's idea of the tripartite soul as man (*The Republic*, IV. 11) and the tripartite World-Soul as God (*Timaeus*, 34f.). The human spirit may be present in one place while the body is in another (1 Corinthians 5:3–5). Even though the human spirit is from God, it is clearly distinguished from the Holy Spirit of God (Romans 8:16). In at least one place the human soul is used as a synonym for the disembodied human spirit (Revelation 6:9–11). In neither the Old Testament nor the New Testament is it possible to establish the unity of human body and human spirit in the human soul so that the idea of a disembodied human spirit can be dismissed.[7] It is simply not true that the human spirit requires a human body.

3. A. S. Peake, ed., *The People and the Book* (Oxford U.P., 1925), pp. 353ff. Cf. H. Wheeler Robinson, *The Christian Doctrine of Man*, Third Edition (Edinburgh: T. and T. Clark, 1920), pp. 11-27.
4. *Inspiration and Revelation in the Old Testament* (Oxford: At the Clarendon Press, 1946), p. 70.
5. *The Vitality of the Individual in the Thought of Ancient Israel* (Cardiff: University of Wales Press, 1949), pp. 7-26.
6. Norman W. Porteous in *The Interpreter's Dictionary of the Bible*, IV, 428f.
7. As is argued in D. R. G. Owen, *Body and Soul* (Philadelphia: The Westminster Press, 1956).

The Influence of the Immortal Soul of Greek Philosophy on Catholicism

Greek philosophy made such an impact on Christian theology that the living soul in Scripture became identified with the soul by nature immortal that is found in the writings of Plato in particular and in much philosophy in general. In a way this is strange, since immortality is always a gift from God beyond death in the writings of Paul (1 Corinthians 15:53–55; 2 Corinthians 5:4). Indeed, God only is by nature immortal in the Pauline Pastorals (1 Timothy 1:17; 6:16). A brief sketch of the influence of philosophy on the biblical teaching will further clarify the problem.

At least three types of Greek philosophy have colored the Christian understanding of the soul. Even Irenaeus of Lyon in the second century, whose theology is often rather biblical, shows the influence of the Stoic view of the soul as an ethereal substance separate from the body, but this is based upon the creation of the soul, not pre-existence (*Against Heresies*, II. xxxiv). In the Latin tradition of the third century Tertullian, the author of the first Christian psychology, this Stoic idea of the soul was further developed (*De anima*, 5–9, 38f.).

Platonism had a pronounced influence on Origen of Alexandria in the third century. Plato had a highly developed set of beliefs on the pre-existence of a soul by nature immortal that not only lived on after death but later returned to live in another body in the future (*The Republic*, X. 608ff.; *Phaedo*, 63–115; *Phaedrus*, 245–257; *Laws*, IV. 720ff., VI. 775ff.; *Timaeus*, 69ff., 89ff.). The fundamental presupposition in Plato seemed to be his belief that the process of learning demonstrated reminiscence (*anamnēsis*) from a previous life of the soul before entrance into the body.

An intimation of the Platonic view has been found in the apocryphal book called *The Wisdom of Solomon* (8:19f.), but this is rejected by competent Roman Catholic scholars.[8] Origen was the major theologian through whom most of the Platonic system gained a footing in Christian faith (*First Principles*, I. viii). Gregory of Nyssa followed Origen and accepted much of Origen's view, but with restraint on pre-existence.

Augustine was the major Latin theologian who made way for the Platonic doctrine of the soul's natural immortality in Christian psychology. This is argued in great detail in *The Immortality of the Soul* (387), the first Christian treatise on the subject in the West, and the Catholic tradition departed little from him until Aquinas. From his understanding of the human mind as an immutable substance, which he developed in greater detail later in *The City of God* and *On the Trinity*, he established a tradition still praised in Roman Catholic scholarship.[9]

The philosophy of Aristotle was followed by that of Thomas Aquinas in the thirteenth century, and he defined the human soul as an individual

8. *The Jerome Biblical Commentary*, XXXIV, 12, 13, 28.
9. Ludwig Schopp, ed., *The Fathers of the Church*, Writings, pp. 3-9.

spiritual substance that was the "form" of the human body. Even though the relationship between soul and body is a unity, he taught that the soul will be separated from the body by death and united again with the body at the resurrection (*Summa Theologica*, Supplement, 69–99). In all of this development the belief in the natural immortality of the soul continued until the condemnation of conditional immortality at the Fifth Lateran Council in 1513 closed the debate in Roman Catholic theology. Yet it seems almost certain that *The Wisdom of Solomon*, to which appeal is often made, taught not the natural immortality of the soul after death but that man may become immortal on the condition that he be in fellowship with God at death (1:15; 2:23; 3:3; 6:19). Again careful Roman Catholic exegesis confirms this fact.[10]

The crisis in theological anthropology in the Roman Catholic Church has not yet been resolved. On the one hand is the historical theology of the Church, and on the other hand is the exegetical theology of the best Roman Catholic biblical scholars. A sign of the tension is evident in the *Theological Anthropology* of Joseph Fichter, O.S.C., in which he begins with a summary of biblical psychology which affirms the unity of man as "embodied soul" and "besouled body," but most of his popular little book is an exposition of Augustine and Aquinas and of other theologians and the councils that supported them. Only at the end does he confront the questions raised by biblical exegesis and modern science. The best he can do is to say: "Still it is too early to reach a definitive conclusion on the matter."[11]

If the signs of the times are read aright, it is almost too late to bring dogmatic theology into line with Scripture and science. As will be elaborated when the doctrine of sin is discussed in detail, the whole of theological anthropology must be delivered from the dead hand of Augustine. When Pope Paul VI appointed a committee to solve some of these problems within the bounds of several traditional guidelines, the result was a report that no solution was possible with such limitations on theological discussion. The problem is still very much at that point as far as the teaching of the Roman Catholic Church is concerned.[12]

The influence of science on the evolutionary theology of Pierre Teilhard de Chardin (1881-1955) makes one wonder how he could be in the same Roman Catholic Church as Pius XII (1876-1958), whose encyclical *Humani Generis* (1950) seemed to condemn some theories associated with this famous Jesuit paleontologist. Teilhard's *The Phenomenon of Man* was not published until 1955, but the manuscript was written by 1937. Until his death he had published only scientific papers, for he was unable to get permission for the publication of his religious and theological works.

The Phenomenon of Man sees the whole universe as an evolutionary

10. *Writings of Saint Augustine* (New York: CIMA Publishing Co., 1947), Vol. 2, pp. 3-9.
11. (University of Notre Dame Press, 1963), p. 97.
12. *Genesis 1–11* (Collegeville, Minnesota: The Liturgical Press, 1967), pp. 76-82.

process passing through stages of increasing complexity, with God as the omega point (see 1 Corinthians 15:28, his favorite text in Scripture). Out of matter comes life, and out of life comes mind until God is "all in all." *The Divine Milieu* (1957) took his thought further by describing all matter as sacramental, in the sense of a panentheism in which all things are in God, although God is more than all things. The whole cosmic process he calls "Christification," the incorporation of all things in God as a consequence of the incarnation of God in Christ (cf. Romans 8:18–25; Colossians 1:15–20).

In this cosmic context Teilhard undercuts the old debate between the traducianists and the creationists by bringing them together in the creative process in which God creates each soul as a unity of spirit and body, a consensus of the supernatural and the natural in the creation of the whole man. This avoids the reduction of God to just *one* of the causes for a *part* of man and sees God as the cause of all causes in the creation of the whole man.[13]

The Struggle for the Living Soul in Protestantism

There was a tendency in Lutheran theology to turn away from the creationism of Catholic theology to the traducianism of Tertullian, which taught that the soul comes from parents, but Calvinism at first retained belief in the natural immortality of the soul created for each human body. The preexistence of the soul and the Catholic doctrine of purgatory were rejected in both Lutheranism and Calvinism, but Calvinism retained belief in an intermediate state in which the soul is awake and aware of God and others between death and resurrection. In fact John Calvin's first theological effort was called *Psychopannychia* (1534), "the alertness of the soul," an attack upon the Lutheran and Anabaptist views on soul-sleeping.

The Lutheran scholasticism of the sixteenth and seventeenth centuries was rather consistent in adopting traducianism when it came to the question of the origin of the soul.[14] Only the soul of Adam was believed to be a direct creation of God. Even the soul of Eve was propagated from Adam! This was the very foundation for believing in the propagation of original sin from Adam. The immortality of the soul was usually identified with the image of God in man, so it has been immortal since creation.[15] The view was noted in Irenaeus.

More recent Lutheran anthropology has all but eliminated the use of the term soul. Resistance to the dualism of body and soul has brought the

---

13. The details of Teilhard's views are in Robert North, *Teilhard and the Creation of the Soul* (Milwaukee: The Bruce Publishing Company, 1967).
14. Heinrich Schmid, *The Doctrinal Theology of the Evangelical Lutheran Church*, tr. Charles A. Hay and Henry E. Jacobs (Minneapolis, Minnesota: Augsburg Publishing House, 1961), pp. 166ff.
15. *Ibid.*, pp. 624-630.

word into such disrepute that one is likely to be regarded as out of date if the word is found on his lips. Lutheranism has all but lost the soul! The idea of the soul is suspect.

A fair example is the systematic theology of the Danish Lutheran Regin Prenter who speaks of "Person and Nature" and relegates most of his discussion of the biblical view of the soul to an excursus "Concerning Biblical Psychology."[16] He defines person as the substantial soul with a theological orientation and he views nature as the elements of humanity, which include the body. Much that he says about man's true orientation toward God, his neighbor and creation agrees with biblical anthropology, but what he says could be made clearer if he used the biblical concept of soul as the unity of human body and human spirit.

The Common Catechism, a joint work by leading Lutheran and Roman Catholic scholars in Europe, says all it has to say on "man in history" without reference to the biblical view of the soul.[17] The discussion of man as historical, social and self-transcending takes account of the biblical insights on man and woman and the image of God in man, but not one word is said about man as a living soul as in Genesis 2:7. This superb view of man is not to be rejected, but what is to be deplored is the failure to use biblical psychology in an unashamed manner and with more insight. As long as the Bible is used in the church, and we hope that will always be, the perversions of ecclesiastical tradition based on Greek philosophy should not require a moratorium on biblical language.

A return to biblical language and concepts seems better than the suggestion by a learned Jesuit biblical scholar that the idea of the soul has become so associated with the dualism of Greek philosophy that it should not be used to translate the Hebrew *nephesh* of the Old Testament.[18] The Revised Standard Version by Protestant scholars tried the term "a living being" in Genesis 2:7, but that term has all kinds of philosophical overtones also. Several other modern translations have this substitute for soul, or terms such as "a living creature" or "a living person." It is better, however, to let biblical anthropology put the biblical meaning into the old term than to rewrite the Bible to fit ecclesiastical tradition. This is most certainly true where biblical authority is more than lip service.

It was not until the impact of recent biblical theology that Calvinism made a clear break from the traditional Platonism and Aristotelianism that taught the natural immortality of the soul with its dualism of body and soul. As in so many other doctrines the great watershed has been most clearly seen in the theological anthropology of Karl Barth. Barth's views

16. *Creation and Redemption* (Philadelphia: Fortress Press, 1967), pp. 259-274.
17. (New York: The Seabury Press, 1975), pp. 397-408.
18. John L. McKenzie, *Dictionary of the Bible* (Milwaukee: The Bruce Publishing Company, 1965), p. 836.

will be stated first, but it is important to note the more satisfactory statements of G. C. Berkouwer, a conservative Calvinist who has no doubt learned much from Barth.

When one turns to Karl Barth expecting help on the harmony of Scripture and science on the soul he will be deeply disappointed. Here, on the doctrine of creation, Barth thinks such discussions are "dilettante entanglements."[19] The simple believer is not always helped by such theological dodging of issues, for the problem of Scripture and science is persistent, but Barth must be understood on his own ground before further criticisms are made.

The wide influence of Barth's theological anthropology makes it necessary to review him in some detail. The best beginning point is his own statement "Man as Soul and Body." He says:

> Through the Spirit of God, man is the subject, form and life of a substantial organism, the soul of his body — wholly and simultaneously both, in ineffaceable difference, inseparable unity, and indestructible order.[20]

As will be seen, every word in this thesis is of great importance.

The wholeness of Jesus, the true man, the man for God wholly dependent upon God for his historical existence and the man in whom the kingdom of God became actual, is one of Barth's important emphases that need not be disputed. His identification of soul, as formulated in the Old Testament, and body, as in the writings of Paul, with the self may be taken as true. However, in Jesus the true man as well as in the human self there is a false identification of Holy Spirit with human spirit. It will blow the minds of Barthians to say so, but Barth's description of the human existence of Jesus borders on a form of Apollinarianism in which there is a unity of the human soul and human body with the Holy Spirit. This criticism is made from the perspective that Jesus *was* a human soul, the unity of human body *and* human spirit. His human spirit was not the Holy Spirit (cf. Matthew 27:50; Luke 23:46; 1 Peter 3:18, RSV). A whole man is body, soul, and spirit, not three substances, but the unity of body and spirit in the living soul (1 Thess. 5:23).

Barth's theology would be more biblical if he had an anthropological Christology rather than a Christological anthropology. He always inverts the pyramid by coming at both anthropology and Christology from above. It is simply not so that biblical theology must await the coming of Christ from above to understand the meaning of a whole man, yet Barth declares that he has an "advantage over the older dogmatics" with this Christological starting point. At this point Berkouwer is better than Barth.

19. *Church Dogmatics*, III/1, p. x.
20. *Ibid.*, III/2, p. 325.

When Barth comes to discuss "the spirit as basis of soul and body" his false anthropology becomes more evident.[21] He begins with the declaration: "Man exists because he has spirit. That he has spirit means that he is grounded, constituted and maintained by God as the soul of his body. In the briefest formula, this is the basic anthropological insight with which we have to start." Later he says plainly: "The spirit is immortal."[22] Is this not what Apollinarius said about Jesus? What does he really mean by the unity of an immortal spirit with a human soul and a human body? This immortal spirit is clearly identified with the Holy Spirit.[23]

In opposition to Barth's interpretation of the living soul we have no desire to deny the Holy Spirit as the source of both earthly and eternal life. This I have made clear in previous writings.[24] The crucial questions come at two points. First, is there no distinction between the human spirit and the Holy Spirit? Both the Old and the New Testaments seem to make a distinction as great as that between creature and Creator. Barth himself catalogues numerous passages about the human spirit, but he always claims that this is the Holy Spirit of God in man. In the *locus classicus* of Psalm 51:10–12, 17 this seems impossible. The human heart is clearly identified with the right or steadfast spirit, the willing spirit, and the broken spirit of man, but the Holy Spirit is the Spirit of God. The *locus classicus* of the New Testament is Romans 8:16 where the Spirit of God is said to bear witness to the human spirit.

At times human soul and human spirit are synonyms (e.g., Luke 1:46f.). Even this much is an admission that spirit is a term used of the creature, but human spirit is at times clearly distinguished from the human soul. The *locus classicus* here is Hebrews 4:12 which says that the word of God divides the soul and the spirit of man, but even here Barth says, "Obviously in such a way that the spirit comes to stand on God's side and the soul on man's," so that the spirit is "the discerner of the thoughts and the intents of the heart."[25] However, it is the living word of God, sharper than a two-edged sword, that discerns the heart. In Hebrews the human spirits of the righteous live on in the heavenly Jerusalem after the death of the human body (12:23), a belief Barth seems to reject. The plural, spirits, makes it impossible to call this the Spirit of God (cf. 12:9).

The crux of the whole matter is that Barth argues for the unity of body and soul in the Holy Spirit of God whereas the Scriptures seem to find the

---

21. *Ibid.*, III/2, pp. 344-366.
22. *Ibid.*, III/2, p. 355.
23. *Ibid.*, III/2, pp. 362-366.
24. *The Hope of Glory* (Grand Rapids: Eerdmans, 1964), pp. 33-54; *Spirit of the Living God* (Philadelphia: The Westminster Press, 1964), pp. 82-127.
25. *Ibid.*, III/2, p. 355.

unity of the human spirit and the human body in the human soul, all of
which is the creation of the Holy Spirit of God. In his discussion of "Soul
and Body in their Interconnexion" he clearly states the unity of soul and
body in the Holy Spirit.[26] At first he argues for a dualism of soul and body,
using the antithesis between the Creator and the creation as an analogy,
even though the first is relative and the second is absolute. Both monistic
materialism and monistic spiritualism are rejected. Materialism leaves man
soulless, and spiritualism leaves him bodyless. His Christological creationism is a process in which the Holy Spirit creates the soul and the soul as
the principle of life quickens the body. "It is thus the Spirit that unifies him
and holds him together as soul and body."[27] A dynamic traducianism that
unites creation and procreation in process seems more satisfactory when
the unity of human spirit and human body is seen in the living soul.

The particularity of soul and body is his second subordinate problem.[28]
No objection is made to the claim that whatever has life is soul. The Bible
goes beyond Barth's preoccupation with animals and includes fish and fowl!
There is no objection to his emphasis on man as a percipient and partner
of God. This, as far as we know, does indeed distinguish man from animals.
At times the human spirit as human transcendence of the physical organism
is the terminology I would use for man's capacity to perceive God and be
a partner with God, but the major objection to Barth's view of man as the
soul of the body is what sounds like a dualism that is never clearly overcome. He steadfastly protests that he is speaking only of two moments, not
two substances, and that there is no partition, but his insistence on "inef-
faceable difference" between soul and body is difficult to harmonize with
"inseparable unity." He is still struggling at the end when he says: "That
man as the soul of his *body* is the secondary fact which is no less indispensable to real man than the first, namely, that he is the *soul* of his
body."[29] It seems more biblical to say that man is a living soul who *has* a
created human body and a created human spirit living in unity until death
separates them.

When Barth comes to interpret the last phrase in his statement, "in-
destructible order," we come upon a genuine surprise.[30] At the beginning
of his discussion of soul and body he does not hesitate to use such terms
as dualism and antithesis, but now he puts the emphasis on the unity and
even identity of soul and body in his description of man as "a natural being"
(*Vernunftwesen*). Soul without body and body without soul are dismissed
as spiritualism and materialism, for man "can in no case understand himself
as a dual but only as a single subject, as soul identical with his body and

26. *Ibid.*, III/2, 366-394.
27. *Ibid.*, III/2, 393.
28. *Ibid.*, III/2, 394-418.
29. *Ibid.*, III/2, 418.
30. *Ibid.*, III/2, 418-436.

as body identical with his soul."[31] He seems to return to his Christological analogy in which soul and body may be compared to the unity of deity and humanity in the person of the one Jesus. This whole is, as he has labored to say consistently, the unity of Holy Spirit — soul-body. This is his theological anthropology, the only true anthropology, which allows no room for a technological anthropology or any other anthropology that neglects man's orientation toward God. At once this is Barth's strength — and his weakness! Any challenge of Barth must be biblical, for he accepts no other guide. That is why his identification of human spirit and Holy Spirit and related points are rejected.[32]

Some conservative Calvinists today have rejected Platonic dualism in no uncertain terms. This is especially true of the theology of the Dutch Calvinist G. C. Berkouwer. At three special points he reviews the views of the soul in historical theology with his typical thoroughness, but his own views become clear also.

Berkouwer has a long chapter on the meaning of the soul called "The Whole Man."[33] Here he denounces the theory of a "substantial dichotomy" between an immortal soul and a mortal body. Berkouwer rightly argues that the soul is not some "part" of man not subject to death but the whole man subject to the judgment of God and to the redemption made possible by the whole man Jesus Christ. This view, which seems thoroughly biblical, requires a complete rethinking not only of traditional Catholicism but of much Protestantism also. This applies not only to conservative Protestantism before Kant but to the liberalism built on Kantian idealism.

The meaning of the soul rests upon the nature of the soul. Berkouwer's critique of belief in the natural immortality of the soul is as significant as it is Scriptural.[34] At times he argues that "creedal caution" is better than dogmatic theology, but his main thrust is against the theory of belief in an immortal soul independent of God. Only God is by nature immortal, and man's immortality is a gift received in dependence upon the immortal God.

The crucial point for conservative theology is the origin of the soul. In reaction against the theory of evolution, Pope Pius XII, on August 12, 1950, in the encyclical *Humani Generis*, denounced any denial of the historical Adam from whom original sin comes and affirmed the immediate creation of individual souls for each human body. The natural body comes through procreation, but the immortal soul comes through direct creation. This was only making dogma out of dualistic doctrine long taught.

31. *Ibid.*, III/2, 426.
32. For detailed discussion of this point see Arnold B. Come, *Human Spirit and Holy Spirit* (Philadelphia: The Westminster Press, 1959).
33. In *Man: The Image of God*, tr. Dirk W. Jellema (Grand Rapids: Wm. B. Eerdmans Publishing Company, 1962), pp. 194-233.
34. *Ibid.*, pp. 234-278.

Calvinism has of course been free to appeal to Scripture over all dogmas and creeds, but the theory of creationism has often been expounded by Calvinists in agreement with Catholics. Lutherans have been more inclined toward the traducianism that goes back to Tertullian. Berkouwer believes that the long debate between creationism and traducianism has for the most part been "an unfruitful controversy," because both argue on the basis of the belief that the soul is a spiritual substance separate from the body.[35] At only one point does Berkouwer hold back from saying what needs to be said against the traditional view of the soul. It is not enough to reject the theory of the substantial dichotomy of body and soul, or of the substantial trichotomy of body, soul and spirit. It is necessary to say that the dualism of *either* creation *or* evolution must go too, and creative evolution must be put in the center. God is at work in the whole process of the whole man, for there is no point at which man is independent of God. Berkouwer needs only to follow through to the logical conclusion of his argument.

The Recovery of the Soul in Modern Philosophical Theology

The dualism of body and soul that dominated Platonism had a revival in modern philosophy after the Protestant Reformation. René Descartes (1596-1650) made a sharp distinction between mind and matter that opened the door to Plato anew. G. W. Leibnitz (1646-1716), in his *Monadology*, according to which the universe is an infinite number of simple monads or substances, taught that the soul is the primary monad in man. He believed these monads were ever-active and indivisible, so that things could sink to next to nothing in an ascending and descending scale, but nothing could become nothing.

The idealistic tradition bbest represented by Immanuel Kant's critical philosophy has argued for a "transcendental" ego or self. In a chapter on "Deduction of the Pure Concepts of the Understanding" in his *Critique of Pure Reason*, Kant postulated a self that is always subject and never the object of consciousness. The transcendental self takes the raw materials of experience and molds them into the phenomenal self of everyday life. It is the noumenal or inner self that abides beyond the outer self that passes away (cf. 2 Cor. 4:16–18).

British empiricism has a long tradition that even claims empirical verification for the reality of the soul. The position expounded by John Locke in his *Essay Concerning Human Understanding* (1690) and James Ward in his *Psychological Principles* (1918) took a new lease on life a generation ago when F. R. Tennant of Cambridge published his *Philosophical Theology* (Vol. 1, 1927; Vol. 2, 1930). In the context of scientific evolution Tennant believed he could demonstrate the pure ego or abiding soul that is neither

35. *Ibid.*, pp. 279-309.

essence without existence nor existence with essence. He did not hesitate to ascribe substance to this soul beyond the empirical self and personality, but he rejected the Platonic ideas of pre-existence and natural immortality. However, he did not believe there was any scientific reason to disbelieve the soul's continued existence after the dissolution of the body.[36]

After the Second World War this view became the object of attack by those converted and confined to the methods of the logical positivism imported through Ludwig Wittgenstein at Cambridge. This blitz bombing from the British bastion of empiricism left the idea of the soul tattered and torn, but it seems to have survived. Three stages of the battle may be illustrated with reference to the Englishman Gilbert Ryle of Oxford, the Scotsman John Macmurray of Edinburgh, and the Dutchman C. A. van Peursen of Leiden, each of whom has given considerable thought to the subject.

Gilbert Ryle's book *The Concept of Mind* (1949) reduces the "I am" of the self to "I say." The mind, his word for what Tennant would call unabashedly the soul, is what we call the nodal point of ideas and images. It is only an index word to designate a configuration, but it is an unstable, shifting term. The idea of a substantial and abiding "I" behind all experience is rejected. Ryle finds it most difficult to account for past memories and future hopes if mind means no more than "now." Self-transcendence, of which every person is aware, remains a mystery that linguistic analysis has not annihilated.

The empirical personalism of John Macmurray picks up the problem of the self in relation to other persons and explores many of its implications. He too rejects Kant's dualism as he shifts from the "I think" of Descartes and the "I say" of linguistic analysis to the "I do" of a personal realism. In idealism there can be only one subject: I–myself. There can never be a second person.[37] As personal realism puts man's acts in the place of man the thinker, the self is seen as the agent of action in a personal universe.[38] Macmurray develops the dialogue of self in much the same way Reinhold Niebuhr does, but he leaves one in suspense as to what implications this has for life after death. He is better at demolishing Plato's dualistic view of natural immortality than exploring the possibilities for an ultimate community of persons.

The future aspect comes into focus when C. A. van Peursen defines the soul in terms of intention. The "I think" of idealism, the "I say" of positivism and the "I do" of personalism become an "I will" in van Peursen's phenomenology. At the end of his survey of the problem of body, soul and spirit, he concludes with the statement:

36. Vol. 1, pp. 91-104.
37. *The Self as Agent* (New York: Harper & Brothers, 1957), p. 72.
38. *Persons in Relation* (New York: Harper & Brothers, 1961), pp. 206-224.

The mystery of man in this his bodily manifestation lies 'out there' *before* him, in the intentional aspects of his life: in love and hate, in confidence and despair, in faith and in fear. . . .[39]

This is all well and good if these intentional aspects indicate self-transcendence and the transcendent reality of God in which man finds his final rest.

Existential philosophy has laid a foundation in the selfhood of man that points toward the personal immortality of the self or soul in a manner met in the Old Testament. The relationship between self, others and God may be of such a quality that it is not destroyed by the death of the human body. A surprising source for this type of thinking is a little gem by the social prophet Reinhold Niebuhr who thought through the relations afresh while recovering from a stroke that nearly took his life.[40]

Another example of existential implications for understanding the self or the soul may be found in the theology of one of the most competent interpreters of existentialism.[41] In his application of existential philosophy to the problems of Christian theology, John Macquarrie agrees in part with Augustine and in part with Aquinas, but he speaks more in terms of an authentic self than a substantial self. Augustine was right in seeing human existence as the present meeting point of the expected future and the remembered past, and Aquinas was nearer to the true polarities of human existence by following Aristotle in viewing the soul as the form of the body, but the authentic self is known only in a community of selves.

The supreme moment of decision is the moment of death, when unfaith takes a leap in the dark and faith affirms the positive possibilities of the future as the genuine fulfilment of selfhood. Man's relation to Being, to God, at the moment of death makes the difference between Sartre's absurdity and nothingness and the possibility of personal immortality. Macquarrie, with his belief in the universal salvation of all souls, does not take the possibility of nothingness with sufficient seriousness, but his affirmation of "positive potentialities in death" is in full agreement with the biblical understanding of the soul. The shift from substantiality to temporality has been rewarding.[42]

Process philosophy, following A. N. Whitehead, shifts from the individual soul as an actual entity to the soul as a society. The social soul in the theology of John Cobb has much in common with the temporal soul of John Macquarrie, even though Cobb builds on the philosophy of Whitehead and Macquarrie on the philosophy of Heidegger. The social soul is a center

39. *Body, Soul, Spirit: A Survey of the Body-Mind Problem*, tr. Hubert H. Haskins (London: Oxford University Press, 1966), p. 194.
40. *The Self and the Dramas of History* (New York: Charles Scribner's Sons, 1955).
41. John Macquarrie, *Existentialism* (Philadelphia: The Westminster Press, 1972).
42. *The Principles of Christian Theology* (New York: Charles Scribner's Sons, 1966), pp. 64-74, 323-330.

of experience. Whitehead himself said nothing about a substantial soul that pre-existed or that lives after death. That is why he can think of the soul of higher animals.

Some of the stronger points in Cobb's theory of the social soul are almost identical with the living soul in Genesis 2:7. The general character of the soul is consciousness, which is the living person, and the living person is a living soul in process of becoming.[43] Language is seen by Cobb as the distinctiveness of the soul, and this was seen as central in Genesis 2:18-25.[44] The most obvious weakness in the process view of the soul is the approach to life after death. Cobb can speak only of "the *possibility* of life after death, not at all for its actuality."[45]

It is when Cobb ventures beyond his mentor Whitehead that he makes a distinctive contribution to belief in the soul's survival of physical death.[46] The problem of personal identity through time confronts the mystery of memory. The possibility of memory suggests the immediate objectification of all past occasions in the living soul or person. To memory may be added the evidence for mental telepathy as "immediated prehension of the mental poles of another person's experience."

Whitehead's famous statement that "consciousness presupposes experience, and not experience consciousness" raises the question of the unconscious.[47] This opens up the possibility that the brain and the soul are not identical. The brain as object is divisible, but the mind as subject is indivisible, and this leads to the conclusion that "we can conceive of the soul occupying generally the region of the brain, receiving the causal efficacy of every portion of the brain at once, and experiencing its own synthesis of all these influences in its own unified subjective immediacy."[48] The possibility that mind may survive the death of the brain adds to the parallels between Cobb's soul and the living soul of the Bible. It is another instance of why biblical theologians and philosophical theologians should listen to one another!

In dialogue with modern psychology and philosophy and against the background of the historical exegesis of Scripture it becomes abundantly clear that the historical theologies of the churches, both Catholic and Protestant, have followed a view of the soul that is supported neither by the Scriptures nor by science. Yet the dogmatism that is unable to admit error will continue to rant against the belief that the soul is the self and rely upon the old clichés that come more from Greek philosophy than from Scripture.

43. *A Christian Natural Theology* (Philadelphia: The Westminster Press, 1965), pp. 47-56.
44. *Ibid.*, pp. 56-63.
45. *Ibid.*, p. 70.
46. *Ibid.*, pp. 71-91.
47. *Process and Reality* (New York: The Macmillan Company, 1929), p. 83.
48. John B. Cobb, Jr., *op. cit.,* p. 91. Cf. William A. Beardslee, *A House for Hope* (Philadelphia: The Westminster Press, 1972), p. 146.

On the other hand it is good to know that at least some are willing to reexamine the Scriptures and to revise their self-understanding.

35. Eden: Man and Creation

A few years ago John Whale caused a small stir in his popular statement of basic Christian doctrine when he said Eden was no place on the map and the Fall was no date in history.[49] This was not really new. Origen had said much the same in his reply to the pagan Celsus (*Contra Celsum* IV. 37-39), and Tertullian made room for such a view when he said every person is born in the Paradise of innocence and goes out of the garden into a world of guilt at adolescence (*De anima*, 38; *De baptismo*, 18:4).

The problem had been created by Augustine's rather literal interpretation of the Paradise story in Genesis 2-3. There were people in Augustine's time who thought man had lived very long upon the earth, but Augustine argued that man was created "less than 6,000 years ago" (*The City of God*, XII. 13). Furthermore, Adam and Eve lived in a garden that was an actual place and the Fall was a date in history (XII. 27). Before the Fall man possessed Original Righteousness, and after the Fall he and all his descendants were guilty of Original Sin (XIV. 1).

It need hardly be said that St. Thomas Aquinas and all conservative Catholicism stand or fall on this foundation.[50] Protestant fundamentalism did not change this picture. Martin Luther was extravagant in his description of the Primitive State of man, and the more sagacious John Calvin did not change the picture (*Institutes*, II. 1). An upsurge of this theory stands ready to denounce all who deviate from the Augustinian view of the Primitive State of man as heretics that should be excluded from the fellowship of "Bible-believing Christians." Logic and scientific evidence are brought into the battle with the zeal of a holy war. The *avant-garde* is the Creation Research Society.[51]

Any suggestion that Eden in the Scriptures has a very definite and profound symbolic meaning that can be related to modern scientific and historical research without disaster is viewed with suspicion, but that is precisely the approach that is sorely needed today in this new time of warfare between science and religion. A preliminary definition of Eden, before a more detailed examination of biblical texts, says: "Eden symbolized the state of the unbroken fellowship between God and man."[52] The Old Testament presents both a heavenly and an earthly picture of this state.

49. *Christian Doctrine* (New York: The Macmillan Company, 1941), p. 52.
50. G. D. Smith, ed., *The Teaching of the Catholic Church* (New York: The Macmillan Company, 1948), Vol. 1, pp. 321f.
51. A representative book is Henry M. Morris, *The Genesis Record* (San Diego: Creation-Life Publishers, 1976).
52. B. S. Childs in *The Interpreter's Dictionary of the Bible*, p. 23.

Eden and Scripture

Eden in a new heaven and a new earth. Apart from the Paradise story in Genesis 2–3 the Old Testament projects the picture of an earthly Eden into the messianic age of the future. This seems to be independent of the belief in the curse upon all creation after the sin of Adam and Eve.

In any case, according to Isaiah 11:6–9, the peace of creation will prevail in the time of the messianic king when:

> *The wolf shall dwell with the lamb,*
> *   and the leopard shall lie down with the kid,*
> *and the calf and the lion and the fatling together,*
> *   and a little child shall lead them.*
> *The suckling child shall play over the hole of the asp,*
> *   and the weaned child shall put his hand on the adder's den.*
> *They shall not hurt or destroy in all my holy mountain;*
> *   for the earth shall be full of the knowledge of the Lord*
> *   as the waters cover the sea.*

When Zion is restored all creation will see the glory of the Lord, and pilgrims will pass through an earthly Eden as they march to ZION (Isaiah 35). The messianic age is actually called Eden in Isaiah 51:3.

Some have found a picture of Eden in the temptation narrative of Mark 1:13, and it is certain that the Gospels saw the dawn of the messianic age in the works of Jesus (cf. Matthew 11:4–5; Luke 4:18–19 with Isaiah 29:18f.; 35:5f.; 61:1). Apart from the person of Jesus the picture of an earthly Eden is either projected into the future new heaven and the new earth or into the realm of the righteous dead. Jesus promised the thief that on the day of their death the two would be together in Paradise (Luke 23:43). In mystical ecstasy the Apostle Paul was caught up into Paradise, but he located that in the third heaven (2 Corinthians 12:1–4). Only in the future is Eden located on earth in the New Testament (Revelation 2:7; 22:1–5). Only in the light of the future hope, it seems, is a Garden of Eden projected into a Paradise of the present in heaven and a Paradise of the past on earth. A Paradise to be gained is the basis for belief in a Paradise that was lost. In more technical language eschatology is the mother of ktisiology or protology. The future man is father of the first man!

Eden in heaven. The first reference to an Eden in heaven in the prophetic writings is found in the prophet Ezekiel at the beginning of the Babylonian Exile, and it may be that this is the origin of the belief in the Old Testament. None of the pre-Exilic prophets mentions the garden of Eden with reference to either the creation of man or the origin of sin. An approach to the heavenly Eden of the present should begin with Ezekiel's Prophecy on Tyre

(26:1–28:19).[53] The dirge (28:12–19) on the king of Tyre is often called a variation on Genesis 2:4b–3:24, but it is more likely a preparation.

The dirge may be divided into three parts. There is first of all a description of original perfection (28:13–14):

> *You were the signet of perfection,*
>   *full of wisdom and perfect in beauty.*
> *You were in Eden, the garden of God;*
>   *every precious stone was your covering,*
> *carnelian, topaz, and jasper,*
>   *chrysolite, beryl, and onyx,*
> *sapphire, carbuncle, and emerald;*
>   *and wrought in gold were your settings and your engravings.*
> *on the day that you were created they were prepared.*
> *With an anointed guardian cherub I placed you;*
>   *you were on the holy mountain of God;*
>   *in the midst of the stones of fire you walked.*

This original state of perfection is stated in terms of the high priest whose breastplate was adorned with precious stones (Exodus 28:17–20) and the cherubim who covered the ark of the covenant with their wings (Exodus 25:20; 1 Kings 8:7). The location of this state of perfection was in Eden, the garden of God, or God's holy mountain in the far north (cf. Isaiah 14:13).

A second part of the dirge describes the expulsion from Eden when the perfect and blameless state came to an end with the origin of iniquity (28:15–17):

> *You were blameless in your ways*
>   *from the day you were created,*
>   *till iniquity was found in you.*
> *In the abundance of your trade*
>   *you were filled with violence, and you sinned;*
>   *so I cast you out as a profane thing from the mountain of God,*
>   *and the guardian cherub drove you out*
>   *from the midst of the stones of fire.*
> *Your heart was proud because of your beauty;*
>   *you corrupted your wisdom for the sake of your splendor.*
> *I cast you to the ground;*
>   *I exposed you before kings,*
>   *to feast their eyes on you.*

Iniquity, sin, and pride led to the expulsion from Eden, a symbol of the fall of the king of Tyre.

---

53. Exegetical problems are discussed in some detail by H. J. Van Dijk, *Ezekiel's Prophecy on Tyre* (Rome: Pontifical Biblical Institute, 1968).

The third part turns from heavenly language to describe the fall of the king of Tyre in terms of corrupt trade that led to injustice and violence (28:18f.). History has been interpreted in symbolic language.

In the allegory of the cedar tree Ezekiel interprets pride as the cause for the fall of Egypt (31:1–18). The great tree which all the other trees in Eden envied fell to the lowest level of all, *Sheol*. This Eden is also called the garden of God (31:9, 16, 18). The symbolism of the great world tree in the garden of God is also a variant version of the tree of life (Genesis 2:9; 3:24).

The restoration of Israel from the Babylonian Exile is promised in terms of a new age when the wilderness will be turned into an Eden, but this points to the eschatological Eden when heaven and earth become one (Isaiah 51:3). This will be God's holy mountain in the messianic age (Isaiah 11:6–9; Revelation 21:10).

Eden on earth. Eden may be derived from the Sumerian-Akkadian word *edinu*, meaning "wilderness" or "flatland," but the Greek translation of the Old Testament led to the traditional association of Eden with Paradise, the "garden of delight." In at least three places Eden is described as a definite place on earth (Genesis 2:8, 10; 4:16), but in thirteen places it is used in the singular to designate an undetermined location. These two usages are very important for understanding the meaning of the Eden motif in Holy Scripture. A similar usage of Adam and "the man" will be discussed later.

The primary biblical passage on the earthly Eden is Genesis 2:8f.: "And the Lord God planted a garden in Eden, in the east; and there he put the man whom he had formed. And out of the ground the Lord God made to grow every tree that is pleasant to the sight and good for food, the tree of life also in the midst of the garden, and the tree of the knowledge of good and evil."

The symbolism of the two trees points up the possibilities of personal immortality and knowledge. The fact that man does not eat of the tree of life and is later driven from the garden lest he do so indicates that immortality is a gift from God (2:8; 3:22–24). As has been seen, there is no place for the Greek idea of the natural immortality of the soul in biblical theology.

The tree of the knowledge of good and evil has been interpreted in several ways. The popular view that the tree symbolizes carnal knowledge claims the support of Genesis 4:1, but sexual experience is not forbidden in the narrative about the making of the woman (2:18–25). A theory that the story forbids knowledge of the occult is far-fetched, even though the Old Testament does forbid the occult (Deuteronomy 18:14). The most likely interpretation is that man's knowledge of good and evil will doom him to death (2:17). Man is neither immortal nor omniscient by nature.

The symbolism of the four rivers is an additional embellishment of the geography, but only the Euphrates and Tigris rivers can be definitely located

(2:10–14). Behind the passage the symbol of the four world rivers that circle the earth has been suggested, but literal speculation is not very fruitful.[54]

The place of man in the garden as a whole was that of a caretaker (2:15). The prohibition against eating forbidden fruit in this context emphasizes the lordship of God and the stewardship of man. This important teaching in this older creation story has been recovered as a corrective to the false interpretation of man's dominion in the later creation story (Genesis 1:26–31) that has been used to justify man's exploitation of natural resources. Theology is, after all, relevant in ecology.

Even after the exegesis of Scripture is complete the traditional argument resorts to analogy. If Jesus, the Last Adam, lived at a certain time and in a certain place, then the first Adam must have lived at a certain time and in a certain place, it is argued. However, there is one great difference. We know when and where Jesus lived, but we do not know when and where the first man lived. Eden was a place on the map, but we do not know where it was. The first sin was at a definite time in history, but we do not know when. Therefore, the ancient primeval fact can be described only in symbolic language that applies to every man. The details of this approach will follow later.

Eden and Society

This earthly pilgrimage is better described in terms of the Exodus from Egypt followed by the wandering of the people of God through the wilderness of this world. This emphasis on the Exodus motif in biblical theology is abundantly illustrated in the history of theology.[55] In Catholic theology, Paradise is generally located in the realm of the dead, as in Dante's *Divine Comedy*, although the picture of a Paradise in the historical past is retained. This picture is repeated in the Reformed theology of Calvinism, but with the rejection of a Catholic purgatory. The classic expression of Puritan Calvinism, as the poetry of John Milton summed it up, was a balance between Paradise Lost, about 4004 B.C., and Paradise Regained in Christ, both in the present realm of the dead and in the future on earth. However, the earthly Eden was more and more spiritualized under the influence of Calvin's revival of Augustine's amillennialism.

If Genesis 1:1–2:4a teaches that there is no creation without a Creator, then Genesis 2:4b–25 says loud and clear that there is no man without creation. These words are being written at a time when there is much discussion about whether there is any life on the planet Mars. It does not strain the human imagination at all to think of a lifeless planet, but the idea

---

54. B. S. Childs, *The Book of Exodus* (Philadelphia: The Westminster Press, 1974), loc. cit.
55. George H. Williams, *Wilderness and Paradise in Christian Thought* (New York: Harper & Brothers, 1962).

of life without a planet is inconceivable. That earth rolled along for millions of years, at least half her history, with no trace of life is common knowledge for schoolchildren now, but earth life before the earth is unthinkable. These obvious facts come home in a fresh and sobering way when one finds himself alone in the vast ranges of Sinai. All this dust was around before man was made of dust!

A few years ago the word "ecology" was almost unknown to the average person. A prophetic word was spoken by Prince Bernhard of the Netherlands when he said:

> Ecology, in the next 10 or 20 years, may well become the most
> popular of sciences — a household word of those masses who today
> are ignorant of both the word and its meaning.[56]

At the time the word had been used in biology and sociology, but not in theology! Ecology is derived from the Greek word *oikos*, a house.

The idea that the created order all around is our house was quickly accepted, but a relation between ecology and theology was thought to be the rumination of unconventional people like Francis of Assisi. That it should be a part of practical living was a peripheral thought, yet the present ecological crisis has changed the situation. In 1224, after illness left Francis completely blind and St. Clara had nursed him back to sight, he composed the Italian prose poem *The Song to Brother Sun*. How relevant it sounds now to scientific man who has come to see more clearly his dependence on solar energy and the whole realm of creation.

> *Praise to Thee, my Lord, for all Thy creatures,*
> *Above all Brother Sun*
> *Who brings us the day and lends us his light.*
> *Lovely is he, radiant with great splendour,*
> *And speaks to us of Thee,*
> *O Most High.*
> *Praise to Thee, my Lord, for Sister Moon and the stars*
> *Which Thou hast set in the heavens,*
> *Clear, precious, and fair.*
> *Praise to Thee, my Lord, for Brother Wind,*
> *For air and cloud, for calm and all weather,*
> *By which Thou supportest life in all Thy creatures.*
> *Praise to Thee, my Lord, for Sister Water,*
> *Who is so useful and humble,*
> *Precious and pure.*
> *Praise to Thee, my Lord, for Brother Fire,*
> *By whom Thou lightest the night;*
> *He is lovely and pleasant, mighty and strong.*

56. In his "Introduction" to Peter Farb, *Ecology* (New York: Time Inc., 1963, 1967), p. 7.

> *Praise to Thee, my Lord, for our sister Mother Earth*
> *Who sustains and directs us,*
> *And brings forth varied fruits, and coloured flowers, and*
> *plants.*[57]

A theology of nature prepared the way for ecological theology. One of the several places at which the Baptist theologian H. Wheeler Robinson was ahead of his time was in his serious study of the Old Testament view of nature.[58] His student E. C. Rust expanded these explorations and related the biblical understanding to modern scientific theories.[59] Before Rust's book, Alan D. Galloway, under the influence of Paul Tillich, summarized the suggestions on cosmic redemption in historical theology.[60] The climax for cosmic theology came with the death of Pierre Teilhard in 1955, when his forbidden writings could be safely published (sic!).[61] The major theology of nature became Conrad Bonifazi's *Theology of Things: A Study of Man in His Physical Environment*, but he was most interested in philosophical phenomenology.[62]

A call for an ecological theology came out of concern for the ecological crisis. It was claimed that traditional Christian theology had blessed the exploitation of nature by magnifying the dominion of man over the order of creation according to the command of Genesis 1:26–31.[63] By 1970 Frederick Elder, following some insights by Loren Eiseley, divided the theologies of man's relation to nature into the exclusivist and the inclusivist companies.[64] The exclusivist sees man as outside and above the process of nature, exploiting it for his own goals. Inclusivists recognize man's dependence on nature and his involvement in all of its processes. It would seem that reflection on Genesis 2:4b–25 would make this last view obvious, but preoccupation with man's dominion over nature as in Genesis 1:26–31 has distorted man into a predator. Even though Elder's exegesis of Psalm 8 is superficial, this is basically a biblical view of Eden.

---

57. Marion A. Habig, ed., *St. Francis of Assisi: Omnibus of Sources* (Chicago: Franciscan Herald Press, 1973), pp. 1258f.
58. *Inspiration and Revelation in the Old Testament* (Oxford: Clarendon Press, 1946), pp. 1-48.
59. *Nature and Man in Biblical Thought* (London: Lutterworth Press, 1953).
60. *The Cosmic Christ* (London: Nisbet and Company, 1951). Rust later responded to the ecological crisis with a summary of his years of study on earth and science in his *Nature: Garden or Desert?* (Waco, Texas: Word Books, 1971). Kenneth Maah's dissertation (Southern Baptist Theological Seminary) on the Old Testament and ecology is even more detailed.
61. For a good introduction to this unusual man see Doran McCarty, *Teilhard de Chardin* (Waco, Texas: Word Books, 1976). However, it is not clear whether the cosmic is to be redeemed or be only the scene for salvation history.
62. (New York: Lippincott, 1967).
63. An article by Lynn White, "The Historical Roots of our Ecological Crisis," in *Science*, CLV (1967), p. 1207, precipitated several ecological theologies.
64. *Crisis in Eden: A Religious Study of Man and Environment* (Nashville: Abingdon Press, 1970).

In the same year H. Paul Santmire, building on the detailed discussions of creation in Karl Barth's *Church Dogmatics*, advocated a similar view.[65] His analysis of American culture detects a tide of Civilization versus Nature with an undertow of Nature versus Civilization. The surge of Civilization versus Nature was due to Puritan promotion of man's dominion as well as secular concern for wealth. Using the biblical eschatology that includes creation in redemption, Santmire seeks to bring both Nature and Civilization into the Kingdom of God. Man is portrayed as a caretaker of creation and not just a sovereign lord bent on exploitation.

Despite his adoption of Barth's view of body and soul as his major analogy, Santmire sees clearly that nature is independent of man but man is not independent of nature. Nature has a life of its own, but man's life is lived in nature, even though he is also above nature. Viewing flesh and spirit as the living soul would make this point better, but the book as a whole is rather balanced. "Man is not immersed altogether in nature; nor is he separated from it. He exists *in* and *with* nature."[66]

Santmire found "the key to the New Horizon" in a reinterpretation of Romans 8:20 which says the futility of creation is "not of its own will." God made it subject to futility because of man. After pointing out the fallacy of Origen's theory of a cosmic fall before man and giving some praise for the partial insights of both Irenaeus of Lyon and Martin Luther, Santmire makes this significant claim:

> Man definitely has fallen, but the whole of nature has not. Through man's sin a divine curse is placed upon his life in nature. The theme is especially evident in the Yahwistic creation narrative. A cursed nature is the legacy of man when he goes outside of the Garden.[67]

Although Genesis 2–3 may be earlier or later in the Old Testament, this is true regardless of the question about how literal or how symbolic the story should be taken. Even before the impact of modern science Irenaeus of Lyon, Tertullian of Carthage, and Martin Luther left the legacy of a lost key.

If Santmire be correct in his observation, as he seems to be, the Pauline view of the fall of creation is in harmony with what has been said about the fall of man (to be discussed in detail with the doctrine of sin). Sin did enter through one man, but the sentence of death is on all men only because all men, each in his own life and time, "have sinned" (Romans 5:12, AV; cf. 3:23). There is no fallen creation apart from the fall of man (Genesis 3:14–19). To *the man* the Lord God said: "cursed is the ground because of you"

65. *Brother Earth* (New York: Thomas Nelson Inc., 1970).
66. *Ibid.*, p. 133.
67. *Ibid.*, pp. 164f.

(3:17). So, to put it in terms of modern science, there was an ecological balance in the whole realm of creation until man the exploiter disturbed it. The fact that an ecological crisis is required for this to become clear is no argument against it.

Eden and Science

At no point have modern science and biblical criticism made a greater impact on Christian theology than on the concept of Eden. In both Protestant and Catholic traditions some have abandoned all efforts at reconciliation and harmony. Either the theories of modern science and biblical criticism are rejected or the Scriptures are discarded as irrelevant for understanding human origin and destiny. Both postures are unsatisfactory if biblical faith is to survive in the context of scientific and critical thought. It may be helpful to assess the present situation in both Protestantism and Roman Catholicism.

The crisis in Protestantism came in the nineteenth century but the controversy continues in the twentieth. In 1881 the learned Friedrich Delitzsch, in his book *Where Was Paradise?*, attempted to locate Eden about one hundred miles north of Baghdad, but his later book *Babel and Bible* (1902-3) argued that several Old Testament narratives, including the Paradise story, were symbolic reinterpretations of Babylonian culture. These views created such a controversy that he became hostile toward the Orthodox tradition, especially in his book *More Light* (1907).

It may be said that the Babel–Bible controversy divided Protestantism into the two camps that continue until now. As recently as 1976, Harold Lindsell, editor of the widely read *Christianity Today*, called on all conservatives to rally under the banner of biblical inerrancy to defend among other issues the most literal view of the Paradise story. His book *The Battle for the Bible* is a broadside at authors and institutions that were once considered in the conservative camp. Lindsell thinks they have compromised too much with modern science and the historical-critical method of Bible study.

On the issue of Eden, Lindsell joins President J. A. O. Preuss of the Lutheran Church (Missouri Synod) in attacking Professor Walter E. Keller of Valparaiso University for departing from the literal tradition of pre-scientific and pre-critical Lutheranism.[68] However, Lindsell leaves one bewildered on how to relate science and Scripture in the present situation.

Lindsell's useful edition of the *Harper Study Bible* is more moderate and constructive on the Eden issue. He says:

The location of the Garden of Eden has never been precisely determined. Scripture locates it generally on the Tigris (designated

68. (Grand Rapids: Zondervan, 1976), p. 80.

in KJV by its ancient name Hiddekel) and Euphrates rivers where they were joined by the Pishon and Gihon. The last two have never been identified. Tradition has located Eden south of Ur, at a site known as Eridu. British archaeologists excavated the ruins of Eridu in 1918-19. On the other hand, Albright thinks that Pishon and Gihon may have been the Blue and White Nile.[69]

His *Battle for the Bible* lacks this moderate stance.

Since Lindsell speaks for the literal theory of Eden, it may be helpful to note other concessions made by his *Harper Study Bible*. On Genesis 4:22 his note says:

> For nearly three centuries the accepted chronology of the Bible was based upon the assumption that Adam commenced his career around 4004 B.C. This chronology was worked out by Archbishop Ussher in the 17th century. Recent scientific advances, including the carbon dating method, make the Ussher chronology impossible. Many scholars accept interpretations of the biblical text which allow for substantial chronological gaps in the genealogical lists of Gen. 5, 11, thus allowing for an age of man much greater than that suggested by Ussher. Bronze did not become common until 3300-3000 B.C. and iron did not appear until 1500-1200 B.C. Tubal-Cain, the 8th generation from Adam, according to this verse was *the forger of all instruments of bronze and iron*. This, along with scientific data, makes it evident that the biblical chronologies have tremendous gaps in them.[70]

Having gone this far it seems logical to go on to the position advocated by these pages. At least this moderate and irenic approach is more helpful than the belligerent attitude displayed in his *Battle for the Bible*.

The crisis in Roman Catholicism is even more crucial. This is due to the centralized teaching authority of the Roman Catholic Church which requires all scholars to agree with Papal pronouncements. In 1909 the Pontifical Biblical Commission required the most literal interpretation of the Paradise story of Genesis 2–3. The encyclical *Humani generis* of Pius XII (August 12, 1950) condemned any denial of the historical Adam as father of all, whose original sin has been transmitted to the whole human race. This requires all interpretations to accept the limitations of past tradition going back to the ancient Church Fathers, especially Augustine. Original righteousness and original sin by the historical Adam in an earthly Eden were given Papal support.

When this position was challenged by the French Jesuit Stanislaus Lyonnet in his commentary on Romans 5:12, even Pope John XXIII sus-

69. (Grand Rapids: Zondervan, 1965), p. 7.
70. *Ibid.*, p. 11.

pended him from teaching. This created such a stir that Pope Paul VI restored him, but a symposium of distinguished theologians was chosen to deal with the problem. In an address by Pope Paul VI on July 11, 1966, limits were placed within which the problems must be discussed. The limits were essentially those imposed by the Augustinian tradition.[71] No satisfactory report has been noted.

The rift in Roman Catholicism on the Eden issue appears in many writings. In his book *Eden: Golden Age or Goad to Action?* the Dutch Carmelite priest Carlos Mesters remarks:

> All of this shows that without realizing it we are held captive by a predetermined way of seeing and interpreting earthly Paradise. This is the pattern created in our minds by the traditional teaching of the catechism. But science and common sense make us have serious reservations about our traditional approach and give us the feeling that something is wrong somewhere.[72]

The epicenter of this "somewhere" is the incorrect exegesis of Romans 5:12.[73] When Lyonnet exposed Augustine's erroneous translation the traditionalists rushed to crush him if possible. Following the translation adopted by Jerome in the Latin Vulgate that says *in quo* (in whom) where the Greek says *eph' hōi* (because), Augustine developed the theology that we are all sinners by propagation rather than imitation. Out of this the whole tradition of *limbo* developed, so that all unbaptized infants are declared damned. This same theology was defended by Pope Paul VI in his address of July 11, 1966.

The clash of tradition with Scripture is obvious in the correct Roman Catholic translation of this verse in *The Jerusalem Bible*. In Protestantism, the Authorized (King James) Version is also correct, but the weight of the Augustinian tradition is so great that many twentieth-century translations and paraphrases return to the error of the Latin Vulgate. If one checks all the translations and paraphrases of Romans 5:12 he will often see an amazing inconsistency in which the translation of Romans 3:23 is usually correct, but the same words in Romans 5:12 are mistranslated by the simple omission of the "have" in "all have sinned."

This is also true of Ephesians 2:1 where "dead in trespasses and sins" (AV) appears rather than the correct translation "because of your disobedience and sins" (TEV). Even the TEV (*Good News for Modern Man*) has the error in Ephesians 2:5 after translating the same phrase correctly in Ephesians 2:1! The triumph of tradition over Scripture is possible when the best of translations are off guard.

71. The address is in William G. Heidt, *The Book of Genesis 1–11* (Collegeville, Minnesota: The Liturgical Press, 1967), pp. 76-82.
72. Tr. Patrick J. Leonard (Maryknoll, New York: Orbis Books, 1974), p. 8.
73. For details see my commentary on Romans in *The Broadman Bible Commentary* (Nashville, Tennessee: Broadman Press, 1970), Vol. 10, pp. 195ff.

These two examples are chosen to illustrate how the false theology of Augustine has so blinded the eyes of those who read the Paradise story that they see no way out of his trap without feeling they have betrayed Holy Scripture. Romans 5:12 and Ephesians 2:1 are always in their arsenal of proof texts to put down all opponents with the charge of *Pelagian!* The details of the biblical teachings on sin come later, but these references are used to support the ideas of original righteousness and original sin. Adam and Eve alone are necessary in this discussion of Eden.

Eden can be reinterpreted as the model by which every person is to see the meaning of sin as disobedience to God. The original unity between God and man has been destroyed not just in one man Adam and one woman Eve but in every man and every woman who has reached the stage of discretion and accountability to God. Long before the challenge of scientific anthropology this was clearly seen by Tertullian. It is necessary to begin here again.

36. Adam: Man and Mankind

Among conservative evangelical Christians the question of the relation between the Adam of the Scriptures and the first men described in scientific anthropology is far from answered. Accepting both biblical authority and scientific anthropology, the following pages hope to suggest an answer. Neither the retreat of fundamentalism into a pre-critical view of Scripture nor the low view of biblical authority in radical theology that dismisses the relevance of Scripture is satisfactory for understanding human origins.

There are signs that many evangelicals are not fully satisfied with the options of fundamentalism or radicalism. An article in *Christianity Today* by Robert Brow entitled "The Late-Date Genesis Man" dated the so-called Genesis Man around 3900 B.C. and relegated all human forms before that date to the status of animals.[74] Apparently the publication of Erich Däniken's books *Chariots of the Gods* (1970) and *Gods from Outer Space* (1971) stimulated this sensational resurgence of pre-critical and pre-scientific thought. Däniken's *Gold of the Gods* (1973), *In Search of Ancient Gods* (1974), and *Miracles of the Gods* (1976) have inflamed other fantasies in biblical interpretation.

A response to Brow by William Kornfield rejected the theory that all the human forms before 3900 B.C. were animals, but he believed that all were descendants of Adam and Eve. He therefore insisted on an earlier and more uncertain date for his view of a direct creation of Adam and Eve as

74. September 15, 1972, Vol. 16, No. 24, pp. 1128f.

two individuals. His article was therefore called "The Early-Date Genesis Man."[75] The debate was then on between the late daters and the earlier daters, and not even the lamentations of James O. Buswell about this "unnecessary breach" could stop the evangelical feud.[76]

Buswell's big tent view for evangelical creationist fellowship was similar to the one voiced by an English evangelical before the American scrap began. The question asked by E. K. Victor Pearce in 1969 was "Who Was Adam?" In a second edition in 1976 he has stated where the issues are in both science and Scripture.[77] It is soon apparent that Pearce is more advanced in scientific knowledge than in Scripture study. As is frequently the case among evangelicals, he seems to think that any recognition of sources in Genesis 1–11 is a threat to biblical authority, yet his survey of scientific anthropology is helpful for a beginner.

The best that Pearce can do is to make a distinction between what he calls the Adam of Eden or Farmer Adam in Genesis 2f. and a pre-Adamite man in Genesis 1 without any recognition of the view that Genesis 2:4b–3:24 is one source and Genesis 1:1–2:4a is another. Adam of Eden is identified with New Stone Age Man while pre-Adamite man is supported by skeletal remains and especially older tools that are found in greater abundance. It is really the J Adam of Genesis 4:1–26 that is nearest to his Farmer Adam, but there is no discussion of this as a third source. However, there is the realization of the problem presented by what L. S. B. Leakey has called *Adam's Ancestors*.[78] Pearce's theory that Farmer Adam may be identified with New Stone Age Man is appealing. He has made a good beginning.

The question of a man's relation to all mankind is answered in part by investigating the biblical use of Adam (*ādām* in Hebrew, *adam* in Greek). The Hebrew word is probably derived from the common Semitic root *'dm*, to be red. If this is related to the Akkadian word for blood, *adamātu*, then the common expression "red-blooded man" is not far from the original meaning.

The word may mean "man" or "mankind," but biblical thought develops the idea into the two great pillars of biblical anthropology that are summarized by Paul as the First Adam or man and the Last Adam or Second Adam. The Old Testament teachings about the First Adam became a type of which the Last Adam of the New Testament is antitype. A careful study of the two concepts is a key that unlocks the closed door between Scripture and science. It is therefore important to understand man in both.

75. *Christianity Today*, June 8, 1973, pp. 931-934.
76. *Christianity Today*, "Creationist Views on Human Origins," August 8, 1975, pp. 1046-1048.
77. E. K. Victor Pearce, *Who Was Adam?* (Exeter: The Paternoster Press, 1976).
78. Fourth Edition (London: Methuen, 1953).

Adam in Scripture

First Adam as type. In considering Adam as type we will use the term not only to include the Christological meaning, as Paul introduces it in Romans 5:14 (*typos*), but also in the anthropological sense found in Genesis 1–5. Adam is a type of other men as well as Christ.

Since the publication of John A. T. Robinson's influential book *The Body* (1951), the idea of Adam as a type of which Christ is the antitype has been discussed. Robinson suggested the unlikely idea that the relation of both Adam and Moses to the law (Torah) would make Moses, not Christ, the future antitype of Adam.[79] The priority of the Adamic eschatology in the pattern of the two Adams in 1 Corinthians 15:20–28 and the hymn about Adam and Christ in Romans 5:12–21 argues for the traditional view that the antitype is Christ in analogy and in contrast.

The word Adam (*ādām*) is used over five hundred times in the Old Testament. Outside Genesis 1–5 the generic use for the first man is found only in the genealogy of 1 Chronicles 1:1. Some interpret a few other passages in this way, but the interpretation is uncertain (Deuteronomy 4:32; Hosea 11:9; Job 31:33).

Concentration on the generic use in Genesis 1–5 detects at least three different meanings, each corresponding to what have been recognized by some as separate sources belonging to different periods of Old Testament history. These are, to be sure, disputed, but it may be helpful to interpret what is evident to some careful scholars. The following terminology has been coined for lack of better terms: (1) Individual Adam in the J source of Genesis 4, (2) Representative Adam in the JE source of Genesis 2:4b–3:24, and (3) Collective Adam in the P source of Genesis 1:1–2:4a.

The first member of this Adam family, J Adam, is clearly a man, an individual man with a wife named Eve. His son Cain, the farmer, killed his brother Abel, the shepherd. Since Abel was the seed of promise, God appointed him another seed named Seth (4:25). It is assumed that God in this passage is the Lord, *Yahweh*, the word for God in the rest of the chapter (cf. 4:1).

It seems just as clear that Adam and Eve, Cain and Abel were not the only human beings living before God gave them Seth to take the place of Abel. There were members of other tribes who could slay Cain as he became a fugitive and a wanderer on the earth, so a protective mark, perhaps a tattoo, was placed upon him as a warning and as a sign of the Lord's mercy (4:15). The argument that Cain married his sister and that the later sons and daughters of Adam were those who could slay Cain is not evident in

---

79. *The Body: A Study in Pauline Theology* (Chicago: Henry Regnery Company, 1952), p. 35, note 1. Cf. Robin Scroggs, *The Last Adam* (Philadelphia: Fortress Press, 1966), p. 81; J. W. MacGorman, *Romans* (Nashville, Tennessee: Convention Press, 1976), pp. 77-84. My own views on Romans 5:12-21 are in *Broadman Bible Commentary* (Nashville, Tennessee: Broadman Press, 1970), Vol. 10, pp. 195-198.

the story. The claim that children were born in Paradise before Cain and Abel is also without support in the text.

A second evidence that others lived at the same time is indicated by the law of vengeance by which seven members of other tribes would be killed in blood revenge if one of them killed Cain (4:15). This would make little sense if only three persons were left on earth after the death of Abel. The probability that this story was originally used to explain the origin of the Kenites only, or that it exalts seminomadic life over sedentary, does not remove the fact that Adam is one man among many. If there are those who object to this literal following of the text, then let them restrain rigid literalism at other points which have been used to repudiate the evidence of scientific anthropology for the ancient date of man.

To the mark of Cain and the law of vengeance another source adds two other indications that many other people lived at the time of the J Adam family! The old question as to where Cain got his wife is hardly answered by saying she was his sister (4:17). Identification of J Adam with New Stone Age Man is an attractive idea, as the book by Pearce illustrates. Then Cain built a city and named it after his son Enoch, the grandson of J Adam (4:17). Thus after shepherds and farmers a type of city developed. Several ancient cities have been discovered from eight to ten thousand years old, one of the oldest being Jericho of Old Testament fame.[80]

The JE Adam is a representative of every male while his wife Eve is a representative of every female. Some scholars classify Genesis 2:4b–3:24 as J, the oldest source, rather than JE, the source that combines Lord and God and is thus called *Yahweh Elohim* (JE) because of the uniform use of Lord God as the sacred name for deity. S. H. Hooke is perhaps correct in calling the source JE.[81] The term Lord God is found elsewhere in the Pentateuch only in Exodus 9:30. The JE Adam is clearly symbolic since he is mentioned as made before the vegetation and the animals, and his wife Eve comes last of all in the series.

With the exception of 2:20; 3:17, 21, the article appears with *ādām* and should be translated "the man." The absence of the article indicates the identification of Adam with the man. An interpretation of theological symbolism has profound implications for the male's relation to the earth, vegetation, animals, and the female. More about male and female will follow in the next chapter.

The P Adam is the community of mankind, or Collective Adam. A literal translation of the Hebrew requires agreement between Genesis 1:26f. and 5:2. Genesis 1:26f. says "Let us make Adam in our image, after our likeness; and let them have dominion. So God created Adam in his own

80. Dora Jane Hamblin, *The First Cities* (New York: Time-Life Books, 1973).
81. H. H. Rowley and Matthew Black, ed., *Peake's Commentary of the Bible* (London: Thomas Nelson and Sons, 1962), pp. 177, 179.

image, in the image of God he created him; male and female he created them." The same shift from the singular to the plural in deity (us-our-his-he) is found in reference to man. Adam is both "him" and "them." If there is any doubt the literal translation of 5:2 should help: "Male and female he created them and named them Adam when they were created." The AV says Adam rather than man as in the RSV, and yet Adam is mentioned again as an individual in the very next verse (5:3). A complete circle has been made from Adam and Seth in 4:25 to Adam and Seth in 5:3. Adam is both individual man and collective man in the P source.

Second Adam as antitype. Adam is used in all three senses in the New Testament. Adam is just an individual in Luke 3:38 and Jude 14, yet the representative view begins to appear in 1 Corinthians 11:2–16 and 1 Timothy 2:11–15. The Collective Adam of the Old Testament becomes the Corporate Adam of Paul. As there is a Corporate Christ, so there is a Corporate Adam: "For as in Adam all die, so in Christ shall all be made alive" (1 Corinthians 15:22).

The typology of the two Adams, or the two men, is based on Genesis 1, 2, especially 2:7. Paul is apparently reversing the idea of the two Adams in Philo Judaeus, who taught that the man of Genesis 1:27 was a heavenly man who came first and the early man of Genesis 2:7 who was second (*Allegory of the Jewish Law*, I. 31f.; *On the Creation of the World* 134).[82] Paul makes a clear distinction between the First Adam and the Last Adam, the first man and the second man, the man of dust and the man of heaven (1 Corinthians 15:45–49).

When Jesus Christ is called the second man, it certainly does not mean that no man lived between him and the first man. To call Jesus Christ the Last Adam does not mean that no men lived after him. Jesus is the Last Adam in the same sense that the man in Genesis 2:7 is the First Adam, in the communal and corporate sense. As there were men before and after the historical and individual Jesus, so there were men before and after the historical and individual Adam.

The typology of the two Adams in Romans 5:12–21 is crucial for the interpretation of man and his sin in most Latin theology after Augustine. It has led to the assumption that man cannot be discussed apart from his sin. This point of view is hereby rejected, but man's sin will be discussed in detail in a later study.

A second fallacy is the assumption that Adam is to be understood in terms of man's past ancestry and antiquity, whereas the Pauline perspective is focused on the future when God's intention for man will be realized. What was first realized in the perfected humanity of Jesus, so central in

---

82. G. C. Berkouwer, *Man: The Image of God,* tr. Dirk W. Jellema (Grand Rapids: Wm. B. Eerdmans Publishing Co., 1962), pp. 9-36.

the New Testament Letter to the Hebrews, is ultimately to be realized in all who are in the new creation in Christ.[83]

It is not argued here that Paul had all this in mind when he spoke of Adam, but it is permissible on the basis of Genesis 1-5, especially ch. 4. Paul was not confronted by the evidence for the great antiquity of man in scientific anthropology, but his views of man and his sin are not irrelevant in a scientific age if the archaic barnacles of Augustine's fifth-century anthropology are removed from the exegesis of Paul's letters. Biblical anthropology is in difficult circumstances if all that can be done in the presence of such evidence as "Three-Million-Year-Old Lucy," found in 1974 at Hadar, Ethiopia, is hope that it is all a mistake.[84] Little Lucy is forty percent complete with sixty separate pieces of bone all in place, so it becomes more difficult to call all such evidence "boners" based on a few scattered fossils.

Some errors do not prove all the mounting evidence for man's great age upon the earth to be an invention of people hostile to the Christian view of man. Many theologians need to discover that Scripture and science can live together in peace when evidence is followed carefully by students in both fields. It can really become a great adventure in understanding ourselves.

Even Augustine was a wiser man than some of his disciples. He recognized the problem in Genesis 4 when he said:

> Those who find a difficulty here have failed to realize that the writer of the Scriptural story was under no obligation to mention the names of all who may have been alive at the time, but only of those whom the scope of his work required him to mention. All that the writer had in mind, under the inspiration of the Holy Spirit, was to trace the succession in the definite lines from Adam to Abraham and then from the children of Abraham to the people of God.[85]

His solution to this problem argued that Adam was the first human being who ever lived and that all people have descended from Noah and his family. Evidence for the antiquity of human life in America, Europe, Asia and Africa makes this solution impossible. It is surely time for theology to seek a solution for a scientific age unless the choice is made to live in theological isolation from the modern world. A brief survey of scientific anthropology may help to justify this statement.

A consideration of scientific evidence for the *antiquity* of man should keep in mind that this is not the same question as the *ancestry* of man. The theories on the ancestry of man are now in a very fluid state and will remain so until further evidence is available, but evidence for the great antiquity

83. Robin Scroggs, *The Last Adam* (Philadelphia: Fortress Press, 1966), pp. 59-112.
84. *Nature/Science Annual* 1976 (New York: Time-Life Books, 1975), pp. 19-31.
85. *The City of God*, XV. 8.

of man, long before six to ten thousand years ago, increases more and more. Rejection of this evidence by appeal to Scripture is a precarious position for theology. It seems possible to accept this evidence without doing violence to biblical authority. The debate between the advocates of "The Late Date Genesis Man," to use the title of the recent article, and those who accept both the historical study of Scripture and ancient anthropology will no doubt continue, but it should be done on the level of scholarship rather than slander.

A more detailed understanding of the antiquity of man reflected in the Bible requires more space and great patience with tradition. Those who follow the Augustinian literalism about the Creation and Fall of Adam are most likely to do the same with Genesis 5–11. Genesis 9:19 says that the whole earth was peopled from the three sons of Noah. Genesis 10:32 and 11:1 imply the same. If one is unwilling to accept the view of a flood limited to the earth as it was understood around 1500-1200 B.C. a hopeless conflict develops between Scripture and science. This is also a crucial question for understanding the Fall and the transmission of sin, but we will save that for a later discussion. At present the relation between Adam in Scripture and Adam in science is the chief concern. Calmness and patience are required.

Adam in Science

On July 10, 1925, in the small town of Dayton, Tennessee, one of the most bizarre trials in American history took place. A teacher named John Thomas Scopes had agreed to plead guilty of the charge that he had taught the theory of evolution in the public school in violation of a Tennessee law. Clarence Darrow, a noted defender of radicals, was called upon for the defense, and William Jennings Bryan, three times the nominee for President by the Democratic Party, was the prosecutor. The whole nation became involved in debate about "the monkey trial" in which the traditional view of man's origin was being tested.[86]

The First Americans. Bryan died in Dayton, July 26, 1925, after the conclusion of the trial, but had he lived until 1953 he would have been shocked by discoveries at Russell Cave, near Bridgeport, Alabama, down the Tennessee River from Dayton. A record of eight thousand years of Indian life in Russell Cave was laid bare by members of the Tennessee Archaeological Society. Later excavations were so successful that a Presidential proclamation, May 11, 1961, established Russell Cave National Monument to preserve this place of pilgrimage for the first Americans. Research into Indian remains in the Tennessee region put together a story that reached

86. Leslie Henri Allen, *Bryan and Darrow at Dayton* (N.Y.: Russell and Russell, 1967).

back fifteen thousand years ago when small bands of nomadic hunters first saw the untrodden wilderness that had never heard a human voice.[87]

This rocked those who dogmatically dated the first human being at 4004 B.C., but later discoveries were to fill out many details that established the presence of man in North America more than twenty-five thousand years ago. Between thirty-six and thirty-two thousand years ago and again between twenty-eight and thirteen thousand years ago a land bridge existed between Siberia and Alaska. At such times evidence indicates that the ancestors of the American Indians crossed over.[88] Enough information is now available to unfold a fascinating story of a civilization that had no contact with the Old World for generations.[89]

The real turning point for knowledge of Indian antiquities came in 1926 when a black cowboy named George McJunkin noticed some bones on the edge of a deep arroyo near Folsom, New Mexico. Arrowheads were found mixed with the bones of a bison which had vanished with the ice age ten thousand years ago. These discoveries pushed the presence of man in North America back twelve thousand years, and further discoveries and studies have made Indian history a romantic field for research.

Tools, arts and religious practices reveal a very high degree of development. It is hardly possible to lecture in theological classes with brilliant and beloved students without a drop of Old World blood and dismiss them as mere animals! Their ancestors produced messianic movements, and even monotheism flourished in some Indian cultures long before they had contact with biblical religion. Among the Iroquois, who have been called "The Greeks of America" because of their democratic ideas, a saintly prophet named Daganawideh was inspired by a dream that with practical necessities led to "The Great Peace" of the Iroquois League. This was proclaimed as a practical reality by Hiawatha, a Mohawk "apostle" who went from tribe to tribe promoting confederation.[90]

Cro-Magnon Man. Modern man is usually dated from the type of life that existed about twenty-five thousand years ago at Cro-Magnon on the Vézère River in southwestern France. These discoveries, found in 1868, are thought to represent a culture that reached back to forty thousand years ago. The evidence indicates that they were "creative, inventive and reverent."[91] In summary:

87. Thomas M. N. Lewis and Madeline Kneberg, *Tribes That Slumber* (Knoxville, Tennessee: The University of Tennessee Press, 1958), p. 3.
88. Robert Claiborne, *The First Americans* (New York: Time-Life Books, 1973).
89. Peter Farb, *Man's Rise to Civilization As Shown by the Indians of North America from Primeval Times to the Coming of the Industrial State* (New York: E. P. Dutton & Co., Inc., 1968).
90. *Ibid.*, pp. 95-111.
91. Tom Prideaux and the Editors of Time-Life Books, *Cro-Magnon Man* (New York: Time-Life Books, 1973), pp. 27-33.

With the Cro-Magnons, technological man can be said to have come into existence. The people invented the first crude forms of baked pottery, constructing kilns and even burning coal. They presumably were the first to weave baskets as well. They made great strides not only in the preparation and use of stone tools but also in the elaborate development of tools, weapons and implements manufactured from bone, ivory and antler and, undoubtably, wood. They fashioned better clothing, built better fires, constructed bigger dwellings, ate more kinds of food than earlier men had.

Perhaps most important of all the Cro-Magnon achievements was art. On the walls and ceiling of caves, in clay figurines, in decorated artifacts, these people exhibited an unprecedented artistic mastery. Never before had men expressed themselves with the esthetic awareness that the Cro-Magnon artists displayed in even their humblest efforts. The best of their paintings and sculptures still rank among the world's greatest.[92]

At other places the Time-Life volume makes clear that religion played an important part in the life of Cro-Magnon man. There were not only initiation rituals at the age of puberty, but burial customs indicating belief in life after death. "The fear of death, a questioning of what it means and what it leads to, has always been one of the most basic human concerns, one that the Cro-Magnons shared with other men."[93] With technology, art and religion, modern man had indeed arrived.

The Neanderthals. Despite the fact that the traditional view of man's creation had been dated at 4004 B.C., the discovery of Cro-Magnon man was a welcome relief. In 1856 the apelike features of human life in the Neander Valley had been exaggerated, and in 1859 Charles Darwin, in his *Origin of Species*, had propounded the theory of evolution. Any proof that man's ancestors were more human than apes was acceptable to traditionalists, but with reservations.

The Neanderthals, dated between forty and one hundred thousand years ago, were not so primitive as at first described when religious people reacted to "all that monkey business of the scientists." Indeed, the whole story of the adjustment of biblical scholars to scientific anthropology no doubt would have been very different had not these initial ideas been published and popularized by scientists not altogether free from bias and antipathy for religion. As it was, this closed-minded conflict continues to the detriment of both disciplines.

It is now thought that Marcellin Boule, the French paleontologist considered the foremost authority on fossils in the early twentieth century,

92. *Ibid.*, pp. 13f.
93. *Ibid.*, p. 139.

made many blunders in his reconstruction of Neanderthal man. Despite the excellent set of bones from La Chapelle-aux-Saints he used in the French National Museum, more recent studies by Stauss and Cave and others since 1957 have exposed his astonishing errors. The skeleton from La Chapelle-aux-Saints apparently suffered from a severe case of arthritis! One contemporary specialist on the Neanderthals says:

> Boule so misconstructed the bones as to make the Neanderthal appear much like an ape from head to toe. He mistakenly arranged the foot bones so that the big toe diverged from other toes like an opposable thumb; this feature presumably forced the Neanderthal to walk on the outer part of his feet, like an ape. Boule's interpretation of the knee joint was equally incorrect; he declared that the Neanderthal could not fully extend his leg, and that this resulted in a bent-knee gait.[94]

This volume goes on to expose the blunders of Boule and to trace other Neanderthal finds from Rhodesian man to the sensational skeletons found by Ralph S. Solecki at Shanidar cave in Iraq on April 27, 1957.[95]

It is now apparent that the evidence for Neanderthal man from the first finds in the Neander Valley near Düsseldorf, Germany, through more than one hundred finds in Europe, Africa and Asia, reveals an ancestor that one would be willing to accept at a family reunion. It is altogether possible that he would be more welcome than some who have wandered away into stupidity and shame! In technology, art, and religion it is just possible that he would, with modern motivation, be an achiever on a current academic campus. The only embarrassment that he would cause at the old pioneer church would be his antiquity, but little children would no doubt delight in riding on the burly shoulders of Uncle Ugh. He was at least *Homo sapiens* if not *Homo sapiens sapiens*!

His tools, to be sure, did not show the techniques of the Cro-Magnon period, but the fact that he was a tool-maker marked him off from monkeys and made him a man. In care and compassion and their love for peace the Neanderthals were perhaps superior to many modern people! It was necessary for their survival. Survival in the Neander Valley was no doubt difficult, but they were hardly chill-resistant as some scientists in the 1950s speculated! They were intelligent enough to make tools of stone that are difficult to duplicate. It is clear that they were not "thunderstones" formed by lightning, as some French and Scandinavian farmers thought when they put them in walls and doorsills "to ward off lightning, on the dubious theory that it never struck twice in the same place."[96] Since the French customs

94. George Constable, *The Neanderthals* (New York: Time-Life Books, 1973), p. 19.
95. Ralph S. Solecki, *Shanidar: The First Flower People* (New York: Alfred A. Knopf, 1971).
96. George Constable, *op. cit.*, p. 11.

inspector Boucher de Perthes discerned in the 1830s that chipped stones he found in the gravel terraces of the Somme River were made by ancient man, a great quantity of such evidence has been accumulated.

Art had only a beginning among the Neanderthals. A few objects beyond useful tools suggest an appreciation for beauty, but they left no signs of representational engravings or statues. Not a single perforated tooth that might have been used for necklaces has been found. Natural pigments such as red or yellow ocher and black manganese have been noted, but the purpose intended is not clear. The art that only budded had to await the Cro-Magnon man to bloom into the beauty of human imagination.

Religion, a sure sign of human transcendence, did bloom among the Neanderthals. The burial customs reflected both great compassion for the dead and belief in life after death. A form of ritual cannibalism, in which the human brain was eaten, had religious significance, and there were initiation rites with a mixture of mystery and magic.

The most famous religious rite was practiced in a bear cult in which the bear was considered an intermediary between man and the ruling spirits. In winter the bear was sacrificed after a long ceremony, and men drank the blood as the presiding shaman offered prayers to the Creator. Such rites, strange as they may seem to modern people, are signs of a religious stir in the human spirit. Animals do not reach out for contact with the unseen power believed to be both the origin and destiny of man.[97]

The first men. Another giant step in knowledge about the human past took place in 1893 when Eugene Dubois, a Dutch anatomist, announced that he had found the "missing link of Darwin" in Java. He named his discovery *Pithecanthropus erectus*, from the Greek *pithecos* (ape) and *anthropos* (man) and the Latin for erect, a name coined by Ernst Heinrich Haeckel seven years before. Later research was to conclude that he really had found the first true man thus far, *Homo erectus* (upright man), but this was the stimulus for further search, especially in Java, Peking in China, Heidelberg in Germany and Terra Amata in France. By now a fairly clear picture of the early phase of human history about four hundred thousand years ago has been put together. This of course includes other pieces of knowledge.[98]

Little knowledge of his religion, if any, has come to light. Some indications of ritual human sacrifice have been noted, but further light is needed before a decision can be made on this question. *Homo sapiens* was *Homo religiosus* in an impressive manner, but it would be rash to conclude that human awareness or belief in the supernatural arose only a hundred thousand years ago.

How one defines man determines whether these finds point to the "last

97. *Ibid.*, pp. 97-113.
98. *The First Men* (New York: Time-Life Books, 1973), pp. 32-65.

ape" or "the first man." If religion were the criterion, the Neanderthals could possibly be called the first men, but if the use of tools is the criterion, the date could be pushed back to *Australopithecus* or *Homo habilis*, to be described later. They were possibly tool-makers too.

If the use of fire is the criterion for acceptance among men, then *Homo erectus* must be warmly received. His most distinctive contribution to human life was the use of fires set by volcanoes, lightning, and spontaneous combustion, but apparently he did not learn to light fires from stones and sticks. Once he learned to "keep the home fires burning" given to him by natural phenomena, great innovations took place.

First of all, the dominion of man over animals was greatly increased. He learned that animals flee from fire, so he used it for his protection. He also learned to capture more animals for food by building fires around them, as every frontiersman was to remember.

In the second place, he began to cook — distinctive indeed. Whoever saw an ape cook a meal? Cooking his meat so improved man's diet that many physical changes took place in his body. This revolution in eating also prolonged life.

A third result that the use of fire brought was social organization. As long as vegetarianism prevailed, each could "get his own greens," but it took organization to capture and cook the best meats. Even more so, the family fireplace became a social circle. The hearth made the home, and the fire formed the family into a unit. Primitive promiscuity was replaced by family fidelity. One wonders whether ancestor worship did not begin around the family fire, but this is an open question.

Language was also developed around the hearth. As *Homo erectus* moved into the colder climates of the North, the long winter nights were real "family get-togethers," and it would have been a bit dull to glare into the fire at one another and say no more than "ugh." Vocal capacities and vocabularies were developed by such social ties. Objects took on names to take the place of the pointed finger or nodded head or the bristled brow. Once a person knows a ["ah"], i ["ee"], and u ["oo"], he has the foundation for all languages! With language, human speech began.

A leading authority on human origins traces the racial differentiation back to the time of *Homo erectus*. He says:

> For present purposes I am using a conservative and tentative classification of the living peoples of the world into five basically geographical groups: the Caucasoid, Mongoloid, Australoid, Congoid, and Capoid. The first includes Europeans and their overseas kinsmen, the Middle Eastern Whites from Morocco to West Pakistan, and most of the peoples of India, as well as the Ainu of Japan. The second includes most of the East Asiatics, Indonesians, Polynesians, Micronesians, American Indians, and Eskimo. In the

third category fall the Australian aborigines, Melanesians, Papuans, some of the tribal folk of India, and the various Negritos of South Asia and Oceania. The fourth comprises the Negroes and Pygmies of Africa. I have named it *Congoid* after a region (not a specific nation) which contains both kinds of people. The term Negroid has been deliberately omitted to avoid confusion. It has been applied both to Africans and to spiral-haired peoples of Southern Asia and Oceania who are genetically related to each other, as far as we know. Negroid will be used in this book to denote a condition, not a geographical subspecies. The fifth group includes Bushmen and Hottentots and other relict tribes, like the Sandawe of Tanganyika. It is called *Capoid* after the Cape of Good Hope.[99]

The search for the missing link. The debate over whether Dubois' *Pithecanthropus erectus* was the missing link between ape and man or the first man was soon to pass. When Robert Ardrey published his book *African Genesis* in 1961 he was only reporting to the public what scientific anthropologists were finding and discussing about far more ancient Australopithecines in Africa. In 1924 Raymond Dart, a Johannesburg anatomy professor, received a mold and a skull that one of his students had found in a limestone quarry at a place called Taung. It was soon identified and named *Australopithecus africanus* (southern African ape).

Robert Broom, a friend of Dart, announced that *Australopithecus africanus* was two million years old, more than a million years older than *Pithecanthropus erectus* or *Homo erectus*, as Dubois' find came to be called. Broom became the leader of an African ape-manhunt that found enough fossils at five different sites to conclude that there were two species: a heavy-jawed "robust" type with extremely large molars and a slenderer, smaller type with smaller molars.

Louis S. B. Leakey, employed by the Museum in Nairobi, Kenya, began to report on finds made by his family at Olduvai Gorge in Tanzania. His book *Adam's Ancestors* came ten years after Dart's discovery, and he was destined to become the most famous African anthropologist of all. One afternoon in 1959, while Leakey himself was lying in his tent with fever, his wife Mary discovered what they called *Australopithecus boisei*, after the Boise Fund that financed much of his work. This skull turned out to be 1.75 million years old.

The search goes on. Soon after returning from Nairobi and a visit to Olduvai Gorge, I noticed an article in *The Cincinnati Enquirer*, Nov. 10, 1972, announcing that Richard Leakey, the son of Louis and Mary, had found a skull 2.5 million years old at Lake Rudolf in Kenya. The younger

99. Carleton S. Coon, *The Origin of Races* (New York: Alfred A. Knopf, 1963), pp. 3f.

Leakey was quoted as saying: "If there was a Garden of Eden, I would call it the African continent."

One of the last statements made by Louis before his death in 1972 is found in a summary volume on these sensational discoveries. He said:

> The Australopithecines developed away from true man (Homo), who was approximately contemporary. By three million years ago, both forms were present in East Africa.
>
> My finds show that man's ancestral stock separated from that of the great apes more than 20 million years ago. They also show that the genus Homo dates back in East Africa 1.5 to three million years, that a form of Homo erectus was present in Africa before Asia and, finally, that "near man," Australopithecus, was developing in parallel and died out 50,000 to 1.5 million years ago.
>
> The time span of psycho-social man — 40,000 years — represents a moment compared with the 20 million years of hominid existence. We can, therefore, expect a long future ahead if we do not destroy ourselves and the world.[100]

Others claim that man existed in Africa and Arabia as long as five million years ago. The greater antiquity of man is highly probable, but the ancestry of man remains an open question.

Is it possible both to accept those scientific claims and take the Bible seriously as a source of genuine light on human existence? To many in the fundamentalist faith the answer would be to ban all such publications and prohibit all such teaching in the schools of the land. Others would say that the fundamentalist understanding of Scripture is as superficial as their evaluation of scientific anthropology. Indeed, a serious study of both will lead to surprising results that make it possible for science and Scripture to supplement each other in the interpretation of the greatest mystery other than God, man himself.

How then is the believer in the Bible as inspired and authoritative for faith going to relate Scripture and science? The first reaction is usually to reject all scientific anthropology and maintain a pre-scientific stance with bristling brow. Some have had a great time gloating over the Piltdown hoax of 1912, a fake fabricated by putting a modern skull on an apelike jaw, but they seem to forget that scientific anthropology in the early 1950s exposed it as a hoax and helped thereby to bring Neanderthal man into the human family. A so-called Nebraska man turned out to be a pig, but that hardly refutes all other evidence for the antiquity of man before 4004 B.C.

Even those who say scientific anthropology is a series of hoaxes are forced to admit that Cro-Magnon man and Peking man lived "thousands

100. Maitland A. Edey, *The Missing Link* (New York: Time-Life Books, 1972), p. 144.

and thousand of years ago."[101] Such vagueness obscures the basic question: Did the first man live only six thousand years ago? The scientific evidence when sifted in the most critical manner is overwhelmingly to the contrary, and no amount of debunking rhetoric seems able to destroy the evidence surveyed above. Revisions and exposures are sure to come, but a pre-scientific stance is possible only for those who refuse to review the evidence.

A second reaction is to retreat from such controversial issues and to get on with the "main job." Students in science become skeptical when they confront this pious ploy. They often conclude that the theologian is "taking a trip" backward into a pre-scientific land of nostalgia that makes biblical theology irrelevant in the modern world of science. Others, to prove they are *avant-garde*, abandon all efforts to construct a biblical theology in the world of natural and historical sciences. Both views leave students of intelligence and integrity torn by the rifts of reaction and retreat.

Neither hostile reaction nor reductionist retreat is adequate. Very few theologians have made any effort to construct a biblical anthropology congenial with scientific anthropology, but the work desperately needs to be done. If only a few new trails can be explored in this vast wilderness of biblical illiteracy and irrelevance, future study may be able to bring Scripture and science together in a new synthesis. A beginning must be made.

The very idea that there are sources in Genesis arouses some conservatives to a crusade of censorship, yet the book of Genesis itself identifies a major source called "the book of the generations" (5:1). References are made to this source at least ten times (2:4; 5:1; 6:9; 10:1; 11:10, 27; 25:12f., 19; 36:1, 9; 37:2). As to such sources as P which uses the word God, JE which uses the term Lord God, and J which uses the word Lord, it would be simpler for the English reader to call them G, LG, and L. A denial of sources as such does not even take the statements in Genesis seriously. A pre-critical mind-set on Scripture defends a pre-scientific view of man. It is time to study both science and Scripture in a historical manner, and the results will be constructive.

With all good will toward the Creation Research Society, it does not seem possible to put all the evidence for the antiquity of man and his world in a time span of no more than 10,000 years. There is great danger that this approach will drive the many scientific minds completely out of the Christian fellowship. These words are written to keep them within.

37. Eve: Man and Woman

A study of the man-woman relation in the Scriptures takes one from woman as a partner to man in creation to woman as a partner to men in the church.

101. W. A. Criswell, *Did Man Just Happen?* (Grand Rapids, Michigan: Zondervan Publishing House, 1957), p. 91.

However, later interpretations of passages in between brought alien ideas to the Scriptures until concern for the liberation of woman in the church and in modern society has required a fresh exegetical approach to the biblical teachings. The two points of partnership constitute the two divisions around which the biblical material can be discussed.

Man and Woman inside the Bible

The man-woman partnership in creation. In the light of historical exegesis there is no doubt that Genesis 2:18–24 is the foundation for all future biblical teachings. The primacy of the social relation between man and woman is seen in both woman's superiority to all animal life and in the symbolic source from which she was "made." The superiority of woman to animals is unmistakable (2:18–20). The man was formed for social relation, so solitude was "not good" for him (2:18).

The animals were "formed" from the earth as was the man (cf. 2:7–19), but none of them qualified as "a helper fit for him." Even though they are described as "living souls," the same words used for man, they were not fit for man. Solitude must be overcome for man's complete formation, so the Lord God made one similar to the man to supplement his social development. This gulf between woman and animals is behind the Old Testament legislation against sexual relations between animals and men, but the sexual relation is not primary. The naming of the animals underlines the language barrier between man and animals. The animals are only objects toward which man's language points, but language is the means by which social relations between man and woman (and others) are established. The man-woman relation is falling apart when they no longer talk to each other.

The social relation between man and woman is found in the symbolic statement about woman's source (2:21–24). It is said that in 1847 James Simpson, a Scottish surgeon, justified the use of anesthesia by appeal to the "deep sleep" the Lord God caused to come upon the man (2:21).[102] As a defense against heresy hunters such use of Scripture may be justified, but the meaning is more significant than that. Man was no spectator to the miracle by which the Lord God "made," literally "built" woman, and man should not make her in the mystery of her subjectivity a sex object. She is a person, not a thing.

The joy of the subject-subject relation between man and woman is seen in the song of the man when he saw the woman (2:23):

102. A. D. White, *The History of the Warfare of Science with Theology in Christendom* (New York: Appleton, 1955), Vol. II, p. 63.

> *This at last is bone of my bones*
> *and flesh of my flesh;*
> *she shall be called Woman (ishshah),*
> *because she was taken out of Man (ish).*

There may be some sexual significance in the rib from the lower part of the body, and from their becoming "one flesh," but the primary relation was social, not sexual. The social includes sex, but is more than sex relations.

The problem of the Fall for the man-woman relation comes forth in a perplexing way in Genesis 3:20. The threefold curse upon the serpent, the woman and the man had a note of hope in the promise to the woman that her seed would bruise the serpent's head (3:15). Irenaeus taught that this promise was fulfilled in Mary as the Second Eve in the Virgin Birth of Jesus (*Against Heresies*, V. XIX. 1). This has led to the Roman Catholic doctrine of Genesis 3:15 as the Proto-gospel, especially since the Council of Ephesus in A.D. 431 when Mary was declared *Theotokos* ("Mother of God" in English).[103]

Protestant theology has rejected the doctrine of the Perpetual Virginity of Mary and the dogmas of the Immaculate Conception (1854) and Bodily Assumption of Mary (1950) which developed around Genesis 3:15. However, the promise in part is further supported in 3:20, a text notoriously difficult. Gerhard von Rad has rejected the Rabbinic argument that found the origin of the name Eve in the Aramaic *chewyā* ("serpent"). He has followed the explanation in the text which derives the word from *hayah*, to be, to live, and made of Eve a symbol and promise of life beyond the curse of sin.[104] The promise of life in 3:20 is greater than the penalty of death in 3:3 much as the tree of life is greater than the tree of knowledge (2:9). These additions to the text are clues for the finished meaning. The clothing of their nakedness supports this view (2:25; 3:21).

However, the polemic against the place of procreation in the man-woman relation can be pushed too far. Augustine rightly observed that the creation of another male would have solved the social problem (*De Genesis ad litteram*, IX. 5. 9). It is the question of the primacy of the social over the sexual that is central. Sexual relations are periodic, but the social may be and should be permanent.

The sordid view of the man-woman relation that has produced extremes in Christian ethics is rooted in the philosophy of Plato. The famous

---

103. Henricus Renckens, *Israel's Concept of the Beginning*, tr. Charles Napier (New York: Herder and Herder, 1964), pp. 294-304.
104. *Genesis*, tr. John H. Marks (Philadelphia: The Westminster Press, 1961), p. 93. Eve was obviously not the mother of all that has physical life. This would include fish, fowl and animals as well as mankind. She was, however, to become the mother of all who would receive spiritual life through the promise made to Eve, much as Jerusalem can be called "mother of us all" (Gal. 4:26) and Abraham can be called "father of us all" (Rom. 4:16).

myth of Androgyny, from *andros* (man) and *gynē* (woman), described a monster with four arms and four legs that was round and rolled like a barrel. This was enough to create anxiety in Zeus, who split Androgyny into two halves with a bolt from the blue and a threat to quarter him. The result was a longing (*erōs*, sexual love) that tried to unite the two halves as man frantically looked for his "better half" (Plato, *Symposium*, 189a-193d).

The meaning of the myth is obvious. The distinction between male and female is the result of a curse and the relation is primarily sexual. Gregory of Nyssa read the androgynous idea into the Paradise story in Genesis 2:4b–3:24 (*The Making of Man*, XVII. 2, 4). This clearly contradicts the primacy of the social in the partnership of man and woman in the purpose of God, but this view corrupted the sexual ethics of Eastern Christianity down to the theology of the famous Nicolas Berdyaev who defended the androgynous idea with zeal.[105] Augustine believed in the primacy of procreation, and Roman Catholic theology has followed him most of her history, but he roundly rejected the androgynous idea that based the sexual distinction between male and female on the Fall rather than creation (*The City of God*, XV. 21).

The second creation story in Genesis 1:1–2:4a, P, forms a new introduction and relates the creation of male to female and to man's dominion over all creation and human procreation. All of this belongs to God's good creation, and procreation has his blessing (1:26–28). The significance of the image of God in man is the subject of a later chapter, but let it be noted here that it has a vital relation to both male and female (1:27):

> *So God created man in his own image,*
> *in the image of God he created him;*
> *male and female he created them.*

It has already been noted that man here includes both him and them, both male and female. A dispute has arisen as to whether the passage says plainly that the female is also in the image of God.[106] The dispute must go on, for later Scripture does not clarify it (cf. 1 Corinthians 11:7).

Some, especially Paul King Jewett, have made the idea of both male and female in the image of God the decisive point for biblical theology, but this is hardly the case in either the Old Testament or the New Testament. This is further clarified when the partnership of male and female is applied to life in the church.

The man-woman partnership in the church. The unity of male and female in Christ Jesus was and is basic for the meaning of Christian baptism (Galatians 3:27f.):

105. *The Destiny of Man* (London: Geoffrey Bles, 1954), pp. 61-67, 79-87.
106. Paul King Jewett, *Man as Male and Female* (Grand Rapids: Wm. B. Eerdmans Publishing Co., 1975), p. 30.

> *For as many of you as were baptized unto Christ have put on*
> *Christ.*
> *There is neither Jew nor Greek,*
> *there is neither slave nor free,*
> *there is neither male and female;*
> *for you are all one in Christ Jesus.*

The translation follows the observation of Paul King Jewett, who points out that the neither-nor of most translations does not apply to male and female, but Jewett has pushed his point too far when he engages in polemic against Karl Barth's argument that there is equality of male and female with a difference.[107] The failure to recognize the difference is a denial of the biblical teaching that recognizes the male-female distinction in creation. There is more than one way to be androgynous! Charlotte von Kirschbaum, whose book on "the real woman" Jewett mentions with praise, and rightly so, was long Karl Barth's secretary.[108]

The biblical view of woman does indeed reflect the patriarchal age in which it was written, but this hardly proves it unworthy.[109] The failure to recognize the male-female difference and the responsibility of the male for his family has introduced some weird results in modern society. Unisex is basically a reflection of sexual confusion and lost identity. The acceptance of one's sexuality is a first step toward a healthy society in the family, the church, and the whole of humanity.

Paul's discussion on the role of woman in public worship is a transition from the man-woman relation in creation to the man-woman relation in the church and an introduction to the solidarity of the human household and of the household of God (1 Corinthians 11:2–16). It unites the two creation stories in Genesis 1–2. Paul does not draw the conclusion advocated by Paul King Jewett. In fact Jewett thinks there is a contradiction between Paul's declaration in Galatians 3:28 and the interpretations of the creation stories of Genesis 1–2 in 1 Corinthians 11:2–16.[110] It is not necessary to draw such a radical conclusion.

A statement by Paul that reflects Genesis 1:27, Jewett's favorite Old Testament text, says that man "is the image and glory of God" and that "woman is the glory of the man" (1 Corinthians 11:7). This is indeed subordination in the male-female relation, but Jewett insists that subordination implies inferiority in some unworthy ways. Any emphasis on difference is apparently denigration to him. The comments by Paul on the creation story of Genesis 2:4b–24 are far more consistent.

---

107. *Ibid.*, pp. 35ff., 43ff., 69ff.
108. *Ibid.*, p. 121, n. 93.
109. See especially O. J. Baab, "Woman" in *The Interpreter's Dictionary of the Bible*, IV, 864-867.
110. Jewett, *op. cit.*, pp. 51-57 and in a dozen other places.

The first parenthetical comment, based on the story of Genesis 2:18–24, says: "For man was not made from woman, but woman from man. Neither was man created for woman, but woman for man" (1 Cor. 11:8f.). What else could be said on the basis of the Old Testament text already examined? A second parenthetical comment modifies the meaning in terms of life in the body of Christ: "Nevertheless, in the Lord woman is not independent of man nor man of woman; for as woman was made from man, so man is born of woman. And all things are from God" (1 Cor. 11:11f.). In terms of a hymn that follows immediately after Jewett's favorite New Testament text, even the Son of God "was born of woman" (Gal. 4:4–6).

Paul does not mean that unmarried people are less than persons. Since the social relation is primary and the sexual relation is secondary, the sexual relation may be sublimated to the social. Paul's preference for the single life, however, was vocational rather than pagan. The single life was best for him and he recommended it to all who had "the gift" of celibacy (1 Corinthians 7:7f., 38, 40). The revolt against celibacy is now a major problem in the Roman Catholic Church, and the attitude that looks upon celibates as super-Christians needs to be modified by Paul's question about himself and Barnabas, both celibates. He asked: "Do we not have the right to be accompanied by a wife, as the other apostles and brothers of the Lord and Cephas?" (1 Cor. 9:5). An affirmative answer to his question, which he expected, would greatly change the traditional views of celibacy, the doctrine of Perpetual Virginity, and the prohibition against married popes!

The solidarity of woman in the solidarity of a human household is a major New Testament theme. In the case of a household divided between believers and unbelievers, the believing woman is to relate herself to her husband as Sarah obeyed Abraham (1 Peter 3:1–6). The "total woman" movement, in resistance to the "woman's liberation" movement, has at times overstated this view, but it no doubt often makes a believer of the husband. This is not always the case, so Paul has some realistic words about why a believer is no longer bound to the unbeliever when the unbeliever desires to separate (1 Corinthians 7:12–16). Here again the right of woman to remain a virgin or to marry is left as a vocational option (7:25–38). The same rule applies to a second marriage for a woman after the death of her husband (7:39f.). Christians, however, should never initiate a divorce.

Paul's view of a united household in which all are believers is fundamental for the Christian family (Colossians 3:18–4:1; Ephesians 5:21–6:9; Titus 2:1–10). A recent study of a table of rules for the Christian household (*Haustafel*) has pointed out the origin in Hellenistic Judaism and its importance in "orthodox" Christianity as a defense against paganism.[111] The expansion of the section on the Christian wife reaches the highest peak

---

111. James E. Crouch, *The Origin and Intention of the Colossian Haustafel* (Göttingen: Vandenhoeck & Ruprecht, 1972).

possible when the husband-wife relation is compared to the relation between Christ and the church, i.e. a relation of submission and love (Eph. 5:21–33).[112] The best argument in favor of this view of the man-woman relation is that it seems to work far better than the modern contracts some people are choosing today.

The solidarity of woman in the household of God at times approached the Ephesian heights. The emphasis on women in the ministry of Jesus and in the early church is a special feature in Luke–Acts. The prominence of Priscilla, the wife of Aquila, noted by both Luke and Paul, points the way in the New Testament (Acts 18; 1 Cor. 16:19; Rom. 16:3f.; 2 Tim. 4:19). The most prominent woman in the New Testament church was perhaps Phoebe (the radiant), deaconess in Cenchreae, whose role in the ministry of Paul is described in official terms (Rom. 16:1–2). It is possible that she was a collector of Paul's letters to Thessalonica and Corinth as well as the carrier of Romans to Rome. The ministry of seven other Christian women is mentioned in Romans 16. Perhaps it will do for women what Philemon did for slaves, but the problem is not the same. Marriage and parenthood are essential, but slavery is not.

We are not arguing that women in the New Testament got beyond the office of deaconess, but many churches have not reached that point. It is rather clear that the functions assigned to elders were denied women. A floating text that may be found in manuscripts at two different places in 1 Corinthians is perhaps a later addition to the text (1 Cor. 14:33b–36), but the prohibition is beyond doubt in 1 Timothy 2:8–15. The reason given was first stated in 2 Corinthians 11:3, but now the deception of Eve by the serpent is made a part of church order. This rule without other New Testament teachings on woman has made "the woman problem" for the modern church. Jewett tries to solve the problem by appeal to Genesis 1:27 and Galatians 3:28. The teachings of the New Testament show that women should be given a greater role in the ministry of the church through the office of deaconess, as Phoebe was.

The most obvious point in this story of Eve's origin is the emphasis on how she comes from Adam, not from the soil. Adam comes from *adāmāh* (the soil) and so do the animals, but Eve comes from Adam. This is to underline the oneness of man and woman (*îsh* and *ishshāh* in Hebrew). The later source in Genesis 1:26f. goes so far as to call both male and female by the one name Adam, and Adam is created in the image of God, an idea to be discussed in a later chapter. Eve is no stranger to Adam, but he is to have dominion over her. Yet this teaching about Eve as the completion of man in creation is always in collision with Eve as the source of

112. A beautiful exposition of this passage is by Markus Barth, *Ephesians* (Garden City, N.Y.: Doubleday & Company, 1974), Vol. II, pp. 607-753.

the curse. Genesis 1, 2 is at war with Genesis 3.

Man and Woman outside the Bible

References to historical views on the man-woman relation have been made in the above discussion, but it may be of further interest to focus on the interpretations of Eve in the different cultural situations in which Christians have reflected on the right man-woman relations. Generalizations can distort, but an examination of Eve in Christian tradition does permit definite trends in interpretations of Eve and womanhood.

Eve in the Catholic tradition. The roots of Catholic tradition are most clearly seen in the first thousand years of the undivided church. In the Greek source the dominant trend is *the exaltation of Eve* by emphasis on virginity and the feminine principle.

In the days before "the conversion of Constantine" women had a surprising role in the life of the church. At times this becomes extremism, as in the charismatic sect that came to be known as Montanism. Even though Montanus was a man, the most charismatic prophets were two women named Prisca and Maximilla. After the conversion of Constantine, when the church, once persecuted, began to persecute, this movement was violently denounced, as one can see in the *Church History* by Eusebius (V. xvi. 7).

Even the most orthodox made much room for the ministry of women before Constantine. A third-century writing called *Didascalia* describes in detail the duties of deaconesses as well as deacons (Ch. XVI). This ministry of deaconesses, to be sure, was confined to women, as the ministry of deacons was confined to men. The duties performed restricted the deaconesses more than any sense of inferiority. The deaconesses were "required to go into houses of the heathen where there are believing women, and to visit those who are sick, and to minister to them in that of which they have need, and to bathe those who have begun to recover from sickness" (XVI. iii.12).[113]

The exaltation of Eve as the type of womanhood grew out of the idea that the Virgin Mary was the Second Eve, i.e. the view of Irenaeus of Lyon in the second century, as mentioned above. It does not appear an accident that the doctrine of the Virgin Mary as the one who bore God (*Theotokos*) gained sanction at the Council of Ephesus in A.D. 431. The Double Church of the Council was a short distance from the Temple of Artemis, the female deity worshipped in Asia.

---

113. *Didascalia Apostolorum* by R. Hugh Connolly (Oxford: At the Clarendon Press, 1969), p. 148.

A "monumental" manifestation of this exaltation of the Second Eve is the Church of *Hagia Sophia* (Holy Wisdom) in Constantinople, dedicated to the Virgin Mary. When this magnificent structure was built, on the patronage of Justinian (527-565), building materials were brought from the Temple of Artemis to be included in the church exalting the Second Eve. In many ways the Virgin Mary took the place of the goddess Artemis and became a goddess herself.[114]

At the beginning of the Latin tradition there was a definite trend toward the subordination of Eve and womanhood. Eve was more of a seducer than a goddess, and the seducer needed to be subordinated to her husband.

Punic patriarchal culture was in the background, but appeal was made to the Paradise story in Genesis 3. The great Carthaginian named Tertullian laid the foundation for anti-feminism in the Latin church. His writing *On Apparel of Women* (about A.D. 202) has the reminder that says (I.1):

> And do you not know that you are [each] Eve? The sentence of death on this sex of yours lives in this age: the guilt must of necessity live too. *You* are the devil's gateway: *you* are the unsealer of that forbidden tree: *you* are the first deserter of the divine law: *you* are she who persuaded him whom the devil was not valiant enough to attack. *You* destroyed God's image, man. On account of *your* desert — that is, death — even the Son of God had to die.

This is not an isolated statement, for from such sources the stream of Latin anti-feminism has been fed to this day. As the curse on Canaan was used to suppress black people, so the curse on creation was used to subordinate women.

This phobia against the feminine found full expression in Jerome, the translator of the Latin Bible in the fourth century and one of the most influential monks of all time. He himself had a problem with sexual passion, about which he wrote freely. In his famous letter to Eustochium, the daughter of Paula, he described his struggle with sex while he lived in the Syrian Desert (*Letters* XXII. 7):

> Now, although in my fear of hell I had consigned myself to this prison, where I had no companions but scorpions and wild beasts, I often found myself amid bevies of girls. My face was pale and my frame chilled with fantasy; yet my mind was burning with desire, and the fires of lust kept bubbling up before me when my flesh was as good as dead.

Against the background of his own sexual frustrations the subordination of woman as the temptress of man became a basic belief.

114. See Dimitri Kessel, *The Splendors of Christendom* (Lausanne: Edita, 1964), pp. 21-33 for an impressive presentation of this architectural symbolism.

The letter to Eustochium contained caustic criticisms about the worldliness of the Roman clergy, so much so that Jerome, under pressure, soon left for Bethlehem where Paula and Eustochium joined him in a newly founded monastery where they lived out their lives. It was there many years later, after Jerome had become more and more the champion of virginity and celibacy, that he disclosed how he began the study of Hebrew in his younger years, because it was more useful than fastings in restraining sexual passion (*Letters,* CXXV. 12).

Jerome's extremes on the sublimation of sex involved him in doctrinal deviations that have made problems for those who would retain a more biblical and practical faith. Jerome's Scripture twisting reached new stages as he tried to answer a Latin lay theologian named Helvidius who rejected the rising doctrine that the Virgin Mary was forever a virgin. The doctrine of her perpetual virginity ran into many exegetical problems when confronted with references to Jesus as Mary's firstborn, the evidence of the four brothers and at least two sisters of Jesus, and other statements.

Jerome's efforts to explain these references have remained standard for conservative Catholicism, and marriage has been reduced to a secondary form of the holy life. Virginity and celibacy are required to scale the heights of holiness. Under the later influence of Ambrose and Augustine, Jerome declared that Jesus passed through the wall of Mary's womb in the same way he passed through the wall of Joseph's tomb.[115] There the deviation remains as an obstacle to Christian unity.

Another controversy involved an attack on a Roman monk named Jovian who denied that virginity is a higher state than marriage. As the "champion of chastity," as J. N. D. Kelly describes Jerome, Jerome did further Scripture twisting as he argued that Adam and Eve embarked upon marriage only after their sin and that their marriage was intended only to "replenish the earth" while virginity would "replenish Paradise" (*Against Jovian,* I. 16). A careful reading of J. N. D. Kelly's standard work indicates how much Jerome's subordination of Eve and womanhood is a handicap to biblical and practical Christianity.[116]

A pathetic picture is given when Paula abandons her little boy Toxotius, sobbing on the quay, while "she herself turned her dry eyes heavenwards, overcoming her love for her children by her love for God."[117] The halo of Augustine goes into eclipse as one reads how he abandons the mother of his son after his "conversion." She was only his concubine in "the mere bargain of a lustful love" (*Confessions* IV. ii. 2). With a theology that sees only the subordination of woman in the symbol of Eve, it is not surprising to read his advice to another young man: "What is the difference? Whether

115. J. N. D. Kelly, *Jerome* (New York: Harper and Row, 1975), p. 106, n. 10.
116. *Op. cit.,* pp. 179-194.
117. *Ibid.,* p. 117. Kelly is quoting Jerome.

it is in a wife or a mother, it is still Eve (the temptress) that we must beware of in any woman" (*Ep.* 243, 10).[118]

One of the strongest efforts to salvage the Catholic understanding of woman is the survey by George Tavard.[119] He rightly recognizes two traditions and sources in Genesis 1–3. In Genesis 2:18–24 he finds Eve more of a completion of man than a companion. Both ideas seem to be implied, and it is certainly correct to see woman as the complement of man. Her position at the end of the sequence of Adam, vegetation, animals and woman does not represent repression and inferiority. It is rather as the crown of creation in which woman is both the complement and the companion of man.

The later tradition in Genesis 1:26f. does indeed include both male and female in Adam as the image of God. That will be discussed in a later chapter. Another male in a Jonathan and David relation can provide companionship, but the Genesis narrative makes the normal companion of male a female. God did not create Adam as male and male as some homosexual anthropology would suggest. Homosexuality is always unnatural (Romans 1:26f.). Tavard has some subtle suggestions that seem to favor an androgynous anthropology. He seems to prefer the Greek translation of the Old Testament over the original Hebrew. That comes out even more in his sarcastic analysis of "Protestant Reflections." Tavard later says the image of God in Adam as male and female is too narrow for the monastic tradition, so he argues for a "man with others" relation whether male or female.[120]

Eve in Protestant tradition. Protestant tradition has usually portrayed Eve as womanhood *domesticated*, but radical Protestantism has begun to reject this view in favor of woman *liberated*. Eve as domesticated womanhood was understood at first in the setting of a pre-scientific anthropology that was rooted in Augustine, but neo-orthodoxy embraced scientific anthropology with restatements of the man-woman relation.

When the Saxon monk Martin Luther broke with the Catholic tradition and married the nun Katherine von Bora there were many changes in both thought and action. The belief that virginity and celibacy are superior states to marriage and family life became a broken myth. As Roland Bainton tells the story of Luther's married life in a chapter "The School for Character" he rightly begins with the "domesticity" of woman, and Luther appears in a good light.[121]

118. Quotations from Peter Brown, *Augustine of Hippo* (London: Faber & Faber, 1967), p. 63.
119. *Woman in Christian Tradition* (Notre Dame, Indiana: University of Notre Dame, 1973), pp. 3-12.
120. *Ibid.*, p. 191.
121. *Here I Stand* (Nashville: Abingdon-Cokesbury, 1950), pp. 286-304.

As Tavard, a Roman Catholic scholar, comes to Luther all the quotations on woman are construed in a derogatory manner, yet all of Luther's bad ideas about woman are attributed to people like Augustine, Aristotle and the Nominalist School, all from Catholicism.[122] Luther no doubt had his limitations but his interpretation of the curse on Eve is not even mentioned. Compare these words with the subordination of sex in Jerome and Augustine:

> Therefore truly happy and joyful is this punishment if we correctly appraise the matter. Although these burdens are troublesome for the flesh, yet the hope for a better life is strengthened together with those very burdens and punishments, because Eve hears that she is not being repudiated by God. Furthermore, she also hears that in this punishment she is not being deprived of the blessing of procreation, which was promised and granted before sin. She sees that she is keeping her sex and that she remains a woman. She sees that she is not being separated from Adam to remain alone and apart from her husband. She sees that she may keep the glory of motherhood, if I may use the phrase. All these things are in addition to the eternal hope, and without a doubt they greatly encouraged Eve. Above all, there remains also a greater and more genuine glory. Not only does she keep the blessing of fruitfulness and remain united with her husband, but she has the sure promise that from her will come the Seed who will crush the head of Satan.[123]

This and many similar statements are far more typical of what Luther believed than the quotations by Tavard. Luther saw three traditions in Genesis where Tavard saw only two. To creation and the curse Luther added redemption, the distinctive emphasis in the New Testament.

Tavard is correct in seeing a more refined and delicate presentation of woman in John Calvin than in Martin Luther. It is also true that much of Calvin's anthropology was not against other Western thinkers, but a considerable concession is made when it is said: "This was well in line with the prevailing emphasis of Western thought, though Calvin more underscored it than was usual before him."[124] Calvin did not *underscore* the superiority of virginity and celibacy to marriage and family, a view that prevailed in the West from the fourth century to the sixteenth. Partnership was put prior to procreation in the purpose of marriage, and that did not and does not prevail in Catholic theology. Domesticity did prevail in Calvin as in Luther, and that has been the major emphasis of Protestantism.

122. *Op. cit.*, p. 174.
123. *Luther's Works*, edited by Jaroslav Pelikan (Saint Louis: Concordia Publishing House, 1958), Vol. I, p. 199.
124. *Op. cit.*, p. 175.

In the setting of scientific anthropology Emil Brunner and Karl Barth have added comparable influences to that of Luther and Calvin. Brunner is much nearer the Reformers Luther and Calvin by putting his emphasis on the order of creation and the Old Testament. For Brunner the profoundest psychological distinction is that of male and female. Because of sin all sex has a taint of shame. Genesis 2–3 are clearly in the background here, yet Brunner did not take the story of Paradise and the Fall as literal history. In all male-female relations there is "a certain super- and subordination."[125]

Karl Barth faces the man-woman relation from a Christological perspective that is more in the context of New Testament teachings on love. The man-woman relation is one of fellowship in freedom, especially in Christian marriage. All unisex mythology is repudiated. Barth says:

> It belongs to every human being to be male or female. It also belongs to every human being to be male and female: male in this or that distant relationship to the female, and female in a similar relationship to the male. Man is human, and therefore fellow-human, as he is male or female, male and female.[126]

Just why Tavard calls this "very biblically inspired" yet unsatisfactory is not clear. Fellowship of male and female in freedom seems the best of all human relations. It seemed obvious that this high standard of male-female relations was more than theory with Barth. His secretary Charlotte von Kirschbaum, who wrote her book *The Real Woman* before Barth made his own classic statement, summed up the relation in these words:

> On the one hand, the obedience of woman and her subordinate position must witness that Christ is the prototype of all subordination; on the other, Christ glorified, the head of all domination and authority, is at the source of authority assigned to man. The assertion that man is the head of woman is acceptable, as long as it is not separated from its Christological context.[127]

A liberated Eve that transcends all male-female distinctions belongs to heaven, but not to earthly existence. Much liberation theology seems also to be based upon a false individualism that forgets that human beings exist in family relations. This does not mean that all must marry to find human fulfillment. It is possible to have an extended family of friends, but this can never be the norm for all. Marriage and family life are the fundamental forms of human existence as male and female. Adam and Eve belong together that they may be "one flesh" in their offspring. Marriage is not for

125. *Man in Revolt* (Philadelphia: The Westminster Press, 1939), pp. 358f.
126. *Church Dogmatics*, III/4, p. 140.
127. Quoted in George Tavard, *op. cit.*, p. 178.

all, but the whole human race would end if all practiced either celibacy or homosexuality.

Appeal for the liberation of woman from cultural limitations can be balanced or unbalanced. The frontal attack upon the Bible that magnifies the female deities outside the Bible as if a return to the fertility cults of Canaanite culture would be progress is most misleading. That is the tone of the book by Merlin Stone called *When God Was a Woman*.[128]

A more balanced approach is by Georgia Harkness, the First Lady of American theology. She has told the story of Eve's emancipation as a prelude to "the next revolution."[129] She is unmarried and an ordained Methodist minister, yet there is no suggestion that her unmarried status makes her superior to married women or that women are inferior to men. Pope Paul VI can declare that all priests must be men since Jesus and the apostles were all men. This assumes that there are only two traditions, to use Tavard's phrase: woman in creation and woman under the curse. But there is a third tradition suggested by the promise that the seed of the woman will bruise the serpent's head (Genesis 3:15). It is the tradition of woman in Christ.

Paul the apostle has been pounded for following some of the Jewish restrictions on woman in the Jewish religion, but authentic Pauline teachings laid the foundation for the third tradition in which the distinction between male and female is transcended in Christ (Galatians 3:28). The outcome of this in actual practice is manifest most in the letter for Phoebe (Romans 16) in which the role of at least eight women in the Roman church is very pronounced. As the covering letter for Colossians, the letter to Philemon, prepared the way for the emancipation of the slave Onesimus and the end of all slavery, so the Romans 16 letter, with Paul's letter to Rome, should now be used to liberate women. Paul VI should have followed the apostle Paul.

It has not yet dawned on many that Luke–Acts by Luke the physician has as a major theme the role of women in the ministry of Christ and of the early church. The mothers of John and Jesus, the home of Martha and Mary, the teaching of Lydia and Priscilla, and the mention of the "women" and the "widows" in the ministry of Jesus and the churches have just been ignored under the influence of the Latin tradition of the church. One of the clearest notes sounded in Luke–Acts is that Jesus came to set free the captives whether they be slaves, the poor, or women. In a fellowship of freedom all are one.

---

128. (New York: The Dial Press, 1976). The history of the feminine deities is told better by J. Edgar Bruns, *God as Woman, Woman as God* (N.Y.: Paulist Press, 1973).
129. *Women in Church and Society* (Nashville: Abingdon Press, 1972), pp. 13-35.

38. The Image of God: Man and God

Man's most distinctive quality is the image of God by which he has dominion over all other creatures and the whole of God's creation. This, however,
is a dynamic process of becoming. At least three perspectives on the image
of God in man may be distinguished in the teachings of the Holy Scriptures.
They are: (1) the image of God in creation which is never lost, (2) Christ
as the image of God in both redemption and creation, and (3) the image of
God in Christ which is bestowed upon the believer in the dynamic process
of transformation in salvation. In the history of Christian theology, at various times and places, the emphasis has often been upon one perspective
to the detriment of another, so the discussion that follows will first attempt
to state the meaning of each and then relate the three in a balanced whole.
After the analysis of the threefold image in biblical theology a brief survey
will be made of the major interpretations in historical theology.

The Image of God in Biblical Theology

The image of God in creation. It has been said that the idea of the image
of God in man is only "on the margin" of the Old Testament teaching, but
it is more like the summit of the Old Testament view of man than the
margin. The oldest account of man's creation in Genesis 2:4b–3:24 (JE)
does not hesitate to speak of man as a living soul along with the animals
(2:7, 19), but the later account in Genesis 1:1–2:4a (P) speaks of fish and
birds and animals as living souls, "living creatures" in the RSV. Man alone,
however, is described as in the image of God (cf. 1:20f., 24).

The dominion of man over all creation dominates the first reference to
the image of God in creation, but there are other elements of importance
(Genesis 1:26f.). The basic meaning of the image of God appears at the
very beginning when "after our likeness" is added by way of explanation.
Likeness to God is the image of God, but one's view of God determines the
view one holds of the image. In the context of Genesis 1:1–2:4a the central
concept of God is that of the Creator who rules not only over all nations,
as in Isaiah 40–55, but over all creation. Man is the crown of creation, and,
under the dominion of God the Creator, man has dominion over all other
creatures: fish and birds, cattle and creeping things (1:26). The creation of
man as male and female (1:27) has already been discussed in detail in
chapter 37.

The blessing of God upon man's dominion has been perverted in two
directions (1:28). Too much emphasis on replenishing the earth leads to
overproduction and overpopulation, and too much emphasis on subduing
the earth leads to exploitation and the rape of natural resources, but man
remains the lord of creation. It is only when he forgets that his dominion

is exercised under the dominion of God that disaster follows. Technology without theology leads to tyranny over God's good creation.

The continuity of the image of God in man is obvious in the second reference (Genesis 5:1-3, P). The likeness of God remains as the central meaning of the image of God. Man as both male and female, as both body and spirit, is included again in the image of God. However, the creation of man in the image and likeness of God is not confined to the first male and the first female. Every male and every female is created in the image and likeness of God. Immediately after the Priestly Writer repeats the view of Genesis 1:26f., he says: "When Adam had lived a hundred and thirty years, he became the father of a son in his own likeness, after his image, and called him Seth" (Genesis 5:3). The image and likeness of God in creation is now transmitted to Seth through human procreation and divine creation working together. Adam and Eve plus God bring Seth into the world. The idea of a lost likeness is unknown in the passage.

The dignity of man as the image of God is the thrust of the third reference in the Old Testament (Genesis 9:6). Man may make food of both vegetation and living creatures, but the blood of life must first be drained from the living creatures. Life is in the blood, so the life must first be removed, but it is forbidden to shed the blood of man for the reason that he is made in the image of God. "Whoever sheds the blood of man, by man shall his blood be shed; for God made man in his own image." From primitive blood feuds to modern capital punishment the emphasis has been put on the negative side of this great principle. It is now time to put forth the positive emphasis on the dignity of man and the sacredness of life.

It is true that the likeness of God is not mentioned in this third passage on the image of God in man, but this does not justify the conclusion that man lost the likeness and retained the image by a historical Fall. The Priestly Writer has no doctrine of the Fall, but he of course adds his views to those of the older account on which the doctrine of a historical Fall is based.

Man as the link between invisible and visible reality is found in the majestic Psalm 8 that uses neither the term image nor the term likeness, but is based upon the Priestly view of man. After magnifying the majesty of God in the heavens above, the Psalmist comes to the question of man (v. 4). How can one so majestic even think of man, much less care for him?

> Yet thou hast made him little less than God,
>   and dost crown him with glory and honor.
>   thou hast given him dominion over the works of thy hands;
>   thou hast put all things under his feet,

> *all sheep and oxen,*
> *and also the beasts of the field,*
> *the birds of the air, and the fish of the sea,*
> *whatever passes along the paths of the sea (5–8).*

Man's dominion under God could hardly be stated with greater clarity. This applies to Everyman, not just to the First Man. More than the creatures and less than the Creator: that is man's glory and honor. To mix ancient and modern ideas, man is less than the angels and more than the apes.

The very words "glory and honor" summarize man's likeness. Man was made to make present the reality of God. The glory of God is the Presence of God, and man is the reflector of this glory even more than the glory in the heavens. The soul, not the stars, is the summit of God's creation. Man, not the majesty of the earth, is the crown of all creation. Renckens is no doubt right when he sees "the primacy of spirit over matter" in this Old Testament view of the image of God in man.[130]

Some of the apocryphal writings expand the view of man in Psalm 8. The *Wisdom of Sirach* elaborates the dominion of man and assigns the authority to the image of God. It says (17:3):

> *He endowed them with strength like his own,*
> *and made them in his own image.*

The destiny of man is described in the majestic words of *The Wisdom of Solomon* which say (2:23):

> *God created man for immortality,*
> *and made him in the image of his own eternity.*

Many other references indicate man's ultimate destiny as God's image (cf. 1:15; 3:3; 6:19).

This lofty Old Testament view of man's dominion over all creation is not discarded in the New Testament. In general one may say that the image of God in the Old Testament is likeness to God, and the image of God in the New Testament is likeness to Christ, but there is an overlap. In the Jewish Christianity that is found in the wisdom of James the same reason is given for not cursing man as the Old Testament gives for not killing him: All men "are made in the likeness (*homoiosis*) of God" (3:9). It is impossible to find a lost likeness in this passage.

A second writing from Hellenistic Jewish Christianity reminds us that the dominion of man is a process that has reached perfection only in Jesus. Hebrews 2:6–8 is a quotation of Psalm 8:4–6 LXX, and the commentary that follows is a reminder that God's intention has not been fully realized in men. All things are not yet subject to men, and the glory and honor of

---

130. Henricus Renckens, *Israel's Concept of the Beginning*, tr. Charles Napier (New York: Herder and Herder, 1964), p. 126.

God can be seen perfectly only in Jesus who tasted death for everyone (2:8f.). On this Barnabas, the author of Hebrews, builds his great Christology in which complete humanity and complete deity are united in the incarnation. Renckens is again right when he sees the deepest meaning in the creation of man "as a preparation for and prefiguration of the incarnatio Dei."[131]

One passage in Paul is based upon a merger between the two accounts of creation in Genesis 1–3, and in this passage the image of God in Christ is also merged with the image of God in creation (1 Cor. 11:2–16). The hierarchy of God-Christ-man-woman already discussed is likened to the idea of the image of God (11:9).

> He (man) is the image and glory of God;
> but woman is the glory of man.

If woman derives her glory from man, does she also derive her image from him? That puts a question to the text that can't be answered despite Genesis 5:3 in which Seth's image and likeness is derived from Adam. Paul would be more popular today had he answered all the questions he raised on this point. In any case the image and glory of God are to be found in any person.

If one tries to reach a conclusion as to the meaning of the image of God in creation, that of David Cairns, the author of a little classic on the subject, is good enough. He says:

> My own conclusion is that 'P' means by existence in God's image
> a personal responsible existence before God, and that this implies
> what Barth and Brunner read into it, though I very much wonder
> how deeply 'P' saw into the societary nature of personal being,
> both divine and human.[132]

It was Augustine who built his doctrine of the Trinity on the image of God in man in which love became his chief category. Karl Barth has revived this in modern theology. However, it is right to follow out implications for both the incarnation and the Holy Trinity if one does not claim that 'P' had all this in his own mind.

Christ as the image of God. As the major description in the Old Testament of the image of God in creation does not use the term, so the profoundest statement in the New Testament on Christ as the image of God uses other terms to express the idea. R. H. Fuller has said that Hebrews 1:3f. is part of a Christological hymn.[133] The first stanza says:

131. *Ibid.*, p. 127.
132. *The Image of God in Man*, Revised Edition (London: Collins, 1973), p. 32.
133. *The Foundations of New Testament Christology* (New York: Scribner's, 1965), pp. 220f.

> *Who being the radiance (apaugasma) of his glory*
> *and the very stamp (charaktēr) of his substance,*
> *upholding all things by the word of his power.*

Apaugasma and *character* imply the very likeness of Jesus to God in both spirit and body, deity and humanity.

A background passage does use the term image of God (*Wisdom of Solomon* 7:26). Speaking of wisdom it says:

> *For she is a reflection of eternal light,*
> *a spotless mirror of the working of God,*
> *and an image of his goodness.*

It is in the Pauline letters that these ideas designate Jesus as the image of God. The first great passage states the difference between the earthly man Adam and the heavenly man Jesus in terms of creation and consummation (1 Corinthians 15:49):

> *Just as we have borne the image of the man of dust,*
> *we shall also bear the image of the man of heaven.*

The image of the man of dust included both body and spirit as in Genesis 5:3. This image has never been lost, and all men have borne it. The image of the man of heaven has not yet been borne by all men. It belongs to the eschatological hope when body and spirit are included in the spiritual body of the resurrection.

This emphasis on the inclusion of the body in the future image is particularly strong in Romans 8:29. After stating his hope that both God's creation and God's children will be liberated in a cosmic redemption that includes human bodies (Rom. 8:18–25), he hastens on to say (Rom. 8:29):

> *For those whom he foreknew he also predestined*
> *to be conformed to the image of his Son,*
> *in order that he might be the first-born*
> *among many brethren.*

What has already happened to Jesus, the Son of God, is a clue to what awaits the children of God in the eschatological future (cf. Philippians 3:21).

Christ is the image of God in both redemption and creation. That is in the background of the Great Thanksgiving of 2 Corinthians 2:14–7:4. At two different places Christ is called the *eikōn* (image) of God (2 Cor. 3:18; 4:4), and in each instance the *eikōn* is closely related to the *doxa* (glory). In 1 Corinthians 11:7, too, man is said to be both *eikōn* and *doxa* of God. In Psalm 8:5, where man is said to be crowned "with glory and honor" in his dominion over all the works of God, glory is almost a synonym for the image of God as seen in Genesis 1:26f.; 5:1–3; 9:6. With his profound "doxological" view of the dignity and destiny of man, Paul has put the idea of glory in the center of his perspective. Man's dignity and destiny is to share in the glory of Christ (Romans 5:2).

Christ as the image of God in creation is the first theme in the Christological hymn of Colossians 1:15–20. As the Firstborn of God, Christ is the Firstborn (*prōtotokos*) in both creation (vv. 15–17) and reconciliation (vv. 18–20). The title Firstborn, introduced by Paul in Romans 8:29, does not mean that Christ in his pre-existence was the first creature God created, as later Arianism and the modern Jehovah's Witnesses claim. J. B. Lightfoot long ago (1875) made it clear that the title is deeply rooted in the Old Testament view of the authority and inheritance of the first son to be born in a family.

It is interesting to note that Isaac, who was not the first son to be begotten by his father, received the authority and the inheritance from Abraham (Gen. 17:19–21). He could even be called Abraham's only son (22:12), the sense in which Jesus is called God's only Son (John 1:14, 18; 3:16, 18).[134]

A good example of the meaning even before it is applied to Jesus is Psalm 89:27, which by all means should be read in context:

> *And I will make him the first-born,*
> *the highest of the kings of the earth.*

This identification of "the image of the invisible God" with "the first-born of all creation" expresses priority to and authority over all creation. That the primate (*prōtotokos*) has primacy (*prōteuōn*) captures some of the play on words found in the Greek (Col. 1:18).[135]

By way of summary it can be said that the identification of "the image of the man of heaven" (1 Corinthians 15:49), "the image of his Son" (Romans 8:29), "the same image" (2 Corinthians 3:18), "the image of God" (2 Corinthians 4:4), and "the image of the invisible God" (Colossians 1:15) with the crucified and risen Lord was a point in Pauline theology which lifted the idea of the image of God to the highest level and shifted it from the past bestowal in creation to the dynamic process that begins in the present and is brought to completion in the consummation when man in body and spirit will be the *likeness* of God because he is in the *likeness* of Christ.

It has already been noted that this process of perfection was applied to both man and Christ in Hebrews (cf. 2:8–18; 5:1–10; 12:1f.). In 1 John the destiny of likeness to God is also expressed without using the terms image and likeness of God (3:2). It is assumed that the "him" of 1 John 3:2 has reference to God (cf. 2:29). However, too much should not be made of the difference between the Christ-mysticism of Paul and the God-mysticism of John, true as the distinction may be. A dignity and a destiny that is the image and likeness of God, or of Christ, is for the Christian the same.

---

134. J. B. Lightfoot, *St. Paul's Epistles to the Colossians and Philemon*, pp. 140-156.
135. For further details see *The Interpreter's Dictionary of the Bible*, II, 270-272.

At times this grand theme of Christ as the image of God has been better expressed in song than in sermon. A prime example of this is Charles Wesley's "Hark the Herald Angels Sing," which addresses this prayer to Jesus in the pietistic devotion so characteristic of his evangelical faith:

> Come, Desire of nations, come!
> Fix in us Thy humble home.
> Adam's likeness now efface,
> Stamp thine image in its place.
> Second Adam from above,
> Reinstate us in thy love.

In the Old Testament, man's dominion over God's creation is the central emphasis in the term image of God, but the coming of Christ has deepened, not excluded, this idea into existence in the love of God for us and our love for God and for one another. In this way the distinctive view of God as *agapē* (love) and of the good life as love for God and man has become the very heart of the Christian faith.

The image of God for those in Christ. The image of God in Christ, i.e. the image of God as it is bestowed on those who believe and are in Christ Jesus, is both a future goal and a present process. In the passages about "the image of the man of heaven" (1 Corinthians 15:49) and "the image of his Son" (Romans 8:29) the image of God is that which is the destiny of the Christian, something to be borne or something to which he is to conform in the future. The transformation or renewal of man into the image of God in Christ is also a dynamic process of the present.

The present process of transformation or metamorphosis of the soul, i.e. the self, is the result of turning to the Lord or repentance.[136] "And we all, with unveiled face, reflecting the glory of the Lord, are being changed into his image from one degree of glory to another; for this comes from the Lord who is the Spirit" (2 Corinthians 3:18).

This translation, which adopts the reading of the footnote in the RSV and retains the literal translation of *eikōn* as image, not likeness, is very important in seeing the image of God in Christ as the imitation of Christ or Christ-likeness. Here, as in 2 Corinthians 3:16, the TEV is right in saying all who turn to the Lord "reflect the glory of the Lord."[137]

This statement follows a comparison of the two faces of Moses in the

---

136. *The Metamorphosis of Apuleius*, c. A.D. 150, describes the initiation of Lucius into Isis mysteries at Cenchreae in language that has a superficial parallel to Paul. If Paul used the language of mystery he transformed the meaning by his emphasis on the cross and repentance. 2 Corinthians 3 is based upon the Old Testament account of the giving of the law to Moses in the light of the gift of the Spirit at Pentecost. See David Cairns, *op. cit.*, pp. 61-65.

137. Cf. G. C. Berkouwer, *Man: The Image of God*, tr. Dirk W. Jellema (Grand Rapids: Wm. B. Eerdmans, 1962), p. 111.

old covenant and the dispensation of death and of the believer in the new covenant and the dispensation of the Spirit who gives life. The veiling of the face of Moses (Exodus 34:29–35) is interpreted as a sign of the transiency of life under the law. The first covenant is to be fulfilled in a second and new covenant and the dispensation of the Spirit.

The two covenants and the two dispensations become the framework of New Testament faith. The old is promise, and the new is the beginning of fulfillment. Until one turns to the Lord a mask is on the mind when the old covenant is read. When one turns to the Lord the mask is removed. The Lord in Exodus 34:34 represents the role of the Spirit in the new covenant. The TEV has caught the meaning of 2 Corinthians 3:17 with the translation: "Now, 'the Lord' in this passage is the Spirit; and where the Spirit of the Lord is present, there is freedom." In this freedom of the Spirit a process of transformation begins and continues until the whole self, body and spirit, is in the image of God. This transformation of human existence into a life of love for God and others is the true image of God, the likeness of Christ.

The Christian *halakah*, rules for Christian living, in Colossians 3:10, speaks of the new man (*neos anthrōpos*) as one "which is being renewed in knowledge after the image of its creator." "The image of its creator" is the same as the image of God. Renewal (*anakainōsis*) seems to be a better way to express this transformation (*metamorphosis*) of the soul into the likeness of God and Christ.

This new man puts Christ above all racial distinctions such as Greek and Jew, all religious ceremonies such as circumcision, all cultural barriers such as Barbarian and Scythian, and all social distinctions such as slavery. This social ethic is supported by a personal ethic in which the new man is Christ-like. The personal imperative is: "Put on then, as God's chosen ones, holy and beloved, compassion, kindness, lowliness, meekness, and patience, forbearing one another and, if one has a complaint against another, forgiving each other; as the Lord has forgiven you, so you also must forgive. And above all these put on love, which binds everything together in perfect harmony" (Colossians 3:12–14). It is hardly true to say Christianity is dogma and Judaism is Torah in the light of such Christian *halakah*. Christian doctrine and Christian conduct are inseparable. The will and the mind are in the process of renewal.

The renewal of the mind appears in a parallel Christian *halakah* in Ephesians 4:1–5:20. At the end of the second "walk" is an imperative that is seldom translated with meaning. Ephesians 4:23 in the RSV says "be renewed in the spirit of your minds." There is no Pauline parallel to the idea of "the spirit of your minds." If it is translated as follows there is good background: "Keep on being renewed (*ananeousthai*) by the Spirit in your mind." The idea of the Holy Spirit at work in the human mind is called "the mind of the Spirit" in Romans 8:6, 27.

The main difference is the word for mind, mind-set (*phronēma*) in Romans and mind (*nous*) in Ephesians. In Colossians 3:10 the result was the *neos anthrōpos* (new man) and in Ephesians 4:24 it is *kainos anthrōpos* (new man), but the basic difference between *neos* and *kainos* is that the latter emphasizes quality of life.

The Image of God in Historical Theology

In the history of Christian theology two major views of the image of God have developed. Under the influence of Greek philosophy a twofold view was developed in Catholicism in which the image of God came to focus on man's reason and the likeness on immortality. At the time of the Protestant Reformation the new emphasis on biblical theology did not make a distinction between image and likeness, so Martin Luther identified the image of God with a lost Original Righteousness which is restored in Christ by justification. John Calvin also saw that the likeness is a parallel with the image, but he argued for a relic after the Fall of man from the Original Righteousness of a historical Paradise. A brief survey of the two views will be made.

The image of God in Catholicism. It seems that Philo Judaeus, the Jewish Hellenistic philosopher (c. B.C. 20-A.D. 54), first distinguished the man of Genesis 1:26f. as ideal man from the man of Genesis 2:7 as material man. The Valentinian Gnostics of the second century A.D. found a difference between the image (*selem*) and the likeness (*demut*) in Genesis 1:26.

This distinction between image and likeness was accepted by Greek theology under the influence of Irenaeus of Lyon (*Against Heresies* III, 18, 1; 23:1f.; IV, 38, 3f.; V, 1, 3). The first passage by Irenaeus says both image and likeness were lost by the Fall, and both are restored in Christ. The next two passages refer to Adam before the Fall, and the fourth and fifth have reference to man in Christ.

The dominance of reason in the image of God shows the influence of Greek rationalism, but the emphasis on the incarnation is a rejection of Greek dualism. Reason is not lost at the Fall, but man does become irrational in his opposition to God. "But man, being endowed with reason, and in this respect like to God, having been made free in his will, and with power over himself, is himself the cause to himself, that sometimes becomes wheat and sometimes chaff. Wherefore also he shall be justly condemned, because, having been created a rational being, he lost the true rationality" (IV. 4, 3).

The likeness of God in man is lost through the Fall and restored by the gift of the Spirit. Before the gift of the Spirit fallen man is only body and soul, but the gift of the Spirit makes him a tripartite person in the likeness of God. "But if the Spirit be wanting to the soul, he who is such is indeed of an animal nature, and being carnal, shall be an imperfect being,

possessing indeed the image in his formation, but not receiving the simili-
tude through the Spirit; and thus is this being imperfect" (V. 6, 1).

In the Latin tradition the image of God is identified with the rationality
of the immortal soul. On the basis of belief in the image of God, Augustine
argued from a trinity of memory, understanding and will in man to a Holy
Trinity in God. "We may say then neither that we shall have the image of
God in that trinity which does not exist at present, nor that we have it now
in the trinity which then will exist no longer. We must find, in the rational
or intellectual soul of man, an image of its Creator planted immortally in
its immortal nature" (*De Trinitate* XIV. iv. 6). The image of God in man
and the Holy Trinity in God are both immortal.

Thomas Aquinas was the first Catholic theologian to describe the image as an endowment. Out of this endowment man may act in love, both
in present grace and future glory. In this way Aquinas tries to do justice to
the image of God in both creation and redemption. "Whence the image of
God can be considered three ways in man. In one way, according as man
has a natural aptitude for understanding and loving God, and this aptitude
consists in the very nature of the mind, which is common to all men. In
another way, according as man by act of habit knows God and loves him,
but imperfectly, and this is the image by conformity of grace. And a third
way according as man knows and loves God in act perfectly, but this is the
image according to likeness of glory" (*Summa Theologica* I, 93, 4).

The second and third references in Aquinas are really the present and
the future of the same thing. This twofold distinction is very close to the
biblical view, but the rationalism of Aristotle dominates. Reason has not
been damaged by the loss of immortality in the Fall, and a two-story theology of the natural and the supernatural results.

The image of God in Protestantism. In the Protestant orthodoxy of Martin
Luther there was a violent attack on the rationalism of the universal image
and the image by conformity of grace, between a public and private likeness,
but both are interpreted in terms of the relation of love for God. His commentary on Genesis 1:26; 9:6 rejected the distinction between image and
likeness that had been a part of the Catholic view since Irenaeus in the
second century A.D. The image of God had only one meaning for Luther.

Luther does not reject Augustine's speculation on memory, understanding and will in terms of hope, faith and love, but the dynamic relation of
future hope in 1 Corinthians 15:48 and the present process of renewal in
Ephesians 4:23 leads him to identify the image and likeness of God with
the state of Original Righteousness before the Fall. The image was lost in
the Fall, according to Luther.

Yet he recognized that Genesis 9:6 speaks of man's dignity after Adam
and Eve. Man has dominion over the animals, but for Luther this is only
a "relic" of a lost image, if his sermon on Genesis 1:26 is taken as a norm

for the image of God as Original Righteousness which is lost by the Fall and restored in Christ.[138]

John Calvin makes more of this "relic" of Original Righteousness in man, but he retains the idea that the image is more of a relation than reason. This is a twofold relation to the creator and to creation. Obscure lineaments or a remnant of this image is retained after the Fall. This does not mean there is some part of man untouched by sin, but man is related to God and his creation as a responsible being even in his sin. Perhaps Calvin's view is best stated in his commentary on Genesis 1:26–28 where he says: "But now, although some obscure lineaments of that image are found remaining in us, yet they are so vitiated and maimed that they may truly be said to be destroyed. For besides the deformity which everywhere appears unsightly, this evil is added, that no part is free from the infection of sin."[139] It is most difficult to see how there can still be obscure lineaments that have been destroyed. In his *Institutes* Calvin says the image of God in man was "obliterated" by the Fall (II. 1. 5).

After reading the ambivalent and unsatisfactory exegesis by both Luther and Calvin it is not difficult to see how both Emil Brunner and Karl Barth, locked in battle like theological dinosaurs, could both claim support from Luther and Calvin. The neo-orthodoxy of both Brunner and Barth rejected the idea of a state of Original Righteousness in a primitive Paradise that was enjoyed by only a primal pair called Adam and Eve, yet they often confuse the issue by using the pre-scientific and pre-critical language that goes back to Augustine.

The debate between Brunner and Barth began when Brunner published his small book *Nature and Grace* in 1933 in which he spoke of a "formal" image of God that remains in man even in his sin, and that this is the point of contact (*anknüpfungspunkt* in German) or the possibility by which man can understand the word of God to him (*Wortmächtigkeit*). There is also a "material" image of God that is lost by a transcendental Fall, and this is restored when man in Christ hears the Word of God. In 1937, under the influence of the I–Thou philosophy, Brunner developed the dimension of personal relation to both God and man in his Olaus Petri Lectures on *Truth as Encounter*, but the chief source for understanding his final formulation is *Man in Revolt* (1939), perhaps Brunner's greatest book. However, this amounts to no more than a refinement of language.

Karl Barth's retort to Brunner's *Nature and Grace* was called *Nein! Antwort an Emil Brunner* (*No! Answer to Emil Brunner*). In 1919, Barth, in his *Commentary on Romans*, taught a transcendental Fall much like that in Emil Brunner, yet he later repudiated this in his *Church Dogmatics* I/1

---

138. *Luther's Works*, edited by Jaroslav Pelikan (Saint Louis: Concordia Publishing House, 1958), I, 62-65.
139. Quoted by David Cairns, *op. cit.,* p. 138.

in 1932.[140] In a milder manner than in 1934 Barth rejects Brunner's views on a "point of contact." Faith, he argued, is the only contact with God. In his discussion of "the Word of God and Faith" he says:

> This point of contact is, therefore, not real outside faith but only in faith. In faith a man is created by the Word of God for the Word of God, existing in the Word of God, not in himself, not in virtue of his humanity and personality, nor from the standpoint of creation, for what is possible from the standpoint of creation from man to God has actually been lost through the Fall.[141]

This goes beyond the relic doctrine of Luther and Calvin. No other theologian has so clearly rejected the Old Testament view of the image of God in man from creation. It is also far from clear as to what Barth means by "the Fall."

It was against the background of his own radical pronouncements that Barth made his blast at Brunner in 1934. As late as 1938, in his Gifford Lectures, Barth was defending the radical view that the image of God in man was "annihilated" by "the Fall." With gusto he used the Scottish Confession of 1560 which has the statement that "the image was utterly defaced in man." He was even willing to appeal to the Latin Vulgate which used the words *"ad imaginem et similitudinem ipsius"* (to be the image and likeness of himself) to make the point that God alone could restore his image in man.[142]

After all this over-kill in attacking Emil Brunner, it is astonishing to see Barth take a third position which leads logically to the position of Emil Brunner. Seven years after his Gifford Lectures Barth reversed his radicalism. In his discussion of "Creation as the External Basis of the Covenant" he comments on Genesis 1:26f. as follows: "He would not be man if he were not the image of God. He is the image of God in the fact that he is man."[143] Surely Barth does not mean to say that those outside of Christ are not men at all. Barth is right on target when he sees in the man-woman relation the primary example of the relationship of man to others and the relationship to God as the supreme human relation.

Three years later, in 1948, Barth was coming to grips with scientific anthropology and saying things impossible to harmonize with his heated statements about the annihilation of the image of God by "the Fall." At the close of his discussion of "Humanity as Likeness and Hope" are statements like these:

140. Preface, p. vii.
141. *Op. cit.,* p. 273.
142. *The Knowledge of God and the Service of God* (London: Hodder & Stoughton, 1938), pp. 40-51.
143. *Church Dogmatics*, III/1, p. 184. Cf. pp. 191f.

> God created him in His own image in the fact that He did not
> create him alone but in this connexion and fellowship. . . . God is
> in relationship, and so too is the man created by Him. This is his
> divine likeness. When we view it in this way, the dispute whether
> it is lost by sin finds a self-evident solution. It is not lost.[144]

The image of God includes the *reason* of Catholicism, but the twofold
relation to God and man (and the whole creation) sums up the image of
God in man from the creation.

The long debate between Brunner and Barth was not as fruitless as
the faint-hearted sometimes say. It is doubtful that Brunner would have
otherwise written his great book *Man in Revolt*, and it is almost certain
Barth would not have wrtten his massive work on "the Doctrine of Creation" had the issue been dismissed lightly. Laborious as the reading may
be, there is great reward at the end. Brunner was no doubt right when he
was finally able to rejoice that Barth and he were in agreement.[145] It must
go down as one of the great debates on one of the great ideas of biblical
theology and Christian anthropology.[146]

As long as theology contends for a special salvation history in which
God has disclosed or will disclose himself in a unique historical continuum
of time and space, the position to which David Cairns has brought the
discussion seems most biblical and most valuable. The radical alternative
in which the image of God is no more than human historicity in which man
creates himself is a typical reaction by previous disciples of the early Barth.
It is really a sophisticated example of cradle kicking that leads to an atheistic anthropology that thinks that man can be understood independent of
God.[147] A theistic anthropology is able to avoid both extremes and make a
positive contribution to man's self-understanding in relation to God.

In creation and redemption man exists in relation to God. As image of
God in creation he is responsible to God even in his sin. As image of God
in redemption he reflects the very presence of God. As man exists in love
he reflects the likeness of Christ who is the image of God.

39. Conscience: Man and Morality

Conscience is the human capacity by which the principles of moral responsibility are grasped. It forms a threshold between the animal and the human.

144. *Church Dogmatics*, III/2, p. 324.
145. "The New Barth" in *Scottish Journal of Theology*, Vol. 4, 1951, No. 2, pp. 123-135.
146. Further details with which I have only minor reservations are in David Cairns, *op. cit.*
The conclusion reached by G. C. Berkouwer, *op. cit.*, pp. 100-118, that the image of God
means the imitation of God or the imitation of Christ is correct if lordship over creation
(dominion) is included with the relation of love for God and man. The Old Testament view
is not to be excluded in the interest of the New Testament emphasis.
147. An example of radical historicity is Gordon Kaufman, *Systematic Theology* (New
York: Charles Scribner's Sons, 1968), pp. 329-351.

That is why James Breasted could describe the beginning of human culture and civilization as *The Dawn of Conscience*. Is this also the entrance of sin into the world (cf. Rom. 5:12)? A survey of some biblical teachings and historical theories on conscience may suggest its importance for the understanding of human existence.

The Greek Syneidēsis

The Greek dramatist Menander (342/341-291 B.C.) has a line that says "to every mortal his conscience is a god" (*Monostichoi*, 654). It is possible that the *daimonion* which gave pain or regret to Socrates (469-399) had this idea in mind, but the biblical meaning of conscience seems to employ a more popular concept shaped by Christian experience. A recent study of conscience in the New Testament argues that the statement of Paul in Romans 13:5 is normative not only for Romans but for the whole new Testament.[148] However, the passage is more important for understanding the wrath of God, and a better suggestion for a *locus classicus* in the New Testament on conscience must surely be found in Paul's statement about Gentiles who did not know the law of Moses (Romans 2:14–16):

> *When Gentiles who have not the law do what the law requires,*
> *   they are a law to themselves,*
> *   even though they do not have the law.*
> *They show that what the law requires is written on their hearts,*
> *   while their conscience also bears witness*
> *   and their conflicting thoughts accuse them*
> *   (or perhaps excuse them on that Day when,*
> *   according to my gospel,*
> *   God judges the secrets of men by Jesus Christ).*

The combination of their hearts and their thoughts with the concept of conscience requires some background considerations in both the Old and New Testament.

The moral meaning of the heart has roots in the Old Testament. The article by R. C. Dentan in *The Interpreter's Dictionary of the Bible* says that the heart is generally corrupt, undependable, and evil, but this is hardly true. In Deuteronomic theology one is commanded to love the Lord God with all his heart and to keep God's words in his heart, yet the heart may be lifted up in forgetfulness and pride (Deuteronomy 6:5f.; 8:14). Therefore, it is necessary to turn back to the Lord with the whole heart, for the heart can do what the word of the Lord commands (30:10, 14). The good heart is one that is perfect, yet the tender heart may turn away from the Lord and become hardened (1 Kings 8:61; 11:2; 2 Kings 22:19; Zechariah 7:12).

---

148. C. A. Pierce, *Conscience in the New Testament* (London: SCM Press, 1955), p. 67.

The heart may, therefore, be circumcised or uncircumcised (Jeremiah 4:4; 9:26). It may become desperately corrupt (17:9). Before God the heart should be upright, clean and blameless, and in the time of sin broken and contrite (Psalms 32:11; 34:18; 51:17; 73:13; 119:80). Man may secure a renewed heart from the Lord (Jeremiah 31:33; Ezek. 18:31; 36:26; Psalm 51:10). There seems to be no deviation from the two major possibilities of the heart in the Old Testament (Numbers 15:39; Prov. 23:26; 2 Chronicles 12:14).

The New Testament writers make no radical departures from the Old Testament concept of the heart. The heart can be pure or hard (Matthew 5:8; 19:8). The word of God is held fast by the honest and good heart (Luke 8:15), yet Satan can fill the heart, and it can be so "uncircumcised" that it resists the Holy Spirit (Acts 5:3; 7:51). An evil and unbelieving heart can lead to apostasy from God (Hebrews 3:12).

Paul is the pivotal New Testament source for understanding the meaning of the heart, the mind, and the conscience. As for the heart, it can receive the guarantee of the Holy Spirit and become the realm of light in a world of darkness (2 Corinthians 1:22; 4:6). It is impossible to portray the human heart as a cesspool of corruption when a balanced picture is given. The heart can of course be impure, but the Holy Spirit can flush it clean with love (Romans 1:24; 5:5). The true Jews and the true circumcision are a matter of the heart (2:29). Paul's desire for his Jewish brothers was that they might be saved, but salvation is a matter of the heart (10:1, 9f.). The peace of Christ rules in the Christian heart, Christ dwells there by faith, and the Christian servant serves not his earthly master but the Lord in singleness of heart (Colossians 3:15; Ephesians 3:17; 6:5).

The Johannine writings also retain the Hebrew view of the heart. The devil entered the heart of Judas after he brooded on the betrayal of Jesus for a year (John 6:70; 13:2). On the other hand one of the tests by which one may know he possesses eternal life is that the heart does not condemn (1 John 3:19–22).

The Greek concept of mind (*nous*) in the New Testament is used very much in the sense of the Hebrew use of heart (*lev*). In fact the Septuagint translates *lev* (heart) with both *nous* (mind) and *kardia* (heart). Paul uses the terms as parallels (2 Corinthians 3:14f.; Philippians 4:7). The hardening of the mind and the hardening of the heart are the same (cf. 2 Corinthians 3:14; 4:4; 11:3 with Romans 1:21; 2:5; 16:18). In the same context this is true. In the darkness of their "senseless minds" the Gentiles give themselves up to "the lusts of their hearts" (Romans 1:21, 24).

The meaning of mind differs from that of heart much as knowing and willing do in the English language, yet one may speak of both "the purposes of the heart" and "the secrets of the heart" (1 Corinthians 4:5; 14:25). The Greek concept of mind really has difficulty in displacing the Hebrew concept of heart, but by the time Paul's great letter to the Romans was written in A.D. 55 that dominance was established.

By his mind man is able to perceive (*nooumena*) invisible reality in the visible, although the mind may become reprobate because of the absence of God (Romans 1:20f., 28). Rudolf Bultmann is no doubt correct when he singles out Romans 7:23 for the "full meaning of *nous*."[149] The passage identifies the inner man or inmost self with the mind: "For I delight in the law of God, in my inmost self, but I see in my members another law at war with the law of my mind and making me captive to the law of sin which dwells in my members" (7:22f.). This explication of the two laws refutes the tradition that the heart or mind of man is *by nature* reprobate and depraved. The mind *becomes* reprobate by yielding to "the law of sin" and excluding the light of God's presence.

The mind may be renewed when it makes room for God. "Do not be conformed to this age but be transformed by the renewal of your mind, that you may prove what is the will of God, what is good and acceptable and perfect" (Romans 12:2). This function of proving (*dokimazein*) means making a judgment on what is worthy to be called the will of God. As to the observance or non-observance of holy days Paul says: "Let every one be fully convinced in his own mind" (Romans 14:5).

As Christian anthropology developed in history the concept of conscience became more central for understanding the moral responsibility; thus more complete consideration will be given to the New Testament meaning of this word. Afterward the theological and philosophical modifications of the New Testament teachings will be explored.

The concept of conscience in the New Testament is an adaptation of popular usage in the context of the Christian understanding of God. Conscience as such is the sense of moral responsibility and does not give content to right and wrong. Discernment of what is right and what is wrong is conditioned by experience, education, and environment. Conscience says do the right and reacts against any deviation from one's standard of right and wrong, but conscience without conditioning does not tell what is right. With this preliminary statement the teachings of the New Testament will be examined in six major topics followed by a summary.

1. Conscience in relation to love is a topic in 1 Corinthians. The statement by C. A. Pierce that conscience is "the catchword of Corinth" is made in a derogatory manner, and his prejudice comes to the surface when he insinuates that "disruptive tendencies within the church have made a battle-cry of conscience."[150] An examination of the two passages in 1 Corinthians does indicate that immature Christians and unbelievers have consciences

---

149. *Theology of the New Testament*, tr. Kendrik Grobel (New York: Scribner's, 1952), Vol. I, p. 212.
150. C. A. Pierce, *op. cit.,* p. 65.

that are easily offended, but there is no denigration of the importance of conscience.

In the case of the weak brother in 1 Corinthians 8 there is an impressive description of how Christians may live on one of three different levels. The one who lives on the level of conscience has only recently escaped from the worship of pagan idols, so his conscience is weak and he may not be able to distinguish between eating meat that has been offered to idols and his former idol worship. The associations of sacred meals are powerful, and it takes time for one to overcome such associations.

The one who has advanced from conscience to knowledge (*gnōsis*) knows that the so-called "gods" and "lords" of paganism are unreal, so he does not associate eating meat offered to an idol with the actual worship of the "gods" and "lords" represented by the idol. His real problem is that his pride makes him insensitive to what his example does to a weak brother. His bad influence leads the weak brother to go back to idol worship and perish (1 Cor. 8:11).

The highest level on which a Christian can live is neither conscience nor knowledge, but love (*agapē*), a New Testament term more distinctive than conscience (*syneidēsis*). *Agapē* does not wound the weak brother. Those who live by *agapē* will neither eat meat nor drink wine if such actions cause a brother to stumble and fall back into the pagan life (cf. Romans 14:13–23). Knowledge does indeed puff up but love builds up (1 Cor. 8:1).

As Paul comes to discuss the difference between a communion meal and common meal in 1 Corinthians 10 he forbids participation in the pagan sacrifice when worship is intended (10:14–22), but in the case of a common meal with a pagan unbeliever there is no barrier until the pagan implies that eating the meat is pagan worship. In this case the conscience of the unbeliever becomes involved and the believer should refrain even though he has no personal reason on the grounds of his own conscience (10:23–30). All of this indicates that believers and unbelievers alike have conscience, but experience, education, and general environment give each man's conscience a different content. These passages in 1 Corinthians have far more value than C. A. Pierce has ascribed to them.

2. Conscience in relation to the world is further developed when 2 Corinthians ascribes this moral responsibility to every man. Paul can without hesitation speak to the Corinthians of "our conscience," "every man's conscience," and "your conscience" (1:12; 4:2; 5:11). His own conscience allows him to boast that he has "behaved in the world, and still more toward you, with holiness and godly sincerity, not by earthly wisdom but by the grace of God" (1:12). One can hardly imagine a better way to describe the Christian content of conscience over against the standards accepted in the world.

He commends himself "to every man's conscience in the sight of God" (4:2). It could be argued that this is limited to believing men, but the previous use of conscience in 1 Corinthians 10:29 permits a universal interpretation in which the medium of the Christian becomes the message to the world. The man of the world can see in the messenger how much difference the gospel makes in the manner of one's life.

His appeal to the conscience of the Corinthians is in the same tone. "Therefore, knowing the fear of the Lord, we persuade men; but what we are is known to God, and I hope it is known also to your conscience" (2 Cor. 5:11). These standards of conduct are possible (others, self, God), but the final judge is God. Self is superior to others, but God is superior to both (cf. 1 Cor. 4:1-5).

The older source (1-4, 9-11) in Romans, containing what is perhaps a typical Pauline sermon in a synagogue setting, points up in a powerful way how the Christian conscience is formed by Christ and the Holy Spirit. Absence of pain in the heart can hardly be the sign of a Christian conscience. Indeed, Paul's conscience gave him great sorrow as he pondered "the Jewish problem" of his day. In a moving testimony reminiscent of Moses in Exodus 32:32, Paul says (Romans 9:1-3): "I am speaking the truth in Christ, I am not lying; my conscience bears me witness in the Holy Spirit, that I have great sorrow and unceasing anguish in my heart. For I could wish that I myself were accursed and cut off from Christ for the sake of my brethren, my kinsmen by race."

3. Conscience in relation to the Gentiles has fuller expression in Paul's letter to the Romans. One wonders if his very high view of conscience among the Gentiles and his favorable view toward Roman government was not influenced by his knowledge of such great Roman officials as the Spaniard Gallio and his brother Seneca who had just come to a position of great power at the time Romans was written for Paul by the Roman Tertius (Romans 16:22). Be that as it may, the passages in Romans are most instructive.

Already Romans 2:14-16 rather than 13:5 has been suggested as the *locus classicus* on conscience in the New Testament. Whether Paul was conscious of agreement with Stoicism or using a popular concept is of secondary importance. The high value he places on conscience among Gentiles who did not know the law of Moses is the important point. Whether Paul was trying to convince others or himself or both does not discount what he really says.

With all his qualifications and reservations C. A. Pierce concludes that the Gentiles are "a law unto themselves," a natural moral law. This is shown by three things:

First; their behaviour, their overt acts, reveals that they have accepted standards of some sort for conduct, not entirely other than
those of the Jewish Law: secondly; they suffer this pain, conscience, which warns them that they have done or are doing something morally wrong; and thirdly; their reasons pass judgment on
their conduct (or, perhaps, in their rational discussions with one
another they agree in calling some things right and other things
wrong).[151]

This negative function of conscience does not go beyond the theory
expounded by Emil Brunner in his controversy with Karl Barth. It is true
as far as it goes, but Paul says the conscience of the Gentiles could also
excuse them "on that day when, according to my gospel, God judges the
secrets of men by Jesus Christ" (Romans 2:15f.).

As the Gentiles have the law of conscience, apart from the law of
Moses, so the Christian has the law of a Christian conscience, conditioned
by love, apart from the law of the sword, ordained by God for order and
justice and interpreted as the wrath of God (Romans 13:1–5). The pressure
of the sword does deter disorder and injustice, but this outward restraint
does not promote good citizenship equal to the loyalty of a Christian conscience in the apostolic instruction that says: "Therefore, one must be subject, not only to avoid God's wrath but also for the sake of conscience"
(Romans 13:5). The concept of the state described in Romans 13:1–7 does
not always prevail, for the Christian citizen is at times confronted by the
beast of Revelation 13, but as long as the state is "the servant of God to
execute his wrath on the wrongdoer" (13:4) the Christian conscience is
superior to any military pressure of the state. It is strong enough to rise up
in defiance when the state is unjust.

4. Conscience has a vital relation to faith in the Pastoral Letters of
Paul. This is hardly the place to discuss the question of the Pauline authorship of the Pastorals. The Pauline authorship is far from a closed issue,
as every informed person knows.[152] It is assumed here that these letters
were composed for Paul, while he was alive, by Luke the beloved physician
about A.D. 66-67 (2 Timothy 4:11). Furthermore, the views on conscience
are very close to the brief references in Acts 23:1 and 24:16, written about
A.D. 60.[153]

With these explanations we should take note of some statements on
conscience in Acts. The very terms "good conscience" (23:1) and "clear
conscience" (24:16) prepare the way for the Pastorals. To his Jewish breth-

151. *Ibid.*, p. 85.
152. A good introduction to the problem is that by Glenn Hinson in *Broadman Bible
Commentary* (Nashville: Broadman Press, 1971), Vol. 11, pp. 299-305.
153. See my essay, "A New Chronology for the Life and Letters of Paul," *Perspectives in
Religious Studies*, Vol. III, Number 3, Fall 1976, pp. 248-271.

ren of the Sanhedrin Paul could say: "Brethren, I have lived before God in all good conscience until this day" (23:1). To Felix, the "law and order" Roman governor of Palestine, he broadened his claim to say: "So I always take pains to have a clear conscience toward God and toward men" (24:16). As a Christian and as a Roman citizen his conscience enabled him to declare, this time before Festus, who in A.D. 57 arrived to replace Felix: "Neither against the law of the Jews, nor against the temple, nor against Caesar, have I offended at all" (25:8). That is the meaning of a good and clear conscience.

Conscience has both a positive and a negative function in the Pastorals. The positive function of a good conscience makes it, like the sources of the Jordan, one of the tributaries of love along with a pure heart and sincere faith. The importance of the Hebrew idea of the heart has already been discussed, but here it is associated not only with conscience but with a faith that is free from hypocrisy (1 Timothy 1:5).

When the good conscience is rejected, faith is shipwrecked (1 Timothy 1:19). The pure intentions of the heart may be corrupted; the conscience that knows no more consciousness of sin no longer exists; and faith becomes hypocritical palaver that is professed but not practiced. This is not only possible, for Hymenaeus and Alexander have suffered shipwreck, and Paul excommunicated them by delivering them to the realm of Satan where they would hopefully be taught not to blaspheme. The context would suggest that they had also received the ministerial charge that had been given to Timothy. Still there are those who pretend that such ministerial tragedy does not happen.

The clear or clean conscience is required of deacons (1 Timothy 3:9). There is no apparent difference between a good (*agathē*) and a clear (*kathara*) conscience. In both instances it means that those with such a conscience are free from the charge that they have led others astray. In the case of the deacon he is to be free from the charge that he has a double tongue, or is addicted to much wine, or is greedy for gain (3:8).

This clear conscience Paul claimed for himself (2 Timothy 1:3). This claim takes one back to his defense before Felix where the word used is *aproskopos* (blameless). The context in Acts 24:10–21 makes it abundantly clear that Paul believed he had never deviated from the faith of the patriarchs and prophets. Here C. A. Pierce, raising no questions about the theories of date and authorship embraced by critical orthodoxy, says the writer "appears to have been familiar with St. Paul's mind in the matter."[154] He does indeed!

The negative function of conscience is a description of how one may deviate from the faith. The conscience may become corrupt or defiled (Titus 1:15). The verb *memiantai* used here is the perfect passive of *miainō*, meaning defile or contaminate, as in the ritual defilement of John 18:28.

---

154. *Op. cit.*, p. 95.

The context indicates how it is the very opposite of pure (*kathara*). "To the pure all things are pure, but to the corrupt and unbelieving nothing is pure; their minds and consciences are corrupted." Cf. 1 Corinthians 8:7 where the Greek word *molynō* is used to describe the defiled conscience of the weak brother.

It can hardly be argued that this defilement and deterioration of conscience happens only in the case of those who were never believers. 1 Timothy 4:1–3 should put an end to such argument, but tradition dies hard, especially when it can claim the support of both Augustine and Calvin. The reader will have to argue with Paul, not me, for it was he who said: "Now the Spirit expressly says that in later times some will depart from the faith by giving heed to deceitful spirits and doctrines of demons through the pretensions of liars whose consciences are seared, who forbid marriage and enjoin abstinence from foods which God created to be received with thanksgiving by those who believe and know the truth."

The seared conscience is a better translation of the Greek *kaustēriazō* than the branded conscience. It means that conscience has been burned with a hot iron to deaden the nerve ending, calloused. This cauterizing is done by false doctrine that leads away from the apostolic faith. Strangely enough the doctrines here designated as "doctrines of demons" (i.e. celibacy and abstinence from certain foods) were later imposed upon the faith as obligations under certain circumstances. Such again is the power of ecclesiastical tradition to triumph over the apostolic tradition. The conscience can indeed be cauterized to the point that the false is considered true.

5. Conscience is especially related to God in 1 Peter 2:19; 3:16, 21. The Revised Standard Version obscures the meaning of conscience in 2:19 with the translation "mindful of God." This is perhaps a correct interpretation of the meaning, as is the TEV rendering "because you are conscious of his will," i.e. the will of God. The reason for such paraphrases is found in the bewilderment that a literal translation of "conscience of God" would produce. "Conscience toward God" would be better, for God does not have a conscience, but the essential idea is that one who is conscious of his moral responsibility toward God will endure persecution before he will violate his conscience.

The clear conscience of 3:16, 21 is literally the same words translated elsewhere as good conscience (*syneidēsis agathē*), but a literal translation would be awkward in 3:16. The conscience is kept "good" or clear by a reverence for Christ as Lord in a heart that is willing to suffer for the sake of righteousness, even as Christ has left an example (2:18–25; 3:13–22).

The pledge of this clear or good conscience in Christian initiation appears in the same context of suffering but it has reference to the pledge made to God as one died and rose with Christ in the paschal liturgy of baptism. A pledge was made on the basis of belief in the death and resurrection of Christ. The good Christian is defiled when this confession of faith is abandoned or made in a hypocritical fashion. In Acts, the Pastorals, and 1 Peter the good conscience has the dominant idea of no deviation from the truth or the faith.

6. Conscience in relation to sin is the special emphasis in Hebrews. C. A. Pierce has rightly seen that Hebrews integrates all the ideas associated with the theme of conscience.[155] He has also pointed out that the five passages on conscience in Hebrews constitute five stages of deliverance, but his prejudice against the very concept of conscience delivers him into absurd statements about the negation of conscience in redemption.[156] He claims that Christ delivers one from conscience rather than from the guilt or pain of conscience. Conscience and pain are inseparable in his exposition, but one may have a conscience free from pain.

The first stage recognizes that gifts and sacrifices "cannot perfect the conscience of the worshiper" (9:9). It is the perfection of maturity of conscience that is needed, not the negation of conscience.

The second stage is the sacrifice of Christ by which the conscience may be purified "from dead works to serve a living God" (9:14). Hebrews does not speak of a "conscience *of dead works*," as C. A. Pierce argues, but of the purification of conscience cluttered with dead works.

The third stage is the cleansing of the conscience from sin (10:2). A literal translation of the Greek would be the "conscience of sin," much as the genitive in 1 Peter 2:19 would be the "conscience of God." As "conscience of God" means "consciousness of God," so "conscience of sin" means "consciousness of sin," as the RSV says. The TEV rightly paraphrases: "they would not feel guilty of sin any more." Pierce still persists with "the negation of conscience"!

The fourth step is the free access to God "with a true heart in full assurance of faith, with our hearts sprinkled clean from an evil conscience and our bodies washed with pure water" (10:22). The context of exhortations on faith, hope, and love with the reference to "bodies washed with pure water" may indicate Christian initiation by baptism. In any case it is not a state of deliverance from conscience but "from an evil conscience."

The fifth and final step is the clean conscience in which conduct and confession do not deviate from Christian truth (13:18). The author, perhaps Barnabas about A.D. 69-70, is not without a conscience when he says: "Pray for us, for we are sure that we have a clear conscience, deserving to act honorably in all things." The adjective translated clear in the RSV is *kalos*, and the emphasis on purification in Hebrews certainly justifies the translation (1:3).

155. *Ibid.*, p. 100.
156. *Ibid.*, pp. 101-103.

The Latin Conscientia

As the New Testament views on conscience were developed in the history of the church, at least two views may be detected. At first the Catholic tradition labored to relate conscience to the classical concept of reason in both Greek and Latin thought. After the Protestant Reformation conscience became the foundation for faith and freedom in opposition to authoritarianism and rationalism. The two developments constitute much of the history of Christianity.

Conscience and reason. The Latin word *conscientia* means "knowledge with one another" or "knowledge within oneself," and the general usage indicates moral judgment. The judgment may be reflection or reaction on past performance or the capacity to discern right and wrong in general even before performance. The Latin *conscientia* gives more emphasis to the future direction given by conscience than the Greek *syneidēsis*, but the future reference is not altogether missing in the New Testament use of *syneidēsis* (cf. Romans 2:14–16; 1 Peter 2:19; 3:21).

The Greek fathers used *syneidēsis* in a positive way much as in 1 Peter 2:19. Justin Martyr spoke of a Christian who was willing to be castrated to refute the calumnies circulated against Christians. When the Prefect refused his offer, it is said that he "remarried as he was, content with the approval of his conscience and that of his fellow-believers" (*Apology* 29:3).

Clement of Alexandria spoke of conscience as a positive gift from God (*Stromateis* 2:6:29). It is true that the old pagan idea, in which regret and remorse dominate, is to be found in Clement (*Stromateis* 4:6:37; 7:4:27), but a more balanced view of the negative and positive functions of conscience may be found in his description of conscience as a game in which fouls are avoided but the victor's crown is awarded to the Christian athlete "with a good conscience" for his positive performance (*Quis dives salvetur*, 3:6). Love, according to Clement, reinforces this positive will of the good conscience (*Stromateis* 7:12:79).

Origen of Alexandria pushed this positive concept toward a perfection that claimed for the Christian "the freedom of speech that a clear conscience gives" and that could challenge the devils to convict him of sin (on John 8:46 where this is the challenge of Christ). This sinless perfection needs to be restrained by progressive sanctification, but such statements in the Greek fathers refute the idea that the positive direction of conscience is the product of the Latin *conscientia*.

Jerome did indeed teach that the positive function of conscience was not extinguished by the Fall. In his allegorical manner he saw lust, anger, and reason as the first three figures of Ezekiel 1:5, but the fourth figure "which the Greeks call conscience" remained in Cain when he left Paradise.

Jerome also, through a copyist's error of *synderesis* for *syneidēsis*, became the source for the medieval distinction between general principles (*synderesis*) and particular applications (*conscientia*). This second idea, which laid the foundation for a systematic statement on conscience, was developed in his commentary on Ezekiel 6.

Augustine, following Jerome, thought a good conscience could become the restoration of Paradise upon the earth (*De Genesis ad litteram*, 12:34). Unfortunately he did not follow his Latin predecessor Tertullian who believed a child is born in this Paradise of innocence and experiences guilt only when he or she reaches the age of accountability (*De baptismo*, 18; *De anima*, 38f.).

Alexander of Hales, the founder of the Franciscan school of theology, argued that decisions made by an erroneous conscience were binding until there was further enlightenment. This was based upon the belief that good could be used for evil ends (alms, prayer, fasting) and bad could be used for good ends (visiting a brothel to help the inmates). This "situation ethics" of medieval Catholicism actually absolutized conscience, for all one needed to do was to be conscientious. Anything agreeing with conscience, however erroneous, was right (*Summa*, 2-2ae:3:3:3).

Bonaventure and other Franciscans used the concept of *synderesis* to designate the natural inclination of the will or affections toward good, even though reason, blinded by the error of heresy or the sin of passion, could block this "drift" toward good and end in damnation. For him conscience was the result of habit, an act of the will, voluntarism (II *Sent.* 39:2:1c).

Albert the Great, Thomas Aquinas and other Dominicans taught that conscience was the result of a rational judgment in which general principles were applied to particular situations. This rationalism of Aquinas, built on the philosophy of Aristotle, defined *synderesis* as habitual knowledge of moral action, while *conscientia* is the application of the moral law of nature to particular actions (III *Sent.* 24:2:23). Knowledge corrects the erroneous conscience of Alexander of Hales. This application includes both the inclination toward good and aversion to evil, the positive and negative functions of conscience.

The rationalism of Thomas was greatly modified when confronted by the so-called invincible ignorance of pagan people. The Spanish Jesuit theologian Francisco de Suarez found it necessary to go beyond both the Franciscans and the Dominicans by recognizing that people ignorant of truth may do good, but this seems nearer to the voluntarism of the Franciscans than to the rationalism of the Dominicans (*De bonitate et malitia actuum*, 6:1:12). The good thing is the good will. This prepares the way for the Reformation debate on grace and free will.[157]

157. *A Catholic Dictionary of Theology*, II, 100-102.

Conscience and freedom. A new note was sounded when Martin Luther wrote, as one of his three so-called "Reformation writings" of 1520, a stirring call entitled *The Freedom of the Christian Man*. The freedom came from justification by faith without the works of the law and the performance of good works. At the heart of this experience was release from a tortured conscience, and the result was peace with God.

At the Diet of Worms in 1521 the distinguished secretary, John Eck, tried to persuade Luther to recant with the words: "Lay aside your conscience, Martin; you must lay it aside because it is in error and it will be safe and proper for you to recant."[158] These were the words that set off the explosion that rocked the Christian world. About the last thing Luther could do was to lay aside his conscience. It is really astonishing how often the works of Luther speak of this quest for a quiet conscience.

The quiet conscience was the flower of Christian freedom. The guilty conscience is in bondage to sin, and God alone, in his great act of justification by faith, can set the conscience free. In his book *The Bondage of the Will* (1526), attacking the rationalistic view of freedom in Erasmus' book *The Freedom of the Will*, he says: "So you bid adieu meanwhile to God and to conscience — for how does it concern Erasmus what God wills in these matters and what is good for the conscience . . . ?"[159] For Luther the conscience is bound only by the commandment of God, not by laws, religious or civil. His attack on Erasmus is perhaps his clearest statement on the freedom of conscience, but the value of conscience is well summarized in his *Table Talk*, December, 1532, when he said: "The greatest gift is to have a conscience pacified by the Word. For this did God permit his Son to die, that we might have a good conscience."[160]

In a more systematic manner John Calvin also discussed conscience in the context of freedom. His definition of conscience has shaped the popular meaning of the term. "The definition must be sought in the etymology of the word. For as men, when they apprehend the knowledge of things by the mind and intellect, are said to know, and hence arises the term knowledge or *science*, so when they have a sense of the divine justice added as a witness which allows them not to conceal their sins, but drags them forward as culprits to the bar of God, that sense is called *conscience*. For it stands as it were between God and man, not suffering man to suppress what he knows in himself; but following him on even to conviction" (*Institutes* III. XIX. 15). With this definition Calvin goes on to discuss the New Testament passages on conscience (*Institutes,* III. XIX. 16).

At another place in the *Institutes* Calvin found it necessary to return to this definition of conscience with the references in the New Testament.

158. *Luther's Works* (Philadelphia: Fortress Press, 1958), Vol. 32, p. 130.
159. *Ibid.*, Vol. 33, p. 48.
160. *Ibid.*, Vol. 54, p. 64.

Some of his readers were puzzled by Romans 13:5, a passage used much by Luther to support civil authority, but Calvin makes a distinction between what he calls "the external forum and the forum of conscience" (IV. X. 3-5). Ecclesiastical and civil law are never superior to conscience. The forum of conscience has reference to God, and nothing must be allowed to come between the conscience and God. The dictates of conscience have become a challenge to all future dictators, ecclesiastical or civil. The very foundations of democracy and "the free world" have been laid down by the French Reformer in Geneva.

Calvinism, however, did not always live up to the high ideals of freedom of conscience, and Lutheranism was more in opposition to the tyranny of Rome than to the domination of the state. The principle of *cujus regio, ejus religio*, by which a ruler determines the religion of his subjects, meant to change your religion when you change your flag. On English soil Thomas More, at his trial in 1535, tried to put conscience above the state, but Henry VIII had him beheaded at the Tower of London. The Catholic More had expressed a true leaning toward Calvin's doctrine of conscience when he said: "Ye must understand that in things touching conscience every true and good subject is more bound to have respect to his said conscience and to his soul than to any other thing in all the world beside; namely when his conscience is in such sort as mine is, that is to say, where the person giveth no occasion of slander, of tumult, and sedition against his Prince, as it is with me; for I assure you that I have not hitherto this hour disclosed and opened my conscience and mind to any person living in all the world."[161] A Calvinist would not have kept so quiet!

When the Baptist Thomas Helwys began to circulate his *Declaration of the Mystery of Iniquity* (1611-12) with its plea for religious toleration and the freedom of conscience in man's relation to God there was great opposition from the state, and Helwys met his death in obscurity. His call for religious liberty was too much for the King James to whom the Authorized Version of the Bible (1611) was dedicated. Said Helwys:

> The king is a mortall man, and not God, therefore hath no power over the immortal soules of his subjects, to make Lawes and Ordinances for them, and to set spiritual Lords over them. If the king have authority to make spiritual Lords and Lawes, then he is an immortall God and not a mortall man.[162]

In New England where Congregational Calvinism became dominant, freedom of conscience was rejected when Roger Williams came in search of religious liberty. Williams was expelled from Massachusetts and took

---

161. From *A Catholic Dictionary of Theology* (London: Thomas Nelson and Sons, 1967), II, 102.
162. *The Mistery of Iniquity* (1612), published by The Baptist Historical Society (London: The Kingsgate Press, 1935), after p. XXIII.

refuge among the Indians in Providence in 1636, where he founded the first Baptist church in the colonies. On his return to England to procure a charter he wrote *The Bloody Tenent of Persecution for the Cause of Conscience* (1644). Other settlers in Massachusetts were imprisoned for preaching on religious liberty based on belief in the freedom of conscience in matters related to God.

William Penn the Quaker wrote a tract, *The Great Case of Liberty of Conscience* (1670). Penn defined religious liberty as "not only a mere liberty of mind in believing or disbelieving this or that principle or doctrine but the exercise of ourselves in a visible way of worship, upon our believing it to be indispensably required at our hands that if we neglect it for fear or favour of any mortal man we sin and incur divine wrath."[163]

These popular documents on conscience led to philosophical theories on the subject. The *Sermons, Dissertation on Virtue and Analogy of Religion* by Bishop Joseph Butler (1692-1752) developed the idea of conscience as a safe guide to action. By intuition the honest man knows what is good and what is bad. Butler argued that true morality is living in accordance with human nature, the basic elements of which are self-love, benevolence, and conscience. He attached supreme authority to conscience as a gift from God along with the Bible. The two parts of his *Analogy of Religion, Natural and Revealed to the Constitution and Course of Nature* anticipated much that was to appear later in the moral philosophy of Immanuel Kant (1724-1804).

Kant called conscience the categorical imperative. This he defined as an absolute moral law unconditionally binding on every rational being. His *Metaphysics of Morals* (1785) began with the declaration: "There is nothing wholly good without qualification either in the world or without it except the good will." The absoluteness of the moral imperative enabled Kant to argue for God as the moral law-giver, for freedom to obey its demands, and for immortality as the possibility for perfection when demand and obedience are one. Much of Protestant liberalism has been an elaboration of Kant's concepts, and some moralists have used the moral judgment as the basis for a whole religious philosophy. A. E. Taylor's Gifford Lectures on *The Faith of a Moralist* (1930) is a prime example.

The conflict between the absoluteness of the human conscience and external authority was a problem with which John Henry Newman (1801-1890) wrestled most of his life. Catholics have called him *doctor conscientiae*.[164] He believed every man could hear the voice of conscience, and he was to obey it, but a man should not confuse his conscience with God. It could lead into error, especially when each person regarded his own conscience as absolute.

163. From *A Catholic Dictionary of Theology*, II, 103.
164. *A Catholic Dictionary of Theology*, II, 103.

Conservative Protestantism did not trust the authority of conscience as did Protestant liberalism. The almost absolute authority of conscience sounded too man-centered for God-centered conservatism. The New Testament teachings on conscience were recognized, but the Catholic idea of a *synderesis*, an organ untouched by "the Fall" and inclined toward the good, was rejected. There was and is a distinct tendency to think only of the negative function of conscience, with the commandments of God as the chief source of conviction for sin. As Newman modified the authority of conscience with the authority of the church, so conservative Protestantism falls back on the authority of Scripture. The doctrine of human corruption aroused doubt about the trustworthiness of conscience as the voice of God.[165]

Much modern thought has discounted the importance of conscience. Speaking rather of moral judgment, the authority of conscience has been made as fallible as human reason and experience. A more radical tendency has all but discarded the very idea. Friedrich Nietzsche (1844-1900) thought he could trace the idea of conscience to biological evolutionism which viewed a bad conscience as animal instincts thwarted by human civilization. Sigmund Freud (1856-1939) saw conscience as the product of unconscious activity that was never allowed to become conscious. This imperfect development he called the Super Ego, i.e. the internalization of moral standards approved by parents, teachers, and other authority figures. Martin Heidegger (1889-1976) and other existential philosophers eliminated the moral quality of conscience and looked upon it as the self-seeking realization. This is more like Freud's description of the Ego.

When all of these ideas are added together there is still a picture of man's moral nature by which he *feels* that he should do what is right, although his reasoned views of right and wrong are conditioned by all his experiences both conscious and unconscious. The authority of Scripture and the authority of society, ecclesiastical or civil, are able to appeal to man because there is this point of contact that the New Testament and other Christian writings call conscience. Without this there is no man. This has led to the most important question in modern thought: What is man?

40. What is Man?

The answers to this question in modern thought have been numerous, but the light thrown on this question in biblical theology is often hidden under an intellectual bushel. As in most theology that I have advocated, the procedure has been first of all a careful study of some crucial biblical concepts on man in his many relations, then soundings into theology, philosophy,

---

165. G. C. Berkouwer, *Man: The Image of God*, tr. Dirk W. Jellema (Grand Rapids: Wm. B. Eerdmans, 1962), pp. 171-177.

and the sciences to illustrate the realism of biblical thought and its relevance to human existence.

When Psalm 8 raised the question used as the title of this chapter there was little doubt in the mind of the author as to the answer. His question was an exercise in wonder at his position in the great panorama of creation and in worship of the majestic Name that had disclosed himself as the source of man's dignity and the hope of man's destiny. His orientation was thoroughly theological, but that does not discount the value of his perspective for the understanding of technological man. It is indeed the light that further illuminates man's darkness. It is the major perspective that makes man more than a monkey.

Before we examine details, we will survey some answers to this question that have dominated and still do shape man's self-understanding. There is almost no end to these so-called answers, but the major options offered modern man follow.

Special attention will be given to the "big four" among the options, but other light will be used when available. Many Christian theologians have been able to incorporate these answers in a theological anthropology, but no one option is complete and adequate for man's understanding of his true self without the "light from above."

Biological Man

The major movement in modern thought that marked the boundary between pre-scientific and pre-critical views of man and the movements which studied both man and the Bible in a historical manner was and still is the theories of evolution. Evolution is not one uniform theory. The central problem is man's relation to the whole of reality which includes not only nature but also God. For this reason at least two general types of theories may be distinguished at the very beginning. They are the naturalistic and the theistic.

The naturalistic theories have adopted the agnosticism of Darwinism which neglected man's relation to God. Although Charles Darwin (1809-1882) himself at one time contemplated the vocation of a clergyman, the belief in an environment of man that included God never gained a dominant place in his theories. His works *The Origin of Species* (1859) and *The Descent of Man* (1871), therefore, stirred up "a storm in a Victorian teacup," as C. E. Raven once called the controversy.[166]

The ideas of natural selection and the survival of the fittest have remained the central concepts in one set of theories down to this day. Unfortunately these are the only theories associated with the term evolution in the mind of the average conservative Christian.

166. *Science, Religion, and the Future* (New York: The Macmillan Company, 1944), pp. 33-50.

A very different cluster of evolutionary concepts comes to the fore in the development of theistic evolution. A leading figure in the new currents of evolutionary thinking was the French Jew Henri Bergson (1859-1941). His works *Time and Free Will* (1889), *Matter and Memory* (1896), *Creative Evolution* (1907), and *Two Sources of Morality and Religion* (1932) challenged static naturalism and intellectualism at the very foundation of knowledge. Bergson believed that intellect is subordinate to both instinct in animals and intuition in man. Reality is dynamic and progressive and makes room for freedom and creativity. At the root of all reality is the impulse or life-force, which he called *élan vital* in French.

A system of this type does not exclude either morality or religion. Many Roman Catholic theologians who were dissatisfied with traditional theology embraced this vitalism, but they were formally condemned as "modernists" by Pope Pius X in his decree *Lamentabili*, July 3, 1907.[167] However, theistic evolutionary theories in the Roman Catholic Church did not die as the comprehensive evolutionism of the French Jesuit Pierre Teilhard de Chardin (1881-1955) indicates.[168]

The polarization of thought over naturalistic evolution surfaced only one year after Darwin's *Origin of Species* was published. At the Oxford meeting of the British Association in 1860 Thomas Henry Huxley clashed with Samuel Wilberforce, Bishop of Oxford, on the controversial issue. Wilberforce suggested that Huxley descended from a monkey, but Huxley retorted that this would be more honorable than descent from a dishonest clergyman. The name of Huxley is still a term of reproach for bad boys among the pious.

Happily the great Henry Drummond, scientific friend of D. L. Moody and author of many writings on science and religion, turned the theory of evolution into an apologetic for belief in the purpose of God and the immortality of man. Conservative reactionaries may well be admonished to read Drummond's sober reflections in *The Ascent of Man* (1894), an obvious response to Darwin's book *The Descent of Man* (1871).

One of the most profound probings of this line of thought is the all too neglected writing of John W. Oman, *The Natural and the Supernatural* (1931). Much in the spirit of Rudolf Otto's classic *The Idea of the Holy* (1917), Oman describes man as an amphibian with both a natural and a supernatural environment. As man can develop his awareness of the natural, so can he arrive at an authentic awareness of God. Both Otto and Oman were indebted to the *Speeches on Religion* (1799) by F. D. E. Schleiermacher. The advanced students of the late W. O. Carver of Southern

---

167. A brief summary may be found in the article "Modernism" in *The Oxford Dictionary of the Christian Church*.
168. There is now a Teilhard Centre for the Future of Man in London that publishes regularly *The Teilhard Review*. Some of the leading anthropologists of the world sponsor this publication.

Baptist Theological Seminary were required to master Oman. Carver was very sympathetic with what he called "creative emergent evolution."

The views of Julian Huxley, a grandson of T. H. Huxley, are much wider than the narrow naturalism of the nineteenth century, but they do not go beyond evolutionary humanism.[169] His book *New Bottles for New Wine* (1957) put the new wine of humanistic culture into the new bottles of creative evolution, using Henri Bergson's theory of the three levels of matter, life, and mind. These steps led him toward a new cultural synthesis. In the context of scientific cosmology the level of matter is the slow cosmic process that began about five billion years ago as physical and chemical interaction. With the appearance of life the cosmic process quickened into biological complexity and transformation. The emergence of mind marks the beginning of the third level of psychosocial interaction and even greater complexity.

If the question is asked why there is this movement from the lower to the higher in apparent stages of progress, the best Julian Huxley can do is to say this is due to "a self-operating, self-transforming process which in its course generates both greater variety and higher levels of organization."[170] References to a "self" in a naturalistic process is a foreign language that sounds more like pantheism than atheism. The prospect for a further level beyond the psychosocial is not entertained by Huxley as a possibility. Man himself is the crown and completion of the evolutionary complexity and further transformation in human culture.

At the very point where Julian Huxley runs into a *cul-de-sac* Pierre Teilhard makes his distinctive contribution as a scientist and as a Christian. Teilhard de Chardin includes all the phenomena on which Julian Huxley based his theory of humanistic naturalism, but Teilhard sees a purpose running through all progress. In no sense did Teilhard show hostility toward scientists and scientific data. He was in fact a personal friend of Julian Huxley. He even tried to separate his scientific observation from his Christian beliefs. This is best seen in his two most important books.

His scientific observations are best summarized in *The Phenomenon of Man* (1955). The whole universe is seen as a progressive unfolding of the purpose of God. The three levels of creative evolution move from simplicity to greater and greater complexity and are described as *lithosphere*, the stage of matter alone, the *biosphere*, when life develops to the threshold of consciousness, and the *nousphere* in which mind more and more takes control of the process and directs the natural laws toward ultimate purpose. The final stage is the omega point when all things are gathered up into God (cf. 1 Cor. 15:28).

---

169. Perry LeFevre, *Understandings of Man* (Philadelphia: The Westminster Press, 1966), pp. 29-44.
170. *Ibid.*, p. 30.

Teilhard's theological insights led him to use such New Testament terms as Christification for the process and *plērōma* (fulness) for the final outcome (cf. Romans 11:12, 25). The vision has been criticized as too optimistic in the light of natural and moral evil, but Teilhard is speaking of the process as a whole in the light of the final prospect. It really sounds much like Paul writing in the context of modern science (cf. Romans 8:28).

This theological context of the natural process is further elaborated in a devotional writing called *The Divine Milieu* (1927 in French). How the Apostle Paul would have been at home with these words by Teilhard: "Thanks to the multitude of individuals and vocations, the Spirit of God insinuates itself everywhere and is everywhere at work."[171] In this light the whole universe is a sacrament in which the lower levels are used to point to the higher and ultimate intention of God. The central fact in this process is the incarnation of God in a man. At the center of the evolutionary process and at the consummation is the true man.[172]

Political Man

The inhumanity of man to man in modern industrial society has contributed to the explosive revolt of communism with its distinctly social view of human nature. As evolution brought on discussion as to man's relation to nature, so communism stimulated new questions on man's relation to man.

The central figure in communism is still a German Jew, reared as a Christian, named Karl Marx (1818-1883). In many ways the political theories of Marx reflect his experiences as a rebel against European society. In his early life in Germany he was greatly influenced by the philosophical idealism of G. W. F. Hegel while a student at the University of Berlin, and in 1842-43 he wrote a critique of Hegel's *Philosophy of Right*. His view, expressed through the *Rheinische Zeitung*, which he edited, resulted in his two years of exile in Paris in 1843-45.

In 1845 his *Theses on Feuerbach* reflected a radical reversal of the philosophy of Hegel. Hegel began with the thesis of an Absolute Spirit that evolved into the antithesis of matter and moved toward the synthesis of mind with matter in a panentheism of self-realization. When applied to social conditions the right-wing Hegelian viewed the Prussian state as the realization of the ideal society. Left-wing Hegelians who saw the faults of Prussian society argued for a future synthesis that required more revolution than evolution.

The philosophy of Ludwig Feuerbach, whose *Essence of Christianity*

171. *The Divine Milieu* (New York: Harper & Brothers, 1960), p. 85.
172. For a further summary of Teilhard's view of man see Perry LeFevre, *op. cit.*, pp. 45-62; Doran McCarty, *Teilhard de Chardin* (Waco, Texas: Word Books, Publisher, 1976), pp. 65-71. For a survey of evolutionary philosophies see E. C. Rust, *Evolutionary Philosophies and Contemporary Theology* (Philadelphia: The Westminster Press, 1969).

was published in 1841, caused Marx to reject Hegel's philosophy. Marx adopted Feuerbach's notion of materialistic or economic determinism and the ideas of God and religion in general as an expression or projection of man's alienation from the fruits of his labors in a capitalistic society. Marx also read the ideas of the British economist Adam Smith whose *Wealth of Nations* (1776) was the capitalist "Bible," and he revolted violently against this accumulation of wealth from another man's labor. He was also a careful student of the French socialist Claude Saint-Simon (1760-1825) whose main thesis was the organization of society for the brotherhood of man.

By 1845 Marx was no longer welcome in Paris, so he spent the years 1845-49 in Brussels. During this period his economic determinism found expression in other works: *The Holy Family* (1845), *The German Ideology* (1846), written with Friedrich Engels, and *The Poverty of Philosophy* (1847). In 1848 he and Engels published the *Manifesto of the Communist Party*, and after the failure of several efforts at revolution he was forced into his third exile, this time in London where he lived and wrote in poverty for the rest of his life. His *Critique of Political Economy* was published in 1859, but his most substantial writing was his attack on capitalism, *Das Kapital* (1867f.), the "Bible" of Communism.

The ideas he and Engels called "scientific socialism" began to develop away from the Hegelian idea of alienation toward a more positive proposal by which the dilemma of capitalism could be overcome. All evil seemed to him to be concentrated around private property. At least he did not advocate the abolition of money and the return to a primitive society with no specialized labor. He advocated the overthrow of capitalism and the dictatorship of the working class, the proletariat in French, which he devoutly believed would lead to a classless society in which each person would contribute according to his ability and receive according to his need. He certainly did not visualize the permanent dictatorship that developed in Stalin's Russia, and he failed to see how decentralized private property could remedy the sense of man's alienation and create the genuine community toward which he aimed.[173]

Some Christian realists who never became converts to atheistic materialism and the scientific socialism of Marx were able to see the problem of alienation and the need for more human communities that played such a role in the raging soul of the radical Jew. It was really the method of violent revolution that they rejected, not the cry for community.

In the most highly industrialized area of America, Reinhold Niebuhr (1892-1971) formulated what he called Christian realism, and he offered

---

173. Further summaries and brief guides to Marx are in David Cairn's *The Image of God in Man*, Second Edition (London: Collins, 1973), pp. 214-232; Perry LeFevre, *op. cit.*, pp. 63-75; Leslie Stevenson, *Seven Theories of Human Nature* (Oxford: Clarendon Press, 1974), pp. 46-60.

little comfort for those who without conscience watch the rich get richer and the poor get poorer. Niebuhr was always fascinated by the socialist dream of a brotherhood of man that was so much a part of the Social Gospel of liberal Protestantism, but he had a more realistic view of human sin, his name for alienation! His students will never forget how he introduced them to some of the very social radicals that fascinated Marx. The Levellers, The Diggers, The Fifth Monarchy Men and other radicals opposed to Puritan dictatorship in the age of English Puritanism became familiar to students from well-heeled homes, and many of them rallied around "old Reiny" to challenge complacent social conservatism in the Protestant pew.

The voices of the biblical prophets were heard afresh in his writings *Does Civilization Need Religion?* (1928), *Moral Man and Immoral Society* (1932), *Beyond Tragedy* (1938), *The Nature and Destiny of Man* (1941-43), *Faith and History* (1949), *Christian Realism and Political Realism* (1954), *The Self and the Dramas of History* (1955), *An Interpretation of Christian Ethics* (1956), and *Man's Nature and His Communities* (1965). The Christian realism of his greatest work, *The Nature and Destiny of Man*, the title of his Gifford Lectures for 1939, and his final testimony in *Man's Nature and His Communities* (1965) are genuine reassurances of the relevance of the Christian faith when one has just been baked with the blistering criticisms of Protestant capitalism in Marx's *Critique of Political Economy* and *Das Kapital*.

The Nature and Destiny of Man penetrates the pride and alienation of man as no Marxist had ever done. In jest students of Niebuhr often said he sincerely believed in "the Fall of Man in Adam" but the Adam was Adam Smith! Indeed, Niebuhr believed much of man's alienation from himself and others may be found in industrial society, but man's deepest alienation is from God. Even though he rejected the pre-scientific, pre-critical view of a One Man–One Sin Fall about six thousand years ago, he saw in the Paradise story of Genesis 2–3 a profound paradigm of what happens to every male and every female in their relation to God.

Man's attempt to overcome his finitude in his freedom by putting himself in the place of God grows out of anxiety. His pride is the basic source of his estrangement, which manifests itself in so many ways in society. Out of this self-love and the resultant guilt man attempts to escape by abandonment to various forms of sensuality. He was sharply critical of Sigmund Freud for locating self-love in the *id* rather than in the conscious *ego* where self-interest is supreme.[174]

Love and justice were never separated in Niebuhr's prescriptions for healthy communities. Love alone in liberal theology leads toward a naive sentimentalism in which the social norms for justice are neglected. Situation

---

174. *The Nature and Destiny of Man* (New York: Charles Scribner's Sons, 1941), Vol. I, pp. 178-240.

ethics, as the liberal ethic was later called, is not the social ethics of Niebuhr's Christian realism. Niebuhr shows the relevance of *agapē*-love to man in his social relations and makes it a corrective to communist dictatorships. A balance of power is a prerequisite for justice, and the mutuality of love makes this balance possible.

Among the many places where Niebuhr summarized and revised his thought, two are of special interest for his understanding of man. *The Self and the Dramas of History* (1955) has details on the dialogue of the self with itself, others and God. *Man's Nature and His Communities* (1965) is a review of his major views. The first was written as he recovered from a serious illness, and in the second he was conscious that this could be the last effort of an old man to express his major ideas.

As he reflected on the changing perspectives in his thought, he confessed a movement away from Protestant individualism and an increasing appreciation for the communal concerns in both Judaism and Catholicism. A little quip from the social-gospel Episcopal Bishop of Detroit, Charles Williams, helped him to express his social ethics and the communal relations of man. Williams was often quoted as saying: "In the weightier matters of social justice, there are only two Christians in Detroit, and they are both Jews."[175]

The long chapter that gives this last book its title is a review of major political theories in European history. A dialectic that attempts to balance belief in individual freedom in idealism with the concrete communal relations recognized by realism runs through all that he says. His final paragraph contains the gist of his thought.

> This final ironic culmination of the dreams of the ages for the fulfillment of a universal community, consonant with the obvious universality of the human spirit, reveals the whole scope of the relation of human nature, with its finite and indeterminate dimensions of human freedom, to the organization of human communities. They are always more limited than the projects of human imagination. They reveal that, while man may be universal as free spirit, he is always parochial and tribal in the achievement of organized community. Thus we are witnessing a final revelation of the incongruity of human existence.[176]

This is the central concern of his Christian realism.

Details of man's inhuman tribalism including race, language, and class distinctions expose the dilemma of American culture where the greatest goals of the human spirit are hampered by historical realities of human nature.[177] The relevance of Christian realism to this human situation re-

---

175. *Man's Nature and His Communities* (New York: Charles Scribner's Sons, 1965), p. 18.
176. *Ibid.*, p. 83.
177. *Ibid.*, pp. 84-105.

quires a return to the real self in both its self-seeking and self-giving paradox. Protestant individualism may lead to social disaster if it is not restrained by more Christian communal concerns.[178]

Criticisms of Niebuhr's polemic against pietistic sectarianism are often justified, but his searching analysis makes one aware that where there is no self-giving love in social relations there is no evidence that the human experience is that of the Holy Spirit of the living God.

Psychological Man

Psychoanalysis is a term invented by Sigmund Freud (1856-1939), who may be called the founder of a movement that has shaped a new understanding of man's relation to society and religion in general and of himself in particular. The development of the theory may be understood in the light of personal development, one of the fundamental concepts of Freud. At least three periods are clearly marked.[179]

The first period was physiological in orientation. Born of Jewish parents in Freiberg, Moravia, Freud lived in Vienna most of the time between the ages of 4 and 82. The last year of his life was spent in exile in London. As a medical student he worked first for E. W. von Bruecke in a physiological laboratory and then for T. H. Meynert in a psychiatric clinic. He started practice as a neurologist in 1886 to make money for his marriage, but this was to be his work for the rest of his life. A year of study in Paris in 1885 under Jean Charcot had turned him toward this practice.

The decisive direction in his theories came from his contact with Josef Breuer, a Viennese physician, who told him of an extraordinary experience of hysteria in which a girl in a state of hypnotic somnambulism was able to relate impressions about her relations with a sick father. This led to her recovery. In 1895 Breuer and Freud published *Studies on Hysteria*, an explanatory theory which they called *catharsis*.[180] This became the starting point of what became psychoanalysis.

The physiological orientation in this period appears in *Project for a Scientific Psychology*, written about the same time but published in 1950. His scientific psychology had the weaknesses of Marx's scientific sociology in its subordination to positivism. Freud made an abortive attempt to find a material basis for psychology in the brain. David Cairns has rightly emphasized the lingering legacy of naturalistic determinism in the writing of Freud.[181]

Soon Freud switched from hypnotism to free association as his method of analysis. This enabled him to study the patient's resistance when repressed experiences were uncovered, and the transference of emotion to the

178. *Ibid.*, pp. 106-125.
179. Leslie Stevenson, *op. cit.*, pp. 61ff.
180. See the article "Psychoanalysis" by Freud in *Encyclopedia Britannica*.
181. *Op. cit.*, pp. 233-252.

analyst. Beginning in 1897 Freud used his method on himself, and this approach has remained a practice in training professional psychoanalysts.

The second period of development turned more toward normal mental life. This normative period began with the publication of *The Interpretation of Dreams* (1900), the writing Freud regarded as his best contribution. *The Psychopathology of Everyday Life* (1901) attributed everyday errors to "Freudian slips," as they have been called. The *Three Essays on the Theory of Sexuality* (1905) led to the superficial view that sexuality means no more than the desire to copulate, after having passed already through the oral and anal stages, but Freud broadened the idea to include all forms of pleasure. Many students of Freud regard the *Five Lectures on Psycho-analysis* (1909) as the best introduction to his thought, and the Pelican book *Two Short Accounts of Psycho-analysis* includes these lectures plus a later work *The Question of Lay Analysis* (1926).[182] Others would include the summary of his theories in the *Introductory Lectures on Psycho-Analysis* at the University of Vienna, 1915-17.

The major concept in Freud's most mature thought was that of the *unconscious* mental state. The unconscious is the inner life of repression, suppression and sublimation that must be distinguished from the preconscious and the conscious. The preconscious can be recalled almost at will, but the unconscious requires psychoanalysis. The conscious is only the tip of the iceberg above the great mass of the unconscious life. There is no doubt that the concept of the unconscious is a great contribution to man's self-understanding.[183]

The third period of Freud's development shifts to social questions. The application of his theories to anthropology in *Totem and Taboo* (1913-14) indicated a new trend, but this becomes more pronounced after the First World War. There seems to be even an "unconscious" religious interest in *Beyond the Pleasure Principle* (1920) in which the death instinct was introduced alongside the fundamental postulate of a life instinct of sex and self-preservation. During this period Freud discovered he had cancer, the major cause for his death.

It is true that his *Group Psychology and the Analysis of the Ego* (1921) seems to forget the instinct of death, but that is due to a new interest in the structure of the self. This was most fully developed in *The Ego and the Id* (1923) in which Freud developed his earlier instinct theory into the tripartite structure of *id* or the factor of desire, the *ego* or reason and the *superego* or moral conscience. The development of the pleasure principle collides with the reality principle of the objective world. The *ego* is confronted with

---

182. Leslie Stevenson, *op. cit.*, p. 63.
183. A philosophical study is Alasdair MacIntyre, *The Unconscious* (New York: Humanities Press, 1958).

the task of holding the *id* and *superego* within the bounds of reason! The *ego* is the referee between two irreconcilable enemies.

A sociological analysis of religion found fullest expression in *The Future of an Illusion* (1927) in which belief in a heavenly father is reduced to a projection of the image of the earthly father. Freud did not develop a death of God theory, but the application of the sexual idea of the Oedipus complex would lead logically to this conclusion. In the Greek myth Oedipus killed his father and married his own mother.

The idea of the death instinct returns on a cosmic scale at the end of *Civilization and Its Discontents* (1930), a writing in which the conflict between the pleasure principle and the reality principle ends in tragedy for mankind. He says:

> The fateful question of the human species seems to me to be whether and to what extent the cultural process developed in it will succeed in mastering the derangements of communal life caused by the human instinct of aggression. In this connection, perhaps the phase through which we are passing deserves special interest. Men have brought their powers of subduing the forces of nature to such a pitch that by using them they could now very easily exterminate one another to the last man. They know this — hence arises a great part of their current unrest, their rejection, their mood of apprehension, aggression and self-destruction. And now it may be expected that the other of the two "heavenly forces," eternal Eros, will put forth his stength so as to maintain himself alongside of his equally mortal adversary.[184]

Eternal Eros, Plato's word for sexual energy, did not put forth his strength as Freud hoped. The Jewish holocaust was not far away, so the old man came to the end of his days in exile, much as Marx. His last book, on *Moses and Monotheism* (1939), was a psychoanalytic study of the history of his Jewish people.[185]

It would be folly to ignore the "drives" of sex and self-preservation that have been uncovered by psychoanalysis. Out of the Vienna School many significant studies have come. A recent representative is Konrad Lorenz whose analysis of innate aggression argues that our "little partial drives" are often at the disposal of one or more of the "four big drives" of feeding, reproduction, flight, and aggression, which are all related to self-preservation.[186]

184. From Perry LeFevre, *op. cit.*, pp. 91f.
185. The classic biography is Ernest Jones, *Life and Work of Sigmund Freud* (London: Penguin, 1964).
186. *On Aggression*, tr. Marjorie Latzke (London: Methuen, 1966), pp. 74-76. Cf. Leslie Stevenson, *op. cit.*, p. 115.

It is also folly to conclude that reason and conscience will restrain all human aggression without a higher motivation than preservation. Society does have a suicide instinct when animal drives dominate. Even the eternal Eros of Plato does not express the sacrificial Agape, love, that is so distinctive in the Christian faith. If Freud is to be faulted it is on the grounds that his "scientific psychology" was not scientific enough and that he looked with contempt upon belief in the reality of God who is Agape.

Christians have often responded with contempt for psychoanalysis, or any probing around in the underworld of the unconscious. But this is immature. The most rigorous scientific research on man should be welcomed, and examples of exact study with Christian conclusions are not lacking. A good example of this is the recent book by J. Z. Young, Professor of Anatomy at the University of London, entitled *An Introduction to the Study of Man*. After his detailed survey of the many levels of research from the beginning of life to human behavior he draws some conclusions on human action, especially the possibilities of human co-operation as a restraint on human aggression. He says:

> So far as we can plan, we should do so on the basis that man's special genius is for co-operation. This is not simply optimism, as some people seem to wish to show, but a rational forecast based upon the evidence. Men and women have tendencies to love and help much more than to hate each other: we are not fallen angels but risen apes, getting better![187]

However, co-operation is a behavior that must be learned if man is to overcome his innate aggression. As with Cain, there is a beast in his breast that must be tamed if he is to love his brother (1 John 3:11–18).

Some psychologists have rejected the methods of psychoanalysis as unproven superstition. The whole concept of the unconscious has become suspect. Neither the study of consciousness, as advocated by the questionnaire approach of Wilhelm Wundt and William James, nor that of the unconscious is acceptable to some scientific study. This scientific method is concerned with psychological behavior that is subject to control and can be conditioned by environment. This is really a return to the behaviorism of Ivan Pavlov, the Russian physiologist who experimented with dogs, and J. B. Watson, the American psychologist who coined the term.

The best-known behaviorist in America is no doubt B. F. Skinner of Harvard. His experiments with rats and pigeons led to some sweeping conclusions about environmental determinism but little reflection on who would *determine* the environment by controls and conditionings. His book *Behavior of Organisms: An Experimental Analysis* (1938) explored the techniques of conditioning. A novel, *Walden Two* (1948), portrays the Par-

187. (Oxford: Clarendon Press, 1971), p. 630.

adise that behavior modification and reinforcements can achieve with the Skinner spirit walking through the garden to keep the serpent away.

Science and Human Behavior (1953) applied this theory to human behavior in general, and *Verbal Behavior* (1957) attempted to explain human language as nothing more than the adaptation of the organism to environment. Just why human language is learned by human beings alone is not clear. His grand plan by which all society, all but the Skinner schemers, is to be put in a Skinner box of behaviorism was *Beyond Freedom and Dignity* (1971), and answers to his critics are in his book *About Behaviorism* (1974).

Despite the narrowness of this almost universal determinism there are positive values in the recognition that human behavior can be changed. Too much emphasis has been given to irrational and unconscious drives as explanations for irresponsible behavior. No doubt a Skinner box is at times needed, but a determinism that goes so far is bound to get both unconscious and conscious reaction, and that is the major meaning of the expression of existential freedom.

Philosophical Man

A fourth movement in modern thought that has challenged the Christian understanding of man is existentialism. The term is derived from Søren Kierkegaard (1813-1855), a Danish philosopher and devout Lutheran Christian. Kierkegaard, however, launched an attack on the Established Church, because he thought it had catered to human desires.

On the philosophical level Kierkegaard was impatient with the compromise between Christianity and the official philosophy of Hegelianism that was later turned upside down by Karl Marx. In his major philosophical works *Either-Or* (1843), *Philosophical Fragments* (1844), and *Concluding Unscientific Postscript* (1846) as well as the more theological writings such as *The Concept of Dread* (1844) and *The Sickness unto Death* (1849), he repeatedly stated that "truth is subjectivity" as an alternative to the objective "system" of doctrine based on Hegelian dialectic.

The subjectivity of the individual before God is not some superficial life of isolation from God and man. Subjectivity is achieved only in stages through suffering. The first stage toward this Christian existence takes one beyond the aesthetic life of inertia and indecision into the ethical stage that decides between good and evil. The third stage is the religious in which man finds a relation to God in his own inner life and not in the rules of the ethical life. But there are two forms of the religious life. Commitment to Christ takes one from Religiousness A to Religiousness B. This identification with Christ by faith enables man to overcome his anxiety and despair, but it is a way of life rather than a system of thought.[188]

---

188. *Stages On Life's Way*, tr. Walter Laurie (Princeton University Press, 1940).

His views on a consciousness of God's immanence (Religiousness A) were hardly the first floor of Thomism's two-storey Catholicism, but his personal passion and emphasis on God's transcendence and justification by faith (Religiousness B) reflect his return to original Lutheranism. His devotional writings *Works of Love* (1847), *Christian Discourses* (1850), and *Training in Christianity* (1850) reveal his personal piety and his understanding of the cross of Christ.[189]

At the other extreme existentialism has been used to describe the verbose reflections of Jean-Paul Sartre (1905-1980), a French atheist, and there is the popular notion that atheism and existentialism are one and the same. A term coined by a passionate theist has become a label for man's loneliness in a world without hope and without God. The one thing Sartre has in common with Kierkegaard is the quest for meaning in human existence, which Sartre does not find, and the affirmation of individual freedom, which both defend with a passion. At least this is some relief from the naturalistic determinism that dogged the thoughts of Darwin, Marx, and Freud. It is a commentary on modern cynicism, however, that the writings of Jean-Paul Sartre have become so widely known. The philosophical writings *Imagination* (1936), *Sketch for a Theory of the Emotions* (1939), *The Psychology of the Imagination* (1940), and *Being and Nothingness* (1943) are most difficult to comprehend. Perhaps his popular and superficial lecture *Existentialism and Humanism* (1945), his novel *Nausea* (1938), and the trilogy *Roads to Freedom* have gained him attention as an advocate of human freedom, a lonely theme in modern politics and religion.[190]

It is far more valuable to compare the atheistic existentialism of Martin Heidegger (1889-1976) with the Christian existentialism of Rudolf Bultmann (1884-1976), as John Macquarrie saw in his excellent study a few years ago.[191] One hesitates to call Heidegger an atheist, but he convinced himself that he was when he renounced traditional Catholic theology and left a Jesuit Seminary to study philosophy under Edmund Husserl at Freiburg University in Germany. After teaching as a colleague with both Paul Tillich and Rudolf Bultmann in the Protestant University of Marburg he became Husserl's successor in 1929. His masterful writing *Being and Time* (1927) had made for him a name. Unfortunately his membership in the Nazi party wrecked his career, and he never wrote another book equal to his classic *Being and Time*. Husserl's phenomenology prepared the way for Heidegger's reflection on human consciousness, and this led to his metaphysic of the human person. He thought the self of Kantian idealism removed man from history, so he undertook to examine man in his human existence in history. Therefore, *Dasein*, being there, became his key word

189. See LeFevre, *op. cit.*, pp. 93-106 for a brief survey of Kierkegaard.
190. See Leslie Stevenson, *op. cit.*, pp. 78-90 for a short study.
191. *An Existentialist Theology* (London: SCM, 1955).

for understanding man in all his temporal relations as he faces death and nothingness. Sartre's *Being and Nothingness* was a poor imitation of Heidegger.

Heidegger's later writings seem to make the existentialism of his early writings a form of inauthentic existence over against a more authentic existence that puts intuition above reason as a way of knowledge. The poet becomes the guardian of Being, as his writing *Hölderlin and the Nature of Poetry* (1936) suggests.[192] His *Introduction to Metaphysics* (1953) worked out some of the implications of this point of view.

On these concepts of authentic existence and Being his old friends Bultmann and Tillich built their respective systems of thought, and neither ever felt that he was an atheist. With the distinction between the inauthentic existence in the alienation of sin and the threat of death Bultmann penetrated into Paul's view of man as no previous writer had done.[193] By defining God as Being Itself, Paul Tillich constructed a most satisfactory beginning point for understanding man's existence in relation to the Being of God.[194]

Existentialism has been used by John Macquarrie not only as the foundation for his understanding of man but also for the whole of the Christian faith. His analysis of human existence expounds three ideas: polarity, disorder, and selfhood.[195] Man's polarities include the possibility of freedom over against the facticity of finitude, rationality over against the threat of the irrational, the need of community among individuals, responsibility of conscience in the midst of moral impotence and the final absurdity of death itself. All of these are means by which man may exist, i.e. stand out from nature. This is a clear rejection of all naturalistic determinism.

The polarities of life make possible disorders in human existence. Macquarrie prefers to call this disorder an "imbalance" between the potential and the actual. Man falls short of his goal in God by refusal to accept the facticity of finitude, so he tries to put himself in the place of God. He then retreats into forms of sensuality as an escape from guilt and despair. This view is almost identical with Reinhold Niebuhr's view of human sin.

Life between its possibilities and actualities is the meaning of selfhood. Genuine selfhood is found only in faith. "Existence fulfills itself in selfhood. An authentic self is a unitary, stable, and relatively abiding structure in which the polarities are brought to fulfillment."[196] After a survey of theological views of man, it will be shown that this view is very close to the biblical view of the soul.

192. This is included in *Existence and Being*, tr. Werner Brock (London: Vision, 1959), pp. 291-315. Cf. J. M. Robinson and John B. Cobb, Jr., eds., *The Later Heidegger and Theology* (New York: Harper & Row, 1963).
193. *The Theology of the New Testament*, tr. Kendrik Grobel (New York: Charles Scribner's Sons, 1951), Vol. 1, pp. 185-366.
194. *Systematic Theology* (Chicago: University of Chicago Press, 1951), Vol. I, pp. 163-289.
195. *Principles of Christian Theology* (New York: Charles Scribner's Sons, 1966), pp. 53-74.
196. *Ibid.*, p. 64.

Theological Man

The passing of such giants as Teilhard de Chardin, Barth, Brunner and Niebuhr from the drama of man's reflection on himself was a great loss, but recent thought has not been without worthy successors on the stage. In 1962 Wolfhart Pannenberg of Munich published a brief theological anthropology called *What is Man?*[197] Answers to the question are sought basically outside theological disciplines by dialogue with biology, sociology, history, psychology, and philosophy.[198]

Pannenberg's central concept is that of the openness of man, an idea that has deep roots in the existential revolt against scientific determinism. Skinner's emphasis upon man's environment would be no threat to Pannenberg, but Skinner's universal determinism is at the opposite pole from Pannenberg's observation of modern man as the ruler of his environment. This assertion of his freedom has indeed brought man to the brink of extinction.

Man's egocentricity relates him to the animals, but animals apparently do not experience the predicament of man's polarity between instinct and freedom. Natural man thus becomes historical man who can change his environment and in part shape his own destiny. This is his dignity and his danger. Ultimately, Pannenberg believes, man's historical fulfillment is found in his relation to Jesus Christ the true man.

Man's first escape from egocentricity is seen in his openness to the world. Man's transforming activity transforms the world. There are no fixed limits. The limits of animal instincts are transcended as man exercises his dominion over the world in his culture and technology. Man ventures into the mysteries beyond the horizon.

Man's openness to the world should and does lead to openness toward God. This is really man's true orientation, his goal for eternity.

> The animal's bondage to its environment corresponds, not to man's relation to the world of nature or to his familiarity with his structural world, but to his infinite dependence on God. What the environment is for animals, God is for man. God is the goal in which alone his striving can find rest and his destiny be fulfilled.[199]

This restatement of man as an amphibian of his natural and spiritual environment, as John Oman saw so clearly years ago, is surely a valid biblical perspective, but Pannenberg's perspective has the value of dialogue with the present situation in the world.

This openness of man to God goes beyond the present and points to

---

197. English tr. Duane A. Priebe (Philadelphia: Fortress Press, 1970).
198. A good summary may be found in E. Frank Tupper, *The Theology of Wolfhart Pannenberg* (Philadelphia: The Westminster Press, 1973), pp. 70-76.
199. *Op. cit.,* p. 13.

the future fulfillment at the consummation of history. Man lives in community in this life, but the human community is not eternal. If man's relation to God is not eternal, then death ends all. Man lives in hope that there is a fellowship with God and with others beyond death, and this is what the New Testament calls the resurrection of the dead.

As Pannenberg has put the emphasis on man's openness to the world and to God, Jürgen Moltmann has pointed up the need for openness to man in all social relations. This was the special burden of his book entitled *Man* (1971),[200] written as Moltmann was shifting his emphasis from the future in his *Theology of Hope* (1964)[201] to the identification of God with man in his sufferings, past and present, in *The Crucified God* (1972).[202] His theological trilogy is now complete with *The Church in the Power of the Spirit* (1976); it supplies the note missing thus far in his theology of hope.

Moltmann's main theme is the implications of man's question about himself asked in many different settings. Historical man is questionable, able to ask questions and seek answers about himself. Questions about himself are never asked in the abstract but always in comparison with some other person, place, or thing. Four fundamental comparisons are with animals, men, God, and the God-man Jesus Christ.

When man is compared to the animals the answer to the question of man is in the context of biological anthropology, but this is not the answer in a different context with a different set of relations. It is important to know that man lives by his intelligence while animals live by their instincts, but this does not furnish a complete answer to the question of man as a whole.

In comparison with other men the answers of cultural anthropology are added to the answers of biological anthropology. Differences in race, religion, class, and nations were noted long before common human rights were recognized. Ethnocentricity is much nearer to egocentricity than to an open society. It is only in the context of a common culture that men discover their common humanity. The making of a nation out of the American melting pot and the difficulties encountered in efforts at world community seem to illustrate Moltmann's meaning.

It is in comparison with the divine that the human comes to mean more than biological and cultural anthropology can discover. Even the religious anthropology of Greek mythology has answers to the question of man that comparisons with animals and men could never give. Men are mortal, while the gods are immortal. The monotheism of the Old Testament that arrives at the belief that man is in the image of God, yet never God, adds self-knowledge to the knowledge of God.

Christian anthropology includes all that biological, cultural, and reli-

200. English tr. John Sturdy (Philadelphia: Fortress Press, 1974).
201. English tr. James W. Leitch (New York: Harper & Row, 1967).
202. English tr. R. A. Wilson and John Bowden (New York: Harper & Row, 1974).

gious anthropologies have to offer, but it is more. It sees man in the mirror of the Crucified.

> Just as one cannot tell of a skull whether it comes from a rich man or a poor man, from a righteous or from an unrighteous man, so too in human misery which becomes manifest in the crucified Jesus and to which the love of God is given, which becomes real in the crucified, those differences are done away with by which men divide themselves from one another.[203]

Out of this anthropology of the cross comes the political theology of Moltmann that began behind barbed wire when he was a prisoner of war in England and reached a climax in his book *The Crucified God*. That is why he finds it relevant to do dialogue with both communism and capitalism on behalf of the rejected people of the earth.

203. *Man*, p. 20.

VI. SIN

41. The Question of Sin

When John Whale discussed the Christian doctrine of sin, in some widely-read lectures at Cambridge in 1941, he lamented the smug complacency of modern optimism with a story ascribed to T. E. Hulme: "It is as if you pointed out to an old lady at a garden party that there was an escaped lion twenty yards off, and she were to reply. 'Oh, yes,' and then quietly take another cucumber sandwich."[1] He then goes on to introduce the renewed emphasis on human sin made popular for awhile by the realism of Reinhold Niebuhr.

As late as 1973, however, a well-known doctor aroused considerable comment when he raised the question anew: *Whatever Became of Sin?*[2] Against his broad background in counseling and psychiatry Karl Menninger made a survey of sin, crime and mental illness in modern society. It becomes obvious that something is wrong in human society whatever the terms to designate the malady may be. His classifications of corporate and individual sins stimulate many to make a personal inventory of wrongness and responsibility for this wrongness.

Menninger's most meaningful statement for theological understanding came at the end of his detailed catalogue of individual sins both traditional and more recent. He said:

> If one wanted to find a germinal word to link all sins,
> perhaps *hate* would do it. In terms of action, however,
> the long term consequences of hate are self-destruction.
> Thus the wages of sin really are death.[3]

On the basis of clinical evidence he has reached one side of the conclusion with which the Scriptures begin. Sin is the disruption of man's relation with both God and others. Where there is no God, there is no sin,

1. *Christian Doctrine* (New York: The Macmillan Co., 1941), pp. 35f.
2. The title of a book by Karl Menninger (New York: Hawthorn Books, Inc., 1973).
3. *Ibid.*, p. 172.

for sin is man's broken relation with God. Before the details of this broken relation are discussed, it will be helpful to begin with three central pictures of sin prominent in three parts of the Old Testament Scriptures.

Sin and Creation

The first is from the Pentateuch, the Law of Moses. In the Paradise story of Genesis 3 the presence of God is described as a voice in the cool breeze of the evening, a *qol* (voice) in the *ruach* (the wind). Adam and Eve hear the voice and flee from the presence of the Lord God. The fear of God's presence is due to their disobedience to God's command. Sin is indeed, to use a term coined by Norman Snaith, *"theofugal,"* a fleeing from God.[4]

The poet Francis Thompson has explored many of the emotions and thoughts associated with this fleeing from God in his poem "The Hound of Heaven." It begins with these lines:

> *I fled him down the nights and down the days;*
> *I fled him through the arches of the years;*
> *I fled him down the labyrinthine ways*
> *Of my own mind; and in the midst of tears*
> *I hid from him and under running laughter.*[5]

The threefold temptation of the lust of the flesh, the lust of the eyes and the vainglory of life led to the threefold curse (Gen. 3:6). Temptation came to Jesus in the same threefold manner (Matt. 4:1–11; Lk. 4:1–13). I John 2:16 uses this threefold temptation to summarize the meaning of the godless *kosmos* (world).

This state of sin is described as expulsion from the presence of the Lord God. "God drove out the man; and at the east of the garden of Eden he placed the cherubim, and a flaming sword which turned every way, to guard the way to the tree of life" (Gen. 3:24). Sin is a state of spiritual death that leaves man without access to the tree of life. Men are indeed "alienated from the life of God because of the ignorance that is in them" (Eph. 4:18).

The Cain and Abel story reinforces the picture of sin as a state of alienation from the presence of God "east of Eden" (Gen. 4:16). It was the hate that Menninger mentioned that caused Cain, the farmer, to slay his brother Abel, the shepherd. This time sin is not like a serpent but like a beast in his breast that sprang to life so that "Cain rose up against his brother Abel, and killed him" (Gen. 4:8).

According to the Johannine teaching of the New Testament Cain cut his brother's throat. Western Christianity, both Catholic and Protestant,

4. *The Distinctive Ideas of the Old Testament* (Philadelphia: The Westminster Press, 1946), p. 75.
5. *The Complete Poetical Works of Francis Thompson* (New York: The Modern Library, n.d.), p. 88.

has rightly looked upon sin as a disruption of the perpendicular relation with God, but this horizontal human disruption should not be neglected. Anti-social behavior is an index of man's relation to God. As I John 3:10b–12 says:

> Everyone who does not do righteousness is not of God,
>   and anyone who does not continue to love his brother,
> because this is the message which you have heard from the
>   beginning,
>   that we should continue to love one another;
> and not be like Cain who was of the evil one
>   and cut the throat of his brother.

So goes the most literal translation.[6]

As the Pauline picture uses the Adam and Eve model for sin, the Johannine picture employs the Cain and Abel model. Both will later be discussed in further detail as this broken relation with both God and man is developed.

Sin and the Covenant

A picture of man's rebellion against God, ignorance of God and estrangement from God may be found at the beginning of the book of Isaiah. In short summary sin is described as the breach of the father–son relation. As Isaiah 1:2 says:

> Sons have I reared and brought up,
> but they have rebelled against me.

Rebellion is the very root of man's ignorance. The oracle about ignorance in Isaiah 1:3 says:

> The ox knows its owner,
>   and the ass its master's crib;
> but Israel does not know,
>   my people do not understand.

This ignorance is not the need of knowledge about God but a breach of the covenant with God. It is the lack of a personal knowledge of God that can be remedied only through personal obedience to God. No amount of rational assent to propositions about God can be substituted for this personal relation with God.

Another oracle begins with the reproach against Israel's estrangement from God (Isa. 1:4):

6. Dale Moody, *The Letters of John* (Waco, Texas: Word Books, 1970), pp. 66f.

Ah, sinful nation,
  a people laden with iniquity,
offspring of evildoers,
  sons who deal corruptly!
They have forsaken the Lord,
  they have despised the Holy One of Israel,
they are utterly estranged.

This estrangement from the covenant relation with God is made acute by the awareness of the holiness of God.

Estrangement from God as the Holy One, the only God, has been given new emphasis as the sense of guilt has been explored. Conviction for sin and cleansing from sin find classic expression in the call of Isaiah where he says (Isa. 6:5): "Woe is me! for I am a man of unclean lips, and I dwell in the midst of a people of unclean lips; for my eyes have seen the King, the Lord of hosts!"

Rudolf Otto ranked the experience of Job 38–42 as among the most remarkable in the history of religion for the display of mystery. Here Job confesses (Job 42:5):

I have heard of thee by the hearing of the ear,
  but now my eyes see thee;
therefore I despise myself,
  and repent in dust and ashes.[7]

Inside and outside the Bible this is the authentic human response when confronted by the Holy God.

In the New Testament, Peter, when confronted by the holiness and mystery of Jesus, pleads (Lk. 5:8): "Depart from me, for I am a sinful man, O Lord." Before the risen Lord Jesus, John fell as one dead (Rev. 1:17). And so runs the theme of biblical teachings and all other authentic teachings about the sinfulness of man before the holiness of God.

There is hardly a page in the Bible that does not have a synonym or a suggestion about sin, but three terms used in the Old Testament point to the very heart of the human problem. Isaiah 59:12–13 has the three terms in the order of their importance:

For our transgressions are multiplied before thee,
  and our sins testify against us;
for our transgressions are with us,
  and we know our iniquities:
transgressing, and denying the Lord,
  and turning from following our God,
speaking oppression and revolt,
  conceiving and uttering from the heart lying words.

---

7. *The Idea of the Holy*, tr. John W. Harvey (Oxford: Oxford University Press, 1923), p. 80.

It is clear that transgressions, used in parallel with both sins and iniquities, is the leading idea and the most profound word for human wrong. It means to rebel against the will of God. It is wilful disobedience, rebellion, not just a mistake or a failure growing out of ignorance and weakness. The words translated sin in both the Hebrew and the Greek mean "to miss the mark," but this may mean no more than spiritual or moral failure. Iniquities overstep the word, command, law, or covenant of the Lord, but the word "transgressions" penetrates the human problem most.

The Apostle Paul makes a profound distinction between sin and transgression, but this comes later. However, Isaiah (59:13) follows his discussion of transgressing with some strong statements about man's rebellion against God in thought, word, and deed: "denying," "turning," "speaking," "conceiving" and "uttering."

Sin and Confession

Perhaps the best-known summary of sin in the Old Testament is found in the seven Penitential Psalms (6; 32; 38; 51; 102; 130; 143). The blessings of forgiveness reveal the relation between transgressions as rebellion, sins as missing the mark, and iniquities as moral crookedness in man and the action of God by which they are forgiven or covered or no longer imputed (Ps. 32:1f.).

Psalm 51:3–5 has the confession:

> For I know my transgression,
>   and my sin is ever before me.
> Against thee, thee only, have I sinned,
>   and done that which is evil in thy sight,
> So that thou art justified in thy sentence
>   and blameless in thy judgment.
> Behold, I was brought forth in iniquity,
>   and in sin did my mother conceive me.

It is not necessary to accept some later misinterpretations of this passage to see that the Psalmist has gone beyond the three words for sin to describe a state of sin from the moment of his conception and in the whole context of his life.

These Old Testament teachings answer the question raised by Karl Menninger. Since the Fall sin has been a crucial factor in the life of man, but it has been ignored by man in his vain hope that there is no God to whom he is presently and finally accountable. It is significant that the question of sin is being raised again, but many of the historical answers need to be re-examined in the light of the Scriptures and the experience of all mankind.

42. The Nature of Sin

Against the background of the Old Testament the teachings of Jesus on sin are to be understood, but his emphasis was more on the forgiveness of sin and the triumph over sin in the coming kingdom of God.[8] It is in the Pauline and Johannine writings that major movements of thought beyond the Old Testament teachings are made.

The nearest to a New Testament *doctrine* of sin is Romans 1:18–32. In fact, most of the major questions about a *doctrine* of sin are suggested by statements in Paul's great Roman letter, and the order of that letter is followed in the next six sections. Therefore, the nature, universality, origin, transmission, wages, and power of sin will be surveyed before a concluding chapter on the dominion of darkness, i.e. the devil and the demons.

Sin as Ungodliness

The nature of sin is summarized in the use of the words *un*godliness and *un*righteousness (Rom. 1:18). Ungodliness is the broken relation with God, and unrighteousness is the broken relation with others. The ungodly and unrighteous "suppress the truth" which restores and establishes the right relations with God and man.

Ungodliness is first of all ignorance of God. Again it is personal knowledge, not propositional knowledge, that Paul has in mind when he says:

> For what can be known about God is plain to them, because God has shown it to them. Ever since the creation of the world his invisible nature, namely, his eternal power and deity, has been clearly perceived in the things that have been made. So they are without excuse; for although they knew God they did not honor him as God or give thanks to him, but they became futile in their thinking and their senseless minds were darkened. Claiming to be wise, they became fools, and exchanged the glory of the immortal God for images resembling mortal man or birds or animals or reptiles.

This ignorance results from a rejection of the knowledge of God made possible by a general revelation "since the creation of the world." Any effort to restrict this knowledge to Gentile believers who have been confronted by the special revelation of God in Jesus Christ is special pleading in the interest of a preconceived conclusion, yet that effort is made by Markus Barth in his effort to defend his father's rejection of a general revelation of God apart from the special revelation of God in Jesus Christ.[9]

The rejection of this general revelation leads to personal estrangement from God and idolatry. Idolatry is a God substitute: "because they exchanged the truth of God for a lie and worshipped and served the creature rather than the Creator; who is blessed forever!" (Rom. 1:25). Ungodliness is on the one hand ignorance, the negative side, and on the other idolatry,

8. Frederic Greeves, *The Meaning of Sin* (London: The Epworth Press, 1956), pp. 100-124.
9. *The Scottish Journal of Theology* (September, 1955), pp. 280ff.

the positive side. As Martin Luther saw so clearly, a person turns away from God by the four "stages of perdition": ingratitude, vanity, blindness, and idolatry.[10]

On the grounds of existential philosophy John Macquarrie has seen the relationship between religious ignorance and idolatry.[11] He identifies idolatry with what Martin Heidegger called "forgetting of Being" or taking the place of Being, Macquarrie's basic meaning of God. The imbalance of life in modern anthropolatry, human existence organized around man himself, has reached its most destructive form in modern technology that turns away from God and idolizes man.

Sin as Unrighteousness

Unrighteousness may be manifested in either the defilement of the human flesh or the defilement of the human spirit, to use the terminology of Paul in II Corinthians 7:1. The most obvious defilement of human flesh in Paul's time was the practice of homosexuality (Rom. 1:26f.). Several emperors had their "boy" for sexual enjoyment, but female homosexuality was about as common as that of males.

At the present the so-called "gay movement" has declared itself and advocated homosexuality as a "sexual preference" on par with heterosexuality. This has come forth with suddenness. When *The Interpreter's Dictionary of the Bible* was first published in 1962 the subject was briefly treated by O. J. Baab, but later "gay explosions" provoked an extensive survey by M. H. Pope in the Supplementary Volume of 1974.

There is no question that both biblical and historical theology have spoken with one voice in condemning homosexuality as a major sin by which the human body is defiled, but other forms of sexual abuse, excessive use of drugs, intemperance in drink and food have not been overlooked. Homosexuality has some interesting company in Paul's list of ten sins that can deprive one of the kingdom of God (I Cor. 6:9f.).

Many now brand the biblical perspective as bias toward those who are homosexuals by nature or choice. The majority of studies have concluded that most homosexuals have chosen this deviation and that it is not incurable. This is in agreement with the apostle Paul, who plainly says that some of the saints of Corinth were former homosexuals (I Cor. 6:10). What Christian counselor has not known a number of people who have departed from this deviation by deliberate choice and by the help of God? It is perhaps not true that "once a homosexual always a homosexual," and Christian groups are seldom mature enough to hear a testimony on "my homosex-

---

10. Wilhelm Pauck, trans. and ed., *Luther: Lectures on Romans* (Philadelphia: The Westminster Press, 1961), pp. 25f.
11. *Principles of Christian Theology*, Second Edition (New York: Charles Scribner's Sons, 1977), pp. 259-261.

uality and how I overcame it," but case studies of this type are sorely needed for the encouragement of others (cf. 1 Cor. 6:11).

It hardly needs to be said that these words are being written with as much compassion for homosexuals as for alcoholics, yet there is not as much help available for the former as for the latter. As for the question of congenital or constitutional homosexuals, the compassionate person needs to keep an open mind until there is sufficient knowledge to discern whether heterosexuality is a possibility for all.[12] Even now it is possible to say that celibate life is, by the grace of God, a possibility for both the homosexual and the heterosexual, and many beautiful people have chosen that way. That is surely a Christian choice with apostolic blessings on it (I Cor. 7:25–35; 9:1–5).

Sins of the human flesh are manifested in the defilement of the body, but sins of the human spirit defile the mind (Rom. 1:28). Three times the apostle Paul said "God gave them up" (Rom. 1:24, 26, 28): "in the lust of their hearts," "to dishonorable passions" and "to a base mind." It is through the base mind that the sins of the human spirit are manifested in anti-social attitudes (Rom. 1:29–31).

They were filled with all manner of wickedness, evil, covetousness, malice. Full of envy, murder, strife, deceit, malignity, they are gossips, slanderers, haters of God, insolent, haughty, boastful, inventors of evil, disobedient to parents, foolish, faithless, heartless, ruthless.

The New Testament often catalogues sins according to whether they are manifested in body or mind. These lists are never more important than the condition of ungodliness in estrangement from God as manifested in ignorance and idolatry, but Jesus did not hesitate to specify individual sins. He spoke not only of sin in general but of specific sins.

L. H. Marshall pointed out that inordinate self-love seemed to be the root of all sin in the teaching of Jesus, but he goes on to classify the sins of the flesh and the sins of the spirit in the teachings of Jesus, much as has been noted in the teachings of Paul.[13] It is therefore false to put the teachings of Jesus over against those of Paul as if Paul was the pessimist and Jesus the optimist about mankind.

12. Clinical study of homosexuality will no doubt develop more in the future, but the following books have been helpful to shape the attitude here expressed: D. S. Bailey, *Homosexuality and the Western Christian Tradition* (New York: Longmans, Green, 1955); Lawrence J. Hatterer, *Changing Homosexuality in the Male?* (Philadelphia: The Westminster Press, 1971); W. Dwight Oberholltzer, ed., *Is Gay Good?* (Philadelphia: Westminster Press, 1971); Weinberg and Williams, *The Male Homosexual* (Oxford University Press, 1974); John Drakeford, *A Christian View of Homosexuality* (Nashville: Broadman, 1977).
13. *The Challenge of New Testament Ethics* (New York: The Macmillan Company, 1974), pp. 36-52.

Eastern Christianity has emphasized most the sins of the flesh, but Western Christianity, both Catholic and Protestant, has followed the teachings of Augustine who classified sins as "carnalities" and "animosities," those of the flesh and those of the soul. Even though Augustine was more Platonic than Pauline in his understanding of the soul, his understanding of sin was much in line with that of Paul.

After his distinction between "carnalities" and "animosities" was clearly made he gave this remarkable summary of sin: "It was not the corruptible flesh that made the soul sinful, but the sinful soul that made the body corruptible" (*The City of God*, XIV. 3). Much that Augustine said about Original Sin will be later rejected, but his emphasis on animosities as the chief sins is valid.

Perhaps the classic discussion on human sins in the history of theology is to be found in the Gifford Lectures for 1939 by Reinhold Niebuhr.[14] Niebuhr rejected the emphasis on the primacy of sensuality in Eastern Christianity. He points up pride as the primal sin, whether among angels or men. Indeed, if sensuality were the primary form of sin, sin among angels would be impossible.

Eastern views of the Fall look upon sin as sensuality. For Clement of Alexandria the serpent was a symbol of "the power of pleasure," especially sexual pleasure (*Protrepticos* XI, iii). Origen of Alexandria taught the Platonic idea of a pre-historical Fall by which the soul fell into the body, but he also believed in an historical Fall by which sexual relations between Eve and the serpent took place. The serpent for him was a phallic symbol. Gregory of Nyssa, the most influential Eastern theologian of all, adopted the Platonic idea that the distinction between male and female was the result of the Fall (*On the Making of Man* XVIII, 4). Until the twentieth century this obsession with the evil of sex has dominated Eastern Christianity, as one can see in the androgynous theology of Nicolas Berdyaev.

It is all but impossible for Eastern Orthodoxy to accept the Western view of pride as the primary sin. From Augustine to Thomas Aquinas in Catholic theology and from Luther to Niebuhr himself in Protestant theology this primacy of pride over pleasure is pointed out. It was when Niebuhr became a critic of the pride of power, knowledge, virtue, and religion and portrayed sensuality in luxury, drunkenness, and sex as an escape from the sinful self that he became the social prophet that he was. Of all twentieth-century theologians who convicted the modern conscience of sin, there has been none superior to Niebuhr.

In all of this probing into the nature of sin the relevance of the Pauline view of unrighteousness has been vindicated.

14. *The Nature and Destiny of Man* (New York: Charles Scribner's Sons, 1941-1943), pp. 178-240.

43. The Universality of Sin

The traditional Augustinian distinction between Original Sin and Actual Sin made too much of the first sin to be useful in the context of scientific anthropology. It is much better to speak of the universality of individual and corporate sin, in that order. Using these terms Gustaf Aulén saw the relationship between universality and solidarity when he spoke of interdependence and interrelatedness in the total human situation.[15]

Individual Sin is Universal

Traditional Augustinianism has so emphasized man's inherited guilt for the first sin committed by the individuals Eve and Adam that the sense of personal responsibility for individual sins declined. In Paul's Roman letter the universality of individual sins is stated first as an empirical fact, with reference to the sin of the First Adam coming later as a corollary to the redemption that is in Jesus Christ, the Last Adam.

With six Old Testament passages, none of which has reference to Adam, Paul composed a hymn on the empirical evidence that every person is a sinner. The three stanzas give evidence that all have sinned in thought, word and deed, and this has been made clear in *The New English Bible*, which says in Romans 3:10b–18:

> *There is no just man, not one;*
> *no one who understands, no one who seeks God.*
> *All have swerved aside, all alike have become debased;*
> *there is no one to show kindness; no, not one.*
>
> *Their throat is an open grave,*
> *they use their tongues for treachery,*
> *adders' venom is on their lips,*
> *and their mouth is full of bitter curses.*
>
> *Their feet hasten to shed blood,*
> *ruin and misery lie along their paths,*
> *they are strangers to the high-road of peace,*
> *and reverence for God does not enter their thoughts.*

These words from the Old Testament make no reference to individual sins being caused by the sin of Adam and Eve because the idea never appears in the Old Testament. The sin of Adam and Eve appears in the New Testament only in the writings of Paul. This will be discussed in the next two sections.

At present the evidence that all have sinned is the main point. Evidence for the Old Testament view is abundant outside the Bible. The primitive

15. *The Christian Faith* (Philadelphia: The Muhlenberg Press, 1948), pp. 270-277.

religions of Africa present always a picture of man's estrangement from a remote and hostile God with whom he must make peace because of his sins.

After a catalogue of sins typical in African religion, sins very much the same as those in the Bible, a leading authority on the subject makes this interesting summary:

> By nature, Africans are neither angels nor demons. They can be as kind as the Germans, but they can be as murderous as the Germans; Africans can be as generous as the Americans, but they can be as greedy as the Americans; they can be as friendly as the Russians, but they can be as cruel as the Russians; they can be as honest as the English, but they can be as equally hypocritical. In their human nature Africans are Germans, Swiss, Chinese, Indians or English — they are men.[16]

It may be added that they are not only men but sinners, with both goodness and sinfulness universal for all.

The same universality of sin is manifested in the more highly developed religions. It is more important to distinguish between the views of Eastern and Western religions on evil than it is to remember the primacy of pleasure in Eastern Christianity and of pride in Western Christianity. The Eastern religions are man-centered, while the Western religions are God-centered, so the sense of sin against a personal God does not exist in the religions that originated in India and China. It is hardly correct to refer to their views of evil as "Eastern Equivalents" as Shirley Sugerman does in what is a helpful introduction.[17]

The two major religions that originated in India understand evil as the struggle of the self. In Hinduism the self is identified with the cosmos. But by knowledge of his identity with the cosmos the self climbs over the wall to self-transcendence by identification with the cosmos. Evil is therefore ignorance.

Buddhism originated in India, but it has become an international and missionary religion that seeks to overcome suffering and sorrow (*dukkha*) by walking the Noble Eightfold Path with no help from a transcendent God. Theravada Buddhism, the most extreme form, recognizes no ego and no Other. The self is completely overcome.

The Chinese religion of Confucianism is more social and practical than Hinduism and Buddhism. Self-transcendence is achieved by the five cardinal virtues symbolized by a flowering tree: moral perfection as the root, righteousness by justice as the trunk, religious and moral ways of acting as the branches, wisdom as the flower, and faithfulness as the fruit.[18]

16. John S. Mbiti, *African Religions and Philosophy* (London: Heinemann, 1969), p. 210.
17. *Sin and Madness: Studies in Narcissism* (Philadelphia: The Westminster Press, 1976), pp. 88-127.
18. *Ibid.*, p. 115.

The Taoism of China is more concerned with man's relation to nature than society. Man is an agent of nature. Evil as separation from this Source in the cosmic order leads to the destruction of Being and the well-being of man.

All Eastern religions recognize a condition of estrangement from the ultimate, but the idea of sin as transgression of the will of a personal God is missing. Only in the monotheistic religions of Judaism, Christianity and Islam is the sense of transgression found. Christ takes Christianity beyond law into the dimension of belief or unbelief. The law brings the knowledge of sin, but faith overcomes the world by trust in the grace of God in Christ.

Corporate Sin is Universal

The corporate sin of the tribe or nation is a basic belief in the Old Testament. The collective guilt of the nation because of the sin of Achan is only one of the many examples in the Old Testament. Israel was frustrated at Ai, or, as some say, Bethel, because one man violated his oath to destroy Jericho. Therefore, the Lord said: "Israel has sinned: they have transgressed my covenant which I commanded them; they have taken some of the devoted things; they have stolen, and lied, and put them among their own stuff" (Josh. 7:11). Yet the individual guilt of Achan is recognized in the sentence of Achan which says: "And he who is taken with the devoted things shall be burned with fire, he and all that he has, because he has transgressed the covenant of the Lord, and because he has done a shameful thing in Israel" (Josh. 7:15).

This polarity between collective and individual guilt was pronounced in some of the classical prophets. The prophet Jeremiah looked forward to the time when they would no longer say (Jer. 31:29f.):

> The fathers have eaten sour grapes, and the children's teeth are
> set on edge. But every one shall die for his own sin; each man who
> eats sour grapes, his teeth shall be set on edge.

The old proverb is repudiated with vigor as the prophet Ezekiel develops more fully the idea of individual responsibility (Ezek. 18).

Historical theology has often failed to give due consideration to this prophetic protest against collective guilt as the explanation for misfortunes and sin. This comes out most clearly in the history of the English Bible. The same words are translated the same way in the Authorized (King James) Version of Romans 3:23 and 5:12. In both passages the words are rightly translated "all have sinned," yet most other translations leave out the word "have" in Romans 5:12. In that way the guilt is shifted away from each individual to Adam as the individual who "sinned" for all. The disastrous consequences of this misunderstanding will be later discussed in more detail, but it is used here to illustrate how belief in collective sin can weaken individual responsibility and guilt.

Corporate sin is universal, but each individual is responsible for his personal involvement in the consequences. Paul views man's *nature* in terms of his conformity to the world, the devil and the flesh. The Authorized (King James) Version is not so correct in the translation of Ephesians 2:1 where man is said to be "dead in trespasses and sins." The Revised Standard Version says the Gentiles "were dead through the trespasses and sins," but "the" should be "your"! In other words the nature that brought spiritual death was a consequence of trespasses and sins, not one sin by one man in the distant past.

The presupposition that man is dead "in trespasses and sins" rather than *because* of trespasses and sins is so persistent in theological tradition that *The Good News Bible* (TEV) has the translation correct in Ephesians 2:1 but incorrect in Ephesians 2:5! In Ephesians 2:3 *nature* grows out of action not action out of nature. Yet Western theology, both Catholic and Protestant, has usually followed the false translation in the interest of theological tradition. All responsible men are, before the experience of grace, "children of wrath," but this is *because all have sinned*, not solely because one man sinned.

The Johannine concept of the *world* supports the Pauline concept of *nature*. In that classic collection of early Christian hymns called I John, sin is described in three cycles as defilement (1:5–2:2), disobedience to the love commandment (2:28–3:10a), and spiritual death (5:14–17).

In Paul Ricoeur's detailed study *The Symbolism of Evil* the phenomenon of defilement is described prior to the concept of sin.[19] Apparently I John thinks of defilement as the primal condition of sin, but John would hardly disagree with Ricoeur's statement that: "With defilement we enter into the reign of Terror."[20]

With the knowledge of the love commandment "sin is lawlessness" (I John 3:4), Cain, not Adam, is the cardinal sinner for John. It was Cain who cut his brother's throat because of the hate that was in him. This was, according to John, inspired by the devil (I John 3:8). According to the Gospel of John those who hate and murder have chosen to be the children of the devil rather than the children of God (John 8:39–46). The fact that Adam is never mentioned in the Johannine Writings should remind one that the sin of Adam and Eve, to be discussed later, is not the only dimension of universal sin.

The climax to sin as defilement and disobedience is spiritual death. I John is very emphatic about love for the brethren in the family of God as a sure sign that one has passed out of spiritual death into spiritual life (I John 3:14). *Eternal* life is his usual adjective, but he is just as emphatic about the possibility that a brother may pass again into spiritual death

19. (Boston: Beacon Press, 1967), pp. 25-46.
20. *Ibid.*, p. 25.

(I John 5:16). There are those who argue that the passage from life to death in I John 5:16 refers to physical death, but I John 5:11–17 when read as a whole does not support this view. Physical death is a form of judgment in I Corinthians 11:30, but this does not seem to be the case in I John.

The victory of the children of God over the world in I John is a passage from darkness to light (2:12–17), from hate to love (4:1–6) and from death to life (5:1–13), all in the terms of fellowship (*koinōnia*), but the children of God must continue to resist darkness, hate and death in their pilgrimage out of the *KOSMOS* (world) into the *KOINŌNIA* (fellowship).[21]

The fellowship of God's children with God and with one another is nourished most by the concepts of *nature* in Paul and *world* in John, but there is some existential verification of these concepts. Martin Heidegger has coined the philosophical concept of "das Mann" (the Man), and John Macquarrie, in his usual manner, has seen this as a parallel to the Christian understanding of the universality of sin.[22] The I is set over against "they," the impersonal and anonymous mass, in which the individual is dragged along to destruction and death. The "system" overwhelms the individual who has been caught in the social trap that I John called "the world." Whether "the Man" or "the world," it is the catching of the individual in the web of the world that makes it impossible to speak of the universality of individual sin or corporate sin in isolation from one another. Liberal theology has magnified the individual and conservative theology the corporate, but the two need to be studied in the tension of polarity.

44. The Origin of Sin

As the Pauline approach to the universality of sin began with the particular evidences for individual sins and projected this understanding backward toward the recognition of corporate sin, so the question of the origin of sin begins with the Pauline concept of the flesh and moves logically toward an understanding of the Fall. This is intended to correct the imbalance of the Augustinian tradition which gave undue emphasis to the fall of the first man and woman and neglected the Pauline teachings on the fall of every man and woman.

The Flesh

The personal origin of sin in the flesh does not have reference to the physical flesh. That was the mistake of the Greek philosophy of Plato and much of Eastern Christianity that read this meaning into the letters of Paul. Flesh is at times used by Paul to represent the physical, but when flesh is used

---

21. For further details on I John see my commentary on *The Letters of John* (Waco: Word Books, 1970).
22. *Principles of Christian Theology*, Second Edition (New York: Charles Scribner's Sons, 1977), p. 262.

to designate the origin of sin a psychological meaning is intended. Flesh has reference to man's self-centered life as he turns away from God. It is egocentricity. Three current ideas on the personal origin of sin need to be defined.

The Pauline view of the flesh, as has been said, is man's self-centered orientation in which all is organized around his ego. When Paul asks the Galatians if they are going to begin the life of faith in the Spirit and end up in the flesh, he has no reference to the physical meaning of flesh (3:3). He means that they are about to be bewitched to turn away from Christ as the center of their lives to the Jewish ceremony of circumcision. He warns them not to use the flesh as an opportunity by which to turn away from their freedom in Christ to become slaves again (4:8f.; 5:1, 13). To crucify the flesh is to die with Christ in order to live with Christ (2:20; 5:24).

His profound probing into the personal origin of sin makes the confession: "For I know that nothing good dwells in me, that is in my flesh. I can will what is right, but I cannot do it" (Rom. 7:18). This contradiction of the will is the conflict between that which is the creation of God and the condition of one who is centered in himself rather than in God. This is very near to the Rabbinic teachings on the good impulse in conflict with the evil impulse, the *yeser ha-tob* and the *yeser ha-ra* in Hebrew.[23]

The philosophical view of radical evil in Immanuel Kant's last large-scale work has a striking parallel to the Pauline view of the flesh, but he rejected the Augustinian belief that this had a temporal origin and was inherited. In defense of human freedom he posited a state of innocence for every person and left the explanation of man's evil propensity in the realm of the inscrutable.[24] This will be further discussed in the next section.

The existential description of sin in the ethics of Reinhold Niebuhr also leaves the explanation of man's inevitable sin without an answer. All he can say is that out of finitude and freedom man's anxiety leads him to turn away from God and turn in on himself in self-love.[25] Historical conditioning behind this anxiety destroys for him the radical nature of sin, but there is more to be said than he and Kant have said. Man is conditioned by his inheritance, but this does not remove all his freedom and responsibility.

The Fall

The Pauline approach to the ultimate origin of sin alone uses the Old Testament teachings on Adam and Eve in the interpretation of man's fallen

23. Detailed studies on the Pauline meaning of the flesh may be found in W. D. Davies, *Paul and Rabbinic Judaism* (London: S.P.C.K., 1948), pp. 17-35; W. David Stacey, *The Pauline View of Man* (London: Macmillan and Co., 1956), pp. 154-180.
24. *Religion Within the Realm of Reason Alone* (1793), tr. Theodore M. Greene and Hoyt H. Hudson (Chicago: The Open Court Publishing Co., 1934), pp. 15-39. Emil Brunner, *Man in Revolt*, tr. Olive Wyon (Philadelphia: The Westminster Press, 1947) owes much to the distinction between man as he is and man as he ought to be.
25. *Op. cit.*, pp. 241-264.

condition that requires redemption as a remedy. Paul's teachings on the Fall of man must first of all be distinguished from the teachings of the Greek philosopher Plato, and Paul's use of the Old Testament teachings depends more upon his present experience than on past events.

First of all the Platonic idea of an immortal soul that fell from a pre-existent state into a mortal body has no place in Paul. A consistent use of Plato leads to the transmigration of the immortal soul from one mortal body to another. Only a few Christian theologians like Origen of Alexandria went all the way with Plato, but the modified Platonism of both Roman Catholicism and conservative Protestantism identified the image of God in creation with Plato's idea of the natural immortality of the soul. There is no support for this identification in the Bible.[26]

Paul's view of the Fall is historical, but he moves first from the present to the past in his letters. In this way his interpretation makes room for the fall of each man and woman as well as for the first man and woman.

The first reference to this present tense approach is I Corinthians 15:22 which establishes the principle:

> For as in Adam all die,
> so in Christ shall all be made alive.

He does not say "in Adam all died," as one often hears. In the present each person dies as he becomes estranged from God by his own action. In the future all in Christ will be made alive, but only on the condition that the act of faith identifies them with Christ. If "all" means every human being with no reference to human response then the universalism of Karl Barth is the result, so that every person is damned in the First Adam and every person is redeemed in the Last Adam. This is not the conclusion reached by the apostle Paul, for he was no universalist (cf. Rom. 2:8f.).

It has already been noted that the conclusion of Romans 3:23 is based upon an observation of Gentiles and Jews alike in their conduct. The principle is verified by evidence: "For there is no distinction: since all have sinned and fall short of the glory of God." *The Good News Bible* leaves no doubt about the meaning of the passage when it rightly adopts the interpretation which says: "everyone has sinned."

In a consistent manner *The Good News Bible* translates the key passage in Romans 5:12 as follows: "Sin came into the world through one man, and his sin brought death with it. As a result, death has spread to the whole human race because everyone has sinned." *The Authorized (King James) Version* and *The New English Bible* support the interpretation in *The Good News Bible*. All are consistent with the original Greek in both Romans 3:23 and 5:12, yet many, with minds programmed by tradition,

---

26. See Krister Stendahl, ed., *Immortality and Resurrection* (New York: The Macmillan Co., 1965) for a modern debate on this conflict of ideas.

still interpret Romans 5:12 as if it said, not "because everyone has sinned," but "because Adam sinned."

Romans 5:19 is often advanced as support for the false interpretation because it says that "just as all people were made sinners as the result of the disobedience of one man, in the same way they will all be put right with God as the result of the obedience of one man" (TEV). Exactly so, but how does the disobedience of one man make all people sinners and the obedience of one man put them right with God? The analogy is obvious, when reversed. The obedience of Jesus Christ puts all people right with God who respond in the obedience of faith, and the disobedience of one man makes all people sinners when they respond in the disobedience of unbelief. If one is solely the work of God, so is the other, and all people that are sinners will be made righteous in universal salvation; but this is not the teaching of the passage.

We take the correct approach to this problem when we see the experience of the first man and the first woman as pictures of what happens to every man and every woman. Paul saw this pattern in his own experience when he said: "I myself was once alive apart from the law; but when the commandment came sin sprang to life, and I died" (Rom. 7:9f.). What does he mean by this if not that he relived history from Adam to Moses until he experienced spiritual death at the age of accountability in his life, and under the law he relived history from Adam to Christ? He was born alive, not dead, but the law brought spiritual death to him until Christ made him alive again. The Old Testament also places the beginnings of the evil imagination of man's heart at adolescence (Gen. 8:21).

How then did traditional theology go so far astray by teaching only two stages, from death to life, rather than the three stages of life to death and back to life? It takes only a brief survey to discover the debacle that took place in the theology of Augustine.

Irenaeus, the greatest and most biblical theologian among the Greeks of the second century, saw Adam as "nothing more than a little child" who "little by little — ascends to perfection" (Against Heresies IV, 38, 1-3). Tertullian, the father of Latin theology, pictures every person in this way at the beginning. Every person is born and lives in the paradise of innocence until the age of puberty, at which time a person leaves paradise for the world of guilt (On the Soul, 38f.). For this reason Tertullian rejected infant baptism, which was believed to remove guilt (On Baptism, 18).

Augustine painted a very different picture in the fifth century. For him Adam was perfect from the beginning. He had Original Righteousness, interpreted as possessing immortality, until it was lost by Original Sin. Baptism, according to Augustine, removed Original Sin and restored immortality to man. It takes very little study in Genesis 2-3, I Corinthians 15 and Romans 5, where the Bible links Adam to sin, to discover that all of this primitive perfectionism and sacramentalism is from the speculation of Augustine and those who followed him.

When Genesis 1–11 is approached from the Pauline perspective and with the original meaning, there is a rich relevance to these passages which have been distorted by the idea of primitive perfectionism, about which Martin Luther could speak with such extravagant speculation.

There are really many models of fallen humanity in Genesis 1–11. Paul makes most of the model of Adam, but at least three more models of sin drawn from Genesis 1–11 are found in Paul's letter to the Romans. First, Noah's sons showed disrespect for their father (cf. Rom. 1:30 with Gen. 9:20–27). Second, there is a general corruption of mankind (cf. Rom. 3:9–20 with Gen. 6:11). And third, the evil imagination brings guilt at the age of adolescence (cf. Rom. 7:9 with Gen. 8:21).

There are three more models of sin drawn from Gen. 1–11 in New Testament writings outside of Paul. The Petrine writings make the fallen angels into models of the sin of *hybris* (pride) in sex (cf. I Pet. 3:18–22; II Pet. 2:4 with Gen. 6:1–4). The Lukan writings view the effort to build the tower of Babel as a model of the *hybris* of science and technology that divide the human race (cf. Acts 2:5–11 with Gen. 11:1–9). The Johannine writings use Cain as the model for sin as hatred for our brother (Jn. 8:44; I Jn. 3:11 with Gen. 4).

These seven models may be called in a new way "the seven deadly sins" in Genesis 1–11 that form models of man's sinful condition in antiquity and today. This new style does not put Genesis 1–11 in opposition to the valid discoveries of scientific anthropology, and at the same time it is a view of sin based on biblical revelation.

45. The Transmission of Sin

The question of sin moves more and more toward the most difficult topics thus far, but the previous preliminary review must be kept in mind as sin is now first related to guilt and then to grace. Responsibility raises the question of guilt as restoration in Christ requires a consideration of grace.

Sin and Guilt

Since the time of Augustine, Western theology, both Catholic and Protestant, has been troubled by the belief that the human race is so depraved, as a result of Adam's sin, that even infants without baptism are guilty and deprived of the blessings of heaven. Augustine coined the term limbo as the eternal abode of unbaptized infants (*Contra Julianum* II. 40; *Enchiridion,* 95).[27] All that has been said on sin thus far is obviously a repudiation of this view, but the question of guilt remains.

27. The history of this problem has been surveyed in my book *Baptism: Foundation for Christian Unity* (Philadelphia: The Westminster Press, 1967).

How then does man become guilty before God? If the answer is sought in Holy Scripture it is always the same: man is guilty before God because of his personal sin, not because he has inherited an alien guilt that goes back to the first man and first woman. The Old Testament proof text used from Augustine to the present to support the theory of inherited guilt is Psalm 51:5, but the text has nothing whatsoever to say about the damnation of the Psalmist because of Adam's sin. The sin of Adam is mentioned in the Old Testament in Genesis 3 only. The protest of Jeremiah 31:29f. and Ezekiel 18 against guilt for ancestral sin has already been mentioned. If anything is clear in Psalm 51 it is that the Psalmist recognizes his guilt for his personal sins: "my transgressions" (vv. 1, 3), "my iniquity" and "my sin" (v. 2), "I have sinned" (v. 4).

Augustine was able to support his theory of inherited guilt in the letters of Paul only on the basis of a false translation of the original Greek of Romans 5:12. The original Greek says that death passed upon all men "*because* all have sinned (*eph' hōi pantes hēmarton*)," but Augustine used a Latin text that substituted *in quo* (in whom) for "*eph' hōi*" (for, because, on the condition that).[28]

It is almost incredible to see reputable scholars, Catholic and Protestant alike, holding to the Augustinian idea of inherited guilt on the basis of traditional confessions alone.[29] Without a flaw the French Jesuit Henri Rondet traced the history of the error from Augustine to the present, yet for him the pronouncements of Councils and Popes in favor of inherited guilt settled the issue for Roman Catholics.[30]

When Stanislas Lyonnet, another French Jesuit, challenged this historical error in 1960 he was promptly suspended from his teaching position at the Pontifical Biblical Institute in Rome. This was done by none other than the "ecumenical" Pope John XXIII. Not even the Vatican Council of 1962-65 settled the dispute, so Pope Paul VI restored Lyonnet to his teaching position and appointed a symposium of leading scholars on July 11, 1966 to consider the problem within the limits and in agreement with the guidelines laid down in his address on "The Mystery of Original Sin."[31] The problem has not yet been resolved, and when it is resolved in favor of the supremacy of Scripture over tradition, the Roman Catholic doctrine of sin will have to be reinterpreted. Indeed a German Catholic has already altered the doctrine in a book not translated into English.[32]

The learned Lutheran scholar Joachim Jeremias has never been willing

28. A. T. Robertson, *Word Pictures in the New Testament* (Nashville, Tenn.: Sunday School Board of the Southern Baptist Convention, 1931), Vol. 4, p. 358.
29. This is fully discussed in my book *Baptism: Foundation for Christian Unity*, pp. 113-161.
30. *Original Sin*, tr. Cajetan Finegan (Staten Island, N.Y.: Alba House, 1967).
31. An English translation has been provided by William G. Heidt, *The Book of Genesis, Chapters 1-11* (Collegeville, Minnesota: The Liturgical Press, 1967), pp. 76-82.
32. Urs Baumann, *Erbsünde?* (Freiburg: Herder, 1970).

to say that the Augustinian link between inherited guilt and infant baptism is an error.[33] Calvinism has followed Lutheranism in defense of inherited guilt.[34] G. C. Berkouwer, the conservative Dutch Calvinist, fully recognizes the difficulties associated with the theory, but the best he can do is rehash the Pelagian controversy and appeal to Protestant confessions of faith to support the theory.[35] If ever there was a triumph of erroneous tradition over the teaching of Scripture, here is exhibit A.

This is no denial of inherited sin when inherited sin is interpreted as a state of sin in which there are tendencies that later lead to actual transgression. Romans 5:13f. is very clear in distinguishing sin from transgression. Knowledge of the law is always the basis for transgression. "Where there is no law there is no transgression" (Rom. 4:15; cf. 5:13; 7:8). Yet this distinction between the inheritance of a sinful nature and actual transgression is rejected by G. C. Berkouwer as if it were a liberal deviation from the true tradition. The Calvinistic confession composed by Baptists in 1677 made this distinction (Second London Confession, ch. VI). The Abstract of Principles of Southern Baptist Theological Seminary of 1859 put it succinctly by saying those who inherit a sinful nature become actual transgressors "as soon as they are capable of moral action" (VII). This statement is not superior to Scripture, as some creedalists want to make it, but it is a departure from the corollaries of infant guilt and infant baptism.

Now that the Pauline distinction between sin and transgression, or, in the language of historical theology, inherited sin and imputed sin, has replaced the theory that identifies the two, a second question remains. How does one inherit the tendencies that condition man's actual transgression so that he is not "as mean as the devil and his angels" who are beyond the possibility of redemption? Notice that the heading of this section speaks of the transmission of sin, not transgression. Transgression is personal, not inherited, yet transgression as imputed sin is conditioned by inherited sin.

With this clarification the biological transmission of sinful tendencies is not ruled out. Tertullian's so-called traducianism, which taught that the soul as well as the body is transmitted through the parents, did not teach that guilt is transmitted (*On the Soul*, 23-41). As has been said already, Tertullian taught that the child is in the paradise of innocence until the age of puberty when it goes forth into the world of guilt. The creationism of Catholicism, which teaches that an immortal soul is created for each mortal body that comes through procreation, is difficult to harmonize with any form of inherited guilt, yet both are taught.

F. R. Tennant believed that the Christian doctrine of man and his sin

---

33. This has been discussed personally with him at length and his defense is summarized in my book *Baptism: Foundation for Christian Unity*, pp. 113-161.
34. *Ibid.*, pp. 45-112.
35. *Sin*, tr. Philip C. Holtrop (Grand Rapids, Mich.: Wm. B. Eerdmans Publishing Co., 1971), pp. 424-435, 466-484.

is not difficult to harmonize with the animal ancestry of man, but he said that "sin may be defined as moral imperfection for which an agent, in God's sight, is accountable."[36] That is the meaning of guilt as defined above, but Tennant taught that inherited animal instincts conditioned moral imperfection. The ridicule of Tennant-type sin in the study by Frederic Greeves would be justified if Tennant did not take this animal ancestry so seriously.[37] Indeed, the story of Cain and Abel, without exposure to scientifc anthropology, saw sin as a beast in the breast that must be conquered (Gen. 4:7).

The psychological transmission of sin was advocated by R. S. Moxon. He said sin "is being influenced by the subconscious instincts, tendencies, desires and habits when the time has come to pass under the higher rule of reason and conscience."[38] Greeves also ridicules this psychology of the subconscious as a theory nobody would accept, but this too is an aspect of life that many disciples of Carl Jung would use.[39]

The social transmission of sin has special relevance when Christian criticism is brought to focus on systems of social injustice sanctified by tradition and time and they are recognized as stubborn forms of inhumanity. Sin is a form of social servitude that often destroys human freedom and dignity. Insight into this form of sin is the major contribution of the social gospel in America.[40] The defense of social injustice by self-righteous religion is super-sin.

Sin and Grace

The recognition of human responsibility for sin does not for one moment lessen the sense of guilt and the need for God's redeeming grace. Indeed, the recognition of human responsibility deepens the sense of guilt. This sense of the repetition of the pattern of Genesis 2–3 in the experience of every person was recognized by the author of 2 Baruch 54:19 who said: "Each one has been the Adam of his own soul."

In Pauline theology the sin of Adam is repeated in each individual but reversed in Jesus Christ. With a clear eye Karl Barth saw that Paul's doctrine of sin in Romans 5:12–21 begins with the grace of Christ as the Last Adam. The origin and transmission of sin must be understood in this Christocentric way. His little classic *Christ and Adam* (1952) has made a great impact on modern theology, both Catholic and Protestant, so much so that Rudolf Bultmann tried to answer him with a typical anthropocentric argument called *Adam and Christ* (1959).

The crowning Pauline passage on the liberation of man from the servitude of sin by God's grace in Christ is Romans 8:1–4:

36. *The Concept of Sin* (Cambridge University Press, 1912), p. 245.
37. *The Meaning of Sin* (London: The Epworth Press, n.d.), pp. 52-65.
38. *The Doctrine of Sin* (London: Allen & Unwin, 1922), p. 229.
39. *Op. cit.,* pp. 49f.
40. Charles Howard Hopkins, *The Rise of the Social Gospel in America* (New Haven: Yale University Press, 1940.

There is therefore now no condemnation for those who are in Christ Jesus. For the law of the Spirit of life in Christ Jesus has set me free from the law of sin and death. For God has done what the law, weakened by the flesh, could not do: sending his own Son in the likeness of sinful flesh and for sin, he condemned sin in the flesh, in order that the just requirement of the law might be fulfilled in us, who walk not according to the flesh but according to the Spirit.

The recapitulation theory of Irenaeus of Lyon (c. 130-c. 200) was based on Ephesians 1:10 where the purpose of God to unite all in Christ is stated as the theme of Ephesians, but the graphic elaboration of Irenaeus is in agreement with Scripture. His writing *Against Heresies* (II. XXII. 4) says:

> . . . He came to save all through himself; all, that is, who through him are born into God, infants, children, boys, young men and old. Therefore he passed through every stage of life: he was made an infant for infants, sanctifying infancy; a child among children, sanctifying those of this age, an example also to them of filial affection, righteousness and obedience; a young man amongst young men, an example to them, and sanctifying them to the Lord. So also amongst the older men; that he might be a perfect master for all, not solely in regard to the revelation of the truth, but also in respect of each stage of life. And then he came even unto death that he might be "the firstborn from the dead, holding the preeminence among all" (Col. i.18), the Prince of Life, before all and preceding all.

This theme has been stated in detail by Gustaf Wingren in his classic study of the biblical theology of Irenaeus.[41] Between the passage from life to death and then from death to life is the act of God in Christ. Christ, the incarnation of God, is the true image of God, and in Christ man is by grace renewed in the image of God. This is the most personal of all relations.

The problems attached to the substantial views of sin and grace could be more easily corrected by restoring the biblical view of God as Spirit to the incarnation. This has been done in a significant way in the Bampton Lectures of 1977.[42]

The crux of the question is the debate over the meaning of sin and grace in Western Christianity.[43] Roman Catholicism has taught that the inherited guilt that brings damnation even to infants is removed by an infusion of grace (*gratia infusa*). The two ideas of inherited guilt and infused

---

41. *Man and the Incarnation*, tr. Ross Mackenzie (Edinburgh: Oliver and Boyd, 1959).
42. G. W. Lampe, *God as Spirit* (Oxford: Clarendon Press, 1977).
43. A good survey is in Jaroslav Pelikan, ed., *Twentieth Century Theology in the Making* (New York: Harper and Row, 1970), Vol. II, pp. 161-233.

grace are a consistent disaster in which both are reduced to a substance physically transmitted. This "stuffy" view has obscured the dimension of the personal which is central in covenant faith.

At the time of the Protestant Reformation, Philip Melanchthon, Martin Luther's co-worker, interpreted sin as a broken relation and grace as the unmerited favor of God (*favor Dei*) that restores this broken relation between man and God. Protestant theology has not always followed Melanchthon, but this is the New Testament view. Pauline theology is especially strong on this doctrine of grace, but the rest of the Bible is based on the covenant concept of a personal relation between God and his people. Personal sin is overcome only by the restoration of a personal relation to God. Man's sin is overcome by God's grace (Eph. 2:4-7).

46. The Wages of Sin

The doctrine of death is so confused in Christian theology that it is necessary to disentangle three different theories in historical theology before we examine three New Testament theologies of death. While the three theories are inconsistent with one another the three theologies are complementary.

Historical Theories of Death

The first historical theory that has influenced historical theology and has been most often confused with the biblical understanding of death may be called the *idealistic* view. The classical expression of this view is found in the dialogues of the Greek philosopher Plato (427-347 B.C.).

In simplified form this theory has three points. First, the soul existed before the body and is by nature immortal. Second, this immortal soul comes to live in a mortal body at birth so that the soul is in the body as an oyster is in a shell (*Phaedrus*, 250). Third, according to Plato, at death the immortal soul leaves the mortal body and returns to its source to live in another body at another time. According to this view, the circular movement goes on forever, and there is no redemption or resurrection of the body.

A Platonic myth focusing on the pre-existence of the soul is that of the chariot driver (*Phaedrus*, 246). Reason drives the two winged horses of flesh and spirit across the vault of heaven until they all fall into the world below. Reason desperately tries to return to the original source. This is the myth of the pre-existent soul that falls into a body until released from the body below. While the soul is in the body the relation is one that Plato described as *sōma-sēma* (body-tomb) because the body is the tomb of the soul (*Gorgias*, 493). The best example of the return of the soul to its source in the world soul is the calm death of Socrates (*Phaedo*, 58-64). These views are supported by five arguments: the superiority of life over death, the existence of the soul before the body, the simplicity of the soul that makes it impossible for it to disintegrate, the participation of the soul in life, the self-existence of the soul as eternal motion (*Phaedo*, 61e, 70c-72e, 103b-107b; *Phaedrus*, 245c-246a; *Laws*, 893-896).

In medieval Catholicism and modern idealism these ideas have been so thoroughly mixed with biblical language that many a pious parson takes his text from the Apostle Paul while his source of ideas is the philosopher Plato. Some good examples used at many a funeral are *Intimations of Immortality* by Wordsworth and *Crossing the Bar* by Tennyson. William Wordsworth (1770-1850) said in his *Intimations of Immortality*:

> *Our birth is but a sleep and a forgetting:*
> *The Soul that rises with us, our life's Star,*
>   *Hath had elsewhere its setting,*
>   *And cometh from afar:*
>   *Not in entire forgetfulness,*
>   *And not in utter nakedness,*
> *But trailing clouds of glory do we come*
> *From God, who is our home.*

This same Platonic philosophy of the pre-existence of the soul found expression in *Crossing the Bar* by Alfred Lord Tennyson (1809-1892) when he wrote:

> *Sunset and evening star,*
>   *And one clear call for me!*
> *And may there be no moaning of the bar,*
>   *When I set out to sea,*
> *But such a tide as moving seems asleep,*
>   *Too full for sound or foam,*
> *When that which drew from out the boundless deep*
>   *Turns again home.*

Those and other utterances on the pre-existence and natural immortality of the soul have been substituted for biblical views of the immortality of God from whom men may receive immortality as a gift (I Cor. 15:53, 54; II Cor. 5:4).

The idealistic view of death was not unchallenged even in Greek philosophy. The naturalistic challenge of Epicurean materialism questioned the idea of a pre-existent soul that is by nature immortal by viewing all things as a form of matter. Even though the name is from the Greek philosopher Epicurus (342-270 B.C.), the classic discussion may be found in the Roman poet Lucretius (96-55 B.C.) who said that everlasting death awaits all (*On the Nature of Things*, III, 1094). This was continued in Cicero, *De nat. Deor*. I. 24, 66; Epictetus, *Dis*. II. 8 and Seneca, *Ep. Mor*. XII.

Renaissance humanism revived the naturalistic view of death. The famous lines of Shakespeare about life being a brief candle (*Macbeth*, V. v) and the cynicism of the grave diggers who thought of death as a return to clay (*Hamlet*, V), lines learned by most students of English literature, are examples of the naturalistic view of death. The modern nihilism of Jean-Paul Sartre that sees human existence as an end in itself with no exit, a *cul de sac*, has become the mood of many secular people even if they do not verbalize their feelings. This is what C. E. M. Joad called "Decadence" in our culture.

The biblical view of death — which should be the Christian view — is neither optimistic idealism nor pessimistic naturalism. Biblical realism sees man as a living soul whose body and spirit are created by God at the beginning of each life, not only the first man as in Genesis 2:7 but every man as in Job 10:9–11, as already discussed under the doctrine of man.

The physical termination of life does indeed belong to the natural cycle of life, as argued by naturalism. There are limits to physical life, whether the limit be 70, 120 or a thousand years. Therefore, the result of sin in Genesis 2:17 was spiritual death. Man cut himself off from the tree of life (Gen. 3:22–24) on the very day he disobeyed.

Those who argue for physical death as the result of sin have difficulty in explaining who was right; the Lord who said Adam and Eve would die "in the day" they ate of the tree or the serpent who said "you will not die" (3:4). If the wages of sin is physical death, then it seems that the serpent was right, but if the result is spiritual death, then the Lord was right. Efforts to explain Genesis 2:17 with such linguistic arguments as "they began to die," so that physical death within a thousand years is meant, or they were sentenced to die hardly fit the context and mislead later biblical interpretation. Man may indeed eat of the tree of life, but that belongs to the life to come and the age to come. This is later discussed under the topic of immortality.

The curse on creation in Genesis 3:14–19 is the result of man's sin. The instinctive hostility between men and the serpent may indeed be a result of the disruption of the harmony between man and reptiles, but serpents were around before sin. Childbirth was a part of the Lord's original intention for mankind (Gen. 2:21–24); thus it is the disruption of the natural cycle of birth that makes childbirth an ordeal (Gen. 3:16). Similarly, the curse on the earth is the drudgery of work. Finally, as the result of sin, man's body returns to the earth. Man's return to dust belongs to the natural cycle of physical life (Gen. 3:19). Not even the concept of cosmic redemption in Romans 8:18–25 assigns the termination of physical existence on the earth to sin. The redemption of the body is the restoration of the original intention that the transition from the natural body to the spiritual body should be a departure rather than "the fear of death" (cf. Heb. 2:15). Without spiritual death Enoch would be the example for all (Heb. 11:5).

Biblical Theologies of Death

It is not always certain whether a New Testament text, when considered out of context, has reference to physical or spiritual death, but it is almost always clear when the usage in the whole document is considered. At least three theologies of death may be distinguished.

In the general epistles the reference to spiritual death as the result of sin is often obvious. It would be possible to interpret physical death as the result of sin in James 1:15 if it were not for the clearer reference to spiritual death in James 5:10, 20. The first passage says that "desire when it has conceived gives birth to sin; and sin when it is full-grown brings forth death." The interpretation spiritual death is strengthened by the second passage which says: "My brethren, if any one among you wanders from the truth and some one bring him back, let him know that whoever brings back a sinner from the error of his way will save a soul from death and will cover a multitude of sin." It is clear that the spiritual death of the soul is in mind.

A similar picture of physical and spiritual death appears in the Petrine writings. It is said that Jesus was "put to death in the flesh but made alive in the spirit" (I Pet. 3:19). Physical flesh is here in mind, and it is the human spirit, not the Holy Spirit, that is made alive so that Jesus can preach to fallen angelic spirits in prison, i.e. Tartarus (II Peter 2:4). Physical death is perhaps in mind in I Peter 4:5-6, but it is the human spirit again that is made alive. Some indeed insist that the "dead" here are those spiritually dead, but that would require an interpretation of flesh out of line with I Peter 4:1-2. Physical death even here is not interpreted as a result of sin but what is common for man, "like men" (4:6).

A final example of spiritual death in the general epistles is in Hebrews. The emphasis on the humanity of Jesus in Hebrews 2:9, 14-15 could confine the sufferings of Christ to physical death, but this would assign physical death to the power of the devil. Jesus tasted total "death for every one," and it is total death that holds man in the bondage of fear. It was not just physical "death" from which God "was able to save" Jesus (5:7), but deliverance from total death by resurrection from the dead. The paraphrase of 5:17 in *The Living Bible* gives a peculiar picture of Jesus' prayer by interpreting death in a physical sense. If death were confined to the termination of physical life in Hebrews, the statement about Enoch not seeing death would be a contradiction (11:5). He terminated his physical life, but he did not see death. This is a picture of "what might have been for all" had spiritual death as alienation from God not entered into human experience. As it is, the termination of life is a lonely ordeal for those who are spiritually dead already.

The Pauline view of death in relation to sin makes it possible to say that "in Adam all die" and that death is "the last enemy" (I Cor. 15:22, 26).

This is the total death in the present which is finally overcome by the resurrection of the dead. Those who have terminated this life in Christ have only "fallen asleep" (I Thess. 4:14, 15; I Cor. 15:6, 20, 51). It is not clear whether baptism for the dead is for those physically dead or spiritually dead (I Cor. 15:30).

In the "pillar epistle" of Romans the distinction between physical death and spiritual death is of decisive importance. If the line pursued thus far is correct, then it was spiritual death that entered into the world in Adam. This spiritual death spread to all men "because every one has sinned" (5:12 TEV; cf. AV, NEB, JB with ASV, NASB, RSV, LB, etc.). If the translation adopted here is correct this would make the consequence of sin a movement from spiritual life to spiritual death. Spiritual death comes "through one man's trespass" when there is disobedience to God, as spiritual life comes "through the grace of that one man Jesus Christ" when there is the obedience of faith (5:15–20).

This movement from spiritual life to spiritual death is precisely the point made in that much neglected text in Romans 7:9 where Paul says:

> I was alive once apart from the law,
> but when the commandment came,
> sin revived and I died.

Any effort to confine this meaning to the first man ignores the frequent use of "I" or is forced to say that "I" is Adam! It is clear that Paul believed he was alive until the knowledge of the tenth commandment brought spiritual death to him (Rom. 7:7-8). Paul also believed one could pass from spiritual life back into spiritual death (Rom. 8:12f.). This is a tradition advocated by Tertullian in the early church and adopted by some Baptists later, and it is a tradition true to the Scriptures. We have had enough of Augustinian Manichaeism that teaches that little infants come into the world spiritually dead, guilty and worthy of damnation.

The "prison letters" of Paul take a second step by adding a movement from spiritual death to spiritual life after the movement from spiritual life to spiritual death. This was suggested by Paul's exhortation to the Romans to consider themselves "dead to sin but alive to God in Christ Jesus" (6:11), but this belief first appears in full bloom in Colossians 2:12–13. Here again the *New English Bible* and the *Good News Bible* are correct while many other translations lead astray by saying we were spiritually dead "in trespasses" (RSV) rather than "because of your sins" before "you were raised to life" (2:13, 12 NEB).

The second "prison epistle" to teach this movement from spiritual life to death before the movement from spiritual death to spiritual life is Ephesians. Here the *New English Bible* strangely reverses its correct translation of Colossians 2:13 by saying "you were dead in your sins" or "we were dead in our sins" (2:1, 5). The *Good News Bible* has 2:1 correct and 2:5

wrong. Here it is the Revised Standard Version that is correct in saying "through" rather than "in," but the "your" is left out in 2:1 while the "our" is rightly retained in 2:5. He who says theology does not color translation should compare the various versions of Colossians 2:12, 13 and Ephesians 2:1, 5. Most follow the AV blunder based on the theology of Augustine.

The Johannine theology on the relationship between sin and spiritual death is the richest and most extensive in the New Testament. There is no explanation, to be sure, as to why one was spiritually dead in the first place before he was made spiritually alive when he "has passed from death to life" (Jn. 5:24). Apparently all those who live in the godless world (*kosmos*) of darkness and hate are spiritually dead, but this "passage" from life to death is never mentioned.

The chief additions to the theology of death in the Johannine writings are the ideas of mortal sin and second death. The passage from spiritual death to spiritual life is made manifest by brotherly love (I Jn. 3:14). He who practices brotherly love demonstrates that he has come out of darkness into light and has eternal life (cf. 1:7).

Life is used in three different ways in I John 3:11–18. "We know that we have passed out of death into life (*zōē*), because we love the brethren" (3:14). It would be absurd to say that "we know we have passed out of physical death into physical life because we love the brethren." Unfortunately there are all too many who are physically alive but do not love their brothers.

One who is spiritually alive manifests his brotherly love by his willingness to lay down his physical life (*psychē*) for his brother (I Jn. 3:16). Even if he is not called upon to make this sacrifice of himself he will manifest eternal life by his willingness to share the means of this earthly life (*bios*, 3:17) with his needy brother. If there is no brotherly love, there is no light from God and eternal life in a person. There is no way to water down this Johannine teaching. It has already been noted that Paul taught a passage from spiritual life to spiritual death (Rom. 8:12f.). There is also no way to water down the Johannine teaching on mortal sin (RSV), "a sin unto death" (AV), or the "sin that leads to death" (TEV) in I John 5:16. It would be positively absurd to say: "He who has the Son has physical life; he who has not the Son of God has not physical life" when reading I John 5:12. Again it is unfortunate that many are physically alive who do not have the Son. The contrast in I John 5:16 as in 3:14 is between spiritual or eternal life and spiritual death. It is only a preconceived notion that refuses to face a dangerous possibility by trying to reduce death in I John 5:16 to physical death. Physical death may be a chastisement for sin, as in I Corinthians 11:30–32, but that does not fit the context of I John 5:16 (cf. 3:14; 5:11–13).

This becomes even clearer in that second death in Revelation 2:11; 20:14; 21:8 has reference to spiritual death. The second death is after the resurrection and the final judgment. It means, as in Genesis 2:17, to be cut off from the tree of life (2:7; 22:2, 14), to lose the crown of life (2:10), to be blotted out or never to have been in the book of life (3:5; 13:8; 17:8; 20:15; 21:27; 22:17) and to have no access to the water of life (21:6; 22:1, 17). Second death is spiritual death as eternal life is spiritual life. All spiritual death is the wages of sin.

47. The Power of Sin

The relationship between sin and the law was introduced by the Apostle Paul when he spoke of the power of sin as the law (I Cor. 15:56). This relationship was further explored soon afterward in Galatians, A.D. 54, and Romans, A.D. 55. Indeed these two "pillar epistles" were destined to become the fundamental New Testament writings that stimulated the revolt against legalism at the time of the Protestant Reformation.

In brief these letters teach that the *function* of the law is to bring to man (1) the knowledge of sin over against the holiness, righteousness, goodness, and spirituality of the law on the one hand, and (2) the increase of sin in actual experience on the other. That is why righteousness comes to man by faith and not by the works of the law. Faith becomes the *fulfillment* of the law through (1) the sending of God's Son into human history and (2) the sending of God's Spirit into the human heart that believes.

Here is the place where the systematic theologian will find far more help by a careful reading of Galatians and Romans than in most of the historical theology of both Catholicism and Protestantism. Protestantism has made this issue the main criticism of Catholicism, but extreme reaction has often bordered on an antinomianism with a biblical imbalance. It is, therefore, necessary to consider the biblical teachings first, before going into the thicket of the controversies between Catholicism and Protestantism and between Lutheranism and Calvinism later.

The Function of the Law

How did Paul reach the conclusion that the first function of the law is the knowledge of sin rather than the means of salvation? In the apostolic confrontation between Cephas (Simon Peter) and Paul in Antioch the issue of justification by faith threatened the unity of the churches (Gal. 2:11–21). If the gospel was preached to Abraham before the law was given to Moses, what then is the relationship between gospel and law (Gal. 3:6–9)? If the Spirit is received by faith and not by the works of the law, why then is the law important for believers (3:1–5). If Christ came to redeem those who are under the curse of the law, what is the function of the law for a Jewish believer (3:10–14)? It is clear that the promise to Abraham is much older than the proclamation of the law (3:15–18).

Two questions arise. First question: "Why then is the law? It was added because of transgression, till the offspring should come to whom the promise had been made; and it was ordained by angels through an intermediary. Now an intermediary implies more than one; but God is one" (3:19f.).

Second question: "Is the law against the promises of God? Certainly not; for if a law had been given which would make alive, then righteousness would indeed be by the law. But the scripture consigned all things to sin, that what was promised to faith in Jesus Christ might be given to those who believe" (3:21-22).

The law then is reduced to the role of a *paidagogos*, a custodian who has charge of a child until he comes of age (3:23-4:3). The law is related to both transgression and sin, for it is through the law that sin becomes known as transgression.

If the argument in Galatians is not clear on how the law brings the knowledge of sin, the expansions of the argument in Romans should help. It should not be forgotten that the human conscience may enable one to do by nature what the law of Moses requires, but it is the law of Moses that deepens sin into actual transgression (2:14-16). "For no human being will be justified by the law, since through the law comes the knowledge of sin" (3:20). Indeed, "where there is no law there is no transgression" (4:15). What then is the relationship between sin and transgression? The answer: "Sin indeed was in the world before the law was given, but sin is not counted where there is no law" (5:13). There was a state of sin and spiritual death before the law was given, but this was not like Adam's transgression (5:14).

This leads to the second function of the law. "Law came in to increase the sin" (5:20). Again it is hardly necessary to explain what Paul means by the increase of sin, for his own testimony is clear enough. Law turns one inward and makes him more and more egocentric. That is the meaning of "flesh" when used in a psychological way. It is as important here to distinguish between physical flesh and psychological flesh as it was in the previous section to distinguish between physical death and spiritual death.

Apart from the references to "me" and "my" the egocentric "I" appears thirty-six times in Romans 7:7-25. The first paragraph describes man's exit from the Paradise of innocence into spiritual death by knowledge of the law (7-12). The second paragraph depicts a state of slavery because the law brings unconscious sin into consciousness to make man an actual transgressor (13-20). A third paragraph declares man's utter despair as the knowledge of sin reduces him to wretchedness (21-25).

At the time of the Protestant Reformation the function of the law became a central issue. In protest against the legalism of Roman Catholicism there was the definite tendency in Lutheranism to magnify only the negative function of the law as outlined above. This often went so far that there developed a sort of new Marcionism in Lutheranism that restricted the law to a negative function only.

In Calvinism the positive function of the law, especially the Decalogue, was magnified as a model of the good life. Some Lutheran theologians have seen in this a legalism that allows for life under the law when man obeys it. There is no doubt about Calvin's positive emphasis on the goodness of the law, but instruction alone, without the negative function of failure *under the law*, was never the intention of Calvinism despite the legalism that developed.

This debate about the negative and positive function of law has been brought into fresh focus by the conservative Dutch Calvinist G. C. Berkouwer in his response to the charges by the conservative Lutheran theologian Werner Elert.[44] Lutheran reaction against legalism has gone too far when Luther declares the Letter of James "an epistle of straw" and then emends the text of Romans 3:28 with *allein* to make it read "faith alone." This puts Romans 3:28 in contradiction with James 2:24 which says that "a man is justified by works and not by faith alone." The references to "the perfect law" (James 1:25) and good works (2:26) contradict Paul's teachings on "the law of Christ" (Gal. 6:2, cf. 5:23) only when read through Lutheran lenses.

There is nothing in Paul that contradicts the summary of the law in I Timothy 1:8–11:

> Now we know that the law is good, if any one uses it lawfully, understanding this, that the law is not laid down for the just but for the lawless and disobedient, for the ungodly and sinners, for the unholy and profane, for murderers of fathers and murderers of mothers, for manslayers, immoral persons, sodomites, kidnapers, liars, perjurers, and whatever else is contrary to sound doctrine, in accordance with the glorious gospel of the blessed God with which I have been entrusted.

The Fulfillment of the Law

Fulfillment of the law is not possible under the law. Under the law one is a slave, but in Christ one becomes a son. By (1) the sending of God's Son into human history and (2) the sending of God's Spirit into the human heart the great deliverance takes place. "Christ redeemed us from the curse of the law, having become a curse for us" (Galatians 3:13). Until then demonic powers, "the elemental powers of the universe," dominated our lives (4:3).

As the hymn in Galatians 4:4–5 says:

44. G. C. Berkouwer, *Sin* (Grand Rapids, Mich.: Wm. B. Eerdmans, 1971), pp. 157ff.

> *But when the time had fully come,*
>   *God sent forth his Son,*
> *born of a woman,*
>   *born under the law,*
> *to redeem those who were under the law,*
>   *so that we might receive adoption as sons.*

The second step is the sending of his Spirit into human hearts (4:6–7):

> *And because you are sons,*
>   *God sent the Spirit of his Son into our hearts (crying, "Abba!*
>   *Father!")*
> *So through God you are no longer a slave but a son,*
>   *and if a son then an heir.*

Having received the Spirit by faith, not by the works of the law (3:3), a turning again "to the weak and beggarly elemental spirits" is indeed foolish (3:1–6; 4:8–11; 5:1, 4, 7). Living under the law leads to the work of the flesh, but walking by the Spirit, i.e. being led by the Spirit, is manifested by the fruit of the Spirit (5:16–24).

It is all but impossible to ignore the parallels between Galatians and Romans when the relationship between sin and the law is considered. Romans 8:1–27 again expands Galatians with the repetition of (1) the sending of God's Son and (2) the sending of God's Spirit. There are advances in thought at several places, but the threefold use of law in Romans 8:1–4 is of special importance in stating the relationship between sin and the law.

The relationship between sin and spiritual death is seen in the *law* of sin. The failure of the *law* of Moses in the realm of human egocentricity, i.e. the flesh, made necessary the sending of God's Son so that the *law* of the Spirit of life could bring freedom to those under the law of Moses. The contrast between the "likeness of sinful flesh" in Jesus and his death "as a sin offering" (footnote) is very much the same as that between him "who knew no sin" and him who was made "to be sin" or a sin offering in II Corinthians 5:21. In both passages the sinless Son is the sacrifice for those in bondage to the law of sin and death and under the law of Moses.

48. The Dominion of Darkness

God, according to Paul, "has delivered us from the dominion of darkness and transferred us to the kingdom of his beloved Son" (Col. 1:13). This dominion includes the principalities and powers over which God was victorious in Christ (Col. 2:15). But what does all this mean in terms of modern thought? Do the biblical teachings on the devil and demons have meaning today? These questions can best be answered after a presentation and the interpretation of the biblical beliefs.

The Devil

In the earliest part of the Old Testament the source of man's temptation that is identified with neither man nor God is represented as a subtle serpent (Gen. 3:1–15). The curse of the Lord upon the serpent gave what at times had been a friendly figure the evil reputation reflected in later teachings.[45]

The so-called Deuteronomic historians spoke of this sinister power manifested in the insanity of Saul as "an evil spirit from the Lord" that tormented him when "the Spirit of the Lord departed from Saul" (I Sam. 16:14). Belief in the sovereignty of the Lord over all spirits will not allow for dualism of two independent powers, so the "evil spirit" is said to be "from the Lord."

In the postexilic writings, when the term Satan was adopted for the adversary or prosecutor of man before the Lord, no dualism is detected. Satan is permitted to test the integrity of Job, but he is subordinate to the Lord (Job 1–2). He challenges the fitness of Joshua to serve as high priest, but this is a role in the divine tribunal (Zech. 3:1–2). In II Samuel 24:1, the incitement to take a census of the people is ascribed to the anger of the Lord, but in I Chronicles 21:1 Satan has been assigned this role. Developments in the understanding of the Lord and of Satan are evident, but there is still no ultimate dualism.

When the Old Testament was translated into Greek the usual translation of Satan was *diabolos*, the devil, and this is the most widely used term in the New Testament. In the New Testament the devil is the adversary of both Christ and man. The temptation of Jesus recognized the source of evil neither in Jesus nor God (Matt. 4:1–11; Luke 4:1–13).

In Acts the source of human oppression and evil is ascribed to the devil (10:38; 13:10). In Hebrews the devil has the power of death (2:14), but in other sources for Hellenistic Jewish Christianity he is primarily the adversary that man must resist and guard against lest he be deceived and seduced (James 4:7; I Pet. 5:8).

The earlier writings of Paul use the term Satan, but the later ones adopt the term devil. Ephesians portrays the devil as the ruler of the whole dominion of evil (4:27; 6:11), and the Pastoral letters warn believers lest they fall as the devil did (I Tim. 3:6f.; II Tim. 2:26).

The Johannine writings depict the dominion of the devil as the whole realm of darkness over against the light that came into the world in Jesus (6:70; 8:44; 13:2). Hate is a special manifestation of the devil, and Cain, not Adam, is the cardinal sinner (I Jn. 3:8, 10). Yet in all the Johannine writings there is no ultimate dualism. The devil, identified by several other names, will be defeated (Rev. 2:10; 12:9, 12; 20:2, 10).

45. *The Interpreter's Dictionary of the Bible, Supplementary Volume* (Nashville: Abingdon, 1976), pp. 816f.

If biblical references to the devil are followed there is no question about the reality of the devil, yet there are those who have announced the death of the devil in theology much as the death of God was announced a few years back.[46] H. A. Kelly, himself a Roman Catholic, has ridiculed the role of Satan in religious thought and called for his demise, especially in his own church which he regards as the most demon-ridden of all. In the same emotional and sensational manner, a dispensational Protestant has declared and attempted to demonstrate that "Satan is alive and well on planet earth."[47]

The meaning of the diabolical in human life has not been ignored in more profound theological reflection. Some have assigned the devil to the subjectivity of God and others to the subjectivity of man. Paul Tillich is a good example of the first, although he posits dipolarity in man as well. The effort to locate the devil in man's subjectivity turns man into a devil and puts him beyond redemption.[48] It seems much better to say the devil belongs neither to the nature of God nor man and that he is both subjective and objective. That is why he is to be overcome by both God and those who abide in God.

The real merit in the several works by James Kallas is to be found in his emphasis on this final victory over the devil in biblical faith. To locate the devil in the nature of God or man would make this victory impossible.[49] The devil is the adversary of both man and God, not an attribute of either.

What, then, can be said between these extremes of interpretation? In the Old Testament, and to some extent outside the Scriptures, it seems clear that many phenomena of evil are demonic to such an extent that they do not fit into what is believed about God or man. A third power is posited to account for this diabolical dimension in what is believed to be God's good creation.

In the New Testament Scriptures the temptation of Jesus, the sinless Son of God, accentuates this third power even more. How can one in unique relation to God be tempted in the manner described in the Gospels if there is not a diabolical dimension that is in harmony with what is believed about Jesus and God?

46. Henry Ansgar Kelly, *Towards the Death of the Devil* (London: Geoffrey Chapman, 1968).
47. The title of a book by Hal Lindsey (Grand Rapids: Zondervan, 1972).
48. This has been done by Howard Van Pendley, III, *Views of the Demonic in Recent Religious Thought* (Th.D. dissertation, Southern Baptist Theological Seminary, 1975), 224 pp. Ruth Nanda Anshew, *The Reality of the Devil* (New York: Harper & Row, 1972) presents Satan as the evil inherent in man and the universe. This is a power equal to God that seeks to preserve the individual for itself.
49. James Kallas, *The Satanward View* (Philadelphia: The Westminster Press, 1966); *Jesus and the Power of Satan* (Philadelphia: The Westminster Press, 1968); *The Real Satan* (Minneapolis: Augsburg Publishing House, 1975). This last book is very helpful for the beginner.

Reaction to superficial alibis such as "the devil made me do it" may blind one to the fact that there is a dominion of darkness from which man needs to be delivered. The abundance of biblical evidence should not be dismissed because of bizarre interpretations.

The Demons

About the time pronouncements were being made on the death of both God and the devil, a rash of popular books began to be published on demons and the demonic. A favorite text among fundamentalists was I Timothy 4:1–5 until it was noted that the text teaches the possibility of apostasy, falling away from the faith. Nonetheless there was a resurgence of belief in "deceitful spirits and doctrines of demons."

Belief in demons, like belief in the devil (Satan), is deeply rooted in the Old Testament. The worshippers of other gods were looked upon as demon worshippers. Deuteronomy 32:17 declared:

> They sacrificed to demons which were no gods,
>   the gods they had never known,
> to new gods that had come in of late,
>   whom your fathers had never dreaded.

Some would raise the question whether this identification of demons with what were no gods does not lead to the conclusion that there are no demons. The Scriptures of the Old and New Testaments do not draw this conclusion. The fact that demonic powers in the Old Testament are described as both animals and angels should caution against extreme literalism, but this does not remove the possibility of evil spirits. The evil spirits are, however, described at times as demons in serpent forms (Gen. 3:1–3; Num. 21:6, 8), fiery flying serpents (Deut. 8:15; Isa. 14:29; 30:6) and seraphim (Isa. 6:1ff.). Seirim are hairy demons (Lev. 17:7; Isa. 13:21; 34:14; II Kings 23:8; II Chron. 11:15), and the special Azazel (the scapegoat) made symbolic atonement for Israel through its release into the wilderness (Lev. 16:8–26). Azazel is the leader of the fallen angels in apocalyptic literature (I Enoch 6:7; 9:16; 10:4–6). To these may be added the night demon Lilith (Isa. 34:14; Ps. 91:5) and the mighty ones (Shedim, Deut. 32:17; Ps. 106:37f.).[50]

Belief in demon possession and the possibility of exorcisms, casting out demons in the name of Jesus, is especially prominent in the New Testament. The most pointed statement on the presence of the kingdom of God in the ministry has reference to the casting out of demons (Matt. 12:28 = Luke 11:20). This power was given to the twelve (Mark 3:15), and it is later manifested in the ministry of Paul (Acts 16:18; 19:11–17).

Some would assign the phenomena to what are called complexes to-

---

50. Edward Langton, *Essentials of Demonology* (London: The Epworth Press, 1949).

day.[51] A few see both spiritual causes and cures.[52] Still more see both natural and spiritual causes and natural and spiritual cures.

The beliefs behind the Beelzebub controversy in the ministry of Jesus are basic for understanding other New Testament passages. In the Old Testament Beelzebub was the Philistine god of Ekron in II Kings 1:22ff., a Hebrew spelling meaning "lord of flies," but he has become the prince of demons in the teachings of Jesus (Mark 3:7–35, parallels). Many now explain the origin of the term Beelzebub from the fertility god in Ugaritic writings who was called "prince, lord of the earth." Thus the New Testament preserves the original meaning that made it a logical word for Satan or the devil.

In any case, the last part of the Gospel of Mark pictures this age as a demon-infested house over which Satan rules. Into this house the Spirit enters to cast out Satan and the demons of his domain. Gehenna, the place of final punishment, is prepared especially for the devil and the demons who are called his angels (Matt. 25:41). For this reason, there is no New Testament suggestion that the devil and the demons are to be redeemed. They can only be cast out from those who are redeemed.

The Pauline perspective on demons is in agreement with the Old Testament teaching that identifies demons with heathen deities. Pagan sacrifices are offered to demons, not to God, and those who participate in pagan sacrifices worship demons, not the true God revealed in Jesus Christ (I Cor. 10:20–21).

The most highly developed demonology of the New Testament is in the Pauline writings. Demons are "the rulers of this age" who worked through those who crucified Jesus (I Cor. 2:8). They are the elemental spirits of the world, the *stoicheia*, from whose bondage Christ has redeemed those who have status as sons of God (Gal. 4:3, 8). Above all they are the principalities and powers of the invisible world who are manifested in visible rulers of evil intent (Rom. 8:38; Eph. 6:12).

The present activity and future subordination of the demonic powers are the chief concerns of the New Testament. The final defeat of demons is a special concern in the book of Revelation (16:4; 18:2). However, the logical conclusion that they must have fallen in the past from a previous state of goodness is not overlooked (Jude 6; II Pet. 2:4).

Responses to biblical demonology parallel those to the devil. Many regard this as a part of the ancient world view that needs to be demythologized.[53] Others adopt Paul Tillich's idea of the demonic as the exaltation of the finite to the level of the infinite.[54] Tillich's successor at Union Theological Seminary, John Macquarrie, had more difficulty with the fallen an-

---

51. S. Vernon McCasland, *By the Finger of God* (New York: Macmillan, 1951).
52. Charles Moeller, *et al.*, *Satan* (New York: Sheed and Ward, 1951).
53. John Macquarrie, *The Scope of Demythologizing* (New York: Harper & Brothers, 1960).
54. *Systematic Theology* (University of Chicago Press, 1963), Vol. 3, pp. 102-106.

gels than with the good angels, but he is not willing to close the door completely on these elemental spirits.[55] Such reservations are understandable in these days when heinous crimes are ascribed to demon possession for which there is no human responsibility, but the status of good and evil spirits that never lived in bodies is the same as that of those which have. Both appear as possibilities and actualities.

The victory of Christ over the dominion of darkness at one time bore the brunt of liberal levity, but the little classic by Gustaf Aulén translated *Christus Victor* (S.P.C.K., 1931) has changed all that. Aulén claimed that the victory of the kingdom of God over the dominion of darkness, the devil, demons and death was not only the classic view of the atonement in the New Testament, the Church Fathers and Martin Luther, but that it is still the most dramatic description of what God has done and is doing in Jesus Christ for the redemption of man from sin.

There are indeed passages in the New Testament that describe Jesus as Victim of God's justice and also as the Vicar or helper of man in his need, but Christ as Victor over the dominion of darkness dominates the classic view of the death of Jesus. It is hardly possible to do justice to the work of Jesus Christ whose death delivers us from sin, death and the demonic without serious reflection on the relevance of belief in the devil and the demons that loom so large in the biblical revelation. It is therefore to the work and the person of Jesus Christ that we now turn.

55. *Principles of Christian Theology*, Second Edition (New York: Scribner's, 1977), pp. 237f., 262f., 318f., 325f. See the conservative Calvinist G. C. Berkouwer, *op. cit.,* pp. 99-129, for another example of ambivalence on the demonic. See also *The Christian Hope* or *The Humanity of God.*

VII. SALVATION

49. The Nature of Salvation

The way of salvation is the road of life eternal. It is, as John Bunyan put it, "the pilgrim's progress, from this world to that which is to come." This salvation is so great that Hebrews 2:1–4 becomes a solemn warning to all who hear the good news of this welcome journey to "the saints' everlasting rest" (Richard Baxter). The author of Hebrews raises a question for which there is no answer: "How shall we escape, if we neglect so great a salvation?" There is no answer because there is no escape for those who fail to give heed to the dangers of drifting and disobedience, in their refusal to believe that which "was declared at first by the Lord, and it was attested . . . by signs and wonders and various miracles, and by gifts of the Holy Spirit distributed according to his own will" (Heb. 2:3–4). This salvation may be described as one way with two sides and three stages.

The One Way of Salvation

The New Testament opens with good news about the way of the Lord. John the Baptist appears in the wilderness as the messenger of Malachi 3:1 and as the voice of Isaiah 40:3. As the messenger, he goes before the Lord to prepare the way (Mark 1:2; Matt. 11:10; Luke 7:27); and as the voice, he cries in the wilderness: "Prepare ye the way of the Lord, make his paths straight" (Mark 1:3; Matt. 3:3; Luke 3:4). Preparation is made in order that all flesh could see "the salvation of God" (Luke 3:6).

Christ is the way. In the "inspiration" Christology of the Synoptic Gospels and Acts, Jesus is recognized, even by those who would entrap him, as one who did truly teach "the way of God" (Mark 12:14). He taught with authority that "the gate is narrow and the way is hard that leads to life, and those who find it are few" (Matt. 7:14). His preaching and teaching centered on the main theme of the kingdom of God. The preaching that saves is both an act and a message.

308

The apostolic message of the early church proclaimed that "there is salvation in no one else, for there is no other name under heaven given among men by which we must be saved" (Acts 4:12). In this Name they went forth to make disciples of all nations and to baptize all in that name (Acts 2:38; 19:5).

This does not mean that knowledge of the historical Jesus in whom the name was fully manifested was necessary for this salvation to be found. Even though God allowed past generations to walk in their own way, "he did not leave himself without witness" in nature (Acts 14:17). In all history, God has been present so "that they should seek God, in hope that they might feel after him and find him" (Acts 17:27). What it does mean is that the God who revealed himself supremely in Jesus is the only God who saves.

The "incarnation" Christology of John makes the same universal claim. Even though the eternal Word of God or Son of God has always been in the world he made, the fullest manifestation was in the incarnation of the Word in the flesh of Jesus (Jn. 1:10, 14). That is why it is possible to say that the "I Am," manifested to Moses and supremely in Jesus, was "before Abraham" (Jn. 8:58; cf. Ex. 3:14). Jesus could therefore say: "I am the way, the truth, and the life: no one comes to the Father, but by me" (John 14:6).

Christianity is the way. In Palestinian Jewish Christianity, Saul of Tarsus persecuted the disciples of Jesus as "the Way" (Acts 9:2; 22:4). Later the Jews of Ephesus spoke "evil of the Way" (Acts 19:9), and among the pagans there "arose no little stir concerning the Way" (Acts 19:23). The possessed girl of Philippi was therefore right when she proclaimed Paul and his companions "servants of the Most High God, who proclaim to you the way of salvation" (Acts 16:17).

In the Hellenistic Jewish Christianity from which Hebrews came, the Son of God incarnate in Jesus is proclaimed as the one who, through the shedding of his blood, opened up "the new and living way" into the sanctuary of God (Heb. 10:20). There were those led astray by false prophets even after they came to know "the way of truth" or "the way of righteousness" (II Pet. 2:2, 21). Salvation is always a road that must be walked to the end.

The Two Sides of Salvation

Salvation is by grace through faith. These are the two sides of salvation: God's grace and man's faith. John 1:16 proclaims God's side as "grace upon grace," and Romans 1:17 says man's side is "faith unto faith." There is no contradiction in these two pictures. John looks at salvation from top to bottom ("grace upon grace") and sees grace all the way from God to man. Paul looks at salvation from start to finish ("faith unto faith") and sees faith all the way from man to God. By grace the fulness of God is received; by faith the righteousness of God is revealed. Grace has been the emphasis in Calvinism and faith in Lutheranism. Both are in the New Testament.

Grace is both an event and an experience. The event proclaims the reign of God, and the experience proclaims the riches of God. God's reign is described in Romans 5:12-21, where the picture is one of sin and grace in conflict. Sin reigns in death (12-14), but grace reigns in life (15-17). Two kingdoms are here locked in mortal conflict. Since Adam, sin has reigned in death and no power has been able to break the power of his kingdom. Law tried to topple him from his throne but failed, but "God has done what the law, weakened by the flesh, could not do" (Rom. 8:3). He did this by sending his Son as a sin-offering to condemn sin in the flesh, the very realm where sin had never been defeated. Through the victory of Christ over the kingdom of sin, grace now reigns, "so that, as sin reigned in death, grace also might reign through righteousness to eternal life through Jesus Christ our Lord" (Rom. 5:21). Anders Nygren, more than any other, has seen the importance of this teaching of Paul on the two kingdoms of death and life.[1]

God's riches are described in Ephesians 2:1-10. In this passage the condition of man by nature (2:1-3) is put in contrast to the condition of man by grace (2:4-10). By nature man is dead because of sin, and as a son of disobedience he is under the wrath of God. His deeds are "trespasses and sins"; he is dominated by "the prince of the power of the air"; and his desires spring from the flesh. By grace man is first made alive (2:5) and then made to sit (2:6) in the new realm of the grace of God. God has done this "that in the coming ages he might show the immeasurable riches of his grace in kindness toward us in Christ Jesus" (2:7).

Man's faith is both inward and outward. It is inward trust and outward confession. The two are like the two sides of a door; the door opens in outward confession because of the act of inward belief. No passage in the Scriptures has made this clearer than Romans 10:8-10:

> But what does it say? "The word is near you, on your lips and in your heart" (that is, the word of faith which we preached); be-cause, if you confess with your lips that Jesus is Lord and believe in your heart that God raised him from the dead, you will be saved. For man believes with his heart and so is justified, and he confesses with his lips and so is saved.

This reflects the confession of faith made at baptism. Multitudes have tested these words and found them true.

1. Anders Nygren, *Commentary on Romans*, tr. Carl C. Rasmussen (Philadelphia: Muhlenberg Press, 1949), pp. 16-26, 206-229.

The Three Stages of Salvation

Salvation is past, present, and future for the Christian. It has often been said that the Christian has been saved from the penalty of sin, is being saved from the practice of sin, and is yet to be saved from the presence of sin. A survey of the Scriptures shows this to be a true summary of the Christian experience of salvation, when viewed as a whole.

The past stage of salvation points to the personal experience by which the believer passed from spiritual death to spiritual life, from darkness to light, from the power of sin to the power of God. Jesus said to a sinful woman: "Your faith has saved you" (Luke 7:50). Paul said to a scared jailor: "Believe in the Lord Jesus, and you will be saved, you and your household" (Acts 16:31). There is no doubt that Ephesians 2:8 teaches salvation as an accomplished fact: "by grace you have been saved." Again, in Titus 3:5 the appearance of the goodness and loving-kindness of God "saved us."

The present stage of salvation is also taught in Scripture. Writing to the saints in Philippi, Paul says:

> Therefore, my beloved, as you have always obeyed, so now, not only as in my presence but much more in my absence, work out your own salvation with fear and trembling; for God is at work in you, both to will and to work for his good pleasure (Phil. 2:12–13).

It has been quaintly but correctly said that "God works in" and "man works out" in the process of salvation. This present experience of salvation is the basis for saying that "the word of the cross is folly to those who are perishing, but to us who are being saved it is the power of God" (1 Cor. 1:18).

The future stage of salvation is as clearly taught in Scripture as are the past and present stages. Romans 13:11–15 and I Peter 1:3–9 would be difficult to explain if this future aspect were not recognized. Salvation is V-Day for God, and it "is nearer to us now than when we first believed" (Rom. 13:11). God guards us "through faith for a salvation ready to be revealed in the last time" (1 Pet. 1:5), and that is why the salvation of our souls is the "outcome" of our faith (1 Pet. 1:9). As was pointed out at the beginning, salvation in Hebrews always reaches into the future (1:14; 2:3, 10; 5:9; 6:9; 9:28).

Much of the theology of the Apostle Paul can be discussed without a departure from this pattern of salvation as past, present and future.[2] Most of the great words used by Paul to describe God's deliverance of man from sin are elaborations of salvation. To understand the gospel of Paul is to understand the full scope of salvation.

2. C. Anderson Scott, *Christianity According to Paul* (Cambridge: Cambridge University Press, 1927); A. M. Hunter, *Interpreting Paul's Gospel* (London: SCM, 1954). For a survey of salvation in the Scriptures and in the New Testament world see E. M. B. Green, *The Meaning of Salvation* (Philadelphia: The Westminster Press, 1965).

50. Salvation and Repentance

Repentance means to change one's mind. That is why the Old Testament can speak about God repenting (Gen. 6:6f.; Ex. 32:12, 14). In the same chapter it can be said that the Lord repented, in one sense, yet the Lord does not repent, in the sense of human repentance (1 Sam. 15:11, 29, 35).

It is in the sense of human repentance that the term can be used as a prerequisite for salvation. The Old Testament speaks of a ritual of repentance of all the people when there is a great coming back after seasons of sin (1 Kings 21; Neh. 9). Liturgies of repentance have been preserved (Hos. 6:14; Isa. 63:7–64:12; Dan. 9:4–19).

In the New Testament there are two words in the language of repentance that have often been identified when they should be distinguished. The Greek *metamelomai* means regret or remorse, but this does not lead to salvation (Matt. 21:29, 32; 27:3). *Metanoeō*, noun *metanoia*, meaning to change the mind, is the more frequent term, and it is the change of attitude toward God and sin that leads to salvation.

These teachings in the Gospel may be compared to the practice of church discipline in the letters of Paul (II Cor. 2:7–11). A classic study on repentance has clarified the difference between repentance and regret, by making II Corinthians 7:8–10 the pillar passage.[3] The apostle Paul wrote a severe letter to the Christians of Corinth that plunged them into sorrow, but this sorrow led to repentance, and repentance to salvation. This Paul called a godly sorrow, but a worldly sorrow would have led to regret and to spiritual death.

The repentance that leads to salvation has two basic relations: *toward* God and *from* sin. When repentance is interpreted as toward sin the result is regret and spiritual death, but when it is *from* sin and *toward* God, the way of salvation has begun (Mark 1:1–4).

Repentance toward God is preparation for the kingdom of God and the reception of the Spirit of God. The theme of the Gospel of Mark was on the lips of Jesus at the beginning of the gospel when he said: "The time is fulfilled, and the kingdom of God is at hand; repent and believe in the gospel" (1:14f.). The orientation to the past has been shifted toward the new age of the future. Cf. Matthew 3:2; 4:17.

Repentance toward God is also followed by the reception of the Spirit of God. John the Baptist announced that his repentance baptism in water would be followed by a baptism in the Spirit by one mightier than he (Mark 1:8). A baptism in fire awaits those who do not repent (Matthew 3:11; Luke 3:16). This unity between water baptism and Spirit baptism becomes the norm after Pentecost (Acts 2:38; 11:16; 19:1–7).

3. W. D. Chamberlain, *The Meaning of Repentance* (Philadelphia: The Westminster Press, 1943).

The unity between repenting and believing is obvious in Acts.[4] Repenting or believing always goes before forgiveness (5; 10:43; 13:39). Repentance should be before baptism in water, and baptism in the Holy Spirit is never received before repentance. Repentance with faith is the one thing always associated with baptism in the Spirit. Speaking in tongues, water baptism, and laying on of hands are at times present, but each is at times not mentioned, in the Acts of the Apostles, when the Spirit is received.[5]

Repentance from sins requires one to forsake sins. That was the meaning of the repentance baptism proclaimed by John the Baptist (Mark 1:4). According to the Gospel of Matthew, John required fruit that "befits repentance" before baptism (4:8). According to the Gospel of Luke, these fruits were expanded and made more specific for the multitudes, tax collectors and soldiers who came to receive his repentance baptism in water (3:10–14). The disciples of Jesus were taught by the risen Lord Jesus "that repentance and the forgiveness of sins should be preached in his name to all nations" (24:47).

Repenting and believing are so inseparable in experience that one may include the other. This was true in the preaching of both Peter and Paul (Acts 10:43; 13:39).

Repenting and confessing are also rather close in meaning. In fact, a confession seems to take the place of repentance in the Johannine writings. "If we confess our sins, he is faithful and just, and will forgive our sins and cleanse us from all unrighteousness" (1 Jn. 1:9).

In later baptismal theology, the act of renunciation became an impressive part of the liturgy. According to the *Apostolic Tradition* of Hippolytus of Rome (c. 170-c. 236), the presbyter or elder was to instruct the one to be baptized to say: "I renounce thee, Satan, and all thy service and all thy works" (xxl. 9). According to the *Mystagogical Catecheses* by Cyril of Jerusalem (c. 315-86), this renunciation of Satan was to be performed while one faced west at the break of day, when there is still darkness, the darkness symbolizing all that pertains to Satan (I. 4–9). The lists got longer along with the liturgy in most of the later renunciations, East and West, until infant baptism made some sins irrelevant.[6] If Catholicism has put too much emphasis on the confession of sins, Protestantism has put too little. It is amazing how many people seem to think that confession of sins is a doctrine for Roman Catholics only!

Repentance and Calling

The call to repentance does not always result in salvation. "For many are called, but few are chosen" (Matt. 22:14). Even so, the gospel is to be

---

4. See my book *Spirit of the Living God*, Second Edition (Nashville: Broadman Press, 1976), p. 79.
5. *Ibid*.
6. E. C. Whitaker, *Documents of the Baptismal Liturgy* (London: S.P.C.K., 1960).

preached to all nations before the end of the age (24:14). The disciples of Jesus are commissioned to "make disciples of all nations" (28:19), yet it is recognized that many individuals will go away into Gehenna (25:31–46). The one thing sure is that the call is to all, but not all will be saved.

Calling has a special place in the theology of Paul. An apocalyptic passage distinguished between those who will "suffer the punishment of eternal destruction and exclusion from the presence of the Lord and from the glory of his might" and those for whom he prayed that God would make "worthy of his call," yet there is not a word about double predestination. Those "worthy of his call" are clearly "all who believed, because our testimony was believed" (II Thess. 1:9–11).

The called in Corinthians seem identical with the saints who have believed, but one looks in vain for any suggestion that there is an irresistible call (1 Cor. 1:1, 2, 24, 26). There are many stations in life in which the called are to serve the Lord, but the call to serve is the same as the call to be saved (7:20–22). It is a distortion of the gospel to teach that all are called to be saved but only a few to serve. The called are those who have heard and believed, but there is no suggestion that some who heard were predestined in a predetermined way to unbelief.

The campground of Calvinism with its doctrine of an irresistible call has been Paul's letter to Rome. The first reference to the called is much as those already noted in Corinth (1:1, 6), but two passages call for special examination. Romans 8:28 says that God "co-operates for good with those who love God, and are called according to his purpose" (NEB), yet for centuries now the KJV of 1611 has been followed which says "all things work together for good," as if human co-operation is excluded from God's purpose. The human co-operation of faith, hope and love has been blasted as *synergism*, yet Paul uses the Greek verb *synergei*! Then Romans 8:29f. is interpreted as if predestination, foreknowledge, calling, justification and glorification were an iron chain of cause and effect, yet Paul makes it very clear that those known by God can turn back to the state of slavery from which they came (Gal. 4:8–11).

The last-ditch stand of determinism is at Romans 11:29, where the RSV says "the gifts and the call of God are irrevocable." Here the KJV is preferred when it says "the gifts and calling of God are without repentance," for the Greek *ametameleta* means "unrepented." The point is that God has not changed his covenant with Israel and transferred all his promises to the church, a view advocated by conservative Calvinism. God has a purpose in both Israel and among the Gentiles, but his plan includes the human response of faith before it can be completed. When the patience of God is related to a correct understanding of Paul's doctrine of predestination, there is the collapse of the Calvinistic citadel of determinism. Human responsibility can hardly be more magnified than in Paul's own statement on how the patience of God seeks to lead people to repentance. Romans 2:4–10 requires no alien ideas for clarity. It is quoted in full in the next paragraph.

> Or do you presume upon the riches of his kindness and forbearance and patience? Do you not know that God's kindness is meant to lead you to repentance? But by your hard and impenitent heart you are storing up wrath for yourself on the day of wrath when God's righteous judgement will be revealed. For he will render to every man according to his works: to those who by patience in well-doing seek for glory and honor and immortality, he will give eternal life; but for those who are factious and do not obey the truth, but obey wickedness, there will be wrath and fury. There will be tribulation and distress for every human being who does evil, the Jew first and also the Greek, but glory and honor and peace for every one who does good, the Jew first and also the Greek.

The later section on salvation and predestination will continue the discussion on patience and predestination in the purpose of God in Romans 9:22. Romans 2:4–10; 8:28–30; 9:22; 11:29 must be read as a unit.

It is most instructive to note that Paul instructs Timothy to use the type of pastoral patience that God himself uses to bring people to repentance (II Tim. 2:24–26). This is hardly irresistible patience, for there is the danger that even a bishop who is a recent convert can have the same destiny as the devil (1 Tim. 3:6f.). No doubt some of the mystery plays of the middle ages were correct when they so portrayed some pompous bishops! Proud prelates and professors of the present are not beyond this possibility. Even the apostle Paul did not think he was (1 Cor. 9:27).

The call of God is upward and onward toward the prize, but Paul felt he had to press on (Phil. 3:14). Paul begged his readers to live in a manner worthy of the calling with which they had been called (Eph. 4:1). This is to be based on the beliefs that unify, one of which is "the one hope that belongs to your call" (4:4). God has "saved us and called us with a holy calling," but this does not exclude the possibility that some may turn away from the call (II Tim. 1:9, 15).

The Hebrew believers to whom Hebrews is written were "holy brethren, partakers of a heavenly call" (3:1), as they were "partakers of the Holy Spirit" (6:4), yet there was the possibility that the immature among them might commit apostasy (2:1–4; 3:12–14; 5:11–6:20; 10:26–31; 12:12–17).

If one is not to forget that he was cleansed from his old sins and go spiritually blind, he must confirm his call and election by growth in grace (II Pet. 1:5–11). If he makes his calling and election sure in Christian maturity he will never fall away from the way of truth and righteousness (1:10; 2:2, 21).

To recognize that "we are called into the fellowship of his Son Jesus Christ our Lord" (II Pet. 2:9) does not require the conclusion that others could not answer the call. The effort to confine II Peter 3:9 to the elect only requires exegesis that is not obvious. God would be patient only with the elect and not willing that any of the elect perish, according to that limiting interpretation. On the contrary, it seems that God is patient with all people while he calls any and all to repentance.

When calling is considered in the New Testament writings, free from the creeds of Calvinism, there is no need for the refined distinctions between an external call in general revelation and the preaching of the gospel in an "effectual, irresistible call."[7]

There is only one call from God in general revelation and in the preaching of the special revelation in Scripture, and whenever man hears the call it can be made effectual when there is the response of repentance and faith (Acts 20:21).

Repentance and Conversion

Since the Old Testament speaks of repentance as a possibility for both man and God, the repentance of man is described as a turning of man from sin to God. The Hebrew word for turning is *shub*, and it is widely distributed. Israel is called to return to the Lord as Gomer returned to Hosea after years of unfaithfulness (Hos. 14:1). Exhortations in Jeremiah call God's faithless children back to their master (3:14). Idolatry was a special symbol of sin and the need to turn back to the Lord (Ezek. 14:6). The priestly history has the promise: "If my people who are called by my name humble themselves, and pray and seek my face, and turn from their wicked ways, then will I hear from heaven, and will forgive their sin and heal their land" (II Chron. 7:14). And there are many more.

This relationship between repentance and conversion continues in the New Testament. Jesus put a little child in the midst of the disciples and said: "Truly I say to you, unless you turn and become like little children you will never enter the kingdom of God" (Matthew 18:3). Isaiah 6:9f. is quoted to explain why the Jews did not turn to be healed (Jn. 12:40). Peter preached to the Jews: "Repent therefore, and turn again, that your sins may be blotted out, that times of refreshing may come from the presence of the Lord" (Acts 3:19). Unnamed evangelists arrived in Antioch: "And the hand of the Lord was with them, and a great number believed and turned to the Lord" (11:21). At Lystra Paul resisted the pagan worship of the Lycaonians with the admonition for them to "turn from these vain things to a living God" (14:15). Before King Agrippa he testified that he had been sent to the Gentiles "to open their eyes, that they may turn from darkness to light and

7. J. Norval Geldenhuys in Carl F. H. Henry, ed., *Basic Christian Doctrine* (Grand Rapids: Baker Book House, 1962), pp. 178-184.

from the power of Satan to God, that they may receive forgiveness of sins"
(26:18) and "that they should repent and turn to God and perform deeds
worthy of repentance" (26:10).

The forgiveness of sins is a major result of repentance and conversion. It
is interesting to note how the New Testament consistently speaks of the
forgiveness of sins, not the forgiveness of sin. Confession of sins is therefore
a central practice in repentance baptism (Mark 1:4f.; Matt. 3:5f.). Sins have
accumulated like an unpaid debt, but the debt is removed by forgiveness.

At this point an interesting discussion has developed on the meaning
of forgiveness. Some have identified forgiveness with restoration to fellowship and reconciliation.[8] Others have argued that forgiveness is removal of
the barrier that makes restoration and reconciliation possible.[9] Since the
New Testament speaks so consistently of the forgiveness of sins as well as
the forgiveness of sinners, but never of the reconciliation of sins, it does
seem that there is a difference. Reconciliation is therefore considered separately in a later section. Forgiveness is both objective and subjective.
Therefore we pray:

> *And forgive us our debts,*
> *As we have forgiven our debtors (Matt. 6:12).*

The preaching of repentance and the forgiveness of sins is not enough.
What is preached must be practiced. The practice of forgiveness is a cardinal teaching of Jesus. Failure to forgive others forfeits our own forgiveness
(Matt. 18:15–27; Luke 17:3). The frequency of forgiveness is to be measured by the patience of God with us (Mark 11:25). In teaching and in
practice Jesus is the model of forgiveness and prayer (Luke 11:4; 23:34).

The power of forgiveness resides in the followers of Jesus as they
minister in his name. In his name people are bound and set free from the
bondage of sins (Matt. 16:19; Jn. 20:22f.). His followers are instead the
forgiven and the forgiving community.

Forgiveness and grace are so closely related that Paul could use *char-
izomai*, to be gracious, as a synonym for forgiveness (Col. 3:12f.; Eph.
4:31f.).

There is, however, a limit to forgiveness. Blasphemy of the Holy Spirit
is unforgivable in this age and the coming age of Glory (Mark 3:28f.; Matt.
12:22–27; Luke 12:10). Apostasy and the sin that leads to death are other
ways to describe this state that is unforgivable, but this will be considered
later (Heb. 6:4–6; 10:26–31; 12:14–17; 1 Jn. 5:16).

8. E. Basil Redlich, *The Forgiveness of Sins* (Edinburgh: T. & T. Clark, 1937); Morris
Ashcraft, *The Forgiveness of Sins* (Nashville: Broadman Press, 1972), pp. 12f.
9. Vincent Taylor, *Forgiveness and Reconciliation* (London: Macmillan and Company, 1941),
pp. 25f.; William Klassen, *The Forgiving Community* (Philadelphia: The Westminster Press,
1956), pp. 12f.

Fellowship of the saints is the fellowship that believers have in the Son (1 Cor. 1:2, 9). Fellowship with God and man follows the forgiveness of sins.[10] As with the word forgiveness, a study of fellowship includes much of the Christian life. The Christ-mysticism of Paul, as Albert Schweitzer would call this union with God in Christ, includes much of Paul's theology.[11]

Around the major metaphor of the church as the body of Christ those who are in fellowship with God in Christ are said to be a new creation *in Christ* (II Cor. 5:17). Those in the new creation were crucified *with Christ* so that Christ could live in them (Gal. 2:20). The visible sign of entrance *into Christ* is baptism (Gal. 3:27).[12]

This fellowship is possible by mutual participation in the Holy Spirit (II Cor. 13:14). It is first of all a fellowship of grace, but full expression of this fellowship includes a fellowship of goods (cf. II Cor. 8:9 with 9:23; also Phil. 1:7–2:1 with 2:25–30 and 4:10–20). A shallow subjective feeling needs to be deepened into a tangible form of fellowship as it was in the Jerusalem church (Acts 2:44; 4:32; cf. James 2:14–17).

The God-mysticism of John does not exclude fellowship with Christ. In fact fellowship with the Father is not possible without the Son (1 Jn. 1:3; 4:1–6). Fellowship in light, life and love is fellowship with the Father who has revealed himself most fully in Jesus Christ (1:5, 7; 3:15; 4:16).

51. Salvation and Regeneration

Regeneration, according to the New Testament teaching, may be a new order, as in Matthew 19:28, or a new life, as in Titus 3:5. It is in this second sense that the word is used in this section. Renewal is a parallel with regeneration when Titus 3:5 says that God saved us

> *By the washing of regeneration*
> *and renewal in the Holy Spirit.*

The dynamic unity between outward washing and inward renewal is "in the Holy Spirit." The Holy Spirit is "poured out upon us richly through Jesus Christ our Savior, so that we might be justified by his grace and become heirs in hope of eternal life" (Titus 3:6f.). The radical distinction between "baptismal regeneration" and "mere symbolism" that developed later, destroys this dynamic unity in Christian initiation, but it needs to be restored. This will be discussed in more detail when baptism is the main topic.

10. Vincent Taylor, *op. cit.*, pp. 109-143; A. Raymond George, *Communion with God* (London: Epworth Press, 1953).
11. Albert Schweitzer, *The Mysticism of the Apostle Paul*, tr. William Montgomery (New York: Henry Holt and Co., 1931), p. 5; James Stewart, *A Man in Christ* (New York: Harper & Brothers).
12. Ernest Best, *One Body in Christ* (London: S.P.C.K., 1955), pp. 44-82.

Here the concept of regeneration with its two major corollaries, sanctification and justification, is the main concern. A hymn in 1 Corinthians 6:11 serves as an outline.

> And such were some of you.
>> But you were washed,
>> You were sanctified,
>> You were justified,
> in the name of our Lord Jesus Christ and in the Spirit of our
>> God.

The Concept of Regeneration

In regeneration believers are begotten of God, born of the Spirit and normally grow from immature newborn babes into mature and full-grown followers of Christ. Those begotten by God are brothers (and sisters!) to one another and children of God.

The relation by which those begotten by God are brothers may be described as a reception of the *implanted* word by the believer. In The Letter of James in which believers are saluted as "the twelve tribes in the Dispersion" (1:1), the collective term is twelve times that of brothers (1:2, 16, 19; 2:1, 5, 14; 3:1, 12; 4:11; 5:7, 12, 19).

The process by which the implanted word is received is interpreted after the analogy of natural conception and in comparison with the genealogy of spiritual death. Spiritual death is the offspring of desire and sin (1:15):

> Then desire when it has conceived gives birth to sin;
> and sin when it is full grown brings forth death.

The new life originated from God, for (1:18, 21)

> Of his own will he brought us forth by the word of truth
> that we should be a kind of first fruits of his creatures.
>
> Therefore, put away all filthiness
> and rank growth of wickedness
> and receive with meekness the implanted word,
> which is able to save your souls.

As the seed of the male is implanted in the womb of the female and conception and birth follow, so the word of truth is implanted in the heart of the receptive believer to bring into existence the process of spiritual conception and birth in the new life.

It should not be assumed that conception and birth are all there is to regeneration. After birth there is the need to grow in the process by which the soul is finally saved. It is possible for the immature brothers to wander away from the truth. That is why the twelfth salutation of the brethren says (5:19f.): "My brethren, if any one among you wanders from the truth and some bring him back, let him know that whoever brings back a sinner from the error of his way will save his soul from death and will cover a multitude of sins." Death is here spiritual, as in 1:15. That is why it is contrasted with the salvation of the soul (cf. 1:21 with 5:20). Physical death is out of the question.

In The First Letter of Peter the *implanted* word by which conception and birth into the new life comes into existence is called the *imperishable* seed, and this is identified with "the living and abiding word of God" (2:23). The imperishable inheritance is for those who are born of imperishable seed (cf. 1:4 with 1:23). By the mercy of God "we have been born anew to a living hope through the resurrection of Jesus Christ from the dead, and to an inheritance which is imperishable, undefiled, and unfading, kept in heaven for you, who by God's power are guarded through faith for a salvation ready to be revealed in the last time" (1:3–5). Salvation is to be completed in the future, while a living hope and faith sustain us in the present (cf. 1:5, 9f.; 2:2).

It is the imperishable seed that is the living and abiding word of God. The new life produced by the imperishable seed needs spiritual growth after conception and birth. "Like newborn babes, long for the pure spiritual milk, that by it you may grow up to salvation" (2:2). Spiritual birth without spiritual milk to sustain it ends in death.

A comment on 1 Peter 1:23 by Ray Summers says that one who is of the imperishable seed is imperishable and will not die, but this depends on the conditions for spiritual growth after birth.[13] It is therefore no surprise to read a further statement by Summers in his comments on the parable of the sower in Luke 8:4–18 that the parable should not be applied to salvation.[14] To do so would ruin his argument that those who receive the seed will not die, for some who receive the seed "believe for a while and in a time of temptation fall away" and the fruit of others "does not mature" (8:13f.). Only those who hear the word and "hold it fast in an honest and good heart" are able to "bring forth fruit with patience" (8:15). These alone are finally saved.

It is necessary to supplement faith with such evidence of growth as virtue, knowledge, self-control, steadfastness, godliness, brotherly affection and love, according to the Second Letter of Peter, if one is to grow in grace and reach the place where he will not fall away (1:3–11; cf. 3:18). When Summers comes to the warning about false teachers who entice those who have "barely escaped from those who live in error" (2:18), he has nothing to say, but he does not hesitate to use what he calls the "strange fable" in Luke 11:24–26 to explain how those who have "escaped the defilement of

---

13. *Broadman Bible Commentary* (Nashville: Broadman Press, 1972), Vol. 12, p. 154.
14. *Commentary on Luke* (Waco, Texas: Word Books, 1972), p. 94.

the world through the knowledge of our Lord and Saviour Jesus Christ"
can be "entangled in them and overpowered" so that "the last state has
become worse for them than the first" (2:20). He explains the house which
was "swept and put in order" in Luke 11:25 with the distinction between
"reformation without regeneration" and true regeneration, but nothing in
the passage says that.

Furthermore, 2 Peter 2:21 is very clear when it says that "it would
have been better for them never to have known the way of righteousness
than after knowing it to turn back from the holy commandments delivered
to them." This does not require corny dog and hog stories unless one is
determined to explain away these plain words about one whose last state
is worse than the first. The explanation was stated in II Peter 1:9 when one
who never supplemented faith with growth is described as "blind and short-
sighted and has forgotten that he was cleansed from his old sins." Summers
makes no attempt to explain II Peter 1:9 and his efforts on 2 Peter 2:10–
22 do not convince.[15]

After the picture of those begotten by God as brothers in James and
1 Peter (2:17; 5:9), those so described in the Gospel of John and the First
Letter of John are called God's children. The Johannine writings never speak
of those begotten as *sons* of God. It is always God's *children* who are
begotten of God, never the Son of God, Jesus Christ; and those who are
begotten participate in eternal life and become children of God. A correct
translation of John 1:12f. should read: "But to all who received him [i.e.
Christ], who believed in his name, he gave power to become children of
God; who were begotten not of the blood nor of the will of the flesh nor of
the will of man, but of God."

It is also necessary to retranslate John 3:3–8 and emend the text, in
the light of evidence, to get a clear picture of the teaching.[16] The need for
regeneration is stated in two stanzas of three lines each in the following
translation of 3:3–5:

> *Jesus answered and said to him,*
> *Amen, amen, I say to you,*
> *unless one is begotten from above,*
> *he cannot see the kingdom of God.*

Nicodemus said to him, "How can a man be begotten when he is
old? Can he enter a second time into his mother's womb and be
begotten?"

> *Jesus answered,*
> *Amen, amen, I say to you,*
> *unless one is begotten of the Spirit,*
> *he cannot enter the kingdom of God.*

15. *Broadman Bible Commentary*, Vol. 12, pp. 182-184.
16. For details see my book *Spirit of the Living God*, pp. 154f.

The begetting from above and of the Spirit means the same, and it is necessary for seeing and entering the kingdom in the future.

The nature of this spiritual begetting by God is explained in 3:6–8.

> *That which is begotten of flesh is flesh*
>   *and that which is begotten of Spirit is spirit.*
> *Do not marvel that I said to you,*
> *"You must be begotten from above."*
> *The wind blows where it wills,*
>   *and you hear the sound of it,*
> *but you do not know where it comes from or whither it goes.*
> *so is every one who is begotten of the Spirit.*

It is possible to see a pattern of progressive regeneration from spiritual begetting to spiritual birth and growth to maturity, but two things in traditional Calvinism must be rejected. First, the idea of infant regeneration claimed for children of the covenant makes it possible to say infants are baptized because they are already regenerated, but it requires regeneration before repentance and faith. This second error is indeed followed in traditional Calvinism as regeneration is discussed before repentance and faith.[17]

In the light of the contrast between the eternal and unbegotten Son of God, who has no beginning before or in time, it is astonishing to find the false idea of the begotten Son of God repeated in what is claimed as "evangelical thought" and that in the form of adoptionism. It is hard to believe that this quotation comes from one reputed to be a conservative and evangelical scholar and edited by the so-called "dean of evangelical theologians." In commenting on "water and Spirit" in the uncritical text of John 3:5, none other than Otto Michel said: "That occurred primarily in Jesus Himself, who was declared by the voice of God to be begotten of God. Jesus' begetting by God sustained His life and constituted His messianic mission."[18] It is heresy to say Jesus was begotten by God at his baptism, and it has no basis in Mark 1:11 whatsoever.

However, the teaching on the begotten children of God does not neglect the teaching on the begotten ones as brothers bound together by love (1 Jn. 2:29; 3:9; 4:7; 5:1, 18).

The Corollaries of Regeneration: Sanctification

In the light of 1 Corinthians 6:11 it is possible to speak of sanctification and justification as corollaries of regeneration. The three are too closely related to be separated as has so often been done in Christian thought.

---

17. L. Berkhof, *Systematic Theology* (Grand Rapids: Eerdmans, 1941), pp. 415-509. Cf. Carl F. H. Henry, ed., *Basic Christian Doctrine* (Grand Rapids: Baker Book House, 1971), pp. 158-212.
18. Carl F. H. Henry, ed., *op. cit.*, pp. 189f.

Regeneration has been the characteristic emphasis of Calvinism, sanctification of Methodism, and justification of Lutheranism, but these are unbalanced developments.

Sanctification is past, present and future in the New Testament teachings. These three tenses are also used in the designations possessive, progressive and perfected sanctification. The concept of the primitive wholeness of holiness in the Old Testament is continued in the New Testament teaching. In the Old Testament even the ground is made holy by the presence of God (Exod. 3:3), yet the whole people of God is called to be "a holy nation" (Exod. 19:6). A day is holy when set aside for the worship of God (Gen. 2:3). Whatever belongs to God is holy, whether property or people (Lev. 27:14–26; Ps. 149:1, 5, 9).

The Petrine picture of the people of God linked the holiness of God's people to the Levitical concept of the holiness of God and to the covenant call for the nation to be a holy priesthood (1 Pet. 1:16; 2:5, 9). The pilgrimage of the priesthood from paganism to the fulfillment of the promise is a highway of holiness, from the past to the future.

In Pauline thought it is possible to say that Christ is our sanctification from the very beginning of the Christian life (1 Cor. 1:30). This includes all who belong to the temple of God, the church (1 Cor. 3:16f.; 2 Cor. 6:14–17:1). Against the background of the Old Testament teaching on all things that belong to God being holy, it is possible to say the baby and the unbelieving companion of the Christian believer are holy, but it is hardly possible to say belief is not required of both before their experience can be described as regeneration (1 Cor. 7:12–14). It is, therefore, not possible to speak of one in whom regeneration has begun without saying sanctification has begun also. Sanctification has begun in all believers, and all believers are saints (1 Cor. 1:2).

As regeneration is progressive from spiritual conception to spiritual maturity, so sanctification is progressive from the beginning of the holy life of a saint to the completion of sanctification at the resurrection of the dead.

This possessive sanctification was recovered after centuries of neglect when Martin Luther discovered anew that a mother in her kitchen was as much of a saint as the most ascetic monk in his cell. Out of this developed the teaching that sanctification is both indicative and imperative, both a present gift and a future task, both acceptance and anticipation.[19] This agrees with the most basic idea of sanctification in the Scripture, yet the substitution of the word consecration for sanctification in the first printing of the Revised Standard New Testament set off protests from many holiness groups that tend to think of sanctification as a second work of grace after regeneration and justification.

19. Adolf Köberle, *The Quest for Holiness*, tr. John C. Mattes (New York: Harper & Brothers, 1936).

Progressive sanctification agrees with the possessive view that puts perfection in the future, but much emphasis is given to the need to grow in grace in the present. This view too can claim support in Scripture.

The progressive sanctification of the human body as the temple of the Holy Spirit is a special concern for the Apostle Paul. Even though the husband already possesses his own wife, literally "possess his vessel," this relationship needs to be guarded and to grow in relation to God. Paul is speaking about a progressive relation not a second blessing when he says: "For this is the will of God, your sanctification: that you abstain from immorality; that each one know how to take a wife for himself in holiness and honor, not in the passion of lust like heathen who do not know God; that no man transgress, and wrong his brother in this matter, because the Lord is an avenger in all these things, as we solemnly forewarned you. For God has not called us for uncleanness, but in holiness. Therefore whoever disregards this, disregards not man but God, who gives his Holy Spirit to you" (1 Thess. 4:3–8).

This progressive sanctification of the human body is further elaborated as Paul confronts the contradiction in the practice of fornication among Christians. One joins the Lord with both body and spirit, and it is a contradiction to claim that one is joined to the Lord with his spirit and to a prostitute with his body (1 Cor. 6:9–20).

It is indeed with the human spirit that the highest relation with the Holy Spirit is established, but the body is never neutral in the Christian life. There is therefore the call: "Strive for peace with all men, and for the holiness without which no one will see the Lord" (Heb. 12:14). This favorite text among holiness movements is a call to go on lest we fall away rather than a challenge "to seek the second blessing."

Progressive sanctification has been the characteristic emphasis in the Augustinian-Calvinistic tradition. Sanctification, for Augustine, is God's work in man, but it is never perfected in this life. It is at present only "advancing the growing day by day" (*On Man's Perfection in Righteousness*, 39). Calvin put much emphasis on the Holy Spirit as Sanctifier, but this is a gradual process in the church where "the Lord works day by day in smoothing out the wrinkles and purging out the spots" (*Institutes* IV. I. XVII). This in general is the view of evangelicals in the Calvinist tradition.[20] It includes most Baptist confessions.[21]

Perfect sanctification is good to pursue, but self-righteousness is sure to follow any claim that it has been achieved. The balance between the progressive sanctification of the present and perfect sanctification in the future promotes healthy growth and a quest for holiness in body and spirit.

20. J. C. Ryle, *Holiness* (London: James Clarke, 1952), pp. 15-50.
21. W. L. Lumpkin, *Baptist Confessions of Faith*, Revised Edition (Valley Forge: Judson Press, 1969), p. 395.

Against the background of a cluster of Old Testament promises that call the people of God to a life of separation from the world, the famous yoke passage of 2 Corinthians 6:14–7:1 has this conclusion: "Since we have these promises, beloved, let us cleanse ourselves from every defilement of the body and spirit, and make holiness perfect in the fear of God" (7:1).

Perfect sanctification is also conditional. Only those who continue in the faith perfect holiness. Christ will "present you holy and blameless and irreproachable before him [i.e. God], provided that you continue in the faith, stable and steadfast, not shifting from the hope of the gospel" (Col. 1:22f.). The fact that Paul expects this to take place in the Colossian believers, as the Greek grammar indicates, does not preclude the conditional nature of the presentation before God. Christians can backslide. However, in the consummation, after the church as the body of Christ is cleansed, she may be presented "without spot or wrinkle or any such thing, that she might be holy and without blemish" (Eph. 5:27; cf. Phil. 3:12; Col. 1:28).

The lack of balance between the past, present and future in the process of sanctification has led to false ideas of Christian perfection. Under the influence of Greek Gnosticism, Clement of Alexandria developed the theory of the elite Christian Gnostic who lives by love rather than by mere faith (*Stromateis* IV. 21-26). The belief in the special saints who have already seen the Beatific Vision was promoted by the extreme asceticism of the Franciscan tradition. The devotional perfectionism that found expression in Lutheran Pietism from P. J. Spener's *Pia Desideria* (1675) through F. D. E. Schleiermacher's *The Christian Faith* (1821-22) was looked upon as a threat to the Lutheran doctrine of justification by faith even in nineteenth-century liberalism. Albrecht Ritschl, the leading Protestant liberal, wrote his three-volume *History of Pietism* (1880-86) to displace the Pietistic preoccupation with experience. Ritschl's emphasis was on ethics rather than experience and metaphysics, but experience and ethics belong together.

The tensions of Lutheranism appeared often between the conservative and liberal wings of Methodism. Evangelism and ethics have a difficult time living together. John Wesley was convinced that God had given to Methodists "a full and clear knowledge" of justification by faith, of which Catholics were ignorant, and of sanctification, of which Lutherans were ignorant.[22] Even though he agreed with the Calvinists on much that they said on progressive sanctification, he believed firmly in the possibility of "entire sanctification" in this life.[23]

The Corollaries of Regeneration: Justification

The term justification is used here only because of its long tradition in the Latin Vulgate, its repeated use in English translations of the Bible, and the

22. Albert C. Outler, ed., *John Wesley* (New York: Oxford University Press, 1964), pp. 107f.
23. *Ibid.*, pp. 167-172.

fact that most theologies still have sections on the subject. If ever a mistranslation twisted theology this translation of the Greek *dikaiōsis* based on the Hebrew *sedeq* is one. A return to biblical exegesis requires a translation that denotes relationship rather than a legalistic declaration.

Righteousness is a better translation, but there is no verb current, such as rightwise, that is available. The TEV translation of "set right" is helpful. Old Testament studies have shown beyond much doubt that this righteous relation is obedience to the covenant relation.[24] The faithfulness of God calls for the faithfulness of man.

When it is remembered that the most important New Testament writings on justification focus on the prophetic passage in Habakkuk 2:4, then this return to the Old Testament from Roman legalism seems "justified!" Habakkuk 2:4 says:

> Behold, he whose soul is not upright in him shall fail,
> but the righteous shall live by his faith.

It is perhaps better to follow the footnote in the Revised Standard Version which substitutes "faithfulness" for "faith." This is more in line with the idea of obedience to the covenant relationship.

The confrontation between Paul and Peter in Antioch led to the most crucial clarification of justification through faith (Galatians 2:11–21). It will be noted that the Revised Standard Version suggests the translation "reckoned righteous" rather than "justified" (2:1b) and "righteousness" rather than "justification" (2:21). The testimony of Paul states the true meaning of justification through faith and what a covenant relation with Christ really means. He says: "I have been crucified with Christ; it is no longer I who live, but Christ lives in me; and the life I now live in the flesh, I live by faith in the Son of God, who loved me and gave himself for me" (2:20).

The long defense of justification through faith that follows appeals to the experience of the Holy Spirit, received by faith and not by the works of the law (3:1–5), the example of Abraham in the Scriptures, who was reckoned righteous before the law was given (3:6–18), and the Christ event by which he was delivered from the bondage of sin into the freedom of faith (3:19–29). Note here how Habakkuk 2:4 is used to explain how faith sets one in a right relation to God (3:11).

The example of Abraham is followed again in Paul's Letter to the Romans (4:1–25), but the great step forward is the further clarification of faith and grace. The Old Testament use of salvation and righteousness as synonyms is abundantly evident in the theme of Romans which says: "For I am not ashamed of the gospel: it is the power of God for salvation to every one who has faith, to the Jew first and also to the Greek. For in it a

24. A good summary is the article by E. R. Achtemeier, "Righteousness in the Old Testament" in *The Interpreter's Dictionary of the Bible* (New York: Abingdon Press, 1962).

righteousness of God is revealed through faith for faith; as it is written, 'He who through faith is righteous shall live.' " Notice how Habakkuk 2:4 is the Old Testament passage behind justification through faith in Romans as well as in Galatians.

Two things in Romans 1:16f. call for special comment. First of all God's righteousness is revealed "through faith for faith" or "from faith to faith," which means that the right relation to God is one of obedience to the covenant from the beginning to the end. It is no accident that Paul uses the expression "the obedience of faith" (1:5; cf. 5:10; 6:16; 16:19, 26). Faith is obedience to the covenant relation, and disobedience to the covenant relation is unbelief (cf. Heb. 3:7–4:13).

In the second place faith is a way of life. This is brought out clearly by the improved translation of Romans 1:17 which supports the teaching that the right relation to God is one of continuous trust rather than a once-for-all legal transaction by which one is declared righteous. The right relation to God is faithfulness, obedience to the covenant relation.

The further clarification of the relationship between justification and grace in Romans is found in two Pauline hymns. After the detailed discussion on the need for God's justification because of the universal situation of sin (1:18–3:10), God's means of justification in Jesus Christ is stated (3:21–4:25).[25] The section on the means of justification is introduced with a three-stanza hymn that has a beautiful balance between man's response in faith and God's revelation and justification by grace (3:21–26). In order to bring out the meaning of the Greek original my own translation is offered.

> *But now apart from the law God's righteousness has been*
> *   manifested,*
> *being borne witness to by the law and the prophets,*
> *God's righteousness through faith in Jesus Christ,*
> *to all who continue to believe*
> *   (for there is no distinction, since all have sinned*
> *   and fall short of the glory of God);*
> *being set right freely by his grace,*
> *through the redemption which is in Christ Jesus,*
> *whom God put forward as a mercy seat*
> *through faith, in his blood;*
> *toward a demonstration of his righteousness,*
> *through the passing over of former sins in the forbearance of*
> *   God,*
> *for the demonstration of his righteousness in the present time,*
> *that he himself is righteous and the one who sets right those*
> *   who have faith in Jesus.*

25. See my commentary on *Romans* in *Broadman Bible Commentary* (Nashville: Broadman Press), Vol. 10, pp. 169-191.

After restating some of the basic beliefs about justification through faith and the example of Abraham's faith before circumcision and the law, the death and resurrection of Jesus are declared the basis for the justification of those who trespass the law (4:25). Faith is reckoned as righteousness for those who believe in God who raised Jesus from death, Jesus

> *who was delivered up for our trespasses*
> *and raised for our justification.*

Many other references are made on how justification is by grace through faith, especially in the three-stanza hymn on Adam and Christ in Romans 5:12–21 which was discussed at length in the part on sin, but the necessity for a subjective response *through* faith in obedience to Jesus Christ as Lord in order to experience the blessings of the objective justification *by* grace that triumphs over sin must be stated again and again. Where there is no human obedience in faith there is no justification by grace.

According to the Roman Catholic theology of Thomas Aquinas, God *makes* a person righteous and then bestows the gift of sanctifying grace. At the time of the Protestant Reformation Martin Luther interpreted justification as a forensic act in which a person is declared to be righteous on the grounds of faith alone. Not even Calvinism with emphasis on regeneration and sanctification was able to discard this Latin legalism. James Buchanan, in his Cunningham Lectures of 1867 on *The Doctrine of Justification*, was still working with the false antithesis of justification either as making man righteous or declaring man righteous. The biblical theology of the twentieth century finally discarded the bondage of legalism for the dynamic view of righteousness as the obedience of faith.

52. Salvation and Reconciliation

Now for an examination of the four passages on reconciliation in Paul's letters that Leon Morris said should not be exaggerated.[26] "Reconciliation," according to Vincent Taylor, "is a peace with God made possible by the sacrifice of Christ. It is not only the removal of disharmony and enmity, but also a state of abiding concord which extends to things in the heavens as well as things upon the earth."[27] When reconciliation is recognized as peace with God it becomes a major theme in much of the Bible and a cardinal concept in Christian theology.[28]

Reconciliation is no more a doctrine solely for peace groups such as Mennonites than regeneration is solely for Calvinists, sanctification for Methodists and justification for Lutherans. All of these terms point to es-

26. *The Cross in the New Testament* (Grand Rapids: Wm. B. Eerdmans, 1965), p. 248.
27. *Forgiveness and Reconciliation* (London: Macmillan and Co.), p. 89.
28. John Macquarrie, *The Concept of Peace* (London: SCM, 1973).

sential teachings about man's relation to God that is made possible by grace through faith.

Among the many points on man's reconciliation to God two may be mentioned at the beginning. First, the message of reconciliation declares God the subject and the universe focused on man as the object to be reconciled. Second, the ministry of reconciliation includes participation both in the sufferings of Christ and in the Spirit of God.

The Message of Reconciliation

One of the first voices in the twentieth century to recover the New Testament concern with reconciliation was James Denney (1856-1917). In his commentary on Second Corinthians he wrestled with the relation between reconciliation and propitiation because he followed the mistranslation of 1 John 4:10 in the English Revised Version.[29]

However, Denney struck a better balance in his later book, *The Death of Christ*. He said: "When reconciliation is spoken of in St. Paul, the subject is always God, and the object is always man. The work of reconciling is one in which the initiative is taken by God, and the cost is borne by Him; men are reconciled in the passive, or allow themselves to be reconciled or receive the reconciliation. We never read that God has been reconciled. God does the work of reconciliation in or through Christ, and especially through his death."[30]

The tension between God as the subject of reconciliation and as the object of propitiation remained until the end of his life. In The Cunningham Lectures of 1917, the year of his death, he still had this problem.[31]

Denney has been claimed by competing camps. Fred Fisher, without giving the source, quotes Denney's commentary where it says there is "something in God as well as something in man which has to be dealt with before there can be peace."[32] Fisher strongly insists that there is "a mutual change of attitude" in both God and man in reconciliation, yet he rejects the penal view of the atonement.[33]

The debate on reconciliation and propitiation continued between Vincent Taylor and Leon Morris. Taylor repeatedly argues that the New Testament never says God needs to be reconciled by the death of Christ to forgive man of his sins, yet man needs to be reconciled to God.[34]

29. *The Expositor's Bible* (New York: Funk and Wagnalls, 1900), pp. 210-223.
30. Second Edition (New York: A. C. Armstrong and Son, 1903), pp. 143f.
31. *The Christian Doctrine of Reconciliation* (New York: George H. Doran Co., 1918), pp. 152f., 161f.
32. *Commentary on 1 and 2 Corinthians* (Waco, Texas: Word Books, 1975), p. 344. The quotation is on p. 211 in Denney's Commentary.
33. *Ibid.*, pp. 344-346.
34. Taylor's definitive book was *Forgiveness and Reconciliation* (London: Macmillan and Co., 1941).

Morris goes to great length to defend the idea of propitiation, yet the four texts on which his argument is based are almost certainly mistranslated in the New American Standard Bible (Heb. 2:17; Rom. 3:25; 1 Jn. 2:2; 4:10). All but Hebrews 2:17 were mistranslated in the Authorized (King James) Version, and that is due to the false translation in Jerome's Latin Vulgate. It is difficult to understand why Morris advocates this questionable exegesis. On this as on so many other related matters Vincent Taylor seems correct.

When one turns to II Corinthians 5:18–21 it is very clear that God is the subject of reconciliation — the reconciler, not the one reconciled. "All this is from God, who through Christ reconciled us to himself and gave us the ministry of reconciliation" (5:18). God as the source did not reconcile himself but us to himself through Christ. Indeed, "in Christ God was reconciling the world to himself, not counting their trespasses against them, and entrusting to us the ministry of reconciliation" (5:19).

This message of reconciliation calls all people to "be reconciled to God" (5:20). The offering for this has already been made by one who knew no personal sin, that through faith "in him we might become the righteousness of God" (5:21).

That man is the object of reconciliation has already been made clear by the emphasis on "us" and "the world" (5:18f.), but Romans 5:1–11 is an elaboration on this emphasis. The nature of reconciliation as peace with God is described as a human response of faith, hope and love (5:1–5). "God's love has been poured into our hearts through the Holy Spirit which has been given to us" (5:5). The gift of love again emphasizes God as the subject and source of reconciliation.

When Paul comes to the need of reconciliation, God as subject and man as object is beyond question. Special pleading is obviously at work in minds that argue that "we" in Romans 5:6, 8 means you and I while "we" in 5:10 means God and I. It would be impossible to say God and I were weak or God and I were sinners in 5:6, 8, yet Fred Fisher argues that "we were enemies" in 5:10 means God and I were enemies. We were indeed enemies of God before "we were reconciled to God by the death of his Son," but nothing is said about the reconciliation of God. To follow this false logic would require one to say that God was not only reconciled but "saved," for "we" means the same all three times in 5:6, 8, 10. Reconciliation is "received" by us, but it is given by God (5:11).

Fisher follows the efforts of others to salvage the theology of a reconciled God by appeal to both Romans 5:10 and 11:28. His appeal to W. T. Conner for the argument that "being enemies describes the attitude of God toward sinners rather than their attitude toward him"[35] only compounds the error. The Greek does not have "of God" (11:28), as in the Revised

35. *Op. cit.*, p. 345.

Standard Version. Israel's rejection of Jesus left them under the law of wrath, but God shows his love for those under his wrath (5:8f.).[36]

The object of reconciliation is described as cosmic, personal, universal and social. The reconciliation of the world, the *kosmos*, is focused on man, but it includes more than man. The focus on man may be seen in the use of "us" and "them" along with "the world" in 2 Corinthians 5:18f. Personal reconciliation is more pronounced in Romans 5:6–11 where "we" and "our reconciliation" are used. However, reconciliation is not confined to humanity in Colossians 1:19 when the object of reconciliation is *ta panta* (all things). *Ta panta* is the universe, all that has been created by the cosmic Christ and that coheres in Christ (1:15–20). The social reconciliation removes the hostility between Jews and Gentiles in the body of Christ where it is impossible to be reconciled to God through Christ without reconciliation to all those who are in Christ (Eph. 2:11–21).

The Ministry of Reconciliation

The ministry of reconciliation is the gift of God to all who have received reconciliation (II Cor. 5:18, 20). This ministry includes the sufferings of the fleshly body of Christ. The sufferings of Christ "in his body of flesh" have already reconciled those in his body, the church, but there is suffering yet to be done by the members of his body. God's reconciliation in Christ is continuous: "In Christ God was reconciling the world to himself" (II Cor. 5:18). Participation in the body of Christ is also continuous, because participation depends upon a continuation in the faith (Col. 1:23). Paul believed he must suffer in his flesh as Christ suffered in his flesh in order "to complete what is lacking in Christ's affliction for the sake of his body, that is, the church" (1:24).

This paschal note in Colossians reflects the belief in Christ as the Passover sacrifice. It is possible that the letter was composed for Paul by Timothy during the time of Paul's imprisonment in Herod's palace at Caesarea about Passover, A.D. 57 (cf. Acts 23:35).[37] The letter follows the pattern of a seder with a thanksgiving and intercession (1:3–14) after the salutation (1:1–2) followed by three hymns (1:15–20; 2:9–15; 3:1–5), three lessons, and the epilogue (4:7–18). Reconciliation through the sufferings of Christ is the theme of the first hymn and lesson, but all of the letter reflects the event of Christ's death and resurrection.

The ministry of reconciliation also includes participation in the Spirit of God. Spirit (*pneuma*) appears fourteen times in Ephesians, and at least eleven have reference to the Spirit of God. It is possible that this is the letter to Laodicea mentioned in Colossians 4:16 and that it was composed

36. See my commentary on Romans in *Broadman Bible Commentary*, Vol. 10, p. 246.
37. See my essay "A New Chronology for the Life and Letters of Paul," in *Perspectives in Religion Studies*, Volume III, No. 3, Fall 1976, pp. 248-271.

for Paul by Luke on the framework of a Pentecost seder about A.D. 57, within fifty days after Colossians. Tychicus took both letters to the churches in the Lycus valley (Col. 4:7; Eph. 6:21).

Social reconciliation overcame the state of estrangement between the Jews and the Gentiles. Through the sacrifice of Christ the Gentiles who were far off from God have been "brought near in the blood of Christ" (2:13).

The reconciliation of Jews and Gentiles in the one body of Christ is described in a hymn about "the dividing wall of hostility" that was demolished by the death of Christ (2:14–18). It was not until A.D. 70 that the dividing wall between the Gentiles and the Jewish women was literally demolished, but there is good reason to believe that Paul saw a symbolic anticipation of that event as he composed the hymn about the Broken Wall soon after he was almost lynched when the rumor spread that he had taken the Greek Trophimus of Ephesus beyond that wall (Acts 21:27–36). It is possible that the Stone of Warning now in the Istanbul Museum was attached to that wall.

The hymn on reconciliation in 2:14–18 closes with the claim that through Christ both Jews and Gentiles "have access in one Spirit to the Father" (2:18). The shift from the hymn to the commentary (2:19–22), from the first person to the second person, changes the metaphors from that of a body to that of a building in which the Gentiles and the Jews have been "built into for a dwelling place of God in the Spirit" (2:22).[38]

53. Salvation and Liberation

Liberation is the act by which God in Christ has set man free from the slavery of sin and for a life of love for God and others. It is not to be confused with the more limited meaning in recent radicalism that thinks little about the biblical meaning of freedom and most about groups to be liberated in social action. In the wider theological sense liberation will first be surveyed in the New Testament Scriptures and then in modern theology.

Definition of Liberation in Scripture

There is a distinct theology of freedom in both Pauline and Johannine theology in the New Testament. Pauline theology has teachings on both freedom from death and freedom for life in Christ.

Liberation as redemption. Freedom from death is the meaning of redemption. In the Old Testament the concept of national redemption leads to the

---

38. For a detailed discussion of Ephesians 2:11–22 see the important commentary by Markus Barth, *Ephesians* (Garden City, N.Y.: Doubleday & Company, 1974), pp. 253-325.

hope of personal redemption from death.[39] Job's answer to the problem of suffering and death was (19:25):

> For I know that my redeemer lives,
>   and at last he will stand upon the earth;
> and after my skin has been thus destroyed,
>   then without my flesh I shall see God,
> whom I shall see on my side,
>   and my eyes shall behold, and not another.

This vindicator of Job became the victor also in Jesus Christ.

Personal redemption in Christ is both a present liberation of the human spirit and a future liberation of the human body. Christ is our redemption (1 Corinthians 1:30). He has bought us in the *agora* of agony as one would purchase a slave in the marketplace (6:20), and he should be glorified in the human body as well as in the human spirit. This redemption means freedom, and God's free people do not become the slaves of men (7:23).

Redemption from death is redemption from the law which is the power of sin that causes spiritual death. "Christ redeemed us from the curse of the law, having become a curse for us" (Gal. 3:13).

> But when the time had fully come,
>   God sent forth his Son,
>   born of a woman,
>   born under the law,
> so that we might receive adoption as sons (4:4f.).

Liberation through redemption is life in Christ (Rom. 3:24; Col. 1:14; Eph. 1:7). His intention is to "redeem us from all iniquity and purify a people for his own who are zealous for good works" (Tit. 2:14).

Future redemption is the liberation of the human body. Those who have received the first-fruits of the Spirit wait for the redemption of their bodies (Rom. 8:23). The oldest collection of Paul's letters, P 46, does not have the Greek word for adoption in Romans 8:23, and that agrees with Romans 8:15 and Galatians 4:5. This redemption of the body is part of the liberation of the whole creation in the cosmic redemption of the future (Rom. 8:21).

Belief in the redemption of the body at the time of the redemption of the whole creation reveals the unity between the human body and God's good creation which has been exploited by man and made subject to human bondage. The total self and the total creation are inseparable in sin and in redemption. God has given the Spirit as a guarantee that we are his present

---

39. H. Wheeler Robinson, *Redemption and Revelation* (New York and London: Harper & Bros., 1942), pp. 220-228.

possession, and that future day of redemption awaits those who do not rebel and grieve His Holy Spirit (Eph. 1:14; 4:30).

Liberation as sonship. Sonship is used here in the sense of Galatians 4:6 and Romans 8:15. Freedom is a paradox in the Christian life. Against the background of human slavery it may be stated thus:

> *For he who was called in the Lord as a slave is a freedman of the Lord.*
> *Likewise he who was free when called is a slave of Christ*
> *(1 Cor. 7:22).*

The source of this freedom is the life-giving Spirit who is the Lord (1 Cor. 15:45). As one turns to the Lord, as did Moses on Sinai, the process of transformation into the image of Christ begins, and this is the freedom of the Christian. "Now the Lord is the Spirit, and where the Spirit of the Lord is, there is freedom" (II Cor. 3:17).

This new freedom in Christ is a freedom for our neighbor. By faith life in the freedom of the Spirit begins, and by faith this freedom continues (Gal. 3:1–5). Christ has brought us out of the bondage of spiritual slavery into the freedom of sonship (Gal. 4:4–7). That is why any tendency to return to the state of slavery is viewed with such alarm (4:8–11). "For freedom Christ has set us free," Paul warned the Galatians, "stand fast therefore, and do not submit again to a yoke of slavery" (5:1).

Positive use of this freedom is love for others. "For you were called to freedom, brethren; only do not use your freedom as an opportunity for the flesh, but through love be servants of one another" (5:13). Love for our neighbor is the fulfillment of the law, and thus is possible only in the positive use of the Spirit's freedom (5:14). The witness of the Spirit is the assurance of sonship, and walking in the Spirit in neighborly love is the true life of freedom (5:16–26).

Freedom in the Spirit is also freedom from spiritual death. The paradox of freedom is relevant here also. "When you were slaves of sin, you were free in regard to righteousness. But then what return did you get from the things of which you are now ashamed? The end of those things is death. But now that you have been set free from sin and have become slaves of God, the return you get is sanctification and its end, eternal life. For the wages of sin is death, but the free gift of God is eternal life in Christ Jesus our Lord" (Rom. 6:20–23).

The freedom of sonship is the work of the Spirit from beginning to end. At the beginning there is victory over spiritual death and God's gift of freedom; at the end is the liberation of the human body and the whole creation (Rom. 8:1–27). "For the law of the Spirit of life in Christ Jesus has set me free from the law of sin and death" (8:2). Life in Christ is life in the Spirit, and life in the Spirit is a life of liberation for our neighbor and for God and from sin, the law, death and the coming wrath of God.

The Johannine theology of freedom is liberation from the lie by the truth, but liberation from the lie is liberation from death (Jn. 8:31–59). This discourse about Jesus and Abraham describes the lie from which the truth in Jesus would make them free. The discourse interprets the statement:

> *If you continue in my word,*
>   *you are my disciples,*
> *and you will know the truth,*
>   *and the truth will make you free (8:31b–32).*

The truth is the disclosure of human freedom, God as Father and eternal life. The lie is slavery, the devil and death. The discourse of the word liberates one from the slavery of sin (34–38), the hate of the devil manifested in Cain's murder of Abel (39–47), and the spiritual death that is the absence of eternal life (48–59). Freedom is a state of openness toward God as our Father and man as our brother made possible by the disclosure of truth in Jesus Christ.

Debate on Liberation in History

The fact that freedom has been used more than liberation brings into focus the problem debated in the history of Christian theology. When the focus is on the freedom of the will there is always the implication that freedom is the essence of man, but when the focus is on the freedom of grace there is the presupposition that freedom belongs to the essence of God. If God's grace is the source and agent of the freedom to love God and our neighbor, the freedom of God is the primary theological question, but the problem of freedom of choice remains.

Liberation has become a key idea in modern theology as justification, regeneration, sanctification and reconciliation have at other times. There was first a theological debate, then the ethical application to various groups that were considered oppressed.

The theological debate has been surveyed in Robert T. Osborn's book *Freedom in Modern Theology*, a study that gives special attention to Rudolf Bultmann, Paul Tillich, Karl Barth and Nicolas Berdyaev.[40]

The existential approach to the question of freedom is well illustrated in the effort made to bring existential philosophy into a friendly relation with New Testament teachings. Rudolf Bultmann is perhaps the best example to consider.[41] Remembering his Lutheran heritage it is not surprising that the teachings of Galatians on freedom to love our neighbor are to the fore. Freedom for the neighbor is freedom for God, for God is loved

40. (Philadelphia: The Westminster Press, 1967).
41. *Ibid.*, pp. 25-70.

only through the neighbor. Love is togetherness (*miteinandersein*) with the neighbor and God. Authentic human existence, according to Bultmann, can be detached from the past and the future but never from the present relation with the neighbor and God.

Freedom from the world in the Johannine teachings supplements the concept of a new creation in II Corinthians 5:17. The past, sin, law and death no longer hold the liberated man in bondage. However, Bultmann braces himself against the use of the Johannine writings to support extreme predestinationism. It may be that Bultmann can be charged with teaching that self-understanding is self-determination and self-determinism is self-salvation, but man's responsible existence is never surrendered.

The freedom of God is preserved along with the freedom of man. This is supported by appeal to the hiddenness of God who reveals himself in the cross of Christ in contradiction to the wisdom of this age, much as in 1 Corinthians 1, 2, so that God is wholly other than his creation. On the other hand, there is still room for belief in a natural revelation of God in human existence.

The real problem in Bultmann's existential approach is the difficulty he has in relating the individual to the historical Jesus and the lack of a future eschatology. Attachment to the past events of the gospel and anticipation of the consummation of history limit human freedom, to be sure, but this limited liberation leaves room for the obedience of faith in response to the grace of God.

The ontological approach to human freedom in Paul Tillich attempts to find a foundation for freedom in human existence, but Tillich's symbolism reduces the significance of the historical Jesus and lacks a future orientation about as much as Bultmann. Tillich is especially weak on the freedom of God. In his emphasis on man's ontological freedom, man is almost liberated from God. Man's *courage to be* turns out to be a venture as lonely as in Bultmann.[42]

Lutheranism has finally come to an anchor in the past, present and future in the theology of hope of which Jürgen Moltmann is the chief spokesman. His emphasis on the special resurrection of Jesus and the general resurrection of the future in *The Theology of Hope* (1964) needed the theology of the cross that goes back to Luther, but this he supplied in *The Crucified God* (1972). There was still the need for the freedom of the Spirit, but the completion of his trilogy in *The Church in the Power of the Spirit* (1975) has pointed in the right direction.

The ethical stage in the rebirth of liberation theology has many applications.[43] Liberation from creedalism, racism, poverty, chauvinism, cultural mores, and capitalism has been proclaimed under the banner of hope if not

---

42. *Ibid.*, pp. 71-115.
43. Peter C. Hodgson, *New Birth of Freedom* (Philadelphia: Fortress Press, 1976).

always in love. Unlimited liberation may lead, and has already led, to oppression by the liberators who want others to surrender more than they want freedom. This will continue until freedom *for* balances freedom *from*. True liberation always includes freedom to love God through our neighbor as well as freedom from the powers that oppress the human spirit.

When one turns from Lutheranism to Calvinism it is necessary to begin with the freedom of God. This has found classic expression in both the God-centered liberation of John Calvin himself and in the Christ-centered liberation of Karl Barth in the last generation. As Calvin comes to discuss "The Way in Which We Receive the Grace of Christ: What Benefits Come to Us from It, and What Effects Follow" (Bk. III) there is an unusual chapter on "Christian Freedom" (XIX) that was added in the fifth and last edition, 1559. Read by itself the discussion on liberation from the law is for the most part a clear exposition of the teachings on this subject in Galatians and Romans, but the question of the loss of this freedom is passed by. Liberation from sin, death and the devil is also lacking. The problem of the relation of predestination to liberation or reprobation follows soon (XXI).

Karl Barth's Christ-centered discussion of liberation relates both predestination and liberation to the freedom of God in Christ in such a way that the real freedom of man to reject or receive the grace of God is removed. Damnation for some and liberation for others, as in traditional Calvinism, leads either to double predestination, the majority view, or to universalism, the minority view and that of Karl Barth. In Barth all are liberated and not one is lost.[44] There is no way to do justice to all the New Testament teachings and to human responsibility as long as this Calvinist-Barthian theology is followed. That is why the biblical teachings on both predestination and apostasy must be reexamined.

54. Salvation and Predestination

Many human minds seem to be programmed like a modern computer. Punch a button and a whole system of ideas comes out. This is especially true in theology when certain code words are used.

Take for example the perfectly good New Testament word "predestination." Say it and you can never be sure the New Testament meaning will be aroused in the minds of the listeners. Many, perhaps most, see a picture of an arbitrary tyrant on his hellish-heavenly throne watching mankind march by. Number six — you are in a fix! Number seven — you go to heaven! Why? God just decreed that all number sixes go to hell and all number sevens go to heaven.

This, of course, is not the New Testament teaching at all, but human

---

44. See the criticism of Karl Barth by Emil Brunner, *The Christian Doctrine of God*, tr. Olive Wyon (Philadelphia: The Westminster Press, 1949), pp. 346-353.

tradition has programmed that picture into many minds. That is why it is necessary to begin with a New Testament study of the word, and of the idea of predestination, before historical interpretations can be understood.

Predestination of Christ

In the New Testament predestination is first presented as a description of what happened in the ministry of Christ. In the Acts of the Apostles the predestination of Christ becomes the clue to the interpretation of all history. In the crucifixion of Christ, more than at any other point, the sovereignty of God and the responsibility of man are revealed.

The picture portrayed in the Gospels is far from that twisted theology that reduced Jesus to a robot. According to the Synoptic Gospels, the first three Gospels, Jesus went forth in Galilee to call Israel back into the fold of God. The lost sheep of the house of Israel were to be a light to the Gentiles. This was God's original intention for Israel. What a drama of suspense unfolds as he and his disciples proclaimed the nearness of the kingdom that would be established by the coming of the Son of Man in glory. This was a conditional promise. The coming of the Son of Man in glory to establish God's kingdom was conditioned on the repentance of Israel.

Israel did not repent. The Son of Man did not come in glory. The kingdom of God was postponed until the conditions for its coming were met. The kingdom has not yet come in glory, although it is present in the power of the promise and also in the presence of the Holy Spirit.

A second act in the drama portrays his journey to Jerusalem to die on a cross. He predicts his death and the destruction of Jerusalem. The very generation that saw his death lived to see the fall of Jerusalem as prophesied by Jesus in Mark 13:30. From Galilee to Gethsemane and from Gethsemane to Golgotha there is the suspense of the decision to submit to God's will rather than to do his own will. His was a voluntary sacrifice, not the resignation of a mindless, will-less robot. God's sovereignty and man's freedom work together.

Peter's preaching at Pentecost put God's sovereign plan and man's personal responsibility in proper relation. Here are the words of Acts 2:22f.: "Men of Israel, hear these words: Jesus of Nazareth, a man attested to you by God with mighty works and wonders and signs which God did through him in your midst, as you yourselves know — this Jesus delivered up, according to the definite plan and foreknowledge of God, you crucified and killed by the hands of lawless men."

There is not the slightest suggestion that there is a contradiction between God's "definite plan and foreknowledge" and the guilt of men who "crucified and killed" Jesus. God is sovereign in his rule over the final outcome of history, but he does not deny the freedom of man to make his own decisions even to his own destruction.

Peter's preaching at Solomon's Portico repeated this same balance between God's sovereign plan and human responsibility and freedom. He declared in Acts 3:13–15: "The God of Abraham and of Isaac and of Jacob, the God of our fathers, glorified his servant Jesus, whom you delivered up and denied in the presence of Pontius Pilate, when he had decided to release him. But you denied the Holy and Righteous One, and asked for a murderer to be granted to you, and killed the Author of Life, whom God raised from the dead."

Any talk that attributes to God the pussy-footing of Pontius Pilate is sheer nonsense. The people were not puppets when they clamored for the crucifixion of Jesus and called for the release of the murderer Barabbas. Their free choice killed the Author of Life, but God's sovereign will and power raised Jesus from the dead.

This perfect balance between God's sovereign will and man's responsibility and freedom continues to pervade the interpretation of the cross in the Jerusalem church. On the release of Peter and John from prison the people prayed: "Sovereign Lord, who didst make the heaven and the earth, and the sea and everything in them, who by the mouth of our father David, thy servant, didst say by the Holy Spirit,

Why did the Gentiles rage,
and the people imagine vain things?
The kings of the earth set themselves in array,
and the rulers were gathered together,
against the Lord and against his Anointed —

for truly in this city there were gathered together against thy holy servant Jesus, whom thou didst anoint, both Herod and Pontius Pilate, with Gentiles and the people of Israel, to do whatever thy hand and thy plan had predestined to take place. And now, Lord, look upon their threats, and grant to thy servants to speak thy word with boldness, while thou stretchest out thy hand to heal, and signs and wonders are performed through the name of thy holy servant, Jesus" (Acts 4:24–30).

That prayer puts the responsibility for the death of Jesus on about every person mentioned in the Gospels save Judas Iscariot, but his betrayal is also in the background. The quotation from Psalm 2:1–2 allows people to imagine vain things and to act according to their imaginations, but God rules over all their intentions in the drama of redemption. Their vain imaginations are stimulated by human sin, not by the act of God, and it is this human sin that makes them guilty.

The high priest protested that the preaching of the apostles was intended to bring the blood of Jesus upon the members of the Sanhedrin and the Jewish people. The response of Peter and the other apostles was: "We must obey God rather than man. The God of our fathers raised Jesus whom you killed by hanging him on a tree. God exalted him at his right hand as

Leader and Savior, to give repentance to Israel and forgiveness of sins"
(Acts 5:29–31). This clearly indicates that the blood of Jesus was already
upon the Sanhedrin and the Jewish people, and the only remedy for the
responsibility was repentance.

There is much discussion about the meaning of Gamaliel's speech to
the Sanhedrin, but it seems to me that his closing remarks are in harmony
with the biblical view of predestination. Gamaliel said: "So in the present
case I tell you, keep away from these men and let them alone; for if this
plan or this undertaking is of men, it will fail; but if it is of God, you will
not be able to overthrow them. You might even be found opposing God"
(Acts 5:38f.). God allows man to make his vain plan, but in the end it does
not succeed. Only the plan of God succeeds in the end.

All the talk about man not being able to resist God falls flat before the
preaching of Stephen before he was stoned. After a summary of the drama
between God's sovereignty and man's freedom in the up and down history
of Israel, Stephen makes the final charge: "You stiffnecked people, you
always resist the Holy Spirit. As your fathers did, so do you. Which of the
prophets did not your fathers persecute? And they killed those who announced beforehand the coming of the Righteous One, whom you have now
betrayed and murdered, you who received the law as delivered by angels"
(Acts 7:51–53). Surely one does not insist that all this is the predetermined
plan of God for which man has no responsibility.

With the salvation history of Jesus as the clue, all history may be seen
as a conflict between God's sovereignty and human freedom. Preaching to
the primitive people of Lycaonia, Paul said: "In past generations he allowed
all the nations to walk in their own ways" (Acts 14:16). Their ways were
surely not God's ways, but he allowed them to worship the vanity of nature
rather than the living God.

This sovereignty of God over universal history comes forth more clearly
in Paul's sermon on the Unknown God in Athens. According to Paul, God
"made from one every nation of men to live on all the face of the earth,
having determined allotted periods and the boundaries of their habitation,
that they should seek God, in hope that they might feel after him and find
him" (Acts 17:26f.). This allotment of periods and boundaries does not
attribute to God all the evil of invasions and wars in human history. It does
not mean that all who seek after God find him. If it did all would be saved,
and not even Calvinism holds that view of predestination.

The early proclamations about the death of Jesus in the pattern of
predestination seem rather clear. God does have a goal in human life and
history toward which he is working. He has put limits to man's freedom,
but these limits do not eliminate human responsibility. They do deny human
sovereignty. Man does not have the final decision over the outcome of history and of human destiny. Any effort of man to be sovereign is an effort
to be God, and that can only bring condemnation and human destruction.

God's sovereignty brings all responsive persons to fulfillment, but human sovereignty ends in frustration.

The predestination of Christ that is so prominent in Acts is continued in Paul's writings. This is what Paul called "a secret and hidden wisdom of God, which God decreed before the ages for our glorification" (1 Cor. 2:7). It relinquishes neither the sovereignty of God nor the responsibility of man. It does not confuse the perpendicular act of God with the horizontal acts of man. Even Augustine, who led us astray so often, was correct on this point. He says clearly that "the most illustrious Light of predestination and grace is the Saviour Himself, — the Mediator Himself between God and man, the man Christ Jesus."[45]

Christ is the Predestined One in his death and resurrection. In his death he is both rejected and accepted by God. There, at the cross, he stands as both a rejected sinner and the accepted Son of God. He was rejected because he bore our sins. He was accepted because he knew no sin of his own. In him God says both No and Yes to man.

As the Roman general returned in triumph from battle the incense of the priests in the procession had two meanings: to the vanquished it meant death, but to the victors it meant life. For the Christian, Christ is the triumphant Conqueror whose knowledge is to be spread everywhere like a fragrant smell, but the aroma means death to those who reject it and life to those who accept. As Paul the Apostle says: ". . . to one a fragrance from death to death, to the other a fragrance from life to life" (II Cor. 2:16).

Predestination in Christ

Thus far God's predestination of Christ himself has been central. This must always be first. When the interpretation of predestination shifts away from Christ to creation, all thought becomes confused. This I believe to be the most crucial question on the problem of predestination.

Now, let us turn from the predestination *of* Christ to predestination *in* Christ. Ancient sailors dreaded the journey between the rock on the Italian coast called Scylla and the whirlpool on the opposite coast of Sicily called Charybdis. It took the best pilots to avoid disaster. Both Paul and Peter are called aboard to help us sail between the Scylla of God's sovereignty and the Charybdis of man's freedom.

Paul's first statement on predestination must ever be kept in mind. "For God has not destined us for wrath, but to obtain salvation through our Lord Jesus Christ" (I Thess. 5:9). Paul relates predestination to foreknowledge in what has been called single predestination. Single predestination is the predestination of those who are being saved in Christ. One of the classic texts is Romans 8:28–30. It reads: "We know that in everything God works for good with those who love him, who are the called according

45. *On the Predestination of the Saints*, 30.

to his purpose. For those whom he foreknew he also predestined to be conformed to the image of his Son, in order that he might be the first-born among many brethren. And those whom he predestined he also called; and those whom he called he also justified; and those whom he justified he also glorified."

The translation quoted above is that of the *Revised Standard Version*. *Today's English Version (Good News for Modern Man)* says much the same. The best translation of Romans 8:28 that we have noted is that of the *New English Bible*. It says God "cooperates for good with those who love God and are called according to his purpose." This is just right, the way the Greek reads, but this understanding has been denounced as synergism. The Greek word for "work with" is *synergei*, and from this word synergism was formed. It is strange indeed to hear people declaring they believe in the verbal inspiration of the Holy Scriptures, yet at the same time they denounce this verb! They seem to find an increase in zeal as they butt their heads in an obstinate way against the very language of the Bible. What really do they mean when they speak of the inspiration and authority of Scripture, if the words of the Bible are forbidden?

A little knowledge of Protestant history throws light on this predicament. At the time of the Protestant Reformation, Erasmus of Rotterdam first challenged the extreme denial of human freedom in the early writings of Martin Luther. Erasmus could see no value in the commandments of Jesus if man did not have freedom to do them, and he said so in his book *On the Freedom of the Will* published in 1524. The next year Luther retorted in a tirade called *The Bondage of the Will*. He declared that man is no more than a donkey ridden either by God or the Devil. It seems to me that at that moment Luther was really the donkey. Jaroslav Pelikan, the distinguished editor of *Luther's Works*, a Lutheran himself, has put it more politely by saying that the more he reads Luther the more he likes Erasmus.

Even within the Lutheran camp the debate was heated. Philip Melanchthon, Luther's closest friend, ventured to say three agencies cooperate in human conversion to Christ. These three agencies are the Holy Spirit, the Word of God, and the human will. Melanchthon was especially fond of Philippians 2:13 which says: "God is at work in you, both to will and to work for his good pleasure." The very word "work" put Melanchthon at the mercy of Luther's followers who denounced this teaching as synergism. Luther was great and the Protestant Reformation was not all in vain, but this denial of human freedom has not helped Lutheranism in the evangelistic task of the Church. Holy Scripture is more precious than human tradition, even Protestant tradition.

A second point in Romans 8:28–30 about which there is confusion is the meaning of foreknowledge itself. Medieval theology argued as if foreknowledge meant no more than God knowing beforehand that certain things would happen. The conclusion was drawn that prescience, that is fore-knowledge, could mean nothing less than predeterminism.

On the basis of belief in irresistible grace Augustine (354-430) built his doctrine of single predestination. He argued as follows: "Between grace and predestination there is only this difference, the predestination is the preparation for grace, while grace is the donation itself."[46] If God foreknew those that would be saved, he certainly knew what he would do to save them, so argued Augustine. Therefore, all who are foreknown are foreordained to eternal life. The rest of mankind is left in what Augustine called "the mass of perdition," some of whom had capacity to believe that did not hear and others who heard but refused to believe.[47] It became even worse in a Saxon monk named Gottschalk (805-868?). Gottschalk drew what seemed to him a further logical conclusion. He reasoned that irresistible grace would lead not only to the predestination of the saved but of the lost as well. Even though he was opposed by the learned John the Scot of Ireland, he maintained his gloomy doctrine through condemnation as a heretic and even in imprisonment itself. His poetry reflects the belief that all his tragic life was ordained of God. Even though this sounds more like Islam than New Testament Christianity, such ideas were destined to return in the doctrine of double predestination later expounded in Calvinism. It is often assumed even now that the word "foreknowledge" means no more than knowing beforehand what is to be, and that what is to be will be regardless of human freedom. In the New Testament, however, foreknowledge means that God loves man before man loves God. Knowing and loving mean much the same, as Paul makes clear when he says "if one loves God, one is known by him" (I Cor. 8:1). The classic passage that states God's initiative in terms of God loving us before we love God is I John 4:7–21, a beautiful hymn of Perfect Love that stimulated the great revival under John and Charles Wesley. May this prevenient love prevail.

Paul is very clear on human freedom in relation to foreknowledge. In the great Galatian letter, written perhaps shortly before Romans, Paul describes how those who have come out of slavery into freedom may be in danger of returning to slavery again. This is a possibility even for those God has come to know and who have come to know God. This is the way he puts it in Galatians 4:8–9: "Formerly, when you did not know God, you were in bondage to beings that by nature are no gods; but now that you have come to know God, or rather to be known by God, how can you turn back again to the weak and beggarly elements of the world and become slaves all over again?"

This surely does not mean that foreknowledge rules out freedom. It is not predetermined that foreknowledge will always be followed by predes-

46. *On the Predestination of the Saints*, 19.
47. *Ibid.*, 35.

tination, calling, justification and glorification as were the words at the end of Romans 8. That is the normal sequence, but the sequence can be broken at any point by turning again to slavery. Even Lutheranism agreed on this point, but Calvinism stubbornly and mistakenly held to an unbroken sequence. It was an iron chain. Here again one must choose between the Holy Scripture and human tradition. God indeed has a program, but it is not programmed without a place for human freedom either before faith or after faith.

A second classic passage on Paul's view of predestination is Romans 9:22–24. This passage asks the question: "What if God, desiring to show his wrath and to make known his power, has endured with much patience the vessels of wrath made for destruction, in order to make known the riches of his glory for the vessels of mercy, which he has prepared beforehand for glory, even us whom he has called, not from the Jews only but also from the Gentiles?"

My interpretation of the whole context in Romans 9–11 may be read in Volume 10 of the *Broadman Bible Commentary*, but space does not permit such a detailed statement here. This centers around the debate on double predestination. Double predestination is the belief that God predestines not only the redeemed in Christ but also the damned outside Christ. This second side is often called the decree of reprobation.

The doctrine of the double decree was not so disastrous in the Saxon monk Gottschalk, but the return of the doctrine in the theology of John Calvin was disastrous, for the French Reformer got a following! According to Calvin, even Augustine was afraid to draw the logical conclusion. Augustine depended too much on the ideas of foreknowledge and permission in the "hardening" and "blinding" of sinners, and Calvin found it necessary to answer with what he called "a simple confession of the truth." He replied in the somber words: "We answer, therefore, that it operates in two ways. For, since, when his light is removed, nothing remains but darkness and blindness; since, when his Spirit is withdrawn, our hearts harden into stones; since, when his direction ceases, they are warped into obliquity; he is properly said to blind, harden, and incline those whom he deprives of the power of seeing, obeying, and acting aright. The second way, which is much more consistent with the strict propriety of language, is when, for the execution of his judgements, he, by means of Satan, the minister of his wrath, directs their counsels to what he pleases, and excites their wills and strengthens their efforts."[48] Wherever they have prevailed, evangelism and missions have not even begun, but wherever they have been repudiated in the light of a "whosoever" gospel the fires of evangelism and missions have been lighted.

Calvin's "simple confession" leads to the dismal conclusion that defines

---

48. The fatal words are found in Calvin's *Institutes*, II. iv. iii.

predestination in terms of the double decree. He makes the point clear in these words: "Predestination we call the eternal decree of God, by which he has determined in himself, what he would have to become of every individual of mankind. For they are not all created with a similar destiny; but eternal life is foreordained for some, and eternal damnation for others. For every man, therefore, being created for one or the other of these ends, we say, he is predestinated either to life or to death."[49] How could a statement be more the language of determinism?

The mistranslation and false interpretation of Romans 9:22–24 has led some to denounce the Apostle Paul himself. C. H. Dodd, an English Congregationalist and universalist, protests that "a man is not a pot" and that this parable of the potter is "the weakest point in the whole epistle to the Romans." William Barclay, the prolific and popular Presbyterian of Scotland, gets on Dodd's horse and rides off in all directions at once and leads us into a wilderness of confusion.

A few more careful commentators, notably C. K. Barrett, calmed the British mutiny against what they think is the hyper-Calvinism that required young ministers to declare they were willing to be damned for the glory of God. Franz J. Leenhardt, one of Calvin's most notable successors in Geneva, turns down the heat and increases the light considerably. Leenhardt rightly declares that the parable is concerned with neither Calvinistic rigidity nor anti-Calvinistic absurdity. It is a defense of the freedom and mercy of God rather than an attack on the freedom and responsibility of man.

The first major misunderstanding that stimulated such heated protests pertains to the "vessels for mercy" and the vessels "for menial use." Traditional Calvinism has applied double predestination to the text and comes forth with the idea that one vessel was made for salvation and the other for damnation. This was carried to even greater extremes by Two-Seed-in-the-Spirit Predestinarian Baptists. There really are Baptists by that name!

Paul's point is well made in a later letter which revives the parable and points up human responsibility. II Timothy 2:20 says: "In a great house there are not only vessels of gold and silver but also of wood and earthenware, and some for noble use, and some for ignoble." The Greek words for "noble" and "ignoble" are the same as those translated "mercy" and "menial," but the important point is that one can *purify himself* by consecration to the "master of the house" (II Tim. 2:21).

The second misunderstanding is even more serious. The theory of double predestination has been applied to the "vessels of wrath" and the "vessels of mercy." The passage may be so translated that God is pictured as enduring the vessels of mercy with patience while he himself prepares the vessels for destruction. This, to say the least, gives an odd picture of God. If one shifts from the passive voice to the middle voice (it is the same word

49. *Ibid.*, III. xxi. v.

in Greek), the passage says God patiently endures the vessels of wrath while they prepare themselves for destruction by resistance against God.

James Moffatt's translation seems to have this in mind when it says: "What if God, though desirous to display his anger and show his might, has tolerated most patiently the objects of his anger, ripe and ready to be destroyed?" They get ripe and ready for destruction by resistance to God's grace.

It seems that Lutheranism has led many astray by a false exegesis of Romans 8:28 and that Calvinism has done much the same with Romans 9:22. This, we say again, does not mean that the Reformation was in vain, but it means that Holy Scripture must be put above all human traditional exegesis, even Protestant exegesis. Tradition is of value, but it must never be allowed to be the controlling principle in the interpretation of the Bible.

Paul not only relates predestination to foreknowledge, he relates it also to election. This may also be seen in the details of Romans 9-11, but it is most clearly summarized in Ephesians 1:3-14. Ephesians 1:3-5 makes it clear that Christ is the Chosen One and we are chosen in Christ. We are in Christ by faith, but it is only in Christ that we are chosen or elected. God's grace must be accepted by human faith. Election is a two-sided dialogue, not a one-sided monologue by either God or man.

In this light read carefully Ephesians 1:3-5 and note that it is in Christ before creation, not in creation, that we are chosen. "Blessed be the God and Father of our Lord Jesus Christ, who has blessed us in Christ with every spiritual blessing in the heavenly places, even as he chose us in him before the foundation of the world, that we should be holy and blameless before him. He destined us in love to be his sons through Jesus Christ, according to the purpose of his will. . . ."

Let us use a simple illustration to make this point. I often go to the airport to take a plane from Louisville, Kentucky to Atlanta, Georgia. The airline has a plan. I can read it in the schedule. The jet plane is predestined for Atlanta. It says so in the flight plan. The call goes out for all to board who want to go to Atlanta. I get on and relax and feel predestined. It is a very reliable airline. The pilot says he knows where he is going before he gets there. This gives me a sense of security. Of course I know I can open my emergency exit at any time and jump out. I am not so silly as to think that it is predetermined that once aboard, always aboard.

That is the way we are predestined in Christ. Christ is not only reliable, he is predestined for glory. In him I am predestined for glory too. If I do not remain in him, my destiny will not be glory just as jumping out of the emergency exit would make my destiny some place other than Atlanta. The longer I abide in Christ the more secure I feel, but Christ has not bound me to himself by irresistible grace, but as a free man in the bonds of love and in the experience of grace received by faith. In brief the system of Calvinism cannot be patched with new cloth. The new wine cannot be put in old wineskins. That is what too many do when they try to torture the texts of the Bible to agree with some creed or confession of the past. I cannot say this too strongly.

Paul has been our pilot thus far, but Peter has his contribution also. I Peter 2:8 is another text that the theory of deterministic double predestination has claimed for its support. I think they have made a false claim. Peter's view on predestination seems identical with what has been seen in Paul. Neither of the two great Apostles teaches the absolute and deterministic views of predestination developed in the traditions of Augustine and Calvin. We simply must choose between Paul and Peter on the one hand, and Augustine and Calvin on the other hand. Both Paul and Peter teach that there is a human condition attached to predestination, and that condition is the free response of faith, God's grace and man's faith. Conditional predestination is taught in the New Testament, but absolute predestination is a human tradition and an unfortunate perversion of the language of the Bible.

Now let us return to I Peter for the last part of the pilgrimage of predestination. Again Christ is the Predestined One as seen in Acts. In I Peter 2:6 Christ is the Chosen One, "a cornerstone chosen and precious." I Peter 1:2 uses the same word for those "chosen and destined by God the Father and sanctified by the Spirit for obedience to Jesus Christ and for sprinkling with his blood." This is the single predestination of Christ and for those in Christ.

Double predestination is taught also in I Peter 2:8, but it is a predestination based upon the conditions of obedience or disobedience. As the obedient are predestined to salvation, so the disobedient are predestined to damnation. God did not predestine the disobedient to stumble, but they stumbled because they were disobedient. To the obedient, Christ is the cornerstone in God's spiritual house, but for the disobedient, he is the stumbling stone by which men fall to their own destruction.

They stumble as they disobey the word,
as they were destined to do.

At bottom the conflict between God's sovereign will and man's free will is a problem of the fundamental relationship of God to man and of man to God. Ancient Stoicism reduced God to nature so that whatever happened in nature was interpreted as the will of God. God and nature, after all, are one, according to this view.

The traditions rooted in Augustine, Luther and Calvin come very near to reducing nature and man to God by a deterministic emphasis on predestination. Even though the beginning point is God, the result is much the same as in ancient Stoicism. God and nature are one. There is no room for natural evil and human sin, to say nothing about human responsibility and freedom.

It is no wonder that one of the truly great interpreters of Christian history was tried for heresy by the Calvinists. This was the great Philip Schaff. More than any other he taught me that history is the testing ground for theological ideas. His summary of the conflict between the two major movements stimulated by Calvin is classic. He said: "The Bible gives us a theology which is more human than Calvinism, and more divine than Arminianism, and more Christian than either of them."[50] It is the Bible which we consider inspired and authoritative, that we have sought to follow in this survey of predestination as the problem of God's sovereign will and man's free will. I pray that those who would refute the argument that has been made will do so by appeal to Holy Scripture and not by appeal to human tradition.

55. Salvation and Apostasy

The question of apostasy has been left until the end in the discussion of faith and salvation. This has been done for a number of reasons. First, since the time of Augustine it has been, if possible, more controversial than the question of predestination. Second, after seeing in the introduction that the nature of salvation includes the past, present and future of the Christian life, in all terms used to describe God's deliverance of man from sin the question of apostasy between the beginning and the end of salvation forms the best conclusion to the meaning of salvation in the New Testament.

What does the New Testament mean by apostasy and related terms? A Scriptural approach begins with the central issues and only then sets forth secondary questions of Scripture and tradition. After the meaning of apostasy as a New Testament teaching is clarified, then the controversies in church history may be evaluated.

Apostasy is not a term imposed upon the New Testament; it is a New Testament term used in both a special and a general sense. The special sense in which the apostasy of many in the latter days ends in the great apostasy, or falling away, before the return of Christ, is discussed in the section on the consummation (see II Thess. 2:3 and I Tim. 4:1 for this sense). It is the possibility of apostasy that is ever present between immaturity and maturity in the life of faith that is the subject of this section (see Heb. 3:12 for this sense). This alone is the concern at present.

Apostasy in Scripture

Backsliding in the Old Testament is a general background for understanding the New Testament teachings on falling away from a personal faith in the

---

50. *History of the Christian Church* (Grand Rapids: Wm. B. Eerdmans, 1882-1910), VIII, 816.

Lord Jesus, but the New Testament should be interpreted in terms of the New Covenant. In the Old Covenant the unfaithfulness of Israel to the covenant may be called national apostasy as those who had turned to the Lord turned away from him. This was a special concern of the prophet Jeremiah. The nearest thing in the Old Testament to the New Testament teaching on apostasy would be willing sins or high-handed sins for which there were no sacrifices.[51]

There are several warnings in the Synoptic Gospels about the danger that disciples may fall away, but perhaps the plainest passage is Luke's interpretation of the Parable of the Sower (8:9-15). Some only hear the word of God without believing it, but those in a second group "believe for a while and in a time of temptation fall away" (8:13). A. T. Robertson comments: "Ostensibly they are sincere and have a real start in the life of faith."[52]

Superficial believers are not the only type that falls away. The thorny ground in the Parable of the Sower represents those who hear the word of God, "but as they go on their way they are choked by the cares and riches and pleasures of life, and their fruit does not mature" (8:14). Those who hold fast the word of God "in an honest and good heart" are the only ones that "bring forth fruit with patience" (8:15). It is amazing how preconceived dogmas blind so many to the realism of this parable. It happens before their eyes in so many ways, but they refuse to see what is so obvious.

The Acts of the Apostles records the story of Ananias and Sapphira who were smitten dead because they lied to the Holy Spirit of God (5:11). Simon Magus "himself believed," but Peter pronounced the curse of God upon him. Paul was aware that "fierce wolves" would pounce upon the believers of Ephesus and "draw away disciples after them" (Acts 20:30). On this last passage A. T. Robertson has the salty statement: "There is a false optimism that is complacently blind as well as a despondent pessimism that gives up the fight."[53]

The letters of Paul contain passages that are brushed aside today as unworthy of serious study. Yet the primary letters of 1 and 2 Thessalonians take note of the idle, fainthearted and weak who need to be admonished so that they may be sound and blameless at the second coming (I Thess. 5:14, 23). Even before the great apostasy and the revelation of the man of lawlessness there was the danger that false teachers would lead them astray so that some would refuse to obey Paul (II Thess. 1:1-2; 3:14f.).

At one place he warns those who live on the level of knowledge, the

---

51. I. Howard Marshall, *Kept by the Power of God* (Minneapolis, Minnesota: Bethany Fellowship, 1975), pp. 29-38.
52. *Word Pictures in the New Testament* (Nashville: Sunday School Board of the Southern Baptist Convention, 1930), vol. II, p. 114.
53. *Ibid.*, vol. III, p. 355.

Gnostic notion of knowledge that puffs up, that they can by their example destroy the faith of a weak brother who lives on the level of conscience (I Corinthians 8:11). Paul believed that even he, after preaching to others, could become disqualified, a castaway in the AV, *adokimos* in Greek (I Cor. 9:27). A. T. Robertson has this observation: "Most writers take Paul to refer to the possibility of his rejection in his personal salvation at the end of the race. . . . It is a humbling thought for us all to see this wholesome fear instead of smug complacency in this greatest of all heralds of Christ" (cf. I Cor. 8:11; 10:12).[54] This smug complacency continues among those who ignore the possibility that they may become castaways. The reference of Robertson to I Corinthians 10:12 has the warning: "Therefore let anyone who thinks he stands take heed lest he fall." Paul actually believed his readers could become reprobates, and "fail to meet the test" (II Cor. 13:5). Yet cheap preaching and compromise with sin have made such texts forbidden for serious study.

The Galatian letter of Paul has only one chapter without a serious warning about falling from grace, yet the phrase is forbidden language for some. What does Paul mean when he says: "I am astonished that you are so quickly deserting him who called you in the grace of Christ and turning to a different gospel" (1:6)? What does he mean by beginning in the Spirit and ending in the flesh (3:3)? Why does he fear that those who come out of slavery into sonship (4:1–7) will turn back to the weak, beggarly elemental spirits (4:8–11), if this is impossible? It is nonsense to say these passages have Peter and Barnabas in mind (cf. Gal. 2:12), but it is correct to see "the circumcision party" as the danger to believers.

Surely he would not warn the Galatians against putting on the "yoke of slavery" again, if that were not a real danger. All these questions are answered by the blunt statement: "You are severed from Christ, you who would be justified by the law; you have fallen away from grace" (5:4). A. T. Robertson translates the Greek to say "ye did fall out of grace."[55] J. W. MacGorman rightly says: "To turn to the law as in any way necessary to effect the right standing with God is to turn one's back on Christ . . . nothing more, nothing less."[56] They were running well until somebody hindered them (5:7).

The conclusion needs only to be read to be understood:

> *Be not deceived;*
> *God is not mocked,*
> *for whatever a man sows,*
> *that he will also reap.*

54. *Ibid.*, Vol. IV, p. 150.
55. *Ibid.*, Vol. IV, p. 309.
56. *Broadman Bible Commentary* (Nashville: Broadman Press, 1971), Vol. 11, p. 114.

> *For he who sows to his own flesh*
> *will from the flesh reap corruption;*
> *but he who sows to the Spirit*
> *will from the Spirit reap eternal life.*
> *And let us not grow weary in well-doing,*
> *for in due season we shall reap,*
> *if we do not lose heart (6:7-9).*

Those who flee from these Pauline passages and look for shelter in Romans 8:39 do well provided they understand that nothing will separate us from the love of God if we are "in Christ Jesus our Lord." This does not apply to those who are severed from Christ. Before the precious promise in 8:39 is the warning and promise in 8:12f. which says: "So then, brethren, we are debtors, not to the flesh — for if you live according to the flesh you will die, but if by the Spirit you put to death the deeds of the body you will live." Brothers can keep on living according to flesh and die! Warnings noted in I Corinthians 8:11; 9:27; 10:12 are in Romans 14:13-23. A bad example can lead to the spiritual ruin of a brother for whom Christ died, even "destroy the work of God" (14:15, 20). Scripture should not be read with selective inattention. All of it is inspired and all of it is to be heard and heeded.

The warnings against perils continue in Paul's prison letters. When shelter from the danger of spiritual disaster is sought in Paul's confidence that he who began a good work among the Philippians "will bring it to completion at the day of Christ" (Phil. 1:6), there should be no selective inattention when they are called to work out their salvation with fear and trembling (2:12) and warned about those whose end is destruction (3:19). Paul's security was based on the fact that he pressed on toward perfection (3:12-16; cf. 2:16).

It has already been noted that the presentation of the reconciled and the sanctified to God is conditional, "provided that you continue in the faith" (Col. 1:23). There is nothing in Colossians 3:3 to contradict this. It is strange that appeal is often made to Ephesians 4:30 as if it says the Holy Spirit seals believers "until the day of redemption" when it really says the seal is "unto the day of redemption," i.e. present possession of the Spirit points to the full redemption of the future (cf. 1:13f.). When it is noted that the saying is based on Isaiah 63:10 the meaning is clear. In Isaiah 63:10 the Israelites got all the way to Kadesh-barnea,

> *But they rebelled*
> *and grieved his holy Spirit;*
> *Therefore he turned to be their enemy,*
> *and himself fought against them.*

Paul apparently means that his readers can turn back into the wilderness and perish (cf. I Corinthians 10:12 where the setting is the same as in Isaiah 63:10). Ephesians 1:13f. and 2:8–10 have nothing to refute this when compared with Philippians 2:12.

Paul's pastoral letters mention specific persons who fell away from the faith. The Cretans needed a sharp rebuke from Titus "that they may be sound in the faith, instead of giving heed to Jewish myths or to commands of men who reject the truth" (1:13f.). Hymenaeus and Alexander were among those who made shipwreck of their faith and were delivered to Satan (I Timothy 1:19f.), and in the future many will "depart from the faith" (4:1). Phygelus and Hermogenes turned away from Paul, and it is likely that they turned away from the faith that he preached. Demas, once as prominent as Luke, "in love with this present world," forsook Paul also (II Tim. 4:10). Paul's teachings on the faithlessness of man and the faithfulness of God are summarized in the following statement:

> *If we die with him, we shall live with him;*
>
> *if we endure with him, we shall reign with him;*
>
> *if we deny him, he also will deny us;*
>
> *if we are faithless, he remains faithful (II Tim. 1:11–13).*

Some of the general letters and Hebrews seem to be from Hellenistic Jewish Christianity. James thought his brethren could wander from the truth and be in danger of spiritual death (5:19f.). I Peter teaches that even those "who by God's power are guarded through faith" need the admonition: "Be sober, be watchful. Your adversary the devil prowls around like a roaring lion, seeking some one to devour" (1:5; 5:8). II Peter teaches that those who do not grow in grace may forget they were cleansed from their old sins and that the last state can be worse than the first (1:9; 2:20–22). Jude wrote against those who "deny our only Master and Lord, Jesus Christ" and gave several examples of apostasy (3–16) before he concluded with a summary of apostolic Christianity and a benediction on God's ability to keep those who continue in faith, hope and love (17–25). It is unrealistic to ignore this distinction between apostate and apostolic Christianity.

If one follows the teachings of Hebrews all the other teachings on apostasy in the New Testament present no problems. It is when one tries to twist Hebrews to fit a traditional system based on false philosophy and dogma that difficulties arise. Few passages in the New Testament have been twisted with more violence than the five warnings on apostasy in Hebrews.

It is not crucial for interpretation, but it does seem that Tertullian of Carthage was right when he thought Barnabas was the author of this treatise. A good guess for the destiny and date would be Rome, Passover, A.D. 70. The theme of the letter is the finality of the gospel (1:1–4), but there are subordinate themes such as the priesthood of Christ, the world-mission of Christianity, and the Christian life as a pilgrimage.[57]

The first of the five warnings in Hebrews on the possibility of apostasy has two major statements that are decisive (2:1–4). The first says. "Therefore, we must pay closer attention to what we have heard, lest we drift away from it" (2:1). In order to limit the theme of the letter to world-mission and to exclude any reference to personal salvation, H. H. Hobbs advances a novel interpretation of the passive subjunctive of *pararuōmen*, translated "we drift." He argues, against all other translators and commentators known, that the translation should be "drifted by." The passive of *pararreō*, to flow by, would be drift, but Hobbs wants to make God in his world-mission the drifter, leaving the "readers standing on the bank."[58]

A second statement has been used to limit the message to world-mission. It is the question: "How shall we escape if we neglect such a great salvation" (2:3)? By adopting the Roman Catholic distinction between justifying and sanctifying grace already mentioned, Hobbs limits salvation "to launching out into the river of God's world-mission of redemption."[59] He limits the meaning of salvation in most of the other passages where it is used in Hebrews (1:14; 2:10; 5:9; 6:9; 9:28). Salvation seems always to be the pilgrimage from Egypt to the promised land, past, present and future, but Hobbs usually limits it to either present sanctification or future glorification. Only at 2:10 and 5:9 does he allow for salvation in the "full sense of justification, sanctification and glorification." This exegetical hop-scotch is obviously special pleading to defend the dogmatic theory of eternal security. The whole system of thought that limits justification and regeneration to the beginning of salvation and glorification to the future with sanctification in the present has already been pointed out as the product of the conflict between Christian traditions. It is time to put them together again as parallel ways of describing the process of salvation from beginning to end.

The second warning on the possibility of apostasy in Hebrews is even more difficult to explain away (3:7–4:13). The whole passage reads like a stirring sermon on Psalm 95:7–11, but 3:12–14 is the crucial part on apostasy. Since most commentaries interpret the aorist infinitive *apostēnai*, falling away, to mean apostasy, the transliteration of the Greek into English,

---

57. Cf. I. Howard Marshall, *op. cit.*, pp. 137f. My own views on apostasy in Hebrews were first formulated in 1941, under the influence of the writings of A. T. Robertson, but this doctoral thesis at the University of Aberdeen in 1963 vindicates my conclusions at every point. If Marshall is in error, he should be refuted with sound exegesis, not with emotional ranting.
58. H. H. Hobbs, *How to Follow Jesus* (Nashville: Broadman Press, 1971), p. 17.
59. *Ibid.*, p. 19.

it is well to continue the dialogue with Hobbs, who argues that the Greek does not have the same meaning in English as it does in Greek.[60] Unbelief (3:12, 19) and disobedience (3:18; 4:6, 11) seem to be used as synonyms for falling away. There is a play on the word sounds in Greek: *apistia*, *apeitheia*, *apostasia*.

Hobbs is correct in seeing the root meaning as rebellion or renunciation of the covenant relation and that the turning back of the Israelites at Kadesh-Barnea is the Old Testament paradigm for the whole passage, but he has clearly limited the meaning when he says rebellion against God means no more than "refusing to become an active part of his world-mission." The Old Testament paradigm speaks of those who perished in the wilderness, not of returning to Egypt, as Hobbs' defensive words assert.[61] I am at least one of those mentioned who objected to his limited interpretation when he stated it in conversation.

The third warning on the possibility of apostasy in Hebrews has suffered most from "the sacred art of Scripture twisting" (6:1–29). A volume could be written on 6:4–6 alone. The synonym for *apostēnai* is the aorist participle *parapesontas*, having fallen away, from *parapiptō*, to fall alongside. Again, Hobbs is correct in the interpretation of the first four aorist participles about "those who have once been enlightened, who have tasted the heavenly gift, and have become partakers of the Holy Spirit, and have tasted the good word of God and the powers of the age to come" being Hebrew Christians.[62] However, his effort again to limit the falling away to their failure at fulfillment of their world-mission is due to his belief that the teaching of apostasy would contradict other New Testament passages. All but the Johannine passages mentioned have already been examined, and they will be discussed next.

Hobbs is here clearly limiting the penalty for the sin of falling as he has limited the meaning of salvation. On Hebrews 6:4–6 A. T. Robertson, after explaining the meaning of the Greek text, retorts: "*Adunaton* ["impossible"] bluntly denies the possibility of renewal for apostates from Christ (cf. Heb. 3:12; 4:2). It is a terrible picture and cannot be toned down."[63] Hobbs, however, does not agree with his great teacher and labors hard lest these loud tones awake his readers from dogmatic slumber. The curse and the burning of the soil that bears thorns and thistles is, according to the persistent theory of Hobbs, no more than the loss of rewards.[64]

---

60. *Ibid.*, pp. 38f.
61. *Ibid.*, pp. 19, 38.
62. *Ibid.*, pp. 59f. See also my book *Spirit of the Living God* (Nashville: Broadman Press, 1976), pp. 188-190. R. E. Glaze, *No Easy Salvation* (Nashville: Broadman Press, 1966), made the unbelievable claim that the experience of unbelieving Jews is here described!
63. *Op. cit.*, Vol. V, p. 375.
64. *Op. cit.*, pp. 62f.

The fourth warning on apostasy Hebrews describes the penalty in dreadful terms (10:19–39). The fate of the wilful sinner (10:26–31) is "a fearful expectation of a fiery judgment, and a fury of fire that will consume the adversaries" and is still, according to Hobbs, the destiny of redeemed people. Their rebellion or wilful sin by which they spurned the Son of God, profaned the blood of the covenant by which they were sanctified, and outraged the Spirit of God is also, according to Hobbs, the deed of redeemed and "good for nothing Christians" who are "against God's will in evangelism and missions."[65] There seems to be no language that Hobbs is unable to tone down. Even the fearful falling into the hands of the living God in 10:31 is only the penalty for "refusal to accept their place in his mission of world redemption."[66] If all this is the destiny of the redeemed, redemption has lost all meaning. Hobbs agrees that Hebrews 10:26 is "a terrible but simple verse" for those who believe in apostasy, but he again does not follow his teacher A. T. Robertson, who recognized that the destiny of "apostates from Christ" is here described.

The fifth and last warning on apostasy in Hebrews (12:1–29) declares for a third time that there is no remedy for this sin. In 6:4–6 it was said that "it is impossible to restore again to repentance those who have once been enlightened, who have tasted the heavenly gift, and have become partakers of the Holy Spirit, and have tasted the goodness of the word of God and the powers of the age to come, if they then commit apostasy, since they crucify the Son of God on their own account and hold him up to contempt." In 10:26 it was said that "if we sin deliberately after the knowledge of the truth, there no longer remains a sacrifice for sin, but a fearful prospect of judgment, and a fury of fire which will consume the adversaries." Now, believers are warned not to follow the example of Esau who sold his birthright and found "no chance to repent, though he sought it with tears" (12:17). "The author presses the case of Esau as a warning to the Christians who were tempted to give up Christ" (A. T. Robertson).

By the time that one has reached this point in the exposition of Hebrews three things stand out: (1) it is possible to press on to maturity and full assurance (6:1, 11; 10:22); (2) it is possible for believers who do not press on to maturity to commit apostasy; and (3) there is no remedy for the sin of apostasy. Many, like Martin Luther, would like to drop Hebrews out of the canon of Scripture, some for the second reason and others for the third, but this is out of the dogmatic bias that goes back to Augustine, not to other Scriptures.

Often those who reject the teachings on apostasy do so because they believe certain passages in the Johannine writings teach otherwise. They

65. *Ibid.*, p. 106.
66. *Ibid.*, p. 107.

really misinterpret the Johannine passages by reading them through the colored glass of tradition. The Johannine writings do have a great emphasis on God's preservation of those who abide in Christ, but one may cease to abide in Christ. In their game of theological chess the trick question is often put: "can a person be unborn?" John 3:3-8 is usually in mind. They would never say that a friend who died "got unborn." The trick question grew up by ignoring the plain statement in I John 5:16 which teaches that it is possible for a Christian brother to die a spiritual death. This is not a case like I Corinthians 11:30. Death in I John 5:16 has the same meaning as in 3:14. It should be noted that John 3:16 speaks of those who do not perish as those who continue to believe. The Greek tense behind believeth is present linear, not past and punctiliar.

The next move is almost sure to be John 5:24, which speaks of those who believe as passing from spiritual death to eternal life so that they will not come into judgment, but again it must be pointed out that I John 5:16 says one can pass from eternal life back into death (cf. I Jn. 5:11-13). They work with the false assumption that the adjective "eternal" is an adverb, as if it says the brother eternally has life. It is the life that is eternal, not one's possession of it. Eternal life is the life of God in Christ the Son of God, and this life is lost when one departs from Christ (cf. Jn. 5:26). Eternal life is possible only in the Son of God.

The third move is to John 6:37 where it is said: "All that the Father gives me will come to me and him who comes to me I will not cast out." True! Those who come or keep on coming will not be cast out, but Judas was given to Jesus by the Father, yet he became the son of perdition (John 17:12). That is precisely the teaching of John 6. After the threefold promise that he will at the last day raise up those given by the Father (6:39, 40, 44), "many of his disciples drew back and no longer went about with him" (6:66). Simon Peter then speaks for those who did not go away, for to do so would forfeit eternal life, and Judas is singled out as one among the Twelve who was to go back into perdition (6:67-71). The whole of John 6 is built on the model of the Israelites who got all the way to Kadesh-barnea and turned back to perish in the wilderness. That is why there is the frequent reference to murmuring against Christ (Jn. 6:41, 43, 61; cf. I Cor. 10:10 based on Exod. 16:7, 8, 9, 12; Num. 14:27; 17:5, 10).

Eternal life is the life of those who continue to follow Jesus. No one can retain eternal life who turns away from Jesus. John 10:28 is frequently used as a security blanket by those who ignore many of the New Testament warnings about going back or falling away, but a literal translation of John 10:27-28, all of the sentence, hardly needs explanation, for it is a promise to those who continue to follow Jesus. Not for one moment do I doubt this literal translation: "My sheep keep on hearing my voice, and I keep on knowing them, and they keep on following me: and I keep on giving them eternal life, and they shall never perish, and no one shall snatch them out of my hand." Some read the passage as if it says: "My sheep heard my voice, and I knew them, and they followed me, and I gave to them eternal life." The verbs are present linear, indicating continuous action by the sheep and by the Shepherd, not the punctiliar fallacy of the past tense.

Obviously, those who follow Jesus will not perish, but what about those disciples who "drew back and no longer went about with him?" The allegory on Jesus as the Vine and the Father as the Vinedresser in John 15:1–11 answers that question. "Every branch of mine that bears no fruit, he takes away. . . . If a man does not abide in me, he is cast forth as a branch and withers; and the branches are gathered, thrown into the fire and burned" (15:2, 6). Surely one will not appeal to some passage like I Corinthians 3:15 to prove that the words in the Gospel of John mean nothing more than the loss of reward by a saved person, yet that is just what is often done to defend the dogmatic theory of eternal security, which is never mentioned in the New Testament. It would hardly make sense for Jesus to say he taught his disciples to keep them from "falling away" (16:1) if it were not possible for them to fall away.

In the Letters of John the strong emphasis in the Gospel of John on God's preservation of believers who abide in Christ is continued, but there is still the possibility of mortal sin (I Jn. 5:16). I John 2:19 is also used as a security blanket to cover all cases that depart from following Jesus and the Christian fellowship. It is often read as if it says the antichrists "went out from us" because "they never were of us," but the Greek would also allow for the interpretation and translation that they "went out from us because they were no longer of us." In fact, that is the interpretation A. T. Robertson gives to the passage. It is true that one does not continue in sin as long as the seed *(sperma)* of God abides in him (I Jn. 3:9), but the words of Jesus must remain in him (cf. Jn. 15:7).[67]

This surely is more in agreement with the statement about the brother who can commit mortal sin in I John 5:16. "Sin unto death," as said before, is the sin that leads to spiritual death, not physical death.[68] This agrees with the danger of the deceivers who do not abide "in the doctrine of Christ" (II Jn. 7–11). That is why it is so very important to "follow the truth" (III Jn. 3f.).

The Revelation of John has an abundance of warnings to churches that

---

67. See my commentary, *The Letters of John* (Waco, Texas: Word Books, 1970), pp. 50, 111, for further exegesis of I John 2:19; 3:9; 5:16. Surprisingly, after much wavering, W. T. Conner says the "sin unto death" in I John 5:16 is possibly the same as "blasphemy against the Holy Spirit" (Matthew 12:31ff.) and "the wilful sin" of Hebrews 10:26ff. at an early stage; *The Epistles of John*, Second and revised edition (Nashville: Broadman Press, 1957), p. 131.
68. *The Letters of John*, p. 111.

they can be removed as lampstands in the *menorah* of the living Christ (1–3). The Old Testament speaks of sinners being blotted out of God's book (Exodus 32:33), and Revelation has the promise that the overcomer will not be blotted out (3:5). Those who claim that originally all names were in the book of life and only those who never come to believe are blotted out have not read Revelation carefully (13:8; 17:8). There is also no doubt that one can lose his share in the tree of life (22:19).

The Revelation of John along with the Gospel of John and the Letters of John has a strong emphasis on God's preservation of the faithful through the ordeals of this world. If one means by "the perseverance of the saints" that only those who persevere are saints, then there is no debate, but what do we call all those who do not persevere? Revelation has some strong names for them (22:14f.). The term "perseverance of the saints" never appeared in the English Bible until the New American Standard Bible used the phrase in Revelation 14:12 which says: "Here is the perseverance of the saints who keep the commandments of God and their faith in Jesus" (cf. 13:10). This was the teaching of Jesus (Mark 13:13). With this one may fully agree, but the use and meaning of this term in Christian tradition must be further examined if it excludes the possibility of apostasy in the New Testament teachings.[69]

Apostasy in Tradition

Warnings against the danger of falling away from faith may be noted in every New Testament writing but Philemon, which has no doctrinal discussion at all! Why then has this teaching been excluded in much of the Christian theology of the West? The answer on examination comes home loud and clear: tradition has triumphed over Scripture. At least three distorted traditions and interpretations may be noted in Western theology.

The first was *Augustinianism*. In 429, Augustine, the Catholic Bishop of Hippo, wrote his last two books, *On the Predestination of the Saints* and *On the Gift of Perseverance*. These books, like the Vandal armies who at the time threatened the Christian world, were destined to cast a shadow over Christian life and theology down to this day.

In his battle with the Pelagians over the doctrines of original sin and God's grace, Augustine worked with a logic that later became a system in Calvinism. (1) To him the human race was a mass of perdition so depraved,

---

69. For detailed discussion of all New Testament passages on falling away, especially in Johannine writings, see Robert Shank, *Life in the Son* (Springfield, Missouri: Westcott Publisher, 1960, 1961); *Elect in the Son* (Springfield, Missouri: Westcott Publishers, 1970). Apart from Ch. XIX in the first volume these books are as helpful as the later book by I. Howard Marshall, *op. cit.*, as a refutation of the Augustinian-Calvinistic tradition that has twisted Scripture for centuries. If Shank and Marshall are in error, they should be answered by appeal to Scripture, not ignored or rejected by majority vote as was done in the case of the Remonstrants at Dort in 1618.

as a result of Adam's Fall, that little unbaptized infants would be justly damned in limbo. (2) On no condition due to man, God had chosen to redeem a number of souls that would equal the number of the fallen angels. (3) For this elect group Jesus Christ came to earth to die, and (4) God would save them by his unmerited and irresistible grace. (5) By the gift of perseverance the elect were joined to God forever. He was indeed, as his biographer said, a man predestinate (*Life*, Preface, 2). As the Vandals closed in on him and his flock in Hippo, he prayed that they would be able to persevere to the end (*Life*, XXIX. I).

The second tradition to distort the New Testament teaching on apostasy was *Calvinism*. The logic of Augustine was greatly modified in the history of Catholic theology, but his doctrines of predestination and perseverance were revived again by the French Reformer John Calvin. Calvin believed that God regenerated all elect infants before their baptism, so this softened some of the harshness on infant damnation, but Calvin hardened the doctrine of predestination into a double decree by which God was not only the author of salvation for the elect but of damnation for the non-elect (*Institutes*, III. xxi).

He also believed the elect are given assurance of their election, either at the time of repentance or before they die. This third point prepared the way for later debate on the doctrines of assurance and the second blessing, some holding that assurance came with faith and others that it came later.

As in Augustine, Calvin's doctrine of the perseverance of the saints is a part of his doctrine of predestination. "By predestination," said Calvin, "we mean the eternal decree of God, by which he has decided in his own mind what he wishes to happen in the case of each individual. For all men are not created on an equal footing, but for some eternal life is pre-ordained, for others eternal damnation" (*Institutes* [1539], III. xxi). Even the apostasy of those who experience all that the elect experience, is predestined for reprobates.[70] Calvin followed Augustine in appealing to John 6:37; 17:6 to support his doctrine of perseverance. In his debate with the Roman Catholic scholar A. Pighe, d. 1542, Calvin erected a Johannine fortress using John 6:37; 10:28; 17:6–11 and other passages.[71] A reading of the old Augustine and the old Calvin raises the question whether old men should discuss predestination, perseverance and apostasy at all!

The crucial time for Calvinism was their condemnation of Arminianism at the Synod of Dort in Holland in 1618. Since the condemnation of the Remonstrants, as the disciples of James Arminius were called, their statements have been for the most part vindicated in the modified traditions of Calvinism. The five points that were condemned were:

70. John Calvin, *Hebrews*, tr. John Owen (Grand Rapids: Eerdmans, 1948), p. 136.
71. *Concerning the Eternal Predestination of God* (1552), tr. J. K. S. Reid (London: James Clarke & Co., 1961), p. 56.

I. That God, by an eternal and unchangeable purpose in Jesus Christ his Son, before the foundations of the world were laid, determined to save, out of the human race which had fallen into sin, in Christ, for Christ's sake and through Christ, those who through the grace of the Holy Spirit shall believe on the same his Son and shall through the same grace persevere in this same faith and obedience of faith even to the end; and on the other hand to leave under sin and wrath the contumacious and unbelieving and to condemn them as aliens from Christ, according to the word of the Gospel in John 3:36, and other passages of Scripture.

II. That, accordingly, Jesus Christ, the Saviour of the world, died for all men and for every man, so that he has obtained for all, by his death on the cross, reconciliation and remission of sins; yet so that no one is partaker of this remission except the believers [John 3:16; I John 2:2].

III. That man has not saving grace of himself, nor of the working of his own free will, inasmuch as in his state of apostasy and sin he can for himself and by himself think nothing that is good — nothing, that is, truly good, such as saving faith is, above all else. But that it is necessary that by God, in Christ and through his Holy Spirit he be born again and renewed in understanding, affections and will and in all his faculties, that he may be able to understand, think, will and perform what is truly good, according to the Word of God [John 15:5].

IV. That this grace of God is the beginning, the progress and the end of all good; so that even the regenerate man can neither think, will nor effect any good, nor withstand any temptation to evil, without grace precedent (or prevenient), awakening, following and co-operating. So that all good deeds and all movements towards good that can be conceived in thought must be ascribed to the grace of God in Christ.

But with respect to the mode of operation, grace is not irresistible; for it is written of many that they resisted the Holy Spirit [Acts 7 and elsewhere *passim*].

V. That those who are grafted into Christ by a true faith, and have thereby been made partakers of his life-giving Spirit, are abundantly endowed with power to strive against Satan, sin, the world and their own flesh, and to win the victory; always, be it understood, with the help of the grace of the Holy Spirit, with Jesus Christ assisting them in all temptations, through his Spirit; stretching out his hand to them and (provided only that they are themselves prepared for the fight, that they entreat his aid and do not fail to help themselves) propping and upholding them so that by no guile or violence of Satan can they be led astray or plucked from Christ's hands [John 10:28]. But for the question whether they are not able through sloth or negligence to forsake the beginning of their life in Christ, to embrace again this present world, to depart from the holy doctrine once delivered to them, to lose their good conscience and to neglect grace — this must be the subject of more exact inquiry in the Holy Scriptures, before we can teach it with full confidence of our mind.

These Articles thus set out and delivered the Remonstrants deem agreeable to the word of God, suitable for edification and, on this subject, sufficient for salvation. So that it is not needful, and tends not to edification, to rise higher or to descend lower.[72]

About the only points that would now be questioned by evangelical Christians are the five quotations from Scripture raised as a question at the end of article V, yet the question is a composition from Hebrews 3:14; II Timothy 4:10; II Peter 2:22; I Timothy 1:19; Hebrews 12:15. A scholar as able as G. C. Berkouwer has exercised all his strength to bring Hebrews into line with Calvinism and to defend the Calvinistic doctrine of election and predestination.[73] He really reduces the warnings to bluffing.

Despite the abundance of Scripture surveyed above, the strict Calvinists have defended the doctrines of predestination and perseverance imposed on Scripture by Augustine and Calvin. A study of the English Calvinist John Owen is an ordeal of verbosity in defense of the thesis that apostates were predestined to fall away by the decree of God.

Besides his books *The Doctrine of the Saints' Preserverance* and *The Nature of Apostasy*, John Owen wrote a commentary on Hebrews of 3,500 pages, and even then he was unable to bring the writing into line with his rigid Calvinistic system. Like so many since, he could discern the threat, but he was unable to twist the content. It is a strange spectacle to see so much energy expounded in the effort to make Scripture support a false tradition.

The third movement that found problems with the New Testament teachings on apostasy cherishes the name *evangelical*. By the nineteenth century, under the impact of evangelism and missions, the doctrine of the perseverance of the saints was falling into disrepute. In two branches of evangelical Christianity the terms that began to replace "the perseverance of the saints" were "the security of believers" and "eternal security." The biblical term predestination dropped into the background, the non-biblical

---

72. Quoted from Henry Bettenson, *Documents of the Christian Church*, Second Edition (London: Oxford University Press, 1963), pp. 377-379.
73. *Faith and Perseverance* (Grand Rapids: Eerdmans, 1958); *Divine Election* (Grand Rapids: Eerdmans, 1960). Cf. C. H. Spurgeon's sermon of June 24, 1877.

terms "security of the believer" and "eternal security" took the place of the non-biblical terms "the gift of perseverance" and "the perseverance of the saints," and tradition continues to triumph over Scripture. All this was done by people who appealed to the Scriptures where their terms are never found.

On August 5, 1841, a funeral oration on John 6:37 by Edward Steane, on the occasion of the death of John Dyer, was called *The Security of Believers*.[74] The term was introduced into Southern Baptist Landmarkism by J. R. Graves whose editorial on May 3, 1873 rejected the term "the perseverance of the saints" and proposed the term "security of believers."[75] This was the title of a book by W. P. Bennett in 1895.[76] A sermon by J. M. Carroll on "The Eternal Security of Blood-Bought Believers" preached in Ashland Avenue Baptist Church in Lexington, Kentucky, was widely read and reprinted.[77] The same old arguments were warmed over by Earl Anderson of Dallas.[78] A decade later R. E. Glaze, of New Orleans Baptist Theological Seminary, in response to my much publicized views, was defending the thesis that those warned in Hebrews about the danger of falling away were unbelieving Jews.[79] Some articles by R. T. Kendall of Florida, now pastor of Westminster Chapel in London, tried to solve the problem posed to Calvinism by Hebrews 6:4-6 and other passages, but the argument for the apostasy of those illuminated but not regenerated does not go beyond John Owen.[80] Kendall later became my student with the avowed purpose to refute my views in class and church, but recent reports indicate that he holds my view that Hebrews was written to Hebrew Christians in danger of apostasy. *Highlights*, April, 1978, a publication by the European Baptist Convention, reports him as saying that Hebrews "is an exhortation to Christians to keep them from apostasizing" and that "the purpose of Hebrews was to encourage Hebrew Christians, many of whose friends had apostasized from the faith and left them staggered." That is a good start for understanding apostasy in Hebrews, but it must not be forced into the straitjacket of John Owen's Calvinism.

The voice of written and oral tradition was kept alive also in the growing camp of Dispensationalism. The apostasy of unbelievers was defended in the notes of the *Scofield Reference Bible*, 1909, 1917, 1967. L. S. Chafer,

---

74. London: G. B. Dyer, 1841.
75. *The Baptist*, IV, no. 34, p. 4.
76. (Owensboro, Kentucky: Messenger Job Printing, 1895).
77. *The Sword of the Lord*, edited by John R. Rice, July 26, 1963.
78. *The Eternal Security of Believers* (Dallas: American Guild Press, 1956).
79. *No Easy Salvation* (Nashville: Broadman Press, 1966).
80. *The Redeemer's Witness*, "The Gospel of Full Assurance" (September-October, 1966), pp. 1-4; "Understanding our Modern Dilemma" (January-February, 1967), pp. 1, 3; "Apostasy and Backsliding" (March-April, 1967), pp. 1, 3. See also Robert Tillman Kendall, "The Rise and Demise of Calvinism in the Southern Baptist Convention" (Unpublished M.A. thesis, The Southern Baptist Theological Seminary, Louisville, Kentucky, 1973).

later founder of Dallas Theological Seminary, in the very city where Scofield did his first edition of the reference Bible, devoted two chapters to the doctrine of eternal security in a book still widely used.[81] Seven years later H. A. Ironside, once pastor of Moody Memorial Church, was lending his great weight to the ideas that go back to John Owen.[82] By 1936, J. H. Strombeck was switching emphasis from John 6:37 to John 10:28, but he was saying the same old things.[83]

Some Baptist thinkers in the twentieth century found it difficult to harmonize the Greek New Testament with the Augustinian-Calvinistic-Evangelical (Landmark Baptist-Dispensational) tradition. The roots of resistance go back to the renowned Baptist Greek scholar A. T. Robertson of Southern Baptist Theological Seminary in Louisville, Kentucky.

As early as 1909, Robertson was doing plain talk on falling from grace. The believers in Galatia, he said, "have fallen away from grace and gone back under the bondage of the law" (5:3f.). "They were Gentiles and had tasted the freedom of Christ."[84]

In a comment on II Corinthians 6:1 he said: "Paul does not pause to parlay over the abstract question whether those who have the grace of God can make it null and void. He advises the Corinthians not to experiment with their eternal souls. He took no chances himself."[85]

Robertson was using the term apostasy for his views when he expounded Philippians at Moody Bible Institute in 1917. He said: "There are always timid souls who lose heart in times of persecution. Some even go to the extent of apostasy when the cause seems lost. The early Christian centuries furnish examples of those who renounce Christ for Caesar under the pressure of the Roman state."[86]

By 1922 he was using Judas Iscariot as an example of apostasy. He said: "It is a high and holy privilege to be allowed to come into the inner circle of Christ's followers. It is a dread catastrophe to see such a one sink back into the pit from which he was digged."[87]

Robertson saw no conflict between the conditional faith in Colossians 1:23 and the strong statement on security in Colossians 3:3. On the first passage he says: "Failure to remain firm on the foundation and unshaken

81. *Salvation*, 1917 (Grand Rapids: Zondervan, 1965), pp. 96-137.
82. *The Eternal Security of the Believer* (New York: Loizeaux Brothers, 1924).
83. *Shall Never Perish* (Moline, Illinois: Strombeck Agency, 1936; Chicago: Van Kampen, 1948). See also James T. Draper, Jr., *Foundations of Biblical Faith* (Nashville, Tennessee: Broadman Press, 1979), pp. 150-160.
84. *Epochs in the Life of Paul* (New York: Charles Scribner's, 1909; Nashville: Broadman Press, 1974), pp. 203f.
85. *The Glory of the Ministry* (New York: Fleming H. Revell, 1911), pp. 213f.
86. *Paul's Joy in Christ* (New York: Fleming H. Revell Company, 1917), pp. 78f.
87. *Types of Preachers in the New Testament* (New York: Fleming H. Revell, 1922), pp. 203f. Cf. *Keywords in the Teaching of Jesus* (Philadelphia: American Baptist Publication Society, 1906; Nashville: Broadman Press, 1977), p. 107.

by the Gnostic winds of doctrine will turn them away from the hope held out by the gospels."[88] In the second passage he says: "This is our security, Christ is locked in the bosom of the Father. We are locked together with Christ in God. . . ."[89]

Robertson's comments on the seal of the Spirit recognized this as a sign of ownership, but he did not note the importance of Isaiah 63:10 for the interpretation of grieving the Spirit in Ephesians 4:30.[90] Those who appeal to the seal of the Spirit as a shield from the numerous passages on apostasy in the New Testament can hardly call on Robertson for support.

There are several other passages scattered throughout Robertson's many writings that indicate that he never thought within the confines of Calvinism on the question of apostasy, but his crowning work *Word Pictures in the New Testament*, from which frequent quotations were made in the first part of this chapter, brought all of these up to date before he died in 1934. Calvinism has no claim on him. If one thinks solely in the context of the New Testament Robertson's views create no problem, but the effort to force the New Testament into the dogmatic straitjacket of Calvinism creates the dilemma that so many have faced.

According to official confessions of faith, Baptist theology really began its departure from strict Calvinism in The New Hampshire Confession of Faith of 1833 which said in Article XI (of the perseverance of saints):

> [We believe] that such only are real believers as endure unto the end; that their persevering attachment to Christ is the grand mark which distinguishes them from mere professors; that a special Providence watches over their welfare; and [that] they are kept by the power of God through faith unto salvation.[91]

Baptist Landmarkism alone, in 1955, rejected the term "perseverance of the saints" and adopted the term "eternal security of the believer."[92] The Baptist Faith and Message of 1925 adopted the statement of The New Hampshire Confession of Faith with no significant change. The 1963 revision of the 1925 confession tried to harmonize statements from the older Calvinism that go back to The Westminster Confession of Faith of 1647 by Presbyterians and The Second London Confession of Faith of 1677 by Baptists, but there is no clarification on the question of apostasy. Nothing is said about those who do *not* "endure to the end." Cf. Mark 4:17.

88. *Paul and the Intellectuals* (Nashville: Sunday School Board of the Southern Baptist Convention, 1928), p. 88.
89. *Ibid.*, p. 146.
90. *Word Pictures in the New Testament*, Volume IV, pp. 519f., 541.
91. W. L. Lumpkin, *Baptist Confessions of Faith*, Revised edition (Valley Forge: Judson Press, 1969), p. 365.
92. *Ibid.*, p. 380.

It is indeed time to put the plain teachings of Scripture above all human traditions, for, as The Baptist Faith and Message of 1963 does rightly say, the Scriptures "will remain to the end of the world, the true center of Christian union, and the supreme standard by which all human conduct, creeds and religious opinions should be tried."[93] To this I fully subscribe.

93. *Ibid.*, p. 393.

VIII. CHRIST

A. JESUS AS THE MESSIAH OF ISRAEL

56. Jesus as Prophet

The belief that Jesus is the Christ, the one uniquely anointed by God for the fulfillment of his promise to Israel and through Israel to the world, is the central doctrine of the Christian faith. Christians are those who believe that Jesus is *the* Christ, not just a Christ.

In brief this belief may be explained in three steps. First, Jesus is the Messiah of Israel; second, Jesus is the mystery of godliness; and third, Jesus is the unique mediator between God and man. Under these three headings most of the basic beliefs about Jesus as the Christ can be summarized.

Since the time of Eusebius of Caesarea, it has been said that Jesus is priest, king, and prophet. In discussing the relation between the prophets, kings, and priests of the Old Testament and Jesus, Eusebius said: "And it has actually come down to us that some also of the same prophets have by anointing become typically Christs, so that they may be referred to the true Christ, the divine and heavenly Word, who is the only High Priest of the universe, the only King of creation, and the only supreme Prophet among His Father's prophets" (*H. E.* I. 8).

It was, however, in Reformation Christology that the "threefold office" of Christ found fullest expression. At times the situation gets out of balance, especially when the role of prophet is discussed in a minor manner in conservative Calvinism and in a major way in liberal Lutheranism.[1]

---

1. Cf. Charles Hodge, *Systematic Theology*, 1871 (Wm. B. Eerdmans Publishing Co., 1946), Vol. II, pp. 462f. on the "prophetic office," pp. 464-595 on the "priestly office," and pp. 596-609 on the "kingly office" with Albrecht Ritschl, *The Christian Doctrine of Justification and Reconciliation*, 1870-74), Vol. III, tr. H. R. Mackintosh and A. B. Macaulay, Second Edition (Edinburgh: T. and T. Clark, 1902), pp. 442-452, where the priestly office is made a part of the prophetic vocation of Jesus as Revealer of God. The first volume of Ritschl is a critical history of the theories of atonement and the second volume has the biblical materials, but the systematic statements in Vol. III state clearest Ritschl's prophetic and ethical theory of vocation.

The saving work of God in Jesus Christ has already been surveyed, with human experience at the center. It has become traditional to discuss Christ between sin and salvation, but this has been changed in the previous two parts. It seemed more logical to continue with human salvation after human sin before speaking of the saving work of God in Christ. It is also better to begin with the work of Christ than with the person of Christ. This is a major difference between Reformed and Roman Catholic Christology.

In Emil Brunner's first major statement on Christology, *The Mediator* (1927), he began with the person of Christ, but twenty-two years later (1949) he began with the work of Christ, in his *Dogmatics*, Vol. II. Perhaps it is not immodest to say I am the "theological colleague" mentioned in the preface of his *Dogmatics*, Vol. II. There are some points in Brunner's Christology with which I still disagree, but on the centrality of the work of Christ there is agreement.[2]

With a change in order and an expansion of the office of king the work of Christ may be outlined as prophet, priest, and potentate. In the words of the Revelation of John, Jesus Christ is "the faithful witness, the firstborn from the dead, and the ruler of kings on earth" (1:5).

The Prophetic Mission of Jesus Christ

Even though the "messianic consciousness" of Jesus becomes more and more pronounced in the life of the historical Jesus, it is evident that he had also what may be called a "prophetic consciousness." In all of the Four Gospels the role of Jesus as a prophet is on the lips of Jesus himself (Mark 6:4 = Matt. 13:57 = Luke 4:24 = John 4:44; Luke 13:32f.).[3]

Others — not only the disciples, but the multitudes who heard Jesus, and even such enemies as Herod Antipas — saw in him a prophet (Mark 6:15; 8:28 = Matt. 16:14 = Luke 7:16, 39; 24:19; John 9:17).

When Jesus and Moses are compared there are points of similarity and other points at which Jesus is superior to Moses. One of the major messianic prophecies spoke of a prophet like Moses (Deut. 18:15f., 19), and the early church applied this to Jesus (Acts 3:22). Moses and Jesus were prophets because both were sent from God (cf. Exodus 7–12; Deut. 34:10–12 with John 3:2). The Gospel of John puts special emphasis on Jesus being sent

2. See Emil Brunner, *The Christian Doctrine of Creation and Redemption, Dogmatics*: Vol. II, tr. Olive Wyon (Philadelphia: The Westminster Press, 1952), pp. 271-321. Some Roman Catholic scholars have made the historical Jesus, Jesusology, the foundation for understanding the Christ of faith, Christology. See Edward Schillebeeckx, *Jesus* (1974), tr. Hubert Haskins (New York: The Seabury Press, 1979). Walter Kasper, *Jesus the Christ* (1974), tr. V. Green (New York: Paulist Press, 1976).
3. R. H. Fuller, *The Foundations of New Testament Christology* (New York: Charles Scribner's Sons, 1965), pp. 102-141 denies some titles to the historical Jesus, but not that of "eschatological prophet."

from God. What Moses was to Old Testament prophecy, Jesus was to New Testament prophecy.[4]

Both Jesus and Moses were known by their signs. The Gospel of Matthew draws numerous parallels between Jesus and Moses. Moses received the Torah, but Jesus gave the New Torah as it appears in the five teaching sections of Matthew's Gospel.[5] The Gospel of Luke was greatly influenced by the parallels with Moses.[6]

There are parallels between the cultic prophets and Jesus. The sons of the prophets in the Former Prophets, from 1 Samuel–2 Kings (1 Sam. 10:5, 10; 19:18–24, etc.), are not unlike the seventy sent forth by Jesus. Jesus himself saw visions and experienced ecstasy (Luke 10:18, 22).[7]

Jesus was even more like the Latter Prophets from the eighth century onward. The call of the classical prophet is often given in detail, and all of the Gospels record the descent of the Holy Spirit on Jesus at his Baptism. It does not detract from the uniqueness of Jesus to recognize that Jesus had a great religious experience after John the Baptist baptized him. A few years ago Rudolf Otto did not hesitate to talk about Jesus as a charismatic.[8] At last this quality in the role of Jesus as a prophet has come forth fully.[9]

The Word of the classical prophet was a second characteristic with which that of Jesus can be compared. A classical prophet had a word from the Lord, and Jesus had no less. He *was*, to be sure, the Word made flesh, but he also had a Word to proclaim. Perhaps no other writer has seen this more clearly than Joachim Jeremias who thinks the relation of Jesus to God as Abba and of the pronouncements of Jesus with Amen constitute the clue to the proclamation of Jesus as a message from God.[10]

Jesus was most like John the Baptist, the last and greatest of all the prophets. Jesus' eulogy of John makes it unmistakable that the law began with Moses and the prophets concluded with John the Baptist. This made Jesus like John but greater than John (Matt. 11:2–19 = Luke 7:18–35).

In Luke's "Gospel of the Infancy" (chs. 1, 2). there are at least seven parallels between the birth of John the Baptist and the birth of Jesus.

The first five chapters of John's Gospel make it clear that there was a

4. H. A. Guy, *New Testament Prophecy* (London: Epworth Press, 1947), pp. 83-85.
5. Sherman E. Johnson, "The Gospel According to Matthew," *The Interpreter's Bible*, ed. George Buttrick (New York: Abingdon, 1951), Vol. 7, pp. 231-265; Krister Stendahl, *The School of Saint Matthew* (1954) (Philadelphia: Fortress Press, 1968).
6. Cf. C. F. Evans, "The Central Section of St. Luke's Gospel," in D. E. Nineham, ed., *Studies in the Gospels* (Oxford: B. Blackwell, 1955), pp. 37-53.
7. James D. G. Dunn, *Jesus and the Spirit* (Philadelphia: The Westminster Press, 1975), pp. 68-92.
8. *The Kingdom of God and the Son of Man*, tr. Floyd V. Filson and Bertram Lee Woolf (London: Lutterworth, 1938), pp. 333-381.
9. James D. G. Dunn, *op. cit.,* pp. 11-92.
10. *New Testament Theology: The Proclamation of Jesus*, tr. John Bowden (New York: Charles Scribner's Sons, 1971), pp. 35-37.

vigorous discussion between the disciples of John and the disciples of Jesus as to which was the Messiah (cf. Luke 3:15).

The prophetic mission of Jesus has come into full focus as modern Christology begins from "below" with the historical Jesus. This does not mean that Jesus was "no more than a prophet," but it does mean he was "not less than a prophet." Jesus was "more than a man," but he was also not less than a man.[11] The prophetic mission of Jesus was a great achievement, but the mission and message of Jesus are inseparable.[12]

The Prophetic Message of Jesus Christ

The form of Jesus' message was very similar to that of the classical prophets. The student who first reads Amos or any of the Old Testament prophets in the Revised Standard Version is surprised that there is more poetry than prose. The same is true of the teachings of Jesus in the Gospels, but most translations obscure this point. C. F. Burney was one of the first scholars to recognize the poetic structure in much that Jesus did.[13] Joachim Jeremias used this method to penetrate behind the Greek translations to the original Aramaic that Jesus spoke, and the result has been most rewarding not only in the light that is thrown on the meaning of a saying but on the role of Jesus as a prophet.[14]

The parables of Jesus also follow the prophetic form of speaking. A good example is the use Jesus made of "the song of the vineyard" in Isaiah 5 when he came to interpret his own mission and destiny as the Son of God (Mark 12:1–12 = Matt. 21:33–46 = Luke 20:9–19). Jesus used parables more than the Old Testament prophets, but his form of teaching no doubt was in the prophetic tradition.[15]

The content of Jesus' message continued to follow the prophetic forms. It has long been recognized that the Old Testament prophets uttered prophecies of both woe and weal, of doom and deliverance. This was also true of both John the Baptist and Jesus, even though John had more woe than weal and Jesus had more weal than woe.

The pronouncements of doom in the teachings of Jesus sound much like the prophet Amos (5:18–20). At the end of his ministry in Galilee there are woes upon the cities on the northern shore of the Sea of Galilee (Matt. 11:20ff.). Seven woes against the religious leaders in Jerusalem oc-

---

11. Cf. Russell Aldwinckle, *More Than Man* (Grand Rapids, Michigan: Eerdmans, 1976).
12. See R. H. Fuller, *The Mission and Achievement of Jesus* (London: SCM, 1954) for a watershed in the study of New Testament theology. For a good summary see also Otto Betz, *What Do We Know About Jesus?*, tr. Margaret Kohl (Philadelphia: The Westminster Press, 1968).
13. *The Poetry of Our Lord* (Oxford: At the Clarendon Press, 1925).
14. *Op. cit.*, pp. 1-41.
15. For a detailed study of the parabolic method of Jesus see Joachim Jeremias, *The Parables of Jesus*, tr. S. H. Hooke (New York: Scribner's, 1955).

cupy a prominent place in Matthew's Gospel (23:1–36). These are hardly redactions that have no basis in the life and teaching of the historical Jesus.

The proclamation of good news included variations on the kingdom of God.[16] As the righteousness of God was the major theme of Amos, the mercy of God of Hosea, the holiness of God of Isaiah and the glory of God of Ezekiel, so the kingdom of God was the major theme of Jesus.

The gospel of the kingdom elaborates the good news predicted in Isaiah 40:9; 52:7; 61:1ff., and the book of Isaiah seems to be the source of the very word translated gospel or good news. It is no wonder that the Synoptic Gospels are called Gospels.

The Gospel of Mark has as its theme: "The time is fulfilled, and the kingdom of God is at hand; repent, and believe the gospel" (1:15). The proclamation of the kingdom of God by Jesus marked the end of the law and the prophets and the beginning of a new age with Jesus. This was good news indeed. The coming kingdom had arrived in Jesus and was offered to all who would repent and believe.

The Gospel of Matthew elaborates the apocalyptic gospel of the two ages. At one place seven parables are collected around the theme of the mystery of the kingdom (Matt. 13). In all of them past, present and future stages of the kingdom of God are central. The parable of the sower is a model in which there is a time of sowing, a time of growing and a time of harvest.

The Gospel of Luke has as its theme the proclamation of Jesus in the synagogue of Nazareth (4:16–30). It was Isaiah 61:1–2 that Jesus read before he announced the good news that all of those things were being fulfilled in him. In the Acts of the Apostles where the miracle of Pentecost is a parallel to the proclamation in the synagogue of Nazareth, the proclamation of the good news of the kingdom finally reaches Rome (28:30f.).

The signs of the kingdom were the miracles of Jesus.[17] The major Old Testament source for this was Isaiah 35:5f. (cf. Matt. 11:4–6). In fact most that is said about the kingdom of God in the teachings of Jesus has reference either to the gospel of the kingdom or the signs of the kingdom. This will be examined in Part X.

There were other prophetic themes in the preaching of Jesus that include both woe and weal, condemnation and salvation.[18] The three predictions of the passion of Jesus have been denied Jesus because the increasing details are so much like the passion narrative that follows (Mk. 8:31; 9:30f.; 10:33f.). This raises the whole question of predictive prophecy. If there is

---

16. Jeremias, *New Testament Theology*, pp. 141-158.

17. *Ibid.*, pp. 85-92; Walter Kasper, *Jesus the Christ*, tr. V. Green (New York: Paulist Press, 1976), pp. 89-99. Both Jeremias and Kasper reduce the claim for miracles in the ministry of Jesus, but they think it impossible to eliminate the evidence. For further discussion of miracles see Part IV.32.

18. Jeremias, *New Testament Theology*, pp. 122-141.

no predictive prophecy the objections are sustained; but if Jesus did foresee his coming death and resurrection a new light is thrown on how his prophetic consciousness deepened into a messianic consciousness.

The same problem arises anew in the six predictions of Jesus on the fall of Jerusalem in A.D. 70 in the Gospel of Luke. The major reason many date the Gospel of Luke after the fall of Jerusalem rests on these predictions. This whole scheme has been challenged by one who hardly belongs to the fundamentalist fold.[19] Much of the language Jesus used was used by Jeremiah (ch. 6), and Old Testament scholars do not deny that Jeremiah predicted the fall of Jerusalem. Why should not Jesus have as much insight as Jeremiah?

If the Gospel of Luke was composed before the fall of Jerusalem in A.D. 70, then the Oracle on the Wisdom of God found at six places in Luke is a major example of the role of Jesus as a prophet as well as the Son of God (11:29-32, 49-51; 13:34f.; 19:41-44; 21:20-24; 23:28-31). These prophetic words were perhaps circulated as a separate oracle before Luke included them in his Gospel by the year A.D. 60, and there is every reason to attribute them to Jesus rather than to some later Christian prophet.[20]

The two synoptic apocalypses, for the most part, contain prophecies not yet fulfilled, but that does not mean that Jesus was mistaken. He was not mistaken on predictions about his own death and resurrection and the fall of Jerusalem, now in the past, so there is no cogent reason for giving up the hope that Jesus will return as the Son of Man, the Messiah, to establish God's kingdom upon the earth. That is the theme of both the Marcan apocalypse (13:1-27 = Matt. 24:1-25:46 = Luke 21:5-36) and the Lucan apocalypse (17:20-37).[21]

There is then really no solid reason for rejecting the belief that Jesus understood himself to be a prophet, *the* prophet, from God and that all the Gospel writers understood him that way also. The role of prophet does not exhaust his meaning. He was no less than a prophet, but he was far more.

57. Jesus as Priest

Jesus was also a priest, but far more than any other priest. The most conservative Christology does not hesitate to magnify this office. Even though Jesus was the Messiah of Israel, he was a priestly Messiah. In the New Testament and in church history, there is no lack of evidence for this. That is one reason why Christ as priest is given far more space in traditional theologies than Christ as prophet.

19. John A. T. Robinson, *Re-dating the New Testament* (Philadelphia: The Westminster Press, 1976), pp. 86-117.
20. For a similar dating see John A. T. Robinson.
21. Jeremias, *New Testament Theology*, pp. 122-127. See Part X for further details.

In the New Testament two major Old Testament categories are used to portray Jesus as priest. In the Synoptic Gospels, Acts and 1 Peter Jesus is interpreted primarily as the suffering Servant of the Lord in Isaiah 53, but in the rest of the New Testament some form of sacrifice is used to interpret the death of Jesus.

New Testament Interpretation

Jesus as Servant. In the Mark–Matthew teachings the Servant Jesus is a *victim.* The second half of the Gospel of Mark (8:27–16:8) shifts from the Messianic secret of the first half (1:1–8:26) and has as a framework for the words and deeds of Jesus the Messianic sufferings. The three predictions of his passion and the passion narrative tell the story that finds full focus in the so-called ransom saying of Mark 10:45: "For the Son of man also came not to be served but to serve, and to give his life as a ransom for many." There is no doubt that this saying identifies Jesus with the suffering Servant of the Lord in Isaiah 53:11f.[22]

The saying of Jesus on the cross, the so-called cry of dereliction, underlines the death of Jesus as a sacrificial victim (Mark 15:37 = Matt. 27:46). The classic study by Vincent Taylor does not shrink back from the picture of utter desolation when Jesus cried: "My God, my God, why have you forsaken me." After a review of views that seek to soften the picture, Taylor rightly says that "the saying expresses a feeling of utter desolation, a sense of abandonment by the Father, an experience of defeat and despair. . . . The feeling of desolation is temporary, but it is real, and it is due, so far as it can be explained at all, to preoccupation by Jesus with the fact and burden of sin."[23]

The Gospel of Matthew does not modify the Markan portrait of the death of Jesus in any essential point. Matthew also identifies Jesus with the Servant of Isaiah 42:1–4, the first Servant song in which the emphasis is more on the Spirit than sacrifice (12:18–21), but the predictions of the passion and the cry of dereliction in Mark are repeated.

It is interesting to note how the "Theology of Hope" associated with Jürgen Moltmann balanced the emphasis on the resurrection with Moltmann's surprising statements on how Jesus died a "god-forsaken" death for "god-forsaken" people.[24] There is no doubt that Jesus died under some circumstances that afflict all of the oppres ed people of the earth. Death on a cross was the most shameful death that one could die, and the best-

22. Vincent Taylor, *Jesus and His Sacrifice* (London: Macmillan and Co., 1937), pp. 99-105; William Manson, *Jesus the Messiah* (Philadelphia: The Westminster Press, 1946), pp. 182-185.
23. *Jesus and His Sacrifice*, p. 161.
24. *The Crucified God*, tr. R. A. Wilson and John Bowden (Philadelphia: The Westminster Press, 1974), pp. 145-153.

established fact in the Gospels is the crucifixion of Jesus.[25] Jesus was a victim.

Jesus was also a *victor*. God raised him from the dead. Even the Jewish scholar David Flusser said: "There is no doubt that the Crucified 'appeared to Peter, then to the twelve. Then he appeared to more than five hundred brethren at one time. . . . Then he appeared to James, then to all the apostles.' Last of all, he appeared to Paul on the road to Damascus (1 Cor. 15:3–8)."[26] It is a strange turn of events when a Jew writes a book on Jesus and affirms the historical resurrection of Jesus to correct a Lutheran theologian like Rudolf Bultmann who also wrote a book on Jesus and reduced the appearances of Jesus to mythology![27]

The resurrection was not objective in the sense of the crucifixion, but it was an event that cannot be reduced to existential subjectivity. Details of the resurrection will be discussed later in the chapter on "The Post-existence of Jesus," but the conclusion reached by R. H. Fuller may be stated here. "God raised Jesus from the dead. This meant, in apocalyptic language, that the total being of Jesus, his concrete psychosomatic being, the whole man, was translated into eschatological existence, and thereby transformed."[28] The Roman Catholic scholar Raymond E. Brown adds: "Small wonder that he [Paul] speaks of a mystery! In our fidelity to proclaiming the bodily resurrection of Jesus, we should never become so defensively governed by apologetics that we do not do justice to this element of transformation and mystery. Christian truth is best served when equal justice is done to the element of continuity implied in bodily resurrection and the element of eschatological transformation."[29]

The victory of Jesus, the Lord's Servant, is the major motif in the apostolic preaching in the Acts of the Apostles. The death of Jesus as a victim of historical circumstances is expressed in such stark terms as "crucified and killed at the hands of lawless men" (2:23; cf. 3:15; 4:10), "killed by hanging" (5:30), "betrayed and murdered" (7:52), but God raised Jesus from the dead and "made him both Lord and Christ" (2:36). The victim became victor by an act of God.

Jesus, as God's Servant, is most of all *vicar* for those who believe. His suffering and death were vicarious. To say his crucifixion was vicarious means that he suffered, died and was raised from the dead and others are

---

25. See Martin Hengel, *Crucifixion*, tr. John Bowden (Philadelphia: Fortress Press, 1977) for the horrors of that history.
26. *Jesus*, tr. Ronald Walls (New York: Herder and Herder, 1969), p. 122.
27. English title, *Jesus and the Word*, tr. Louise Pettibone Smith and Erminie Huntress (New York: Charles Scribner's Sons, 1934), pp. 213f.
28. *The Formation of the Resurrection Narratives* (New York: The Macmillan Company, 1971), p. 185.
29. *The Virginal Conception and Bodily Resurrection of Jesus* (New York: Paulist Press, 1973), p. 128.

able to benefit from what he did. First Peter seems almost certain to be a
Passover letter in the form of a Christian Passover worship service.[30]

There can be no doubt that the hymn in 1 Peter 2:21-25 is built on
Isaiah 53, for there are at least four direct quotations. In the first stanza
Jesus is vicar, for he suffered or died on our behalf (21-23), but the second
stanza does not forget that he was also a victim (23-25). He is both our
example and our shepherd. Any effort to separate the exemplary and substitutionary suffering of Jesus in this hymn is futile.

The themes of Jesus as victim, victor and vicar are all included in the
hymn included in 1 Peter 3:18-22 and perhaps 1:20 and 4:6. This is most
obvious in the lines here translated literally.

> 18 *Christ once for all concerning our sins died,*
> *that he might bring us to God,*
> *having been put to death in the flesh,*
> *having been made alive in the spirit,*
> 22 *Who is on the right hand of God,*
> *having gone into heaven.*

It will be noted that three comments are not parts of the hymn, but
they too reinforce the meaning of the saving death of Christ. The phrase
"the righteous on behalf of the unrighteous" (3:18) is the key thought of
1 Peter. The long comment on the descent of Jesus into the nether regions
describes what Jesus did between his death and resurrection and will be
further discussed in a later chapter (3:19-21). The victory of Jesus over all
demonic powers at the end of 3:22 is a frequent theme in New Testament
Christology. Christ was victor not only over sin and death but even over
the devil and the demons. See Part VI.48.

Jesus as sacrifice. The use of sacrificial language in Paul's understanding
of the death of Jesus Christ may be summarized in the four Rs: revelation,
reconciliation, righteousness and redemption. These four concepts are included in Paul's "pillar epistles" of 1, 2 Corinthians, Galatians and Romans.

Revelation is the key concept in 1 Corinthians. The true wisdom of
God is disclosed in the cross — so Paul proclaimed in what appears to be
a Christian interpretation of Jesus Christ as the sacrifice for the Day of
Atonement (1:18-4:21). Jeremiah 9:24, quoted in 1:31, was read on Yom
Kippur as the High Priest went into the Holy of Holies to offer a sacrifice
for his own sins and the sins of the people. This is still the holiest day in
the year for Judaism, and with Rosh Hashana (New Year's, ten days earlier)
it is called a High Holy Day. The Day of Atonement has not been celebrated

---

30. F. L. Cross, *1 Peter a Pascal Liturgy* (London: A. R. Mowbray, 1954). See also Joseph
A. Fitzmyer in *Jerome Biblical Commentary* (Englewood Cliffs, N.J.: Prentice-Hall, 1968),
p. 363.

in the Temple since A.D. 70, when it fell. There is no need, for the perfect sacrifice of Jesus Christ himself for the sins of the whole world has been offered once for all.

The true worship of God is a celebration of the sacrificial love revealed in the death of Jesus Christ. This celebration of the Lord's Supper includes the idea of Jesus also as the Passover lamb (5:6–8). The 1 Corinthian letter was written between Passover and Pentecost, about A.D. 53, so it is also possible that another example of apostolic preaching is to be found in the symbolism of 1 Corinthians 5–6.

Communion and the Lord's Supper are also participation (*koinōnia*) in the body and blood of Jesus. The communion service described in 1 Corinthians 10:1–11:1 applies numerous symbols from the Passover in stating the difference between a communion meal (10:1–22) and a common meal (10:23–11:1). The Lord's Supper, communion with a meal between the bread and the cup, is also in the context of a new covenant (11:2–33). Further discussion of these points follows in Part IX.

The other three Rs (reconciliation, redemption and righteousness) used to interpret the saving work of Christ have already been discussed in Part VI in relation to salvation, and Jesus as some type of sacrifice for sin is central in all of them. Sacrifices are offerings to God to remove the barrier of sin between man and God and to restore fellowship. That seems to be Paul's theology of the cross of Christ.[31]

Jesus as the sacrifice for sins as a fulfillment of the Day of Atonement is the theme of the whole treatise called The Letter to the Hebrews. Written by Barnabas within a few months before the fall of the Temple in A.D. 70, this is the profoundest interpretation of the death of Christ in the entire New Testament.[32] Even if Calvin was wrong in believing that God predestined some to commit apostasy, he was right in finding Hebrews the Christian classic on the sacrifice of Jesus.

The office of Jesus as High Priest is the theme of Hebrews 1–7. As in 1 Peter the portrait of Jesus as victim, victor and vicar is in perfect balance in Hebrews 2:8–18. As victim Jesus is king (8f.), as victor he is leader (10–13), and as vicar he is High Priest (14–18). Melchizedek is the model for his priesthood because his sacrifice is once for all and has no end in the provision made for believers.

The oblation of Jesus is the theme of Hebrews 8–13, and the model for this is the Levitical priesthood. Jesus, however, offers a better priesthood (8–10) because he has a better sanctuary (8:1–5), a better covenant (8:6–13) and most of all a better sacrifice (9:1–10:18). Jesus also has a better promise because he leads into the city of God (11–13).

---

31. For details see Vincent Taylor, *The Atonement in New Testament Teaching* (London: Epworth Press, 1940), pp. 54-100.
32. Again see John A. T. Robinson, pp. 200-220, on historical matters.

In the Letter to the Hebrews and in the history of atonement theories the key text is 9:22. Often the statement "without shedding of blood is no remission" is quoted as if it means that God could not forgive sin *before* the sacrifice of Christ. This is clearly a contradiction of Old Testament texts such as Psalm 51:16f. and of the practice of Jesus himself. In the New Testament, in the whole of Luke–Acts, there is no requirement for forgiveness other than repentance.

A correct translation of Hebrews 9:22 should be: "And almost all things are by the law purged with blood; and without shedding of blood is no remission" (AV). Two modifiers qualify the last statement. The first is the word "almost," *schedon* in Greek, and that does not mean always. The second is the phrase "by the law" (*kata ton nomon* in Greek), and that does not mean by the grace of God. God does forgive sin without the shedding of blood and outside the law. However, the God who forgives is the one who has most fully revealed himself in the death of Jesus.

The death of Jesus is the first of the three appearings of Jesus. At present he appears in heaven in the presence of God on our behalf (9:24), but he has already appeared the first time "to put away sin by the sacrifice of himself" (9:26). In the future he will appear a second time on earth without sin to bring salvation to those who are expecting him (9:28). The High Priest appeared in the presence of God once each year in the Holy of Holies, but Jesus appears in the presence of God on behalf of believers until he comes again. Jesus brings eternal redemption (9:12) with the promise of an eternal inheritance (9:15).[33]

In the Johannine writings it is the Passover festival that furnishes the frame of reference for understanding the glory of God in the death of Jesus. The Gospel of John not only points to Jesus as the Lamb of God "who takes away the sin of the world" (1:29; cf. 1:36), but three Passovers, not one as in the Synoptic Gospels, are mentioned (2:13; 6:4; 12:1).

Jesus' sacrifice as the Lamb of God was a voluntary "laying down" of his life, as seen in three references to Jesus as the Good Shepherd (10:11, 15f., 17f.). The references to Peter (13:37f.) and to the love of a friend (15:13) substantiate this voluntary nature of Jesus' death. A second description of the death of Jesus calls the sacrifice a "lifting up." Three of the seven Son of Man sayings speak of the Son of Man being lifted up so that crucifixion becomes exaltation (3:13ff.; 8:28; 12:32f.). This laying down and lifting up underscores the role of Jesus as both victim and victor.

The meaning of Jesus' death is stated as both a sign and as a sacrifice. The subjective side of his death as a sign comes forth eloquently in the

---

33. For a clear interpretation of the finality of Jesus' death and the problem of falling away from this final revelation and redemption see William Manson, *The Epistle to the Hebrews* (London: Hodder and Stoughton, 1951). See also Vincent Taylor, *The Atonement in New Testament Teaching*, pp. 111-130.

speech following the fourth of the seven signs (6:51–57). The objective significance comes forth clearly in the seven "my hour" sayings because the death of Jesus is thereby anchored to a point in time (2:4; 7:30; 8:20; 12:23, 27; 13:1; 17:1).

The Revelation of John speaks of Jesus as the Lamb of God twenty-eight times. The sacrifice of the Lamb as a victim at the hands of sinners was a slaying (5:6, 9, 12; 13:8). The blood of the slain Lamb of God rules out all Gnostic notions that would deny the humanity of Jesus (1:5; 7:14; 12:11). The Lamb as victor through suffering, and the followers of the Lamb, the martyrs who are also victims of sinners, share in the victory of the Lamb (2:10; 3:10; 4:1; 11:12; 5:8, 10; 6:11b; 13:10b, 15b). The martyrs became priests and kings because they followed the Lamb (6:9–11; 8:1–5; 14:1–5; 20:4–6).

The interpretation of the death of Jesus in 1 John is a fitting summary and conclusion to the Johannine view (1:1–4). The flesh of Jesus is the realm of manifestation (3:5, 8) and incarnation (4:1–6). The blood of Jesus is the means of purification (1:7) and expiation (2:1f.; 4:10). The theory of propitiation in the Latin translation of 2:1f.; 4:10 has no place in any New Testament interpretation. It is clearly a pagan idea read into the New Testament. God loved the world *before* Jesus died. Indeed, it was the love of God that *sent* Jesus into the world.[34]

Historical Theories

The historical theories of atonement often pick up some major points of New Testament teaching on the death of Jesus and develop them. At times alien ideas are added and important New Testament ideas are neglected, but always some biblical authority is claimed.

In general the dominant idea in the Patristic period is that of Jesus as victor over Satan. There was a time when the so-called Patristic ransom theory was the object of liberal jests, but the tide has changed since the publication of Gustaf Aulén's study in 1930 of the three main ideas of the atonement. To the consternation of conservatives and liberals alike, Aulén argued that the view of the incarnation and redemption behind the vivid Patristic imagery was more authentic than the later theories.[35] The recapitulation theory of Irenaeus was rightly praised.

In the Middle Ages and much conservative Protestantism the idea of Jesus as a victim to satisfy the justice of God became the major motif. Where Jesus was victor over Satan in Patristic theories Jesus became the victim of God's wrath among those who elaborated the satisfaction theory of Anselm of Canterbury (1033-1109).[36] Jesus was called upon to satisfy

---

34. Taylor, *The Atonement in New Testament Teaching*, pp. 81-100.
35. *Christus Victor*, tr. A. G. Hebert (New York: The Macmillan Co., 1954).
36. *Ibid.*, pp. 81-100.

and vindicate the divine honor that had been offended by man's sin. The moral influence theory of Peter Abelard (1079-1142) softened the harshness of the medieval theories, but the official theology followed the merit system of St. Thomas Aquinas (1224-1274).

Reformation theories, even Luther's, were often a mixture of the Christ as victor and Christ as victim views.[37] The penal substitutionary theory of John Calvin often thinned out into a governmental theory, as in the *Defense of the Catholic Faith Concerning the Satisfaction of Christ* (1617) by Hugo Grotius or in the propitiation theory that is still stoutly defended by Leon Morris.[38] It is unfortunate that efforts to look to Jesus as an example were advocated mostly by the followers of Laelius Socinus (1525-1562), whose theology was thin on other issues.

It was not until modern theology that the efforts to see the death of Jesus also in terms of his impact on man were crowned with any success. The Jesus versus Satan and Jesus versus God views were not always neglected. Jesus was victor, victim *and* vicar in the most balanced views, but it is difficult to maintain this balance in conflict with tradition. The modern theories of atonement are bewildering in variety, but *The Atonement and the Sacraments* by Robert S. Paul comes as near as any thus far.[39] The death of Jesus was related to Satan, God and the community of mankind: "In Christ God was reconciling the world" (2 Corinthians 5:19, RSV note). Any theory that neglects any relation is out of balance.

Often the hymns we sing are more balanced than our theories and sermons. Isaac Watts no doubt believed that Jesus was a victim as much as Luther believed he was a victor, but Christ as vicar whose love demands all has seldom been expressed better than in Watts' great hymn entitled "When I Survey the Wondrous Cross." If Watts is not enough, try one of Charles Wesley's greatest, his "Love Divine." Perhaps adoration in the presence of mystery is after all the best response to the love of God revealed in the death of Jesus.

58. Jesus as Potentate

This title is not so much a striving after alliteration with Jesus as prophet and Jesus as priest as it is the search for a new word to broaden the traditional references to Christ as king. It is drawn from 1 Timothy 6:15 which speaks of our Lord Jesus Christ as "the blessed and only Potentate, the King of kings, and Lord of lords" (AV). Potentate means Sovereign as

37. Cf. J. S. Whale, *Victor and Victim* (Cambridge: At the University Press, 1960).
38. *The Cross in the New Testament* (Grand Rapids: William B. Eerdmans Publishing Company, 1965), pp. 348ff. There is much to be learned from this book, but his rigid defense of propitiation qualifies its value.
39. (New York: Abingdon Press, 1960). See the briefer effort by Fisher Humphreys, *The Death of Christ* (Nashville: Broadman Press, 1978).

in the RSV. In the Old Testament both kingship and lordship are ascribed to God, so both are ascribed to Jesus in his unity with God. The sovereignty of Jesus grows out of his unity with God as disclosed in the resurrection.

King of Kings

The Son of David as king. The roots of Israel's hope for a King–Messiah were expressed in several titles. The first and most highly developed hope looked for a Messiah who would be the Son of David, the scion of Israel's ideal king. After the anointing of Saul by Samuel (1 Samuel 10:1), King David was the Lord's Anointed, the representative of the kingship of God among his people. At many places in the Old Testament this hope was very much alive.

The Hebrew text of the Torah, the Pentateuch, looked for the Shiloh in Jacob's blessing of Judah (Genesis 49:10) and for the Star out of Jacob mentioned in the oracle of Balaam about the latter days (Numbers 24:17). Even after the coming of Jesus, there were those who welcomed one as the Son of the Star, Bar Kokhba, the leader of the Jewish revolt against Rome in A.D. 132-135.[40] Until this day Jewish young people are often an easy prey for the charlatan Sun Myung Moon, who claims Jesus appointed him to complete the work Jesus failed to accomplish.[41]

The prophets of the eighth century B.C. looked beyond the failure of the kings of Israel and Judah to an ideal ruler from the line of David (Isaiah 7:10-16; 9:1-7; 11:1-9; Micah 5:2-4). A century later Jeremiah had not abandoned that hope (23:5f.), and Ezekiel kept alive the Davidic hope even in Exile (34:23f.).

The Psalms have a group of royal Psalms that are now believed to go back to the period of the United Monarchy, and there the ideology of Davidic kingship finds full expression (2, 20, 21, 45, 72, 89, 110, 132).[42] They are later used to shape belief in the kingship of Christ.

The hope of the Messiah as a priestly figure gained prominence in the priestly writings after the decline of the monarchy, but the idea of priesthood is combined with the idea of kingship in some post-exilic prophets (Hag. 2:23; Zech. 3:8-10; 4:7; 6:9-14). The Qumran writings mention two Messiahs, one kingly and one priestly.[43]

At several major places the Gospel of Mark portrays Jesus as the Son of David. The confessions of Peter at Caesarea Philippi (8:27-33) and of Jesus before Caiaphas in Jerusalem (14:61f.) indicate how much the belief

---

40. Yigael Yadin, *Bar Kokhba* (London: Wiedenfeld and Nicolson, 1971), pp. 18f.
41. Sun Myung Moon, *Divine Principle* (New York: Holy Spirit Association for the Unification of World Christianity, 1973), pp. 497-536.
42. For details see Sigmund Mowinckel, *He That Cometh*, tr. G. W. Anderson (New York: Abingdon Press, 1954); Aage Bentzen, *King and Messiah* (London: Lutterworth Press, 1955).
43. R. H. Fuller, *The Foundations of New Testament Christology*, pp. 28f.

in Jesus as the Messiah was a part of the faith in Hellenistic Jewish Christianity, even though the title Son of David is not used.

Some Son of David passages are: the healing of blind Bartimaeus (10:46–52 = Matt. 20:29–34 = Lk. 18:35–43), the question about David's son (12:35–37 = Matt. 22:41–46 = Lk. 20:41–44), and the inscription on the cross (15:26). It is not likely that the early church invented these stories despite R. H. Fuller's arguments.[44]

The hope for a Davidic Messiah persisted in both Palestinian and Hellenistic Judaism, and hymns in Luke's "Gospel of the Infancy" give abundant evidence that the early church viewed Jesus in the same way, as the Son of David (1:32f., 69). The birth of Jesus in Bethlehem added to this interpretation (2:10f.). The Gospel of Matthew has the Davidic descent of the Messiah also (1:18–25; 2:1–12). In fact, the Gospel of Matthew accentuates the Son of David theme taken from Mark.

Davidic Christology penetrated into the apostolic preaching in the Acts of the Apostles (2:22–36; 13:16–41). Perhaps the best summary of Jesus as the Son of David is found in the confession with which Paul's Letter to the Romans begins (1:3):

> Born of the seed of David;
> Declared Son of God by his resurrection from the dead.

This means that Jesus, the Son of David, was "pre-destined to be the eschatological judge at his second coming." Here Fuller is correct.[45]

The Son of God as king. Jesus as the Son of God has the same roots as Jesus as the Son of David. One of the royal coronation hymns already mentioned blended the concepts Son of David with Son of God (Psalm 2:7). The Former Prophets had this same point of view (2 Sam. 7:14).

This does not mean that Jesus was adopted as God's Son at his baptism or at his resurrection, as some have argued on the basis of Romans 1:3. R. H. Fuller is correct in rejecting the views of his former colleague John Knox.[46] Israel was the son of God by adoption (Ex. 4:22f.; Hos. 11:1), and the kings of Israel were too (Ps. 2:7; 2 Sam. 7:14), but this is never the relation between Jesus and God.

If the Gospel of Mark wanted to portray Jesus as the Son of God by adoption, the opportunity was missed in the prologue (1:11) where the reference to begetting in Psalm 2:7 is replaced with the conflation from Isaiah 42:1. Jesus as the Son of God is dramatically proclaimed in Mark by a voice from heaven twice (1:11; 9:7), voices from demons twice (1:24; 5:7), sayings by Jesus twice (12:6; 13:32) and finally by a Roman centurion

44. *Ibid.*, pp. 108-114.
45. *Ibid.*, pp. 166f.
46. Cf. the previous reference from Fuller with John Knox, *The Humanity and Divinity of Christ* (Cambridge: At the University Press, 1967), pp. 5ff., 12ff., 19f., 36f., 55ff., 94ff.

(15:39). Mark does indeed dramatize these declarations in his Gospel, but it is unlikely that this is all "church-formation," as Fuller argues.[47] In any case the kingly roles of Jesus as Son of David and Son of God converge at the resurrection from the dead, as in Romans 1:3f.

Returning to Luke's "Gospel of the Infancy" again, the merging of Son of David with Son of God in the kingly portrait of Jesus is most obvious in "the gospel of Gabriel" to the Virgin Mary. The first stanza in the hymn of annunciation declares Jesus to be Son of David (1:32f.), but the second stanza declares him Son of God (1:35).[48] At his conception and at his coronation in heaven Jesus is the Son of David and the Son of God. In the New Testament the begetting of the Son is always at his coronation, never at his conception (Acts 13:33; Heb. 1:5; 5:5, the only three passages in the New Testament in which Ps. 2:7 is quoted without change).

Jesus as Son of God is used in a sense other than a kingly role in the high Christologies of Paul, Hebrews and John, but that is discussed elsewhere.

The Son of Man as king. Kingship is the chief concern when the Messiah is designated Son of Man. Much has been written on the background to the idea in Jewish apocalypticism that begins with the prophet Ezekiel and reaches a climax between the second century B.C. and the second century A.D. and the Iranian dualism that modified prophetic eschatology over that period.[49]

The one general agreement that has been reached is that the major source for the term on the lips of Jesus is the kingly vision in Daniel 7:13f. which reports the coming of the Son of Man before the Most High God, the Ancient of Days.

> *I saw in the night visions,*
> *and behold, with the clouds of heaven*
> *there came one like a Son of Man,*
> *and he came before the Ancient of Days*
> *and was presented before him.*
> *And to him was given dominion*
> *and glory and a kingdom,*

47. Pp. 114f.
48. Cf. Raymond E. Brown, *The Birth of the Messiah* (Garden City, N.Y.: Doubleday & Co., 1977), pp. 310-316.
49. H. H. Rowley, *The Relevance of Apocalyptic*, Revised Edition (New York: Association Press, 1964); S. B. Frost, *Old Testament Apocalyptic* (London: Epworth Press, 1952); Walter Schmithals, *The Apocalyptic Movement*, tr. John E. Steeley (New York: Abingdon Press, 1975); Paul D. Hanson, *The Dawn of Apocalyptic* (Philadelphia: The Fortress Press, 1975).

> *that all peoples, nations, and languages*
>   *should serve him;*
> *his dominion is an everlasting dominion,*
>   *which will not pass away,*
> *and his kingdom one*
>   *that shall not be destroyed.*

This coming of the Son of Man in the clouds of glory is the third of three ideas associated with the term in the Gospel of Mark. If one reads through the Gospel of Mark as it is, the Son of Man is first used to describe the authority of the historical Jesus. This, however, is in the context of the first five of ten controversy stories (2:1–3:6; 11:27–33; 12:13–37), and both references to the Son of Man seem to be comments by Mark who believed Jesus as Son of Man had authority to forgive sin and was lord even of the sabbath (2:10, 28).

The sufferings of the Son of Man in Mark have already been noted, with the conclusion that Jesus did identify himself with both the suffering Servant of Isaiah 53 and the Son of Man in Daniel 7:13 who is destined to come in the glory of the Father after he suffered many things.

The kingly role of the Son of Man appears more frequently in Mark than in any other Gospel. In Mark 8:38 a distinction is made between Jesus of whom men can be ashamed "in this adulterous and sinful generation" and the Son of Man who will be ashamed of such men "when he comes in the glory of the Father." This, with the parallel in Luke 12:8f., has been used by Rudolf Bultmann and others to deny Jesus' identification of himself with the Son of Man, but H. E. Tödt, R. H. Fuller and others have argued there is a soteriological continuity between the two.[50] Tödt accepts five other future sayings on the Son of Man that sanction the challenge of Jesus. They are Matthew 24:27 par.; 24:37 par. (Q); Luke 17:30; Matthew 24:44 par. (Q). Once these sayings, mostly Q, are accepted, it is difficult to see why Mark 8:38; 13:26; 14:62 should be denied to Jesus.

The central passage in Mark on Jesus as king is the combination of Psalm 110:1 and Daniel 7:13 in the response of Jesus to the question of the high priest Caiaphas (14:62). It is fashionable to deny that Jesus called himself the Messiah, but this passage says he replied "I am" to Caiaphas when asked if he were the Messiah, the Son of the Blessed (14:61). Jesus did use reservations in 8:29, but that was earlier in the Galilean ministry when the Messianic secret was hidden.

After Peter's confession of Jesus as the Messiah the secret is more and more revealed until this confession of Jesus before Caiaphas. It was the last straw for the high priest to charge him with blasphemy. It is difficult to

---

50. R. H. Fuller, *The Foundations of New Testament Christology*, pp. 122f.

understand the charge by the high priest and the inscription on the cross of Jesus if no such confession was made by Jesus.[51]

The resurgence of the kingship of Christ in modern theology has been sensational. The Stone Lectures at Princeton Theological Seminary in 1947 revealed how the struggle of the church with Nazism led to the recovery of this "office" in European theology.[52] Unfortunately this recovery was viewed by many followers of the German Rudolf Bultmann as the reaction of a Dutch Calvinist. It was not until a German Lutheran named Ernst Käsemann delivered his famous lecture on how apocalypticism was the Mother of Christian theology that the relevance of this theme was more fully realized.[53]

Lord of Lords

Among the eight royal Psalms already mentioned, Psalm 110:1 proved most useful for interpreting the authority of Jesus as the risen Lord. His lordship is well summarized in the statement:

> The Lord says to my lord:
> "Sit at my right hand,
> till I make your enemies your footstool."

In the Hebrew text, as indicated in the RSV, the Lord is the tetragrammaton YHWH revealed to Moses (Ex. 6:3), but the second lord is the king, *adonai*. The LXX uses *Kyrios* for both, and this is the general practice in the Old Testament. Jesus was confessed as *Kyrios* in both the functional and the ontic Christology of the New Testament. Functional Christology is concerned only with the action of God in Jesus, while ontic Christology includes Jesus in the eternal Being of God.

Jesus as Lord in functional Christology. When Jesus was challenged about his authority it was to Psalm 110:1 that he appealed in the last of his ten great controversies already mentioned (Mk. 12:36 par.). It has already been noted how the confession of Jesus as the Messiah in Mark 14:62 par. combined Psalm 110:1 with Daniel 7:13.

The beginnings of a developed Christology in the Acts of the Apostles quote Psalm 110:1 with the comment that "God has made him both Lord and Christ, this Jesus whom you crucified" (2:35f.). This is not adoptionism,

---

51. Cf. David Flusser, *Jesus* (New York: Herder and Herder, 1969), p. 122. For an up-to-date defense of the discussion see William L. Lane, *The Gospel According to Mark* (Grand Rapids, Michigan: William B. Eerdmans Publishing Co., 1974), pp. 536f.
52. W. A. Visser 't Hooft, *The Kingship of Christ* (New York: Harper and Brothers, 1948).
53. Käsemann's lecture was delivered on October 20, 1953, and it has become a watershed for the recovery of apocalyptic in theology. The English translation is "The Problem of the Historical Jesus," *Essays on New Testament Themes*, tr. W. J. Montague (London: SCM, 1964), pp. 15-47. See also James M. Robinson, *A New Quest of the Historical Jesus* (London: SCM, 1959) for a survey of the situation.

but it does identify Jesus with *Kyrios* and Messiah from his ascension and resurrection. His reign in heaven has begun.

John A. T. Robinson argues that an older Christology in Acts did not include a reign in heaven. According to Robinson, Acts 3:12–26 reflects a stage in Christology when it was believed that Jesus was only *received* in heaven after his resurrection and that he was only appointed to reign as the Messiah at his return.[54] There is no doubt that the earliest church expected a future reign of Jesus Christ on earth after the *parousia*, but this does not rule out his present reign in heaven.[55] The two were combined in Mark 14:62, but Robinson argues that the coming in the clouds is the same as the reign![56]

A good case has been made for the Hellenistic origin of belief in Jesus as *Kyrios*, since the Aramaic Palestinian community called him *maran(a)*, not *adonai*, but both languages were perhaps used in Jerusalem from the beginning. Robinson does not take account of this recent evidence.[57] However, there is no doubt that Acts 2:36 speaks of Jesus reigning as Lord. This confession of Jesus as reigning Lord was the proclamation of the Hellenistic Jewish missionaries (Acts 11:20; 14:3; 51:31) and a requirement for baptism (8:16; 11:17; 19:5).

Jesus as Lord in ontic Christology. Ontic Christology includes pre-existence and the participation of Jesus in the eternal Being of God. The functional Christology or lower Christology is not excluded, but a second step forward is taken. The confession of Jesus as Lord has become both formalized in 1 Corinthians (12:3) and a part of belief in the Holy Trinity (12:4–6).

The lordship of Jesus Christ both in the present in heaven and in the future on earth are firmly united in the pillar letters of Paul. First Corinthians 15:20–28, building again on Psalm 110:1, speaks of the reign of Christ since his exaltation continuing into a period between the *parousia*, the Second Coming, and the end, the consummation of all things in God (1 Cor. 15:24f.).

The teaching of the lordship of Jesus Christ continues in Paul's letters. The confession of Jesus as Lord is both a part of his baptismal theology (Rom. 10:9) and a part of the hymnology of worship (8:34). Romans 8:31–39 is a four-stanza hymn, but 8:34 is based on Psalm 110:1. Paul's prison letters also have an ontic Christology of the lordship of Jesus.

A hymn in Philippians 2:6–11, to be discussed later, has the whole universe joining in the praise of Jesus Christ as Lord (2:11), but there is no

54. "The Most Primitive Christology of All?" *Twelve New Testament Studies* (London: SCM Press, 1962), pp. 139-153.
55. Eduard Schweizer, *Lordship and Discipleship* (London: SCM Press, 1960), p. 57.
56. *Jesus and His Coming* (London: SCM Press, 1957), pp. 45-48.
57. *Ibid.*, pp. 184f.

direct reference to Psalm 110:1. However, the exaltation of Jesus as Lord is the same Christology in a cosmic and ontic setting.

Another hymn, in Colossians 3:1–4, speaks of Christ "seated on the right hand of God" (3:1), and Ephesians 1:20 has the same idea included in a hymn (1:20–23) which is part of a prayer (1:15–23). By this time belief in the lordship of Christ based on appeal to Psalm 110:1 has become central in Christian worship.

The Christian interpretation of the Day of Atonement in the Letter to the Hebrews, about A.D. 70, has a dozen references to Psalm 110. Six of the references are to Psalm 110:1 where the emphasis is on Jesus reigning as a High Priest at "the right hand of God" (1:3, 13; 8:1; 10:12f.; 12:2), and the other six say the reign as High Priest is one that is eternal after the order of Melchizedek (5:6, 10; 6:20; 7:3, 17, 21).

The lordship of Jesus Christ continues as a theme in the Johannine writings of the New Testament. The Gospel of John comes to a climax with Thomas' confession of Jesus as "My Lord and my God" (20:28), much as the Gospel of Mark has the confession of the Roman centurion that Jesus is God's Son (15:39).

The Revelation of John, about A.D. 68-70, describes the departed saints singing to the Lamb (5:9):

Worthy art thou to take the scroll and open its seals,

for thou wast slain and by thy blood didst ransom men to God

from every tribe and tongue and people and nation,

and hast made them a kingdom and priests to our God.

This will come to pass when Jesus Christ, the crucified and risen Lord, returns in glory with all the saints to rule upon the earth (20:4–6). Then all will know that Jesus is "King of kings and Lord of lords" (19:16).

The relevance of the lordship of Jesus Christ to modern politics was seen clearly by courageous German Christians who resisted Adolf Hitler as their *Führer* (leader) because they believed that Jesus Christ is *Führer*. For them leadership was lordship. One can forgive the Scot D. M. Baillie for chiding Karl Heim for using this term, for Scots and Germans were not on good terms when he published his excellent Christology.[58] It took as much courage to confess Jesus as *Führer* as Scots and Germans displayed in their tragic and crucial battle in North Africa.

---

58. See D. M. Baillie, *God Was in Christ* (New York: Charles Scribner's Sons, 1948), 98-105.

B. JESUS AS THE MYSTERY OF GODLINESS

59. The Post-existence of Jesus

What really happened to the historical Jesus after he died? Since the sixth century many churches have repeated the Gallican form of the so-called Apostles' Creed which says:

> *He descended into hell,*
> *rose again on the third day,*
> *ascended unto heaven,*
> *sat down at the right hand of the Father,*
> *thence he is to come to judge the living and the dead.*

With the exception of the doctrine of descent into hell "The Old Roman Creed" of the fourth century has essentially the same beliefs.[59]

In recent years many have found it impossible to "repeat the creed" with sincerity. Some modern theology, especially since 1941 when Rudolf Bultmann published his essay on the "New Testament and Mythology," has reduced all that is said about Jesus after the cross to mythological language that must be demythologized to discover the existential meaning relevant in the modern world.[60]

The French Jesuit Xavier Leon-Dufour has applied the Bultmann process of demythologization to all of the details of the traditional views on the post-existence of Jesus with the result that all beyond the cross is myth and legend. Historicity is completely theologized.[61]

Even Anglican theology, which is often more empirical and traditional, has found it necessary to wrestle with this problem. G. W. Lampe argued that the continuing presence of the Spirit of Christ does not depend upon evidences for the "physical" resurrection of Jesus. Lampe lampooned the arguments for the post-existence of the historical Jesus that are based upon prayer, the presence of Christ in the eucharist and the future hope of his *parousia*.[62]

Others have observed this radical process of demythologizing is due to the deistic dualism that undergirds such views of God's relation to the world. In defense of the historicity of both the resurrection of Jesus from the dead and his ascension into heaven, T. F. Torrance has made some

---

59. Henry Bettenson, ed., *Documents of the Christian Church*, Second Edition (London: Oxford University Press, 1963), pp. 33f. For details see J. N. D. Kelly, *Early Christian Creeds* (London: Longmans, Green and Co., 1950), chs. IV, XII.
60. See C. A. Braaten, *History and Hermeneutics* (Philadelphia: The Westminster Press, 1966) for a survey of the situation.
61. *Resurrection and the Message of Easter*, tr. R. N. Wilson (New York: Holt, Rinehart and Winston, 1971).
62. *God as Spirit* (Oxford: Clarendon Press, 1977), pp. 145-175. Cf. Don Cupitt, *Christ and the Hiddenness of God* (Philadelphia: The Westminster Press, 1971), pp. 154-167.

caustic criticisms of the presuppositions that rule out any post-existence of the historical Jesus.[63]

In response to such efforts to detach the Christ of faith from the Jesus of history, all the elements of the creed need examination in their logical relation. Briefly stated the logic of the historical belief in the post-existence of Jesus has been: (1) belief in his descent into hell, the realm of the dead and fallen angels, has been an answer to the question about what Jesus did between his death and his resurrection on the third day; (2) belief in the empty tomb and his resurrection on the third day was based on the appearances of Jesus to the disciples on several occasions; (3) when he no longer appeared to the disciples in their worship, belief in his permanent ascension into heaven and his enthronement at the right hand of God became firmly established; and (4) the hope of his return will complete the salvation begun at his first coming. It is clear that the historicity of his appearances is the central issue, but each item will be examined in chronological order.

He Descended into Hell

The first creedal references to Jesus' descent into hell are the Fourth Creed of Sirmian of 359 and those of Nike and Constantinople in 360, all of Arian origin. This has raised questions as to the New Testament support for the doctrine, but the belief that Jesus descended into the realm of the dead between his death on the cross and his resurrection from the dead is reflected in several New Testament passages. According to the Gospel of Mark, Jesus died a God-forsaken death, but nothing is said about his post-existence between death and resurrection. The Gospel of Matthew does speak of his victory over the powers of death, the gates of Hades (12:29, 40; 16:18), and how some "who had fallen asleep" were raised when Jesus died and appeared to others after Jesus' resurrection (27:51–53). Some have thought those ideas were out of line with the Lukan promise to be with the thief in Paradise (Luke 23:43), but the Lukan Acts records the belief that Jesus was in Hades between his death and resurrection (2:27–31). This perhaps reflects the belief that Paradise was in Hades until the resurrection of Jesus. The Gospel of John says Jesus went away at death to prepare a place for his disciples (14:2), but the Revelation of John speaks also of his victory over Hades by his resurrection from the dead (1:18).

When Paul's letter to the Romans asks the question who can descend into the abyss to bring Christ back from the dead, there is the implication that Jesus did descend into the abyss at death (10:7). The call for "things under the earth" to confess Jesus as Lord indicates their deliverance by Jesus' descent and exaltation (Phil. 2:10). The reference to Jesus' descent

63. *Space, Time and Resurrection* (Grand Rapids, Michigan: Wm. B. Eerdmans Publishing Co., 1976).

"into the lower parts of earth" has been interpreted, following the view of the Gnostic myth, to mean into the earth down below heaven, but this is not accepted by others (Eph. 4:9).[64]

Those who reject the descent doctrine in the early Christian hymn in 1 Timothy 3:16 get thoroughly confused in their expositions. If the hymn is interpreted as six events in historical sequence, the meaning is clear, but this requires belief in Jesus' descent into the realm of fallen angels and the dead. It is strange how English translations miss the three parallels.

1 *He was manifested in the flesh,*	1 Peter 3:18a
2 *vindicated in the spirit,*	3:18b
1 *seen by angels,*	3:19
2 *preached among the nations,*	4:6
1 *believed on in the world,*	
2 *taken up in glory.*	3:22

The RSV has only one error, Spirit for spirit, but the printing is misleading.

The references to 1 Peter indicate how five of the six lines in 1 Timothy 3:16 are in 1 Peter. Those who think these parallels fancies do so more out of Protestant presuppositions than objective exegesis. The angels in 1 Timothy 3:16 are the spirits in prison in 1 Peter 3:19, and the nations in 1 Timothy 3:16 are the dead in 1 Peter 4:6. The two passages together furnish the firmest New Testament evidence for belief in Jesus' descent into hell.[65] The view that one adopts will depend more on one's cosmology and ontology than on exegesis. Since I reject cosmic dualism and accept the God as Being, I do not find belief in Jesus' descent into a realm remote from God any more absurd than the belief that he came into the world to save sinners.

He Rose Again on the Third Day

If Jesus arose from the dead on the third day, as the Christian faith has always confessed, then the question of his descent into the realm of the dead is most logical, unless one applies the doctrine of soul sleep to him. That Jesus was raised from the dead is the basic belief of New Testament Christianity. The two types of evidence that support belief in his resurrection are (1) the empty tomb and (2) Jesus' appearances to his disciples. The arguments that require no evidence usually conclude with no historical resurrection.

The empty tomb is central in the short text of Mark (16:1–8). There is evidence that Mark anticipated an appearance in Galilee (14:28; 16:7),

---

64. Markus Barth rejects the descent doctrine, but see his note on those who do in *Ephesians* (Garden City, New York: Doubleday & Co., 1974), p. 433.
65. For guidance to an extensive bibliography see the *Oxford Dictionary of the Christian Church*, Second Edition, p. 395.

but the appearances in the long reading seem to be later additions from other sources, as the note in the *New Oxford Annotated Bible* clearly explains. The fact that Matthew's Gospel reports an alternate explanation for the empty tomb is really evidence. If the body of Jesus could be produced there would be no need for the guards to be bribed to say the body was stolen (28:11-15).

It may be that Matthew used Mark's account of the empty tomb, although that is doubtful, but it is almost certain that Luke and John are separate sources. With all four Gospels telling about the empty tomb, it is difficult to believe it was an invention growing out of belief in the appearances. At least three separate witnesses furnish strong evidence (Mark 16:1-8; Matthew 28:1-8; Luke 24:1-12; John 20:1-10). Then there is the reference to Jesus' burial in Paul (1 Cor. 15:4).[66]

It is with Paul that the positive evidence of the appearances are added to the negative evidence of the empty tomb. At the very beginning it should be noted that in Paul's earliest account there is a clear distinction between a physical body which is not raised and a spiritual body which is raised (1 Cor. 15:35-58). Yet Bultmann's bias is obvious when he speaks of "the resuscitation of a corpse," and Lampe's lampoon is little better with its frequent reference to Jesus' resurrection body as a "physical" body.[67]

R. H. Fuller, who can hardly be brushed off as a fundamentalist, cogently argues, after one of the most detailed examinations of the resurrection narratives, that the empty tomb should be understood "not as the resuscitation of Jesus' earthly body, but as the transformation of his whole being into the new mode of eschatological existence."[68]

The positive evidence of Jesus' post-resurrection appearances begins with the letters of Paul. Although the paschal passages in 1 Thessalonians 1:10 and 4:14 seem to be aware of the same pre-Pauline baptismal confession, the greatest details are to be found in 1 Corinthians 15:1-11. Few Pauline passages have received more attention in the twentieth century than the various parts of the formulary.[69] Always the crucial issue is the question of historicity over against mythological reductionism.

R. H. Fuller finds four formulae: I: the death (15:3b); II: the burial (15:4a); III: the resurrection (15:4b); and IV: the appearances (15:5-7).[70] The first two bring the existence of the historical Jesus to a close, but the

66. For further details see John E. Alsup, *The Post-Resurrection Appearance Stories of the Gospel-Tradition* (London: S.P.C.K., 1975), pp. 85-117.
67. R. Bultmann, "New Testament and Mythology," in *Kerygma and Myth*, Vol. I, ed. H. W. Bartsch, tr. R. H. Fuller (London: S.P.C.K., 1953), p. 39; G. W. H. Lampe, *op. cit.*, pp. 145-157, 159f.
68. *The Formation of the Resurrection Narratives* (New York: The Macmillan Co., 1971), p. 170. Cf. pp. 17f., 21, 49, 185.
69. A recent review of great value for guidance to other literature is to be found in John Kloppenberg, *The Catholic Biblical Quarterly*, Vol. 40, No. 3, July, 1978, pp. 351-367.
70. *Op. cit.*, pp. 15-30.

second group are evidence for his post-existence, not in the sense of the resuscitation of the earthly body and the historical Jesus but in the sense of transformation into a new mode of eschatological existence.

Fuller also follows the theory of Adolf von Harnack which divided the appearances into two groups of which Cephas (Peter) and James were at the head. The first group had "church-founding significance," and the second group had "mission-inaugurating significance."[71]

No geography is given in the six appearances in 1 Corinthians 15, but the appearances in the Gospels have two locations: Jerusalem and Galilee. The arguments against historicity have made much of these two locations, as if the answer must be either Jerusalem or Galilee.[72]

The crucial question of the Gospel appearances is one of chronology. If the Jerusalem appearances are first and the Galilee appearances are later an either/or conclusion is not necessary. A clue to the solution may be found in 1 Corinthians. The appearance to Cephas was no doubt earlier than the one to James. There is no reference to an appearance to James in the Gospels. Furthermore, if Paul was converted in A.D. 36, as seems probable, there was a seven-year interval between the appearance of Jesus to Cephas in Jerusalem and his appearance to Paul on the Damascus road. The appearances in Paul are not dated and located, but they did take place between "the third day" after the crucifixion and the final appearance to Paul.

Where the Gospels' accounts are read in this longer time frame many of the so-called "contradictions" disappear. Things have a different look when the Gospels' appearances are read in the order of John, Luke, Mark 16:1–8, Matthew. The theory that over a period of time the resurrection body of Jesus went through a process of glorification, from the material to the spiritual, has been discarded by some, but a reading of the four Gospels in the above order does give that impression.

In John, Mary Magdalene can grasp Jesus before his ascension, and Thomas can see his wounds. After the eight days, when, at the Sea of Tiberias, Jesus appears to the disciples for the third time, Jesus has breakfast with the disciples.

In Luke–Acts, Jesus breaks bread in Emmaus and has flesh and bones and eats fish in Jerusalem on the First Day, but, after his ascension on the Fortieth Day, seven years later one hears a voice and sees a bright light, but no material manifestation is mentioned.

In Matthew, at some undated time, the appearance to the eleven, on a mountain in Galilee, has no references to a material act. It seems that a better solution is found when the Johannine, Lukan and Matthean narratives

71. *Ibid.*, p. 41.
72. Cf. Xavier Leon-Dufour, *op. cit.*, pp. 79-104.

are read in that order. It is interesting to note that the long ending in Mark 16:9-20 follows this order![73]

He Ascended into Heaven

Many who would affirm the historicity of the resurrection and the appearances pass as gently by the ascensions or the ascension as they do the descent into hell. This is also unnecessary when special attention is given to the Johannine view of ascension as well as the Lukan.

Ascension is prominent in the Gospel of John (3:13; 6:62; 14:2; 16:7, 16; 20:17). The last reference indicates that there was an ascension on the First Day of the resurrection. The Spirit was also given on the First Easter Evening (20:22). These have been seen as a contradiction to the Lukan view of ascension and the gift of the Spirit, but this too is unnecessary.

There is also an ascension in Luke on the First Day of the resurrection (Luke 24:50f.), and Acts 1:2 indicates that Jesus taught the disciples "through the Holy Spirit" over a period of forty days until he was taken up into heaven. This ascension after the Forty Days certainly did not rule out the appearance to Paul seven years later (Acts 9:1-19; 22:6-21; 26:12-23).

There is no doubt that the concept of the ascensions of Jesus Christ needs further exploration and reinterpretation. A few helpful studies have already been done.[74]

He Sat Down at the Right Hand of the Father

The exaltation of Jesus to the place of authority with God the Father is often expressed in terms of Psalm 110:1. This is symbolic language, as is the three-story universe in the doctrines of the descent and the ascension, but it is the post-existence of Jesus in the sense of eschatological transformation and glorification. In both functional Christology and ontic Christology the exaltation of Jesus is the last step before his return in glory.

Functional Christology does not mention pre-existence and incarnation, but it does portray the post-existence of Jesus with the position of the authority of God over the lives of his disciples (Mark 12:36 = Matt. 22:44 = Lk. 20:42; Mk. 14:62 = Matt. 26:64 = Luke 22:69; Matt. 28:16-20).[75] In what has been called the earliest Christology and eschatology in this

---

73. For more details on the appearances the books by Fuller and Alsup are most useful. Good, brief studies are Joachim Jeremias, *New Testament Theology* (New York: Charles Scribner's, 1971), pp. 300-312; Raymond Brown, *The Virginal Conception and Bodily Resurrection of Jesus* (New York: Paulist Press, 1973), pp. 69-129. The trans-historical nature of the events is more likely than the mythological and legendary views.

74. A. W. Argyle, "The Ascension," *The Expository Times*, LXVI, No. 8 (May, 1955), pp. 240ff. J. G. Davis, *He Ascended into Heaven* (London: Lutterworth Press, 1958); T. F. Torrance, *op. cit.*, pp. 106-158.

75. Cf. John A. T. Robinson, *The Expository Times*, LXVI, No. 11 (August, 1956), pp. 336-340.

early church, the exaltation of Jesus is central (Acts 3:19–21; cf. 2:29–36; 5:31; 7:55f.; 13:33–37).

Ontological Christology includes both the exaltation of Jesus in his post-existence as well as the pre-existence of the Christ who indwelt Jesus. The three major traditions are in Paul, Hebrews and John.

Jesus as head in Paul. The exaltation of Jesus is the climax after the descent into hell, resurrection, and ascension (Romans 1:3; 8:17, 34; 14:19). However, the central picture is of the exalted Jesus as head of the church, his body (Phil. 2:9; Col. 1:17; 2:9f.; 3:1; Eph. 1:22f.; 4:15).

Jesus as high priest in Hebrews. Nothing is said in Hebrews about Jesus' descent into hell or ascension, but his resurrection comes in the benediction (13:20f.). However, the concept of exaltation includes all events between the death of Jesus and his exaltation as high priest (1:3; 2:9; 10:12; 12:2). See also 1 Peter 3:22.

Jesus as king in John. The descent, resurrection, and ascension of Jesus are all taught in the Johannine writings (Rev. 1:18; Jn. 20). The exaltation of Jesus in the Gospel of John telescopes everything between the cross and the consummation into the concept of Jesus being lifted up from the earth (3:14; 8:28; 12:32, 34). If any picture of Jesus' exaltation is central in Revelation it is that of rule of the kings of the earth (1:3–7; 3:21; 5:6; 19:11–16).

Thence He Shall Come to Judge the Living and the Dead

This Johannine portrayal leads logically to the fifth point in the Apostles' Creed, Jesus' coming to judge the living and the dead, but this is discussed in detail in Part X. It is not claimed that the biblical writers had a modern scientific view of the world, but that which they portrayed as the post-existence of Jesus can be interpreted in the world of modern science without reducing all beyond the cross to myth and legend.

When all evidence is examined the conclusion reached may seem very conservative, but here it is. Jesus did appear to his disciples over a period of seven years. These appearances gave meaning to the empty tomb and the cessation of appearances. Since he is now the Risen One, he will return. These events are supported by the apocalyptic teaching of the Old Testament and the historical Jesus.

60. The Pre-existence of Christ

The pre-existence of the Messiah is not found in the Old Testament. Some indeed have interpreted such passages as Micah 5:2 as references to pre-existence, but this is doubtful exegesis. The note in the *New Oxford Annotated Bible* is perhaps correct when it says that the statement that the ruler from Bethlehem will be one "whose origin is from of old" "could mean from the days of David, rather than pre-existence from the beginning of time."

The pre-existence of Christ is not even taught in the Synoptic Gospels and Acts. G. W. Lampe, who takes a dim view of pre-existence in Paul, Hebrews and John, suggests that Christology would have fewer problems if the Spirit-Christology of Luke–Acts had been followed in the history of Christianity.[76] It is true that neglect of the Holy Spirit in the Christological debates of church history was unfortunate, but the ontological questions posed by high Christology are required in a complete Christology. In Lampe's view only a low Christology of the relation of the man Jesus to God is possible. Low Christology and high Christology are both required.

The ontological post-existence of Jesus was noted in the high Christology of Paul, Hebrews and John. It is in these same New Testament writings that the pre-existence of Christ, who became man in the existence of Jesus Christ, is taught. This includes (1) the Wisdom of God Christology of Paul, (2) the Word of God Christology of John and (3) the Son of God Christology of Hebrews.[77]

Christ as the Eternal Wisdom of God

The identification of Jesus with the wisdom of God is found in the Synoptic Gospels, especially Matthew's Gospel which portrays Jesus as the new Torah.[78] However, Lampe is perhaps correct when he says the "assimilation of 'Logos-Wisdom' to 'Son-Jesus Christ' appears to begin with Paul."[79] The background of the identification of Jesus Christ with the eternal wisdom of God is found in abundance in Rabbinic Judaism.[80]

The pre-existence of Christ in Paul's "pillar epistles." This identification of the crucified Jesus with God's eternal or pre-existent wisdom finds classic expression in Paul's first letter to the Corinthians, about A.D. 53. The importance of this letter becomes clear when it is compared to Paul's first letter to the Thessalonians, about A.D. 50. 1 Thessalonians has no reference to the pre-existence of Christ, but at least four references are found in 1 Corinthians.

Christ is first identified with the wisdom of God (1 Cor. 1:24, 30), then with the pre-existence of wisdom (2:6–9). This wisdom of God was "hid-

76. *God as Spirit* (Oxford: Clarendon Press, 1977), p. 144.
77. Fred B. Craddock, *The Pre-existence of Christ* (New York: Abingdon Press, 1968), pp. 81-150.
78. M. J. Suggs, *Wisdom, Christology and Law in Matthew's Gospel* (Cambridge: Harvard University Press, 1970). For all three of the Synoptic Gospels see Felix Christ, *Jesus Sophia* (Zurich: Zwingli-Verlag, 1970).
79. *Op. cit.,* p. 123.
80. W. D. Davies, *Paul and Rabbinic Judaism* (London: S.P.C.K., 1948), pp. 147-176. Cf. G. W. H. Lampe, *op. cit.,* pp. 128f.

den" (2:6–9), then revealed through the Spirit in the Crucified One (2:10–13), and received by those who possess the Spirit (2:14–16). The continuity of the Spirit of God in the church is indeed important, but the identification of Jesus with *Sophia* (wisdom) is the central concern of Paul. The possibility that 2:10f. is a six-line hymn adds to its centrality in Pauline Christology. Hymnology often formulates Christology.

It is even more likely that the liturgical formula in 1 Corinthians 8:5–6 was already used in Christian worship to express the pre-existence of Christ. The concept of Christ as the agent of creation goes beyond all low Christology. The Crucified One is related not only to redemption but also to creation, for the very Being of God is most fully manifested in Jesus. Therefore, Christian worship confesses:

> *There is one God, the Father,*
> *from whom are all things*
> *and for whom we exist,*
> *and one Lord, Jesus Christ,*
> *through whom are all things*
> *and through whom we exist.*

Even though this confession is framed on a Stoic formula of "from-through-unto," there is a great difference in the view of God's relation to Christ and creation. Stoicism taught that all things *are* God, pantheism, but Paul taught that all things are *in* God, panentheism (1 Cor. 15:28). This binitarianism proclaims the pre-existence of Christ before the existence of the historical Jesus. When this binitarianism is added to the function of the Spirit in 2:10f., the result is trinitarianism (12:4–6; cf. 2 Cor. 13:14).

Christ as the Crucified One and as Creator was also the Christ of Israel's history. Lampe rightly singles out 1 Corinthians 10:4 and says: "The most striking passage which might suggest that Paul believed that the pre-existent person of Christ made himself known to men before his human birth is his assertion that the people in the wilderness wandering 'drank from a spiritual rock which followed them, and the rock was Christ.' "[81] This then is developed into one of the most powerful warnings about the danger of apostasy.[82]

The reference to Jesus as the Man from Heaven in 1 Corinthians 15:47 comes in the midst of Paul's Adam Christology in which Jesus is identified with "the second man from heaven" (15:47) or "the man of heaven" (15:49). Even though the thrust of the argument is on the future when "we shall also bear the image of the man of heaven," the reference to "the man from heaven" seems to imply his pre-existence, although it may have reference to the *parousia* (Second Coming).

81. *Op. cit.*, p. 123. Philo identified the Rock in the wilderness with Wisdom (*Leg. alleg.* II, 21).
82. Cf. Fred B. Craddock, *op. cit.*, pp. 113-119.

It is hardly possible to support the claim that the statement about "him who knew no sin" in 2 Corinthians 5:21 has reference to the pre-existent state of Christ, but the beautiful statement about "the grace of our Lord Jesus Christ, that though he was rich, yet for your sake he became poor, so that by his poverty you might become rich" (2 Cor. 8:9) does. Christ was rich in his state of pre-existence, but he became poor for us in his historical existence. As Paul Tillich says in the language of existentialism: "Essential God-Manhood has appeared within existence and subjected itself to the conditions of existence without being conquered by them."[83]

In our discussion of 1 Corinthians 8:6 we noted that Paul was a pan-entheist, not a pantheist, for he taught that all things are *in* God, not that all things *are* God. Furthermore, as in 1 Corinthians 15:28, Paul is no unitarian who believes only in the second person of the Trinity. The formula is: "All this is from God, who through Christ reconciled us to himself" (2 Cor. 5:18). He does not say "God was Christ" but that "God was *in* Christ" or, as the footnote in the RSV says, "In Christ God was reconciling" (5:19).

God's sending of his Son in the fulness of time includes more than a prophetic vocation (Gal. 4:4). Out of eternity into time the Son of God came on a mission of redemption. The parallel of the two sendings, of the Son into history and of the Spirit, suggests the same origin. God's Son and God's Spirit originate in the Being of God (4:4–7).

The pre-existence expressed in the parallelism between God's sending of his Son into human history and of his Spirit into the human heart is continued in Romans 8:1–4, written from Corinth about a year after Galatians 4:4–7 from Ephesus in A.D. 54. The poetic structure of both passages indicates that they were first used as hymns. At least the pre-existence of the Son and the Spirit in the very Being of God is in both.

The pre-existence of Christ in Paul's "prison epistles." The pre-existence of Christ in both redemption and creation, as already noted in Paul's "pillar epistles," continues in his "prison epistles." If these "prison epistles" are dated between A.D. 55 and 57, in Caesarea, as seems most likely, then there is no need to invent another author. Some differences in style are to be noted in the "pillar epistles," but this is due to the amanuensis, Sosthenes in 1 Corinthians, Timothy in 2 Corinthians, unknown in Galatians, and Tertius in Romans. Timothy is again the amanuensis in Philippians and Colossians, the two "prison epistles" with passages on pre-existence. Timothy seems always to indicate he is the amanuensis by adding his name to Paul's in the salutation.

---

83. *Systematic Theology* (Chicago: University of Chicago Press, 1957), Vol. II, p. 98.

Philippians 2:6–11 has long been recognized as a hymn.[84] The next section will discuss this great hymn in more detail, but the first line is noted now as a statement on the pre-existence of Christ. Literally translated it says (2:6a):

In the form of God subsisting.

Subsisting in the form of God means participation in the very essence of God before coming under the conditions of human existence.[85]

Colossians 1:15–20 has also been widely recognized as a hymn.[86] The first stanza of this hymn on God's Firstborn proclaims Christ as pre-existent in creation (1:15–17, my translation):

He is the image of the invisible God,
the Firstborn of all creation;
for in him were created all things (in heaven and on earth,
the visible things and the invisible things,
whether thrones or dominions
or principalities or authorities).
All things through him and for him were created,
and he is before all things,
and all things in him cohere.

The Firstborn is the Son of God who has the authority and the inheritance of the Father, as in Exodus 4:22. It does not mean that before creation God had no Son, as was taught in ancient Arianism and by the modern Jehovah's Witnesses. Firstborn in Colossians is a term of precreation, not procreation.

The second stanza in this hymn on God's Firstborn proclaims Christ as pre-existent in reconciliation (1:18–20, my translation):

And he is the head of the body (the church);
he is the beginning,
the Firstborn from the dead
(that in everything he might have primacy);
for in him all the fullness was pleased to dwell,
and through him to reconcile all things to himself
(having made peace through the blood of his cross,
[through him] whether on earth or in heaven).[87]

84. The standard study is Ralph P. Martin, *Carmen Christi* (Cambridge: Cambridge University Press, 1967). Charles H. Talbert, "The Problem of Pre-existence in Philippians 2:6–11," *JBL*, 86 (1967), pp. 141-153, denies that the passage has any reference to pre-existence, but his argument has not been widely accepted. See also George Howard, "Phil. 2:6–11 and the Human Christ," *CBQ*, Vol. 40, No. 3 (July, 1978), pp. 368-387.
85. Martin, *op. cit.*, pp. 99-133.
86. The standard work is Hans Jakob Gabathuler, *Jesus Christus: Haupt der Kirche-Haupt der Welt* (Zürich: Zwingli Verlag, 1965). See also Nicholas Kehl, *Der Christushymnus in Kolosserbrief* (Stuttgart: Verlag Bibelwerk, 1967).
87. Cf. this translation with the Greek in Gabathuler, *op. cit.*, p. 131.

The primary statement on pre-existence in reconciliation is "the beginning" (*archē*). Since Christ belongs to precreation, not to procreation, he was present when all created things began; the Beginning always participated in the very Being of God.

The pre-existence of Christ in Paul's "pastoral epistles." In the "pastoral epistles" a "faithful saying" declares that "Christ Jesus came into the world to save sinners" (1 Tim. 1:15). This again is more than a prophetic vocation, for this coming into the world is an *epiphany* of the very essence of God under the circumstances of human existence (2 Tim. 1:10). In the "pastoral epistles" the Greek word for epiphany (*epiphaneia*) is the word often used for the Second Coming (Titus 2:13; 1 Tim. 6:14; 2 Tim. 4:1, 8), so that makes the use of the word for the First Coming of Christ significant indeed.

The identification of the pre-existent Christ with eternal wisdom was misinterpreted after New Testament times. An early Christian heresy argued, by appeal to the created wisdom of Proverbs 8:22, that Christ was the first creature of God. However, in Proverbs 8:22, Wisdom is God's action personified, not a being distinct from God.

The Wisdom heresy, and many other heresies, was often traced back to Simon of Samaria (cf. Acts 8:9–25).[88] Orthodox theologians continued to identify the pre-existent Christ with Wisdom, but so much ambiguity attended the term, especially in Origen of Alexandria, that Arius and his followers boldly taught that Christ was a creature between the Creator and the creation.[89] After Arianism was officially condemned as a heresy, Wisdom became less popular as a Christological term. However, it has continued in Eastern Orthodoxy down to modern times.[90]

Christ as the Eternal Word of God

The threefold use of the Word of God in the Scriptures was sketched in Part II.10. Here the relationship between the personal Word of God and the pre-existence of Christ is the chief concern.

Christ is proclaimed as the pre-existent Word of God in the prologue of 1 John (1:1–4). My own translation attempts to bring out the three steps of pre-existence, manifestation and proclamation in what appears to be one of the twelve Christian hymns that constitute what is called the First Letter of John.

88. Jaroslav Pelikan, *The Christian Tradition* (Chicago: University of Chicago Press, 1971), Vol. I, pp. 23f.
89. *Ibid.*, Vol. II, pp. 191f.
90. Sergius Bulgakov, *The Wisdom of God* (New York: Paisley Press, 1937). See also W. M. Horton, *Contemporary Continental Theology* (New York: Harper & Row, 1938), pp. 31-36, and the articles "Santa Sophia" and "Bulgakov, Sergius," in *The Oxford Dictionary of the Christian Church*, Second Edition.

1 *That which was from the beginning,*
   which we have heard,
   which we have seen with our eyes,
   which we have looked upon
   and touched with our hands,
   concerning the Word of Life —
2 *And the Life was manifested,*
   and we have seen,
   and we are bearing witness,
   and we are proclaiming to you
   the eternal life which was with the Father
   and was manifested to us —
3 *that which we have seen and heard we are proclaiming to*
      you,
   in order that you may have fellowship with us;
   and our fellowship is with the Father
   and with his Son Jesus Christ,
4 *and these things we are writing to you,*
   in order that our joy may be complete.[91]

The Prologue to the Gospel of John (1:1–18) will be discussed in more detail in the next section, but the doctrine of pre-existence is very much the same as in the prologue of 1 John. At this point there is the transformation of other terms by the doctrine of pre-existence. It will perhaps be best to translate here the hymn about the Word that is a part of the prologue in John 1:1–18.

1 *In the beginning was the Word,*
   and the Word was with God,
      and the Word was God.
3 *All things through him were made,*
      and apart from him was nothing made.
4 *That which was made in him was life,*
      and the life was the light of men.
5 *And the light shines in the darkness,*
      and the darkness has not overcome it.
10 *He was in the world,*
      and the world was made through him,
         and the world knew him not.
11 *He came to his own home,*
      and his own people did not receive him.

91. *The Letters of John* (Waco, Texas: Word Books, 1970), p. 19.

14 *And the Word became flesh,*
   and dwelt among us;
and we have seen his glory,
   glory as of the only Son from the Father.
18 *No one has ever seen God;*
   the only God,
Who is in the bosom of the Father,
   he has made him known.

The first part of the hymn declares the pre-existence (1), the creativity (3, 4), and the illumination of the Word (5) before the Word came to exist as Jesus. The second part of the hymn elaborates the ideas in the prologue of 1 John 1:1–4, which spoke mostly of the incarnation. The Word was rejected by the world (10) and Israel (11), but the disciples saw the glory of God dwelling among them in the flesh of Jesus (14). This dwelling of the Word in the flesh of Jesus reveals a unique relation with the Father (18).[92]

In the pre-existence of the Son of God as the Word of God, the Gospel of John does not hesitate to call the Son God without the article, meaning he participated in the eternal Being of God before and after the Word became flesh (1, 18). The distinction between the Father and the Son is never obscured before or after the incarnation. It is this binitarianism that leads to trinitarianism, and that is why the doctrine of pre-existence is a prerequisite to the doctrine of incarnation.

The Word of God is not mentioned after the prologue of John (1:1–18), but other terms for the pre-existence and eternal Son of God agree with this view. This is especially true in (1) the seven "Son of Man" sayings, (2) the seven "My hour" sayings, and (3) the seven "I am" sayings.

The seven Son of Man sayings are John 1:51; 3:13f.; 6:27, 53, 62; 9:35; 12:23.[93] In the first Son of Man saying, the ascending and descending upon the Son of Man is done by angels (1:51), but in the second saying it is the Son of Man who ascended into heaven because he first of all "descended from heaven" (3:13). His descent from heaven is into the world of flesh and blood, but afterwards he ascended to where he was before (6:27, 53, 62). The same Son of Man is confessed in his life (9:35) and glorified in his death (12:23).

The glory of the Son of Man is seen especially in his seven "My hour" sayings (2:4; 7:30; 8:20; 12:23, 27; 13:1; 17:1).[94] It is only in the context of the seventh saying that the pre-existence of Christ is proclaimed, but

92. For detailed analysis see Julius Sheril Jones, "A Literary Analysis and Exposition of the Prologue of John's Gospel," Th.M. thesis, SBTS, 1956.
93. For detailed analysis of these sayings see Paul Davis Early, "The Conception of the Son of Man in the Fourth Gospel," Th.D. thesis, SBTS, 1952.
94. For details see Harold Lee Moore, "The 'My Hour' Sayings in the Fourth Gospel," Th.M. thesis, SBTS, 1951.

there it is clear when Jesus says: "Father, glorify thou me in thy own presence with the glory which I had with thee before the world was" (17:5).

The pre-existence of Christ is proclaimed also in the seven "I am" sayings. The first "I am" saying compares Jesus with Moses. Jesus identified himself with the true bread that came down from heaven so that one could partake of him by faith and live forever (6:35, 38, 41, 48, 51). The bread that Moses gave them in the wilderness sustains only the natural life, as descent from Abraham.

In the second "I am" saying Jesus is compared with Abraham. Jesus declared: "I am the light of the world" (8:12). Natural descent from Abraham helps no more than the physical bread that Moses gave them. To be children of Abraham by natural descent did not make God the Father of the Jews. Jesus said to the Jews: "If God were your Father, you would love me, for I proceed and come forth from God; I came not of my own accord, but he sent me" (John 8:42). That is why he could say: "Truly, truly, I say to you, before Abraham was, I am" (8:58).

In the other five "I am" sayings the pre-existence of Christ is not always as emphatic as in the first two, but it is always assumed. They are: "I am the door" (10:7), "I am the good shepherd" (10:11), "I am the resurrection and the life" (11:25), "I am the way, the truth and the life" (14:6), and "I the true vine" (15:1).

The Apocalypse (Revelation) of John continues to proclaim the pre-existence of Christ as seen in 1 John and the Gospel of John. In fact the declaration of God as the Alpha and the Omega, the beginning and the end, is the same as the declaration of the risen Lord Jesus as the first and the last (cf. 1:8; 4:8; 21:7 with 1:17; 3:14; 22:13). As in the Gospel of John, Jesus is declared to be the Word of God in the Apocalypse of John (19:13).

The Word of God Christology in John was even more important for the development of the doctrine of the Trinity than the Wisdom of God Christology of Paul. The first steps toward a Greek triad in God were taken by Theophilus of Antioch who described God as one Being with a *Logos endiathetos*, the Word within, which became the *Logos prophericos* when Jesus came into human history. (See also Part III.20.)

Christ as the Eternal Son of God

The pre-existence of the Son of God in Hebrews unites the Wisdom of God Christology of Paul and the Word of God Christology of John. In all three pre-existence means that the very Being of God was united to human existence in Jesus Christ.

Jesus as the first and the last in the Apocalypse of John is introduced in Hebrews as the Son of God "whom he appointed the heir of all things, through whom also he created the world" (1:2). The present activity of the

Son, which unites the future and the past, is the theme of the Christological hymn (1:3–4):[95]

> *Who being the radiance of glory*
> *and the stamp of his substance,*
> *upholding all things by the word of his power,*
> *having made purification for sins,*
> *he sat down at the right hand of the Majesty on high,*
> *having become as much superior to the angels.*

Many call attention to the parallel of this passage in the Wisdom of Solomon 7:25–27, but the identification with the Word of God and the Son of God makes Hebrews 1:3f. more personal. Therefore, in Hebrews the saints live by faith, not wisdom.

Apaugasma, found only here in the New Testament, is found frequently in Philo, but some translate it reflection rather than radiance. However, the Greek *apaugasma* seems to have the meaning of the Hebrew *Shekinah*, meaning God's Presence as in the cloud of glory in the Exodus. Therefore, "the radiance of glory" expresses the source of the Son in God. *Charaktēr*, translated stamp, means the exact likeness of the eternal reality, the *substantia* in Latin, *hypostasis* in Greek. He, the Son, is the agent of creation, the heir of all things and the present sustainer of the universe. Pre-existence in the very Being of God beyond all created existence can hardly be put with greater power. Pre-existence, purification for sin and exaltation are inseparable.

Since the Son of God belongs to precreation and has always participated in the eternal Being which is God, the worship of created angels is forbidden, as in Paul's Colossian letter. The author of Hebrews, perhaps Barnabas around A.D. 70, does not hesitate to apply passages about God to the post-existent and exalted Jesus (1:8).-As Lord, he was also the agent of all creation (1:10). Therefore, in the light of his pre-existence and post-existence, he was made lower than the angels only "for a little while" (2:7). The "while" is a quotation from the Septuagint, not the Hebrew of Psalm 8:5.

The idea of Christ as the radiance of God was also used in early Christianity as an illustration of God as an ontological Trinity. Tertullian of Carthage used many illustrations, and one of his favorites seemed to be that of the Father as the sun, the Son of God as the beam from the sun, and the Holy Spirit as the inward illumination (*Against Praxeas*, 8). Neglect of this sun-beam-light view in the interest of the *personae*, the modes at first and three individuals later, led to forms of tritheism that still make for problems when explaining to Jews and Moslems why Christians also believe in one God.

95. R. H. Fuller, *The Foundations of New Testament Christology* (New York: Charles Scribner's Sons, 1965), pp. 220f.

In unexpected places a denial of the distinction between the Eternal Father and the Eternal Son can also be found. J. R. Graves, the founder of the Southern Baptist movement known as Landmarkism, declared the very distinction between the Eternal Father and the Eternal Son "inadmissible" and "manifestly of human coinage."[96] A proper understanding of the pre-existence of Christ rules out both tritheism and strange forms of unitarianism. God is Father, Son and Spirit in eternal relations.

61. The Existence of Jesus Christ

A philosophical title is used for this chapter to relate it more obviously to the chapters on the post-existence of Jesus and the pre-existence of Christ. In New Testament terms the concern is with what Paul called "the fulness of time." If the epiphany of Jesus Christ had not been traditionally used of his baptism, some such term as the first epiphany (appearing) of Jesus Christ could be used (cf. 2 Tim. 1:10; Heb. 9:26).

In the inspiration Christology of G. W. Lampe the term "the Christ-event" is used.[97] Many others find this term sufficient for a functional Christology that is shy of the post-existence of Jesus and pre-existence of Christ. Inspiration or functional Christology says many things that need not be rejected. No question is raised about the work of the Spirit in creation, Christ and the church. It is the Christology in much of the New Testament (Mark–Matthew, Luke–Acts), but it is incomplete, from a New Testament point of view, until the questions of the pre-existence of Christ and an incarnation Christology are considered. Incarnation Christology is ontological and relates Jesus to the very Being of God. A description of Jesus as a Spirit-filled man is true but inadequate and incomplete.

In a broader sense, incarnation Christology includes the humiliation of the pre-existent and exalted Christ as in Paul, the incarnation of the eternal and abiding Word as in John and the perfection of the eternal Son of God who appeared as Jesus in Hebrews. The pre-existence of Christ as a presupposition throws new light on the historical Jesus as prophet, priest and potentate.

The Humiliation of a Slave

In Paul's Christology of the cross the humiliation and exaltation of the historical Jesus is seen in the light of his subsistence in the very Being of God, "Light of Light, true God of true God" in the Nicene Creed. The Christological center of this question, however, is in the New Testament, especially in the hymn on the humiliation of the Christ in Philippians 2:6–

---

96. *The Seven Dispensations*, 1883 (Texarkana, Ark.-Tex.: Baptist Sunday School Committee, 1928), pp. 61f.
97. *God as Spirit*, pp. 95-119.

11.[98] Interpretations of the hymn are too numerous to trace here, but some positive conclusions need to be noted as a preparation for present application of the view.

An adaptation of the structures suggested by Joachim Jeremias and Ralph P. Martin seems to be an antiphonal hymn with six parallels in three stanzas.[99] This is nearer to the view of Ernst Lohmeyer and others who understand the hymn against a Jewish background, but at places the thought reflects the Hellenistic background explored by Ernst Käsemann and others. There are really elements of both in the hymn.

I. Heavenly Pre-existence

6 *(Who), in the form of God, subsisting*

    did not think equality with God a thing to be grasped,

7 *but he emptied himself,*

    taking the form of a slave.

II. Earthly Humiliation

    Being born in the likeness of men

    and being found in fashion as a man,

8 *he humbled himself,*

    becoming obedient unto the death

    (even death on a cross).

III. Heavenly Exaltation

9 *Therefore, God has highly exalted him*

    and given him the Name which is above every name,

10 *that at the Name of Jesus every knee should bow*

    (in heaven and on earth and under the earth),

11 *and every tongue confess that Jesus Christ is Lord*

    (to the glory of God the Father).

R. H. Fuller has described this as a "three stage Christology."[100] He is indeed correct, but his three-line structuring and some of his interpretations need revision. The structure of six parallels and two synonymous lines seems more correct. Therefore, we will follow the structure above in our search for meaning.

---

98. The major studies of the structure and meaning of the hymn are Ralph P. Martin, *Carmen Christi* (Cambridge: Cambridge University Press, 1967) and Otfried Hofius, *Der Christushymnus Philipper 2:6-11* (Tübingen: Mohr, 1976).
99. Cf. Ralph P. Martin, *op. cit.,* pp. 36f.
100. *The Foundations of New Testament Christology*, pp. 203-214.

The effort to exclude the doctrine of pre-existence is interesting but unconvincing.[101] As has already been noted in the discussion on the pre-existence of Christ, the very first line is a summary statement on pre-existence. Today's English Version, *The Good News Bible*, has made a correct paraphrase with the statement: "He always had the very nature of God" (2:6a).

The Good News Bible has also paraphrased the parallel line with: "But he did not think that by force he should try to become equal with God" (2:6).

This is possibly a Second Adam Christology in which Christ is contrasted to the First Adam who snatched the forbidden fruit (Gen. 3:6). Jesus received equality by way of the cross.

Here R. H. Fuller has failed to see that the first line has to do with the essence, the very being of Christ in his pre-existence, but the second line has reference to his equality with God at his exaltation. Even *The Good News Bible* retains the incorrect idea by saying "he gave it all up" (2:7a) rather than "he emptied himself." Equality in Paul and in the entire New Testament is always what Jesus receives at his exaltation (2 Thess. 1:12; Rom. 8:5; Tit. 2:13; Acts 20:28; Heb. 1:8, 10 and 2 Pet. 1:1 can be so interpreted, but only John 20:28 and Phil. 2:6, 9-11 seem sure).

To say that Christ emptied himself at the cross, as Joachim Jeremias does, is pushing the analogy of Isaiah 53:7 too far. The passage does say the Servant, *pais* in Greek, "poured out his soul to death," but the Greek word in Philippians 2:7b is *doulos*, slave, not *pais*, servant (cf. Acts 3:25, 27, 30). There is not one passage in Paul that interprets Jesus as the suffering Servant. All that is in Mark–Matthew, Luke–Acts and 1 Peter.

The earthly humiliation of the Christ as a slave is described in the second stanza of the hymn (2:7b-8). Stanza one (2:6-7a) is about pre-existence and incarnation. The Christ emptied himself into the man Jesus and appeared among men as God's slave. Existing in "the likeness of men" and being found "in fashion as a man" (2:7b) is the same Christology already noted in the discussion of the pre-existence of Christ (2 Cor. 8:9 and Rom. 8:3). This time the emphasis is very much on the humiliation of the poor Jesus ("he humbled himself, existing in obedience to death").

Here begins the servitude of a slave, as R. H. Fuller makes so clear in his rejection of the curious claim of Jeremias that this happened when Christ "emptied himself" at the cross. Jeremias has confused the meaning of "he

101. Charles F. Talbert, "The Problem of Pre-Existence in Philippians 2:6–11," *Journal of Biblical Literature*, 86 (1967), pp. 141-153. Frank Stagg, "Philippians," *Broadman Bible Commentary* (Nashville: Broadman Press, 1971), Vol. 11, pp. 195ff. George Howard, "Phil. 2:6–11 and the Human Christ," *Catholic Biblical Quarterly*, Vol. 40, No. 3 (July, 1978), pp. 368-387. For criticism of Talbert, see R. G. Hamerton-Kelly, *Pre-Existence, Wisdom, and the Son of Man* (Cambridge: At the University Press, 1973), pp. 156-159.

emptied himself" as if it means the same as "he humbled himself." Fuller, following Ernst Käsemann, observes that taking on the form of a slave (*doulos*) corresponds with previous Pauline passages on "thralldom to the powers of evil (*doulei*)." Cf. Galatians 4:3–8; Romans 8:21, and Colossians 2:20.

Obedience to death is the final act in the humiliation of God's slave, Jesus Christ. The phrase "even death on a cross" is distinctively Pauline and may be considered a comment on the hymn (cf. 1 Cor. 1:17–2:5; Gal. 2:20; 5:14). The hymn itself may be pre-Pauline, but nothing makes that conclusion necessary.

The heavenly exaltation of God's obedient slave is the theme of the third stanza (2:9–11). Each of the four lines in 2:9–11 expounds and clarifies the meaning of equality with God in 2:6b. The comment on the three-storied universe does not seem to be a part of the hymn either. Jeremias, Martin and others are not doing exegetical surgery at all. As to the doxology at the end, George Howard may be right in saying it should be sung at the end of each antiphonal couplet or stanza, but it does not belong to the couplet itself. Jeremias, Martin, and Fuller, against the background study of Johannes Weiss, have greatly illuminated this great hymn, but the above sketch will illustrate why none of them is completely satisfactory. In the one point that the existence of Jesus Christ in Paul's writings is most fully stated here, most would agree.

The *kenosis* (emptying) of Philippians 2:7 should be understood in relation to the *plerosis* of Colossians 2:9f. *Kenosis* is from the side of man, and *plerosis* is from the side of God. Looking at the existence of Jesus Christ in one way, Christ emptied himself into the man Jesus, and at the same time the man Jesus was filled with the Christ. It is more than God in a human body, as Cyril of Alexandria taught in the fifth century and many have repeated since. It is a Spirit-filled, God-filled man, complete and perfect man, the humiliation and incarnation of the Christ, the Son of God.

The Incarnation of the Word

In the discussion of the pre-existence of Christ the two divisions of the Johannine hymn about the Logos, "in the beginning" and "in the world," were noted (John 1:1, 10). In the last four lines two couplets about the dwelling of the Logos (Word) in Jesus (1:14) introduce two main themes in the Gospel of John: (1) the revelation of glory and (2) the uniqueness of the Son.

The revelation of the glory is seen in the two divisions of the Gospel of John: (1) the Book of Signs (1–11) and (2) the Book of the Passion (12–20).[102] The signs in Galilee were the turning of water into wine (2:1–11),

---

102. William E. Hull, "John," *Broadman Bible Commentary* (Nashville: Broadman Press, 1970), Vol. 9, pp. 206-208.

the healing of an official's son (4:46–54), the feeding of the five thousand (6:1–15) and the walking on the water (6:16–21). On such occasions Jesus "manifested his glory" (2:11), i.e., he revealed the fact that the Shekinah glory had come to dwell in him. "We beheld his glory" (1:14).

The three signs in Jerusalem were the cure of a lame man (5:1–9a), restoring sight to a man born blind (9:1–12) and the raising of Lazarus from the dead (11:1–54). At the tomb of Lazarus Jesus said to Martha: "Did I not tell you that if you would believe you would see the glory of God?" (11:40). The whole event of Jesus' Passion, his death, resurrection, appearances and ascension was his glorification (7:39), but the cross was the crucial moment (17:1–5).

The unique relation between the Father and the Son was nothing less than the indwelling of God in the man Jesus. The incarnation of the Word in the flesh of Jesus was an act of complete indwelling in which the Word remained Word and Jesus remained a true man. When the water became wine, there was something added, but the water did not cease to be water. The same word, *ginomai*, is used in 2:9 that was used in 1:14. If the Word ceased to be the Word by indwelling Jesus the result was a metamorphosis as in Greek mythology, but if the Word continued as the Word and Jesus continued to be a man in whom the Word came to dwell, then there was an incarnation in which the Father is in the Son and the Son is in the Father. Several dialogues in the Gospel of John should make this clear.

When the Jews said Jesus made himself equal with God (5:18), the response was: "Truly, truly, I say to you, the Son can do nothing of his own accord, but only what he sees the Father doing; for whatever he does, the Son does likewise" (5:19f.). The dialogue continues with the distinction between the Father and the Son always clear and never confused (5:21–28).

The unity of the Father and the Son is not identity. Jesus said indeed that "the Father and I are one" (10:30), but this is explained in the words: "that the Father is in me and I am in the Father" (10:38). The Father and the Son are one, but not the same.

To Philip Jesus said: "He who has seen me has seen the Father; however, you say, 'Show us the Father'? Do you not believe that I am in the Father and the Father in me? The words that I say to you I do not speak on my own authority; but the Father who dwells in me does the works. Believe me that I am in the Father and the Father is in me; or else believe me for the sake of the works themselves" (14:9–11).

Perhaps the clearest statement of all on incarnation as indwelling, first of the Father in the Son, then as the Father in the Son continuing the incarnation in all the disciples, is found in the high-priestly prayer of 17:20–26.

I do not pray for these only, but also for those who believe in me through their word, that they may all be one; even as thou, Father, art in me, and I in thee, that they also may be in us, so that the world may believe that thou hast sent me. The glory which thou hast given me I have given to them, that they may be one even as we are one, I in them and thou in me, that they may become perfectly one, so that the world may know that thou hast sent me and hast loved them even as thou hast loved me. Father, I desire that they also, whom thou hast given me, may be with me where I am, to behold my glory which thou hast given me in thy love for me before the foundation of the world. O righteous Father, the world has not known thee, but I have known thee; and these know that thou hast sent me. I made known to them thy name, and I will make it known, that the love with which thou hast loved me may be in them, and I in them.

The Perfection of the Son

Perfection may sound strange when applied to the sinless Son of God, but it is a characteristic term in the Letter to the Hebrews and is applied to both Jesus as the Son of God and to believers as sons of God. Jesus passes through all the stages and temptations of human life without sin (4:15), but the process of being made perfect describes his existence in the mission of redemption.

The perfection of Jesus was reached through suffering. "For it was fitting that he, for whom and by whom all things exist, in bringing many sons to glory, should make the pioneer of their salvation perfect through suffering" (2:10). Christ was both the agent of creation and the agent of salvation.

The perfection of Jesus was reached also through perfect obedience to the will of God. "In the days of his flesh, Jesus offered up prayers and supplication, with loud cries and tears, to him who was able to save him from death, and he was heard for his godly fear. Although he was a Son, he learned obedience through what he suffered; and being made perfect he became the source of eternal salvation to all who obey him" (5:7-9). It is difficult to state the true humanity and true deity of Jesus in stronger terms.

The law was unable to accomplish perfection (7:19), but the sacrifice of Jesus through perfect obedience and suffering accomplished eternal perfection for him and all who obey him.

"For it was fitting that we should have such a high priest, holy, blameless, unstained, separated from sinners, exalted above the heavens. He has no need, like those high priests, to offer sacrifices daily, first for his own sins and then for those of the people; he did this once for all when he offered up himself. Indeed, the law appoints men in their weakness as high priests, but the word of the oath, which came later than the law, appoints a Son who has been made perfect for ever" (7:27f.). There is certainly no conflict between sinlessness and the process by which Jesus was "made perfect."

The followers of the perfect pioneer and priest become in the end a perfect people. Christian maturity may be reached in this life (5:1). By the sacrifice of Jesus the conscience of the worshiper can be made perfect (9:9; 10:1, 14), but complete perfection is reached when all are made perfect together in the consummation (11:40; 12:23). Saints are to persevere toward perfection, "looking to Jesus the pioneer and the perfecter of our faith" (12:2).

Even though Irenaeus used the language of Ephesians 1:10 as he expounded his view of recapitulation, the description of the redemptive work of Jesus was very similar to the process of perfection in Hebrews. He said:

> He came to save all through himself; all, that is, who through him are born into God, infants, children, boys, young men and old. Therefore he passed through every stage of life: he was made an infant for infants, sanctifying infancy; a child among children, sanctifying those of this age, an example also to them of filial affection, righteousness and obedience; a young man amongst young men, an example to them, and sanctifying them to the Lord. So also amongst the older men; that he might be a perfect master for all, not solely in regard to the revelation of the truth, but also in respect of each stage of life (*Against Heresies*, II, xxii, 4).[103]

He then goes on to repeat this theory in terms of the Word of God, the Son of God, and the Son of Man, all of which are in the Gospel of John and Hebrews (III, xviii; V, xxi, 1). In a cosmic and ontological Christology it is difficult to imagine more helpful models today. The New Testament models need to be explained and applied in a scientific age. They are as relevant today as ever.

C. JESUS CHRIST AS THE MEDIATOR OF GOD AND MAN

62. The Deity of Jesus Christ: Truly God

Under the heading of Jesus as the Messiah of Israel, the traditional "three offices" of Christ as prophet, priest and king were discussed in a broader context. The so-called "three states" of Christ were surveyed under the divisions post-existence, pre-existence, and existence in the mystery of godliness. A review and reappraisal of "the two natures" of Christ, so much

---

103. Quoted from Bettenson, *op. cit.*, p. 43.

under fire in much of modern theology, is now in order. More and more an appreciation for Patristic Christology, rightly understood and interpreted, has emerged; so, unashamedly, the questions of the Definition of the Council of Chalcedon in 451 form the outline of the last three sections under the heading of Jesus as the Mediator of God and man: truly God, truly man, one and the same Christ.[104]

The formulation of belief in the exalted Jesus as truly God was established in Patristic Christology, but a clarification of belief in the earthly Jesus as truly man has been delayed until the modern historical study of the Scriptures. A satisfactory model for the unity of Jesus Christ as truly God and truly man in one and the same Christ has not yet gained the status of a consensus.

Some New Testament passages that speak of the exalted Jesus as God have already been noted (2 Thess. 1:12(?); Rom. 9:5(?); Tit. 2:13(?); Heb. 1:7f.(?); 2 Pet. 1:1(?); Acts 20:28(?); John 1:1, 18(?); 8:58; 10:31–39; 20:28). It will be noted that only in the Gospel of John are there passages beyond question in translation or interpretation. It is also important to remember that it was the Logos Christology of John that led to the Patristic affirmation that Jesus is truly God.

The Patristic affirmation developed against the background of attacks from without and of heresies within the church. The major attack from the outside was by a second-century pagan critic named Celsus, about A.D. 178, who confronted the church with the dilemma that "either God really changed himself, as they say, into a mortal body — or he himself is not changed, but makes those who see him think that he is so changed. But in that case he is a deceiver and a liar."[105]

Origen of Alexandria, the great Christian genius of the third century, prepared the way for later controversies in Christology in his effort to answer Celsus. Grillmeier well summarized the situation when he said: "The question was whether God had really entered history while still remaining God, the same problem with which contemporary theology is still engaged, though in a different way, in its debate with Bultmann. The substance of Christianity was at stake."[106]

The heresies of docetism and gnosticism reflected in the criticism of Celsus developed within the church. Docetism denied that Christ had a human body, and gnosticism interpreted Christ in terms of philosophy and theosophy, very much as some attempt to do today. The old controversies

---

104. A classic account in Aloys Grillmeier, *Christ in Christian Tradition*, tr. John Bowden (Atlanta: John Knox Press, 1975), pp. 343-557.
105. Origen, *Contra Celsum* IV, 18, from Grillmeier, *op. cit.*, p. 105.
106. *Ibid.*

are far from irrelevant now, as a study of a recent gnostic library brings to light again.[107]

A second heretical movement went the other way by putting so much emphasis on the unity of God that Jesus was portrayed as God in a human body. This became known as monarchianism. The model forms were the patripassianism that identified Jesus with the Father and the Sabellianism that taught one God in three temporary manifestations. A second form called dynamic monarchianism, associated with Theodotus of Byzantium, held with the Ebionites that Jesus was a mere man adopted as God's Son when he was endued with God's power at his baptism.[108]

The formulation of Chalcedonian Orthodoxy had roots reaching back to Irenaeus of Lyon (c. 130-c. 200) and Athanasius of Alexandria (c. 296-373). Irenaeus believed that Jesus Christ summed up all humanity in himself by the union of God and man. This was his theory of recapitulation.[109]

In many ways Athanasius of Alexandria prepared the way for what later became Chalcedonian Orthodoxy when he wrote his little gem called *The Incarnation of the Word* (318).[110] The fact that the Latin translation speaks of *incarnatione*, meaning in flesh, and the Greek speaks of *enanthrōpēseos*, meaning in a man, reflects the two types of Christology that Grillmeier has so brilliantly called Logos-sarx and Logos-anthropos Christologies.

The formulation of the Definition of Chalcedon was the main subject in the first four ecumenical councils of the church.

The Council of Nicaea, 325

The first ecumenical council of the church was called at Nicaea in 325 to settle the dispute over the teachings of Arius (c. 250-c. 336), a presbyter in the church of Alexandria. He taught what may be called a creature Christology that denied the preaching of Pope Alexander of Alexandria who said: "God always, the Son always; at the same time the Father, at the same time the Son; the Son co-exists with God, unbegotten; he is ever-begotten, he is not born by-begetting; neither by thought nor by any moment of time does God precede the Son; God always, Son always, the Son exists from God himself."[111] Arius believed that "the Son has a beginning."[112]

The response of the Council of Nicaea in 325 has many ramifications,

---

107. James M. Robinson, ed., *The Nag Hammadi Library* (New York: Harper and Row, 1977).
108. Some sources for these heresies are mentioned in Henry Bettenson, *Documents of the Christian Church*, Second Edition (London: Oxford University Press, 1963), pp. 42-55.
109. Henry Bettenson, *op. cit.*, pp. 42f.
110. A handy Greek text is edited by F. L. Cross, *Athanasius De Incarnatione* (London: S.P.C.K., 1939). There is also a beautiful English translation with an introduction by C. S. Lewis (New York: The Macmillan Company, 1946).
111. From his letter to Eusebius, Bishop of Nicomedia, in Henry Bettenson, *op. cit.*, p. 55.
112. *Ibid.*, p. 56.

but the crux of the controversy is found in the Creed of Nicaea. The revisions of the Creed of Caesarea, which are underlined below, have two phrases and two participles that have shaped Christology until the present.

> We believe in one God the Father All-sovereign, maker of all things visible and invisible;
> And in one Lord Jesus Christ, the Son of God, *begotten of the Father*, only-begotten, *that is, of the substance of the Father*, God of God, Light of Light, *true God of true God, begotten not made, of one substance with the Father*, through whom all things were made, *things in heaven and things on earth*; who for us men and for our salvation *came down* and was made flesh, *and became man*, suffered, and rose on the third day, ascended into the heavens, is coming to judge the living and the dead.
> And in the Holy Spirit.

The two phrases destined to become decisive are "of the substance of the Father" (*ek tēs ousias tou patros*), meaning "from the inmost being of the Father," and "of one substance with the Father" (*homoousios tō patri*), meaning sharing one being with the Father.[113]

The two participles are "was made flesh" (*sarkō thentas*), from the Creed of Caesarea, and "was made man" (*enanthrōpēsanta*). The first participle was elaborated in the Logos-flesh Christology of Alexandria and the second in the Logos-man Christology of Antioch.[114]

If one thinks this is so much ecclesiastical politics that has no influence today, a look at Southern Baptist Landmarkism will be a surprise. J. R. Graves, the founder of Landmarkism, made a statement very much like the view of Arius.[115] This is also the view advocated by the Jehovah's Witnesses and perhaps others.

The Council of Constantinople, 381

The second ecumenical council was called at Constantinople in 381 to clarify the controversy caused by the composition Christology of Apollinarius, Bishop of Laodicea. Apollinarius apparently over-reacted against the creature Christology of Arianism and promoted teachings that undermined the full humanity of Jesus.

Apollinarius misused 1 Corinthians 15:45–47 to support his claim that Jesus was a heavenly man unlike the earthly man Adam and all other men. At times he taught a dichotomy of flesh and divine Logos for Jesus and flesh and human spirit (or mind) for other men. The same combination is

---

113. *Ibid.*, p. 35.
114. Grillmeier, pp. 167-442.
115. *The Seven Dispensations*, 1883 (Texarkana, Ark.-Tex.: Baptist Sunday School Committee, 1928), pp. 61f.

also stated in terms of a trichotomy of body, soul and Logos for Jesus and body, soul and spirit for others. This clearly made the historical Jesus a hybrid of half-man and half-God or two-thirds man and one-third God but not truly man. He even compared Jesus to a mule who came from a horse and a donkey.

This heavenly man had only one nature (*mia physis*), and that nature was divine. Two natures in one person was, according to Apollinarius, impossible. He said:

> The created body does not live in separation from the uncreated Godhead, so that one could distinguish a created *physis*, and the uncreated Logos does not dwell in the world in separation from the body, so that one could distinguish the *physis* of the uncreated.[116]

The one nature and the one person were for Apollinarius closely connected.

If the refutation of Apollinarius by Gregory Nazianzus can be trusted, the true humanity of Jesus has been sacrificed in defense of true deity. Expressing later orthodoxy, Gregory said:

> If any one has put his trust in him as a man without a human mind, he is himself devoid of mind and unworthy of salvation. For what he has not assumed he has not healed; it is what is united to his Deity that is saved.[117]

If this refutation by Gregory Nazianzus seems remote from current Christology more attention should be given to the thought of popular piety. Often the views of Apollinarius have been given to candidates for ordination as a test question and many have subscribed to them. That is what they have understood older preachers to be saying. On one occasion a controversy was created by a Bible lesson based on Luke 2:52 that described how Jesus must have learned in his youth. Emotional critics seemed to think that any description of Jesus as "a learner" undermined his deity, despite the hymn in Hebrews 5:7–10.

The Council of Ephesus, 431

The third ecumenical council was called at Ephesus in 431 to consider the conjunction Christology of Nestorius, Bishop of Constantinople. Nestorius compared the union (*synapheia*, conjunction) between Jesus and Christ to that between husband and wife. This Christological question is from the side of the school of Antioch rather than the side of the school of Alexandria, as in the case of Apollinarius. Nestorius was accused of teaching that there were two separate persons in Christ.

116. *Ibid.*, p. 334.
117. Henry Bettenson, *op. cit.*, p. 64.

Following his teacher Theodore of Mopsuestia, Nestorius defended the full manhood of Jesus as well as his full Godhood. In the process he rejected the term *theotokos*, meaning God-bearer, as it had been used by followers of Origen of Alexandria who introduced the term. Nestorius taught that Mary was the mother of Jesus by a virginal conception, but he refused to say that Mary was the mother of God, as much piety today interprets the term. In Latin the term is *Dei Gentrix*, not the more exact translation *deipara*. *Christotokos*, meaning Christ-bearer, was suggested in the place of *theotokos*.

Cyril of Alexandria defended the *theotokos* with zeal and stirred up opposition to Nestorius of Constantinople. Ecclesiastical politics, as usual, got mixed with theology, and the outcome is still a debated question. Theodore of Mopsuestia and Nestorius have been defended as far more in agreement with the Council of Chalcedon twenty years later than was Cyril of Alexandria, although the Council of Ephesus condemned and banished Nestorius.[118]

The Council of Chalcedon, 451

The fourth ecumenical council, at Chalcedon in 451, became crucial for Christology for centuries to come. It was precipitated by the confluent or coalescent Christology of Eutyches, an elderly monk of Constantinople whose anti-Nestorian zeal caused him to conclude that Jesus Christ was *from* two natures but *in* one nature. This was another resurgence of the Christology of Alexandria which emphasized the deity of Christ at the cost of his humanity.

The following statement by Eutyches was the chief cause of his condemnation as a heretic.

> I admit that our Lord was of two natures before the union, but after the union one nature — I follow the doctrine of the blessed Cyril and the holy fathers and the holy Athanasius. They speak of two natures before the union, but after the union and incarnation they speak of one nature not two.[119]

The Council did not agree with his interpretation of Cyril and Athanasius and formulated a definition that affirmed the incarnation with two natures. This was based on a tome by Leo, Bishop of Rome, and came to be known as the Definition of Chalcedon.

This Definition of Chalcedon is so important as a summary that it is quoted below.

---

118. R. A. Norris, *Manhood and Christ: A Study of the Christology of Theodore of Mopsuestia* (Oxford University Press, 1963); cf. A. R. Vine, *An Approach to Christology* (London: Independent Press, 1948).
119. *Ibid.*, p. 69.

(1) Therefore, following the holy Fathers, we all with one accord teach men to acknowledge one and the same Son, our Lord Jesus Christ, at once complete in Godhead and complete in manhood, truly God and truly man, consisting also of a reasonable soul and body; of one substance [ὁμοούσιος] with the Father as regards his Godhead, and at the same time of one substance with us as regards his manhood; like us in all respects, apart from sin; (2) as regards his Godhead, begotten of the Father before the ages, but yet as regards his manhood begotten, for us men and for our salvation, of Mary the Virgin, the God-bearer [θεοτόκος]; (3) one and the same Christ, Son, Lord, Only-begotten, recognized IN TWO NATURES, WITHOUT CONFUSION, WITHOUT CHANGE, WITHOUT DIVISION, WITHOUT SEPARATION;* the distinction of natures being in no way annulled by the union, but rather the characteristics of each nature being preserved and coming together to form one person and subsistence [ὑπόστασις], not as parted or separated into two persons, but one and the same Son and Only-begotten God the Word, Lord Jesus Christ; even as the prophets from earliest times spoke of him, and our Lord Jesus Christ himself taught us, and the creed of the Fathers has handed down to us.[120]

The part of the definition marked (1) is a refutation of both Arianism and Apollinarianism with a distinctive Chalcedonian statement. The reference to Jesus as "complete in Godhead and complete in manhood, truly God and truly Man" is the basic affirmation of Chalcedon, but the reference to "a reasonable soul and body" is a refutation of Apollinarianism which denied that Jesus had a human mind.

The part marked (2) is a refutation of Nestorianism as the Council understood Nestorius. It has statements difficult to harmonize with New Testament teachings. The statement about Christ being "begotten before the ages" reflects neo-Platonic philosophy and can be interpreted in agreement with Arianism. The *theotokos*, God-bearer, could be clearer by saying Mary bore the one in whom God fully dwelt. She did not give birth to God, and the Son of God, not God, died on the cross.

The part marked (3) is very satisfactory with the exception of the further reference to "only-begotten." The idea that Christ was begotten "before the ages" is a mistranslation of the *monogenēs* of the New Testament and a misunderstanding of the Johannine teaching of the eternal Son of God and the uniqueness of Jesus in relation to God. In Johannine teachings it is

*ἐν δύο Φυσεσιν, ἀσυγχύτως, ἀτρέπτως, ἀδιαιρέτως ἀχωπίστως.
120. *Ibid.*, p. 73.

the children of God who have a beginning and are begotten, but the Son of God is eternal and never begotten.[121]

The strong affirmation of Jesus Christ as "complete in Godhead and complete in manhood, truly God and truly man" is fully clarified by the recognition of Jesus Christ as "IN TWO NATURES, WITHOUT CONFUSION, WITHOUT CHANGE, WITHOUT DIVISION, WITHOUT SEPARATION," but the unsatisfactory statements in the definition led to an emphasis on Jesus Christ as "truly God" at the expense of the belief that he was "truly man."

After Chalcedon two movements developed that revealed the loss of the true humanity of Jesus. One was the monophysitism which taught that the Incarnate Son of God had only one nature and that divine. This came into existence after Chalcedon and in opposition to Chalcedon. It really represented an advanced type of the Christology of Cyril of Alexandria who worked so hard to get Nestorius condemned. Nestorius accepted the Definition of Chalcedon as his own before he died in 451.[122]

The second movement was the monotheletism that taught the two natures but denied the two wills of Jesus and God. Only one mode of activity (*mia energeia*) was recognized, and this was later interpreted as one will.[123] A man without a human will is no better than a man without a human mind. It was this tendency in Patristic Christology that made it necessary to recover the full humanity of Jesus in modern thought.

63. The Humanity of Jesus Christ: Truly Man

The balanced Chalcedonian Christology continued in creedal language, but in actual thought and practice the belief that Jesus was "truly God" triumphed over the belief that he was also "truly man." More and more the Virgin Mary was viewed as a goddess and Jesus as a god.

It was not until the modern view of ideal humanity gained prominence that a search for the historical Jesus began. Even then the historical Jesus was subordinated to the view of humanity that the particular writer embraced. This was abruptly brought to a halt by the publication of Albert Schweitzer's *Von Reimarus zu Wrede* in 1906.[124]

A brief retreat from the quest took place under the influence of the neo-orthodoxy of such writers as Karl Barth, Emil Brunner, Rudolf Bultmann and Paul Tillich between the two world wars, but a new thaw began

---

121. See my article "Only Begotten" in *The Interpreter's Dictionary of the Bible* (Nashville: Abingdon Press, 1962), Vol. 3, p. 604.
122. *Oxford Dictionary of the Christian Church*, Second Edition (London: Oxford University Press, 1974), pp. 931f.
123. *Ibid.*, p. 932.
124. Translated into English by W. Montgomery as *The Quest of the Historical Jesus*, Second Edition (London: A. and C. Black, 1910); cf. C. C. McCowin, *The Search for the Real Jesus* (New York: Charles Scribner's Sons, 1940).

after the Second World War. One of the first signs of spring was *God Was in Christ* by D. M. Baillie in 1948.[125] The floods came after the publication of "The Problem of the Historical Jesus," which was first delivered as an address by Ernst Käsemann to a gathering of Rudolf Bultmann's friends and students.[126] Of course, arguments against the historicity of Jesus still appear, but few take them seriously.[127]

Against the background of the new search for the historical Jesus, a new emphasis on Jesus as "truly man" has begun, and the place to begin is with the witness of the New Testament. What does it mean to be "truly human"? It would be most interesting to know how many answers would be given to this question, but a preliminary answer should be given here to avoid misunderstanding of much that follows. Here it is, straight out of the New Testament. A true man is one who loves God with all his heart, soul, strength and mind and his neighbor as himself. If these familiar New Testament words need translation, perhaps a statement about complete openness of life before God and man will help.

The Christian faith seems in many ways to be saying that Jesus was the only perfect man who ever lived out his life to the end in complete devotion to both God and others. He was truly the man for others to imitate and follow in order to fulfill their humanity. This does not mean "he was as much God as if he were not man and as much man as if he were not God," as is so often said, but that God is most fully known in relation to man and man in relation to God. Apart from man God is not fully revealed and apart from God man is not fully realized. With God in a man, Jesus Christ, it may be said, in the words of the creed of Chalcedon: "We all with one accord teach men to acknowledge one and the same Son, our Lord Jesus Christ, at once complete in Godhead and complete in manhood, truly God and truly man." In the light of New Testament teachings and its relevance to the human situation, it seems best to explore now the affirmation that Jesus was truly human, the man for others and the man for God.

Jesus as the Man for Others

How can one say Jesus was one of us, without sin against man or God? The Gospels portray this oneness and openness in three basic ways which we will discuss in reverse order: his birth, his temptation, and his death.

The humanity of Jesus is manifested most of all in his death on the cross. It has already been noted how the Gospel of Mark is a passion narrative with an introduction. Jesus died as a God-forsaken man and with-

125. (New York: Charles Scribner's Sons).
126. James M. Robinson, *A New Quest of the Historical Jesus* (London: SCM, 1959); Leander E. Keck, *A Future for the Historical Jesus* (Nashville: Abingdon Press, 1971).
127. Herbert G. Wood, *Did Jesus Really Live?* (London: SCM, 1938); G. A. Wells, *Did Jesus Exist?* (London: Elek Books, 1975).

out the resurrection he was a victim of human circumstances and nothing more. With his resurrection he was a man who died for others, and this was the supreme revelation of his humanity *and* his deity.

The Gospels of Matthew and Luke repeat the portrayal of Jesus as one who died as other men die, but the temptation of Jesus as a man and as the Messiah destined to save men is expanded in details not found in Mark (Matt. 4:11 = Luke 4:1–13). The order of details is slightly different in that Luke gives the temptations in a different order from Matthew, but both make clear that he was victorious over the threefold temptation of the lust of the flesh, the lust of the eyes and the pride of life as displayed in Genesis 3:1ff. and summarized in 1 John 2:16.

The Gospel of Luke goes beyond the Gospels of Mark and Matthew in its emphasis on Jesus as a Spirit-filled man who was able to overcome temptation and live a victorious life. As it is summarized in Acts, his ministry in Galilee and in Jerusalem was made possible because "God anointed Jesus of Nazareth with the Holy Spirit and with power" (10:38). It is not possible to reduce the passion of Jesus to a Spirit Christology alone, but it is surely an important point in his true humanity.[128]

The Gospels of Matthew and Luke also focus on the birth of Jesus. They testify that his birth was due to a virginal conception, but the major point is that he was born as other men are born. It is unfortunate that the term virgin birth has been used rather than the term virginal conception or miraculous conception, for the theory of the perpetual virginity of Mary, the mother of Jesus, denies that Jesus was born as other men are born. Jerome, who first formulated the doctrine of the perpetual virginity of Mary, taught that Jesus passed through the wall of Mary's womb in the same way he passed through the wall of Joseph's tomb, and that sounds more like Greek mythology than New Testament Christology (Jerome, *Against Helvidius*, 2; *Against Jovinianus*, I. 31).

It is really strange to see Protestant Christians defending the Roman Catholic view of the virgin birth, yet Martin Luther and many of his followers taught the perpetual virginity of Mary. Many years ago, when there was a controversy raging over the translation of Isaiah 7:14 in the RSV, I wrote a number of articles that proposed the term "miraculous conception" as a more exact way to describe the birth of Jesus, but there was considerable reaction about dropping the Roman Catholic term virgin birth.[129] It is interesting indeed to see a Roman Catholic scholar using the term virginal

128. G. W. Lampe, "The Holy Spirit and the Passion of Christ" in *Christ, Faith and History*, edited by S. W. Sykes and J. P. Clayton (Cambridge: Cambridge University Press, 1972), pp. 111-130.
129. *Review and Expositor*, LI, No. 4 (Oct., 1954), pp. 495-507; LII, No. 1 (Jan., 1955), pp. 44-54; LXI, No. 2 (July, 1955), pp. 310-324.

conception in what is a careful statement of his case.[130] The miracle did take place at conception nine months before birth. There was no human father in Nazareth, but the birth itself in Bethlehem was as natural as any other birth. The four sons and at least two daughters of Mary were conceived in a natural way.[131]

In the early church the emphasis on the virginal conception of Jesus was intended to refute the Gnostic denial of the complete humanity of Jesus. The Gallican version of the Apostles' Creed in the sixth century has seven assertions that make the true humanity of Jesus a bulwark against heresy.

> I also believe in Jesus Christ his only son, our Lord, conceived of the Holy Spirit, born of the Virgin Mary, suffered under Pontius Pilate, crucified, dead and buried; he descended into hell, rose again the third day.

Actually all three parts of the Apostles' Creed intend to put an end to Gnosticism.

In modern theology attacks have been made upon belief in the virginal conception of Jesus. This has been a part of the skepticism toward the miraculous in general, the use of Isaiah 7:14 in Matthew 1:23, the lack of references outside of Matthew and Luke, and belief in the humanity of Jesus.[132] The reasons for belief in miracles was discussed in Part IV. The belief in the virginal conception of Jesus does not depend upon the translation of Isaiah 7:14. Most of all, the importance of the birth of Jesus in the New Testament and the early church grew out of concern for his humanity over against Docetism and Gnosticism.[133]

Jesus as the Man for God

The ontic Christology of pre-existence and incarnation continues to emphasize the full humanity of Jesus in his birth, temptation and death. The humanity of Jesus manifested in his birth is a special concern in the writings of Paul. Nothing is said about a virginal conception but the hymn in Galatians 4:4–6 makes much of the Son of God becoming man by being born of a woman and born under the law. Under the law the curse of God was upon him in his death (3:13).

130. Raymond E. Brown, *The Virginal Conception and Bodily Resurrection of Jesus* (New York: Paulist Press, 1973), pp. 21-68.
131. For a review of the problems involved see my article "Virgin Birth" in *The Interpreter's Dictionary of the Bible* (Nashville: Abingdon Press, 1962), Vol. 4, pp. 789-791 and the additional article on the subject by Raymond E. Brown in the Supplementary Volume (Nashville: Abingdon Press, 1976), pp. 940f. The classic study on the birth narratives in Matthew and Luke is Raymond E. Brown, *The Birth of the Messiah* (Garden City, New York: Doubleday & Company, 1977).
132. Thomas Boslooper, *The Virgin Birth* (Philadelphia: The Westminster Press, 1962).
133. Hans von Campenhausen, *The Virgin Birth in the Theology of the Early Church*, tr. Frank Clarke (London: SCM, 1964).

The hymn in Romans 8:1–4 says that God sent forth his Son in the likeness of human flesh. This does not mean that Jesus was guilty of personal sin. This has been argued on the basis of 2 Corinthians 5:21, but that contradicts the claim that Jesus was made an offering for sin, although he "knew no sin." Nels Ferré repeatedly made the superficial claim that rebellion is a first necessity for freedom.[134] The very opposite seems to be true, for true freedom is found in obedience and lost in disobedience. Jesus lived a life of perfect freedom because of his perfect obedience to the Father's will. Sin is not essential to full humanity. The truly human involves obedience and love.

Karl Barth asserted that Jesus had a "fallen human nature" and that is what Paul meant when he said the Son of God came in the likeness of human flesh. D. M. Baillie is not too severe when he identifies this with Spanish adoptionism, the theology of the early nineteenth century represented by Gottfried Menken of Bremen, Germany, and the views of the Scottish Edward Irving, founder of a charismatic and chiliastic sect in nineteenth-century London.[135] It was the sinless humanity of Jesus that made him the only true man who ever lived. If man is made for God, as Augustine said so eloquently at the beginning of his *Confessions*, then it is only in obedience to God that man is fully human. Jesus was a man and the Man for God.

The fullness of humanity is found only in the fullness of deity. True man is man truly indwelt by God. That Jesus Christ was, and in him the fullness of our humanity is realized. "For in him dwells the whole fullness of deity bodily, and you have come to fullness of life in him, who is the head of all rule and authority" (Col. 2:9f.).

The general epistles of the New Testament proclaim the sinless humanity of Jesus in obedience to God. The paschal letter called 1 Peter portrays Jesus as a Lamb "without blemish" (1:19) and as one "who committed no sin" (2:22).

At no place in the New Testament is the true humanity of Jesus more fully stated than in the Letter to the Hebrews. God's intention in man was not fulfilled until Jesus came (2:5–18). In the life of Jesus that was obedient unto death, true humanity was first fully realized. The apostle Paul called Jesus "the first-born among many brethren" (Rom. 8:29), but a full portrait of Brother Jesus is painted in him who was made perfect in suffering (Heb. 2:10–18).

If so many did not follow the false teaching of M. R. De Haan, it would hardly be worth mentioning, but such nonsense is proclaimed from the lips of many a Fundamentalist preacher. On the basis of a note in the Scofield Reference Bible on Hebrews 2:14 De Haan asserted that the Greek word *metechō* means "to take part but not all." Consequently, De Haan declares,

---

134. *Evil and the Christian Faith* (New York: Harper & Brothers, 1943), pp. 34f.
135. *God Was in Christ* (New York: Charles Scribner's Sons, 1948), pp. 16f.

"The blood was the result of supernatural conception."[136] This not only sounds like the Greek mythology which spoke of gods eating ambrosia and drinking nectar to produce ichor in their veins, it undermines the statement that Jesus became like his brethren "in every respect" (*kata panta*, 2:17). The RSV has clarified the meaning with the translation: "Since therefore the children share flesh and blood, he himself likewise partook of the same nature" (2:14).

The one point where Jesus was different from his brethren was manifested in his temptations. "For we have not a high priest who is unable to sympathize with our weakness, but one who in every respect has been tempted as we are, yet without sinning" (4:15). This *chōris hamartias* (without sinning) has the same meaning as *mē gnonta hamartian* (not knowing sin) in 2 Corinthians 5:21. Jesus was "without blemish" (Heb. 9:14; cf. 1 Pet. 1:19).

The true humanity was most manifest in his experience. Before the cry of dereliction on the cross (Mark 15:34), Jesus in Gethsemane said to his disciples: "My soul is very sorrowful, even to death" (14:34). This theme of true humanity finds celebrated expression in a hymn in the Letter to the Hebrews (5:7–8):

> *In the days of his flesh,*
> > *Jesus offered up prayers and supplications*
> > > *(with loud cries and tears)*
> *to him who was able to save him from death,*
> > *and he was heard for his godly fear.*
> *Although he was a Son,*
> > *he learned obedience through what he suffered.*

The humanity of birth and temptation was most fully revealed in death.

The true humanity of Jesus in the Johannine writings follows the pattern of birth in the flesh, the emotions of human life and the agony of human death. When the Gospel of John speaks of the Logos becoming flesh it means that the Logos came to dwell in a man, "the only Son from the Father" (1:14). Throughout this Gospel flesh always means what is human (1:13; 3:6; 6:51–63; 8:15; 17:2).

The emotions of the human life of Jesus are mentioned as a matter of course in John's Gospel. Jesus, "wearied as he was with his journey, sat down beside the well" (4:6). At the tomb of Lazarus, Jesus seems as human as Mary and the other Jews. "When Jesus saw her weeping, and the Jews who came with her also weeping, he was deeply moved in spirit and troubled. . . . Jesus wept" (11:33–35).

Three or four of the sayings of Jesus on the cross underline his death

---

136. *The Chemistry of the Blood* (Grand Rapids, Michigan: Zondervan Publishing House, 1943), pp. 35f.

as a human death (19:25–30). What could be more human than the water and the blood that flowed from the side of Jesus when a soldier thrust a spear into his side (19:31–37)? What could be more human than his burial by Joseph of Arimathea and Nicodemus (19:38–42)? Yet the resurrection which followed confirmed him as Son of God and Messiah (20:1–30).

64. The Unity of Jesus Christ: One and the Same Lord

As modern biblical studies began to search for the historical Jesus and recover his humanity, several types of Christology developed in order to relate the historical and human Jesus to the living God his heavenly Father. This concern over the unity of Jesus Christ with God followed three major approaches, all of which claimed support from the New Testament. These may be called (1) the *gnosis* type that focused on the intimate and unique knowledge that related Jesus as Son to God as Father, (2) the *kenosis* type that focused on how the eternal Son of God emptied himself into the historical Jesus, and (3) the *skenosis* type that tried to clarify how the Logos indwelt the man Jesus.

The Gnosis Model

The *gnosis* type tried to recover the Jesus behind the Synoptic Gospels and Acts where there was no talk of pre-existence and the incarnation of an ontological Son. In general the nineteenth century often portrayed Jesus as a God-conscious man, while the twentieth put more emphasis on him as a Spirit-filled man.

The portrait of Jesus as a man with a unique knowledge of God often relied on the Q sayings in Matthew 11:25–27 = Luke 10:21–22, which were believed to be the oldest source in the Synoptic Gospels. This has also been called a Johannine bolt in the Synoptic sky, but this is hardly true, since no reference is made to pre-existence. It does describe Jesus as a man who knew God as Father in a unique way and experienced spiritual ecstasy. This is especially true in the Lucan form that says that Jesus "rejoiced in the Spirit and said:

> *I thank thee, Father, Lord of heaven and earth,*
> > *that thou hast hidden these things from the wise and*
> > > *understanding*
> > *and revealed them to babes;*
> > > *yea, Father, for such was thy gracious will.*
> *All things have been delivered to me by my Father,*
> > *and no one knows who the Son is except the Father,*
> > > *or who the Father is except the Son*
> > > > *and any one to whom the Son chooses to reveal him.*

Nineteenth-century liberalism began with an emphasis on Jesus' unique

God-consciousness. This was especially true in the Christology of F. D. E. Schleiermacher (1768-1834). By the end of the century William Sanday (1843-1920) was teaching that God was present in Jesus' unconscious life in such a way that he was unable to sin but did not know it![137] This, however, relects the influence of the *kenosis* view that follows.

Twentieth-century Christology has seen the development of a Spirit-Christology that sees Jesus as a Spirit-filled man.[138] Joachim Jeremias described Jesus as the prophet in whom the quenched Spirit returned with power.[139] James D. G. Dunn has developed this theme in detail.[140] The most recent exploration into this unity of the Spirit between Jesus and God is the Bampton Lecturers by G. W. Lampe to which reference has frequently been made in the earlier pages of this part.[141] Lampe is more satisfactory on this point than in some of his reductionism in related matters.

The Kenosis Model

The *kenosis* type of Christology tried to recover the unity between the eternal Son of God and the historical Jesus by interpreting the emptying of the Son of God into Jesus Christ in Philippians 2:7 as the laying aside of such attributes as omnipotence, omniscience, and omnipresence in order for Jesus to become man. The three "omnis" were called relational attributes in distinction from the immanent attributes of power, truth, holiness and love, which were retained. This was the teaching of the Lutheran theologian Gottfried Thomasius (1802-1875) in his work *Christi Person und Werk* (three volumes, 1845, 1852-61).

This theme was introduced into British theology in the Cunningham Lectures of A. B. Bruce, *The Humiliation of Christ* (1876). This enabled theologians to recognize a limitation to the knowledge of Jesus on many matters without a denial of the unity of deity and humanity in him, but it precipitated much conflict between critical liberals and conservative orthodoxy.[142]

It also stimulated some profound Christological reflection when there was a shift from metaphysics to morals. One of these was *The Person and Place of Jesus Christ* (1909) by P. T. Forsyth. Forsyth believed that the three "omnis" in *kenosis* Christology were *retracted* in the historical Jesus,

---

137. William Sanday, *Christologies Ancient and Modern* (Oxford: The Clarendon Press, 1910).
138. Cf. my book *Spirit of the Living God*, Revised Edition (Nashville: Broadman Press, 1976), pp. 33-57.
139. *New Testament Theology*, tr. John Bowden (New York: Charles Scribner's Sons, 1971), pp. 76-85.
140. *Jesus and the Spirit* (London: SCM Press, 1975), pp. 11-92.
141. *God as Spirit* (Oxford: Oxford University Press, 1977).
142. J. S. Lawton, *Conflict in Christology* (London: S.P.C.K., 1947). Reference should be made to this volume for most of the theologians involved.

but they remained *potential* so that they could be called forth at any time. To the *kenosis* idea from Philippians 2:7 he added the *plerosis* (fulfilling) idea of Colossians 2:9. To him there was both a self-emptying and a self-fulfillment of the pre-existent Christ in the incarnation. He called this the moralizing of dogma, a reflection of the influence of the nineteenth-century liberalism that exalted ethics above metaphysical speculation.

Kenosis Christology moved beyond both metaphysics and morals when Donald G. Dawe adopted what he called a new key. Building on the theology of Karl Barth who interpreted God in the light of the *kenosis* of Jesus rather than Jesus in the light of God as Being, Dawe followed a view that was not so new, for it was used by the left-wing Hegelians of the nineteenth-century. This was a shift from the mediating theologians who, in order to retain contact with conservative orthodoxy, spoke of the *kenosis* of Christ, to the Hegelian idea of a *kenosis* of God in both creation and redemption.[143] Both Emil Brunner and Karl Barth used this motif, but they well-nigh lost the historical Jesus in the process.[144] A few Christologians such as Norman Pittenger saw the weakness of Brunner and Barth, but there are some who still dance to their tune even after the death of God has been declared.

Pandemonium broke loose when the death of God theologians pushed the idea of the *kenosis* of God to a radical extreme with a gospel of Christian atheism.[145] With the mythological idea of the radical *kenosis* of God, which they accepted, combined with what they called the myth of the resurrection, which was rejected, they were ready for the requiem mass of God. If the transcendent God metamorphosed himself completely into the man Jesus, as the radical *kenosis* of God required, and if there was no historical resurrection of the historical Jesus, then the death of God was a logical conclusion. With Karl Barth's radical *kenosis* of God and Rudolf Bultmann's belief in the resurrection as a myth, a potent potion had accomplished the euthanasia of deity, leaving only humanity for our devotions.

Before fundamentalists engage in premature self-righteousness, let it be said that the idea that Jesus was "God in a bod," an idea reaching back to Cyril of Alexandria, escaped the conclusions drawn by the death of God theologians only because they were not logical. If Mary gave birth to God, as the *theotokos* idea of the Council of Ephesus in 431 asserted, then God

---

143. *The Form of a Servant* (Philadelphia: The Westminster Press, 1963). This book is the best history of *kenosis* Christology.

144. John Thompson, *Christ in Perspective* (Grand Rapids, Mich.: Wm. B. Eerdmans, 1978).

145. See especially Thomas J. J. Altizer, *The Gospel of Christian Atheism* (Philadelphia: The Westminster Press, 1966); *The Descent into Hell* (New York: Lippincott, 1970); *The Self-Embodiment of God* (New York: Harper and Row, 1977). A milder effort on the *kenosis* of God as a controlling principle in theology is John Macquarrie, *The Humility of God* (Philadelphia: The Westminster Press, 1978), but even this raises more questions than it answers.

died on a cross and there was no God left to raise him from the dead. Even if Protestant orthodoxy and neo-orthodoxy have often hitched their theological wagon to the *kenosis* idea, it is doubtful that it is as satisfactory as the *skenosis* (indwelling) idea that follows. It is a dangerous day when the *kenosis* idea is considered *the* Protestant view while the *skenosis* idea is rejected as the Catholic view.

The Skenosis Model

Anglican Christology has led the way in the reinterpretation of the *skenosis* type in Christology. The biblical basis for this has been the Gospel of John, as in the Church Fathers so highly regarded by Anglicans. What is here called the *skenosis* type is anchored to the Johannine text which says (1:14):

> *And the Word became flesh*
> *and dwelt among us,*
> *and we beheld his glory,*
> *glory as of the only Son from the Father.*

This translation intends to emphasize that "became" is to be interpreted in the light of "dwelt" and that the manifest presence of the Logos, the glory, is recalled as the tabernacling presence, the Hebrew *shekinah* (Divine Presence). God fully indwelt a man.

The best example of this effort to unite Jesus to God in English Anglicanism is perhaps found in the writings of the Mirfield monk, Lionel S. Thornton of the Community of the Resurrection, founded by Charles Gore. Thornton attempted a reinterpretation of incarnation that made room for *kenosis*, but it was the *skenosis*, the indwelling of God in a man, that meant most to him. He very early came to grips with the classic cosmology of A. N. Whitehead most fully expressed in his Gifford Lectures at the University of Edinburgh (1927-28) and published as *Process and Reality* (1929).

Thornton accepted Whitehead's organic model for the world until he came to the person of Jesus Christ, but at that point he insisted that Jesus was different. "Jesus Christ," he said, "is not the product of history in its cumulative development. He stands within its succession; but He entered it from beyond."[146] His book *The Common Life in the Body of Christ* (1942) was a work that saw a continuation of the incarnation in the church, and this accounts for his rather "high" view of the church. This point of view is elaborated in his three-volume study *The Form of the Servant: Revelation and the Modern World* (1950), *The Dominion of Christ* (1952), and *Christ and the Church* (1955).

It was this idea of transcendence that was challenged by the American

146. *The Incarnate Lord* (London: Longmans, Green and Co., 1928), p. 164.

Anglican W. Norman Pittenger. Pittenger did not see the need for an intrusion from the beyond because he believed that God's creative action has been immanent in the world from the beginning of creation. He heard a Eutychian ring in Thornton's bell that separated the incarnation of God in the man Jesus from the action of God in the rest of the world.[147]

Pittenger will have no part in the argument that the presence of God in Jesus was of a different "kind" from the incarnation of God in creation, the church and the Christian. The difference is one of degree rather than kind, of focus rather than transcendent intrusion.[148] His humanity was our humanity and his God was our God, but the union was a unique event and a perfect focus in God's revelation of himself in man.

John Knox, an American Methodist who "converted" to Anglicanism, seems to agree with Pittenger's view of the incarnation when he says Jesus was "the historical locus of God's action in Christ."[149] Knox sees the unique event as social, since Jesus was in the midst of his own. This view can adapt to the most radical form of biblical criticism, but this is not necessary. Both Pittenger and Knox do preserve the full humanity of Jesus without sacrificing his unique relation to God.

The American Methodist David R. Griffin has argued that Pittenger destroyed the belief in the incarnation as the supreme act of God. Griffin argued that the very content of God's aims in Jesus was unique, but this could lead to a revival of the Alexandrian Christology of Cyril who all but lost the humanity of Jesus.[150] It is rather Griffin's colleague John Cobb who threatens the uniqueness of Jesus by his preoccupation with Buddhism as a pluralistic parallel with the action of God in Jesus. Cobb seems to call for a merger between Christianity and Buddhism which would result in an ecumenical Eutychianism that would remove the uniqueness of God's action in Jesus altogether.[151]

If there is a Theodore of Mopsuestia in recent Christology it must surely be Norman Pittenger, for Pittenger revives the very marital model of Theodore, who compared the unity between God and Jesus to that of the unity between husband and wife who became one in will and love. For Pittenger God is the great cosmic Lover who lured Jesus on to do his will in every word and deed so that Jesus can be called the incarnation of God in a man. Briefly, according to Pittenger: "The *most complete, integrated* union of Godhead and manhood which is conceivable is precisely one in which by gracious indwelling of God in man and by man's free response in

---

147. *The Word Incarnate* (New York: Harper and Brothers, 1959), pp. 108f.
148. *Christology Reconsidered* (London: SCM, 1970), pp. 111-133.
149. *The Humanity and Divinity of Christ* (Cambridge: Cambridge University Press, 1967), p. 112.
150. *A Process Christology* (Philadelphia: The Westminster Press, 1973), pp. 262f.
151. *Christ in a Pluralistic Age* (Philadelphia: The Westminster Press, 1975).

surrender and love" there is found true unity.[152] This is the heart of the *skenosis* Christology which comes nearest to keeping the person of Christ in balance. It is Chalcedon in a contemporary setting.

In case it has not already become clear by now, let it be said that a firm conviction abides that it was Cyril of Alexandria, not Nestorius, who should have been rejected at the Council of Ephesus in 431. It is also clear that Theodore of Mopsuestia was much nearer the Definition of Chalcedon than was Cyril. A critical Chalcedonian Christology, based on the Johannine Logos, is still the most adequate way to state the unity between God and Jesus Christ.

152. *The Word Incarnate*, p. 188; cf. Gilbert L. Sanders, "The Christology of W. Norman Pittenger: A Summary and a Critique" (SBTS doctoral dissertation, 1978). See Pittenger's own summary in "The Incarnation Process Theology," *Review and Expositor*, Vol. LXXI, No. 1 (Winter, 1974), pp. 43-47. Other essays in this unusual issue on "Christology" are good summaries.

IX. THE CHURCH

65. The Mission of the Church

Mission is basic to the meaning of the church. Indeed, the church is mission, and where there is no mission there is no church. God has called the church out from the world to send her back into the world with a message and a mission.

Mission is a part of the Old Testament covenant concept that prepared the way for the New Testament *ekklēsia*, the word translated church in English. The group of Anglo-Saxon words for church are derived from a late Greek word *kyriakon*, meaning the Lord's house (cf. 1 Corinthians 11:20 where it is used in the Lord's Supper).

The Greek word *ekklēsia* was the name of the classical Greek assembly that gathered together for deliberative purposes (cf. Acts 19:39-41 for the assembly in Ephesus). When the Old Testament was translated into Greek, *ekklēsia* was used to translate the Hebrew *qahal* which with the Hebrew word *edah* signified the religious assembly of Israel; but *edah* is usually rendered by the Greek *synagogē*, synagogue in English.

Even when the disciples were scattered under the pressure of persecution, the church of Jerusalem remained one (Acts 9:31). The first Christian *ekklēsia* was in Jerusalem. This included all the believers in Jesus as the Messiah, but there was no final break between the Jewish assembly in Jerusalem and the Christian assembly until the temple was destroyed in A.D. 70. Until that time the followers of Jesus were looked upon as a sect within Judaism, Nazarenes along with the Sadducees and Pharisees (Acts 5:17; 15:5; 24:5; 28:22).

According to the Gospel of Matthew, the founding of the Christian *ekklēsia* goes back to the ministry of Jesus. For this and other reasons Matthew has been called the "ecclesiastical" Gospel. Concern for the universal mission is obvious in the prologue (1, 2), which begins the genealogy with Abraham. The first of the five "books" (4-7), on discipleship, has a special concern with the Gospel that includes Galilee of the Gentiles (4:15).

Book two (8-10), on apostleship, records the choice of the twelve dis-

427

ciples who were sent forth to call Israel to repentance before the Gospel could be proclaimed to the Gentiles. Book Three (11–13) describes the offer of the kingdom to Israel and the consequences that will follow its rejection.

It is the fourth "book" (14–18), on the church, that comes to focus on the founding and fellowship of the *ekklēsia*. Debate over the primacy of Peter and the claim that the Popes of Rome have been his successors has made Matthew 16:16b–19 one of the most controversial passages in the New Testament, and the issues are by no means settled in the most ecumenical efforts toward unity.[1]

The fact that the saying on the founding of the *ekklēsia* is found only in the Gospel of Matthew by no means rules it out as if it is an unhistorical redaction. The passage is one of the most Aramaic passages in Matthew, and the background of the Dead Sea Scrolls shows that belief in "the assembly of God" *(qehal El)* in a time of apocalyptic hope is not impossible. Furthermore, the identification of Christ with the rock *(petra)* upon which the *ekklēsia* is built is not to be dismissed lightly, especially since 1 Corinthians 10:4 and perhaps 1 Peter 2:8 make such identification.[2]

The teaching section on the fellowship of *ekklēsia* (18) does anticipate an organized and disciplined community, but this too has parallels in the Qumran community (18:15–17).

The fifth "book" (20–25), on the judgment, does have some strong statements about the repudiation of Israel because of their rejection of Jesus as the Messiah. Much is made of Matthew 21:43 which says the kingdom was taken away from Israel and "given to a nation producing the fruit of it." The disciples, the heirs of the kingdom, are therefore, in the epilogue (26–28), commissioned in Galilee to "make disciples of all nations" (28:18, 19).

Emphasis on the rejection of Israel to the exclusion of some future promises has led to shameful anti-Semitism in Christianity. It should not be forgotten that Jesus also taught that before the consummation "the time of the Gentiles" would come to an end (Luke 21:24). This is in harmony with Paul's teaching that God is able to graft the natural branches, Israel, back into the old olive tree, God's people, when they come to recognize Jesus as the Messiah (Romans 11:12, 25–36).

Against the background of God's assembly in the Old Testament and of Christ's assembly in the Gospel of Matthew, the mission of the New Testament church, and all churches that follow a New Testament model, may be summarized in a threefold way: as *martyria* (witness), *diakonia* (service) and *koinōnia* (fellowship).

1. See the collaborative study by both Protestant and Catholic scholars, edited by Raymond E. Brown, Karl P. Donfried and John Reumann, *Peter in the New Testament* (Minneapolis: Augsburg Publishing House, 1973), pp. 83-101.
2. *Ibid.*, pp. 92f.

The Mission of Martyria (Witness): The Petrine Tradition

Witness is the primary mission of the church in all situations, but this is a special concern in the Petrine tradition. This does not mean the Petrine tradition is unconcerned with service and fellowship, but witness is primary. One can hardly miss this motif when reading carefully Acts 1–2, 1 Peter and the Gospel of Mark, the three major sources for the Petrine teachings.

Before the Day of Pentecost the promise was made to the disciples by the risen Lord: "But you shall receive power when the Holy Spirit has come upon you; and you shall be my witnesses in Jerusalem and in all Judea and Samaria and to the end of the earth" (Acts 1:8). Matthias was chosen over Joseph to succeed Judas Iscariot as one of the twelve because, as Peter said: "One of these men must become with us a witness to his resurrection" (1:22).

After Pentecost, Peter preached: "This Jesus God raised up, and of that we all are witnesses" (2:32). On Solomon's Porch, Peter identified Jesus with the suffering Servant of Isaiah 53:12. This belief was based on the fact that God raised Jesus from the dead. "To this we are witnesses," proclaimed Peter (3:15). To their witness about the empty tomb and the appearances of Jesus over a period of forty days, a third witness, that of the Holy Spirit, was added. In summary, Peter said to the Sanhedrin: "And we are witnesses of these things, and so is the Holy Spirit whom God has given to those who obey him" (5:32).

There are six "books" in Acts. Each closes with a summary on the spread of the gospel (6:7; 9:31; 12:24; 16:5; 19:20; 28:30f.). The climax of his crusade was before the household of Cornelius, the first Gentile convert. Peter's preaching was that: "We are witnesses to all that he did both in the country of the Jews and in Jerusalem. They put him to death by hanging him on a tree; but God raised him on the third day and made him manifest, not to all the people but to us who were chosen of God as witnesses, who ate and drank with him after he rose from the dead" (10:39–41). The primacy of the witness of Peter and the twelve was preached by Paul, although he believed he had been chosen as a special witness to the Gentiles (13:31; 22:15; 26:16).

In the second part (2:11–4:11) of the paschal letter of 1 Peter, written by Silvanus for Peter soon after the burning of Rome in A.D. 64, Peter portrays Jesus as the suffering Servant in a hymn (2:21–25) that is almost a composite of Isaiah 53:5–12. After an exhortation to be ready to make an *apologia* (defense) of the faith in times of persecution, a second hymn in the third part portrays the church as the household of God (4:12–19) and the flock of God (5:1–11), and Peter portrays himself "as a fellow elder and a witness of the sufferings of Christ" (5:1).

The Gospel of Mark does not use the word "witness" to describe the preaching of the disciples, as does Luke (24:48), but the whole Gospel is a witness to the belief that Jesus was in his death the suffering Servant (Mark 10:45). The first half of the Gospel is about the secret of the Son of God (1:1–8:26), and the second part identifies Jesus as the Son of God and Son of Man with the suffering Servant (8:27–16:7).

The Mission of Diakonia (Service): The Pauline Tradition

As has been said, the primacy of service in Paul does not rule out the importance of witness and fellowship, but service has a special place in five of Paul's letters.

The Pillar Epistles of 1, 2 Corinthians, Galatians and Romans may well be called the Collection Letters. That is due to the fact that in each one the Great Collection that Paul and his companions took to the poor saints of Jerusalem in A.D. 55 is mentioned.

One of the six questions submitted to Paul by the church of Corinth concerned that collection (16:1; cf. 7:1, 25; 8:1; 12:1; 16:12 for the other five questions). A whole section in 2 Corinthians is on the grace of giving (8, 9). The poor Macedonians had made themselves a model of generosity and grace. They were indeed so much a continuation of the incarnation that one of the most important Christological statements in the New Testament appears as an introduction to the call for a generous contribution from Corinth. "For you know the grace of our Lord Jesus Christ, that though he was rich, yet for your sake he became poor, so that by his poverty you might become rich" (8:9).

In A.D. 46 there was a great famine in Judea (Acts 11:27–30; Josephus, *Antiquities*, xx.ii.5). The next year, A.D. 47-48, was to be a sabbatical year for the Jewish disciples in Jerusalem, and the fields would not be cultivated. This would cause great suffering in Jerusalem, so the church of Antioch displayed true service *(diakonia)* with their offering.

At the Jerusalem Conference, A.D. 49, there was an agreement between James, Cephas and John, the "pillars" of Jerusalem, and Barnabas and Paul, representing the more open attitude toward Gentiles. The Jerusalem pillars agreed to work among circumcised Jews while Barnabas and Paul would go to the uncircumcised Gentiles (Galatians 2:1–10).

One of the conditions was that Barnabas and Paul would make a second collection within the Gentile churches to help the poor saints during their next sabbatical year, A.D. 54-55. If Galatians was written in A.D. 54, one statement is rather significant: "Let him who is taught the word share all good things with him who teaches" (6:6).

The slow response of Corinth, perhaps the wealthiest contributing church, delayed delivery of the great collection until Pentecost, A.D. 55, when Paul and the Gentile Seven took the offering to Jerusalem (Acts 20:1–6; 24:17). It seems that Romans was written about Passover, A.D. 55, and

Phoebe departed immediately for Rome with the letter to prepare the way for Paul (Romans 16:1-2).

This makes the service motif in Romans interesting indeed. Paul had called himself "a servant of Christ" before Romans (Galatians 1:10; 2 Corinthians 3:6), but it is in Romans 1:1 that he identifies himself for the first time as "a servant of Jesus Christ, called to be an apostle." About six months later, if part of Philippians was written from Caesarea around the Feast of Tabernacles, A.D. 55, Paul and Timothy are yoked together as "servants of Christ Jesus" (1:1), and this is in a letter of thanks for a generous contribution (1:1-3:1b; 4:10-20; cf. Colossians 1:23; Ephesians 3:7).

At no other place is the diakonic mission of the church more evident than in Romans 15:7-33. Christ is described as a servant *(diakonos)* not only to the Jewish people but also to the Gentiles (15:8f.; cf. Mark 10:45). His service to the Jewish people was indicative that God had kept the promise that he made to the patriarchs (cf. Gen. 12:3). This included the blessing of the Gentiles. The fact that the word *diakonos* is used also of the Emperor Nero in 13:4 and of Phoebe the deaconess of Cenchreae in 16:1 indicates the broadness of service to God.

Now Paul is performing the services of both priest and apostle as he delivers the great collection from the Gentiles to the poor saints in Jerusalem. At no other place does Paul describe himself as a priest doing priestly service, but that is the meaning of the Greek word *leitourgos* in 15:16 and *leitourgēsai* in 15:27, the first being the person performing the priestly service and the second being the service performed.

Any effort to separate witness and service in the mission of the church contradicts the purpose of Paul. The material blessings from the Gentiles was a thankful response for the spiritual blessings from the Jews. Indeed, there is a beautiful balance between witness, service and fellowship in 15:26f. The contribution itself is called a *koinōnia*, the great word for fellowship, and the Jewish sharing of the gospel with the Gentiles is described with the aorist verb *ekoinōnēsan*, meaning "shared" (15:27). With the completion of this threefold mission in the East, Paul anticipates a mission in the West that will take him to Spain (15:28). This balance between witness, service and fellowship in mission yields "the fulness of the blessing of Christ" (15:29). Then and now, this is the mission of the church.

The Mission of Koinōnia (Fellowship): The Johannine Tradition

It would be a *faux pas* for one to assume that the fulness of mission can be realized by fellowship alone, to the exclusion of witness and service, but it will be helpful to see how important fellowship is when confronted with heresy.

Koinōnia was a vital part of the Petrine tradition after Pentecost (Acts 2:42). It became a vital concept associated with the Holy Spirit in the

Pauline benediction that prepared the way for the earliest formulations of
Holy Trinity (2 Corinthians 13:14; cf. Philippians 2:1).

The *locus classicus* on *koinōnia* is the prologue for the early collection
of twelve Christian hymns that came to be called 1 John.

> *That which was from the beginning,*
> *which we have heard,*
> *which we have seen with our eyes,*
> *which we have looked upon*
> *and touched with our hands,*
> *concerning the Word of Life —*
>
> *And the life was manifested,*
> *and we have seen,*
> *and we are bearing witness,*
> *and we are proclaiming to you*
> *the eternal life which was with the Father*
> *and was manifested to us —*
>
> *That which we have seen and heard we are proclaiming to you,*
> *in order that you may have fellowship with us;*
> *and our fellowship is with the Father*
> *and with his Son Jesus Christ;*
> *and these things we are writing to you,*
> *in order that our joy may be complete.*

The rest of 1 John is an elaboration of *koinōnia*, in three cycles, as
abiding in light (1:5–2:27), life (2:28–4:6) and love (4:7–5:21).[3]

A widely accepted theory speaks of 1 John as a prime example of
"Christ Against Culture," a view later advocated from Tertullian to Tolstoy.[4]
As a general type this may be true, but there are times when the mission
of the church has called for just this confrontation. However, there is always
the danger of a ghetto gospel and a minority complex when fellowship is
isolated from witness and service in the world.

One of the best theological pictures of Christian *koinōnia* describes the
future relationship between God as Father, Christ the Son and the disciples
of Jesus in the threefold way (John 14:20):

> *In that day you will know that*
> *I am in the Father,*
> *and you in me,*
> *and I in you.*

At times the Gospel of John magnifies the Father–Son relationship and at
others the Father–children, but all of this is included in Christian *koinōnia*.

---

3. See my commentary *The Letters of John* (Waco, Texas: Word Books, 1970), p. 19.
4. H. Richard Niebuhr, *Christ and Culture* (New York: Harper & Brothers, 1951), pp. 45-82.

A good example of the Johannine concept of *koinōnia* is the threefold portrait of the disciples as branches in Jesus the vine (John 15:1–11), friends for whom Jesus will give his life (15:12–17) and witnesses to a godless world (15:18–27). A fortress of *koinōnia* does distinguish the disciples from the *kosmos* of darkness, death and hate, but the threefold witness and service of the fellowship are not abandoned.

Another example of true *koinōnia* is the threefold prayer of Jesus in John 17 for himself (1–5), the twelve disciples (6–19) and all who will ever believe the witness of the disciples (20–26). The unity of the fellowship is the major witness to the world. Ecumenical exploitation of this oneness is no excuse for sectarian schism and isolation. The unity between the Father and the Son is to be duplicated by the disciples (17:11), not for the sake of unity alone but as a witness to the world (17:22).

Unfortunately, about the time this prayer for unity was about to be answered, there arose a radical claim that the mission of the church was service only. Radicals to the left under the banner of *diakonia*, and conservatives to the right with the witness of evangelism and missions have become as much a threat to the *koinōnia* of the church as dead denominationalism did in the past. If the manifold mission of the church is to be recovered it will need to be a table with at least three legs if it is to stand in the world: *martyria*, *diakonia*, *koinōnia*.

At different times, as in the New Testament, witness or service or fellowship may need to be emphasized in mission, but any one without the other two is inadequate. It may be that service has been the most neglected part of mission in the economic security of the state church. Jürgen Moltmann, working and writing in the state church situation of Germany, has raised a relevant voice on the mission of the church with his call to service, but he has not neglected the necessity for witness and fellowship.[5]

66. The Structures of the Church

If the mission or missions of the church are to be carried out with all the people of God involved there is a need for organizations and structures. The general structures have not always been the same as a survey of the church in the context of culture reveals. When Christians are in the minority the structure is more the conventicle or congregational, but when this minority approaches a majority a more connectional structure of ecclesiastical power tends to develop. The development has been, as Ernst Troeltsch

5. See especially *The Church in the Power of the Spirit*, tr. Margaret Kohl (New York: Harper and Row, 1977). Ferdinand Hahn, *Mission in the New Testament*, tr. Frank Clarke (London: SCM Press, 1965), has interpreted the mission of the church primarily in terms of service, but the threefold mission outlined above includes all the New Testament and is more balanced and more practical.

observed, a movement from vital groups to more organized and less vital churches.[6] Both Reinhold and Richard Niebuhr, in social ethics, drew heavily on this observation. The following survey is to suggest that a return to some elements of the vital group is in order today.

A few years ago very little was said about the structure of the church. In the centuries since the Protestant Reformation, a multitude of denominational structures developed outside Catholicism along congregational, presbyterian or episcopal lines. At times vigorous debate developed as to which was *the* New Testament polity and pattern. Since all could be found in the New Testament very little was accomplished until ecumenical dialogue displaced denominational debates.

With the coming of Vatican Council II, 1962-1965, the question of structure and the need for restructure became a serious study.[7] The publication of *The Structures of the Church* by Hans Küng in 1964 marked a watershed on this subject.[8] A brief survey of some major developments since the apostolic age may furnish a framework for new perspectives. This will be done along historical lines in which metropolitan, conciliar, denominational and ecumenical structures have developed according to the needs of mission.

Metropolitan Structures

Between the time Jesus gathered his disciples about himself and the Fall of Jerusalem in A.D. 70 the center of the church was Jerusalem. It was there that Jesus died and rose again, according to his own predictions (cf. Mark 8:31; 9:31; 10:33; Luke 9:51; 13:22; 17:11; 18:31; 19:28). Because of his death, the temple of Jerusalem was destroyed and the time of the Gentile domination of the temple area has continued and will continue until the time of the Gentiles comes to an end at the return of Jesus (Luke 11:29–32, 49–51; 13:34f.; 19:41–44; 21:20–24; 23:28–31). According to the Gospel of Luke, the death and resurrection of Jesus in Jerusalem was indeed "the center of time."[9]

The centrality of Jerusalem in the Gospel of Luke continues in the structures of the church in the Acts of the Apostles. Until the founding of the church of Antioch the only church was the Jerusalem church (Acts

6. The title of Troeltsch's most famous book was *The Social Teachings of the Christian Churches and Groups* (1911), but the groups are oddly omitted in the title of the English translation by Olive Wyon (New York: The Macmillan Co., 1931), 2 vols.
7. *Documents of Vatican II*, edited by Walter M. Abbot (New York: Guild Press, 1966).
8. (University of Notre Dame Press, 1968).
9. A literal translation of the German title of an important book by Hans Conzelmann, *The Theology of St. Luke*, tr. Geoffrey Buswell (London: Faber & Faber, 1960). Helmut Flender, *St. Luke*, tr. Reginald H. and Ilse Fuller (Philadelphia: Fortress Press, 1967), rather unsuccessfully attempts to displace Conzelmann's threefold scheme with Jesus in the middle between Israel and the Church. Flender argues for a twofold scheme of victory in heaven, then victory on earth, an obvious Lutheran bias that perpetuates the tensions between Pietistic Lutherans and the anti-chiliastic traditions of Lutheran orthodoxy.

11:26). The temple of Jerusalem was still the center of worship. As there was only one temple, so was there only one church (5:11; 8:1-3). Even when the disciples were scattered under persecution, there was still only the one metropolitan church of Jerusalem. There is strong manuscript support for the reading in Acts 9:31 which says: "So the church throughout Judea and Galilee and Samaria had peace and was built up; and walking in the fear of the Lord and in the comfort of the Holy Spirit it was multiplied." This is one of the three summaries about the growth of the Jewish church in Jerusalem (6:7; 9:31; 12:24).

Even when Gentile Christianity spread from Antioch into many other metropolitan areas, there was still the picture of the mother church in Jerusalem. Luke's scheme of six "books" of five years each adds three more "books" on Gentile churches (16:5; 19:20; 28:30f.), but Jerusalem is the church before which Paul and Barnabas must answer for their liberal rules on the acceptance of Gentiles into newly founded metropolitan churches (Acts 15). For the next six years, A.D. 49-54, Paul was busy gathering the great collection from Gentile churches for the poor saints in Jerusalem. When he finally reached Jerusalem in A.D. 55, it is clear that the model of the mother church prevailed (Acts 21:17).

In the multiplicity of metropolitan Gentile churches there is still only one church in a Greek *polis* (a city). The Greek *polis* becomes the center for mission. Never is there more than one church in a city. At least four steps may be noted. (1) The house church in which believers gathered was the most simple structure of all (1 Corinthians 16:19; Romans 16:5; Colossians 4:15; Philemon 2). (2) The city church composed of all the believers in a *polis* is the usual understanding of the word church (1 Thessalonians 1:1; 2 Thessalonians 1:1; 1 Corinthians 1:2; 2 Corinthians 1:1). (3) The plurality of churches always goes beyond the single metropolitan area. At times the churches are those of a Roman province such as Judea (1 Thessalonians 2:14; Galatians 1:22), Galatia (1 Corinthians 16:1; Galatians 1:2), Asia (1 Corinthians 16:19), or Macedonia (2 Corinthians 8:1). The plurality of churches may also be used in reference to the churches of the Gentiles (Romans 16:4), the churches of Christ (Romans 16:16), or simply churches (Acts 15:41; 16:5; 2 Thessalonians 1:4; 1 Corinthians 4:17; 7:17; 11:16; 14:33; 2 Corinthians 8:1, 18, 19, 23, 24; 11:28; 12:13). (4) The New Testament also speaks of the church as the one body of Christ composed of all true believers in all places, but it never speaks of a plurality of churches in one city (Colossians 1:18, 24; Ephesians 1:22f.; 2:14-21; 3:6-10; 4:4, 12; 5:23-33). It comes as a jolt, but it must be said again that the modern concept of a plurality of churches in one city is never found in the New Testament.

The model of the metropolitan church was dominant in the whole Roman Empire between the Fall of Jerusalem in A.D. 70 and the Council of Nicaea in A.D. 325. The centrality of the metropolitan church before

A.D. 325 has been made obvious in Hans Lietzmann's history of the period.[10] Antioch and Alexandria, Ephesus and Rome, Carthage in Africa, and Lyons in Gaul and Edessa were some of the most important centers where distinctive types of Christianity developed, but no one church took the place Jerusalem held before A.D. 70. Only after a rift between East and West began to develop did Rome and Constantinople rise above the rest, and this led to the later West–East schism.

Conciliar Structures

With the removal of the capital of the Roman Empire from Rome to Constantinople the church council became the supreme authority for all churches. This role was played by Jerusalem in A.D. 49, but the Roman Emperor had no part in this early council. It was the call for a Council at Nicaea by the Emperor Constantine that marked a new period for the structures of the church. The domination of the church by the Emperor really began in the West when the Donatists, in A.D. 313, appealed to Constantine to settle the controversy in Africa. Of the twenty-one ecumenical councils, the first eight were in the East and the rest were in the West.

The first seven ecumenical councils of the East are alone recognized by the Eastern Churches, and the councils are considered infallible. For Eastern Christendom all the problems of Christian unity are easily solved by a return to all the beliefs and practices in the documents of the seven councils, between the fourth and eighth centuries, when the Christian emperors dominated the church. Christian emperors are gone, but the authority of their councils remains, according to Eastern Orthodoxy.

All of the first seven councils were called to clarify issues about the person of Christ. The shift in the church from the historical language of Hebrew thought to the metaphysical language of Greek thought threatened belief in the humanity of Jesus. Arianism claimed that Jesus was neither God nor man but an intermediate creature between God and man. The Hebrew idea of the firstborn who inherited the authority of the father was interpreted to mean that Jesus was the first creature of God, much as in the Christology of the Jehovah's Witnesses today. The Council of Nicaea of 325 declared that in the incarnation Jesus was both truly God and truly man.

In the effort to explain how Jesus could be both God and man, Apollinarianism taught that Jesus had a human body and soul but not a human mind. This was condemned as heresy at the Council of Constantinople in 381.

The Nestorians went so far in defense of the humanity of Jesus that they were charged with the heresy of two persons, and they were con-

10. *The Founding of the Church Universal*, tr. Bertram Lee Woolf (New York: Oxford University Press, 1954), pp. 30-52.

demned at the Council of Ephesus in 431. The declaration of the council that the Virgin Mary was the Mother of God *(theotokos)* laid the foundation for the later doctrines and dogmas of Marianism, and these form one of the major barriers between Catholics and Protestants today.

The logic of the Council of Ephesus really led to Eutychianism, which denied the true humanity of Jesus, so the Council of Chalcedon of 451 was necessary to check this trend. It is very difficult to harmonize the Christology of Ephesus with that of Chalcedon, and this led to the later schism of the monophysite churches which rejected belief in the two natures of Christ. The last three councils of the East were efforts to defend the humanity of Jesus against the mythological trends that tended to make Mary a Greek goddess whose son Jesus was like a Greek god. The Second Council of Constantinople in 553, convened by the Emperor Justinian, compromised Chalcedonian Christology to pacify the monophysites. The Christology of the great Theodore of Mopsuestia was condemned, a thing not done at Ephesus or Chalcedon. Pope Vigilius of Rome was exiled for his defense of Theodore.

Monophysitism, the belief in one nature, was bound to raise the question of monothelitism, the belief in one will, so the Third Council of Constantinople of 680-81 had to be called to correct the child of the Second Council of Constantinople by the reaffirmation of the two natures of Chalcedon and the proclamation of two wills, of God and of Jesus.

Even the Second Council of Nicaea of 787, the seventh ecumenical council in the East, was concerned with the humanity of Jesus. Opposition to the use of icons, iconoclasm, was promoted by the monophysites, who took a dim view of any emphasis on the human Jesus, but the Second Council of Nicaea in 787 defined the use of icons. The iconoclastic controversy put Pope and Emperor on opposite sides and further prepared the way for schism between East and West.

The eighth ecumenical council was in the East, but its authority is recognized only in the West. At the Fourth Council of Constantinople in 869-70 Photius, the Patriarch of Constantinople, was supported by the Emperor Basil. Photius was anathematized in agreement with a council in Rome in 869. This so-called Photian schism between East and West marked the end of the emperor's domination in the church and the increase of Papal authority. All the other thirteen councils recognized by the later church took place in the West.

The next four councils took place at the Lateran palace at the Cathedral of St. John the Baptist in Rome. All of them were concerned with the authority of the Pope. In 1123 it was the investiture controversy, in 1139 the challenge of Arnold of Brescia, in 1179 Papal elections and in 1215 the role of the laity among the Waldenses. All this was far removed from the person of Christ!

The First Council of Lyons in 1245 met the challenge of the Emperor Frederick II, and the Second Council of Lyons, 1274, wrestled with the problems of reunion. At Vienne, near Lyons, in 1311-12, the authority of the Pope against the Templars was defended. At Constance, 1414-17, and at Ferrara-Florence, 1438-39, the unity of the church was the chief concern.

The Fifth Lateran Council, 1512-17, on the eve of the Protestant Reformation, and the Council of Trent, 1545-63 after the Reformation began, were concerned with reform. The First Vatican Council 1869-70, ended with the dogma of Papal Infallibility, and the Second Vatican Council of 1962-65 tried to remedy the damage done by Vatican I and to renew the church.

Conciliarism has left a rift between East and West and the separation between Catholicism and Protestantism in the West. All who take the New Testament teachings on the church as the one body of Christ on earth seriously find Christian schism a contradiction, but much reform and renewal are required to remedy the situation. The model for reunion is a major problem for mission.

Denominational Structures

The roots of Protestant perspectives on the structures of the church reached back to sources long before the actual Reformation. One of the most influential writings was John Wycliffe's writing on the church, *De Ecclesia*, 1377-78. On philosophical grounds Wycliffe made a distinction between the visible and the invisible church. He argued that the visible church had no authority unless it conformed to the invisible pattern he found in the Bible and the Church Fathers. John Huss of Prague incorporated this view in his slashing attack on the visible church in a book (1413) with the same title used by the Englishman Wycliffe.

The Reformation churches were at first inclined toward the free church tradition which magnified the concept of the invisible body of Christ in the eucharist and in the *ekklēsia*, but the circumstances that prevailed turned some of the reformers toward the idea of a state church defended by civil authority.

Martin Luther pined for a return to the church as he found it in the New Testament, and he was at first frustrated by the belief that the people were not yet ready for such a restoration of New Testament patterns and practices. This was especially true in his writing *The German Mass and Order of Service* (1526), but the pressures of the Peasant Revolt, 1524-26, and other factors made him compromise with the state. He did not give in, however, before he had denied the primacy of the Pope and the infallibility of the General Councils of the church.

In the Reformed tradition, Ulrich Zwingli was at first sympathetic with the Anabaptists who wanted to restore the church order of the New Testament, but he withdrew from the movement in favor of a state church. The

Petition of Protest and Defence (December, 1524) by Felix Manz makes plain Zwingli's wavering that led to the shameful treatment of the Swiss Brethren in 1525 and the later intolerance of Calvinism in both Europe and America.[11]

Anglicanism was at first more tolerant toward dissenters, but the wedding between state and church has been an unhappy marriage until this day. Part of the Anglican communion, the Anglo-Catholics, would gladly return to Rome and Catholicism, while others, more loyal to Calvinism, the evangelicals, retain Erastianism with zeal. Erastianism was the teaching of Swiss theologian Thomas Erastus (1524-83), who defended the ascendancy of the state over the church even in ecclesiastical matters. His influential book was translated into English as *The Nullity of Church Censures* (1659), but Richard Hooker's *Ecclesiastical Polity* (1594) taught similar ideas. This has led to such absurd events as the rejection by Parliament of the Prayer Book of 1928, approved by the Established Church. Much illegal praying has resulted!

The free church tradition never had a fair opportunity to prove its benefits for the churches and the Church as the body of Christ until universal religious liberty was first proclaimed in the First Amendment to the Constitution of the United States of America.

It is true that the United States has become the spawning ground for every religious sect vital enough to reproduce, but it can hardly be said that the churches and sects are so dead that they must depend on state aid for support and propagation. If there is a major sin in American Christianity, it is that freedom has been used as an occasion to sin against Christ and one another.

In the atmosphere of freedom the flames of Christian unity have been fanned most fervently. At times the vision of the one body of Christ manifested here and now in history has lifted hopes, but anxious bishops and social activists and rigid conservatives have complicated matters by arousing emotions that hardly manifest the work of the Spirit. There is great danger that concern for position and power may frustrate the purpose of Christ in his Church, but the vision should be kept alive.[12] It is sad to see so many resolved to save the *status quo*.

It is not too late to turn again to the apostolic faith nurtured by the gathered company of committed believers who are willing to move away from national churches and become the pilgrim church again scattered throughout the world for witness, service, and fellowship. People are no

11. John T. McNeill, *The History and Character of Calvinism* (New York: Oxford University Press, 1954), pp. 30-52.
12. A good example of this vision is Ronald E. Osborn, *A Church for These Times* (New York: Abingdon Press, 1965). For the same vision in a British setting see John Huxtable, *A New Hope for Christian Unity* (London: Collins/Fount, 1978).

more ready for this than they were in Luther's day, but the Diaspora structures are necessities for mission.[13]

67. The Nature of the Church*

The nature of the church in the New Testament has been obscured through the conflicts of church history. Augustine's distinction between the earthly city *(civitas terrena)* and the heavenly city *(civitas Dei)* has been perverted in Roman Catholicism by the identification of the historical institution with the heavenly ideal; yet for Augustine the church, while participating in the *civitas Dei*, is not identical with the ideal until the end of history. Likewise the state, while participating in the *civitas terrena*, is not identical with earthly evil; to become identical would mean its own destruction.[14] Calvin's distinction between the visible and the invisible church is strikingly similar to Augustine's distinction between the ideal and the institutional.[15]

This distinction in Augustine and Calvin was a tenet of the Particular Baptists in England. The Baptist Confession of the seven London congregations in 1644, the first Baptist confession of the Calvinistic type, says:

> XLVII. And although the particular Congregations be distinct and severall Bodies, every one a compact and knit Citie in it selfe; yet are they all to walk by one and the same Rule, and by all means convenient to have the counsell and help one of another in all needfull affaires of the Church, as members of one body in the common faith under Christ their onely head.[16]

After the historic Westminster Confession, generally accepted as the classic exposition of Calvinism, was presented to Parliament in 1646, almost all Particular Baptist confessions followed it except in regard to believer's baptism and congregational government. The Particular Baptist Confession of 1677, reaffirmed in 1689, was "adopted by the Baptist Association met at Philadelphia, September 25, 1742," and by both the Charleston Association in South Carolina and the Warren Association in

13. See Jürgen Moltmann, *The Open Church*, tr. M. Douglas Meeks (London: SCM, 1978). *The first edition of this section was prepared as an essay in honor of the late William Owen Carver (1868-1954) and published in *The Review and Expositor*, Vol. LI, No. 2 (April, 1954), pp. 204-216. A second edition appeared in *What Is The Church?*, edited by Duke K. McCall (Nashville: Broadman Press, 1958), pp. 15-27. Other additions have been made in this third edition.
14. Ernest Barker, "Introduction," *The City of God*, tr. John Healey (New York: E. P. Dutton and Co., 1931), pp. xvi-xxxii.
15. John Calvin, *Institutes of the Christian Religion*, tr. John Allen (Grand Rapids: Wm. B. Eerdmans Publishing Company, 1949), II, 269-273.
16. W. J. McGlothlin, *Baptist Confessions of Faith* (Philadelphia: American Baptist Publication Society, 1911), pp. 186f.

Rhode Island in 1767. It represents classic Baptist Calvinism. The nature of the church is described as follows:

> The Catholick or universal Church, which (with respect to internal work of the Spirit, and truth of grace) may be called invisible, consists of the whole number of the Elect, that have been, are, or shall be gathered into one, under Christ the head thereof; and is the spouse, the body, the fulness of him that filleth all in all.[17]

The Charleston Summary of Church Discipline, a document filled with amazing insight, said the church when "considered collectively forms one complete and glorious body" and "is the general assembly and church of the first born."[18]

The priority of the spiritual organism over the institutional organization is obvious in all this great theological stream. It is clearly summarized in the Abstract of Principles adopted by the Southern Baptist Theological Seminary, April 30, 1858. Article XIV of that historic document reads:

> The Lord Jesus is the Head of the Church, which is composed of all his true disciples, and in Him is invested supremely all power for its government. According to his commandment, Christians are to associate themselves into particular societies or Churches; and to each of these Churches he hath given needful authority for administering that order, discipline and worship which he hath appointed. The regular officers of a Church are Bishops or Elders, and Deacons.

It is, therefore, no surprise to read a long and lucid chapter on "The Church Universal" as well as one on "Local Churches" in the first textbook in systematic theology used at the Southern Baptist Theological Seminary.[19] Many Southern Baptists, unaware of the facts of Southern Baptist history and unmoved by the plain teachings of the New Testament, have followed the innovations of Landmarkism which infiltrated the South from the North through such personalities as J. R. Graves and J. M. Pendleton.[20]

Even the preface of the New Hampshire Confession of Faith in 1833 expresses the hope that it would "be blessed by the great Head of the Church to promote still more that delightful harmony of sentiment and ardent brotherly love which now exists in so eminent a degree among our

17. *Ibid.*, p. 264.
18. Chapter I, p. 3 (from the 1850 printing by B. Temple at Raleigh, NC, bound with the Charleston Confession and a catechism).
19. J. L. Dagg, "A Treatise on Church Order," *Manual of Theology,* Second Part (Charleston: Southern Baptist Publication Society, 1859), pp. 74-143.
20. W. W. Barnes, *The Southern Baptist Convention* (Nashville: Broadman Press, 1954), pp. 100-117.

churches."[21] Article XIII defines "a visible Church of Christ" and is therefore not in conflict with the Preface in the use of "the Church."

To use P. T. Forsyth's metaphor, the local congregation is the "outcrop" of the church composed of all true believers. As the "outcrop" is of the same nature as the formation of which it is a part, so the local congregation shares the nature of the body of Christ.[22] Rigid distinction between the local assembly and the general assembly, especially when the general assembly as the body of Christ is rejected, is a case of not being able to see the woods for the trees. The spiritual nature of the local assembly is so identical with that of the general assembly that it is impossible to have a local church if it is not composed of regenerate members of the body of Christ. Local societies not composed of such regenerate members are, in the words of the Particular Baptist Confession of 1677, "Synagogues of Satan." The church is that fellowship of faith created by the living God as Father, Son, and Holy Spirit to the praise of his glory. Apart from God no other agency, in heaven or on earth, is adequate to create, continue, or complete this spiritual organism. "Membership in the church universal," declared the saintly J. L. Dagg, "is determined by God himself."[23]

The Church in Relation to God

The question of the relationship between the church and God is raised by the use of the terms "the church of God" (1 Cor. 1:2; 10:32; 15:9; 2 Cor. 1:1; Gal. 1:13; 1 Tim. 3:5, 15) and "the churches of God" (1 Thess. 2:14; 1 Cor. 11:16) in the New Testament.

First, the church is presented as the people of God. A passage such as 1 Peter 1:3–2:10 relates the concept of the church to the people of God in the Old Testament. Against the background of the work of the Father (1:3–6), the Son (1:7–9), and the Holy Spirit (1:10–12), God's redemption of his people is described in the figures of an exodus (1:13–21), a life (1:22–2:3), and a house (1:4–10). The description of the new exodus made possible by "the precious blood of Christ" (1:19) is filled with allusions to the Old Testament Exodus. The new life, also explained in Old Testament language, is produced by spiritual seed (1:22–25) and nurtured by spiritual milk (2:1–2). And, finally, the new house is described with a constellation of Old Testament quotations (2:4–8). Writing "to the exiles of the dispersion in Pontus, Galatia, Cappadocia, Asia, and Bithynia, chosen and destined by God the Father and sanctified by the Spirit for obedience to Jesus Christ and for sprinkling with his blood," Peter can say:

---

21. *New Hampshire Baptist Register*, January 20, 1833. Quoted from Charles Riley MacDonald, "New Hampshire Declaration of Faith" (unpublished doctoral dissertation in Northern Baptist Theological Seminary, Chicago, May, 1939), pp. 52f.
22. Cf. Ernest A. Payne, *The Fellowship of Believers* (London: The Carey Kingsgate Press, 1954), p. 29, n. 6.
23. J. L. Dagg, *op. cit.*, p. 143.

But you are a chosen race, a royal priesthood, a holy nation, God's own people, that you may declare the wonderful deeds of him who called you out of darkness into his marvelous light. Once you were no people but now you are God's people; once you had not received mercy but now you have received mercy (1 Peter 2:9–10, RSV).

The pilgrim people of God in 1 Peter have a function as a "holy priesthood" (2:5), but this priestly people of God is magnified even more in the Christian *midrash* on the Day of Atonement that is known as Hebrews. The office of Jesus Christ as the great high priest after the order of Melchizedek is magnified in chs. 1–7. Then the oblation of Jesus Christ as a sacrifice that needs never to be repeated is interpreted in chs. 8–13. Believers in Jesus constitute a pilgrim people on the earth who participate in the eternal priesthood of the city of God (13:10–16).

Second, the Church is presented as the temple of God. This figure, evident in 1 Peter 2:4–10, is elaborated by Paul and John. In 2 Corinthians 6:14–7:1 the whole point of the appeal, containing five rhetorical questions and three quotations from the Old Testament, which calls for separation from pagan immorality, is summed up in the statement that "we are the temple of the living God" (6:16, RSV). First Corinthians 3:10–17 expands this "temple" terminology by declaring Jesus Christ the foundation upon which may be built "gold, silver, precious stones, wood, hay, stubble" to be tested by fire in the day of judgment (3:10–15). The frightful thing about spiritual sacrilege, that is, schism in the church, is found in the fact that God will destroy those who destroy his temple. And this temple is composed of those in whom God's Spirit dwells (3:16f.).

A third passage in Paul, Ephesians 2:11–22, brings the temple concept to a climax. Those alienated from God (2:11f.) have been reconciled to God through the blood of the cross of Christ (2:13–16). Christ, who is our peace (2:14) and who makes peace (2:15), preaches peace to those far off and to those who are near (2:17) by breaking down the dividing wall of human hostility (2:14). The result of reconciliation follows (2:19–22, RSV):

So then you are no longer strangers and sojourners, but you are fellow citizens with the saints and members of the household of God, built upon the foundation of the apostles and prophets, Christ Jesus himself being the cornerstone, in whom the whole structure is joined together and grows into a holy temple in the Lord; in whom you also are built into it for a dwelling place of God in the Spirit.

It is highly probable that the Gospel of John, written to persuade the readers "that Jesus is the Christ, the Son of God" (20:31), intends for the reader to see Jesus as the new temple taking the place of the Temple of Jerusalem that is destroyed. The cleansing of the Temple at the first of three Passover feasts (2:13) is not without theological significance. The discussion about the destruction of the Temple in contrast to the death of Jesus is not left ambiguous. John says plainly: "But he spoke of the temple of his body. When therefore he was raised from the dead, his disciples remembered that he had said this; and they believed the scripture and the word which Jesus had spoken" (John 2:21–22, RSV).

The Church in Relation to Jesus Christ

It has been impossible to speak of the people of God and the temple of God apart from Jesus Christ and the Holy Spirit, but a clearer understanding of the relationship between Jesus Christ and the church appears in Paul's use of the metaphors of the body of Christ and the bride of Christ. Indeed, it is not beyond probability that the Gospel of John implies these two relations by the emphasis it gives the miracle of turning water into wine at the marriage of Cana and the prediction about the temple of Jesus' body in the cleansing of the Temple. However that may be, there is no mistake about these metaphors in Paul.

The church as the body of Christ can best be understood against the Hebrew idea of corporate personality, such as is found in the teachings on the Servant of the Lord (Isa. 53), the Son of man (Dan. 7:13–22), and Adam (Rom. 5:12–21). The items of greatest importance to Paul are the members; then the head; and finally the unity of the body with Jesus Christ as the head.

The members of the body come in for special consideration in a number of passages. In 1 Corinthians 6:15f. Paul rebukes immorality among Christians on the basis that the bodies of Christians are "members of Christ" as well as the temple of the Holy Spirit. The fact that Christians constitute one body of which all are members is both the basis for saying the loaf at the Lord's Supper is a participation *(koinōnia)* in the body of Christ and the reason for Christians to separate themselves from pagan sacrifices (1 Cor. 10:14–22). Those who participate in the Lord's Supper are warned to examine themselves that they may not bring the judgment of God upon themselves by failing to discern the body of Christ (1 Cor. 11:28f.). These close associations between the one loaf which represents the body of Christ and the members who constitute the body of Christ have led A. E. J. Rawlinson and a number of other New Testament theologians to conclude that Paul's idea of the body of Christ is derived from the loaf at the Lord's Supper.[24] Unity in diversity in the church is based on the belief that "just as the body is one and has many members, and all the members of the body, though

---

24. J. Robert Nelson, *The Realm of Redemption* (London: The Epworth Press, 1951), p. 71.

many, are one body," this unity may be realized by taking thought that "the body does not consist of one member but of many" (1 Cor. 12:12, 14, RSV). Those who "have died to the law through the body of Christ" not only "belong to another" (Rom. 7:4) but "are one body in Christ, and individually members one of another" in the functions of sober Christian living (Rom. 12:15f.). The body of Christ is nothing less than the presence of Christ himself in the life and service of the Christian community.[25] This does not mean that the church is Christ, but it means that there can be no true church apart from vital union of the members with Christ.

The head of the body is Christ. In Colossians the idea of the church as the body of Christ is continued as Paul rejoiced in the sufferings which "complete what is lacking in Christ's afflictions for the sake of his body, that is, the church" (Col. 1:24). He exhorted the believers to put on love and let the peace of Christ to which they "are called in one body" rule in their hearts (Col. 3:15). In Paul's thought Christ as the head is used in three ways.[26] First, Christ is the head of every man, even as the husband is the head of the woman and God is the head of Christ (1 Cor. 11:3). Second, Christ is the head of all rule and authority (Col. 2:10), having disarmed the principalities and powers by the triumph of the cross (Col. 2:15) and put them under his feet (Eph. 1:22). Third, Christ is the head of the church as his body (Col. 1:18). Those who worship angels are "not holding fast to the Head, from whom the whole body, nourished and knit together through its joints and ligaments, grows with a growth that is from God" (Col. 2:19, RSV).

The unity of the body finds fullest expression in Ephesians. The head of the body, as in Colossians, is seen also in Ephesians (1:22; 4:15; 5:23); but the unity of the body, implicit in other places, becomes very explicit. In Ephesians the headship of Christ is described in reference to the past, present, and future. The great prayer for knowledge in Ephesians 1:15–23 is a petition for spiritual enlightenment (1:15–19a) and spiritual energy (1:19b–23) in the light of the resurrection and exaltation of Christ to the right hand of God. Those who believe that this great reality will be postponed to some future time, as if Christ had a body only at the end of history, greatly err. Christ, here and now, is both sovereign over the church and the one who fills it with his presence, so that it "is his body, the fulness of him who fills all in all" (Eph. 1:23). The past reality of the exaltation of Christ is experienced as a present reality in the life of the body.

The unity of life is grounded in the great sevenfold unity: "One body and one Spirit, just as you were called to the one hope that belongs to your

25. Eduard Schweizer, *Das Leben des Herrn in der Germeinde und ihren Diensten* (Zurich: Zwingli-Verlag, 1946), p. 51.
26. Elias Andrews, *The Meaning of Christ for Paul* (New York: Abingdon-Cokesbury Press, 1949), pp. 112-115.

call, one Lord, one faith, one baptism, one God and Father of us all, who is above all and through all and in all" (Eph. 4:4–6, RSV). The growth of this unity is realized by the exercise of the gifts bestowed by the exalted Lord (Eph. 4:7–11) as the members build up the body in love (4:12–16). This body, after the analogy of any body, has a beginning, a growth, and a completion in the future presentation of the body as the bride of Christ.

The church as the bride of Christ is an idea rooted in the teachings of the Old Testament prophets who spoke of Israel as the unfaithful wife of Yahweh and in poetic passages, such as Psalm 45 and the Song of Songs. Some Old Testament scholars, notably T. J. Meek, see a spiritual marriage in the Song of Songs not far removed from the extreme allegorical teachings of prescientific Old Testament study, and it is not at all sure that the literal interpretation is the clue to the meaning of this book.[27] The nuptial theme appears in the teachings both of John the Baptist (John 3:25–29) and Jesus (Mark 2:18–28; Matt. 22:2; 25:1–13; Luke 14:7–11). Apocalyptic eschatology anticipates "the marriage of the Lamb" when "his Bride has made herself ready" for "the marriage supper of the Lamb" (Rev. 19:7–9), and the bride becomes the wife of the Lamb (Rev. 20:9). But, as with the concept of the Body of Christ, the church as the bride of Christ finds fullest expression in Paul.

Three passages of Paul have a strong nuptial element. The first is Galatians 4:21–31 where two women are an allegory of two covenants, one being Hagar the slave, who represents Mount Sinai, and the other being Sarah the free woman who represents the Jerusalem above and is the mother of all who, like Isaac, are "children of promise." This is preceded by Paul's travail for the Galatians (4:19) and is based on the prophetic teaching in Isaiah 54:1. The second passage is 2 Corinthians 11:2–3. For Paul, Christ is the "Second Adam" and it is logical for the church to be compared to Eve. The Corinthian Christians were betrothed to Christ as "a pure bride to her one husband," but there was always the danger that the serpent who deceived Eve would lead the church away from pure devotion to Christ. The third passage is Ephesians 5:21–23. As in the metaphor of the body, "The husband is the head of the wife as Christ is the head of the church," and the wife is to be subject to the husband as the church is subject to Christ. Here Paul went beyond the relation of husband and wife so far that he ended by talking about "Christ and the church." The husband is to measure his love for his wife by the love Christ had for the church and by the love the husband has for his own body. Not only do Paul's thoughts flow back and forth between the Christ-church and the husband-wife relation but the metaphors of the body and the bride blend into one. The roots of these relations are found in God's intention for the family and the church, as revealed in Genesis 2:24.

27. Claude Chavasse, *The Bride of Christ* (London: Faber & Faber, Ltd., 1940), pp. 27-45.

The Church in Relation to the Holy Spirit

The Holy Spirit transforms the sociological phenomenon, subject to the laws of other social groups, into a spiritual fellowship *(koinōnia)* with a ministry *(diakonia)* of service. The fellowship of the Spirit is a term found only twice in the New Testament (2 Cor. 13:14; Phil. 2:1), but the idea supplements the fellowship with the Father (1 John 1:3) and the fellowship with the Son (1 John 1:3; 1 Cor. 1:9) to give the very essence of the church. Devotion "to the apostles' teachings and fellowship, to the breaking of bread and the prayers" (Acts 2:42, RSV) is something more than voluntary association with one another or participation in the Spirit. It is nothing less than the access through Christ, in the Spirit, to the Father (Eph. 2:18) by all who have been reconciled to God through the blood of the cross of Christ. A thin theology can only lead to a thin ecclesiology.

The fellowship *(koinōnia)* of the Spirit may be summarized with three New Testament terms: the baptism of the Spirit, the gift of the Spirit, and the unity of the Spirit.

The baptism of the Spirit distinguishes the baptism of Jesus from the baptism of John the Baptist (Mark 1:8; Matt. 3:11; Luke 3:16; John 1:33; Acts 1:5; 11:15f.). The two baptisms are closely associated in Acts, but it is evident in the experience of the Samaritans (Acts 8:14–24), Cornelius (Acts 10:44–48), and the disciples at Ephesus (Acts 19:1–7) that the connection is not so inseparable that one must receive the two together. This close association continues in 1 Corinthians 10:1–4; 12:13. Just as the fathers were baptized into Moses and ate the spiritual food and drank the spiritual drink in the wilderness experience of the old Exodus, so now in the new exodus (1 Cor. 10:11) "by one Spirit we were all baptized into one body — Jews or Greeks, slaves or free — and all were made to drink of one Spirit" (1 Cor. 12:13).

The gift of the Spirit (Luke 11:13; John 3:34; Acts 2:38; 8:20; 10:45; 11:17) is closely associated with baptism. God imparts the Spirit in baptism, as in the laying on of hands and the invoking of the name of Jesus Christ. Any effort, however, to chain the gift of the Spirit to any one of these three acts is refuted by the examples in the book of Acts. Slavery of the Spirit to sacramental rituals is not the faith of the New Testament.

The unity of the Spirit (Eph. 4:4) is also a solemn warning to those who would advocate an organic union based on sacramentalism as a substitute for the spiritual unity which only the Spirit can give the body of Christ, the church. This ecclesiastical danger, however, should not be used as a shield for indifference to God's call to walk worthily "with all lowliness and meekness, with patience, forbearing one another in love, eager to maintain the unity of the Spirit in the bond of peace" (Eph. 4:2–3, RSV).

The ministry *(diakonia)* of the Spirit likewise may be summed up with three New Testament terms: the gifts (*charismata*) of the Spirit, the filling of the Spirit, and the sword of the Spirit.

The gifts (*charismata*) of the Spirit are not the same as the gift (*dōrea*) of the Spirit, the first being what the Spirit gives and the second being the Spirit himself. The term *charisma*, found outside of Paul only in Philo (*De leg. alleg.* iii. 30) and 1 Peter 4:10, describes the spiritual endowments bestowed by the Spirit for the ministry of the church (1 Cor. 1:7; 12:4, 9, 30f.; Rom. 12:6; Eph. 4:11).

The filling of the Spirit appears often in Acts (2:4; 4:8; 4:31; 6:3, 5; 7:55; 9:17; 11:24) and takes on special significance in Ephesians 5:18 as Paul moves from the wisdom (5:15–17) of the Christian life to the power of the Christian life (5:18–20). Christians are to avoid drunkenness and debauchery by being filled with the Spirit, which enables them to address one another in psalms directed toward God, hymns directed toward Christ, and songs inspired by the Spirit. It was this spiritual fulness that led some observers at Pentecost to conclude that Spirit-filled men were "filled with new wine" (Acts 2:13), but this filling of the Spirit is the source of power in the worship and work of the church.

The sword of the Spirit (Eph. 6:17) brings the nature of the church to a grand climax. The church pits herself against the world; and the Spirit with which she is filled, like a warrior, wields the living word of God until every power of darkness is vanquished (Heb. 4:12; Rev. 1:16; 2:16; 19:15, 21).

An exalted view of the living God leads to an exalted view of "the church of the living God, the pillar and ground of the truth" (1 Tim. 3:15, ASV). The mystery of godliness in Jesus Christ is the point from which to start both in the understanding of God and of "the household of God" (Eph. 2:19). The highest point in our understanding of God is reached in the formulation of the doctrine of the Holy Trinity, and it is from this perspective that the true nature of the church is revealed.

68. The Ministry of the Church

The tension between laity and clergy in much recent discussion is a part of the larger problem of the proper relation between the charismatic and official elements in the ministry of the New Testament church. The very fact of institutionalism, with an official ministry to preserve and perpetuate the apostolic tradition, has at times been blasted as a misunderstanding of the church.[28]

A milder form of the tension has come from careful New Testament

---

28. Emil Brunner, *The Misunderstanding of the Church*, tr. Harold Knight (Philadelphia: Westminster Press, 1953), pp. 35-46.

studies, but even in these room is made in the primitive church for the roots of all traditions from Quakerism to Catholicism. At one extreme is John and at the other are the Pastorals, with Paul at some point near the middle.[29] Such stimulating theories deserve the most careful study, but a less violent treatment of the basic texts does not demand such diversity.

It is the purpose of this brief essay to focus attention on some of the chief factors that require reconsideration. This may be done by drawing an analogy between the ministry of Christ and the ministry of the church.

The Ministry of Christ

It has been pointed out that "the prototype for the ministry is our Lord Himself" and that "the pattern for all the New Testament has to say about the ministry is what our Lord has to say about His ministry."[30] With this, one must quickly agree, but it is no easy thing to select those characteristics of our Lord's ministry. When the disciples disputed as to which of them was to be considered greatest, they received this answer:

> The kings of the Gentiles exercise lordship over them; and those in authority over them are called benefactors. But not so with you; rather let the greatest among you become as the youngest, and the leader as one who serves. For which is the greater, one who sits at table, or one who serves? Is it not the one who sits at table? But I am among you as one who serves.[31]

The servant motif becomes the link between the ministry of Jesus as the servant of the Lord and the ministry of Christian service, but there are some neglected elements in the ministry of Christ that help relate the charismatic and official ministries of the church.

The first is the anointment of Jesus. This is summed up in the statement that "God anointed Jesus of Nazareth with the Holy Spirit and power" (Acts 10:38), and this recalls the practice of anointment with all the implications involved. The Old Testament recognized three types of person consecrated for service: prophets, priests, and kings.[32] Anointment was used in the consecration of all of these.[33] Ordinarily, as after the anointment of Saul (1 Sam. 9:16; 10:1), "the anointed" was a term associated with kings; but Elijah anointed Elisha to a prophetic role (1 Kings 19:16), and Aaron the High Priest was also anointed (Exod. 29:7, 21; Lev. 6:20; 8:12). All of

---

29. Eduard Schweizer, *Church Order in the New Testament*, tr. Frank Clarke (London: Student Christian Movement Press, 1961), pp. 164f., n. 589.
30. J. K. S. Reid, *The Biblical Doctrine of the Ministry* (Edinburgh: Oliver and Boyd, 1955), p. 1.
31. Luke 22:25–27.
32. J. J. von Allmen, ed., *Vocabulary of the Bible* (London: Lutterworth Press, 1958), pp. 259-262.
33. T. F. Torrance, "Consecration and Ordination," *Scottish Journal of Theology*, Vol. II, No. 3 (September 1958), pp. 225-232.

the roles are related to the anointment of Christ with the Holy Spirit to fulfill his Messianic ministry.

The power *(dynamis)* of Jesus is the basic manifestation of the anointment of Jesus with the Spirit. The summary statement in Acts 10:38 is illustrated many times in the Gospel of Luke in particular. Even the birth of Jesus is made possible by the Holy Spirit coming upon Mary and the power of the Most High overshadowing her (Luke 1:35). After the Holy Spirit descended upon Jesus in bodily form as a dove (Luke 3:22), Jesus is described as returning from the Jordan "in the power of the Spirit" (Luke 4:14). The crucial passage is that concerning the reading of Isaiah 61:1f. in the synagogue at Nazareth (Luke 4:16–21), for after this, Jesus commands the unclean spirits to come out "with authority and power" (Luke 4:36). He healed people because "the power of the Lord was with him" (Luke 5:17), and "power came forth from him and healed them all" (Luke 6:19). Perhaps the most vivid example is the healing of the woman with the flow of blood. On this occasion Jesus said, "Some one touched me; for I perceive that power has gone forth from me" (Luke 8:46). The works God wrought in Jesus were *dynameōn* (Luke 19:37). This power was imparted to the Twelve (Luke 9:1) even when they followed Jesus in his earthly ministry; but after the Resurrection Jesus promised the Father would clothe them "with power from on high" (Luke 24:49). It is this dynamic, pneumatic, and charismatic quality in Jesus that furnished the basis for the charismatic ministry of the church. The power which worked in him was transferred to the church, and this is the theme that holds Luke's Gospel and Acts together.

Along with the power *(dynamis)* Jesus transferred his authority *(exousia)* to the Twelve (Luke 9:1), and Matthew tends to emphasize this quality as Luke emphasized the *dynamis*. This does not mean that Luke presents a dynamic Christ and Matthew an authoritative Christ, for power and authority are found in both pictures; but the special concern of Matthew for the teaching of Jesus in the role of the New Moses does make authority stand out in bold relief. The root idea may be seen in Matthew 11:27, where Jesus declares, "All things have been delivered to me by my Father." Mark's first chapter presents a general picture of Jesus astonishing the people because he "taught them as one who had authority *(exousia)*, and not as the scribes" (vs. 22). And this caused them to exclaim, "With authority *(kat' exousian)* he commands even the unclean spirits, and they obey him" (vs. 27). All three of the Synoptic Gospels record the fact that Jesus refused to answer the question as to the source of his authority (Mark 11:27–33; Matt. 21:23–27; Luke 20:1–8). It remains for Matthew to give the most exalted picture of the authority of Jesus. The six antitheses (Matt. 5:21–48) place the authority of Jesus over against all previous authority with the ringing repetition of the phrase "But I say to you" — six times in this one passage. Such teaching astonished the multitude, "for he taught them as one who had authority, and not as a scribe" (Matt. 7:29). Such authority extended to the forgiveness of sins (Mark 2:10) and the casting out of demons (Mark 3:15; 6:7). The ability *(dynamis)* to forgive sins and the authority *(exousia)* to forgive sins mean almost the same in Mark 2:7 and 2:10, and this helps to avoid a radical distinction between the two.

In addition to the anointment of Jesus and the related ideas of *dynamis* and *exousia*, the appointment of the Twelve furnishes background information for understanding how the ministry of Jesus is transferred to the church. It is impressive to note the concern of the Apostles with the vacancy left by the fall of Judas Iscariot. He lost his share in the ministry *(klēron tēs diakonias)*, and it became necessary for one "to take the place *(topos)* in this ministry and apostleship" (Acts 1:17, 25). There is considerable evidence the *klēros* and *topos* are official terms which designate the ruling places of the Twelve in the renewed Israel.[34] These conclusions are strengthened by the reference to the *klēros* of the presbyters in 1 Peter 5:3. It is, therefore, difficult to see how the New Testament ministry can be so interpreted as to rule out all teachings on an official ministry which begins with the Twelve.

The place of the Twelve in the renewed Israel has both evangelical and eschatological application. Mark 3:14–15 says that Jesus "appointed twelve *(apoiēsen dōdeka)*, to be with him, and to be sent out to preach and to have authority to cast out demons." The verb *poieō* is used in the Septuagint to describe the appointment of Moses and Aaron (1 Sam. 12:6) and priests (1 Kings 12:31; 13:33; 2 Chron. 2:18), and it is difficult to confine this to a purely charismatic calling. The number twelve has reference to the twelve tribes of Israel and becomes Mark's term to designate the group (Mark 4:10; 6:7; 9:35; 10:32; 11:11; 14:10, 17, 20, 43). In the eschatological hope which attended the proclamation of the Kingdom, the promise is made that those who followed Jesus in the "regeneration" *(palingenesia)* would "sit on twelve thrones judging the twelve tribes of Israel" (Matt. 19:28). This statement about an authoritative position strengthens the picture of an official position for the Twelve.

The primacy of Peter presents a peculiar problem that needs renewed consideration. Jesus said to him, "I will give you the keys of the kingdom of heaven, and whatever you bind on earth shall be bound in heaven" (Matt. 16:19). The women at Jesus' tomb were told that they should report the Resurrection to "the disciples and Peter" (Mark 16:7). It was Peter who spoke for the group at Pentecost (Acts 2:14–42). Even Paul says plainly that "Peter had been entrusted with the gospel of the circumcised," as he himself had been entrusted with the gospel of the uncircumcised (Gal. 2:7);

---

34. L. S. Thornton, "The Choice of Matthias," *Journal of Theological Studies*, Vol. 46 (1945), pp. 51-59.

and he calls attention to the fact that Jesus first "appeared to Cephas, then to the twelve" (1 Cor. 15:5). This proves nothing as to whether there is a successor to Simon Peter or not, but it does point to some sort of official ministry.

The position of James in the Jerusalem community needs to be considered also, for Paul says, "Then he appeared to James, then to all the apostles" (1 Cor. 15:7). When Peter appears at the house of Mary he says to Rhoda, "Tell this to James and to the brethren" (Acts 12:17). At the Jerusalem conference it was James who presided (Acts 15:13), and Paul went to James when he arrived in Jerusalem on his last journey (Acts 21:18). Peter and James were the only two Apostles whom Paul visited on his famed fifteen days in Jerusalem soon after he became a Christian (Gal. 1:19), and it was James, Cephas, and John who gave Paul and Barnabas the right hand of fellowship (Gal. 2:9). When men came to Antioch from Jerusalem, it was said they "came from James" (Gal. 2:12). The question is not raised as to the successor of James, but he is as prominent as Peter. His special relation to the Lord and the manner of his conversion perhaps account for this special position in the Jerusalem community.

It may be seen from this brief survey of the ministry of Christ that charismatic anointment and official appointment stand side by side. Adolf von Harnack, Karl Holl, and Max Weber have distinguished the inspired and the institutional leadership much in this manner, but it has become the custom to brush these categories aside as inadequate classifications. Even the great work by Hans von Campenhausen, *Church Office and Spiritual Authority in the First Three Centuries*,[35] which has done so much to illuminate the developing ministry, hesitates to make too much of this division. In the following pages an effort is made to suggest the twofold types anew.

The Ministry of the Church

In an effort to organize the New Testament material on the ministry, two Greek words may serve as guides: *charismata* and *cheirotonia*. Spiritual gifts, or *charismata*, are the characteristic ministries in the Pauline corpus, that is, Paul's letters aside from the Pastoral Epistles. God has bestowed these gifts for the edification of the saints and the building of the body of Christ, the church.

Charismata. A total of nine gifts are listed in 1 Corinthians 12:8–10. The word of wisdom enables those who are spiritual to understand the wisdom

---

35. von Campenhausen, *Kirchliches Amt und geistliche Vollmacht in den ersten drei Jahrhunderten* (Tübingen: J. C. B. Mohr [Paul Siebeck], 1953). English translation by J. A. Baker, *Ecclesiastical Office and Spiritual Power in the Church of the First Three Centuries* (London: A. and C. Black, 1979).

of God hidden from the wisdom of men (1 Cor. 2:6f.). The word of knowledge, even though it is less than love and may puff one up (1 Cor. 8:1), is to be used for spiritual edification (1 Cor. 14:6). The gift of miracle-working faith is also less than love (1 Cor. 13:2), but it is nonetheless God's gift (Rom. 12:3). Physical healings, which James (5:14f.) regulates through the presbyters, is viewed by Paul as one of the *charismata*. The mysterious working of miraculous powers, so common in the Gospels, continues to work in the spiritual body of Christ, which is the church. A type of inspired preaching, exercised by men and women, was also accepted as the gift of God (1 Cor. 11:4f.; compare Acts 21:9f.). In such a charismatic situation there were often false claims to inspiration (compare 1 John 4:1–6), but God had given some the ability to discern the spirits. Along with the gift to speak in ecstatic tongues was the gift to interpret these tongues so that all could be edified (1 Cor. 14:5).

A list of eight spiritual gifts soon follows in 1 Corinthians 12:28–30. The numbering of the gifts would indicate that Paul has some rating of value in mind. God appointed apostles first, but this has to do not with the official apostleship of the Twelve but with a type of charismatic person mentioned several times in the New Testament (Acts 14:4, 14; Rom. 16:7; 1 Cor. 9:2–5; 2 Cor. 11:13; 12:12; Gal. 1:19) and in the *Didache* (11:3ff.). (The *Didache* also mentions the charismatic prophets and lays down some rules by which false prophets can be discovered. If he stays for three days, asks for money, or eats a meal he ordered in the spirit he is a false prophet [*Didache* 11:3–12]). Inspired teachers, among whom were Barnabas and Saul, were also found in the early churches. Powers and healings along with tongues are mentioned again, but in between are the helpers and administrators that some have thought to be identical with the "deacons" and "bishops" of Philippians 1:1.[36] If this thesis be true, these helper-deacons and administrator-bishops are put only one step above those who speak in tongues! But perhaps the shift from the charismatic type to the official type reversed the order to this extent.

The seven gifts of Romans 12:6–8 include prophecy and teaching, but service, exhortation, liberality, ruling, and showing mercy are added. The difficulty confronted in the effort to define these spiritual gifts is some indication that already the charismatic glow has begun to vanish, but the seven gifts become more relevant when they are related to inspired preaching, social service, instruction in faith, pastoral counseling, Christian liberality, administration, and the visitation of the sick.[37] One wonders if all these functions would not be more deeply valued if they were recognized as

36. John Knox, "The Ministry in the Primitive Church" in *The Ministry in Historical Perspectives*, ed. H. Richard Niebuhr and Daniel D. Williams (New York: Harper & Brothers, 1956), p. 10.
37. A. M. Hunter, *The Epistle to the Romans* (London: Student Christian Movement Press, 1955), p. 109.

spiritual gifts. In this suggestion a spark of hope for the renewal of spiritual life may be seen.

The five gifts of Ephesians 4:11 add two new gifts: evangelists and pastors. Philip, one of seven elected to aid the Apostles, is later mentioned as an evangelist in Caesarea, and his four unmarried daughters have the gift of prophecy (Acts 21:9). The only other time the term evangelist appears in the New Testament is found in the exhortation to Timothy to "do the work of an evangelist" (2 Tim. 4:5), but his official capacity is in another direction. The gift of pastor *(poimēn)* is not an office, as Protestant thought since Zwingli's work on *The Shepherd* (1524) has assumed, but a gift and a function. The *laos* is the whole church, but *klēros* is that portion of the church under the care of a presbyter. The picture of Christ as the Good Shepherd (John 10:1–16) and the Great Shepherd (Heb. 13:20) adds much to the gift which finds classical expression in 1 Peter 5:1–4. The New Testament basis for a distinction between laity and clergy is found in 1 Peter *(laos*, 2:10, and *klēros*, 5:3). It seems probable that these references do have some connection with an official ministry, but there is no mention of ordination and office.

Some would raise the question whether the New Testament ever gives a basis for the practice of ordination and the institution of an official ministry.[38] Any conclusion must be reached through an evaluation of the evidence relating to the apostolic ordination of others through the laying on of hands. Some have traced ordination directly to the rite of *semikah*, which was designed to communicate rabbinic authority through the laying on of hands,[39] but the evidence is so uncertain that it seems safer to say the New Testament practice is derived directly from the Old Testament.[40] The term *samak* is used in the Old Testament three times to describe the ordaining of Joshua as the successor of Moses (Num. 27:18, 23; Deut. 34:9); and the act indicated that Moses "put his honor *(hod)* upon him." Another term of special significance is *sim* or *shith*, the two terms being used as synonyms in the act of blessing in Genesis 48:14ff. The question as to which if either of these practices stands behind the practice of ordination in the New Testament remains to be determined. The use of the verb to tend *(poimanate)* and the noun flock *(poimnion)* in 1 Peter 5:2 addressed to presbyters and the use of the same words in a similar passage in Acts 20:28–29 are the closest identification of the gift of pastor with the office of bishop that can be found; yet the link is not complete even here, and one can only conclude

38. Heber F. Peacock, "Ordination in the New Testament," *Review and Expositor*, Vol. LV, No. 3 (July 1958), pp. 262-274.
39. David Daube, *The New Testament and Rabbinic Judaism* (London: Athlone Press, 1956), pp. 224-246.
40. Peacock, *op. cit.*, pp. 224-246. Arnold Ehrhardt, "Jewish and Christian Ordination," *The Journal of Ecclesiastical History*, Vol. V (1954), p. 138.

that the noun pastor *(poimēn)* is never used in an official sense in the New Testament.

Cheirotonia. Ordination is the crucial issue in relating the charismatic and official ministries of the church. The Pauline corpus hardly mentions any type of official ministry, and for this reason a radical distinction has often been made between the Pauline and the Jerusalem view of the ministry. First Thessalonians 5:12 mentions "those who labor among you and are over you in the Lord." *Proistamenous* means "those who stand in front" and may have reference to "the presbyters or bishops and deacons."[41] The Corinthians are told "to be subject" *(hypotassesthe)* to those of the household of Stephanas, but this seems to be due to their devoted service to the saints (1 Cor. 16:15f.). Hebrews mentions a group of leaders *(hegoumenoi)* to whom the believers are to submit because they watch over their souls (Heb. 13:7, 17, 24), and some see here a reference to "bishops, teachers, deacons."[42]

Deacons derive their name from the idea of the servant, a term most closely related to the Messianic ministry of our Lord. Despite this, in the history of this church the diaconate became the lowest of the three main orders of the church.[43] It is generally assumed, although the noun is not used, that Acts 6:1–6 accounts for the origin of the deacons (Phil. 1:1 and 1 Tim. 3:8–13), as they were later known. The ministry *(diakonia)* of the seven was "to serve *(diakonein)* tables," that the Twelve might devote themselves "to the ministry *(diakonia)* of the word." One of the qualifications for this official group was that they should possess charismatic qualities — "full of the Spirit"! Out of the circle of charismatic men the official ministry was to be chosen, and the fact that this has not always been done in the history of the diaconate has often been disastrous.

Were the deacons ordained? After they were chosen by the whole multitude, they were set "before the apostles, and they prayed and laid their hands upon them" (Acts 6:6). Who laid their hands on them? Codex Bezae and the Peshitta support the idea that the Apostles laid their hands on the seven, but many reject this reading and claim this as an instance of lay-ordination such as is seen in Acts 13:3; however, the laying on of hands in this instance is by the prophets and teachers. If the background of this type of ordination is Numbers 8:10, then the Levites become the nearest Old Testament source for the seven. A passage in *The Mishnah* *(Sanhedrin* 1.6), which mentions the permission given to a group of one hundred and twenty

---

41. A. T. Robertson, *Word Pictures in the New Testament* (Nashville: Sunday School Board of the Southern Baptist Convention, 1931), IV, 36.

42. Johannes Schneider, *The Letter to the Hebrews,* tr. William A. Mueller (Grand Rapids: Wm. B. Eerdmans Publishing Company, 1957), p. 127. It is surely more than "the hankering after the Jewish cult" (Schweizer, *op. cit.,* p. 17).

43. Reid, *op. cit.,* pp. 1-3.

men (compare Acts 1:15) to elect a local Sanhedrin of seven, is interpreted as background to "elder-deacons."[44] Again, others have concluded that they were more missionaries than they were either elders or deacons.[45]

When one turns to Philippians 1:1 it seems that the deacons are the assistants of the bishops, and it is generally thought that these bishops are the same as elders. First Timothy does not leave the impression that the deacons of 3:8-13 are identical with the elders of 4:14 and 5:17. Along with the deacons a group of "women" (1 Tim. 3:11) are mentioned, and this raises the question whether they were deaconesses after the manner of Phoebe, the deaconess of Cenchreae (Rom. 16:1). This is about as far as the New Testament evidence goes, but the early church recognized an order of ordained deacons.[46] The evidence for deaconesses is not so plentiful, but as early as the reign of Trajan (A.D. 98-117), Pliny the Younger reports "two maid-servants, who were called deaconesses *(ministrae).*"[47]

The elders or presbyters are mentioned many times in the New Testament (Acts 11:30; 14:23; 15:2, 4, 6, 22f.; 16:4; 20:17; 21:18; 1 Tim. 4:14; 5:17, 19; Titus 1:5; 1 Pet. 5:1-5; Jas. 5:14; 2 John 1; 3 John 1). There will even be elders in heaven (Rev. 4:4, 10; 5:8, 14; 7:13)!

Only Acts 14:23 and Titus 1:5 throw any light on the ordination of elders. At the conclusion of the first missionary journey by Barnabas and Paul it is said: "When they had appointed *(cheirotonēsantes)* elders for every church, with prayer and fasting they committed them to the Lord in whom they believed" (Acts 14:23). It is from the verb *cheirotoneō* (*cheir,* "hand," and *teinō,* "to stretch") that the technical term for ordination, *cheirotonia,* later developed; yet the use of the term in 2 Corinthians 8:19 makes clear that there is a long development before the full idea of ordination is reached. Titus is told to "appoint *(katastēseis)* elders in every city" (Titus 1:5), and the verb *kathistēmi* is the same as that used in the appointment of the deacons in Acts 6:3. The appointment of the elders was a part of the process by which Titus was to set in order *(epidiothosei)* what was lacking in Crete. *Epidiorthoō* (from *orthoō,* "to set straight," *dia,* "thoroughly," and *epi,* "in addition") gives some idea of the necessity of order in the churches, but it adds little to the idea that the appointment is ordination.

The origin of the elders is not specified in the New Testament. They are first mentioned in the churches in Acts 11:30, but they are found also outside the church (compare Luke 22:66; Acts 4:5; 22:5). It is the most general term for members of the Sanhedrin, and the idea reaches back to "the elders of Israel" (Exod. 3:16; 24:1; Num. 11:16). There seems little doubt that they were taken over from the Sanhedrin to the church. In Je-

44. Torrance, *op. cit.,* p. 237.
45. G. H. C. Macgregor in *The Interpreter's Bible* (New York: Abingdon-Cokesbury Press, 1951-57), Vol. 9, p. 90.
46. *The Apostolic Tradition,* IX.
47. *Epistulae,* X, 96.

rusalem the elders have authority alongside the Apostles (Acts 15:2, 4, 6, 22f.; 16:4; 21:18), and they are the only leaders of the churches in 1 Peter 5:1–5 and James 5:14. Even Peter classifies himself as a "fellow elder" *(sympresbyteros)* in 1 Peter 5:1. In James 5:14 they are not only official leaders but they possess the charismatic power of healing.

The office of bishop presents a most difficult problem. At times one finds evidence in the early church to support the idea that "bishops and deacons" were the official ministry (1 *Clem.* 42:4, 5; *Didache* XV.1). This is the picture presented in the New Testament in the earliest reference (Phil. 1:1). It may be that the charismatic helpers and administrators of 1 Corinthians 12:28 have become the "bishops and deacons" of Philippians 1:1. That *episkopoi* has Greek antecedents as *presbyteroi* has Jewish antecedents seems clear from the fact that in Philippi the term *presbyteroi* is not used at all. In Acts 20:28 the term *episkopoi* is used as a synonym of the *presbyteroi* of Acts 20:17, and there is still a plurality as in Philippi.

A shift from the plural to the singular appears in the Pastoral Epistles. In Titus the *episkopos* of 1:7 almost certainly has reference to the *presbyteroi* of 1:5; otherwise the *gar* ("for") makes little sense. Any basis for a bishop beyond the plurality of elders must be found in 1 Timothy.

The real question is: Who occupies the office of bishop *(episkopē)* in 1 Timothy 3:1? Is it the *presbyteroi* of 1 Timothy 4:14; 5:17, 19? It hardly seems possible to draw this conclusion. Timothy is exhorted: "Do not neglect the gift *(charisma)* you have, which was given you by prophetic utterance when the elders laid their hands upon you" (1 Tim. 4:14). This is followed by the suggestion that Timothy would lay his hands on others (5:22). Is Timothy the one who occupies the *episkopē*, and is this that to which the *presbyterion* consecrated him? Ignatius was "bishop of Syria,"[48] Polycarp of Smyrna,[49] Onesimus of Ephesus,[50] Damas of Magnesia,[51] and Polybius of Tralles.[52] Of course this does not prove that Timothy was bishop of Ephesus before Onesimus; but if he is the Onesimus of Philemon 10, there is a clear connection with Paul. The jump between 1 Timothy and Ignatius is not so great as some suppose.

Much has been said about the *charisma* which was given *(edothē)* to Timothy through prophecy *(dia propheteias)* and by the laying on of the hands *(meta epitheseōs tōn cheirōn)* of the presbytery (1 Tim. 4:14). Emphasis on "because of prophecies" (accusative plural) instead of "through prophecy" (genitive singular) hardly explains away the *meta* of accompaniment in *meta epitheseōs tōn cheirōn*. To this must be added the statement by Paul that Timothy should "rekindle the gift *(charisma)* of God" that was

48. Ign. Rom. 2:2.
49. Ign. Poly. 1:1; Magn. 15:1.
50. Ign. Eph. 1:3.
51. Ign. Magn. 2:1.
52. Ign. Trall. 2:1.

in him through the laying on of Paul's hands, *dia tēs epitheseōs* (2 Tim. 1:6). This *dia* must be genitive singular. The idea of *semikah*, or the pouring of one man's powers into another man, is more than imaginary exegesis in 2 Timothy 1:6. At least the official ministry of Timothy is vitally related to the *charismata*. The union of prophetic utterances and the presbytery in 1 Timothy 4:14 comes near to the ideal ministry for which a crippled Christendom waits.[53]

The Ministry of Women

Special ministries that did not require ordination were performed by women in the church of the New Testament and of the early centuries.[54] The probability that there were deaconesses along with deacons in apostolic times has already been mentioned, and it is certain that the office developed into major importance in the third and fourth centuries. It was only the triumph of infant baptism as the almost uniform practice of the church that helped to bring about the decline of this special ministry, for the preparation of women catechumens for baptism and assistance in the administration of immersion were among their particular duties. It was not until the nineteenth century that Protestant churches began to restore the ministry of the deaconesses, but a restoration of believer's baptism with the resumption of their ancient functions would do much to give their role the recognition that is long overdue. Lutherans, Methodists, Anglicans, and Presbyterians have done much in other ways to reestablish the deaconesses, but German Baptists have done most to make them a regular part of the church's official ministry.[55]

The modern nun has a precedent in the ministry of the New Testament virgins. Although it is not certain, the order of virgins may have arisen out of the practice disclosed in Acts 21:9, which speaks of four virgin daughters of Philip, the evangelist, who had the gift of prophecy. The strange practice of spiritual marriage, seen later in the *Shepherd of Hermas* (Sim. IX.11), may also be behind Paul's concern with celibacy in 1 Corinthians 7:25–35. There is no doubt that Paul regarded the celibate life the best life, for this would free both male and female from the anxieties of marriage and enable them to be more consecrated to the Lord. The virgin "is anxious about the affairs of the Lord, how to be holy in body and spirit" (vs. 34). This is obviously a special ministry that only a few can follow, but there is surely

---

53. Paul Rowntree Clifford, "Confronting the Episcopalian Theory of the Apostolic Ministry," *Foundations*, Vol. II, No. 3 (July 1959), pp. 207-220.
54. Jean Daniélou, *The Ministry of Women in the Early Church*, tr. Glyn Simon (London: Faith Press, 1961). C. H. Turner, "Ministries of Women in the Primitive Church: Widow, Deaconess and Virgin," in *Catholic and Apostolic*, edited by H. N. Bate (London: A. R. Mowbray, 1931), pp. 316-351.
55. A survey with sources may be found in F. L. Cross, editor, *Oxford Dictionary of the Christian Church* (London: Oxford University Press, 1958), pp. 377f.

room for this type of life in the body of Christ even in the modern world. The lives of a multitude of noble nuns testify to this point.

Deaconesses and virgins were closely associated with the ministry of widows, but they do not appear to be identical. Very early the widows have a claim on the charity of the church, and their neglect was associated with the necessity of the so-called seven deacons (Acts 6:1). In Joppa the disciple named Tabitha or Dorcas lived with a community of widows connected with works of charity (Acts 9:36-39). A long passage in 1 Timothy 5 (vss. 3-16) brings the widows in full view. Indeed, more is said about this order than is said of deacons, presbyters, or bishops. "Real widows," in contrast to younger widows, are women over sixty whose main ministry is a life of perpetual prayer. Their previous lives in the married state met the highest standards of Christian holiness. The household of God was an extension of the godly households in which each had been a faithful wife and mother. Just as a bishop or deacon was required to be the husband of one wife, a widow was permitted to be the wife of one husband (*henos andros gynē*, vs. 9). Remarriage disqualified them for this honored service to which a widow dedicated herself with a pledge (vs. 12).

Early church leaders mention this order. After greeting Polycarp, bishop of Smyrna, along with the presbytery and deacons, Ignatius of Antioch speaks of the "virgins who are called widows" (*Smyr.* XIII.1). Virgins and widows are apparently merged, as in much later history, but they are clearly marked off from the ordinary laity. Polycarp himself speaks of the widows' chief function in the early church when he says:

> Let us teach the widows to be discreet in the faith of the Lord, praying ceaselessly for all men, being far from all slander, evil speaking, false witness, love of money, and all evil, knowing that they are an altar of God, and that all offerings are tested, and that nothing escapes him of reasoning or thoughts, or of "the secret things of the heart" (*Phil.* IV.3).

In the early church three orders of women developed along with the three orders of men. In the case of men, ordination definitely set them apart from the general laity, although they were still a part of the laity; but the women, too, were in other ways marked off by functions not expected of all Christians.

The picture that develops is one of a large charismatic circle that includes all the people of God, all members of the body of Christ; but some members with unusual gifts and qualifications are set aside for special ministries that have official status. Even those who protest most vigorously against any distinction between the official ministries and ministries that are only charismatic are unable to discount the development of some substitute for these original workers. The very phrase "full-time ministry" — to say nothing of "deacons," "pastors," "executive secretaries," and the like —

exposes the emptiness of this protest. There is no reason why those "who live by the gospel" should not be consecrated to the life to which they have given themselves.[56]

69. Initiation into the Church: Baptism

"Believer's baptism" as a descriptive and definitive phrase is the usual way Baptists and kindred groups designate the primacy of faith in the baptismal act and distinguish themselves from those who practice "infant baptism." Appeal is made to the subjective response in a manner that excludes the *opus operatum* of Roman Catholic theology and other forms of objectivity that permit the administration of baptism to infants and even the unborn foetus that has never breathed the breath of life.

Advocates of infant baptism insist that the subjective response of the parents and the worshipping congregation justifies the practice, but there are many instances where it is administered without these two forms of proxy faith. At the present time serious questions are being raised within the groups that have long practiced infant baptism, and the questions reach so far as to raise theological issues about the practice of child baptism (pedobaptism) among Baptists.

It is obvious that some of the great Christians of the past and present were baptized as infants or as children. The atmosphere of a Christian home and a Christian congregation enabled them to appropriate subjectively what they had previously received objectively, while some who received baptism as adolescents and adults fell by the wayside with little evidence that they died to sin and rose to walk in a new life. It is the purpose of this brief essay to point out factors that focus on the most appropriate time for the administration of baptism and the primacy of faith in baptismal theology. The priority of grace to faith is presupposed.

Baptism and Purification

Some baptismal theology, notably that of Joachim Jeremias, finds the origin of baptism associated with the idea of impurity.[57] In proselyte baptism, Gentiles, who were considered impure by the Hillel school, were initiated by circumcision, baptism, and sacrifice. In the famous debate between R. Eliezer the Shammaite and R. Joshua the Hillelite, the Sages concluded that both the circumcision promoted by the Shammaites and the baptism advocated by the Hillelites were necessary to make one a proper proselyte (b. *Yeb.*, 46a). It is thought by most scholars that the idea reaches back

56. This section was originally published in *Interpretation*, XIX (April, 1965), No. 2, pp. 168-181. Recent debate over the charismatic and official ministries does not require any revisions.
57. *Infant Baptism in the First Four Centuries*, tr. David Cairns (Philadelphia: The Westminster Press, 1960), pp. 24-40.

before the destruction of the temple in A.D. 70, since sacrifice followed circumcision and baptism, but Jeremias dates it before A.D. 30. A passage in the *Mishnah*, attributed to Hillel, is crucial: "He that separates himself from his uncircumcision is as one that separates himself from a grave" (*Pesahim* 8.8). Therefore, the impurity of uncircumcision needs to be washed away as if it were contact with the dead.

Strong opposition to this view has been expressed. Some think there is no suggestion of purification in the rite as described (*Gerim*. I. 1–8; b. *Yeb*., 47a, b), but this is difficult to defend in the light of related passages on purification (b. *Yeb*., 46b; cf. *Ker*., 9a). It seems a false antithesis to say that this baptism was essentially a forward look of initiation rather than a backward look of purification.[58] It was both. Jeremias is obviously inspired by his desire to prove that infant baptism was administered with infant circumcision in both proselyte baptism and Christian baptism, but this should not blind Baptists to the value of his research.

If this brief preface on purification has relevance for Christian baptism it is at the point of John's repentance baptism for the forgiveness of sins (Mark 1:4f.), but the strong stress on the confession of sins *(exomologoumenoi tēs hamartias)* leaves no room for the baptism of those void of repentance and faith. This same note is sounded in the early church, and the promise to children is as future as is the promise to those "far off, everyone whom the Lord your God calls to him" (Acts 2:39).

Repentance baptism is vitally related to ritual purification (1 Cor. 6:11). Paul was commanded: "Rise and be baptized, and wash away your sins, calling upon his name" (Acts 22:16). Ritual purification is always related to repentance and the reception of the word. The word associated with the water in Ephesians 5:26 is perhaps the confessional word that attended baptism (cf. Rom. 10:8–13). The "water with the word" *(hydatos en rhemati)*, not water without the word, is the creating and cleansing act of God. Purification in other New Testament passages does not appear to contradict this claim (Heb. 10:22; Tit. 3:5; John 3:5).

Jeremias is careful to concede that there is no *"direct mention* of the baptism of young proselyte children" before R. Huna (c. A.D. 212-297), but this is a minor, not an infant.[59] The first instance of infant baptism in Judaism is at the end of the third century A.D. when a foundling was baptized in case it was a Gentile, but this was after infant baptism was widely practiced in Christianity. The circumcision of infant males was pre-Christian, but the baptism of infants and children is another matter. Even so, infant baptism in Judaism was practiced only when they were not born in holiness (b. *Yeb*. 11.2). When applied in 1 Corinthians 7:14, as it per-

---

58. G. F. Moore, *Judaism* (Cambridge: Harvard University Press, 1946), vol. I, p. 334; T. W. Manson, *Studies in the Gospels*, edited by D. E. Nineham (Oxford: Basil Blackwell, 1955), pp. 219f.
59. *Ibid.*, pp. 38f.

haps should be, it becomes an argument against the baptism of infants born in the holiness of a home in which at least one parent is holy (i.e., a Christian).

This primitive idea of purification leads to infant baptism only when perverted by the fallacious notion of original guilt. In the second Christian century appeal was made to the innocence of children, not to their guilt.[60] It was not until after A.D. 231 that there was *direct approval* of infant baptism, and original guilt was there assumed. Origen's comments on Leviticus 12:2, Luke 2:22, and Romans 6:5-7 argue for original sin on the basis that infant baptism is being practiced, not vice versa.[61] Tertullian mentioned the practice of infant baptism at the beginning of the third century, but he opposed it on the basis of his belief in two ages: the age of innocence until puberty and the age of guilt after puberty (*De baptismo*, 18; *De anima*, 38. 1).

As long ago as 1924, when N. P. Williams delivered his Bampton Lectures in Oxford, the link between inherited guilt and infant baptism has been greatly weakened. Williams frankly said: "If, then, the insistence of the historic Church upon the permissibility, and indeed necessity, of infant baptism is to be justified, some theoretical basis for this custom other than the idea of 'original guilt' must now be found."[62] Yet Cyprian (*Ep.* 64:2) spread the idea in Latin theology and promoted both infant immersion and infant communion (*De lapsis*, 25). In conflict with the Pelagians, Augustine developed the doctrine into a rigid dogma that assigned saving efficacy to the most indiscriminate forms of infant baptism. The unbaptized infant of a pious mother is damned while the infant of an enemy of Christ indiscriminately baptized is saved (*Contra Julianum*, II. 11), and he argues on the assumption that the unbaptized twin, exposed by a harlot mother, was damned while the twin baptized by a merciful person was saved (*ibid.*, II. 14).

Against this absurd theology the Anabaptists made protest. "Believer's baptism" does not get to the heart of the problem, unless repentance is always assumed as the negative side of faith and baptism is attended by guilt and forgiveness.

> The initial call to believer's baptism stressed, over against pedo-baptism, not the adult capacity to believe but rather to repent. The revival at Zollikon involved the reconception of repentance. To the worn out sacrament of Baptism had been restored the experiential significance of the now displaced sacrament of penance.[63]

60. Kurt Aland, *Did the Early Church Baptize Infants*, tr. G. R. Beasley-Murray (London: SCM Press, 1963), pp. 70-74.
61. The quotes are given in *ibid.*, p. 47, n. 1.
62. *The Ideas of the Fall and of Original Sin* (London: Longmans, Green and Company, 1927), p. 551.
63. George Williams, *The Radical Reformation* (London: Wiedenfeld and Nicolson, 1963), p. 124.

The practice of pedobaptism (child baptism) among Baptists may be said to make room for the faith of innocent children, who later appropriate their baptism, but it is doubtful that it can pass for a repentance baptism that involves guilt and forgiveness. If one must be "saved" before he is baptized and one must be "lost" before he can be "saved," it is as difficult to defend much present practice of pedobaptism as it is to defend infant baptism. Only the transfer of belief from the parents to the child makes the difference between infant baptism and pedobaptism (child baptism). This is the crux of the questions relating belief and baptism, but a briefer survey of some related ideas may be added.

Baptism and Identification

Before turning to the distinctive Pauline view of baptism as a sign of incorporation into the one body of Christ, a kindred idea linked directly as a formula with *baptisthēnai* only in Acts should be considered separately, although many make no distinction between identification with Christ in Acts and incorporation into the body of Christ in the letters of Paul. Since Luke does not use the metaphor of the body of Christ, the teachings in Acts require separate notice.

Acts 2:38 has four steps in Christian initiation: (1) repentance, which was found in the preaching of John the Baptist, (2) baptism in the name of Jesus as the distinctive teaching in Acts, (3) the forgiveness of sins found also in the preaching of John the Baptist, and (4) the reception of the Holy Spirit which had been promised as a future gift of the Messiah by John the Baptist.

The preposition in Acts 2:38 is *epi*, and this is perhaps due to the quotation from the prophet Joel who promised salvation to "whoever calls upon *(epikalesētai)* the name of the Lord" (Acts 2:21). In Acts 8:16 and 19:5 the preposition is *eis*, and this is the preposition in the great commission of Matthew 28:19 where those who are made disciples are, according to the longer text, to be baptized "in *(eis)* the name of the Father and of the Son and of the Holy Spirit." The shorter text says simply to "make disciples in my name," with no mention of baptism. Acts 10:48 uses a third preposition, *en*, but Luke seems to mean the same thing with each preposition.

Some light is thrown on this identification formula by the language of Paul. In 1 Corinthians 1:13, 15 Paul rebukes those who claimed to belong to him when they had not been baptized in his name. This seems clearly to imply that baptism in the name of a person signified that one belonged to that person. The Corinthians had been baptized in the name of Christ, so they belong to Christ, not Paul. 1 Corinthians 6:11 speaks of Christian initiation "in *(en)* the name of our Lord Jesus Christ and by *(en)* the Spirit of our God," and this is further support for the identification formula before Paul used the incorporation formula in reference to the one body of Christ.

Baptism and Incorporation

References to household baptism in the New Testament (Acts 16:15, 31; 18:8; 1 Cor. 1:16),[64] plus the mention of Christian children in the New Testament and in the early church,[65] have been proposed as *indirect proof* that baptism was administered to children before they believed. If they are incorporated into the body of Christ, as Christians, it is argued, they must be baptized, for baptism is incorporation into the body of Christ. Without baptism, even children born into a Christian household would be outside the *Corpus Christi*, in the *Regnum Christi* where the demons and unbelievers are.[66]

In the early church the enrolment of Christian children as catechumens for baptism made them Christians along with adult converts not yet baptized. Even Augustine, with his doctrine of original guilt, reflects this practice at several places (*Conf.*, I. 11; *De cat. rud.*, 50; *De pec. merit. et remis.*, 2, 26). In his words to catechumens, Quodvuldeus states clearly the Latin practice: "For you are not yet reborn in holy baptism, but by the sign of the cross you are conceived in the womb of mother church."[67] In the East, as late as the seventh century, James of Edessa said of catechumens: "The ancient custom was that they remained thus for a long time and during this period were called Christians; then finally they were baptized."[68] Both catechumens and the faithful were within the body of Christ the Church, but the baptism of catechumens, converts and Christian children, was a further incorporation into the body which increased communion until the completion of Christ's mystical body at the resurrection of the dead.

It is not evident that such views were innovations from the baptism of repentance and faith in the New Testament. Baptism as the crucial act of incorporation into Christ's mystical body concentrates on the factor of faith (1 Cor. 12:1–13). It is significant that the letter which is of major importance on the theme of justification by faith has the declaration: "For as many of you as were baptized into Christ did put on Christ" (Gal. 3:27). Luther's doctrine of *sola fides* in justification drove him in defense of infant baptism to a doctrine of *fides infantium*.[69]

Faith-knowledge is a refrain in the great baptismal hymn preserved in

---

64. The Church of Scotland, *Interim Report of the Special Commission on Baptism*, May, 1955, pp. 19-29.
65. Joachim Jeremias, *op. cit.*, pp. 59-86.
66. Oscar Cullmann, *Baptism in the New Testament* (London: SCM Press, 1950), p. 34.
67. From E. C. Whitaker, *Documents of the Baptismal Liturgy* (London: S.P.C.K., 1960), p. 97.
68. *Ibid.*, p. 50.
69. See Anders Nygren, *Commentary on Romans*, tr. Carl C. Rasmussen (Philadelphia: Muhlenberg Press, 1949), pp. 164f. for a summary of *sola fides* and Karl Brinkel, *Die Lehre Luthers von der fides infantium bei der Kindertaufe* (Berlin: Evangelische Verlagsanstalt, 1958) for *fides infantium*. Augustine also taught a theory of infant faith in Letter 98. 10 and infant illumination in *De pecc. merit. et remiso* I. 38. See D. S. Bailey, *Sponsors at Baptism and Confirmation*, pp. 112f.

Romans 6:3–11. Each stanza appeals to what they "know" (6:3, 6, 9). The *locus classicus* for those who would equate circumcision in the Old Covenant with baptism in the New Covenant rules out baptism without belief with the words: "having been buried with him in baptism, wherein you were also raised with him *through faith* in the working of God" (Col. 2:12). The *dia tēs pisteōs* (through faith) is not in harmony with a Christian circumcision received in infancy. Christian circumcision is received in the heart of the believer, not in the flesh (Rom. 2:28f.). It is not necessary to interpret "the circumcision of Christ" as the crucifixion of Christ to refute the appeal to circumcision for the support of infant baptism. Immersion in water through faith is only one act, the crucial act, in the process of Christian incorporation into the body of Christ.

Baptism and Regeneration

Calvin saw clearly this point in his exposition of progressive regeneration. He taught that baptism was administered even to infant children, not *in order* to incorporate and regenerate them, but because, having received the covenant promise, they must be presumed to be in the process already. According to Calvin, children are admitted into the church by baptism on no "other ground than that they belonged to the body of Christ before they were born."[70] Baptism is the sign of both the forgiveness of sins and regeneration, but "regeneration is only begun, and goes on making progress during the whole life."[71] In summary:

> It follows, that children of believers are not baptized, that they
> may thereby then become the children of God, as if they had been
> before aliens to the church, but on the contrary, they are received
> into the Church by the solemn sign, since they already belong to
> the body of Christ by virtue of the promise.[72]

The promise has pushed into the background the necessity of baptism for the removal of original guilt, but the reason for infant baptism has been weakened.

The clash of Calvinism with Catholicism in the Anglican tradition precipitated the famous Gorham case of the nineteenth century. In 1847 the Bishop of Exeter, Henry Philpotts, found the Rev. G. C. Gorham "unsound" on the doctrine of baptismal regeneration because Gorham insisted that baptism was efficacious only when worthily received. Article XXV of the Thirty-Nine Articles, a Calvinistic document, said much the same, but the necessity of a worthy reception raised again the primacy of faith in

70. *Calvin's Tracts and Treatises*, tr. Henry Beveridge, edited by Thomas F. Torrance (Edinburgh: Oliver and Boyd, 1958), Vol. III, p. 275.
71. C. R. XXXV, p. 425.
72. *Institutes of the Christian Religion*, IV. v. 22.

baptism. Present interest in the debate has been precipitated by the problems that still persist.

A baptismal hymn in Titus 3:4-7 is the *locus classicus* on baptism in relation to regeneration, and it is very clear that it concerns those "who have believed in God" (3:8). Christian children are mentioned in Titus, but this is no proof that they were baptized before they believed. In any case, they are "children that believe, who are not accused of riot or unruly" (1:6), and this is not the behavior of babes. Even so, a defense of infant baptism appeals to this passage.[73]

Baptism and Salvation

Baptism in relation to the whole process of salvation brings further focus on the primacy of faith. Another baptismal hymn found in 1 Peter 3:18-22 does indeed declare that, after the antitype of Noah's flood, "baptism now saves" *(nyn sōizei baptisma)*, but it is necessary to note the nature of this saving act. It is not the act of ceremonial washing that saves, for this is not the controlling principle of baptism, but "the interrogation of a good conscience toward God, through the resurrection of Jesus Christ" (3:21). The interrogation *(eperōtēma)* possibly reflects the practice of confessing one's faith as a part of the baptismal rite. It is the same as the *homologia* (confession) of Rom. 10:10, another baptismal hymn.[74] Interrogation and confession not only point up the primacy of faith, but they leave no place for infant baptism.

Baptisma includes both faith and immersion, but it is faith that is the controlling principle. The confession of faith may even in an irregular way lead to salvation without immersion in water, but immersion in water does not lead to salvation without the confession of faith in the saving event of Christ's death and resurrection. It is the act of God in the complex of factors in *baptisma* (faith, immersion, even chrismation, confirmation, and communion)[75] that saves, but the one factor that controls all the rest is faith. Without faith none of the potentialities of the other acts becomes actual and potent unto salvation.

Baptism and Illumination

A sixth approach to the primacy of faith in baptism appears in the Letter to the Hebrews. Reference to those "who were once enlightened" *(tous hapax phōtisthentas*, Heb. 6:4) is generally taken to be connected with baptism (cf. Heb. 10:32), and this is the guiding thought in the baptismal

---

73. The Church of Scotland, *Interim Report of the Special Commission on Baptism*, May, 1955, p. 26.
74. Bo Reicke, *The Disobedient Spirits and Christian Baptism* (Copenhagen: Ejnar Munksgaard, 1946), pp. 182-186.
75. G. W. H. Lampe, *A Patristic Greek Lexicon* (Oxford: At the Clarendon Press, 1961), p. 285.

theology of Justin Martyr (1 *Apology* 61, 65). Instruction before immersion and belief before baptism, as in *Didache* 7, are clearly two of the major steps to the Eucharist. Justin said (1 *Apology* 61):

> As many as are persuaded and believe these things which we teach and describe are true, and undertake to live accordingly, are taught to pray and ask God, while fasting, for the forgiveness of their sins: and we pray and fast with them. They are led by us to a place where there is water, and they are reborn after the manner of the rebirth by which we also were reborn: for they are then washed (or, wash themselves) in the water in the Name of the Father and Lord God of all things, and of our Savior Jesus Christ, and of the Holy Spirit — This washing is called enlightenment, *(phōtismos)*, because those that are experiencing these things have their minds enlightened.

It is this cognitive element in baptism that has been brought to the fore by Karl and Markus Barth. In 1943 Karl Barth's booklet *The Teaching of the Church Regarding Baptism* made no little stir as it called infant baptism into question by placing the cognitive act over the causative act. In 1951 a larger splash was made in the baptismal debate when Markus Barth, in an elaborate and impassioned way, put the question in the title of his book: *Die Taufe — ein Sakrament?* The words *Gebot, Gehorsam, Gebet, Gabe* (command, obedience, prayer, gift) are left ringing in the ears as one plows through the answer to the question: Is baptism a sacrament? A certain imbalance creeps in as the *Gehorsamakt* (act of obedience) crowds out all human instrumentality, but the obedience of faith is given the primacy in all efficacious baptism. Baptismal theology of this type, if taken seriously, is sure to lead to a radical baptismal reform not far from that of the Anabaptists and the Baptists.[76]

70. Fellowship in the Church: The Lord's Supper

If one should witness the celebration of our Savior's sacrifice in all the churches of a large city, he would be amazed at the variety of practices and the different names used to designate the service. This is true as much in the case of the Lord's Supper as in the case of baptism.

On the one hand one would see a small group in an informal meeting in what would usually be a modest building, but they would practice earnest exhortation and self-examination before they ate an unleavened waffle or loaf blessed in the name of the Lord Jesus. They would also use a single

---

76. This was virtually what Karl Barth called for in his last and unfinished volume, *Kirchliche Dogmatik* IV. 4 (Zollikon-Zürich: Evangelischer Verlag, 1967). For detailed exegesis on New Testament passages see G. R. Beasley-Murray, *Baptism in the New Testament* (Grand Rapids, Michigan: Wm. B. Eerdmans Publishing Company, 1962, 1973).

cup or chalice of consecrated wine which had been blessed in the same manner and from which each member reverently drank after the blessing.

On the other extreme he would see a priest with attendants all dressed in colorful vestments before what would usually be a large congregation in a beautiful building. Only the priest would drink from the chalice of wine the substance of which is believed to be the blood of Jesus after the words of consecration: "This is my body" (*hoc est corpus meum* in Latin). The people before the priest would receive only the little white wafers, the substance of which is believed to be the flesh of Jesus after consecration.

In between the two extremes he would see other groups. One would proceed to the altar of the church after prayers to receive the white wafers and to drink from the one consecrated chalice of wine while kneeling, but they would not hold to the belief that the substance of the bread and wine was the flesh and blood of Jesus.

In a typical Protestant community most churches would eat pieces of diced bread and drink grape juice from trays filled with small tots or dram glasses passed to the congregation after the blessing.

The names by which the reverent services are designated would vary also. Some would speak of it as a "mystery," from the Greek word *mystērion* used in such New Testament passages as 1 Corinthians 4:1 ("the mysteries of God"). This is influenced by the religious rites of the so-called "mystery religions" that flourished in the Greek world about the time Christianity began. Orthodox Christians with Greek backgrounds use this word along with others.

Christians with a Latin background may call it the "mass," from the words of dismissal (*missa* = mass) which the priest used. They would also use the word "sacrament," from *sacramentum*, a Latin word meaning "pledge of allegiance" that was used to translate the Greek word *mystērion*.

The congregation influenced by the revival of biblical beliefs and practices since the Protestant Reformation in the sixteenth century would usually call the service the Lord's Supper, a term found in 1 Corinthians 11:20. It is the purpose of this brief discussion to sift the original practices found in the New Testament from the development in later usage in order to deepen appreciation and understanding for what many regard as the central act of Christian worship.

The Sources of the Lord's Supper

Meals of a religious and social nature were customary among the Jews. A special meal for Jewish homes called a *kiddush* was observed weekly in preparation for the Sabbath. Another special meal called a *chaburah*, limited to a small circle of friends, was a close-knit fellowship. The most important was the annual Passover meal celebrated in the home, and this seems to be the occasion for the Last Supper of our Lord with his disciples.

Some New Testament scholars, using statements in John's Gospel, attempt to prove that the Last Supper took place the night before the Passover meal. It is impossible to be dogmatic about this difficult problem, but there are two sources that prepare the way for the Lord's Supper in a special way.

The first is the Love Feast, called *Agape* in Greek (Jude 12). This has a long history, but the primary associations for the first disciples reached back to the days of our Lord in the flesh, to his earthly ministry. It is obvious from reading the Four Gospels that the feeding of the five thousand is of great importance for the early Church — the miracle appears in all four, a unique fact (Mk. 6:30-44; Matt. 14:13-21; Lk. 9:10-17; Jn. 6:1-13).

The elaboration in John 6 suggests great value to early Christian worship, and much has been written on this question. It records that after his resurrection: "When he was at table with them, he took bread and blessed, and broke it, and gave it to them" (Lk. 24:30). After the return of these two disciples to Jerusalem "they told what had happened on the road, and how he was made known to them in the breaking of the bread" (Lk. 24:35). John's Gospel has a special bread and fish story (21:9-14).

In Acts there is no mention of the cup of wine, only "the breaking of bread" (2:42), and that a daily thing "in their homes" (2:46). The weekly celebration at Troas was in an "upper chamber" such as it was in Jerusalem (20:7, 11), and this marks it off as something very different from the temple sacrifice.

The Love Feast has not been continued among all groups of Christians as it was practiced among the Montanists, Moravians, some Methodists, and several modern sects. The typical "church supper," however, has taken on some of the qualities of the ancient *Agape*.

The major source of the Lord's Supper was the Last Supper Jesus had with his disciples in the upper room of Jerusalem (1 Cor. 11:23-25; Mk. 14:22-24; Matt. 26:26-28; Lk. 22:19f.). Whether this was on the evening of the Passover as we believe or on the evening before as others think on the basis of John's Gospel, there is no question that Passover ideas became associated with the Lord's Supper which resulted. *The Eucharistic Words of Jesus* by Joachim Jeremias (English translation, Oxford, 1955) and *The Lord's Supper in the New Testament* by A. J. B. Higgins (S.C.M., 1952) are detailed studies that support the Passover theory of the Last Supper. At any rate the Love Feast and the Last Supper became united in the Lord's Supper, and the consecrated cup of wine representing "the new covenant" in his blood (1 Cor. 11:25; Lk. 22:20) may be traced to this source.

For further study of this point the reader may consult the essays on the Lord's Supper by Oscar Cullmann and F. J. Leenhardt.

The Significance of the Lord's Supper

The historic interpretations of the Lord's Supper, especially as they were represented among the major groups at the time of the Protestant Reformation, are of three types. Catholics look upon it as a sacrifice, holding that the substance of the bread and wine has been changed into the flesh and blood of Jesus by the words of consecration. In contradiction to Scripture they teach that our Saviour's sacrifice is not only remembered but repeated.

At the other extreme Zwingli, following ancient writers such as Chrysostom, Rabanus Maurus, and Berengar of Tours, taught that the elements were symbols eaten as a memorial supper.

A third group, including Luther and Calvin, thought of the bread and wine as more than mere symbols and spoke of them as outward signs of an inward grace. When a Catholic and a Calvinist, therefore, speak of the Lord's Supper as a sacrament, they mean very different things, the Catholic meaning an act by which man offers a sacrifice to God and the Calvinist an act by which God gives a sign to man.

The significance of the Lord's Supper in the New Testament has been discussed in more detail in my essay printed in *What Is the Church?*, edited by Duke K. McCall (Broadman, 1958), but only a brief summary may be given here.

The present significance of the Lord's Supper is indicated by two Greek words: *eucharistia* (thanksgiving) and *koinōnia* (communion or participation). 1 Corinthians 11:24 and Luke 22:19 say that Jesus gave the bread "when he had given thanks," and Mark 14:23 and Matthew 26:27 say that the same was done with the cup. For this reason many Christians refer to the Lord's Supper as the Eucharist, from the Greek word meaning thanksgiving, and the central act of Christian worship may well be considered the Christian thanksgiving service for the blessings of God made available by our Savior's sacrifice for our sins.

The word *koinōnia* has reference also to the present experience of fellowship with Christ and with all who are members of the body of Christ. The most powerful presentation of this is found in 1 Corinthians 10:16f.: "The cup of blessing which we bless, is it not communion in the blood of Christ? The loaf which we break, is it not communion in the body of Christ? Because we are one loaf, we who are many are one body, for we all partake of one loaf." The phrase *heis artos, hen sōma* (one loaf, one body) is the source not only for our understanding of the Lord's Supper as communion or participation but also of our understanding of the church as the body of Christ.

The past significance of the Lord's Supper is brought out by two great words: covenant and remembrance. All four accounts of institution mention the covenant (1 Cor. 11:25; Mk. 14:24; Matt. 26:28; Lk. 22:20), and it is very important to consider the Lord's Supper as a covenant meal in which the Lordship of Christ and our commitment to do his will are brought again and again to the worshiping congregation.

Remembrance or recollection is an important part of the Lord's Supper as the new covenant in his blood. 1 Corinthians 11:24f. and Luke 22:19 use the strong word *anamnēsis*, translated "remembrance" or "recollection," and this is much more significant than the word for "memorial" *(mnēmosynon)* in the case of the woman of Mark 14:9. Remembrance has reference to an event in the past that is recalled with such power that it brings a blessing in the present.

The future significance of the Lord's Supper brings forth two New Testament terms also: the kingdom of God and the coming of Christ. Jesus spoke of the kingdom of God in terms of a great banquet (Matt. 8:11; 22:1; Lk. 13:29; 22:30), and this became associated with the Lord's Supper when Jesus said in the upper room: "Take this, and divide it among yourselves; for I tell you that from now on I shall not drink of the fruit of the vine until the kingdom of God comes" (Lk. 22:17f.).

The kingdom of God comes when Christ comes. It was present in a veiled form while he was veiled in flesh (Lk. 11:20; 17:21, RSV), and the powers of the kingdom are present in the church which is his spiritual body (1 Cor. 4:20; Col. 1:13; Rom. 14:17; Heb. 12:28), but the kingdom comes in glory only when Christ comes in glory. The Lord's Supper joins the two comings of Christ, because in it "you proclaim the Lord's death until he comes" (1 Cor. 11:26).

The Service of the Lord's Supper

It is not absolutely certain, but there is some evidence that the early Church had two services: an early morning service for baptized believers only (1 Cor. 10, 11), and a second service in the evening to which unbelievers and outsiders were invited (1 Cor. 14). The morning service included baptism, instruction, the Lord's Supper, and offerings along with prayer and praise, but the evening service seems to be limited to set and spontaneous prayers, praise of God in psalms, hymns, and spiritual songs, and the preaching of the gospel. It is difficult indeed to restore the New Testament practices on the Lord's Supper unless this pattern is followed. It will help to improve our practices to know some of the history behind them.

The elements of the Lord's Supper are two: bread and wine. For the first thousand years the bread was a waffle baked between clay or stone bread prints, much as a modern waffle is baked between irons. Even the print in the modern waffle goes back to the practice by which figures like a lamb, the cross, or letters like AO (from "I am the Alpha and the Omega" in Rev. 1:8) were used. Several of these bread prints, dating from the fifth through the sixteenth centuries, may be seen in the Museum of Southern Baptist Theological Seminary in Louisville, Kentucky.

Around the ninth century a division arose as to whether the bread should be leavened or unleavened. By the eleventh century both practices were considered valid, but the East maintained the leavened bread over against the unleavened bread of the West. After the rise of the doctrine of transubstantiation, the belief that the words of consecration changed the substance of the bread and wine into the flesh and blood of Jesus, there was a change from the waffle to a little wafer. Each person ate a wafer prepared with wine lest the breaking of the loaf cause crumbs of Christ's flesh to fall to the floor. Even the Lutherans and the Anglicans continued this practice after the Reformation, although this was ridiculed by the Reformed tradition. Many in the Reformed tradition have departed even more from the one loaf or waffle by adopting the innovation of diced bread.

Along with the one consecrated loaf there was also one consecrated cup or chalice of wine until a rural preacher in Ohio invented the tots and trays in 1893. With the discovery of a process by which unfermented grape juice could be preserved there was a shift from the wine also. The temperance movement helped this transition until most Protestant groups outside Episcopalians and Lutherans adopted the diced bread and the dram glasses of grape juice. In other places and at other times mead (a kind of ale), beer, and even banana juice have been substituted for wine, but these changes did not last.

In the Middle Ages the doctrine of transubstantiation led the Catholics to confine the cup to the priest alone and leave the people with only the wafer. Luther restored the cup to the people, but he retained the wafer. Until recently, only among some free church groups has there been a strong sentiment for the return to one unleavened loaf and one cup of consecrated wine as it is found in the New Testament (1 Cor. 10:16f.; 11:23–26). The nearest thing to this practice may be seen among Baptists in some rural churches in Kentucky that have resisted the change which has become almost uniform since the First World War. Many old churches in Kentucky still have the one cup as a museum piece, but some of the older members talk freely of the days of the one loaf and one cup.[77] We believe they are right, despite the arguments over sanitation and convenience.

Discipline at the Lord's Supper, practiced with such earnest zeal by Baptists of the last century, has fallen into neglect today. Self-examination is a necessary practice if the New Testament meaning is to be recovered. Not only should there be fervent prayer and the confession of sins, but each person should examine himself as to his fellowship with Christ and his Christian brothers (1 Cor. 11:27–32).

At times excommunication becomes necessary, as in the case of incest described by Paul in 1 Corinthians 5:1–13. In the early Church the refusal to eat the loaf and drink the cup with a person was a sure sign that the church looked upon the sinning brother as having broken the unity of fel-

---

77. At times more than one cup is used, but the variation is more often three as in the early church in which some relation to the Trinity may be found. Convenience alone was mentioned. Indeed, at times one was for men, one for women, and one for slaves!

lowship symbolized by the one loaf and one cup. The one loaf in particular represents the one body of Christ (1 Cor. 10:16f.; 12:12-27; Col. 1:18, 24; 2:17, 19; 3:15; Eph. 1:23; 2:16; 3:6; 4:4, 12, 16; 5:23, 30). Any unconfessed sin that breaks this unity makes the Lord's Supper a curse rather than a blessing.

The frequency of the Lord's Supper has varied all the way from daily to annually, or not at all among Quakers. Both daily and weekly observances are mentioned in Acts (2:46; 20:7), but pagan practices brought great changes. In A.D. 506 people were required to commune at least on Christmas, Easter, and Pentecost, but by A.D. 1215 at the Fourth Lateran Council this was relaxed to once a year, at Easter. The Presbyterian practice of once a month or once a quarter has been followed by some other denominations, including Baptists, but Lutherans generally, and Episcopalians and Disciples uniformly follow a weekly observance. Some Catholics follow a daily observance. The New Testament leaves no specific instruction but simply says: "For as often as you eat this bread and drink this cup, you proclaim the Lord's death until he comes" (1 Cor. 11:26). It is this proclamation that is primary whatever the frequency.

71. The Worship of the Church

Worship is devotion to that which is of supreme worth. The English word is from the Anglo-Saxon "weorthscipe" which became worthship, then worship. Devotion to God as the one of supreme worth ascribes to him those words and deeds that disclose his worth.

A typical call to worship in the Old Testament Psalms says (29:1, 2):

> *Ascribe to the Lord, O heavenly beings,*
> *ascribe to the Lord glory and strength.*
> *Ascribe to the Lord the glory of his name;*
> *worship the Lord in holy array.*

Christian worship continues with this orientation toward God in gratitude for all his benefits in creation and redemption, but the center of this devotion is Jesus Christ. An ascription to God as Creator reads (Revelation 4:11):

> *Worthy art thou, our Lord and God,*
> *to receive glory and honor and power,*
> *for thou didst create all things,*
> *and by thy will they existed and were created.*

In ascribing redemption to God there is even more concentration on Jesus Christ as the Lamb of God in the song which says (5:9, cf. 5:12):

Worthy art thou to take the scroll and to open the seals,
for thou wast slain and by thy blood didst ransom men to God,
from every tribe and tongue and people and nation,
and has made them a kingdom of priests to our God.
And they shall reign on earth.

It is all but impossible to make sense of biblical faith apart from this orientation of worship. As the people of God in covenant relation worship is essential. Where there is no worship there is no church, for the church is God's people gathered out of the world to celebrate the mighty acts of God in words and deeds. As 1 Peter 2:9 says to the pilgrim people of God, "You are a chosen race, a royal priesthood, a holy nation, God's own people, that you may declare the wonderful deeds of him who called you out of darkness into his marvelous light."

Raymond Abba pointed out four basic principles of Christian worship: response to revelation, worship in spirit, corporate activity, and witness.[78] All of this is true, but the most basic thing in Christian worship seems to be gathering together to celebrate the acts of God in creation and redemption.[79] Coming together for the Lord's Supper was of special significance, but this was not the sole purpose (James 2:2; 1 Corinthians 5:4; 11:17, 20, 33–34; 16:2; Acts 2:1; 4:31; 14:2, 7; 15:6; 20:7–8). However, the assembling together was of major importance (Matthew 18:20; Hebrews 10:25). The meeting continued to be central after the apostles (Justin, *Apology*, 65).

With the abundance of evidence that Christian worship is at the center of Christian faith only a survey of some principles and practices in the Bible and in church history can be made, but the major points are not too difficult to discern.

Biblical Sources of Christian Worship

Next to gathering together, the principle of polarity between the objective system of worship, the cult, and the subjective response of the worshipper belongs to the very origins of Christian worship. Christian worship was a reformation and a renewal of the cultic worship in the Old Testament form.

It is hardly possible to give further details of the cultic attachment to persons before the time of Moses. This has been done in the discussion of "The God of the Patriarchs" (Part III.19). The cultic attachment to places included Sinai, Shechem, Shiloh and particularly Jerusalem, and the conflict between Shechem and Jerusalem is manifested in the tension between the Jews and the Samaritans (cf. John 4:20). The reforms of King Josiah in

78. *Principles of Christian Worship* (New York: Oxford University Press, 1960), pp. 5-14.
79. Cf. Ferdinand Hahn, *The Worship of the Early Church*, tr. David E. Green (Philadelphia: The Fortress Press, 1973), p. 36; Eduard Schweizer, *Divine Service in the New Testament* (Montreal: The Presbyterian College, 1970), p. 15.

622 B.C. centralized worship in Jerusalem, and this increased the crisis when Jerusalem fell in 587 B.C. and also in A.D. 70.

Worship in Spirit was the only way to transcend dependence upon persons and places, and this is the spiritual transformation which is most evident in early Christian worship. This transformation of worship is especially evident in the new meanings for sacrifices and festivals. Sacrifices in the Old Testament become spiritual sacrifices in the New Testament. Spiritual worship is a presentation of the whole self to God, and this transcends the polarity between objective sacrifices and subjective responses.

Some examples of this transformation illustrate this personal aspect. Paul could say: "For God is my witness, whom I serve *(latreuō)* with my spirit in the gospel of his Son, that without ceasing I mention you always in my prayers, asking that somehow by God's will I may now at last succeed in coming to you" (Romans 1:9).

The best-known Pauline passage on spiritual worship is the appeal to the Romans which says: "I appeal to you therefore, brethren, by the mercies of God, to present your bodies as a living sacrifice, holy and acceptable to God, which is your spiritual worship. Do not be conformed to this world, but be transformed by the renewal of your mind, that you may prove what is the will of God, what is good and acceptable and perfect" (12:1, 2).

Almost any service can be described as priestly service to God: the duties of a state official (13:6), the collection for the poor saints in Jerusalem (15:27; cf. 2 Corinthians 9:12), the service of Epaphroditus in bringing an offering from Philippi to Paul in prison at Caesarea (Philippians 2:25, 30). Already Paul's offering of the Gentiles to God as a priestly service has been mentioned (Romans 15:16).

The contrast between the cultic acts which required circumcision in the flesh and the true circumcision of those "who worship God in Spirit" is a polemical presentation of the polarity between the religion of the sacrificial cult and spiritual worship in Christ (Philippians 3:3).

Only in James is the word for cultic religion, *theskeia*, used of Christian service and that in the most practical form (1:27). It is applied otherwise to the Old Testament cult (Acts 26:15) and to the angel worship of the Colossians heretics (2:18). Only in Acts 13:2 is the technical word for worship used to describe Christian worship.

The transformation of the means of the cultic festivals adds to the altered meaning of sacrifice. Had it not been for such theological views as those set forth in the treatise called The Letter to the Hebrews, the Jewish believers would have suffered the trauma of Jewish unbelievers with the fall of Jerusalem in A.D. 70. Written perhaps in A.D. 69-70, about forty years after the crucifixion of Jesus and before the temple worship ceased in late A.D. 70, the new order of priesthood in Jesus (chs. 1–7) and the once-for-all sacrifice of Jesus (chs. 8–13), Hebrews constitutes the most thorough transformation of the meaning of the Day of Atonement.[80]

If a text must be chosen to express most fully the way the sacrifice of Christ transformed cultic worship and perfected spiritual worship, then Hebrews 13:10–16 must be nominated.

> We have an altar from which those who serve the tent have no right to eat. For the bodies of those animals whose blood is brought into the sanctuary by the high priest as a sacrifice for sin are burned outside the camp. So Jesus also suffered outside the gate in order to sanctify the people through his own blood. Therefore let us go forth to him outside the camp and bear the abuse he endured. For here we have no lasting city, but we seek the city which is to come. Through him then let us continually offer up a sacrifice of praise to God, that is, the fruit of lips that acknowledge his name. Do not neglect to do good and to share what you have, for such sacrifices are pleasing to God.

The festival of Passover was also transformed in meaning by the sufferings and sacrifice of Christ. 1 Peter, written perhaps around Passover in A.D. 65, after the burning of Rome, July 18-24, 64 A.D., has been described as a Passover liturgy.[81]

The new birth is described in the first part (1:3–2:10) with a prayer (1:3–12), a baptismal instruction (1:13–21), dedication (1:22–2:3) and a hymn (2:4–10). The second part (2:11–4:11), on the new behavior, is an imitation sermon with teachings on good conduct (2:13–3:12) and a good conscience (3:13–4:11). The good conscience section has one of the most important passages on baptism in the New Testament (3:18–22).

Part three (4:12–5:14), on the new brotherhood, is thought to be a sermon to the congregation (4:12–5:11) with a note from Silvanus the writer (5:12–14). The Passover sacrifice combined with the Messianic picture of Jesus as the suffering Servant penetrates the seven references to the sufferings of Christ and the seven references to the sufferings of Christians, but both ideas have been deepened in meaning by the sacrifice of Christ.

It is also possible that Paul's letter to the Colossians is a Passover letter, written from Caesarea about 57 A.D. The structure, which is made up of salutation (1:1f.), thanksgiving (1:2–8) and prayer (1:9–14) followed by a doctrinal section (1:15–2:7) including a hymn about Christ as the firstborn of God (1:15–20) and a sermon (1:21–2:7), then a polemical section with a second hymn (2:8–15) and a second sermon (2:16–23), and concluding with a practical section (3:1–4:1) that includes a third hymn

---

80. Cf. A. Nairne, *The Epistle of Priesthood* (Edinburgh: T. and T. Clark, 1913, 1915); F. C. N. Hicks, *The Fulness of Sacrifice* (New York: Macmillan, 1930).
81. F. L. Cross, *I Peter: A Paschal Liturgy* (London: A. R. Mowbray & Co., 1954).

(3:1-4), a third sermon (3:5-4:1), and some personal remarks (4:2-18), has many marks of a liturgy and many references to the sacrifice of Christ.

The Pentecost festival celebrated in 1 Corinthians 12-14 has a definite reference to the threefold sermon and is clearly written after Passover (5:7) and before Pentecost (16:8). The section begins with a confession (12:1-3), and this is followed by a hymn (12:12f.) and a sermon (12:14-31), a longer hymn (13:1-13), and a still longer sermon (14:1-54).

The Pentecost festival behind Paul's letter to Laodicea (cf. Colossians 4:16), commonly called Ephesians, has been widely recognized.[82] It is possible that Ephesians was written around Pentecost, 57 A.D., from Caesarea also. The difference in style from Colossians is due to the festival celebrated and the amanuensis, Timothy for Colossians and Luke for Ephesians. The doctrinal section (1:1-3:21) begins with the adoration of God, a doxology (1:3-14) and a prayer for knowledge (1:15-23). The prayer also includes a hymn (1:20b-23). Following a trinitarian pattern, the next part is on the mediation of Christ: resurrection with Christ (2:1-10), including a hymn (2:4-7), and reconciliation through Christ (2:11-22) with another hymn (2:14-18). The third part of the doctrinal section is on the revelation of the Spirit (3:1-21), and includes another hymn (3:5, 7-12) and a prayer (3:14-21) that ends with a hymn of benediction (3:20f.).

The practical section of Ephesians (4:1-6:23), after baptism, has an expansion of the third sermon in Colossians (cf. Colossians 3:5-5:1 with Ephesians 4:1-5:20), and this includes several spiritual songs (4:4-6, 22b-24; 5:2, 14, 25b-27). After the concluding hymn (6:14-18) there is a prayer request (6:19f.) with greetings (6:21f.) and a benediction (5:23f.).

The Jerusalem Bible has taken note of the fact that the Gospel of John is organized around at least three Jewish festivals: Tabernacles, Dedication and three Passovers. In all of these there is the belief that the glory of God, the Shekinah, dwelt in the historical Jesus so that in his incarnation and vicarious sacrifice the cultic religion of the Old Testament has been fulfilled and a new age of the Spirit has begun (John 4:23f.; 7:39).

It is even argued by a leading liturgical scholar that the Revelation to John follows the pattern of a Christian worship service.[83] The twenty-eight references to Jesus as the Lamb of God point toward the Festival of Passover as the season of the year when the revelation was written down. If it was written between the death of Nero, July, A.D. 68, and the fall of the temple, A.D. 70, which seems likely, then the worship of God with the Lamb in the midst of the throne is more meaningful.

Surely all these suggestions are not the result of liturgical fancy. One thing is sure, and that is that the cult of Old Testament sacrifices and

82. John C. Kirby, *Ephesians: Baptism and Pentecost* (London: S.P.C.K., 1968).
83. Massey Shephard, *The Paschal Liturgy and the Apocalypse* (Richmond, Va.: John Knox Press, 1960).

festivals have been transformed by the sacrifice of Jesus Christ in the new age of the Spirit.

The order of Christian worship has indeed a biblical basis. There is no model service of worship in the New Testament, but most of the elements in later liturgies are there.

Priority must be given to prayer and praise, for biblical worship seems impossible without these two elements. *Amen* and *Alleluia* are about the most basic words in biblical worship. The ancient Shechem ceremony in Deuteronomy 27:1–26 is a cultic event in which prayer is the pronouncement of a curse on the disobedient, but there are many forms of prayer (see Part IV. 31). With prayer and the praises of Israel, especially in the Psalter, the foundations of biblical worship are laid. By the time of the prison letters of Paul a distinction can be made between psalms, hymns and spiritual songs, but all of these are melodies of praise to the Lord (Colossians 3:16; Ephesians 5:19).

From the beginning of a canon of Holy Scripture, the reading of Scripture and teaching with applications to present situations were a part of biblical worship. After the return from Babylonian exile Ezra gathered the people at the Water Gate and read the law to the people, and this was followed by the celebration of the Feast of Tabernacles and a great confession of sin (Nehemiah 8, 9).

Reading of Scripture with interpretations and application became a regular part of synagogue worship. Jesus went to the synagogue, "as was his custom, on the sabbath day" and read the Scriptures (Luke 4:16). It is obvious from the New Testament writings that the Scriptures usually meant the Greek Old Testament, the Septuagint, although the original Hebrew and other versions may have been used also.

The reading of Scripture was part of worship in the churches founded by Paul (cf. Acts 13:15; 2 Corinthians 3:14). Among the instructions given to Timothy were such things as "the public reading of scripture" along with preaching and teaching (1 Timothy 4:13). Scriptures were in the home as well as the synagogues and churches because they were accepted as inspired and authoritative (1 Timothy 3:14–17).

All of these forms of worship were practiced in the synagogues; but in the church the prayer and praise were focused on Jesus, and the New Testament Scriptures in time were accepted as the norm by which the Old Testament Scriptures were to be interpreted. To the four synagogue sources were added Baptism and the Lord's Supper. Baptism was in the name of Jesus Christ and the Lord's Supper was in remembrance of his sacrifice.

As a seventh element of early Christian worship the collection should be added. The "offering" was indeed a part of temple worship. God's kingship was celebrated with the call (Psalm 96:8):

Ascribe to the Lord the glory due his name;
  bring an offering and come into his courts!

Jesus did not reject the temple offering (Matthew 5:23f.; 8:4; Luke 17:14). However, even when Paul used the technical word *prosphora* for the Gentile people he offered to God, their contribution for the poor saints at Jerusalem is called the *koinōnia* (cf. Romans 15:16 with 15:26). He also called it simply the *logeia* (collection, contribution, 1 Corinthians 16:1).

Historical Types of Christian Worship

Out of the wealth of ways to worship God in the Scriptures, at least three major types of worship have developed in the Western churches alone.[84] There are also liturgies in the Eastern Churches.[85]

The Catholic type of worship magnifies the idea of Sacrifice. From the time of the *Didache*, around A.D. 80-130, the word for sacrifice, *thysia*, was emphasized for the Lord's Supper, the eucharist as it was called (*Didache* 13:3). By the end of the first century the priestly functions of the clergy are interpreted along the lines of the Old Testament cult (*1 Clement* 50f.). Even though 1 Clement is written to Corinth, the differences between the cultic worship in 1 Clement and the charismatic worship in Paul's first Corinthian letter are unmistakable. By developing the two sources of biblical worship, the Old Testament and the New Testament outlined above, into a twofold mass — the Mass of the Catechumen and the Mass of the Faithful — the foundations for Catholic worship were laid.

Through the centuries the Roman Catholic mass developed, like a great cathedral, until all the acts and words were prescribed and the spontaneity of the Holy Spirit was quenched. All was so beautifully arranged and explained around the sacrificial mass that no surprises were possible. The monumental study *Missarum Sollemnia*, written in 1948 by J. A. Jungmann, was just that, a monument to a dead past with all the fossil fragments explained in detail.[86]

The Anglo-Catholic version of the mass as practiced and believed in much of the Church of England has its own sacramental Cathedral. Gregory Dix, an Anglican Benedictine and Prior of Nashdom Abbey, was working for years parallel with J. A. Jungmann and published his historic volume three years before Jungmann's.[87] These two publications with revised versions of the Divine Offices for the clergy reveal the vast system of Catholic worship which has developed since New Testament times.

---

84. A convenient collection of liturgies is available in Bard Thompson, *Liturgies of the Western Church* (Cleveland and New York: Collins and World, 1962).
85. T. S. Garrett, *Christian Worship*, Second Edition (London: Oxford University Press, 1963), pp. 67-82.
86. The English translation by F. A. Brunner called *The Mass of the Roman Rite* (New York: Benzinger, 1951-55). A one-volume revised and abridged edition was published in 1959.
87. *The Shape of the Liturgy* (London: Dacre, 1945).

Protestant worship shifted from the centrality of sacrifice to the centrality of Scripture. It must never be forgotten that Martin Luther was professor of Scripture at the University of Wittenberg, even though he began as an Augustinian monk. His celebrated writing *The German Mass and Order of Service (Deutsche Messe und Ordnung Gottis Diensts,* 1526)[88] recognized the three forms of worship: the *Formula Missal* of Roman Catholicism, the *German Mass and Order of Service* and a "third kind of Service which a truly Evangelical Church Order should have." Unfortunately Luther settled for the German Mass because he did not think the German people were ready for a radical restoration of the New Testament worship which he described so accurately.[89]

The Calvinistic wing of the Reformation made the ministry of the Word central. John Calvin was a master of Holy Scripture. His commentaries were prepared to be preached, as his *Institutes* were composed as instruction for the people. Interestingly enough, Calvin's major contribution to worship was the pastoral prayer.[90] It is not surprising that a major Calvinist contribution to Christian worship was concerned with the theology of worship as well as its practice.[91]

In both Lutheranism and Calvinism there are voices calling for the charismatic worship characteristic of New Testament. Some people are obviously ready for vitality in worship. Concern for free church worship was the concern in the book by Raymond Abba already mentioned, but he did not give adequate attention to the Holy Spirit and orderly charismatic worship such as is described in 1 Corinthians 14. However, the writings by Ferdinand Hahn and Eduard Schweizer do call for this type of worship. Even though their radical views on the date of the New Testament documents are not satisfactory, this call for spiritual worship is welcome. Only time will tell whether adequate freedom in the Spirit will be given in the future. The vitality of worship will have much to do with the vitality of mission with which this section began.

88. An English translation with introduction is in *The Works of Martin Luther*, Volume 6 (Philadelphia: Muhlenberg Press, 1932), pp. 151-189. Bard Thompson, *op. cit.*, reproduced the text, pp. 123-137.
89. Bard Thompson, *op. cit.*, pp. 125-126.
90. *Ibid.*, pp. 185-210.
91. J. J. von Allmen, *Worship: Its Theology and Practice* (New York: Oxford University Press, 1965).

X. THE CONSUMMATION

72. Hope in History

The consummation of all things in God is the conclusion, not an appendix to Christian theology. The dominant concept in one's view of the consummation may shift from time to time and from age to age, but belief in a consummation of some type has always been a vital part of Christian theology.

In biblical theology there is no question that the Old Testament hope was anchored in the belief that God is sovereign in human life and history. Even before the heyday of a universal monotheism, the worship of one God, monolatry, was based on the belief that God was able to achieve his purpose. God Almighty was the Shield of Abraham, the Fear of Isaac and the Mighty One of Jacob before he revealed himself as Lord to Moses (Exodus 6:3). Universal monotheism makes the sovereignty of God even more explicit (Isaiah 44:6f.; 48:12f.).

Under the shield of God's sovereignty the Old Testament perspectives on the consummation passed through three stages. The personal perspective expressed the hope that life after death would first be realized in one's seed or descendants, then as shades in Sheol, and finally as a resurrection of the body. The historical perspective was first expressed in the prophetic eschatology that saw God rewarding the righteous and punishing the wicked at the Day of the Lord that would take place in this age; then, in apocalyptic eschatology, after the Fall of the First Temple, the Day of the Lord was projected into a new age that would involve not only nations but the whole creation.

In the New Testament the consummation is focused on the Lordship of Christ. Christ is the hope not only of Israel but of the Gentiles also. What had been hidden for ages God revealed to the saints. "To them God chose to make known how great among the Gentiles are the riches of the glory of this mystery, which is Christ in you, the hope of glory" (Colossians

1:27).[1] Commenting on the hymn of hope in Colossians 3:1–4, A. T. Robertson well said: "This is our security, Christ is locked in the bosom of the Father. We are locked together with Christ in God."[2]

The New Testament hope for the consummation expanded the horizon of personal, historical, and apocalyptic or cosmic eschatology. None of these stages was neglected, but later developments in Christian eschatology often vacillated between a two-age apocalypticism and a two-realm ecclesiasticism. Apocalypticism was usually charismatic and chiliastic; ecclesiasticism became conservative and resistant to any change in the light of a consummation. The tension between the two realms and the two ages become the warp and woof of Christian hope.

In the eschatology of the Greek Fathers the motif that came to dominate was belief in the salvation of all that God has created. This universalism does not appear in chiliasm, the belief in the thousand-year reign of Christ on earth, of the more biblical Greek Fathers such as Papias of Hierapolis, Justin Martyr, and Irenaeus of Lyon, with their roots in the theological tradition of Ephesus; but the theologians of Alexandria, under the influence of the Greek philosophy of Plato, concluded that the fire of judgment would finally purify all. Origen of Alexandria and later of Caesarea made the most daring speculations on universalism.[3] Eusebius of Caesarea believed the reign of Christ had been established by the so-called conversion of Constantine the Great, so there was no need for a second coming of Christ to establish the new age (*Church History* X). It was the great Cappadocian theologians, especially Gregory of Nyssa, who established universalism in Greek Orthodoxy.[4] The apocalypticism of two ages is almost completely absent. This acute Hellenization of eschatology led to the most bitter forms of anti-Semitism, especially in the writings of John Chrysostom. This was transmitted to later tradition, and some Calvinistic amillennialists still teach that God has cast Israel off forever.

A dualism between an eternal heaven and an eternal hell took the place of universalism in Latin theology. Latin eschatology also began with a chiliasm or millennialism of two ages. The great Tertullian, the first Christian theologian to write in Latin, agreed with the Ephesian tradition that believed that Jesus Christ would return to reign on earth for a thousand years after the reign of Antichrist during a Great Tribulation (*Against Marcion*, III. 24).

Augustine, the most influential of the Latin theologians, was at first a millennialist like Tertullian, but he later identified the millennium with the

---

1. For further details on this and all that follows see my book *The Hope of Glory* (Grand Rapids: Eerdmans, 1964).
2. *Paul and the Intellectuals* (Nashville: Sunday School Board of the Southern Baptist Convention, 1928), p. 146.
3. Henry Bettenson, ed., *The Early Christian Fathers* (London: Oxford University Press, 1956), pp. 218-227, 352-356.
4. Vladimir Lossky, *The Mystical Theology of the Eastern Church* (London: James Clarke, 1957), pp. 234f.

Catholic church on earth. The millennium for him began with the first coming of Christ, and baptism was the first resurrection. This system, which came to be known as amillennialism, was elaborated in Augustine's most important book, *The City of God* (XX-XXII).

The Catholic theology of the Cathedral schools at first followed Augustine. Millennialism continued among some radical and sectarian believers, and after the Augustinian expectation of the end of the world around the year 1000, at the end of a millennium, did not materialize, a more spiritual millennialism was developed by the Italian monk Joachim of Flora in Calabria. Joachim believed the world would pass through three stages. The age of the Father lasted until the age of the Son began with the first coming of Jesus, but Joachim taught that a third age, that of the Spirit, would begin in the year 1260 (*Apocalypse* 1.5).

This spiritual eschatology of Joachim was believed by some Catholics, especially the Franciscans, but the personal eschatology of Thomas Aquinas continued the dualism of Augustine with little to say on historical eschatology. Using the philosophy of the Greek philosopher Aristotle, as Augustine had used the philosophy of the Greek philosopher Plato, Thomas Aquinas, in his most detailed speculations, advanced Augustine's suggestions of Purgatory with the argument that the soul separated from the body can suffer the pains of a material fire (*Summa Theologica*, I.II. Q. 69-79). He did believe in a cosmic consummation, but he made no effort to relate it to the cosmology of Aristotle.

The weaving back and forth between conservatism and chiliasm burst forth with renewed power at the time of the Protestant Reformation. Like an underground volcano the spiritual church advocated by Joachim was promoted by the Spiritual Franciscans in Italy and France, by Wycliffe and his Lollards in England, by John Huss and his disciples in Prague and by the Anabaptists in the Protestant Reformation.

Luther himself at times agreed with the Anabaptists in their rejection of both Purgatory and Paradise and their emphasis on an apocalyptic resurrection of the dead in the age to come, but the radicalism of the Peasant Revolt (1524-26) drove him into the arms of civil authorities who gladly embraced the church for their own purposes in the struggle for power against the Pope: Belief in a millennial reign of Christ on earth was rejected, and a heavenly millennium became orthodoxy.

Chiliastic apocalypticism was also suppressed in Calvinism. John Calvin did not reject belief in an intermediate state of the righteous in Paradise and of the wicked in Hades, but he did discard the Roman Catholic doctrine of a Purgatory before perfection in Paradise. Some Calvinism went so far as to teach instant perfection at death and even the reception of the spiritual body at death. These beliefs grew out of Calvin's first theological writing, his *Psychopannychia* (1534), meaning soul alertness or the watchfulness of the soul between death and resurrection. However, historical eschatology and cosmic apocalypticism were given little attention in Calvin. Friedrich Nietzsche was right when he said Protestantism made eschatology a foster child.[5]

In general the eschatology of Martin Butzer, a third Protestant Reformer, can be called an eschatology of love, as Calvin's can be called an eschatology of hope and Luther's of faith, but none of the three gets much beyond a personal eschatology in which the righteous go to heaven and the wicked go to hell.[6] The historical eschatology of a consummation of the age with an apocalyptic inauguration of a new age of the ages is hard to find in the Protestant Reformers.

Protestant orthodoxy settled down with a two-realm eschatology in which the future is not a new age but a departure for heaven or hell. It is hard to see why even in this system any teaching about a second coming with a resurrection of the dead and a reign of Christ on earth is needed, and that is precisely the conclusion many reached.

Chiliastic apocalypticism did not die altogether under the weight of ahistorical and acosmic orthodoxy. Among Lutherans a movement known as Pietism began to restore charismatic and chiliastic apocalypticism as a vital part of biblical faith. One of the most extraordinary Pietists was Johannes Albrecht Bengel (1687-1752). He has well been called the father of the historical exegesis of the New Testament. Applying all of himself to the Scriptures and all of the Scriptures to himself, as he said, he produced his penetrating *Gnomon of the New Testament* (1742), which later had a profound influence on John Wesley and is quoted today with respect.

Bengel coined the term *Heilsgeschichte* (salvation history), which has continued as an important approach to eschatology down to Oscar Cullmann and Eric Rust today. Salvation history sees biblical history as the story of salvation in which Christ is the center point between creation and the consummation. The Old Testament is indispensable as a bridge between the general revelation in creation and the special revelation in Christ. Church history as the time of testimony between Christ and the consummation becomes a vital part of Christian eschatology.

The stream of salvation history never ran dry even in the days when liberal Protestantism dominated much of theology. Friedrich Schleiermacher, who is often called the father of modern theology, was nurtured in Pietism, but his experiential eschatology was almost agnostic about a future age. On the basis of the Platonic idea of the natural immortality of the soul,

5. Heinrich Quistorp, *Calvin's Doctrine of Last Things*, tr. Harold Knight (London: Lutterworth Press, 1955), p. 194.
6. T. F. Torrance, *Kingdom and Church* (Edinburgh: Oliver and Boyd, 1956).

Schleiermacher was able to affirm the persistence of personality after death, and his teaching on the reception of a spiritual body at death is hard to harmonize with New Testament teachings on the resurrection of the dead. The consummation is no more than the conversion of the world to Christianity, but this is hardly urgent for Schleiermacher in this age, since he believed in the ultimate salvation of all.[7]

The ethical eschatology of Albrecht Ritschl was centered in a concept of the kingdom of God as the realm of righteousness and ethical values. A kingdom of sin stands in opposition to the kingdom of righteousness.[8] What was Protestant liberalism in the nineteenth century was preached by Protestant conservatives in the twentieth. Using the incorrect translation of Luke 17:21 in the King James Version (cf. RSV), there was much talk about the kingdom of God in the heart rather than on earth and of "the kingdom" composed of "the churches." Programs were promoted as "kingdom enterprises" and every effort was exerted to "expand," "establish," and "extend" "the kingdom." Many a conservative really believed the kingdom would be "brought in" for a thousand years before the return of Christ. This is hardly the imminent apocalypticism of the New Testament, yet that became the language of the establishment.

In the midst of the liberal establishment and just before the First World War marked the beginning of the decline of European civilization, there were those who saw how the nineteenth-century theologians painted Christ after their own fancies. The so-called "consistent eschatology" of Albert Schweitzer proclaimed Jesus as the child of the apocalypticism in the book of Daniel. He claimed that Jesus came to call Israel back to the mission of a light to the Gentile nations before the Son of Man would come before the Ancient of Days and receive a kingdom for his reign on earth. When Israel did not repent he proclaimed his mission as that of the suffering servant of the Lord whose death would be followed by the coming of God's kingdom.[9]

Strangely enough a similar picture of Jesus was painted by a British sectarian movement that began around 1830. In England the charismatic Plymouth Brethren developed a system of Dispensationalism that projected the coming of the kingdom into a seventh dispensation of history yet future.[10] When the ideas were systematized in the notes of the *Scofield Ref-*

7. See his book *The Christian Faith*, tr. H. R. Mackintosh and J. S. Stewart (Edinburgh: T. and T. Clark, 1928), pp. 696-722.
8. *Justification and Reconciliation*, tr. H. R. Mackintosh and A. B. Macaulay (New York: Scribner's, 1900), p. 330.
9. *The Quest of the Historical Jesus*, 1906, tr. W. Montgomery (New York: Macmillan, 1948), pp. 368f.
10. C. Norman Kraus, *Dispensationalism in America* (Richmond, Va.: John Knox Press, 1958); Clarence B. Bass, *Backgrounds to Dispensationalism* (Grand Rapids: Eerdmans, 1960); Dave MacPherson, *The Incredible Cover-Up* (Plainfield, N. J.: Logos International, 1975).

erence Bible (1909, 1917, 1963) and diagrammed in the charts of Clarence Larkin's *Dispensational Truth* (1918), conservative apocalypticism began to spread like a prairie fire. Today it is a major movement in American Christianity. Devout followers of Dispensationalism marvel that "the Holy Spirit" has led so many preachers to the same conclusions when the preachers have used only the same Scofield Bible.

After the First World War, responses to apocalypticism were varied. Rudolf Otto's "anticipated eschatology" restored the charismatic element that is at times lacking in chiliastic apocalypticism. Otto used such passages as Luke 17:20f. to support his picture of the charismatic Christ in whom the coming kingdom of God was anticipated.[11]

The "realized eschatology" of C. H. Dodd shifted the coming of the kingdom of God almost completely into the present.[12] For him the Old Testament was the sowing season for the full harvest in the ministry of the historical Jesus. The German New Testament scholar Rudolf Bultmann reduced eschatology to the personal decisions of the present as the "core of history."[13]

The "theology of hope" has been able to get more attention than the more conservative salvation history of J. A. Bengel, Oscar Cullmann and Eric Rust, but it has not come to grips with science as much as it has with society. The cosmic eschatology of Karl Heim, who was a master of both Scripture and science, needs to be developed more by the radical forms of liberation theology that have grown out of "the theology of hope." Jürgen Moltmann, who coined the term "theology of hope" for the title of his book in 1964 has moved toward the charismatic but not enough toward the cosmic in apocalypticism.[14]

In the pages that follow an effort will be made to keep personal, historic and cosmic eschatology in balance. The scientific, the philosophical and the social relevance of apocalypticism will be noted, but the primary concern is the faithful interpretation and application of a biblical eschatology. This was the concern of my book *The Hope of Glory* (1964), which was written before "the theology of hope" appeared on the scene. Even though more attention is given to the details of biblical exegesis, the orientation toward a future consummation is not on a collision course with the activistic apocalypticism of "the theology of hope."

In a preliminary way "the five points" of Moltmann's eschatology may

---

11. *The Kingdom of God and the Son of Man*, tr. Floyd V. Filson and Bertram Lee-Woolf (London: Lutterworth Press, 1943), pp. 344ff.
12. *The Parables of the Kingdom* (London: Nisbet, 1935), p. 50.
13. *The Presence of Eternity* (New York: Harper, 1957), p. 141.
14. *The Theology of Hope*, tr. James W. Leitch (New York: Harper & Row, 1967); *The Crucified God*, tr. R. A. Wilson and John Bowen (New York: Harper and Row, 1973); and *The Church in the Power of the Spirit*, tr. Margaret Kohl (New York: Harper and Row, 1977) are the major books by Moltmann.

be pointed out. First, the promise of God to the patriarch that has been so central in the Old Testament theology of Gerhard von Rad and others has been used in a creative way that gives all theology a future orientation. This is of positive value.[15]

A second point in Moltmann's eschatology is as important in the New Testament as the Old Testament promise. The emphasis on the historical resurrection of Jesus Christ rejects the Bultmann binge of the last generation that reduces the resurrection to mythology. This is to be applauded.

A third point magnifies the Apocalypse of God in the future as the consummation of all knowledge of God, and this is surely better than the attacks on apocalypticism still current.[16]

In general these three points are welcome signs in eschatology, but some emphases in Moltmann are received with reservations. A fourth point is the extreme contrast between the epiphany revelations of God in the past and present and the apocalyptic revelation of God in the future. This leads to the fifth point in which ontology is disparaged in the interest of an apocalyptic eschatology of the future.

A. PERSONAL ESCHATOLOGY: THE HOPE OF MAN

73. Life

Scripture affirms both earthly life and eternal life as grounded in God, and there is a growing tendency in both modern science and philosophies to say the same.

Earthly Life

The starting point for a comprehensive understanding of the consummation for man, history and the whole creation is the concept of life itself. Life itself is understood in the Scriptures in terms of the living soul. The meaning of the soul has been surveyed in some detail already, so that will not be repeated here (Part V.1).

The living soul of man, however, is the concrete human self in all of its relations (*nepesh chayyah*, Genesis 2:7). This reference, generally called J or JE, forms the foundation for all future development. In the post-exilic priestly sources this concreteness permits the use of the term dead soul, *nepesh mut*, in contrast to the living soul, *nepesh chayyah*.

As in the case of the living soul where the references to animals, fish and birds as *nepesh chayyah* are translated living creatures (Genesis 2:7,

15. Christopher Morse, *The Logic of Promise in Moltmann's Theology* (Philadelphia: Fortress Press, 1979).
16. As in Robert Jewett, *Jesus Against the Rapture* (Philadelphia: The Westminster Press, 1979).

JE; 1:20, 21, 24, P), so *nepesh mut* is translated dead bodies in the priestly sources (Leviticus 19:28; 21:1; 22:4; Numbers 5:2, 6, 11; 9:6, 7, 10; 19:11, 13; cf. Haggai 2:13). This obscures the realism of biblical psychology and opens the door for the body–soul dualism of Greek philosophy.

The prophetic distinction between flesh and spirit is not Platonic dualism. Human spirit is the boundary between God and man (Isaiah 31:3). At the same time it expresses the special relation between man and God (Isaiah 42:5). Man *has* spirit as God *has* Spirit, but the human spirit of man and the Holy Spirit of God are never confused.

This special relationship between the living soul and the living God is especially prominent in the wisdom literature of the Old Testament (Job 27:3; 33:4, 14f.). The Preacher, *Qohelet*, in Ecclesiastes does question "whether the spirit of man goes upward and the spirit of the beast goes down to the earth" (3:21), but in the end the dignity of man's destiny is affirmed. Even though the human spirit is never identified with the Holy Spirit, it is that which returns to God at death when "the dust returns to earth as it was, and the spirit returns to God who gave it" (11:6).

Belief in man as a living soul in his earthly life with the confidence that the relationship between God and man can be established even in worship explains the significance of the Old Testament designation of God as the living God (Psalms 42, 43). This is really the function of the faith, to show that the fullness of life is found in the presence of God (Psalm 16:11). What was quantitative in Deuteronomy 30:15–20 has become qualitative in Psalm 16:11.

The living God who is the fountain of all earthly life is revealed also as the source of the fullness of life. A long life is a blessing of God indeed, but the good life is full of God as well as full of days.

Against the background of the living soul and the living God as corollaries in the Old Testament there is some development in the New Testament, but the Greek dualism of a mortal body and an immortal soul is never found in the New Testament. When a distinction is made between the body and soul, both can be destroyed in Gehenna (Matthew 10:28). When a distinction is made between soul and spirit, it is the Old Testament view that soul relates to all living things as the spirit relates to God (Hebrews 4:12). When body, soul and spirit are used together, body relates to all flesh as soul relates to all life and spirit may relate to all human spirits and to God (1 Thessalonians 5:23).

This lofty view of human life need not fear the scientific phenomenon of life. Karl Friedrich von Weizsäcker's survey *The History of Nature* brings the whole cosmic process to focus on the living soul.[17] Pierre Teilhard de Chardin's *The Phenomenon of Man* (1955) goes even further by describing

17. Tr. Fred D. Wieck (Chicago: University of Chicago Press, 1949).

the whole cosmic process as a movement through the levels of matter, life and mind to the omega point in God.[18]

Philosophy also makes room for the lofty view of life. In existential philosophy the distinction between animal life and human life is central. Man, unlike animals, transcends the natural process and *knows* he must die. Even though John Macquarrie goes too far in his presupposition that there is no Being of God without beings, he is in agreement with the biblical perspective where he grounds human existence in God. Macquarrie's identification of Being with beings leads him into universalism.[19]

Process theology has more difficulty in affirming human life beyond earthly life, but process philosophy does not rule out the living soul and the possibility of human mind in another environment without the human brain.[20] Indeed, the Cartesian claim that man is a thinking substance beyond all space and time is far from a dead issue today.[21] Memory and mind belong to the living soul as well as to the living God.

Eternal Life

Eternal life as a future hope. Implications for the doctrine of eternal life are found at the very beginning of the Bible. The Paradise story of Genesis 2, 3 indicates that man has eaten of the tree of knowledge but not of the tree of life. After the curse pronounced for sin, Eve is declared to be the mother of all living (3:20).

Already in Part VI.46, the claim has been clarified as to why both death and life in the Genesis story should be interpreted as spiritual, not physical, for man's physical death did not take place on the day Adam and Eve ate from the tree of knowledge, and all physical life does not come from one woman. Most physical life is prior to woman, but the promise of eternal life is brought to light by the promise of life given to the woman and manifested in the midst of earthly life in the gospel of Jesus Christ (cf. 2 Timothy 1:10).

It is interesting that literalism is not so literal in the translation of Genesis 3:20. (Cf. *The Berkeley Version*, *The Living Bible*, even *The Good News Bible*.) The meaning of life in Genesis 3:20 is clarified in Genesis 3:22–24. Eternal life as a term does not appear in the Old Testament until Daniel 12:2 where it is used to describe life in the new age after the resurrection from the dead.

---

18. Tr. Bernard Wall (New York: Harper, 1959). See also Doran McCarty, *Teilhard De Chardin* (Waco, Texas: Word Books, 1976) for survey.
19. *Principles of Christian Theology*, Second Edition (New York: Scribner's, 1977), pp. 107-114, 361.
20. William A. Beardslee, *A House for Hope* (Philadelphia: Westminster Press, 1972), p. 146.
21. See Paul Badham, *Christian Beliefs About Life After Death* (London: Macmillan, 1976), pp. 97-146.

In the New Testament eternal life is described as both a future hope and a present possession. In the teachings of Jesus in the Synoptic Gospels earthly life belongs to the present age, but eternal life belongs primarily to the life to come in a future age inaugurated by the coming of the Son of Man in glory (Mark 10:17, 21, 23, 25, 30). Eternal life is the destiny of the righteous as eternal punishment is the destiny of the wicked (Matthew 25:46). Following Jesus in this present age has its compensation in this life, but the major reward is eternal life in the age to come (Luke 18:30).

The teaching on eternal life as a future hope in the Pauline writings continues the use of the concept of the two ages (cf. 1 Corinthians 2:6–8; Titus 3:7), but the primary presentation is in the pattern of the two Adams, a distinctive teaching in Paul (1 Corinthians 15:22; Romans 5:14). Eternal life is both reaped as a result of sowing to the Spirit and received as a gift from God (Galatians 6:8; Romans 6:23). On through the Pastoral Letters of Paul eternal life is portrayed as a future hope (Titus 1:2; 3:7; 1 Timothy 1:16; 4:8; 6:12, 19; 2 Timothy 1:1, 10).

Both the ideas of two ages and two Adams are apocalyptic teachings, so it is no surprise to see eternal life in the Apocalypse of John taught always as a future hope. The tree of life, the crown of life, the book of life, and the water of life are all symbols that belong to the age to come (2:7, 10; 3:5; 13:8; 17:8; 20:12, 15; 21:6, 27; 22:1, 2, 14, 17, 19). Jude has the same teaching about eternal life (21).

Eternal life as a present possession. Old Testament teachings about the fullness of life lived in the presence of the Lord allow for a development toward eternal life as a present possession, but this is not done until we come to the Gospel and the First Letter of John. *Zōē* (life) in the Gospel and First Letter of John means eternal life as a present possession even when the adjective "eternal" is not used.

In the Gospel of John eternal life is manifested in the incarnation of the Son of God in the human flesh of Jesus (John 1:1–18). John the Baptist was a messenger from God to man, but he was not a mediator between God and man. John was a witness but he was not the Word.

Eternal life mediated from God to believers through Christ the Son includes both the present possession of eternal life and the future resurrection of life (5:24–29). The present possession is eternal life for the hour that "now is," while the resurrection of life belongs only to the hour that "is coming."

The present possession of eternal life requires believing in the present tense. Belief in the Gospel of John is always a verb, not a noun, and it includes the present and future, not merely the past. It is the sheep who keep on hearing and keep on following that the Good Shepherd keeps on knowing and keeps on giving eternal life (10:27f.).

As long as one believes, he has eternal life in Jesus. This includes life before physical death and life after physical death. Jesus said: "I am the resurrection and the life; he who believes in me, though he die, yet shall he live, and whosoever believes in me shall never die" (11:25f.). Again: "And this is eternal life, that they may know thee the only true God, and Jesus Christ whom thou hast sent" (17:3). Knowing God and sharing the life of God are inseparable. He who knows lives and he who lives knows.

The First Letter of John has three words for life: *psychē* (earthly life), *bios* (the means of earthly life) and *zōē* (the very life of God imparted to man through the mediation of Jesus Christ). Cf. 1 John 3:14–17 where all three words are used. It has already been noted in Part VII.55 that in First John one can pass not only from spiritual death to spiritual life but also from spiritual life to spiritual death (3:14; 5:11–13, 16).

These teachings on the present possession of eternal life in the Son of God do not contradict the great texts in the Gospel of John. In both, eternal life is mediated from God through the Son of God, so that (1 John 5:12):

> He who has the Son has life;
> he who has not the Son of God has not life.

74. Death

Death, according to Jean-Paul Sartre, "removes all meaning from life."[22] This denial of any passage from earthly life to eternal life now or later is the quiet despair of many modern people. They simply find it impossible to accept the theology of life outlined in the previous section. Albert Camus, speaking at the Dominican Monastery of Latour-Maubourg in 1948, spoke for them when he said to Christian believers: "I share with you the same revulsion from evil. But I do not share your hope, and I continue to struggle against this universe in which children suffer and die."[23] It is to this mood that the Christian existentialist John Macquarrie has addressed his essay on total hope which claims that hope belongs to the very structures of earthly life and that eternal life is the fulfilment of all human existence.[24]

It is to this mood that the biblical revelation is also addressed. Death, according to Scripture, has two faces, both of which are real. Faith hopes that the promise of a friendly interior beyond the hostile exterior is no Janus-faced deception. Faith hopes that death is both the destruction of earthly life and a departure for the eternal life already experienced by abiding in God and anticipated for the life to come. To use the Greek words of the

22. *Being and Nothingness*, tr. Hazel E. Barnes (New York: Philosophical Library, 1956), p. 539.
23. *Resistance, Rebellion, and Death*, tr. Justin O'Brien (New York: Knopf, 1961), p. 71.
24. *Christian Hope* (New York: Seabury Press, 1978), pp. 1-30.

New Testament, death is both *katalysis* (destruction) and *analysis* (departure). "For we know that if the earthly tent we live in is destroyed, we have
a building from God, a house not made with hands, eternal in the heavens"
(2 Corinthians 5:1).

Death as Destruction: Katalysis

The realm of the dead. Death is the great destroyer. It is the disembodiment
of man in his historical and earthly existence, the severance of the self from
its organ of expression. A variety of words are used to furnish a clue to the
Biblical understanding of the state of the dead. The most significant word
is *Sheol*, a word of uncertain origin but used sixty-five times in the Old
Testament. Some think it is derived from the verb *shaal*, meaning "to ask,"
and related to the practice of necromancy. Appeal for this view may be
made to 1 Samuel 28:1–19, although the word *Sheol* does not appear.
Another view relates it to the word *shoal*, meaning "the hollow beneath the
earth."

In post-biblical Hebrew *shaal* means the deep of the sea, and some see
here the picture of the primordial waters which threaten man with chaos
and destruction. Death is viewed as a return to the formless void of *tehom*
(the deep). Some of this idea of *tehom* is suggested by two synonyms for
Sheol used after the time of Ezekiel. The word *bor* or pit is at times associated with the primordial waters, even though the ordinary meaning is a
hole in the earth. Psalm 88:6f. preserves the picture:

> *Thou hast put me in the depths of the Pit,*
> *in the regions dark and deep.*
> *Thy wrath lies heavy upon me,*
> *and thou dost overwhelm me*
> *with all thy waves.*

Waters are symbolic of great dangers that overwhelm men in violent destruction (Ps. 42:7; 124:4f.).

Another synonym, also translated pit, is *shachat*, from *shuach*, to sink
down, and it, too, is pictured as the primordial deep. Ezekiel 28:8 says:

> *They shall thrust you down into the Pit,*
> *and you shall die the death of the slain*
> *in the heart of the seas.*

The dangers of the deep depict the threat of destruction, the loss of all
meaning, and the failure to function according to God's purpose. This chaos
is "without form and void," without the structure of meaning and empty of
all purpose. It is not extinction, a concept never developed in the Bible, but
exclusion from the ultimate purpose of God; yet it is not escape from the

presence of God (Ps. 139:8). *Sheol* is under the dominion of God (1 Sam. 2:6; Amos 9:2).

Abaddon, a word which means destruction, is used six times in the Old Testament for *Sheol*. Job 26:5f. says:

> *The shades below tremble,*
> *the waters and their inhabitants.*
> *Sheol is naked before God,*
> *and Abaddon has no covering.*

In Psalm 88:16f. the danger of destruction is the threat of *Abaddon*:

> *Thy wrath has swept over me;*
> *thy dread assaults destroy me.*
> *They surround me like a flood all day long;*
> *they close in upon me together.*

These terrors of *Tehom*, the dangers of the deep, provide the best picture of what disembodiment in *Sheol* means. Danger, darkness, and despair lurk beneath the deep waters of the formless void. Only the shudder that grips one hurled into the boundless deep can suggest the emotions evoked by the thought of disembodiment in *Sheol*. The loss of the body is the loss of solid ground. Man is "sunk."

The desert was one of the dreadful symbols in the religion of Israel and her neighbors.[25] In the desert theology of the Old Testament this idea of sprawling waste and desolation was an apt symbol of *Sheol* as the realm of the dead (Hos. 13:14):

> *Shall I ransom them from the power of Sheol?*
> *Shall I redeem them from Death?*
> *O Death, where are your plagues?*
> *O Sheol, where is your destruction?*

The plagues and destruction of the desert depict the deprivation that is death, and it is significant that Paul chose this passage in the Old Testament as a picture of the enemy of death that Christ overcame.

Hades in the New Testament preserves much of the Old Testament view of *Sheol*. It is the usual translation of *Sheol* in the LXX, and in the three texts where it is not used *thanatos* (death) appears.[26] *Hades* in relation to men is employed both in a collective and in an individual sense. The whole city of Capernaum can "be brought down to Hades" (Matt. 11:23; Luke 10:15). This clearly reflects the taunt against the king of Babylon in Isaiah 14:13, 15 and adds little to the significance of *Sheol-Hades*. In Luke

---

25. Alfred Halder, *The Notion of the Desert in Sumero-Accadian and West-Semitic Religions* (Uppsala: A. B. Lundequistska, 1950).
26. C. Ryder Smith, *The Bible Doctrine of the Hereafter* (London: Epworth, 1958), p. 88.

16:19–31 only the rich man is seen in *Hades*. Poor Lazarus is across the gulf in Abraham's bosom.

The Old Testament belief that the saint (*chasid*) would not be abandoned to *Sheol* has borne fruit, and *Hades* is left only to the wicked. Typical of the protests of the *chasid* against the destiny of *Sheol* is Psalm 16:10f.

> For thou dost not give me up to Sheol,
>   or let thy godly one see the Pit.
> Thou dost show me the path of life;
>   in thy presence there is fulness of joy,
>   in thy right hand are pleasures for evermore.

This "emotional reaction" of the *chasid* against *Sheol* has become an "emotional conviction" that God will not abandon the righteous in *Sheol*.[27] It is therefore incorrect to say that *Paradise* is a part of *Hades*. *Hades* is the intermediate abode of the wicked alone. There, even though it is the intermediate state, they taste of the torments of *Gehenna* (Luke 16:23–25).

Hades in relation to Christ is also closely related to the protests of the *chasid*. Psalm 16:8–11 is used as the proof text for a part of Peter's Pentecostal sermon in Acts 2:25–28. It is said that the patriarch David spoke of the resurrection of the Christ, that He was not abandoned to *Hades*, nor did His flesh see corruption (Acts 2:31). This clearly reflects the theology of the *chasidim* in the light of Christ's conquest over the powers of death. The same may be said of Matthew 16:18, where *autēs* refers to the rock (*petra*). *Hades* is pictured as a city with gates in the wall ready to swallow men by the powers of death. If "it" means the *petra* upon which the *ekklēsia* is built, the passage possibly has reference to the resurrection of Christ, who is called *petra* in 1 Peter 2:8 and 1 Corinthians 10:4. Matthew 16:21 significantly states that "from that time Jesus began to show his disciples that he must go to Jerusalem and suffer many things from the elders and chief priests and scribes, and be killed, and on the third day be raised." If the more common interpretation that *autēs* has reference to the *ekklēsia* be accepted, it may mean that the powers of death will not swallow up the church, the *chasidim*. On the basis of the Greek language it is possible to take the view that Matthew 16:18, like Acts 2:25–28, has reference to Christ's conquest over the powers of death. Either view leaves the concept of *Hades* about the same.

Christ's conquest over *Hades* is more pronounced in Revelation. In Revelation 1:17b He tells John: "I am the first and the last, and the living one; I died, and behold I am alive for evermore, and I have the keys of Death and *Hades*." In Revelation 6:8 Death and *Hades* are personified as the rider on the pale horse who goes forth "to kill with sword and with famine and with pestilence and by wild beasts of the earth." The twin riders

27. *Ibid.*, p. 64.

will not be able to hold the dead forever, for at the final judgment Death and *Hades* will give up the dead and be thrown into the lake of fire (Rev. 20:13f.). All of this symbolized the belief that death is not the true destiny of man and that *Gehenna* is not God's glory. It is the refuse of the rebels. With the new heaven and the new earth "death shall be no more" (21:4).

The state of the dead. The place of the dead is only a picture of their state. As *tehom* furnished the frame for the picture of a disembodied state, so *rephaim* suggests the conditions of this state. *Rephaim*, the dead, are to be understood as the very opposite of the *chayyim*, the living. The most vivid description of the *rephaim* in *Sheol* is found in Isaiah 14:9–15:

> *Sheol beneath is stirred up*
> >   *to meet you when you come,*
> *it rouses the shades to greet you,*
> >   *all who were leaders of the earth;*
> *it raises from their thrones*
> >   *all who were kings of the nations.*
> *All of them will speak*
> >   *and say to you:*
> *'You too have become as weak as we!*
> >   *you have become like us!'*
> *Your pomp is brought down to Sheol,*
> >   *the sound of your harps;*
> *maggots are the bed beneath you,*
> >   *and worms are your covering.*
> *How you are fallen from heaven,*
> >   *O Day Star, son of Dawn!*
> *How you are cut down to the ground,*
> >   *you who laid the nations low!*
> *You said in your heart,*
> >   *'I will ascend to heaven;*
> *above the stars of God*
> >   *I will set my throne on high;*
> *I will sit on the mount of assembly*
> >   *in the far north;*
> *I will ascend above the heights of the clouds,*
> >   *I will make myself like the Most High.'*
> *But you are brought down to Sheol,*
> >   *to the depths of the Pit.*

The same picture appears in Isaiah 26:14, 19; Job 26:5; Psalm 88:11; Proverbs 2:18; 9:18; 21:16, and Job 3:17–19; 20:20–22. Ecclesiastes 9:5 is a summary of the state.

Contact with the dead raises the question of spiritism. This possibility is suggested by the strong prohibition of the practice in the Old Testament. Deuteronomy 18:10f. forbids the presence in Israel of "any one who practices divination, a soothsayer, or an augur, or a sorcerer, or a charmer, or a medium, or a wizard, or a necromancer." Mediums and wizards (*obot* and *yidde onim*) defile the people and are to be punished by death (Lev. 19:31; 20:6, 27). People should consult God, not the dead, on behalf of the living (Isa. 8:19). When the standard ways of seeking the will of God failed, Saul turned to ask Samuel, who was dead. "The Lord did not answer him, either by dreams, or by Urim, or by prophets," so he found a woman who was a medium (*ob*). By the use of the *ob* Samuel was brought back from the dead as a god (*Elohim*), and one of the things Saul learned was that on the morrow he and his sons would join Samuel in the realm of the dead (1 Sam. 28:1–19). On the basis of Scripture and scientific investigation contact with departed spirits may be considered a definite possibility, but it is regarded as a substitute for seeking God.[28]

Conversion of the dead has been vigorously discussed on the basis of 1 Peter 4:6. It seems impossible to interpret the passage as having reference to those who are spiritually dead. Men must "give account to him that is ready to judge the living and the dead. For unto this end was the gospel preached even to the dead, that they might be judged indeed according to men in the flesh, but live according to God in the spirit" (4:5f., ASV). The dead of verse 5 stand in definite contrast to the living, and there is no good reason to assume that the word has changed its meaning in the very next verse. The departed dead who did not hear the Gospel in the flesh were evangelized (*euēngelisthē*) so that they could be judged on the same basis as men who heard the Gospel in the flesh.

There is no suggestion that they had a "second chance," but it is possible that they were given a "first chance" even after death. Despite the fact that traditional orthodoxy confines this preaching to the "righteous dead" the context would suggest that it was the dead who had no chance to hear the Gospel before they departed from life. It is difficult indeed to believe that God would leave men forever in *Hades* simply because they never had a chance to hear the Gospel. Simple justice would support the belief that "the dead" were not confined to those who died in faith. The NIV tries to avoid this conclusion be adding the word "now," but there is no basis for this in the Greek.

The same conclusion may be drawn from a hymn in 1 Timothy 3:16 (ASV, with my arrangement of the lines):

28. Edmund F. Sutcliffe, *The Old Testament and the Future Life* (London: Burns, Oates & Washbourne, 1946), pp. 25-29.

He who was manifested in the flesh,
  Justified in the spirit,
Seen of angels,
  Preached among the nations,
Believed on in the world,
  Received up in glory.

Manifestation in the flesh includes the life of Christ from birth to death. Justification or vindication in the spirit has to do with the human spirit of Jesus as in 1 Peter 3:18, where it is said that He was "put to death in the flesh but made alive in the spirit." The angels that saw Him are fallen angels to be identified with the disobedient spirits in prison in 1 Peter 3:19f. It then is possible to see the relation between preaching to the dead in 1 Peter 4:6 and preaching to the nations in 1 Timothy 3:16. "Believed on in the world" has reference to His appearance between resurrection and ascension, and the reception in glory is the ascension and exaltation. The elaborate efforts made to avoid this simple chronological order are unnecessary when the two hymns are compared.[29]

Death is not only a future disembodiment, a severance of the human spirit from the human body, it is also a present embodiment, a severance of the sinful soul from God. Even in bodily existence man, alienated from God, is dead. His existence is death incorporated. This mass mortality is based on the solidarity of man in sin: "by a man came death" and "in Adam all die" (1 Cor. 15:21f.). Two corporations are in conflict (Romans 5:12–14).

Sin binds men together in a network of interdependence that makes them a "corporate personality" of mankind in estrangement from God and hostility toward God.

The old self belongs to the old age as the new self belongs to the new age, so that one is delivered from the corporation of death and transformed into a new self by incorporation into the new age and the second Adam who rules in the new age. This incorporation into the new life is the significance of baptism: "For as many of you as were baptized into Christ have put on Christ" (Gal. 3:27). Incorporation into Christ is the crucifixion of the old self and the destruction of "the body of sin" (Rom. 6:6, ASV).

This "body of sin" is the mortal mass of mankind, the mystical unity of sinful humanity in hostility toward God. It is the slavery of sin, the system in which our "mortal bodies" are used as the weapons of wickedness (Rom. 6:12–14). As soldiers serve the state, so sinful men obey the passions dominant in the sinful personality, the self organized and orientated in opposition to God. The work of sinful slavery "leads to death" (6:16). The members of the mortal bodies are employed in obedience to sin so that

29. A detailed study of 1 Pet. 3:18–22 as a hymn of baptism has been done by Bo Reicke, *The Disobedient Spirits and Christian Baptism* (Copenhagen: Ejnar Munksgaard, 1946).

there is "greater and greater iniquity" (6:19); and the increase of this sinful system deepens the estrangement and alienation of men from God. The wages of sin, which is death, is the consequence of remaining in the body of sin (6:23).

The body of sin is also the "body of death" (7:24). Sin is the cause, and death is the effect in this corporate estrangement from God. Paul pictures the wretchedness of the body of death by a series of illustrations. The first is from military life (7:7–12). He was alive before he learned the law, but "when the commandment came, sin revived" and he died. Before he reached the stage of life where he would be responsible to God for his own actions, he was not aware of this involvement in sin. It took the command against covetousness to arouse the latent rebellion against the will of God. Like two soldiers in mortal combat, Paul and sin battle to the fatal finish. Sin, "finding opportunity" (*aphormē*, a military metaphor), deceived and killed Paul. This death was conscious estrangement from God.

The second illustration is from the marketplace (7:13–20). Paul knows that he is "sold under sin" as a slave is sold in the marketplace. In estrangement from God he finds himself helpless to do the good. What a predicament: "I can will what is right, but I cannot do it" (7:18). Sin has become the master of his actions. Sin has come to dwell where the Spirit of God should dwell. It is death incorporated, the body of sin and death in place of the body of Christ. A slave driver has taken the master's place.

The third illustration is from mental experience (7:21–25). In the body of death the law of God in which the inmost self finds delight is opposed by the law of sin. With the law of sin in conflict with the law of the mind, man is reduced to despair. Only the redemptive act of God can deliver man from his misery and wretchedness. Death incorporated is utter despair, man being severed from the source of his life and joy.

Emancipation from this state of estrangement is incorporation into the body of Christ, so that we "may belong to another, to him who has been raised from the dead in order that we may bear fruit for God" (7:4). The law of Moses is able to make us conscious of "the law of sin and death," but only "the law of the Spirit of life in Christ Jesus" can emancipate from this corporate slavery (8:1–4). These are the three laws: the law of sin in which sinful man exists in estrangement from God and in mortality, the law of Sinai through which the complex of sin comes to consciousness, and the law of the Spirit operative in Christ and adequate for deliverance from death. "For God has done what the law, weakened by the flesh, could not do: sending his own Son in the likeness of sinful flesh and as a sin offering, he condemned sin in the flesh, in order that the just requirement of the law might be fulfilled in us, who walk not according to the flesh but according to the Spirit" (8:3, footnote). Apart from God's grace man is "dead through the trespasses and sins," and it is only by the miracle of mercy that he is made "alive together with Christ" (Eph. 2:1, 5). As a primitive song says (Eph. 5:14):

> *Awake, O sleeper, and arise from the dead,*
> *and Christ shall give you light.*

See Part VI.46 for more on spiritual death.

Death as Departure: Analysis

Analysis (departure) is a Greek word used by Paul to describe the other side of death for those in Christ (Phil. 1:23; 2 Tim. 4:6). The biblical revelation begins with the belief that tribal solidarity continues beyond physical death (Gen. 15:15). The second stage expresses the view that the shades of the dead survive in the realm of *Sheol*, the Hebrew word for the realm of the dead (1 Sam. 28:8–14; Isaiah 14:9). Belief in the resurrection of the body will be discussed in the next section, but before that hope was revealed there were prophecies about a future destruction of all death (Isa. 25:8; Hosea 13:14; cf. 1 Cor. 15:24).

Christian tradition has been characterized by conflict on the details of life after physical life comes to an end. It may be helpful to clarify the issues as seen from two different points of view before a summary statement on the present situation is made.

Immortality. Conflict between the biblical view on immortality and that formulated in classical Greek thought has been present since the first collisions between Hebrew and Greek thought. If one could read the Bible without cultural conditioning, it would seem that the biblical view on immortality saw man as a living soul who had eaten from the tree of knowledge but not from the tree of life (Gen. 2, 3; Rev. 2:7; 22:2, 14).

The clearest biblical teachings on immortality are in the writings of Paul. In Paul's so-called "pillar epistles" it is beyond question that he followed the general biblical view that immortality is a garment from God that must be put on.

The resurrection of the body at the Second Coming (*parousia*) is the point at which man's mortal nature will be fully clothed with immortality (1 Cor. 15:51–53). It seems that Paul also believed that the human spirit will be "swallowed up by life" even before the resurrection of the body (2 Cor. 5:4). The idea that these two views are in conflict is untenable, and will be discussed later.

The shift of emphasis from the mortality of man to the immortality of man is even clearer in Paul's letter to Rome. Idolatry is described as an exchange of "the glory of the immortal God for images resembling mortal man or birds or animals or reptiles" (Rom. 1:23). Immortality and eternal life are that for which man must "seek" (2:7).

The "pastoral epistles" of Paul are even more explicit on the immortality of God in contrast to the mortality of man. A doxology has the ascription: "To the King of ages, immortal, invisible, the only God, be honor and glory for ever. Amen" (1 Tim. 1:17).

If there is any doubt about this contrast, a charge and benediction puts it beyond question. "I charge you to keep the commandment unstained and free from reproach until the appearing of our Lord Jesus Christ; and this will be manifested at the proper time by the blessed and only Sovereign, King of kings and Lord of lords, who alone has immortality and dwells in unapproachable light, whom no man has seen or can see. To him be honor and eternal dominion. Amen" (1 Tim. 6:14–16).

The "appearing of our Lord Jesus Christ at his Second Coming" follows the "appearing of our Savior Christ Jesus" at his First Coming when he "abolished death and brought life and immortality to light through the gospel" (2 Tim. 1:10).

If the seven passages of Paul in the above survey are so emphatic on the theme that God alone is by nature immortal and that man is by nature mortal, how did the false idea that man is by nature immortal get accepted in traditional eschatology? The answer is obvious: It was piped into Christian theology from the Greek philosopher Plato, so that preachers, both Catholic and Protestant, take their texts from Paul and preach the philosophical idealism of Plato.

Plato' teachings on the natural immortality of the human soul are elaborated in his dialogue called the *Phaedo*. The first principle is that of an endless cycle from life to death and from death to life (70c-82c).

This leads to a second argument that claims that the soul can remember experiences brought into life from the pre-existence of the soul (72e-77d). This idea of the pre-existence of the soul has been promoted in the poetry of Wordsworth and Tennyson used so often in funeral orations. Cf. Part VI.46.

A third argument says the human soul is "simple" and so unable to fall apart into complexity (80b). This belief in the natural immortality of the "simple soul" really makes man a spark of the divine soul, and medieval mysticism made much of that idea.

A fourth argument develops this identity of man with God by teaching that the soul participates in a life-giving power that does not admit of death (103b-107b). This makes earthly life and eternal life the same and lays the foundation for universalism.

The summary of Plato's "five points" assumes that all that moves is immortal and draws the conclusion that the self-moving soul must be immortal and unbegotten (*Phaedrus*, 245c-246a; *Laws*, 893-896). It is not possible to harmonize these psychological and cosmological ideas with the biblical distinctions between God and man and God and the world, so the outcome has been the loss of the biblical view of immortality in much Christian tradition and modern thought.[30]

The intermediate state. The confusion of the biblical view of immortality with that in Greek philosophy led to the identification of the resurrection of the dead with the natural immortality of the soul. It became easier to say resurrection when one really meant the natural immortality of the soul.

Interpretations and translations in the writings of Paul may best illustrate this. The question is: Did Paul teach the natural immortality of the soul or the resurrection of the dead?[31] It is obvious from reading Paul and Plato that Paul taught the resurrection of the dead, but what is the state of the human spirit between death and resurrection? Is there an intermediate state between death and resurrection in which those in Christ are aware of Christ and others in Christ?

The first of four texts in Paul seems to answer the question in favor of an intermediate state. First Thessalonians 4:14, as usually translated, seems to say that the death and resurrection of Jesus is the basis for the belief that "God will bring with him those who have fallen asleep." *The Good News Bible* alone translates *axei syn* as "take with" rather than "bring with." This supports the doctrine of soul-sleep that rules out awareness between death and resurrection. Appeal is also made to the biblical metaphor of sleep for death. Other texts in Paul do not seem to be in agreement with this novel translation in *The Good News Bible*. The fact that the Lord is descending favors the usual translation.

The most debated text in Paul is 2 Corinthians 5:1–5. Here again translations are confusing. *The New English Bible*, *The Living Bible* and *The Good News Bible* support the view that sees death as moving out of our house to God's house, from a tent into a building, and the building is interpreted as the spiritual body of the resurrection. There would be little need for a *parousia* at the consummation of the age if all this happens at the moment of death. There certainly is no support elsewhere for the belief that the building is the body.

Paul's prison epistle to the Philippians retains the belief that our "lowly body" will be made like the "glorious body" of Christ when the Savior comes back from heaven (3:20f.). If may be that Philippians 1:23 belongs to a later letter to Philippi, but it does lend support to the belief that death is a departure to "be with Christ, for that is far better."

The fourth and final passage in Paul on this problem is 2 Timothy 4:6–8. Death is still viewed as a departure, but reward for faithful living

30. Many details of current debate from the point of view of universalism are in John Hick, *Death and Eternal Life* (New York: Harper and Row, 1976).
31. Krister Stendahl, ed., *Immortality and Resurrection* (New York: The Macmillan Company, 1965) has collected papers on the classic debate at Harvard.

is still associated with the last Day and the Second Appearing of our Lord
Jesus Christ.

Unless there was some inconsistency in Paul's views, it seems that
from 1 Thessalonians to 2 Timothy the belief in an intermediate state was
consistently taught by Paul. This was not Plato's view of the natural immortality of the soul but a coherent view that blended the biblical views on
immortality and resurrection.

This question was seriously debated after the Protestant Reformation.
The intermediate state in Roman Catholic eschatology had been developed
into a doctrine of Limbo and Inferno for the lost and Purgatory and Paradise
for the saved. Martin Luther rejected both Limbo and Purgatory and relegated Inferno and Paradise to a time after the resurrection of the death.

John Calvin was closer to Catholicism, so he taught a present Inferno
and Paradise immediately after death. At times this also raised questions
about the necessity for a consummation and a Second Coming as evangelistic fervor often preached a straight-to-hell and straight-to-heaven view
that made the intermediate state the final state. Careful biblical studies
brought out a more balanced view that set forth a present *Hades* and a
future *Gehenna* for the lost and a present Paradise and a future resurrection
to immortality for the saved.[32]

75. Resurrection

The logical outcome of the Old Testament views on survival after physical
death is the resurrection of the body. Out of the belief in one's survival in
his seed (offspring) in history, hope in God affirmed the survival as shades
in Sheol beyond historical existence. As hope in God increased in relation
to other beliefs, such as the unity of the human soul and the goodness of
creation, the proclamation of total victory over the powers of death was
bound to become a vital part of faith in God. Apocalypticism is not a foreign
element in Old Testament revelation. God's revelation of himself in the
present age became a bridge to belief in an age to come in which the righteous would be raised from Sheol for reward and the wicked would be
called forth for punishment.

The Resurrection to Life

The ground of the belief. The resurrection to life is the Christian answer to
the threat of death. The ground for the belief is found in God, yet not God
in philosophical abstraction, unrelated to man and the world, but in historical action by which He relates Himself to both. In the background are
at least three basic views. The first is the view that man has a corporate

---

32. For further details and documentation see my book *The Hope of Glory* (Grand Rapids,
Michigan: Wm. B. Eerdmans Publishing Co., 1964), pp. 64-77.

existence. The dualism of Plato is foreign to biblical faith, and the idea that death leaves the soul undisturbed as the oyster leaves the shell or as the body leaves the tomb has no place in biblical teaching. Man in his concrete and historical existence is a living soul, made from the breath of God and the dust of the earth (Gen. 2:7).

If there is to be full life beyond death the whole man will need to be redeemed. In the Old Testament, life in *Sheol* is only a shadow of historical existence, and only the shades (*rephaim*), not the disembodied souls, go down to *Sheol*.[33] The Hebrew word for the dead (*rephaim*) denotes weakness, and their existence in Sheol is considered only a weakened form of the present life (Isa. 14:9f.). They can only chirp and mutter (8:19). Paul Althaus has vigorously defended the anthropological grounds for the doctrine of the resurrection, holding that in human existence corporeality and reality belong essentially together.[34]

A second view related to the resurrection of the dead is the goodness of creation. Man's body, being a part of God's good creation, is not essentially evil. It is no prison in which he is confined as a prisoner (Plato, *Phaedo*, 62) and from which he may escape at death, but part of his essential existence and subject to God's redemptive activity. Even though the body is "dead because of sin," the Christian groans "inwardly as [he] awaits the redemption of [his] body" (Rom. 8:10, 23).

Anders Nygren has pointed out that the goodness of creation, the incarnation of the Son of God in human flesh, and the resurrection of the dead are inseparably connected as the three fundamental dogmas of the early Church in her life-and-death struggle against the inroads of Gnostic dualism.[35] If corporeality belongs to God's creation, it may be included in His gracious act of redemption.

The third perspective in the background of the resurrection is the personal reality of God. At many places in the Old Testament, fellowship with God suggests an ultimate triumph over death. "Enoch walked with God; and he was not, for God took him" (Gen 5:24; cf. Heb. 11:5). "God will ransom my soul from the power of Sheol, for he will receive me" (Ps. 49:15). "Thou dost guide me with thy counsel, and afterwards thou wilt receive me to glory" (Ps. 73:24). Elijah was "taken" (2 Kings 2:3, 5, 10) and "went up by a whirlwind into heaven" (2:11). Job believed that he had a living Redeemer and that after his skin was destroyed, without his flesh he would see God (Job 19:25f.). The Psalmist had hope that he would awake and be satisfied with beholding the form of God (Ps. 17:15). In the New Testament, appeal is made to Psalm 16:10 for the resurrection of Jesus Christ (Acts 2:27; 13:35).

---

33. H. Wheeler Robinson, *Inspiration and Revelation in the Old Testament* (Oxford: Clarendon Press, 1946), pp. 94-100.
34. *Die letzten Dinge* (Gütersloh: C. Bertelsmann, 1949), pp. 121f.
35. *Agape and Eros*, tr. Philip S. Watson (Philadelphia: Westminster, 1953), pp. 276-288.

Not too much New Testament teaching should be read into these statements, but it should not be overlooked that Jesus, in opposition to the
Sadducees, appealed even to the written Law (Mark 12:18–27: Matt. 22:23–
33; Luke 20:27–40). The Sadducees knew neither the Scriptures nor the
power of God.[36] Had they known the power of God they would have known
that those who rise from the dead "neither marry nor are given in marriage,
but are like angels" (Mark 12:25); and, had they known what the Scriptures
said about God's personal relation to the patriarchs, they would have concluded: "He is not God of the dead, but of the living" (12:27).

The contrast between the dread and despair that gripped men's souls
in the presence of Sheol, and the jubilant hope aroused by the prospects of
resurrection, is vividly portrayed in the apocalypse of Isaiah (24–27). Isaiah
26:14 says of the wicked:

> They are dead, they will not live;
>   they are shades, they will not arise;
>   to that end thou hast visited them with destruction
>   and wiped out all remembrance of them.

In the same chapter appears the first clear reference to the resurrection of
life. Of the righteous it is said (v. 19):

> Thy dead shall live, their bodies shall rise.
>   O dwellers in the dust, awake and sing for joy!
> For thy dew is a dew of light,
>   and on the land of the shades
>   thou wilt let it fall.

The resurrection of the dead rests on the power and reality of God and
man's right relation to God.

Against this background two major factors stand in the foreground of
resurrection faith.[37] The first is "the first-born from the dead" (Col. 1:18;
Rev. 1:5). In Israel all the inheritance and the authority of the father belonged to the first-born. Israel, destined to rule over the nations of the earth,
was called the first-born of God (Exod. 4:22; Jer. 31:9). As one of the royal
psalms says: "And I will make him the first-born, the highest of the kings
of the earth" (Ps. 89:27). The term therefore has reference more to destiny
than to origin, to pre-eminence than to priority in time. When Christ is
called "the first-born of all creation" (Col. 1:15) and "the first-born from
the dead" (1:18), it is His sovereignty over creation and death that is proclaimed. Paul's famous wordplay makes this plain: "The first-born (prōto-

---

36. William Strawson, *Jesus and the Future Life* (London: Epworth, 1959), pp. 205f. This
theme in the Old Testament has been traced by Robert Martin-Achard, *From Death to Life*,
tr. John Penney Smith (Edinburgh: Oliver and Boyd, 1960).
37. Oscar Cullmann, *Immortality of the Soul or Resurrection of the Dead?* (New York:
Macmillan, 1958), pp. 40-57.

tokos) from the dead, that in everything he might be pre-eminent (*prō-teuōn*)" (Col. 1:18). The same verse calls Christ "head" and "beginning."

In opposition to the idea that Christ was a creature, the early church fathers rightly insisted that Christ was *prōtotokos* (first-born), not *prōtoktistos* (first-created).[38] Those "predestined to be conformed to the image of his Son, in order that he might be the first-born among many brethren" (Rom. 8:29) are those who are to share with Christ in His resurrection. He is the "pioneer of their salvation" as He brings "many sons to glory" (Heb. 2:10).

The historical event by which the Lord Jesus was raised from the dead is the prospective power by which we may believe in our own resurrection. God will bring those back who have fallen asleep in Jesus, "since we believe that Jesus died and rose again" (1 Thess. 4:14). His resurrection from the dead has become the ground of hope that, at the *parousia*, the dead will be raised and the living will be raptured with them.

This is the reason Paul introduces his lengthy discussion of the resurrection of the dead with a vigorous defense of the resurrection of Christ (1 Cor. 15:1–11). His resurrection is preliminary to any clear prospects for our resurrection, and the validity of the gospel is threatened by a denial of the resurrection of Christ.

> Now, if Christ is preached as raised from the dead, how can some of you say that there is no resurrection of the dead? But if there is no resurrection of the dead, then Christ has not been raised; if Christ has not been raised, then our preaching is in vain and your faith is in vain. We are even found to be misrepresenting God, because we testified of God that he raised Christ, whom he did not raise if it is true that the dead are not raised. For if the dead are not raised, then Christ has not been raised. If Christ has not been raised, your faith is futile and you are still in your sins. Then those also who have fallen asleep in Christ have perished. If in this life we who are in Christ have only hope, we are of all men most to be pitied (15:12–19).

Those who are in Christ by faith are not merely hoping; the hope is grounded in the historical event of Christ's resurrection. All stands or falls on this event.

Our resurrection is organically related to His resurrection, so that His conquest of death is the first-fruits of the full harvest at the consummation (15:20–23). If the Lord Jesus is still dead there is no prospect for those who are in Him but the grim reality of death, for His destiny is our destiny. All things, therefore, are worthless compared to the knowledge of Him in

---

38. Cf. Francis W. Beare, *The Interpreter's Bible*, ed. George Arthur Buttrick (New York: Abingdon-Cokesbury, 1955) (hereafter I. B.), XI, 164.

"the power of his resurrection" (Phil. 3:10). Sharing His sufferings and conformity to His death are courageously accepted that we "may attain the resurrection from the dead" (3:11). His actual power is the potentiality for our perfection, the completion of our lives at the resurrection. The whole perspective of the future and possibility of victory over death focuses on Him who has already won the battle at the crucial point.

This prospective power is also proleptic, as in the days when Christ was present in the flesh.[39] The power by which the human body could be transformed was evident in His transfiguration (Mark 9:2) as well as in His resurrection (Matt. 27:52f.), but the power manifest in Him was transmitted to others. He raised the dead (Luke 7:11–17; 8:40–56; John 11), and by the power of the Spirit demonic powers were cast out and destroyed (Matt. 11:5; 12:28; Luke 11:20). The power which was at work in Christ in the days of His flesh became operative in the Church after His resurrection. Unworthy participation in His spiritual body exposed man to the powers of sickness and death (1 Cor. 5:5; 11:29f.), even as worthy participation brought health and final resurrection from the dead (John 6:40, 44, 54).

It is this participation in His proleptic power that opens the way for a deeper understanding of baptism and the Lord's Supper. We share not only in His death to sin but also in the power of the resurrection by which sin and death are defeated. The power of His resurrection is both prospective, looking forward to our resurrection, but also proleptic, at work beforehand in the person of Christ and the fellowship of His Church.

The second factor in the foreground of resurrection faith is "the first-fruits of the Spirit" (Rom. 8:23). In many ways this is inseparable from "the first-born from the dead," for Jesus was "designated Son of God in power according to the Spirit of holiness by His resurrection from the dead" (1:4). The idea of "the first-fruits," like the idea of the first-born, is taken from the Old Testament (Exod. 23:14–17; 34:22–24; Lev. 23:1–44; Deut. 26:1–11; 2 Chron. 31:5). As the first-born of man and beasts were claimed by the Lord (Exod. 13:2), so the first-fruits of the harvest were presented to Him also (Exod. 22:29). In a figurative sense it means the token of the coming harvest. As the first-fruits were a guarantee of the full harvest in the future, so the present possession of the Spirit is a foretaste of full redemption at the resurrection of the body.

It has already been noted that the first four of the spiritual experiences in Romans 8:1–27 are vitally related to the life available in Christ. The last two concepts focus on the resurrection, an essential factor to the fullness of eternal life. The graphic statement on the threefold groan compares the

---

39. Oscar Cullmann, *The Early Church*, tr. A. J. B. Higgins (Philadelphia: Westminster, 1956), pp. 165-173.

bodily sufferings of the present with the glorious redemption of the future.[40] God's creation groans as it longs for deliverance from the bondage of futility in the freedom of the future (8:22). God's children, who have already received the first-fruits of the Spirit, groan for complete sonship in the redemption of the body (8:23).

Sonship is freedom, and sonship is incomplete until freedom is complete. Sonship is a process of perfection until the image of God has been finished in man. God's Spirit groans as He helps our weakness and "intercedes for the saints according to the will of God" (8:26f.). The first-fruits of the Spirit along with the first-born from the dead furnish the foreground for belief in the resurrection.

The first-fruits (*aparchē*) of the Spirit are about the same as the guarantee (*arrabōn*) of the Spirit which God gives to assure us that God will ultimately redeem His possessions from the powers of sin and death (2 Cor. 1:22; Eph. 1:14). God has sealed the believer with the Holy Spirit of promise unto the day of full redemption (Eph. 1:13; 4:30). The present transformation of life in the power of the Spirit constitutes a bridgehead of belief by which the powers of death are defeated and man is delivered from the threat of destruction.

These two factors that constitute the ground for belief in the resurrection are closely related. Both Christ and the Spirit are described as first-fruits (1 Cor. 15:23; Rom. 8:23). Christ, as the last Adam, "became a life-giving spirit" (1 Cor. 15:45). Indeed, "the Lord is the Spirit," and "we all, with unveiled face, beholding the glory of the Lord, are being changed into his likeness from one degree of glory to another; for this comes from the Lord who is the Spirit" (2 Cor. 3:17f.). The complete transformation, when we shall "bear the image of the man of heaven," will be the resurrection of the dead (1 Cor. 15:49).

The goal of the belief. The goal of the redemptive process is the resurrection of the body. The belief that the body, as essential to man's true selfhood, is to be redeemed has both ethical and eschatological significance. This is one of the major differences between the Greek and the Hebrew views of man. The gulf between Paul and Gnostic dualism is vividly illustrated in the conflict over immorality in the Church of Corinth (1 Cor. 6:12–20). The Gnostics were able to justify the most sordid type of sexual behavior with the slogan "all things are lawful for me" (6:12). They assumed that the acts of the body had no effect on the human spirit, so that one could be joined to a prostitute with his body while being joined to the Lord with his spirit.

Paul, looking on man as a psychosomatic entity, was horrified. Those who are united to the Lord not only become one in spirit with Him, but

---

40. Anders Nygren, *Commentary on Romans*, tr. Carl C. Rasmussen (Philadelphia: Muhlenberg, 1949), pp. 329-336.

their very "bodies are members of Christ" (6:15). Man is to glorify God in both body and spirit, not only because they are a unity but also because both are to be redeemed. Appealing to Jewish dietary regulations, the dualism argued: "Food is meant for the stomach and the stomach for food." Paul replies that the food and the stomach have no place in the redeemed body, for both will be destroyed by God.

Paul Althaus rightly points out that the stomach (*koilia*) represents the totality of man's sensual functions which make earthly existence possible and pass away with the world, while body (*sōma*) is "carrier and object of our action, expression, form"; united with the risen Christ, it will be "raised with the personality."[41]

In discussing the Christian attitude towards dietary regulations and Sabbath keeping, Paul sets forth the ethical importance of our union with the Lord in a passage of surpassing poetic beauty. Moffatt's translation preserves much that is in the original Greek (Rom. 14:6-8):

> *The eater eats to the Lord,*
> * since he thanks God for his food;*
> *the non-eater abstains to the Lord,*
> * and he too thanks God.*
> *For none of us lives to himself,*
> * and none of us dies to himself;*
> *if we live, we live to the Lord,*
> * and if we die, we die to the Lord.*

Paul's comment reminds us that "whether we live or whether we die, we are the Lord's. For to this end Christ died and lived again, that he might be Lord both of the dead and of the living" (14:8f.).

The ethical realism of Paul was rooted deeply in his eschatology. Man is to glorify God in his body because the body is to be glorified. But what does he mean by the term body (*sōma*)? In 1 Corinthians 6:13 he implies that food and the stomach have no place in the redeemed body, and he roundly rebukes those whose "god is the belly" (Phil. 3:19). It is in this connection that Paul's heritage needs to be considered.

The Pharisees, among whom Paul was educated, are represented in two different ways. At one place it is said:

> *For the earth shall then assuredly restore the dead,*
> *[Which it now receives, in order to preserve them].*
> *It shall make no change in their form.*
> *But as it has received, so shall it restore them,*
> *And as I delivered them unto it, so also shall it raise them*
> *(II Baruch 50:2).*[42]

41. *Op. cit.*, p. 236.
42. *The Apocrypha and Pseudepigrapha*, ed. R. H. Charles (Oxford: Clarendon, 1913), II, 508.

Yet Josephus, another Pharisee, says they believed that good men are "removed into other bodies" (*Wars*, II.8.14).[43]

Many interpreters find both views in Paul. In 1 Corinthians 15:35–50, both by analogy and appeal to Scripture, he stresses the idea that there is a difference between the psychic or "soulist" body in which man now exists and the spiritual body of the resurrected. His first analogy compares the two bodies to a grain of wheat and that which grows from it. "You sow not the body which is to be. . . . But God gives it a body as he has chosen" (vv. 37f.).

Paul does not intend to teach that this is a natural process in which the powers of germination are in the dead body. He has not abandoned the belief that God raises the dead — "God gives it a body." In his second analogy the difference is similar to that which is seen in the four kinds of flesh (v. 39), but this is not so clear. The same lack of clarity attends the third analogy (v. 40), but the difference between the two bodies is apparently like that between the earthly and heavenly bodies, or the various heavenly bodies. Seed, flesh, bodies — but the most fitting analogy is that of seed.

He appeals to Scripture with what may be a Christian hymn, as the Moffatt translation suggests (15:42–44):

> *What is sown is mortal,*
> *what rises is immortal;*
> *sown inglorious,*
> *it rises in glory;*
> *sown in weakness,*
> *it rises in power;*
> *sown an animate body,*
> *it rises a spiritual body.*

The translation "animate" is literally correct, for neither the word "natural" (ASV) nor the word "physical" (RSV) brings out the full meaning of *psychikon* (psychic, soulish). The animate body is man in his historical existence as a living soul, while the spiritual body is man beyond polarity, the body transformed for spiritual activity in a spiritual state or condition.

The appeal to Genesis 2:7 precipitates the analogy of the two Adams (cf. Rom. 5:12–18). Philo (*On the Creation*, 134; *Allegorical Interpretations*, I. 31) taught that the man of Genesis 1:26 was the ideal man and came first, before the earthly man of Genesis 2:7. Paul repudiates this speculation based on Platonic archetypes and teaches that the earthly man comes first and the spiritual man comes afterward, at the resurrection. Again Moffatt's translation brings out the poetic structure (1 Cor. 15:45–49):

43. *Op. cit.*, p. 676.

> *The first man, Adam, became an animate being,*
> *the last Adam a life-giving Spirit;*
> *but the animate, not the spiritual, comes first,*
> *and only then the spiritual.*

> *Man the first is from the earth, material;*
> *man the second is from heaven.*
> *As man the material is, so are the material;*
> *as man the heavenly is, so are the heavenly.*
> *Thus, as we have borne the likeness of material man,*
> *so we are to bear the likeness of the heavenly man.*

The Christological analogy is again employed in the ethical lamentations of Philippians 3:18-21. Philippi, as a Roman military colony, was directly responsible to the capital in Rome, and her citizens were not subject to the legal political situation (Acts 16:12, 21). With this in mind Paul wrote:

> For many, of whom I have often told you and now tell you even with tears, live as enemies of the cross of Christ. Their end is destruction, their god is the belly, and their glory is in their shame, with minds set on earthly things. But our commonwealth is in heaven, and from it we await a Savior, the Lord Jesus Christ, who will change our lowly body to be like his glorious body, by the power which enables him even to subject all things to himself (Philippians 3:18-21).

Commonwealth (*politeuma*) means "the capital or native city, which keeps the citizens on its registers."[44] From this capital or native city a Savior (the word used for the Roman Emperor since 48 B.C.) will come and change the lowly body or "body of our humiliation" (ASV) "to be like his glorious body" by an energy (*energeia*) which will enable him "to subject all things to himself." The body of humiliation is the psychic body, and the body of glory is the spiritual body. It is by the energy of Christ, not by some innate principle of germination, that this transformation takes place.

In 2 Corinthians 5:1-5 Paul makes a distinction between what he calls "the earthly house (*oikia*) of this tent" in which we now live and the "house (*oikia*) not made with hands, eternal in the heavens" (5:1). The earthly house, which he compares to a tent, appears to be identical with the "earthen vessels" (4:7) and "the outer nature" which "is wasting away" (4:16). Is it possible that the "inner nature" (4:16) is to be identified with "the house not made with hands," so that we already "have a building from God" (5:1)?

Apparently Paul thinks of this further housing as taking place at death,

---

44. Ethelbert Stauffer, *New Testament Theology*, tr. John Marsh (London: SCM, 1955), p. 296.

although the renewal of the inner nature and the putting on of the new nature are prerequisites to this possibility (Col. 3:10; Eph. 4:24; Gal. 3:27). Inner nature, house not made with hands, spiritual body: are they identical, or three stages in the redemptive process? Many commentaries make this identification, at least between the last two, but not one has produced references to prove that the "eternal house" is the same as the "spiritual body."[45] The "white robes" of the martyrs in Revelation 6:11 do not rule out a resurrection in Revelation 20:4. In the Christian apocalypse *The Ascension of Isaiah* there are many references to "garments" (4:11, 16f.; 7:22; 8:14; 9:2, 9, 11, 17f.), but the spirits who are clothed with these garments are always absent from the body. This is precisely the idea of Paul. Those who are clothed are "away from the body and at home with the Lord" (2 Cor. 5:8).

The Resurrection of Judgment

The discussion thus far has been confined to those who will be raised to eternal life with God. This leaves two important questions unanswered, the first of which has already been suggested: are the righteous alone raised? It has been noted that Isaiah 26:19 speaks of the resurrection as a reward for the righteous. II Maccabees 7:14 speaks of those for whom "there will be no resurrection to life!" Josephus reports the Pharisees as teaching that "good men are removed into other bodies" (*Wars*, II.8.14).

Jesus speaks not only of "the resurrection of the just" (Luke 14:14), but of "those who are accounted worthy to attain to that age and to the resurrection from the dead," who "cannot die any more, because they are equal to the angels and are sons of God, being sons of the resurrection" (Luke 20:35f.). At no place do the Synoptic Gospels speak of the resurrection of the wicked, and the same is true of the Pauline Epistles, unless one adopts the highly dubious translation of *telos* in 1 Corinthians 15:24 as "the rest" rather than "the end."

The second resurrection. On the other hand, Daniel 12:2 says: "And many of those who sleep in the dust of the earth shall awake, some to everlasting life, and some to shame and everlasting contempt." It may well be that this particular passage does not teach the resurrection of all but only the resurrection of the conspicuously good and the notoriously wicked, but it does include wicked men as well as righteous. It clearly goes beyond Isaiah 26:19, which speaks only of a single resurrection, namely of the righteous.

John 5:28f. reports Jesus as teaching: "Do not marvel at this; for the hour is coming when all who are in the tombs will hear his voice and come

---

45. Alfred Plummer, *II Corinthians* in *The International Critical Commentary* (New York: Scribner's, 1915), pp. 140-164; Hans Windisch, *Meyers Kommentar* (Göttingen: Vandenhoeck & Ruprecht, 1924), pp. 157-178; Clarence Tucker Craig, I.B., X, 327. Cf. Joachim Jeremias, in *New Testament Studies*, II (Feb., 1956), 151-159.

forth, those who have done good, to the resurrection of life, and those who have done evil, to the resurrection of judgment." In Acts, Paul not only identifies himself as a Pharisee (23:6) but preaches "a resurrection of both the just and the unjust" (24:15).

Must one conclude that the Synoptic Gospels and the Pauline Epistles teach one view and the Acts and the Johannine writings another, or is there a third possibility? The common authorship of Luke 14:14, 20:35f., and Acts 24:15 would make Luke guilty of self-contradiction if the two views are incompatible.

Jesus surely taught a judgment of all men. It will be more tolerable for the people of Sodom and Gomorrah and of Tyre and Sidon on the day of judgment than for those who rejected the opportunity afforded them (Matt. 10:15; 11:22, 24). The men of Nineveh and the queen of the south "will arise at the judgment" to condemn the generation of Jesus (12:41f.). At "the close of the age" the wicked and the righteous are to be separated (13:40f., 49f.), and "all the nations" will be gathered before the Son of Man (25:32).

Paul taught that "every man will receive his commendation from God" when the Lord comes (1 Cor. 4:5), and that "God judges those outside" (5:13). "The saints will judge the world" (6:2), but they are to examine themselves lest they be "condemned along with the world" (11:32). God will judge "every man according to his works: to those who by patience in well-doing seek for glory and honor and immortality, he will give eternal life; but for those who are factious and do not obey the truth, but obey wickedness, there will be wrath and fury" (Rom. 2:6-8).

The second death. The second death has been debated even more than the second resurrection. The term is a Rabbinic expression found in the New Testament only in the book of Revelation (2:11; 20:6, 14; 21:8), but it is identified with "the lake of fire" (19:20; 20:10, 14f.; 21:8), an idea with a variety of apocalyptic associations. It is a great mistake, in reaction to literalism, to brush aside the picture language of the Scriptures as if it is meaningless to modern men. Existential eschatology often employs terms strangely similar to those found in the Bible, even when the interpretations differ.

Two associated pictures merge in the New Testament portrayal of the second death. The first is that of abyss, a term found in the Septuagint translation for *tehom* (deep) in the second verse of the Bible. In the Old Testament the primeval chaos comes to mean the place of intermediate punishment for the enemies of God, and it appears in the New Testament with the same meaning (Luke 8:31; Rom. 10:7; Rev. 9:1; 17:8; 20:3). The place of final punishment is the lake of fire, the second death. Here again it is very important to distinguish between the intermediate state of the godless and their ultimate state.

The second picture is that of *Gehenna. Hades* is the intermediate place of punishment for wicked men (Rev. 1:18; 6:8; 20:13f.), but they are cast into the lake of fire at the final judgment (20:14). The place of the final punishment of wicked men is *Gehenna*, a term used only once in the New Testament outside the teaching of Jesus (Jas. 3:6), but it merges in meaning with the idea of the lake of fire, the second death, in such passages as Matthew 25:41: "Depart from me, you cursed, into the eternal fire prepared for the devil and his angels." There God is able to destroy both body and soul (Matt. 10:28; cf. 5:22, 29f.; 18:9; 23:15, 33). The destruction is compared to "the furnace of fire" (Matt. 13:42), "the outer darkness" (8:12; 25:30), and to "eternal punishment" (25:46; cf. 24:51). The picture of *Gehenna* comes from the valley of Hinnom, the place where the worshippers of Molech burned their children in sacrifice (2 Kings 16:3; 23:10; Jer. 7:31; Ps. 106:31, 37f.; 2 Chron. 28:3; 33:6). This is a fitting description of the final punishment of those, defiled by sin and outside the city of God, who are excluded from the fellowship of God. Man, alienated from God, men and God's whole creation, is a sealed unit.

At other places in the New Testament the wicked are said to "suffer the punishment of eternal destruction and exclusion from the presence of the Lord and from the glory of his might" (2 Thess. 1:9), to be devoured by a consuming fire (Heb. 6:8; 10:27; 12:29), or simply to perish (Rom. 2:12; John 3:16). All of this agrees with the general picture of *Gehenna*.

Gehenna has not always been interpreted as a place of eternal punishment. Origen, the so-called father of universalism, thought of the fire as a process of purification by which man along with the whole of creation would be restored to his original unity with God. The designation *apokatastasis* is found in Acts 3:21, where it has reference to the establishment of "all that God spoke by the mouth of his holy prophets from of old," but Origen appealed more to 1 Corinthians 15:26–28, Romans 5:17, 11:36, and Philippians 2:5–11.

The principles behind his argument revolved around the relation of God and man, and the reincarnation of the soul. The love of God and the freedom of man keep open the possibility that man in his rebellion will finally surrender to the will of God in Christ. The reincarnation of the soul, in the framework of a cyclical view of history, requires the ultimate restoration of souls to their pre-existent state of purity before they return to dwell in other bodies. Origen abandons the idea that choices made in this life have a decisive character, and substitutes a cyclical view of history, characteristic of Greek thought, for the linear view found in Scripture.[46]

The list of universalists could be multiplied, but the Anglican Bishop John A. T. Robinson provides the clearest statement in brief summary of

---

46. Jean Daniélou, *Origen*, tr. Walter Mitchell (New York: Sheed and Ward, 1955), pp. 287-298; Gotthold Mueller, "Origenes und die Apokatastasis," *Theologische Zeitschrift*, 14.3 (Mai-Juni 1958), 174-190. Mueller has collected most of the references.

the so-called "larger hope" that all will be saved.[47] The strength of his statement is found in his attempt to relate the work of God in Christ to the reality of human freedom and the seriousness of hell. His discussion really returns to Origen's teaching on the love of God and the freedom of man. But as long as we think in the context of love and freedom there are always two possibilities.

Irresistible love and forced freedom are nonsense, and if there are no realities to correspond to the possibilities, it is double-talk to say that heaven and hell are being seriously considered. Robinson's one destiny, despite his professed existential viewpoint of subjectivity, is as "objectivized" as the view that sees two possible destinies. One is unable to remain in the realm of impossible possibilities. Robinson fails to see that hell is the place of rejected *agapē*, that *orgē* (wrath) is spurned *agapē*. His supposed subjectivism makes heaven a blur and hell a bluff. It preserves neither the freedom of man nor the seriousness of hell.

A more serious challenge to the doctrine of eternal punishment comes from the camp of conditional immortality. Conditional immortality contends that man is by nature mortal and that those who do not attain immortality or receive immortality as God's gift are extinguished either at death or at some point beyond the final judgment. As early as the time of Justin Martyr the Platonic idea of the soul's natural immortality was rejected (*Dialogue*, V), and Arnobius of Sicca gave even greater stress to immortality as God's boon to mortal souls (*Against the Heathen*, Book II). It was condemned at the Fifth Lateran Council in 1513.

The more difficult decision pertains to the word *kolasis* (punishment). The term "eternal punishment" is used in *The Testament of Reuben* (5:5), but the meaning there adds nothing to the New Testament. *Kolasis*, used in the New Testament only in Matthew 25:46 and in 1 John 4:18 ("fear has to do with punishment"), is derived from *kolazō*, the root meaning of which has reference to lopping off or pruning. The verb with the derived meaning of punishment is other than being lopped off forever. In Matthew 25:46 it must be interpreted in relation to the departure into eternal fire (*to pyr to aiōnion*) in 25:41 and the cutting (*dichotomēsei*) in pieces in 24:51, if any unity to the apocalyptic picture is to be retained. Eternal punishment as the deprivation of eternal life may be sustained by the parallelism of punishment and life in Matthew 25:46 and by parallel passages in Matthew 24:51 and 25:41.

Another apocalyptic passage, Revelation 20:9f., is the most difficult of all. It is said that the beast and the false prophet "will be tormented day and night for ever and ever" (20:10). There is evidence that "for ever and ever" (*eis tous aiōnas tōn aiōnōn*, used also of the great harlot in 19:3), means a time of endless duration, since the same phrase is used of the reign

47. *In the End, God* (London: James Clarke, 1950), pp. 108-123.

of the servants of God in 22:5; but the problem is not so simple as the meaning of torment (*basanisthēsontai*). The verb is used four times in Revelation (9:5; 11:10; 12:2; 14:10), but no additional light is given beyond the literal meaning of "torture in judicial examination" (Arndt and Gingrich), from *basanos*, a dark touchstone used in testing metals. So literally they are put to the touchstone, with eternal consequences.

The grim picture of a final *Gehenna* was a problem even in Judaism. Orthodox Judaism was agreed on a state of endless punishment for the extremely wicked, but both universalism and annihilation were argued as the destiny of those not so wicked. The severe school of Shammai condemned the extremely wicked to endless confinement in *Gehenna*, but the less wicked would be released after a process of punishment and purification. The school of Hillel agreed on endless punishment for the very wicked, but they taught that the less wicked would be annihilated after twelve months and that ordinary sinners would, by the mercy of God, escape *Gehenna* altogether.

Jesus drew the distinction between "a severe beating" and "a light beating" (Luke 12:47f.; cf. 8:18; 19:26), but there is no clear evidence in the New Testament for either the universalist or the annihilationist conclusion. The belief in the mercy of God and the desire for a final harmony of all things in God make one hope for such an outcome, but destruction and the second death confront us under the symbol of "the lake of fire" where all the notoriously wicked "will be tormented day and night for ever and ever" (Rev. 20:10). *Gehenna* was "prepared for the devil and his angels" (Matt. 25:41), but men may end there by spurning the love of God (Rev. 20:14). The Scriptures are not clear on whether eternal torment and second death are identical or degrees of eternal punishment. Augustine identified the second death with eternal torment, and he has been widely followed. However, the Jewish background would suggest that the two phrases refer to two realities.

B. HISTORICAL ESCHATOLOGY:
THE HOPE OF HISTORY

76. The Kingdom of God

At the heart of all historical revelation is historical eschatology. In fact the very concept of biblical history requires the belief in a central historical event related to all creation and pointing toward the consummation. Revelation history and salvation history are one, as Oscar Cullmann has repeatedly demonstrated.[48]

48. See especially *Christ and Time*, tr. Floyd V. Filson, Revised Edition (Philadelphia: The Westminster Press, 1964); *Salvation as History*, tr. Sydney G. Sowers (New York: Harper and Row, 1967).

The major concept of historical eschatology is the kingdom of God, as usually translated, but more exactly the kingship or reign of God. This may be understood as the immediate reign of God in the present known only by faith, as an imminent possibility of the future that constitutes the gospel and is confirmed by signs in the present, or as a future inheritance experienced in the present power of the Holy Spirit and a future disclosure of the glory of God. All of these are fully developed in biblical revelation.

The Immediacy of the Kingdom

The immediacy of the kingdom is a formulation of Old Testament faith that is theocratic, representative and messianic. *Theocratic* kingship was a common belief in most theology of the Near East. *Moloch, Melkart, Milcom*, and *Chemoshmelek* are variations on the Hebrew *melek* (king), but salvation history followed the line of the Hebrew prophets.

The central event that evoked faith in the present reign of the Lord was the Exodus from Egypt (Exodus 15:18). The gathering of the tribes into a unity was possible because of belief in the Lord as their invisible king (Num. 23:21; Deut. 33:5).

Out of theocratic kingship came *representative kingship*, but belief in the Lord as the invisible sovereign never vanished. There was not *absolute* monarchy in Israel, for the Lord alone was the absolute sovereign. After a long history of representative kingship Isaiah thought of the Lord as the real king of Israel. In the vision by which he was called he said: "My eyes have seen the King, the Lord of hosts" (6:5; cf. Zeph. 3:15). Even representative kingship was resisted at first. The irony behind the parable of Jotham indicates how the faith of Israel was rooted in the reign of the Lord (Judges 8:23).

The Deuteronomic historians preserved an early source that did look with favor upon the idea of representative kingship (1 Sam. 9:10–16), but a later source still reflected the prophetic protest against any king but the Lord (1 Sam. 8:1–22; 10:17–27a; 12:1–25).

The priestly history of the Chronicler in the post-exilic period was able to reconcile the two views by representing the house of David as the rightful representatives in the kingdom of the Lord (1 Chron. 17:14; 28:5; 29:23; 2 Chron. 9:8; 13:8).

The worship of Israel in the Psalms never departed from the old belief in the Lord's invisible reign. The so-called Coronation Psalms (47, 93, 96, 97, 99) proclaim the eternal fact: "The Lord reigns." This reign will have no end (Psalm 146:10).

Out of representative kingship, belief in *messianic kingship* was born. Saul and David were indeed the Anointed of the Lord, but most of the kings that followed afterward were poor representatives of a holy God. The house of David became the model for the ideal king of the future in which the reign of the Lord would be fully realized and the people of the Lord would be redeemed (Isa. 7:10-17; 9:2-7; 11:1-9).

This belief in the messianic king of the future was associated with the house of Judah (Gen. 49:8-12) and with the booth of David (Amos 9:11). The royal roots of the Redeemer King of the future reached beyond any historical realization before Jesus Christ.

Other figures of the Redeemer King are found in the later prophets. Jeremiah hoped for a Branch who would "reign as a king and deal wisely" (23:5), and Ezekiel expected a sprig from the top of the cedar tree who would be planted on a high mountain (17:22-24) and would watch over his people like a Shepherd King (34:23f.; 37:24f.). Cyrus the Great was pictured in the role of a Redeemer King (Isa. 45:1ff.), and Zerubbabel was portrayed as the King of the Ages (Zech. 6:9ff.).

The central place where the reign of God will be realized is Mount Zion, the glorified Jerusalem. This eschatological expectation will be realized in the Great Apocalypse of the future which the apocalypse of Isaiah anticipated (24-27).

> *Then the moon shall be confounded,*
> *and the sun ashamed;*
> *for the Lord of hosts shall reign*
> *on Mount Zion and in Jerusalem*
> *and before his elders he will manifest his glory (Isa. 24:23).*

This Zionism stirs zeal in both Judaism and Christianity (cf. Isaiah 29:8; 31:4; 51:11, 20; 59:20 with Revelation 7:1-8; 14:1-5). When Jesus is recognized as the messianic king through whom the Lord will establish his kingdom on earth, the tension between these two monotheistic faiths is removed and the wall of hostility falls down. Where this common hope is discounted anti-Zionism arouses antagonism.

The hope for the Lord's universal reign never dies. The pilgrimage to Jerusalem gives meaning to history (Zech. 12-14). The tension between the present reality of God's sovereignty and the hope of his majestic manifestation in the future is the clue to history. Behind all apocalyptic imagery is the hope for an everlasting kingdom with an everlasting king (Dan. 7:14, 27).[49]

The Imminence of the Kingdom

The words and the works of Jesus were pointers to the coming kingdom of God. His words were called the *gospel* of the kingdom (cf. Isaiah 40:9; 41:27; 52:7; 61:1), and his works were *signs* of the kingdom that is to come (cf. Isaiah 35:1-10; Matt. 11:1-15).

---

49. The above discussion has profited much from Gerhard von Rad, *Basileia*, tr. H. P. Kingdon (London: A. & C. Black, 1957).

The *gospel* of the kingdom has been at the center of recent debate. C. H. Dodd argued that the good news was about a kingdom promised in the Old Testament that arrived with the coming of Jesus. This he called "realized eschatology."[50] Many of the paraphrases in *The New English Bible* (1961) reflect his views, since he was Chairman of the New Testament Committee (see Mark 1:15; Matt. 3:2; 4:17; 10:7; Luke 11:20).

R. H. Fuller subjected Dodd's theory to a rigorous examination and found it inadequate.[51] Although the kingdom of God is present in a hidden way known only to faith, the evidence for the visible realization of God's kingdom in the future seems overwhelming. The kingdom of God is near, but it is not already here in the sense anticipated by the writers of the Old Testament and the New.[52]

The *signs* of the kingdom point to Zion's future glory. They reach back to the prophetic expectation in Isaiah 35:5f. Zion's future was coming:

> *Then the eyes of the blind shall be opened,*
> *and the ears of the deaf unstopped;*
> *then shall the lame man leap like a hart,*
> *and the tongue of the dumb sing for joy.*

The miracles of Jesus were signs of this coming age of messianic salvation. Martin Dibelius rightly summarizes the meaning of these signs when he says: "The powers of the kingdom are already present, yet not as a force that changes the world but as the strength that radiates from One, the only One, who is familiar with it and mediates it. What He makes men see in the form of healing or of encouragement, of criticism and of promise, is not the Kingdom but the *signs* of this Kingdom."[53]

The miracles of Jesus were not used as proof of his Messiahship but as proclamation of the coming messianic kingdom in which the whole created order will participate. The demonology of Mark's Gospel depicts this preliminary eschatological struggle between Jesus and Beelzebul.[54] Beelzebul and the demons under his rule dominate this present evil age, but the powers of a coming age have broken into the satanic system as a sign that these proleptic powers will ultimately triumph. "But no one can enter a strong man's house and plunder his goods, unless he first binds the strong man; then indeed he may plunder his house" (Mark 3:27). Satan is the

---

50. *The Parables of the Kingdom* (London: Nisbet, 1955), pp. 43f.

51. *The Mission and Achievement of Jesus* (London: SCM, 1954), pp. 20-25.

52. W. G. Kümmel, *Promise and Fulfillment* (Naperville, Ill.: Alec R. Allenson, 1957), is a more mediating view.

53. *Jesus*, tr. Charles B. Hedrick and Frederick C. Grant (Philadelphia: Westminster, 1949), p. 88.

54. James M. Robinson, *The Problem of History in Mark* (Naperville, Ill.: Alec R. Allenson, 1957), pp. 33-42.

strong man who occupies the house of the present age, and Jesus has entered to bind him and set his captives free.

Signs as a proof of Messiahship are looked upon as a temptation. The Pharisees demanded of Jesus the type of evidence asked by Satan in the temptation, but He refused to give proof of His own person by saying: "Why does this generation seek a sign? Truly, I say to you, no sign shall be given this generation" (Mark 8:12f.). With the proper distinction made between miracles as a part of the proclamation of the coming kingdom of God and miracles as a proof of the Messiahship of Jesus, the significance of the sign may be assessed.

The typology of Matthew's Gospel elaborates miracles as signs of the kingdom. According to the tradition in the *Mishnah* the miracles of Moses were wonders: "Ten wonders were wrought for our fathers in Egypt and ten at the sea. . . . Ten wonders were wrought for our fathers in the temple" (*Aboth* 5:4f.). Matthew's Gospel reflects this typological pattern by presenting ten miracles of Jesus in Matthew 8 and 9. The miracles themselves were signs of the coming exodus, not the exodus itself, even as the miracles of Jesus were signs of a coming kingdom, not the kingdom itself. Moses wrought his signs by "the finger of God" (Exod. 8:19), and it was by the finger of God that Jesus cast out the demons (Luke 11:20). The portrait of Jesus as the new Moses helps considerably our understanding of how the early Church related the miracles to the coming kingdom which would transform the created order.[55]

The eschatology of Luke's Gospel fills with meaning the interim between the miraculous signs and the future kingdom. Hans Conzelmann's important book *The Center of Time (Die Mitte der Zeit)*[56] inserts three periods into salvation history (*Heilsgeschichte*), thus blazing new trails through the bewildering eschatology of Luke–Acts. The first period, which concludes with John the Baptist, is that of Israel: "The law and the prophets were until John; since then the good news of the kingdom of God is preached, and everyone enters it violently" (Luke 16:16).

The second period is the ministry of Jesus, a ministry free from the activity of Satan from the time "when the devil had ended every temptation" in the wilderness until his return at "an opportune time" to enter into Judas Iscariot (Luke 4:13; 22:3). During this period Jesus so works "in the power of the Spirit" (Luke 4:14) that it may be said that by His exorcisms the kingdom of God had already come (11:20). In His person as well as in His work the kingdom of God was already "in the midst" of the Pharisees even if they were too blind to see it (17:21). Even the relatives of Jesus, along with Herod, wanted to "see" His works but did not (8:20; 9:9).

55. Hans Joachim Schoeps, *Theologie und Geschichte des Judenchristentums* (Tübingen: J. C. B. Mohr, 1949), p. 93; *I.B.*, VII, 336-360.
56. English trans. by Geoffrey Buswell, *The Theology of St. Luke* (New York: Harper, 1960).

This third period is that of the Church, filled with the Spirit to fulfill her mission but pressed on every side by the opposition of the world (*ecclesia pressa*). With power and patience (*hypomonē*) she awaits the delayed *parousia* and looks for the appearance of the kingdom in glory. In the interim Jesus has gone into "a far country to receive a kingdom and then return" (19:12) and "Jerusalem will be trodden down by the Gentiles, until the times of the Gentiles are fulfilled" (21:24). The disciples will not eat the Passover with Him again "until it is fulfilled in the kingdom of God." He will not drink with them again "the fruit of the vine until the kingdom of God comes" (22:16, 18). The powers at work in Jesus do not remove the future hope of "looking for the kingdom of God" (23:51). The ministry of Jesus was a foretaste of the future kingdom which is yet to come in glory. It was only *after* his earthly ministry that Jesus was to "enter into his glory" and come into His kingdom (24:26; 23:42).[57]

The Christology of John's Gospel is dominated by the signs and sayings related to the glory of God. Men must here and now be "born from above" if they expect to "see the kingdom of God" and "to enter the kingdom of God" when it comes (John 3:3, 5). The kingdom of Christ does not belong to this world (*kosmos*, John 18:36), yet glimpses of His glory are seen in all His miraculous signs. This may well be designated the theme of John:

> And the Word became flesh and dwelt among us, full of grace and truth; we have beheld his glory, glory as of the only Son from the Father (1:14).

The signs of His glory are seven in John's Gospel: the turning of water into wine (2:1–11), the healing of the nobleman's son (4:46–54), the healing of the impotent man (5:2–9), the feeding of the five thousand (6:4–13), the walking on the sea (6:16–21), the healing of the man born blind (9:1–7), and the raising of Lazarus (11:1–44). These are signs (*sēmeia*), not wonders (*terata*) that would prove His claims to His opponents. Only once does He refer to miracles as wonders, and that in a derogatory sense (4:48). Some did believe because of the signs (3:2; 7:31; 9:16), but this is not the main purpose.

The main purpose of the signs is to manifest His glory (2:11), but the glimpses of glory did not abide in blinding splendor. The hour had "not yet come" (2:4). These "my hour" sayings in John are also seven (2:4; 7:30; 8:20; 12:23, 27; 13:1; 17:1).[58] It was not until He entered into Jerusalem that it could be said: "The hour has come for the Son of man to be glorified" (12:23), and this hour would be the judgment (*krisis*) of this world (12:31). At the Passover "Jesus knew that his hour had come to depart out of the

---

57. J. R. H. Moorman, *The Path to Glory* (London: S.P.C.K., 1961).
58. These have been expounded by Harold Lee Moore, "The 'My Hour' Sayings in the Fourth Gospel," unpublished thesis at The Southern Baptist Theological Seminary, 1951.

world to the Father" (13:1), and His high-priestly prayer voiced the purpose for which He came into the world: "Father, the hour has come; glorify thy Son that the Son may glorify thee, since thou hast given him power over all flesh, to give eternal life to all whom thou hast given him" (17:1f.). Only after this "hour" can the Spirit be given to the disciples that they may go on their mission in the world (7:39; 20:22f.).

The Inheritance of the Kingdom

The powers of the kingdom. The relationship between the imminence of the kingdom and the inheritance of the kingdom requires a balance between the spiritual presence of Christ here and now and the glorious *parousia* hereafter. This falls within the framework of the two ages, "the present evil age" (Gal. 1:4), dominated by the demonic powers of Satan, and "the age to come" (Matt. 12:32; Mark 10:30). According to the typology of the Exodus, the interim between the *passion* and the *parousia*, between Egypt and Canaan, is the wilderness wandering, and upon those who live in this period "the ends of the ages are come" (1 Cor. 10:11, ASV). Satan is "the god of this world" (2 Cor. 4:4), but one of the elements in present Christian experience is the taste of "the powers of the age to come" (Heb. 6:5). In a much used phrase, "the powers of the age to come" are "proleptically present" even in this evil age. God not only gives bread from heaven and water from the rock, but, as Isaac Watts' familiar lines put it:

> *The hill of Zion yields*
> *A thousand sacred sweets*
> *Before we reach the heavenly fields*
> *Or walk the golden streets.*

Seven texts have been the basis of much debate on this relationship. The first is Mark 9:1: "Truly, I say to you, there are some standing here who will not taste death before they see the kingdom of God come with power." Only a few extremists would claim that the early disciples put the words into the mouth of Jesus.[59] It is generally argued that there is no cause for the Church's attributing these words to Jesus. The interpretations range all the way from Albert Schweitzer's consequent eschatology to C. H. Dodd's realized eschatology. The school of Schweitzer has grouped this passage with Matthew 10:23, Mark 13:30, 14:62 as examples of the unfulfilled expectation of the *parousia* in that generation. At the opposite pole is the school of C. H. Dodd, which understands the seeing (*idōsin*, they see) as spiritual perception and the coming *eleluthuian* as meaning "that some of

---

59. Rudolf Bultmann, *Die Geschichte der Synoptischen Tradition*, 3. Auflage (Göttingen: Vandenhoeck & Ruprecht, 1957), p. 128; Erich Grässer, *Das Problem der Parusieverzögerung in den synoptischen Evangelien und in der Apostelgeschichte* (Berlin: Alfred Töpelmann, 1957), pp. 131-137.

those who heard Jesus speak would before their death awake to the fact that the kingdom of God had come."[60]

Other interpreters have identified the "power" (*en dynamei*) of the kingdom with the transfiguration (2 Pet. 1:16, *dynamin kai parousian*), the resurrection of Jesus when He was "designated Son of God in power according to the spirit of holiness" (Rom. 1:4, *en dynamei*), "sitting at the right hand of power" in the exaltation (Mark 14:62, *tēs dynameōs*), the "power from on high" at Pentecost (Luke 24:49; Acts 1:8, *dynamin*), and "the Son of man coming in clouds with great power and glory" (Mark 13:26, *meta dynameōs*). R. C. H. Lenski, without another "power" proof text,[61] has added the destruction of Jerusalem, and Theodor Zahn interprets the fulfillment to be a combination of all these events.[62]

The polarity of this passage is evident even in the Gospels. Matthew 16:28 follows an apocalyptic understanding and identifies the coming of the kingdom in power with "the Son of man coming in his kingdom." Luke 9:27 is more spiritual and speaks only of seeing "the kingdom of God." J. E. Fison attempts to keep this balance by an eloquent *via media*:

> If, however, we want to know what our Lord meant by his enigmatical statement, then we can see St. Matthew and St. Luke each pointing, like the two sides of a cloud capped mountain, to a hidden reality of love, which is as much future and apocalyptic as St. Matthew asserts and as much present and mystical as St. Luke realizes.[63]

This is all very true, but does it get back to what the saying meant when it was spoken?

The interpretation that seems most plausible is that found in 2 Peter 1:16–18 and accepted by most of the church fathers. They of course assumed that Jesus actually spoke the words and that the Gospels had them in context so that the fulfillment in the transfiguration a few days later is most logical.[64] Jesus took "some" (*tines*, Mark 9:1f., viz. Peter, James, and John) to the high mountain and "was transfigured (*metemorphōthē*, v. 2) before them." Moses and Elijah appeared (*ōphthē*, v. 4), but "as they were coming down the mountain, he charged them to tell no one what they had seen (*eidon*, v. 9), until the Son of Man should have risen from the dead." Even on the mount, after Moses and Elijah disappeared, "they no longer

60. Dodd, *op. cit.*, pp. 53f.
61. *The Interpretation of St. Mark's Gospel* (Columbus, Ohio: Wartburg, 1946), p. 357. Also Norval Geldenhuys, *Commentary on the Gospel of Luke* (Grand Rapids: Eerdmans, 1951), p. 277.
62. *Das Evangelium des Lukas* (Leipzig: A. Deichert, 1913), pp. 381-383.
63. *The Christian Hope* (London: Longmans, Green, 1954), p. 189.
64. The historical details and spiritual meaning of the transfiguration are kept in balance by Heinrich Baltensweiler, *Die Verklärung Jesu* (Zürich: Zwingli Verlag, 1959).

saw (*eidon*, v. 8) anyone with them but Jesus only." This strongly suggests a connection between the *idōsin* in verse 1 and the *eidon* in verses 8f. No less a person than Karl Barth is persuaded of an interpretation including three stages:

> In the transfiguration they see and know him already, although only transitively, as the Resurrected. And in His resurrection they finally see the kingdom come with power, and therefore, in *parte pro toto*, as *arrabōn* and *aparchē*, that which in the *parousia*, as His general revelation, will be comprehensively and conclusively knowable and known as His glory.[65]

The second text relates the imminence and the inheritance of the kingdom in Luke 11:20 (cf. Matt. 12:28): "But if it is by the finger of God that I cast out demons, then the kingdom of God has come upon you." Here C. H. Dodd has made a better case, for it is generally agreed that *ephthasen* (has come) means "has arrived." *Phthanein* clearly has this meaning in 1 Thessalonians 2:16, 2 Corinthians 10:14, Philippians 3:16, and Romans 9:31. It is most instructive to compare 1 Thessalonians 2:16, where *ephthasen* means "has come," with 1 Thessalonians 4:15, where *phthasōmen* means "precede." This would suggest that in the exorcisms of Jesus in Luke 11:20 the powers of the coming kingdom have anticipated, preceded, or arrived in this present evil age. This does not, however, mean that the coming of the kingdom of God is "all over." In 1 Thessalonians 2:16 Paul says, "God's wrath has come (*ephthasen*) upon you at last!," but it is "the wrath to come" (1 Thess. 1:10) that has surprised them in the present. As the coming wrath is so imminent that it may be spoken of as realized, so the exorcisms of Jesus, manifesting the powers of the coming age, make the coming kingdom a present reality.[66]

The third text in the Gospels is Luke 17:21: "Behold, the kingdom of God is in the midst of you." The phrase *entos hymōn* (in the midst of you) was interpreted by Calvin to mean "within you,"[67] but modern exegesis tends more and more to accept the translation "in the midst of you."[68] With the singular the only other example of *entos* in the New Testament does mean "within" (Matt. 23:25), "the inside of the cup," but with the plural (*entos hymōn*) it is best translated "in the midst of you."[69] This means that "there remains only the interpretation that the Kingdom of God has already become effective in advance in Jesus and in the present events appearing in

---

65. *Church Dogmatics*, tr. Harold Knight, et al. (Edinburgh: T. & T. Clark, 1960), III/2, p. 499. Cf. C. E. B. Cranfield, *The Gospel According to Saint Mark* (Cambridge: Cambridge University Press, 1959), p. 288.
66. Fuller, *op. cit.*, pp. 25-27.
67. *Institutes*, II.15.4.
68. There is a brief history by Bent Noack, *Das Gottesreich bei Lukas* (Uppsala, 1948).
69. Bosch, *op. cit.*, p. 65.

connection with his person."[70] United with the exorcisms of Luke 11:20, it may be said that the powers of the coming kingdom of God were already operative in the work and person of Christ.

Some passages in Paul apparently teach that the power of the imminent kingdom is immanent. It seems that a sort of realized eschatology was rampant in Corinth, so that Paul could write with irony: "Already you are filled! Already you have become rich! Without us you have become kings! And would that you did reign, so that we might share the rule with you!" (1 Cor. 4:8). These plutocratic people thought that they had already "brought in the kingdom," that they were, as Augustinian amillennialism later claimed, now in the millennium. The apostle, knowing that this is the time of humiliation, not the time of exaltation, lamented:

> For I think that God has exhibited us apostles as last of all, like men sentenced to death; because we have become a spectacle to the world, to angels and to men. We are fools for Christ's sake, but you are wise in Christ. We are weak, but you are strong. You are held in honor, but we in disrepute. To the present hour we hunger and thirst, we are ill-clad and buffeted and homeless, and we labor, working with our own hands. When reviled, we bless; when persecuted, we endure; when slandered, we try to conciliate; we have become and are now, as the refuse of the world, the offscouring of all things (4:9–13).

Yet it may be that the power of the Spirit is the presence of the kingdom, and that is what Paul means when he reminds them: "For the kingdom of God does not consist in talk but in power" (4:20). For contemporary Christians about to talk themselves to death this is a timely admonition.

The passage in Romans 14:17, as well as 1 Corinthians 4:20, may teach the same thing: "For the kingdom of God does not mean food and drink but righteousness and peace and joy in the Holy Spirit." The *Talmud* says: "In the coming age there is no eating nor drinking nor propagation nor business nor hatred nor competition, but the righteous sit with their crowns on their heads feasting on the brightness of the divine presence" (*shekinah*; *Berakoth*, 17a). This is future, as in Matthew 8:11, when "many will come from east and west and sit at table with Abraham, Isaac, and Jacob in the kingdom of heaven." The presence of the Holy Spirit, even in the present, creates the spiritual blessings of righteousness, peace, and joy. Joy is clearly a fruit of the Spirit (Gal. 5:22), but all three are a foretaste of the coming messianic banquet in God's presence. The kingdom in this passage has reference "to the new order, which is the final reality, but into which as even now partly actualized the Christian has been incorporated."[71]

---

70. Kümmel, *op. cit.*, p. 35. Further documentation is furnished by Bosch and Kümmel.
71. *I.B.*, IX, 627.

One other passage in Paul speaks of the present reality of the kingdom in terms of the body of Christ. "He has delivered us from the dominion of darkness and transferred us to the kingdom of his beloved Son, in whom we have redemption, the forgiveness of sins" (Col. 1:13f.). As a conqueror deports captives from one place to another, so the beloved Son, through redemption and forgiveness, has "transferred us." Therefore they are exhorted: "And let the peace of Christ rule in your hearts, to which indeed you are called in the one body" (3:15). As members of the one body and heirs of the same kingdom they are indeed "fellow-workers unto the kingdom of God" (4:11, ASV), but they have already been transferred from the tyranny of sin into the realm of grace (cf. Rom. 6).

The final reference to the present reality of the kingdom is Hebrews 12:28. Colossians and Hebrews share the same high Christology, and the conception of the kingdom is similar also. The "kingdom that cannot be shaken" is "the heavenly realm of *acceptable worship, with reverence and awe* which is to displace all temporal and shadowy things."[72] Christ "has freed us from our sins by his blood and made us a kingdom, priests to his God and Father" (Rev. 1:5f.), but those around the throne still sing of a future reign, of Him who "hast made them a kingdom of priests to our God, and they shall reign on earth" (5:10). "The kingdom of the world has become the kingdom of our Lord and of his Christ, and he shall reign for ever and ever" (11:15), but this reign is to find fulfillment in the millennium when the saints and martyrs will reign "with Christ a thousand years" (20:4). It is yet future: "They shall be priests of God and of Christ, and they shall reign with him a thousand years" (20:6). All of this is rooted in the wandering people of God to whom the promise was made: "You shall be to me a kingdom of priests and a holy nation" (Exod. 19:6). God's people are now "a chosen race, a royal priesthood, a holy nation" (1 Pet. 2:9), but they are at the same time "aliens and exiles" (2:11) on the earth.

This biblical concept of "a kingdom of priests," along with the other pictures of the present reality of the kingdom of God, is far removed from the evolutionary idea of the kingdom that dominated much of the thought of the nineteenth century and still survives in many quarters of Protestantism, both liberal and conservative. Schleiermacher's theology seeks to separate the *canonical* from the apocryphal by appeal to an evolutionary process that would ultimately lead "to a complete expulsion of the apocryphal and the pure preservation of the canonical."[73] Schleiermacher identified the coming of the kingdom with the increase of religious knowledge even as Richard Rothe put the emphasis on ethical progress.[74] Rothe sought to emancipate

---

72. I.B., IX, 750f.
73. *The Christian Faith*, tr. H. R. Mackintosh and J. S. Stewart (Edinburgh: T. & T. Clark, 1928), p. 603.
74. Paul Althaus, *Die letzten Dinge*, 7. Auflage (Gütersloh: C. Bertelsmann, 1957), pp. 231-250, subjects these two views to a rigorous criticism.

the *ethical* from the *ecclesiastical* and thus separate Christianity from the Church.

Albrecht Ritschl's "kingdom theology" was milder, but the distinction between the Church as the realm of *devotional* action (so central for Schleiermacher's theology) and the kingdom of God as the realm of *moral* action reduced the kingdom to little more than the ethical goals of mankind.[75] To Ritschl "Christianity, then, is the monotheistic, completely spiritual, and ethical religion, which, based on the life of its author as Redeemer and Founder of the Kingdom of God, consists in the freedom of the children of God, involves the impulse to conduct from the motive of love, aims at the moral organization of mankind, and grounds blessedness on the relation of sonship to God, as well as on the Kingdom of God."[76] He clarifies what he means by "the moral organization of mankind" when he says: "The Kingdom of God is the *summum bonum* which God realizes in men; and at the same time it is their common task, for it is only through the rendering of obedience on man's part that God's sovereignty possesses continuous existence."[77] But the dependence of God's sovereignty on the obedience of men is far removed from the biblical view of the kingdom of God.

The glory of the kingdom. The present powers of the kingdom are assurance of the glory that is to be revealed. The sayings and parables of our Lord point toward this glorious manifestation, when that which is now hidden will be made known and the riddles of life will be revealed. The idea of a second exodus frames much of His teaching as well as the rest of the New Testament.[78] One of the vivid examples may be seen in the beatitudes of Matthew 5:1–12, where the blessed live with "one foot in heaven." Moses went upon a mountain to deliver his ten commandments, but Jesus went upon a mountain to bestow his blessings (Matt. 5:3–12).

> *Blessed are the poor in spirit,*
> *for theirs is the kingdom of heaven.*
> *Blessed are those who mourn,*
> *for they shall be comforted.*
> *Blessed are the meek,*
> *for they shall inherit the earth.*
> *Blessed are those who hunger and thirst for righteousness,*
> *for they shall be satisfied.*

75. *Justification and Reconciliation*, tr. H. R. Mackintosh and A. B. Macaulay (New York: Scribner's, 1900), p. 284.
76. *Ibid.*, p. 13.
77. *Ibid.*, p. 30.
78. This has been traced in detail by George Balentine, "The Concept of the New Exodus in the Gospels," unpublished dissertation at The Southern Baptist Theological Seminary, 1961.

Blessed are the merciful,
* for they shall obtain mercy.*
Blessed are the pure in heart,
* for they shall see God.*
Blessed are the peacemakers,
* for they shall be called the sons of God.*
Blessed are those who are persecuted for righteousness' sake,
* for theirs is the kingdom of heaven.*
Blessed are you when men revile you and persecute you
* and utter all kinds of evil against you falsely on my account.*
Rejoice and be glad,
* for your reward is great in heaven,*
* for so men persecuted the prophets who were before you.*

The first part of each beatitude speaks of a condition in this present evil age, but the second part (of nine out of ten) speaks of the reward of the age to come. The present tense in reference to "the kingdom of heaven" (5:3, 10) is to be identified with the "reward" which is "great in heaven" (5:12). The whole "sermon on the mount" (Matt. 5–7) is "the new law, designed for the community whose members will inherit the kingdom."[79] Entrance into the kingdom is in the future (Matt. 5:19f.; 6:10, 33; 7:21).

The "sayings on the road" in Mark 9:30–10:45 agree with the sayings of the Sermon on the Mount. The sayings on stumbling (9:47; 10:14f.) have to do with entering the future kingdom when it comes. According to Mark 9:47 some enter the kingdom at the same time others are thrown into Gehenna, the place of final punishment. The saying at the blessing of the children in Mark 10:14f. speaks of receiving the word of God. It is believing the good news of the coming kingdom in which the simplicity of a child will displace the pride of a man. The sayings on reward in the story of the rich young man in Mark 10:17–31 identify the treasure in heaven (10:17) and the entrance into the kingdom of God (10:23) with the inheritance of eternal life in the age to come (10:17, 30). The request of the sons of Zebedee puts the reward in "glory" (Mark 10:37). Later references to the kingdom of God in Mark (12:34; 14:25; 15:43) are in harmony with this idea of a future reward or inheritance. The saying in Luke 12:32 sums up the reception of the kingdom as a gift from God: "Fear not, little flock, for it is your Father's good pleasure to give you the kingdom."

The parables of our Lord do not depart from the view of the kingdom expressed in the sayings. This is especially true in the sowing parables (Mark 4:2–8, 26–29). The early Church identified the sowing season with the earthly ministry of Christ, the time of growth with the interim between his first and second coming, and the harvest with the end of the age. In the

---

79. I.B., VII, 278.

modern revival of eschatological thinking Albert Schweitzer and his disciples followed this view that the sowing period was the preaching of John
the Baptist and Jesus.[80] C. H. Dodd and his disciples now declare that the
early Church and the consequent eschatology of Schweitzer were in error,
and identify the sowing with the long period of preparation before the great
harvest in the earthly ministry of Jesus.[81] One may agree with Dodd that
there is at least one allusion to the harvest as present (Matt. 9:37f.; Luke
10:2), and that this is elaborated in John 4:35–38, without declaring that
the early Church was in error when it identified the harvest of the sowing
parables with the end of the age. The harvest figure can obviously be used
one way in these sayings and another way in the parables.

The parable of the seed growing secretly (Mark 4:26–27), which is
used as the motto of *The Christian Science Monitor*, has repeatedly been
used to support the evolutionary view of a kingdom which has come in the
past, is growing in the present, and will be consummated in the future. But
the seed that is sown, as in all the sowing parables, is the gospel, not the
kingdom, and the period of growth is of the good news of a coming kingdom,
not the evolutionary development of some kingdom identified with the sum
total of churches. It is the word of God that increases in the interim between
the sowing that began at the first coming and the harvest that takes place
at the second coming of Christ (cf. the six summaries in Acts 6:7; 9:31;
12:24; 16:5; 19:20; 28:30f.).

The parable of the weeds (Matt. 13:24–30), found only in Matthew,
like the parable of the seed growing secretly, found only in Mark, has two
sowers, one of wheat and another of weeds. It seems impossible to dismiss
the eschatological interpretation as a mistake of the early Church (Matt.
13:36–43), but this is done by Dodd with a vengeance: "We shall do well
to forget this interpretation as completely as possible."[82] The parable of the
mustard seed (Mark 4:30–32; Matt. 13:31; Luke 13:18f.), a sowing parable
based on Ezekiel 17:22f.; 31:6; Daniel 4:12, is also forced into the frame
of realized eschatology: "The Kingdom of God is here: The birds are flocking
to find shelter in the shade of the tree."[83]

Along with the picture of the great harvest is that of the great supper.
A series of supper parables in Luke substantiates the teaching of the sowing
parables that there is an interim between the preaching of the gospel and
the coming of the kingdom. Luke 14:15 has included a banquet beatitude
in the parable of the great supper (Luke 14:15–24; Matt. 22:1–10): "Blessed
is he who shall eat bread in the kingdom of God!" This is further framed
by Luke with the parable of the marriage feast (14:7–11) and another
supper parable (14:12–14), the first contrasting present humility with fu-

---

80. *Geschichte der Leben-Jesu-Forschung*, 6. Auflage (Tübingen: J. C. B. Mohr, 1951), p. 403.
81. Dodd, *op. cit.*, pp. 175-194.
82. *Ibid.*, p. 184.
83. *Ibid.*, p. 191.

ture exaltation and the second the reward of the present with the reward "at the resurrection of the just." The parable of the great supper elaborates the banquet beatitude and sets the men who made excuses, perhaps the privileged Jews, in contrast to the rejected, perhaps the Gentiles, who would attend the great messianic banquet. This is the same teaching as in Matthew 8:11f.: "I tell you, many will come from east and west and sit at table with Abraham, Isaac, and Jacob in the kingdom of heaven, while the sons of the kingdom will be thrown into the outer darkness; there men will weep and gnash their teeth." Both the banquet and the casting into outer darkness have to do with the future.

In the teaching of Paul (although 1 Corinthians 4:20, Romans 14:17, and Colossians 1:13 have to do with the power of the kingdom now operative in a hidden way) the inheritance of the kingdom revealed in glory is forcefully put in the future. Believers are "to lead a life worthy of God, who calls you into his own kingdom and glory" (1 Thess. 2:12). Steadfast faith in times of persecution is evidence of "the righteous judgment of God," that the Thessalonians "may be made worthy of the kingdom of God" (2 Thess. 1:5). Those who commit such acts as the catalogue of sins in Galatians 5:19–21 will "not inherit the kingdom of God." Immoral, impure, and idolatrous men have no "inheritance in the kingdom of Christ and of God" (Eph. 5:5).

The most positive affirmation that the unrighteous will not "inherit the kingdom of God" is found in the lofty ethical exhortation in 1 Corinthians 6. 1 Corinthians also affirms that it is at the resurrection, not here and now, that the righteous will inherit the kingdom. Paul plainly says that the resurrection must take place before the kingdom can be inherited: "I tell you this, brethren: flesh and blood cannot inherit the kingdom of God, nor does the perishable inherit the imperishable" (1 Cor. 15:50). At the resurrection, previously discussed, and at the *parousia*, discussed in a chapter by itself, the kingdom will be inherited by the righteous. Meanwhile they live in this "present evil age" tasting "the powers of the age to come."

"Therefore, brethren, be the more zealous to confirm your call and election, for if you do this you will never fall; so there will be richly provided for you an entrance into the eternal kingdom of our Lord and Savior Jesus Christ" (2 Pet. 1:10f.).[84]

77. The Final *Plērōma*

Plērōma, meaning fullness, is first used in Paul's letters for all that fills the earth (1 Corinthians 10:26). It then describes the fullness of time at the

---

84. Historical studies of kingdom of God research have continued in Gösta Lundström, *The Kingdom of God in the Teaching of Jesus* (Edinburgh: Oliver and Boyd, 1963); Norman Perrin, *The Kingdom of God in the Teaching of Jesus* (Philadelphia: Westminster, 1963).

Christ event (Galatians 4:4). A third use has reference to the consummation of God's purpose in Israel (Romans 11:12) which would follow the consummation of God's purpose among the Gentiles (11:25). Later the term is used also of the indwelling of God in Christ and in Christians (Col. 1:19; 2:9; Eph. 1:10, 23; 3:19; 4:13). However, this section uses *plērōma* in the sense of the consummation of God's purpose in Israel and among the Gentiles, as in Paul's letter to the Romans.

The Plērōma of Israel

*Now if their trespass (*paraptōma*) means riches to the world,*
*and if their failure (*hēttēma*) means riches for the Gentiles,*
*how much more will their fullness (*plērōma*) mean!*
(Romans 11:12)

Against the background of the trespass and failure of Israel, her final fullness or full inclusion (*plērōma*) is to be understood. This includes three stages in salvation history.

God's election of Israel. At the very beginning of salvation history is the teaching that God chose Abraham and his descendants for a purpose in universal history. At least two themes express this biblical view of universal history.

The first theme of major importance is the priesthood of Israel (Exodus 19:5f.). This is rooted in the Patriarchal promise that all nations will be blessed or bless themselves through the seed of Abraham (Gen. 12:2f.; 18:17f.; 22:17f.; 26:4; 28:14). In the New Testament all who believe this promise are children of Abraham through Christ as Abraham's seed (Gal. 3:7). Those who become the seed of Abraham through Christ the seed are the "Israel of God" (6:16).

After the failure of the nation as a whole to be a blessing to all nations, the promise of God is renewed for a remnant. God's promise to the remnant is especially prominent in the book of Isaiah, who came to be known as *the* prophet. The faithful remnant is portrayed as the servant of the Lord through whom God's purpose will be fulfilled (42:1-4; 49:1-6; 50:4-9; 52:13-53:12). In the Synoptic Gospels, Acts and 1 Peter in the New Testament Jesus Christ is interpreted as the servant of the Lord (Mark 10:45; Matt. 12:18-21; Acts 8:32f.; 1 Pet. 2:21-25).

Prophetic eschatology proclaimed a pilgrimage of all nations to Jerusalem to receive the blessings of the Lord. This became a second theme of the priesthood of Israel between the Lord and all nations. The temple as the house of the Lord was to become a house of peace for all nations (Isa. 2:2-4; Mic. 4:1-3). It was also to be a house of prayer for all the peoples of the earth (Isa. 56:7; cf. 19:24f.). This proclamation continues after the Babylonian Exile even after the trespasses and failures of Israel as a nation

(Zech. 8:20–23). However, this had to be balanced with belief in the judgment of the Lord upon all nations as it was first proclaimed by the prophet Amos (5:18–20; cf. Zeph. 3:8f.).

God's rejection of Israel. In the New Testament this theme of God's election of Israel for a purpose in universal history is renewed.[85] The promise is still offered, but Israel does not return to the Lord to become a light to the nations. At least four major themes, all from the Old Testament, are used to explain this rejection.

The first is that of the flock. Jeremiah pronounced woe on the shepherds who scattered the flock of the Lord (23:1f.; 25:34f.), and to those oracles of woe were added the hope of weal when the Lord would gather His flock again (3:15–18; 23:3f.; 31:10). This picture is even more pronounced in Ezekiel's prophecy of the Lord God as the Good Shepherd, where the ideal king, mentioned also in Jeremiah 23:5f., is promised as the ruler over the gathered sheep of God (34:1–31). The impending restoration lifts the hope to a crescendo of comfort in Isaiah 40:11, but the Servant Songs mention the straying sheep whose iniquity brings suffering upon the Lord's servant (53:6). In the oracle on the good and worthless shepherds, found in Zechariah 11:4–17, weal has yielded again to woe, and the good shepherd has abandoned the sheep who reject his rule.

Against the background of Israel as the flock of the Lord the particularism of Jesus is made plain. He came to call the lost sheep back into the fold in order that God's purpose of election could be accomplished. His mission charge to the twelve apostles required no elaborate explanation (Matt. 10:5f.): "Go nowhere among the Gentiles, and enter no town of the Samaritans, but go rather to the lost sheep of the house of Israel."

Despite the frenzied efforts to explain Matthew 10:23, made famous by Albert Schweitzer, it seems that Jesus did hope for a return of Israel to the fold and the inauguration of the glory of the Son of Man. This was a conditional prediction that remained unfulfilled, but it illuminates the original hope of the call made to Israel. "When they persecute you in one town, flee to the next; for truly, I say to you, you will not have gone through all the towns of Israel, before the Son of man comes." The careful analysis of the passage made by Jeremias changes some of the wording on the basis of the Aramaic language, but the authenticity and meaning remain intact.[86] The very number of the twelve apostles indicates the concern of Jesus with the unity and ancient hope of Israel.

The activity of Jesus Himself was consistent with the charge to the apostles. A Canaanite woman, addressing Him by the significant title Son

---

85. Joachim Jeremias, *Jesus' Promise to the Nations*, tr. S. H. Hooke (Naperville, Ill.: Allenson, 1958); David Bosch, *Die Heidenmission in der Zukunftschau Jesu* (Zürich: Zwingli Verlag, 1959).
86. Jeremias, *op. cit.*, p. 20.

of David, requested that He deliver her daughter from the possession of a demon. The disciples wanted to send her away, but Jesus replied: "I was sent only to the lost sheep of the house of Israel" (Matt. 15:24). The fact that He responded to her great faith does not remove the fact that He felt confined to the community of Israel and believed that it was the will of God that He should remain so. The initiative was taken by the woman, not by Him. Jesus had "other sheep" to call, but not until He was crucified (John 10:16).

A second figure is that of the temple. Malachi developed the theme of the messenger who would purify the temple and prepare the way for the Lord who suddenly came to the purified temple (3:1). Matthew 21:12-22 (Mark 11:15-17) has this prophecy in mind when it says that Jesus cleansed the temple immediately on entering Jerusalem on Palm Sunday. The house that Isaiah 56:7 had proclaimed "a house of prayer for all peoples" had become, according to Jeremiah 7:11, "a den of robbers." This action of Jesus, so shocking to the religious leaders, was a messianic act of such significance that it can be nothing less than a call to fulfill the purpose of God to the nations. The miracle of the fruitless fig tree which follows represents the failure of Israel to bear fruit even though the outward appearance was one of flourishing religion.

The destruction of the temple is closely associated with the cleansing in both Luke and John. Luke 19:41-44 is a prediction of the destruction of Jerusalem because of her failure to know the time of her visitation. John 2:13-25 has the cleansing of the temple at the beginning of Jesus' ministry. Much has been said about this departure from the chronology in the Synoptic Gospels, but the answer is perhaps more theological than chronological. John presents a contrast between the religion of the Jewish temple, which failed to fulfill the purpose of God, and the new sanctuary, the Church, which would be the agency of God after the death and resurrection of Christ. The destruction of the temple in Jerusalem would not be the defeat of God's purpose in the world.

The temple teaching, along with the parable of the Good Shepherd, gives clear evidence that the Son of Man must be crucified before the Gentile mission could begin. One of the places where this order is most evident is the story of some Greeks who came to worship at the feast in Jerusalem and wanted to see Jesus. It was on this occasion that Jesus was troubled in soul and recognized that the hour of His supreme sacrifice was at hand. When the voice came from heaven Jesus said: "Now is the judgment of this world, now shall the ruler of this world be cast out; and I, when I am lifted up from the earth, will draw all men to myself" (John 12:31f.).

A third figure is that of the vineyard. In Isaiah 5:1-7 there appears a song of the Lord's vineyard, composed perhaps to celebrate the Feast of Tabernacles. It is not necessary to review in detail the complicated question of the authenticity of the parable of the vineyard in Mark 12:1-12 (Matt. 21:33-46; Luke 20:9-19). Much of the confusion and doubt springs from rigid adherence to Adolf Jülicher's theory that Jesus taught in pure parables only, never in allegory. Others have sufficiently rejected this axiomatic restriction and furnished evidence that the allegorical elements of this parable need not be related to the teaching of the primitive Church (*Gemeinde-theologie*).

The teachings of the parable are deeply rooted in Isaiah 5:1–7. God is the owner of the vineyard, the people of Israel. The tenants are the rulers of Israel to whom the servants, the prophets of Israel, were sent (Amos 3:7; Jer. 7:25; Zech. 1:6). After the shameful treatment of the servants, Jesus as the Son was sent to the vineyard, and Him they killed. The parable closes with an Old Testament quotation from Psalm 118:22f., one of the favorite proof texts of early Christian writers (Acts 4:11; 1 Pet. 2:4, 7; Rom. 9:32f.; Eph. 2:20):

> *The very stone which the builders rejected*
> *has become the chief cornerstone.*
> *This is the Lord's doing;*
> *it is marvelous in our eyes.*

Matthew 21:43 draws the obvious conclusion that God has rejected Israel and given the kingdom of God to a nation which would produce fruit. The rulers of Israel knew that the parable was directed at them.

The fourth figure for Israel's failure is that of a banquet. The apocalypse of Isaiah spoke of the time when a banquet of the nations would take place on the mountain of God (Isa. 25:6–8), but the movement was thought of as centripetal. They must come to the holy mountain in order to witness the epiphany of God and enjoy the blessings of Israel. They would come "from afar," "from the north and from the west," to the festal gathering (Isa. 42:12). It is this hope that lies behind Jesus' teachings about a great banquet to which all would be invited; yet the exclusion of Israel was a shocking innovation. In response to the centurion's faith He declared: "I tell you, many will come from east and west and sit at table with Abraham, Isaac, and Jacob in the kingdom of heaven, while the sons of the kingdom will be thrown into the outer darkness; there men will weep and gnash their teeth" (Matt. 8:11f.). Worship of all the people of the earth at the world sanctuary was no new idea, but a picture of "the sons of the kingdom" "thrown into the outer darkness" of total rejection while remote peoples shared the blessings of the patriarchs, must have startled the religious leaders like the crack of doom. The parallel in Luke 13:29 is associated with the saying: "And behold, some are last who will be first, and some are first who will be last" (Luke 13:30). This can only mean that the people once elected are now a people rejected because the fruit of the kingdom has not been found.

The parable of the wedding feast points to the picture of rejection in a still more dismal way (Matt. 22:1–10; Luke 14:16–24). God at first invited Israel to the marriage feast of His Son, but they rejected the invitation delivered by His servants the prophets. This brought the judgment of God upon Jerusalem in A.D. 70 and forfeited the kingdom of the coming age: "The king was angry, and he sent his troops and destroyed those murderers and burned their city" (Matt. 22:7). The parable of the wedding garment is added by Matthew not only to point out the necessity of righteousness and repentance but to prepare for the summary statement: "For many are called, but few are chosen" (Matt. 22:14).

The Plērōma of the Gentiles

Some instances of a centrifugal movement of God's mercy toward the Gentiles may be found in such Old Testament writings as Jonah (4:11) and Malachi (1:11), but the central thrust is centripetal. Through Israel the nations of the earth are to receive their blessings. This is the point of departure for understanding the Gentile mission in the New Testament. This mission may be described first in relation to the twelve and then in relation to the two (Peter and Paul).

The mission of the twelve. The twelve are prominent in Mark's Gospel (3:14; 4:10; 6:7; 10:32; 11:11; 14:10, 17, 43), and this technical use suggests the restoration of God's purpose in Israel. Jesus "appointed twelve, to be with him, and to be sent out to preach and have authority to cast out demons" (3:14). It was to "the twelve" that He gave "the secrets of the kingdom of God" (4:10f.). When "the twelve" were sent out two by two He "gave them authority over the unclean spirits" (6:7), so that the *exousia* (authority) manifested in Jesus was transferred to the twelve. It is "the twelve" who first learned what was to happen to Jesus in Jerusalem (10:32). At Bethany "the twelve" were with Him, but it was one of "the twelve" who betrayed Him (14:10, 43). With "the twelve" He gathered in the upper room (14:17).

The mission to the nations in Mark appears in the Markan apocalypse (13:10): "And the gospel must first be preached to all nations." Believing that this is a condition for the second coming of Christ, many zealous Christians have labored faithfully among the people of all nations. Two able assessments have been made of the interpretation. Joachim Jeremias thinks that "the original reference is not to human proclamation, but to an apocalyptic event, namely, the angelic proclamation of God's final act" (cf. Rev. 14:6f.).[87] David Bosch, in his more detailed discussion, reaches a more conservative conclusion. To him the interim between the passion and the *parousia* is a time of grace in which the gospel may be preached to all nations, not a condition that must be fulfilled before the *parousia* can take place.[88] This is in harmony with the long ending of Mark (16:9-19), although Mark 16:15 can be used only in a secondary sense.

87. Jeremias, *op. cit.,* p. 23.
88. Bosch, *op. cit.,* 132-200.

Matthew's Gospel adds two eschatological emphases, although "the twelve" (10:5; 26:14) are usually described as "the twelve disciples" (10:1; 11:1; 20:17; 26:20) or "the twelve apostles" (10:2). The mission of "the twelve apostles" (10:2) to Israel is elaborated, but they are strictly charged: "Go nowhere among the Gentiles, and enter no town of the Samaritans, but go rather to the lost sheep of the house of Israel" (10:5f.). This may be understood to mean not that there is no concern for Gentiles and Samaritans but that the lost sheep of Israel should be gathered first. To this note of weal is added a note of woe, for the disciples "will also sit on twelve thrones, judging the twelve tribes of Israel" (Matt. 19:28; Luke 22:30).

Matthew's close linking of the twelve with Israel does not exclude a centrifugal movement to the nations. The prologue records that "wise men from the East came to Jerusalem" (2:1) at the birth of Christ, and Book I (3:1–7:28) gives special emphasis to the fact that Jesus fulfilled a prophecy about "Galilee of the Gentiles" when He came to dwell in Capernaum (4:15). Much has already been said about His shocking prophecy that "many will come from east and west and sit at table with Abraham, Isaac, and Jacob in the kingdom of heaven" (8:11). There is no textual question about the Great Commission in Matthew 28:18–20 as there is about the commission in the long ending of Mark (16:9–19), but F. C. Conybeare may have more cogency than most concede when he argues on evidence from Eusebius for the short form of Matthew 28:18–20:

> *All authority has been given to me*
> *in heaven and on earth.*
> *Go therefore and make disciples of all nations,*
> *in my name,*
> *teaching them to observe all*
> *that I have commanded you;*
> *and lo, I am with you always,*
> *to the close of the age.*[89]

This rendering not only harmonizes with baptizing "in the name of Jesus Christ" in Acts (2:38; 8:16; 10 48; 19:5; 22:16), but it also strengthens the evidence for a commission of the twelve to "all nations" so that through the gathering of Israel all nations are to be blessed.

Luke's Gospel speaks frequently of "twelve" (6:3) or "the twelve" (8:1; 9:1, 12; 18:31; 22:3, 30, 47), but only the reference to "the twelve" (8:1) and the ministering women is distinctive. The more distinctive characteristic in Luke is increased emphasis on the Gentile mission. The *Nunc Dimittis* (2:29–32) speaks of "a light for revelation to the Gentiles and for glory to thy people Israel." At the beginning of the travel narrative (9:51–18:14)

---

89. *Zeitschrift für die neutestamentliche Wissenschaft* (1901), pp. 275-288; David Bosch, *op. cit.*, p. 188.

Jesus sent messengers to prepare the way for Him in the villages of the Samaritans, and when James and John wanted to call fire from heaven upon them for refusing to receive Him they were rebuked. The mission of the seventy (10:1–24) has often been thought to have reference to the seventy Gentile nations of Genesis 10, and it is sure that a Gentile mission is entrusted to the faithful eleven in 24:46–49. This commission is renewed in Acts 1:8.

References to "the twelve" have almost disappeared in the Fourth Gospel (6:67, 70f.), but there the strongest universalism is found. John the Baptist identified Jesus as "the Lamb of God, who takes away the sin of the world" (1:29). John 2:23–4:54 is a cycle of three stories in which Jesus ministers to Nicodemus the Pharisee, the woman of Samaria, and a Gentile nobleman.[90] After the conversation with Nicodemus it is said that "God so loved the world that he gave his only Son, that whoever believes in him should not perish but have eternal life" (3:16). The Samaritans say to the woman: "We know that this is indeed the Savior of the world" (4:42). The Gentile nobleman "believed, and all his household" (4:53). Jesus is also "the light of the world" (8:12), and the shepherd who has "other sheep" not of the fold of Israel that must be called so that there will be "one flock, one shepherd" (10:16). Jesus declared: "I, when I am lifted up from the earth, will draw all men to myself" (12:32). Jesus commissions the disciples and imparts the Spirit to them (20:21–23) in order that they may forgive the sins of "any."

The mission of the two. There is some debate as to whether the conference described in Galatians 2:10 took place at the same time as the one in Acts 15, but it is certain that Galatians 2:10 is in the background of Paul's mission to the Gentiles as he outlines it in Romans 9–11. Cf. Part VII.

The mission of Paul to the Gentiles becomes enveloped in mystery as the problem of Israel's rejection deepens. This mystery of Israel is explored to the point of bewilderment in Romans 11:1–36. The remnant of Israel (11:1) believed in Jesus as the Christ, but the rest were blinded (11:7–12). As were the days of Elijah so were the days of Paul: A remnant remained faithful to the promises of God (cf. 1 Kings 19:10, 14, 18). Those who were blinded had the "spirit of stupor" described in Isaiah 29:9f. and their feast had "become a snare . . . a trap" according to Psalm 69:22f. This is summed up in the fascinating play on words:

> *"Now if their fall (*par, paraptōma*) means riches for the world,*
> *and if their failure (*hēttēma*) means riches for the Gentiles,*
> *how much more will their fullness (*plērōma*) mean!"*
> *(Rom. 11:12; my trans.).*

90. R. H. Strachan, *The Fourth Gospel* (London: SCM, 1941), pp. 128-165.

The rejection of Israel (11:13–24) is reasoned by argument and allegory. The argument (11:13–16) is based upon the belief that Israel's rejection made it possible for the gospel to be brought to the Gentiles so that in the end Israel would be provoked to accept what she once had rejected. Israel's rejection means the reconciliation of the world, and her acceptance will be nothing less than life from the dead. Since the fathers of Israel were holy, the whole of Israel has become consecrated: "If the dough offered as first fruits is holy, so is the whole lump; and if the root is holy, so are the branches" (11:16). This assures a future purpose of God with Israel.

The allegory of the olive branches (11:17–24) illustrates the argument of Israel's present rejection and future acceptance. Gentiles are only a wild shoot grafted into a tree from which the natural branches have been lopped off by unbelief. If the Gentiles do not continue in belief they will be lopped off too, even as Israel may be restored "if they do not persist in their unbelief" (11:23). "God has power to graft them in again" (11:23). This is the basis of Paul's *plērōma* hope.

The return of Israel (11:25–36) as an eschatological hope has deep roots in the Old Testament.[91] The deepening mystery of this question leads Paul to the place where debate is precipitated as to whether Paul is a universalist. What does he mean by the *plērōma* (full number) of the Gentiles (11:25)? What does he mean by the *plērōma* of Israel (11:12) or that "all Israel will be saved" (11:25)? Conservative and critical thought have both been concerned with the answers to these questions.[92] The amillennial view found in the writings of John Calvin identifies Israel with "all of the people of God."[93] This he does by appeal to Galatians 6:16 which speaks of "the Israel of God" as the people of God, but this would violate the meaning of "Israel" in the other ten places in the context. The dispensational view that finds modern expression in the theology of L. S. Chafer makes Israel "the nation of Israel" and looks forward to a future restoration during the millennium when all the unfulfilled prophecies of the Old Testament will come to pass,[94] but this is not in harmony with Paul's statement that "not all who are descended from Israel belong to Israel" (Rom. 9:6). The realized eschatology of C. H. Dodd insists that "all Israel" means "the historical nation of Israel" and this combined with "the full number of the

91. Paul Heinisch, *Theology of the Old Testament*, tr. William Heidt (Collegeville, Minn.: Liturgical Press, 1950), pp. 281-284.
92. A conservative survey is by William Hendriksen, *And So All Israel Shall Be Saved* (Grand Rapids: Baker, 1945), and a critical view is presented by Erich Dinkler, "The Historical and the Eschatological Israel in Romans, Chapters 9-11: A Contribution to the Problem of Predestination and Individual Responsibility," *Journal of Religion*, XXXVI (April 1956), 109-127.
93. *Romans*, tr. John Owen (Grand Rapids: Eerdmans, 1948), p. 437. Cf. O. T. Allis, *Prophecy and the Church* (Philadelphia: Presbyterian and Reformed, 1945), pp. 236-255.
94. *Systematic Theology* (Dallas: Dallas Seminary Press, 1948), IV, 310-328.

Gentiles" makes Paul a universalist.[95] This not only contradicts Romans 9:6, but it also requires a future eschatology that is out of harmony with Dodd's realized eschatology.

All three of these views fail to follow Paul's clue in Romans 9:6: "For not all who are descended from Israel belong to Israel." Paul believed that God's ultimate purpose included both the "full number" (*plērōma*) of Israel (11:12) and the "full number (*plērōma*) of the Gentiles" (11:25), but these statements need to be understood against the background of Paul's doctrine of election. When this is done the conclusion becomes clear that he believed that missionary activity would continue until all the elect Gentiles and all the elect Israelites have come to Christ, all the believing Gentiles and all the believing Israelites. Paul was no universalist; he was a missionary. Before this eschatological hope Paul was exuberant with praise: "O the depth of the riches and wisdom and knowledge of God! How unsearchable are his judgments and how inscrutable his ways!" (11:33).

The unity of two apostleships in the consummation is anticipated in the one body of Christ, the Church, where "by one Spirit we were all baptized into one body — Jews or Greeks, slaves or free — and all were made to drink of one Spirit" (1 Cor. 12:13). This anticipation begins in the act of initiation in Christian baptism: "For as many of you as were baptized into Christ have put on Christ. There is neither Jew nor Greek, there is neither slave nor free, there is neither male nor female; for you are all one in Christ Jesus" (Gal. 3:27f.). When the new man is put on, the Gentile and the Israelite become one: "Here there cannot be Greek and Jew, circumcised and uncircumcised, barbarian, Scythian, slave, free man, but Christ is all, and in all" (Col. 3:11). Christ "is our peace, who has made us both one, and has broken down the dividing wall of hostility, by abolishing in his flesh the law of commandments and ordinances, that he might create in himself one new man in place of the two, so making peace, and might reconcile us both to God in one body through the cross, thereby bringing the hostility to an end" (Eph. 2:14–16). Paul's practical application of the principle was a cash contribution from the Gentile Christians to help Jewish Christians in their time of need (1 Cor. 16:1–3; 2 Cor. 8 and 9).

The twofold mission of Peter and Paul became the basis for Luke's structure in the Acts of the Apostles. This Peter–Paul polarity in the salvation history of Acts is pronounced in the great commentary by R. B. Rackham in 1901.[96] Rackham rightly recognized that Acts 1–12 interpreted the acts of Peter and Acts 13–28 the acts of Paul. Each part has three divisions or books clearly marked at 6:7; 9:31; 12:24; 16:5; 19:20; 28:30, 31. Strangely Rackham did not make his divisions of the acts of

---

95. *Romans* (New York: Harper, 1932), pp. 182-187.
96. *The Acts of the Apostles*, "Westminster Commentaries" (London: Methuen & Co., 1901).

Peter at the proper places, but he was correct on the acts of Paul. The Westminster *Study Edition of the Holy Bible* of 1948 got all of the books correct. To these two useful helps in Bible study I owe a lasting debt.[97]

The Johannine vision in Revelation 7 in which God will preserve Israel and the Gentiles has been distorted by the deviations of Dispensationalism. The widely read fantasies in Hal Lindsey's exposition of the Book of Revelation have popularized the theory that the 144,000 from the 12 tribes of Israel are evangelists who convert the great multitude of Gentiles after the church is "raptured" out of the world when the Holy Spirit is removed. There is not one word in Revelation 7 or at any other place in the Bible to support such a theory, but it has captured the imagination of many uncritical people. Others have given highly allegorical interpretations that compound the confusion.

It is interesting to note that a Jewish writer not known for excessive friendship toward orthodox Christianity has rightly identified those in Revelation 7:1-8 with "loyal Israel" and the group of Revelation 7:9-17 as "the redeemed of the Gentiles."[98] Furthermore many other Jewish writers have followed the line of thought that agrees with Paul the Apostle, who most surely believed that the best days for believing Israel are yet to be.[99] In the last generation the Russian Orthodox scholar Nicolas Berdyaev and the Scottish philosopher John Macmurray saw great universal significance in the future role of Israel for history at the consummation of the ages in the kingdom of God.[100]

Very few topics precipitate more searching examination of Jewish-Christian relation than this eschatological question. Some of the most significant Christian thinkers have been Jews, and that number seems to be increasing today.[101] Despite the vilifications experienced by Zionists, both Jewish and Christian, there is a hope that should not be abandoned, for it is a vital part in the purpose of God.

78. The Future *Parousia*

God's greatest revelation is yet in the future. This will be the Great Apocalypse in which God's presence in Jesus Christ will be fully disclosed. There

97. See my survey in *The Hope of Glory* (Grand Rapids: Wm. B. Eerdmans Publishing Company, 1964), pp. 159-165.
98. *The Authentic New Testament*, ad loc.
99. See especially Franz Werfel, *Between Heaven and Earth*, tr. Maxim Newmark (New York: Philosophical Library, 1944), p. 210 and more recently Pinchas Lapide, *Israelis, Jews, and Jesus*, tr. Peter Heinegg (Garden City, N.Y.: Doubleday, 1979).
100. Nicolas Berdyaev, *The Meaning of History*, tr. George Reavey (London: Geoffrey Bles, 1936), pp. 92, 105ff., 107; John Macmurray, *The Clue to History* (New York: Harper, 1939), pp. 54f.
101. See the study by the Jewish Catholic Gregory Baum, *The Jews and the Gospel* (Westminster, Maryland: Newman, 1959).

have been many epiphanies (appearings) of God in salvation history, but there will be only one Great Apocalypse. Jürgen Moltmann's *Theology of Hope* (1964) discounted the importance of "epiphany religion" too much, but he was surely right in giving all theology an orientation toward the future.[102]

At no other point does Christian theology have more common ground with Jewish Messianism than in the belief that the best is yet to be in a Messianic Age. This is especially true when belief in a Messianic Age is linked with belief in a personal Messiah who will establish God's kingdom upon the earth.[103] When this Messiah is identified with Jesus, as the so-called Jesus Jews do, then the bridge between Christianity and Judaism has happily been restored. It was the zeal to build this bridge that gave the Apostle Paul "great sorrow and increasing anguish" in his heart (Rom. 9:2). There is little possiblity that a Christian coronary will take place in the World Council of Churches as long as present perspectives prevail.[104]

The apocalyptic perspective on the *parousia* of Jesus Christ is linked with the prior *parousia* of the Antichrist. The *parousia* of the Antichrist is a counterfeit of the *parousia* of Christ (2 Thess. 2:8–10). Therefore, the *parousia* of the Antichrist will be considered first. As Carl Friedrich von Weizsäcker has said: "Christ renders Anti-Christ possible."[105]

The Parousia of Antichrist

The Antichrist figure in the New Testament is deeply rooted in the historical dualism of the Old Testament. There is no metaphysical dualism in the Bible, for all demonic powers are viewed as fallen creatures originally created good in God's good creation. On philosophical grounds, Nicolas Berdyaev said: "The dualism inherent in Jewish messianic consciousness determined the fateful destiny of the Jews insofar as it combined the expectation of the true Messiah, the Son of God, who was to appear among the Jews, and that of the false Messiah, or Antichrist."[106]

Apocalyptic dualism became dominant in Old Testament eschatology after the time of Ezekiel, at the beginning of the Babylonian Exile of the Jewish people.[107] Against this Old Testament background four biblical apocalypses are of major importance for understanding the idea of the Antichrist.

The first is the Danielic apocalypse that kept hope alive in the time of the great conflict with Antiochus Epiphanes, 167-164 B.C.[108] In the time

---

102. See *Theology of Hope*, tr. James W. Leitsch (New York: Harper and Row, 1967), especially pp. 95-102.
103. Pinchas Lapide, *op. cit.*
104. *Jewish-Christian Dialogue* (Paris: ADAGP, 1975).
105. *The History of Nature*, tr. Fred D. Wieck (Chicago: University of Chicago Press, 1949), p. 189.
106. *The Meaning of History*, tr. George Reavey (London: Geoffrey Bles, 1936), p. 92.
107. Paul D. Hanson, *The Dawn of Apocalyptic* (Philadelphia: The Fortress Press, 1975).
108. Norman W. Porteous, *Daniel* (Philadelphia: The Westminster Press, 1965).

when the Greek Septuagint was the Old Testament of the Church a view developed that is still very popular among Dispensationalists. By combining the kingdoms of Media and Persia, the Greek Fathers were able to interpret the Fourth Monarchy of Daniel 7 as the Empire of Rome. 2 Esdras 12:12 frankly said of Daniel: "But it was not explained to him as I now explain or have explained it to you." This setting aside of the explanation given to Daniel can still be read in *The New Scofield Reference Bible* of 1967 and many less scholarly study Bibles.

The Hebrew Old Testament seems to support the idea that the Fourth Monarchy was Greece and that "the little horn" of Daniel 8:9 was Antiochus Epiphanes. This requires a rejection of the old Patristic interpretation based on the Greek Old Testament. The Seventy Weeks of years in Daniel 9:24–27 have three parts. The 49 years of Daniel 9:24 then become the time between the fall of Jerusalem in 587 B.C. and coming of the anointed as Cyrus the Great in 538 B.C. (cf. Isaiah 44:28; 45:1 with Dan. 9:25). The 434 years become the period between the prediction of Jeremiah 25:11, 12; 29:10 (cf. Daniel 9:2) in 605 B.C. and cutting off the high priest Onias III by assassination in 171 B.C. (Dan. 9:26). It is important to note that the seven years are divided into two periods of 3½ years each (Dan. 9:27).

The Synoptic Apocalypse of the New Testament builds on the Apocalypse of Daniel. The basic form of the Synoptic Apocalypse is in Mark 13:1–36. After the prediction of Jesus about the destruction of the Temple of Jerusalem (13:1, 2), the disciples are instructed on the perils (5–8) and persecutions (9–13) of the present age. The so-called birth pangs are rightly interpreted as marks of the present evil age in the old *Scofield Reference Bible* of 1917, but the *New Scofield Reference Bible* of 1967 shifts to the theory that these are signs of the new age which is about to begin. This has led to a whole series of false predictions about the end of the world. Sensational books by Hal Lindsey with this deviation have been sold by the millions to the publisher's delight.

Two predictions of Jesus follow (13:14–27). The first prediction (14–18) has reference to the Fall of Jerusalem in A.D. 66-70. There is nothing in this prediction that is not reported in Josephus' seven books entitled *The Jewish War*, A.D. 76. Furthermore, the reaction in Luke 21:20–24 makes it clear that this was the Fall of Jerusalem. To avoid this conclusion *The New Scofield Reference Bible* argues that two different sieges of Jerusalem are envisaged — the one in Mark and Matthew in the future but the one in Luke in the past. This is impossible when the Gospels are read in a parallel printing.

The division of the Seventy Weeks of Daniel 9:24–27 into two periods of 3½ years is very important for understanding the shortening of days in the comment at Mark 13:20. At least it is certain that after the Fall of Jerusalem the predictions about the Great Tribulation speak only of the second 3½ years of Daniel's Seventy Weeks (Rev. 11:3; 12:12, 14; 13:5).

After this Great Tribulation the Son of Man will come in glory with the holy angels who will gather the elect (Mark 13:24–27).

The two parables of Mark 13:28–36 speak again of the Fall of Jerusalem (13:28–30) and the coming of the Son of Man in glory (13:31–36). When popular eschatology attempts to interpret the parable of the fig tree as a prediction about the Second Coming of Jesus, there are all sorts of fancy dodges to avoid the conclusion that Jesus was deluded. Only the *Authorized King James Version* and *The New International Version* have translated the passage correctly! The *Good News Bible* is ambiguous on Mark 13:29, but the paraphrase is surely correct on Mark 13:30 which says: "All these things will happen before the people now living have all died." The more literal translation in the RSV rightly says: "Truly, I say to you, this generation will not pass away before all these things take place." A concordance will show that Jesus spoke of "this generation" fourteen times, and each time it means the people who lived at the time of Jesus upon the earth. It is clear that the parable of the journeyman has reference to the coming of the Son of Man in glory at a time known only by God our Father (13:31–36).

The Pauline Apocalypse of 2 Thessalonians 2:1–2 gathers all these ideas about the *parousia* of Jesus Christ and relates them to the *parousia* of the Antichrist. First of all it is said the Jesus Christ will not come to gather the saints (2:1) until the Great Apostasy and the Antichrist take place (2:3). It is desperate exegesis for Kenneth Wuest to argue that the falling away (*apostasia*) is the taking away at the Rapture.[109] The passage says plainly that the *parousia* of Jesus Christ and the gathering of the saints come after the Apostasy and the Antichrist (2:3, 8–10). The other theory that says the present mystery of lawlessness is restrained by the Holy Spirit and that the removal of restraint is the removal of the Holy Spirit before the Great Apostasy and the Antichrist has no basis in the New Testament whatsoever. Jesus is always presented as returning after the Great Tribulation in which Apostasy and Antichrist will be central (Mark 13:24; Matt. 24:29; 2 Thess. 2:3, 8–10; Rev. 13).

Belief in the literal fulfillment of 2 Thessalonians 2:1–12 in the future has led to a Christian Zionism that teaches (1) that Israel will return to the land promised to Abraham, (2) that the Temple destroyed in A.D. 70 will be rebuilt, and (3) that Jesus as the Messiah will return to destroy the Antichrist who will demand that he be worshipped as God. When Jewish Zionism identifies the Messiah as Jesus the "Jesus Jews" of today result. This makes the *parousia* of the Antichrist followed by the *parousia* of the Christ

---

109. *Prophetic Light in the Present Darkness* (Grand Rapids: Wm. B. Eerdmans Publishing Company, 1955), pp. 33-43. Wuest credits this novel interpretation to E. Schuyler English, editor of *The New Scofield Reference Bible*, in which this view does not appear. It is adopted also by W. A. Criswell in *Expository Sermons on the Book of Revelation* (Grand Rapids: Zondervan Publishing House, 1964), Vol. 3, p. 24.

(Messiah) one of the most emotional and explosive beliefs in world politics as well as in eschatology.

The Johannine Apocalypse describes the Antichrist as Nero returning again. If, as I believe, the Johannine Apocalypse was written between the suicide of Nero in A.D. 68 and the Fall of Jerusalem in A.D. 70, then the use of Nero as a type of Antichrist makes good sense. (When *Kaisar Neron* is written in Hebrew the number is equal to 666, as in Rev. 13:18.) Nero was the fifth Emperor, who has fallen at the time of the Revelation (17:10). It does not seem that Jerusalem has fallen (11:8). In any case Nero becomes the type of Antichrist.

In later history many other religious and political leaders, including the Pope himself, have been declared to be the Antichrist. In the light of 1 John 4:1-6, it would perhaps be more accurate to call all this company of candidates some of the "many antichrists," but this does not remove the relevance of the belief in a future Antichrist, the Antichrist, who will be destroyed by the future *parousia* of Christ.

The Parousia of Christ

Belief in the future *parousia* of Jesus Christ is deeply rooted in the Old Testament teaching on the Day of the Lord. This becomes the Day of the Son of Man in the teaching of Jesus and the Day of Jesus Christ in the teachings of Paul. A survey of these three uses of Day will help clarify the use of the word *parousia*, especially in the writings of Paul.

The Day of the Lord. The term Day of the Lord is used many times in the Old Testament. It first appears in the prophet Amos (5:18-20; 8:9-14). The Day of Jezreel in Hosea (1:11) may be a more optimistic reference to the same day. In the Pentateuch there was a fast each year in which there was to be a purification of the people. This was called the Day of Atonement (Lev. 16; 23:27-32). In the future there is to be a time of purification for those who repent and a time of punishment for those who rebel against the Lord.

The prophet Isaiah has a powerful three-stanza oracle in which the first and second stanzas are directed against the haughty (2:6-11, 12-17) and the third is a call to turn to the Lord from idols (2:18-22). This prophetic eschatology thought of the Assyrian Empire under Tiglath-pileser III (734-732 B.C.) or Sennacherib (701 B.C.) as the chief instrument of the Lord in the punishment of the people.

The disciples of Isaiah later saw the Persian soldiers serving God's purpose in the punishment of Babylon for her pride (13:1-12). The destruction of Edom as the enemy of the Lord and his people is seen as the Day of the Lord (34:1-17). Before the Babylon Exile the Day of the Lord is the punishment of Israel, but after the Exile it is the punishment of Israel's enemies and oppressors. This first is more prophetic and historical and the second is characterized by the beginnings of apocalyptic visions in which universal, cosmic events point to an age to come.

The prophet Jeremiah saw the Crown Prince Nebuchadnezzar of Babylon as the instrument of the Lord in the defeat of Pharaoh Neco II at the Battle of Carchemish in June, 605 B.C. His oracle against Egypt is described in terms of the Day of the Lord (46:2–12). This example of the historical and universal judgment of the Lord involved two nations outside Israel.

The doom of Egypt in the Day of the Lord is also a theme in Ezekiel. Again it is Nebuchadnezzar (26:7), king of "the most terrible of the nations" (28:7; 30:11), who will be the instrument of the Lord in the punishment of Egypt (27:6). A real tour of Egypt is offered in the Oracle (30:1–26). The Lord will put his "sword into the hand of the king of Babylon," and the king of Babylon will punish Egypt (30:25).

Perhaps the best summary of the Day of the Lord is in the prophet Zephaniah, about 630 B.C. He saw in the invasion of the barbaric Scythian hordes from the north the judgment of the Lord upon Judah (ch. 1) and the enemies of Israel (ch. 2), with the promise of survival for the righteous remnant (ch. 3).

About 612 B.C., when Nineveh fell to the Babylonians, the prophet Nahum described the Day of the Lord without using the term. Prophetic eschatology sees the Lord at work in this world and in this age as well as in the age to come. When Babylon brought the 150 years of Assyrian domination to an end, Nahum saw this as the vengeance of the Lord against his enemies. There is no absentee God in prophetic eschatology.

The triumph of the cruel Chaldeans made a problem for the prophet Habakkuk between 612 B.C. and 597 B.C., but his theodicy gave the great statement (2:4):

> Behold, he whose soul is not upright in him shall fail,
> but the righteous shall live by his faith.

This was later repeated in the Qumran commentary on Habakkuk and Paul's letter to the Romans.

After Jerusalem fell to the Babylonians in 587-86 B.C. the Day of the Lord was proclaimed for Israel and her enemies. Soon after those perilous days Obadiah saw special punishment for Edom and final deliverance for Israel (15–18).

In the Persian period (539-331 B.C.) Malachi, about 500-450 B.C., saw the Day of the Lord as a time of salvation for true worshippers of God despite the corruption of the temple worshippers of his time. With even greater hope Joel, about 400-350 B.C., saw beyond the warnings of a locust plague (1:1–2:27) to a time when the Spirit of the Lord would be poured out upon Israel (2:28–3:1; cf. Acts 2:17–20).

In the Greek period, ushered in by Alexander the Great as mentioned in a note on Joel 3:6, two oracles attached to Zechariah proclaim the Day of the Lord as a time when Israel will be restored to their land (9-11) and the Lord will reign over all the earth (12-14), a time when the Feast of Tabernacles will be universal. Needless to say these six chapters provoke both joy and rage in modern politics.

In the rebellion against Greek culture the book of Daniel (7:13-14) introduced the hope that the Day of the Lord would be the Day of the Son of Man, and this was a major theme on the lips of Jesus.

The Day of the Son of Man. The preaching of John the Baptist and Jesus may be compared to the prophecies of Amos and Hosea in the eighth century B.C. Amos and John saw the Day of the Lord more in terms of wrath, while Hosea and Jesus had more good news. In the Source Q, found in Matthew and Luke but not in Mark, John the Baptist warned the people of the terrible Day of Wrath that was to come (Luke 3:7, 9, 17). Jesus prefaced all this woe with the promise of weal in the age to come (Luke 6:20-26).

Jesus did teach that there would be a Day of Visitation, but most of all he proclaimed a Day of Vindication. The seven parables collected in Luke 12:35-59 and the seven woes in Matthew 23 are as severe as John. The focus of woe in history was upon Jerusalem. A document in Luke called the Wisdom of God warns at least six times that Jerusalem will fall in the very generation that would witness the rejection of Jesus by the Jewish nation (11:29-32, 49-51; 13:29-35; 19:41-44; 21:20-24; 23:28-31). This is like the historical eschatology found in the proclamation of the Day of the Lord in Amos.

The Day of Vindication in the parable of the unjust judge in Luke 18:1-8 asks: "Will not God vindicate his elect, who cry to him day and night? Will he delay long over them?" And the answer is added: "I tell you, he will vindicate them speedily." To this is added the second question: "Nevertheless, when the Son of Man comes, will he find faith on earth?" This vindication was predicted for the Third Day and the Last Day.

The Third Day was a theme found in Hosea 6:2, but Jesus made the meaning more precise, predicting his own resurrection on the third day after his death. When the Pharisees told Jesus about Herod's threat to kill him he responded: "Go tell that fox, 'Behold, I cast out demons and perform cures today and tomorrow, and the third day I finish my course. Nevertheless, I must go on my way today and tomorrow and the day following; for it cannot be that a prophet should perish away from Jerusalem' " (Luke 13:32f.). This note of culmination was particularly pronounced in the three predictions of Jesus' passion in the Gospel of Mark (8:31; 9:31; 10:34). Belief in the death and resurrection became the major basis for belief that Jesus would return in glory as the Son of Man after he had suffered as the Servant of the Lord.

The vindication of Jesus at his resurrection on the Third Day is not complete until he returns as the Son of Man at the Last Day. The eschatological poem in Luke 17 speaks of three decisive days in salvation history: the days of the Son of Man (22–24), the days of Noah (26f.) and the days of Lot (28–30). In each case the wicked are destroyed and the righteous are left. The disciples are warned against all false prophets that proclaim a secret coming of the Son of Man. "For as the lightning flashes and lights up the sky from one side to the other, so will the Son of Man be in his day" (17:24). The false teaching of a secret Second Coming of Christ in the air at least seven years before his coming to the earth is only one form of this false eschatology in our time.

Ask the average person dipped in Dispensationism to interpret the parallel to Luke 17:26–27, 34–35 in Matthew 24:37–41 in the *Authorized (King James) Version* and inconsistency takes over. Most will say those "taken away" (24:39) in the days of Noah were the wicked. Indeed, Luke 17:33 says they were destroyed. When they are asked to interpret Matthew 24:40f., the very next verses, they will say the righteous are "taken" and the wicked are left for no other reason than that they have "always heard it that way." The idea of a "secret rapture" before the Great Tribulation has been so drilled into their minds that it becomes difficult to point out that "taken" means "destroyed" until the parallel in Luke 17:26–27, 34–35 is studied. The *Scofield Reference Bible* and those who follow it make a false teaching a test of faith and fellowship.

The Day of Jesus Christ. The future *parousia* of Jesus Christ as a historical event is the central teaching in the primary epistles of Paul to Thessalonica. Of the eight *parousia* passages, three speak of weal (1 Thess. 1:9f.; 2:19f.; 4:13–18), three warn of woe (1 Thess. 5:1–11; 2 Thess. 1:7–10; 2:1–10), and two are benedictions (1 Thess. 3:11–13; 5:23f.). This is the usual biblical balance between hope for the righteous and doom for the wicked.

The major comfort passage is the hymn in 1 Thessalonians 4:16f.:

> *The Lord himself,*
>   *with a cry of command,*
>   *with the archangel's call,*
>   *and with the sound of God's trumpet,*
> *Will descend from heaven.*
> *And the dead in Christ will rise first;*
> *then we (who are alive, who are left)*
>   *shall be caught up together with them (in the clouds)*
> *to escort the Lord in the air.*

This translation interprets *eis apantēsin* (to escort) as it is used in Matthew 25:6 and Acts 28:15. The people in Matthew 25:6 most certainly did not go out to spend seven years on the street with the bridegroom, neither did the brethren stay long with Paul at the Forum of Appius and Three

Taverns in Acts 28:15. This explodes the theory that Paul taught a *parousia* in the air seven years before the coming to earth.

The major *parousia* passage on the doom of the wicked in Paul is 2 Thessalonians 1:7–10. The *parousia* will be

> *When the Lord Jesus is revealed from heaven*
> *With his mighty angels in flaming fire,*
> *inflicting vengeance on those who do not know God*
> *and upon those who do not obey the gospel*
> *of our Lord Jesus.*
> *They shall suffer the punishment of eternal destruction*
> *and exclusion from the presence of the Lord*
> *and from the glory of his might,*
> *When he comes in that day to be glorified in his saints,*
> *and to be marveled at in all who have believed.*

The pillar epistles of Paul (1, 2 Corinthians, Galatians, Romans) do not indicate a departure of Paul from the belief in an apocalyptic *parousia*, as is often argued. 1 Corinthians 15 elaborates 1 Thessalonians 4:16f. Romans, the last of the pillar epistles, A.D. 55, speaks of "the day of wrath" (2:5) and the Soldier Song in 13:11–14 looks forward to a day of salvation in the future.

> *Besides this you know what hour it is,*
> *how it is full time now for you to wake from sleep.*
> *For salvation is nearer to us now than when we first believed;*
> *the night is far gone, the day is at hand.*
> *Let us then cast off the works of darkness*
> *and put on the armor of light;*
> *let us conduct ourselves becomingly as in the day,*
> *not in reveling and drunkenness,*
> *not in debauchery and licentiousness,*
> *not in quarreling and jealousy.*
> *But put on the Lord Jesus Christ*
> *and make no provision for the flesh,*
> *to gratify its desires.*

The prison epistles (Philippians, Colossians, Philemon, Ephesians) do not abandon belief in the *parousia* either. It may be that Philippians 3:16–4:9 was an earlier letter by Paul from Ephesus, but it has a powerful hymn on the apocalyptic *parousia* in 3:20f. Even Ephesians, which is often denied Paul, speaks of a day of redemption when God will redeem his heritage (1:11, 14, 18; 4:30).

The pastoral epistles (Titus, 1, 2 Timothy) have at least ten Hymns of Epiphany (Titus 2:11–14; 3:5–7; 1 Timothy 1:17; 2:5f.; 3:16; 4:10; 6:15b–16; 2 Tim. 1:9f.; 2:11f.; 4:1–8). Epiphany is a term often used as a synonym for the apocalyptic *parousia* of our Lord Jesus Christ. There is no good exegetical reason for rejecting any of these letters as Pauline when the circumstances and composers are given adequate attention.

The Johannine Writings have passages on the Last Day and the mystical coming of Christ in the gift of the Spirit in the same selections (cf. John 6:40, 44, 54 with John 14:18–24; 16:16–24). The apocalyptic and the mystical are both present in Revelation (1:10; 4:2; 17:3; 21:10). The belief that God's greatest disclosure of himself is yet in the future at the Great Apocalypse is basic in the Bible.[110]

C. COSMIC ESCHATOLOGY: THE HOPE OF CREATION

79. The Millennium

If the importance of belief in a thousand-year reign of Christ upon the earth were measured by the space it occupies in the Bible, it would be a footnote to discussions on the Kingdom of God; but if the influence of the idea on the history of the Church, both negative and positive, is our guide, then a major role must be assigned to such belief or unbelief. However, the hope that the will of God will be done upon the earth as it is done in heaven belongs to the very foundation of biblical faith.

Premillennialism

After the appearance of the Book of Revelation, perhaps about A.D. 68-70, the vision of Christ's reign upon the earth sustained the disciples of Jesus in times of persecution until the Edict of Toleration under the Emperor Constantine the Great in A.D. 313.

Among Greek-speaking Christians belief in a thousand-year reign of Christ was called Chiliasm, after the Greek word *chilia*, meaning a thousand. Church fathers such as Justin Martyr (about A.D. 100-167), Papias of Hierapolis, whose writings appeared around A.D. 150, and Irenaeus of Lyon (about A.D. 130-202) made much of this belief. A quotation from Papias in the writings of Irenaeus indicates how literally this reign on earth was interpreted, but this need not debunk the view.

> The days will come in which vines shall grow, each having ten thousand branches, and in each branch ten thousand twigs, and in each true twig ten thousand shoots, and in one of the shoots ten thousand clusters, and on every one of the clusters ten thousand grapes, and every grape when pressed will give five and twenty metretes (200 gallons) of wine.[111]

110. For more details see my discussion in *The Hope of Glory* (Grand Rapids, Michigan: Wm. B. Eerdmans Publishing Co., 1964), pp. 171-232. Jürgen Moltmann, *The Theology of Hope*, tr. James W. Leitch (New York: Harper and Row, 1967), pp. 133-138.
111. *Against Heresies*, V. 33. 3. Cf. George Otis, *Millennium Man* (New York: Pillar Books, 1974).

However, the chief concept was the belief that after the time of the Great Tribulation, in which Antichrist would appear, and before the thousand-year reign, Christ would return in glory to establish the Kingdom of God. At times they believed they were already in the Great Tribulation and that Christ would return very soon.

In Latin Christianity belief in the thousand-year reign was called Millennialism, from *mille*, a thousand, and *annus*, a year. The greatest Latin theologian was Tertullian, and his emphasis was very much on teaching that those who died the martyr's death would reign with Christ upon the earth for the complete thousand years. Resurrection for the rest of the believers was for him a process of rewarding in which the saints "rise sooner or later according to their deserts."[112] This eschatology of martyrdom was a major factor in the triumph of Christianity over paganism.

After the long period of Amillennialism between Augustine in the fifth century and the beginning of Protestantism in the sixteenth there was a radical return to the Premillennialism of the first three centuries. Persecution was again a factor in the theology of martyrdom in which many believed the Great Tribulation had begun and that Christ would soon return in glory to establish God's Kingdom upon the earth.

It has not been sufficiently recognized how many biblical roots led the eschatology of the Chiliastic Anabaptists in the sixteenth-century Reformation. It is not necessary to make a strong distinction between Chiliastic Anabaptists and "The Soundly Biblical Anabaptists" as A. H. Newman did.[113] Today the so-called Radical Reformation is getting a new opportunity to be heard as Lutheran Augustinianism finds itself vulnerable to the criticism of Communism.

Historical Premillennialism has had a new revival in recent years. A book by Alexander Reese in 1937 rejected the theory of a Pretribulation Rapture as taught by the Dispensational deviation made popular in the *Scofield Reference Bible* (1909, 1917).[114] Unfortunately he also retained the Amillennial view that identified Israel with the saints of all ages and found it difficult to do justice to such passages as Romans 9–11.

The most scholarly writings on Historical Premillennialism have come from George E. Ladd of Fuller Theological Seminary in Pasadena, California. His book *Crucial Questions About the Kingdom of God* created considerable consternation among those who realized that his challenge to Dispensationalism was solely on the basis of biblical exposition on which Dispensationalism thought it had a monopoly.[115] With a view of biblical inspiration and authority as conservative as any Dispensationalist de-

---

112. *Against Marcion*, III. xxiv.
113. *A Manual of Church History* (Philadelphia: The American Baptist Publication Society, 1931), Vol. 2, pp. 156, 168.
114. *The Approaching Advent of Christ* (London: Marshall, Morgan and Scott, 1937).
115. (Grand Rapids: Eerdmans, 1952).

manded, Ladd shook the very foundations of the Fundamentalism that had swallowed the *Scofield Reference Bible* whole.

Historical background for the debate was supplied by a supplementary book, *The Blessed Hope*, which demonstrated beyond reasonable doubt that Dispensationalism could not be traced beyond the 1830's when the prolific writings of J. N. Darby began to make it popular.[116] Ladd's *Commentary on the Book of Revelation* is very useful for rethinking the relevance of that book for our time.[117] His commentary should be read with great care, even though he still dates Revelation in the time of Domitian rather than in the early reign of Vespasian, A.D. 68-70. This whole question must be rethought.[118]

My own book on eschatology took essentially the same point of view as did Ladd's.[119] A book by Robert H. Gundry has devoted special attention to the passages used by Dispensationalists in support of their theory of a Pre-tribulation Rapture. He found the theory biblically bankrupt.[120]

A book by Dave MacPherson on *The Unbelievable Pre-Trib Origin* (1973) is most irritating to Dispensationalists who argue that the spiritual gift of speaking in tongues has ceased, a view based on a false interpretation of 1 Corinthians 13:3, and that the modern charismatic movement is no more than hypnosis and at times demon possession. The irritation comes from MacPherson's claim that belief in a Pretribulation Rapture can be traced to Margaret MacDonald, a charismatic woman of Port Glasgow, Scotland.[121] The dicussion of this point will be resumed when Dispensationalism is treated in more detail.

Amillennialism

It was not until the so-called conversion of Constantine that *Pre*millennialism ceased to dominate Christian eschatology. When Christianity became the official religion of the Roman Empire there was the widespread feeling that the Millennium had arrived. This became *A*millennialism or Nonmillenialism, as this shift from a future Millennium after the Second Coming of Christ to a present Millennium of triumphant Christianity developed. One of the most obvious examples of this realized eschatology may be seen in the *Church History* of Eusebius, the Bishop of Caesarea. He spoke of the Premillennialism of Papias as the product of "a man of exceedingly

---

116. (Grand Rapids: Wm. B. Eerdmans Publishing Company, 1956).
117. (Grand Rapids: Wm. B. Eerdmans Publishing Company, 1972).
118. John A. T. Robinson, *Redating the New Testament* (Philadelphia: The Westminster Press, 1976).
119. Dale Moody, *The Hope of Glory* (Grand Rapids: Wm. B. Eerdmans Publishing Company, 1964).
120. *The Church and the Tribulation* (Grand Rapids: Zondervan, 1973).
121. The book is now published with *The Late Great Pre-Trip Rapture* (1974), a devastating critique of Hal Lindsey's sensational book on *The Late Great Planet Earth* (1970), as *The Incredible Cover-Up* (Plainfield, New Jersey: Logos International, 1975).

small intelligence."[122] His praise for Constantine as "the most mighty Victor, resplendent with every virtue that godliness bestows" indicates how nearly he identified the Roman Empire with the Kingdom of God.[123]

The transition from Premillennialism to Amillennialism in Latin eschatology came with Augustine, who at first taught the Chiliasm of the early Greek Fathers. In his *First Catechetical Instruction* (*De catechizandis rudibus*) he embraced and followed the view of the *Epistle of Barnabas* (15:4) which taught that world history would last for seven thousand years, corresponding to the six days of creation, with the Sabbath as the last thousand years, the Millennium.[124]

Most of the details of Augustine's Amillennialism may be found in his major work, *The City of God*, Book XX. He interpreted the Millennium in an allegorical manner that led him to believe that he was already living in the Millennium. The first resurrection he interpreted as spiritual, having already taken place for the Christian, while the second resurrection will be the resurrection of the body. Those who sit on thrones judging people are the bishops of the Church, and Gog and Magog represent those who persecute the Church. Those allegorical views have been repeated ever since by both Catholics and Protestants.

The first major crisis in Amillennialism came around the year 1000 when the world did not end, as the followers of Augustine expected. The Benedictine monk Raoul Glaber wrote about this crisis in his *Chronicle*. When the Day of Doom did not come, cathedrals, as touches of heaven upon the earth, began to spring up in many places in gratitude to the Creator.[125]

By the time of Joachim of Fiore (c. 1132-1202) the idea of the Roman Catholic Church as the Millennium was due to go through a radical change. Joachim's commentary on Revelation divided history into three periods: that of the Father down to the time of Jesus, that of the Son which was due to end at the beginning of the third age of the Holy Spirit about A.D. 1260. The Spiritual Franciscans, who lived as if that age had dawned, viewed the Pope as the Antichrist long before Luther. Both of these millennial ideas were in ferment during the age of the Reformation.

Several books advocating the type of Amillennialism found first in Augustine in the fifth century have been published by the Broadman Press in Nashville, Tennessee. This has led to the impression often met outside the Southern Baptist Convention that all Southern Baptists are Amillennialists. A survey would perhaps show that far more Dispensationism is taught in Southern Baptist churches.

A book by Russell Bradley Jones entitled *Things That Shall Be Here-*

122. III, 39, 12f.
123. X, 9, 6.
124. See notes in *The First Catechetical Instruction*, tr. Joseph P. Christopher (Westminster, Md.: The Newman Press, 1962), pp. 123, 136.
125. Dmitri Kessel, *Splendors of Christendom* (Edita Lausanne, 1964), p. 77.

after (1947) illustrates how the Platonic idealism of Augustine is used to resist the realism of the Bible. After the year 1000 Amillennialism of course no longer took the Millennium literally. Jones follows this innovation and speaks of the Millennium as the indefinite reign of Christ between the cross and the consummation. Any belief in a reign of Christ upon the earth is classified as "materialism."

The same tone is found in *The Meaning and Message of the Book of Revelation* by E. A. McDowell (1951), although McDowell was very much under the influence of C. H. Dodd's "realized eschatology" which all but eliminated any future coming of Christ. McDowell spoke of the reign of God and Christ in Revelation 11:15-18 as if it were already here, despite the fact that it is said to be after the Great Tribulation of $3\frac{1}{2}$ years (11:2) and at the time for judging the dead (11:18). Indeed, he believed that we already live in the Millennium of Revelation 20:4-6. He says: "We who live today, therefore, are in the Millennium."[126]

Two books by Ray Summers were more restrained. His commentary on Revelation, *Worthy Is the Lamb* (1951), delayed detailed interpretation of the Millennium until his systematic interpretation in *The Life Beyond* (1959). There the "first resurrection" is interpreted in a symbolic way as the triumph of the martyrs, but the "second resurrection" is said to be literal. This type of exegesis gets out of hand, for it requires the Greek word *ezēsan* (lived) to have two different meanings, without notice or evidence, in the same context (Revelation 20:4f.).

The Cosmic Drama (1971) by H. H. Hobbs followed the symbolic approach of John Wick Bowman's *The Drama of the Book of Revelation* (1955), but the essentials of his view were repeated in *Studies in Revelation* (1971).[127] Hobbs adopted the Amillennial view, although he says he was once a "pre-without-a-program." The old Augustinian idea of the Millennium as the present reign of Christ is advocated, but the reign is said to be in heaven, not on earth. This contradicts Revelation 5:10; 20:8.

The exposition of Revelation by Morris Ashcraft in the *Broadman Bible Commentary* views the reign of Christ during the Millennium as confined to the martyrs.[128]

The Revelation of Jesus Christ by Ray F. Robbins (1975) does place the reign of Christ upon the earth (Revelation 5:10), but the first resurrection is interpreted as spiritual as in Augustine. As in other Amillennial interpretations Revelation is interpreted in a highly symbolic manner that borders on the allegorical method. It is really hard pressed when confronted with biblical literalism.

All six of the above authors are regarded as friends and competent

---

126. *Op. cit.*, p. 200.
127. *The Cosmic Drama* (Waco, Texas: Word Books, 1971); *The Drama of the Book of Revelation* (Philadelphia: The Westminster Press, 1955).
128. *Broadman Bible Commentary* (Nashville: Broadman Press, 1972), p. 349.

scholars, but their exegesis is not convincing. It is devoutly hoped that Millennialism will not be made a test of fellowship among Southern Baptists, but it would be more instructive if Broadman Press would publish more than one point of view.

It is true that *Highlights of the Book of Revelation* by G. R. Beasley-Murray was published in 1972, and the conclusion of this small book has a ringing challenge to return to biblical realism, but Beasley-Murray was British and gave these brief lectures at the Nationwide Bible Conference in Dallas, Texas, March 15-18, 1971.

Another symbolic interpretation by a Southern Baptist with a different publisher interprets the first resurrection as the real resurrection of all believers.[129] This is a departure from the spiritual resurrection or resurrection of martyrs in historical Amillennialism, but a second resurrection for the wicked is denied altogether.[130]

Many others, including myself, have found that Historical Premillennialism is far more literal on Revelation 20 than is Dispensationalism. It offers the best realistic reponse to atheistic Marxism.

Postmillennialism

By the beginning of the eighteenth century a third type of Millennialism began to form. Daniel Whitby (1638-1726), an ardent opponent to Popery, believed that a future Millennium could be brought in by evangelism. To many the revivalism of the eighteenth century, the missionary zeal of the nineteenth century and social reform in the twentieth century kept this hope alive until two World Wars dimmed their vision of the future.

John Wesley was a Postmillennialist. He believed that the Pope was the Antichrist, and that the papal Antichrist would be overthrown by 1836. Jonathan Edwards was influenced by the eschatology of the Spiritual Franciscans. He believed the 1260 years began in A.D. 606 and that he was living in the last days.[131]

Most of the popular commentaries in the nineteenth century followed the theories of Postmillennialism. John Gill had done this in eighteenth century, and his *Annotations on the Bible* was widely read and is reprinted even now.

The English Presbyterian minister Matthew Henry popularized Postmillennialism with his celebrated commentary, *An Exposition of the Old*

---

129. Douglas Ezell, *Revelations on Revelation: New Sounds on Old Symbols* (Waco, Texas: Word Books, 1977), p. 97. This book follows many of the views of II Esdras that Jerome included in the Latin Vulgate and Augustine transmitted to Western Christianity. It also depends much on Austin Farrer, *The Revelation of St. John the Divine* (Oxford: Clarendon Press, 1964), pp. 26-32. For a systematic conservative eschatology based on the Amillennial view see Anthony A. Hoekema, *The Bible and the Future* (Grand Rapids: Wm. B. Eerdmans Publishing Co., 1979).

130. Ezell, *op. cit.*, p. 97.

131. George E. Ladd, *The Blessed Hope*, pp. 33f.

and New Testaments (London, 1708-10). Robert Hall and Charles H. Spurgeon, English Baptists representing different points of view, heaped praise on the work by Henry. Whitefield is said to have read it through four times, the last time on his knees!

Although Henry's friends published his manuscript on the book of Revelation, they no doubt represented his views faithfully. The copy published by the Baptist Book Concern in Louisville, Kentucky, is so sure that the Pope is the Great Harlot of Revelation 18 that the Pope's illustrative medal is added. The text says Satan was partly bound by both Christ and the state, but the complete binding remains in the future when the saints who reign in the Millennium will be those "that had kept themselves clear of pagan and papal idolatry." The first resurrection is again interpreted as spiritual.

The English Methodist Adam Clarke (1762-1832) published an important commentary on the Bible in 1810-26 which also embraced Postmillennialism. The Millennium is not taken literally. "It may signify that there shall be a long and undisturbed state of Christianity; and so universally shall the Gospel spirit prevail, that it will appear as if Christ reigned upon the earth; which will in effect be the case, because the Spirit shall rule in the hearts of man; and in this time the Martyrs are represented as living again; their testimony being revived, and the truth for which they died, and which was confirmed by their blood, being now everywhere prevalent." So Clarke spiritualized.

Later in the nineteenth century (1877) came the commentary by Robert Jamieson (1802-1880), in collaboration with A. R. Fausset and David Brown, all Presbyterians. Fausset was an ardent Postmillennialist, and it is his views that are expressed on the book of Revelation, yet they perhaps reflect the views of Jamieson and Brown also. Again the Papacy is pictured as the Great Harlot, the Millennium will be a time in which Church and State will be co-extensive, and Priest-kings will rule when "all spheres of life shall be truly Christianized within outwardly." Calvin's theocratic kingdom will be fully realized in all the earth.

The movement that began with the tiny Whitby of Salisbury, England, reached its peak with a towering Texan who almost lived to see it vanish. It may almost be said that B. H. Carroll, the Southern Baptist leader and founder of Southwestern Baptist Theological Seminary in Fort Worth, Texas, was the last of the ardent Postmillennialists. Most of his disciples shifted to Amillennialism promoted by conservative Calvinism.

Carroll fervently believed that the Kingdom of God could and would be "brought in" by evangelism, missions and social reform. *An Interpretation of the English Bible*, B. H. Carroll's major work, adopts the view in which the Great Harlot is identified with the Roman Catholic Church and the Millennium is a triumph over Romanism and other forms of human corruption.

It is a victory of the Spirit dispensation through the churches, the ministers and the gospel. It means that Satan has usurped the kingdom of the world for six millenniums, and that the earth shall have in time, and through the gospel, her sabbath millennium — that is, the seventh one — her thousand years of peace and rest and joy and gospel triumph, with no devil to tempt, seduce, and beguile.[132]

The two resurrections of Revelation 20:4-6 are both interpreted as spiritual. For Carroll the resurrection of bodies does not take place until Revelation 20:12f. when Christ returns for judgment.

Dispensationalism

It is often assumed that all Premillennialism is Dispensationalism, but this is far from the truth. Premillennialism is as old as Christianity, but Dispensationalism with the modern form of seven dispensations, eight covenants, and a Pretribulation Rapture is a deviation that has not been traced beyond 1830. Dave MacPherson says that the idea of a Pretribulation Rapture originated with a Scottish charismatic named Margaret MacDonald, but others retort that it was formulated by J. N. Darby (1800-1882).[133] In any case it was unknown before 1830.

Dispensationalism spread rapidly in the United States after the publication of the second edition of the *Scofield Reference Bible* in 1917 and the charts in *Dispensational Truth* by Clarence Larkin in 1918. Dallas Theological Seminary, founded in the very city where C. I. Scofield did his notes between 1903-1909, has been the center from which the system spread, but numerous Bible institutes have followed the Dispensational method of Bible study. For most of them the footnotes in the *Scofield Reference Bible* have been accepted as if they were a part of the inspired autographs.

It has already been pointed out that the scheme of seven dispensations corresponding to the seven days of creation is first found in a second-century writing called the *Epistle of Barnabas* (15:4), but the New Testament speaks of two ages, the present and the future (Matt. 12:32; Gal. 1:4; Heb. 6:5). The idea of eight covenants flatly contradicts the New Testament teaching on two covenants (1 Cor. 11:25; 2 Cor. 3:6, 14; Gal. 4:24; Heb. 8:7, 13). It is ridiculous to see a footnote on eight covenants in Hebrews 8 where the distinction is plainly between old and new, first and second.

The present upsurge of Historical Premillennialism has challenged the Dispensational theory of a Pretribulational Rapture of the Church out of

132. *The Book of Revelation*, edited by J. B. Cranfill (Nashville: Broadman Press, 1947), pp. 224f. The first edition was by Fleming H. Revell, 1913.
133. John F. Walvoord, *The Blessed Hope and the Tribulation* (Grand Rapids: Zondervan, 1976).

the world. Belief in a Pretribulational Rapture is not only a deviation that cannot be traced beyond 1830, it contradicts all the three chapters in the New Testament that mention the Tribulation and the Rapture together (Mark 13:24–27; Matt. 24:26–31; 2 Thess. 2:1–12).

The interpretation of Mark 13:24–27 should be made in the light of the whole chapter. The question put to Jesus by the disciples pertained to the fall of the temple (13:1–4). Before answering the question, Jesus speaks of the perils and persecution of this present age between his death and the end (13:5–13). As an introduction to the Tribulation he speaks of the Fall of Jerusalem which took place A.D. 66-70 (13:14–18).

Then the Tribulation is described (13:19–23), *after* which the Son of Man will come in glory and the elect will be gathered (13:24–27). Dispensationalism makes a desperate effort to support the theory that the angels gather the elect, who are converted after the Pretribulation Rapture, which is not even mentioned!

The rest of the chapter speaks again of the Fall of Jerusalem (13:28–30) and the coming of the Son of Man in glory (13:31–37). Dispensationalism tried to make "this generation" refer to the "terminal generation," as Hal Lindsey calls it, but Jesus always meant the generation that witnesses the preaching and death of Jesus, as any concordance will reveal. If he had reference to the Second Coming, as *The New English Bible* and *The Living Bible* wrongly assume, then he was mistaken. If he had reference to the Fall of Jerusalem, as I believe, he was a true prophet and the Son of God.

Matthew 24–25 includes most of Mark 13, but seven parables of the coming of the Son of Man are added. Dispensationalism interprets the parable of the Twos (in Matt. 24:40f.) as if the righteous are taken and the wicked are left, but this would contradict the previous parable on Noah where the wicked are "taken away" and the righteous are left. Even John F. Walvoord in his commentary on Matthew sees this truth, but many Dispensationalists still try to get a Pretribulation Rapture out of Matthew 24:40f. Walvoord says the Pretribulation Rapture is found neither in the book of Revelation nor in the book of Matthew, but it is to be assumed!

2 Thessalonians 2:1–12 should be decisive in saying the Great Apostasy and the Man of Lawlessness must come before the Second Coming of Jesus and the gathering of the saints. Verse 1 puts our gathering together to meet him after the *parousia* (Second Coming), and verses 7f. speak of the *parousia* of Jesus Christ after the revelation or *parousia* of the Man of Lawlessness (Antichrist). It is difficult to see how it could be plainer. Yet Dispensationalists frantically try to find a Rapture in such words as "falling away" and the removal of restraint or the restrainer.

The theory is so biblically bankrupt that the usual defense is made using three passages that do not even mention a Tribulation (John 14:3;

1 Thess. 4:17; 1 Cor. 15:52).[134] These are important passages, but they have not had one word to say about a *Pretribulational* Rapture. The score is 3 to 0, three passages for a Posttribulation Rapture and three that say nothing on the subject.

It is doubtful that John 14:3 has any reference to the *parousia*. Since Jesus went to prepare abiding places (*monai*), many see the fulfillment of this promise to come again in the coming of the Paraclete (the Holy Spirit) when both the Father and the Son come to make their abode (*monē*, 14:23). This is most likely when read in the context of the dialogue between Jesus and Judas (14:15–31).

Of course the Resurrection of the dead and the Rapture of the living with the dead do take place at the *parousia*, as 1 Thessalonians 4:13–18 clearly teaches. The very word Rapture is derived from the Latin text of 1 Thessalonians 4:17 where "we shall be caught up" is *rapiemur*.

1 Corinthians 15:53 is a restatement of the same teaching. The point is that there is no *parousia* until after the Man of Lawlessness appears as 2 Thessalonians 2:8f. teaches. There can be no Pretribulation Rapture if there is no Pretribulation *parousia*, and there is none in any passage in the New Testament. Pretribulationism is biblically bankrupt and does not know it.

Historical Premillennialism should never be confused with the Pretribulationism taught by the deviation of Dispensationalism. When the Scriptures are interpreted in a realistic way Premillennialism is able to justify itself. As an alternative to all false theories of the future it has no equal. Both the Bible and history are behind it. This has been done on a more philosophical basis by Jürgen Moltmann.[135] Here primacy has been given to the biblical revelation.[136]

80. The New Creation*

The assumption that the cosmos is eternal has been seriously shaken by the progress of natural science. Along with a theological eschatology a scientific eschatology has developed. At no point is this situation more evident

---

134. The most unbelievable effort to defend the theory of a Pretribulation Rapture was introduced into the debate by E. Schuyler English, Editor of the *New Scofield Reference Bible*, but he was unable to get his own committee to agree. He interpreted the "falling away" (*apostasia*) in 2 Thess. 2:3 as the "taking away" of the believers before the revelation of the Man of Lawlessness. This was fully accepted by Kenneth Wuest of Moody Bible Institute. See Kenneth Wuest, *Prophetic Light in the Present Darkness* (Grand Rapids: Wm. B. Eerdmans Publishing Co., 1955), pp. 39f.

135. *Op. cit.*, pp. 261-265.

136. For a good evaluation of current ideas of the Millennium see Millard J. Erickson, *Contemporary Options in Eschatology. A Study of the Millennium* (Grand Rapids: Baker Book House, 1977). For a healthy debate in which all four views are represented see Robert G. Clouse, ed., *The Meaning of the Millennium* (Downers Grove, Illinois: Inter-Varsity Press, 1977).

*The material in this and the following chapter is from my previously mentioned book *The Hope of Glory*.

than in the elaborations of the Second Law of Thermodynamics, a theory that holds that the amount of available energy in the universe is becoming less and less and that finally the whole system will suffer "heat death." The process is called an increase of entropy, from the Greek word *entrepein*, to turn in. The law is thus distinguished from the First Law of Thermodynamics, which has to do with the conservation of energy.

One of the clearest statements of the theory concludes that there is a "historic character" to nature and that "every event is in the strictest sense irreversible."[137] Creation and cosmic end become corollaries. "If events follow upon each other with finite speed, they must run out in finite time. It follows, not only that there is an end in heat death awaiting the events, but also that events must have had a beginning in time."[138]

It is evident that such scientific eschatology is not incompatible with theological eschatology, but cosmic redemption does not depend on cosmic catastrophe. God is not bound by the laws of creation, and there is no assurance that creation will run a gradual course to the end. Cosmic redemption rests on the belief that the living God who created man together with his body and his environment will surely save the same before the ominous threat of oblivion. Holy Spirit linked with human spirit is the motif that finally harmonizes the discords of man and so rescues creation from chaos. If there is no Creator there is no creation, but if things visible rest on things invisible the foundations will not finally fail.

God's ultimate promise is: "Behold, I make all things new" (Rev. 21:5). This includes God's whole creation, things visible and invisible, things as well as persons. The new age that began to dawn in the first coming of Christ into the world will be consummated in eternity, the age of all ages. The new creation is the destiny of the new man and the consummation of the new covenant. A constellation of concepts may be grouped under two major heads: the *futility* of creation, and the *freedom* of creation.

The Futility of Creation

At times the prophet of God, looking into the terrible crystal of judgment, sees only the vision of cosmic destruction, of the whole cosmos reduced to chaos (Jer. 4:23–26):

> *I looked on the earth, and lo, it was*
> *waste and void;*
> *and to the heavens, and they had no light.*

---

137. C. F. von Weizsäcker, *The History of Nature*, tr. Fred D. Wieck (Chicago: University of Chicago Press, 1949), pp. 47, 51.

138. *Ibid.*, p. 59. A detailed study of this problem needs to assess the theories expounded in James Jeans, *The Mysterious Universe* (New York: Macmillan, 1931); Fred Hoyle, *The Nature of the Universe* (Oxford: Blackwell, 1950); A. C. B. Lovell, *The Individual and the Universe* (London: Oxford University Press, 1959); John Macmurray, *The Boundaries of Science* (London: Faber & Faber, 1939). A brief statement is by John Wren-Lewis, "Science and the Doctrine of Creation," *Expository Times*, LXXI (Dec. 1959), 80-82.

I looked on the mountains, and lo, they were quaking,
and all the hills moved to and fro.
I looked, and lo, there was no man,
and all the birds of the air had fled.
I looked, and lo, the fruitful land was a desert,
and all its cities were laid in ruins
before the Lord, before his fierce anger.

At other times, when the Creator and Redeemer, the Lord of all life and history, confronts and comforts His people, the threat of woe is transformed into the hope of weal. The meaningless maze of human and historical contradictions opens into a deeper dimension, a level where all the riddles of life and tragedies of history look new and meaningful before the renewed understanding of the purpose of God. Such is the vision of Isaiah 45:18:

For thus says the Lord,
who created the heavens
(he is God!),
who formed the earth and made it
(he established it;
he did not create it a chaos,
he formed it to be inhabited!);
"I am the Lord, and there is no other. . . ."

The shifting scenes of weal and woe, forming a theater for the drama of redemption and judgment, find ultimate harmony in God and God alone (Isa. 45:7):

I form light and create darkness,
I make weal and create woe,
I am the Lord, who do all these things.

The foundations shake at the onslaught of cosmic fall and frustration, but faith clings to the hope that the high purpose of God to bring His creation into glory will not fail.

The foundation of the cosmos. Never is it argued in Scripture that the creation has a founder. Faith in a sovereign God assumes this as a corollary to the redeeming grace made manifest in history. If His grace is sovereign in salvation, it must also be in creation, for He abides the same in His sufficiency and purpose. This is the fundamental assumption behind the affirmation that God and His purpose are above and beyond the foundation of the world (*katabolē tou kosmou*, Matt. 13:35; 25:24; Luke 11:50; John 17:24; Eph. 1:4; Heb. 4:3; 9:26; 1 Pet. 1:20; Rev. 13:8; 17:8).

This foundation has to do with the absolute beginning when God makes a cosmos from chaos, order from disorder, creation from nothing-ness. The cosmos is created between the living God and a yawning void, between He Who Is and nothingness. Faith follows the path between the possibilities of being and non-being, between destiny and origin.

In biblical thought the cosmos is related to God both as His system and His sign.[139] The Bible begins with the proclamation of the goodness of creation grounded in the goodness of God (Gen. 1:1–2:4a). Order is the most obvious mark of the majestic pavilion that surrounds man in pan-oramic wonder. With poetic power this priestly psalm becomes man's praise of the goodness of God at the turn of each Sabbath rest.

Creation is the act of God alone. The verb *bara* (create) is used only of God's action in the creation, in which He is Lord of all. It is at once the work and word of Him who says: "I am the Lord, that is my name; my glory I give to no other, nor my praise to graven images" (Isa. 42:8; cf. 48:11). And again: "I am the first and I am the last; besides me there is no god" (44:6; cf. 45:5, 21f.; 46:8; 48:11f.). Every man must choose, ultimately, between impersonal polytheism and personal monotheism, between I–It and I–Thou (cf. Isa. 57).

The formless *tohu wa-bohu* is transformed into a theater of action for God in His relation to man. God storms the citadel of chaos with His Spirit (*ruach*), and the meaningless monster *tehom* (the cosmic abyss) trembles before Him, but the preprimeval possibility of chaos and nothingness per-sists. If God's activity ceased for one moment the cosmos would drop back into chaos and nothingness.

The first day celebrates the light of day as a cosmic power that over-comes the chaotic darkness of the night. "While the day is light from the first created original light, night consists in nothing more than that darkness which was eliminated, now limited, to be sure, by wholesome cosmic order. Every night, when the created forms flow together into formlessness, chaos regains a certain power over what has been created."[140] "In the morning the unformed becomes form and then by evening sinks back into formless-ness. The bright polarity of light dissolves into unity with the darkness."[141] This rhythm of weal and woe is the way of God in His creation, who can "form light and create darkness" (Isa. 45:7).

On the second day the firmament, like "a gigantic hemispherical and ponderous bell," is created a stronghold against the chaotic waters. "The heavenly bell, which is brought into the waters of chaos, forms first of all

---

139. H. Wheeler Robinson, *Inspiration and Revelation in the Old Testament* (Oxford: Clar-endon, 1946), pp. 1-16.
140. Gerhard von Rad, *Genesis*, tr. John H. Marks (Philadelphia: Westminster, 1961), pp. 50f.
141. Dietrich Bonhoeffer, *Creation and Fall*, tr. John C. Fletcher (New York: Macmillan, 1959), p. 24.

a separating wall between the waters beneath and above."[142] The Latin *firmamentum* and the German *Feste* rightly translate the Hebrew *raqia*, for it is the mighty fortress against the threat of chaotic waters. It is Heaven in contrast to a meaningless *tehom* of *tohu wa-bohu*.

On the third day the work begun on the second day is completed when the waters under the heavenly dome are gathered together as the seas. The earth as the dry ground is the corollary to the orderly firmament above. Together they fight against chaos. "The origin of the ocean from the dimension of the chaotic is clear enough. The cosmos, therefore, is surrounded entirely and thus threatened on all sides, above, and below, by cosmic spaces, which, to be sure, can no longer be called directly chaotic, but which still permanently preserve something hostile to God and creation."[143]

Organic life first appeared on the third day when plants sprang up from the dry ground, but creaturely life is first suggested by the stars on the fourth day. They are "considered as creatures and as dependent on God's ordering creative will."[144] The two great lights, the sun and the moon, are to "rule" the day and the night as the Creator rules over the creation.

By the fifth day the cosmos is ready for the living creatures. The verb *bara* (create) is again used to designate the divine creativity and the direct relationship between the Creator and His creatures. The mythical sea monsters, symbolized by Leviathan (Ps. 74:14; Isa. 27:1; cf. Dan. 7:21f.; Rev. 11:7; 12:3; 13:1ff.) and Rahab (Ps. 39:10f.), are removed from human understanding but not from the creative will by which God is able to conquer chaos and create cosmos.

On the sixth day the land animals appear as beings related to the realm below. It is "only indirectly" that they "receive the power of procreation from God," but man is the crown of the cosmos, the lord of creation, and the link to that which is above. He is assigned dominion and is the image of the invisible God under whose lordship he rules and subdues.

All is so harmonious in this cosmic order of paradisaical peace that man is assigned only vegetables to eat. Killing and slaughter are excluded in this good creation. Six times it is pronounced "good" (Gen. 1:4, 10, 12, 18, 21, 25), and after the creation of male and female in the image of God it is "very good" (v. 31).[145] However, it is not yet perfect (*tamim*), as man is not yet immortal. Final Righteousness, yes; Original Righteousness, no. The symbolic beauty of this majestic psalm goes far beyond the unhappy

142. Von Rad, *op. cit.*, p. 51.
143. *Ibid.*, p. 52.
144. *Ibid.*, p. 53.
145. Irenaeus of Lyon used the goodness of creation to refute the Gnostic heretics who denied that the Creator and the Redeemer are one. See Anders Nygren, *Agape and Eros*, tr. Philip S. Watson (Philadelphia: Westminster, 1953), pp. 393-412 for a classic statement of this issue.

battles of the days of Babel, but there are still exegetical swamps into which the light has not yet penetrated.

Creation reaches its goal in the eschatological rest of the people of God (Heb. 4), so that the end is more than the beginning. *"Creation in the Old Testament is an eschatological concept.* The fact that God is the creator of the world means that He compasses the complete time process, ruling, determining, and completing all ages. That is why He is called the first and the last, Isaiah 44:6."[146]

The glory of creation blossoms in the biblical *berakah* of Psalm 104. The Lord is blessed for His benefits recounted in the order of Genesis 1:1–2:4a, but there is also a "philosophy of the cosmos."[147] The glory of God in creation is seen as God covers Himself with light and lays the foundation of the earth (Ps. 104:1–9). His preservation is praised for the benefits of springs of water, vegetation, the moon and the sun, the sea and its animals (vv. 10–26). His providential care is over all as He brings them toward their intended goal (vv. 27–30). Wondrous works call for a doxology (vv. 31–35).

The Egyptian "Hymn to Aton," dated from the time of Akhenaton (1380-1362 B.C.), has much of this monotheistic marveling before the greatness of creation. Some have thought that Psalm 104 was actually based on the Egyptian hymn, but the differences are too great. At least it must be said that the glory of God in creation is manifest among the Gentiles also, and the argument that the teachings of Psalm 19 are possible only within the covenant of Israel should be abandoned. The Creator is glorified in His creation even among the Gentiles (Rom. 10:18).

The scriptural teaching is not nullified by scientific investigation. More than once the theology of creation has been translated into a new scientific language without loss of meaning. The "big bowl" view, based on the ancient Babylonian view of the universe, became a "big ball" view in the second century of the Christian era, when Ptolemy of Alexandria expounded a new theory that dominated Christian theology for fourteen hundred years. It is a great tribute to the sanity of the early Church Fathers that this translation was made without heresy trials on Scripture versus science.

Wisdom has not always prevailed in modern times as it did in the Middle Ages. Although Copernicus was able to challenge the cycles and epicycles of Ptolemaic astronomy and die a natural death, Galileo and a great company since have met heavy head winds whipped up by theologians with more zeal than knowledge. Yet theological translation, like biblical translation, wins in the end. Today, as in the time of Newton, a great scientist such as Carl Friedrich von Weizsäcker can write a scientific genesis

146. Ludwig Koehler, *Old Testament Theology*, tr. A. S. Todd (London: Lutterworth, 1957), p. 88.
147. I.B., IV, 550.

(*The History of Nature*) for modern man that gives greater glory to God and makes biblical eschatology as relevant as the biblical belief in creation.

The cosmic order, reflecting as it does the goodness and glory of God, is a sign that points away from the creation to the Creator. This makes for the mystery of creation. The second part of the Elihu speeches in the book of Job (36:1-37:24) leads into the hidden mercy and the haunting mystery of God.[148] God's glory in creation is unsearchable, but His greatness glimmers through the meteorological portents of autumn and winter and in the stillness of the summer's heat. As Lord of autumn (36:26-33) His glory is revealed in providential bounty veiled in the thunderstorm. Grace and judgment are hidden in the weal and woe of the storm. As Lord of winter (37:1-13) the snow and showers add to the glory of the thunderstorm as the hurricane from the south and the cold wind of the north, with frost and ice, make manifest the marvels of God. As Lord of summer (37:14-22) the splendor of God is seen in the stillness and sultriness of the heat.

God Himself speaks to Job out of the whirlwind that veils His majesty (38:1-42:6). The first discourse describes the wisdom of God the Creator (38:1-39:30) in the wonders of the creation of the earth and sea, the days and nights, and the mysteries of the inorganic and organic world. Job is silent before questions so sublime. The second discourse (40:6-42:6) turns from the wisdom to the power of God illustrated by the Behemoth and the Leviathan. Before such cosmic power Job is brought to repentance.

Rudolf Otto has rightly used Job 38 to illustrate the religious experience of the numinous, the *mysterium tremendum et fascinans*, beyond all that is true, good, and beautiful, a mystery that is both awesome and holy, overwhelming and fascinating.[149]

Around A.D. 800 Shankara wrote a commentary on the *Vedānta Sutras* that expounds a unity in all things, but the phenomenal world is reduced to an illusion (*Maya*). In the reinterpretation of Ramanuja around A.D. 1100 the phenomenal world and individual souls have real existence, but they are the body of Brahma. The reality of cosmic redemption vanishes as much in the identity of Ramanuja as in the illusion of Shankara. Some of the wonder of Job is there, but the work of God the Creator and Redeemer is not.

In biblical thought, creation is a medium of revelation, not *Maya*. It is a veil between man and the Creator, but it does not vanish when the Creator is also Redeemer. As a medium, creation may do a service that is both negative and positive, leading to the woe of judgment or the weal of redemption. The wrath of God may be revealed from heaven through the order of creation when men resist God in ungodliness and unrighteousness

148. I.B., III, 1163-1169.
149. Rudolph Otto, *The Idea of the Holy*, tr. John W. Harvey (London: Oxford University Press, 1943), pp. 80-84.

(Rom. 1:18-32). The subjective medium of conscience joins the objective medium of creation to accuse those who reject the law "written on their hearts" (Rom. 2:14-16).

The positive sign may be seen in a religion as primitive as the nature worship of the Lycaonians. Even there God "did not leave himself without witness" (Acts 14:17). Witnessing to the philosophical religion of Athens, Paul holds out for the possibility that men may "seek God" and "feel after him and find him" (Acts 17:27). Even Epimenides, the seventh-century B.C. philosopher and poet in Crete, was not ignorant that "in him we live and move and have our existence" (Acts 17:28, TEV). Aratus, Paul's fellow citizen in Cilicia, knew that men are indeed the offspring of God.

Within the household of faith creation is even more of a sign pointing to the Creator. "That is to say, once we have encountered God in Christ we must encounter Him in all things."[150] The religious art of France in the thirteenth century, a constellation of symbolism singular and superb, would not be possible on any ground outside the biblical belief in "God the Father Almighty, Maker of heaven and earth." Creation and history constitute a monumental medieval mirror that the glory of heaven may be manifest in all the earth.[151]

Plato's principle of plenitude prepared the way for the Christian's more personal encounter with the Creator in His creation. Plenitude presupposed "that it is of the nature of an Idea to manifest itself in concrete existence," "the realization of conceptual possibility in actuality."[153] But the history of thought excludes that principle of emanation which would make the creation an exact image of the heavenly model. Continuity between creation and the Creator is a contradiction, a becoming before the being that is God. "God is the ultimate limitation, and His existence is the ultimate irrationality."[153] The creation is not the realization of the Creator; it is, however, the visible reflection of the invisible God.

The fall of the cosmos. If the creation were the perfect image of the heavenly Creator there could be no cosmic fall, but the creation is contingent and along with free man may fall. Personal freedom, experienced in faith and hope and love, is the perspective from which the contingency and cosmic all of the physical world are understood. God is no longer seen in creation; creation is seen in God. Ultimate relations are interpersonal relations, and the ultimate meaning of the whole cosmic process is seen in the light of the personal relations that emerge. It is our own contingent being as persons

150. Alan D. Galloway, *The Cosmic Christ* (New York: Harper, 1951), p. 250.
151. Emile Male, *The Gothic Image*, tr. Dora Nussey (New York: Harper, 1958).
152. Arthur O. Lovejoy, *The Great Chain of Being* (Cambridge: Harvard University Press, 1950), p. 52.
153. A. N. Whitehead, *Science and the Modern World* (New York: Macmillan, 1925), p. 249. Quoted by Lovejoy, *op. cit.,* p. 333.

in relation that takes theology out of impersonal abstraction and thrusts all thought into an existential situation in which all relations are personal relations. As the human body becomes personalized with the human person whose instrument it is, s the creation becomes a personalized instrument of the Creator in the cosmic process. The I–It becomes I–Thou.

The common assumption that confines the fall to man overlooks the obvious fact that disorders in the creation along with human disobedience are an empirical reality. Things would not be perfect if everyone joined a back-to-nature movement and followed the rule of letting nature take its course. If nature took its course in sex, prolific procreation would turn society into a mass of starving people. This is part of the glaring error in the Roman Catholic resistance to birth control.

Only a few years ago more than four thousand people, in less than ten minutes, were buried beneath an avalanche in Peru. The creation is not essentially evil; it is a good that has been corrupted and distorted by sin. "Nature is not only glorious; it is also tragic. It is suffering and sighing with us. No one who has ever listened to the sounds of nature with sympathy can forget their tragic melodies."[154] "The truly biblical doctrine is that the physical world of Nature is *basically good but distorted by sin*, in very much the same way as human spiritual nature is, so that Nature and mankind *both* stand in need of, and are capable of, redemption."[155]

The biblical doctrine of creation does question the natural order of things. The subjection of the *ktisis* (creation) to futility is found in one of the most spiritual chapters in the Scriptures (Rom. 8:18–25), and it is not possible to dismiss it as a vestige of "unspiritual apocalyptic." It is concern for the disorder and injustices in creation, manifested in unbalanced human suffering, that questions creation in its present state. It belongs to man's vocation now and man's salvation ultimately that disorders of human environment, as well as disobedience of the human will, be brought into harmony with the sovereign grace of a good God.

The present longing (Rom. 8:19) is described with a word which means "to hold out the head, to stretch the neck, in order to observe and keep on the watch in anxious expectation of what one may perhaps see or discover" (*apokaradokia*).[156] "The mystical sympathy of physical nature with the work of grace is beyond the comprehension of most of us. But can we disprove it?"[157] "He is thinking of the inner anxiety, of the conflict and division at the very center of our being, of what we have spoken of as our

154. Paul Tillich, *The Shaking of the Foundations* (New York: Scribner's, 1948), p. 81.
155. John Wren-Lewis, "Christian Morality and the Idea of a Cosmic Fall," *Expository Times*, LXXI (April 1960), 205.
156. Franz J. Leenhardt, *The Epistle to the Romans*, tr. Harold Knight (London: Lutterworth, 1961), p. 219.
157. A. T. Robertson, *Word Pictures in the New Testament* (Nashville: Sunday School Board, 1931), IV, 375.

'brokenness,' the struggle with a threatening meaninglessness, the 'waiting' in which, even if there should be hope, there is also unremitting pain."[158] Through suffering God's sons, like God's Son, are brought through the painful cosmic process of a fallen creation *into the perfection of perfect harmony and heavenly glory*. It is the event of eschatological revelation (2 Thess. 1:7; 1 Cor. 1:7; Rom. 2:5; 16:25).

A past subjection (Rom. 8:20) accounts for this present longing: "The creation was subjected to futility." The third curse in Genesis 3:14–19 includes a cursing of the ground:

> *Cursed is the ground because of you;*
> *in toil you shall eat of it all the days of your life;*
> *thorns and thistles it shall bring forth to you;*
> *and you shall eat the plants of the field.*

However, the subjection to futility is prior to man's sin and the curse. II Esdras 7:11f. is an apocalyptic bridge between the Old Testament and the New Testament, but Paul has taken the cosmic fall to the depths. Man together with his cosmic environment stands in need of redemption.

The hope of future freedom (Rom. 8:21) fills the empty and meaningless process of the present age with the presence and purpose that belong to the age to come. It seems quite impossible to confine this deliverance to the rational realm, for "the whole creation" is restricted to the non-rational.[159] It is that which is other than man and with which man, without redemption, suffers a broken betrothal. "Men prefer to rape the universe rather than to be wedded in organic unity with it."[160]

The *ktisis* (creation), which according to Paul is in subjection to futility, is in John a system (*kosmos*) in hostility to God. "Do not love the world or the things in the world. If anyone loves the world, love for the Father is not in him. For all that is in the world, the lust of the flesh and the lust of the eyes and the pride of life, is not of the Father but is of the world. And the world passes away, and the lust of it; but he who does the will of God abides forever" (1 John 2:15–17). The content of the cosmos brings it into crisis (*krisis*) with God (John 3:14–21), and this is the process of judgment.

The Freedom of Creation

Man was created "a living soul," an organic unity of the breath of God and the dust of the earth (Gen. 2:7). His organic relation to the whole of creation is so real that biblical theology is unable to think of a complete redemption that does not include "the whole creation" (Rom. 8:22), earth as well as man and the animals. One of the leading Old Testament theologians of the

158. John Knox, *Life in Christ Jesus* (Greenwich: Seabury, 1961), p. 103.
159. John Murray, *The Epistle to the Romans* (Grand Rapids: Eerdmans, 1959), I, 301f.
160. Galloway, *op. cit.*, p. 246.

past generation, speaking of the vivid visions of a future transformation of nature, has spoken the solid truth: "These pictures are to be taken realistically, not allegorically; if they seem strangely impossible to us, it is partly because we come to nature with an inveterate prejudice in favor of its fixity and virtual independence of God."[161]

Cosmic redemption presupposes the possibility that creation may be transformed by the same activity from which it finds its source and sustenance. The Redeemer is the Creator and Preserver of "all things." To rule out this possibility is to rule out miracle, and to rule out miracle is to rule out God. We believe in miracles because we believe in God, and belief in "God the Father Almighty, Maker of heaven and earth," is the solid rock on which the doctrine of cosmic redemption rests. In the most realistic way we believe that "the creation itself will be set free from its bondage to decay and obtain the glorious liberty of the children of God" (Rom. 8:21).

What then is meant by miracle, this transforming activity of God? The terms used for miracle, the very vocabulary of Holy Scripture, make manifest the meaning of miracle. A miracle is first of all a power (*dynamis*), a mighty deed or work in which supernatural activity changes the course of creation and the currents of history. It is also a wonder (*teras*), an awesome event that leaves the human participant in the grasp of the incomprehensible glory of God. It is supremely a sign (*sēmeion*), a transformation of creation and history that has significance beyond the event itself. It points to the living God, the ground of all being and the sovereign over all. In summary, miracles are works (*erga* in John's Gospel) that reveal the power and purpose of God.

Miracles may be on any level of encounter between the Creator and His creation. Some may be primarily supernatural events that change the order of creation, the so-called nature miracles of healing of body or mind or both, the type found most frequently in the ministry of Jesus. Israel, Christ and the Church are miracles of history, a complex of events in which the clue to God's purpose, from creation to consummation, is disclosed.

The truth of miracles is not ruled out by the facts of scientific investigation. The closed system of causal connection has been shaken by science itself. Even in the realm of physics there is talk of a law of indeterminacy, and it is scientific dogmatism to rule out the unexpected. Natural selection no longer rules supreme in organic science, and whole systems of thought are built around belief in the emergence of the new. Psychological behaviorism is widely recognized as a vestigial wonder that would change free and responsible man into a meaningless machine. This "open universe" does not prove miracle, but neither does it rule out miracle on *a priori* grounds. Belief in miracle is based on man's encounter with God, sovereign and free, on whom man and the whole creation depend for their origin and

161. H. Wheeler Robinson, *op. cit.*, p. 29.

sustenance. If God brings His creation into being He can bring it to its consummation.

Miracles are signs of the new creation breaking into the old order that has been corrupted by sin and is in "bondage to decay" (Rom. 8:21). The moving metaphors of Holy Scripture suggest the splendor of this consummation and the sordid corruption of the present creation. The consummation is a new order and a new creation, even a new heaven and a new earth.

The new order. The new creation is a new order, a regeneration that is both personal and cosmic (Tit. 3:5; Matt. 10:28). Personal regeneration is a rebirth (*palingenesia*), a radical transformation of the human soul, wrought by the grace of God, that is at once a bath that washes clean from defilement and renews to spiritual life by the Holy Spirit. Cosmic regeneration is likewise a transformation that inaugurates and consummates the new order of Christ. Cosmic judgment accompanies cosmic redemption. The transformation has its beginning in historical revelation, but the consummation includes the cosmic also. The transformation of the Stoic concept does not exclude the Stoic insight into the cosmic process.

The new order is also a restoration. Malachi 4:5f. promised that Elijah the prophet would restore "the hearts of fathers to their children and the hearts of children to their fathers," and this promise is raised as a question in Mark 9:12 (cf. Matt. 17:11). This longing lingered in the minds of the disciples, as the question in Acts 1:6 indicates, and this pre-tribulation prophecy is in the background of Peter's call to repentance in Acts 3:19–21. Yet the question is raised as to whether the famous phrase *apokatastaseōs pantōn* (establishment or restoration of all) does not have cosmic as well as historical content.

H. A. Guy eliminates the cosmic connotations, even doubting that there is a *parousia* expectation in the passage.[162] It would seem, however, that the reception in heaven ("whom heaven must receive") before the "establishment of all" would require two events, two comings of the Christ.

As to the meaning of *apokatastaseōs pantōn*, F. F. Bruce has taken the view that it is identical with *palingenesia* (regeneration) of Matthew 19:28 and that "the idea of restoration is not excluded" because "the final inauguration of the new age is accompanied by the renovation of all nature."[163]

God's new order is above all *a rest* (Heb. 3:1–4:13). On the basis of Psalm 95:7–11 the subtle symbolism of Hebrews moves majestically from the Exodus as a type to the Sabbath as a type. In Deuteronomy 5:12–15 the Sabbath is a celebration of the Exodus, and the typology of a Second Exodus (Isa. 51:9–11; 1 Cor. 5:7; 10:2; Luke 9:31; 2 Pet. 1:13–15) leads

---

162. *The New Testament Doctrine of 'Last Things'* (London: Oxford University Press, 1948), pp. 90f. Cf. C. H. Dodd, G. B. Caird!
163. *The Book of Acts* (Grand Rapids: Eerdmans, 1954), p. 91, n. 36.

logically to a future Sabbath rest. All who maintain their confession (*homologia*, Heb. 3:1) or confidence (*parrēsia*, 3:14) "share in a heavenly call," "share in Christ," and they are exhorted to "hold fast," or "hold firm" lest "an evil, unbelieving heart" lead them "to [apostatize] from the living God" (3:12). Faith is the title-deed to the promised land (11:1).

Cosmic considerations enter by appeal to God's Sabbath rest in Genesis 2:2 (Heb. 4:4). Two days typify the future Sabbath rest. The first day (Heb. 4:1–5) is the age of the old covenant and the law, in which Moses the servant of God is God's spokesman, but this did not enable the household of God to enter the rest. Psalm 95:7–11, written much later, is evidence against any such claim. The second day (Heb. 4:6–10) is the age of the new covenant and the gospel, in which Jesus is God's spokesman (1:1f.), and this new covenant will be consummated with a new creation. God spoke of "another day" (4:8) because no rest was reached in the day of Joshua. "So then, there remains a sabbath rest for the people of God; for whoever enters God's rest also ceases from his labors as God did from his" (4:10).

The cosmic Christology of Hebrews will not allow us to confine this redemption to human history. God's spokesman in the new age is God's speech. Christ is God's Word, "living and active, sharper than any two-edged sword, piercing to the division of soul and spirit, of joints and marrow, and discerning the thoughts and intentions of the heart" (4:12). "He reflects the glory of God and bears the very stamp of his nature, upholding the universe by his word of power" (1:3). He is the one "for whom all things (*ta panta*) and by whom all things (*ta panta*) exist" (2:10). "By faith we understand that the world was created by the word of God, so that what is seen was made out of things which do not appear" (11:3). In the new creation He has prepared for the faithful, the "strangers and exiles on the earth," "a homeland" in "a better country" in which "he has prepared for them a city" (11:13–16).

The new creation. The new order is a new creation, *a recreation*. Christ the Redeemer is Christ the Creator. The bipartite confession in 1 Timothy 2:5f. expresses belief in Christ Jesus as the "one mediator" between the "one God" and men, but an earlier bipartite confession conceives clearly that the relation between the "one God the Father" and the "one Lord Jesus Christ" makes the person manifest in the flesh of Jesus, the one mediator of creation (1 Cor. 8:6):

> We, however, have one God the Father,
> from whom are all things, and we to him,
> and one Lord Jesus Christ,
> through whom are all things, and we through him.[164]

164. J. N. D. Kelly, *Early Christian Creeds* (London: Longmans, Green, 1950), p. 19.

Over "the present evil age" rules "the god of this age" who "has blinded the minds of the unbelievers, to keep them from seeing the light of the gospel of the glory of Christ, who is the likeness of God" (2 Cor. 4:4). Christ as the image of God recalls the original creation of man in the image and likeness of God (Gen. 1:26), suggesting that the new creation, surpassing the old, is ruled by one who truly reflects the glory of God. As God commanded the light to shine out of the darkness at the beginning (Gen. 1:3), so, in the new creation that inaugurates the end, God "has shone in our hearts to give the light of the knowledge of the glory of God in the face of Christ" (2 Cor. 4:6).

The cosmic implications of this new creation are heard in the declaration: "Therefore, if any one is in Christ, he is a new creation; the old has passed away, behold, the new has come. All this is from God, who through Christ reconciled us to himself and gave us the ministry of reconciliation, that is, God was in Christ reconciling the world to himself, not counting their trespasses against them, and entrusting to us the message of reconciliation" (2 Cor. 5:17-19). This is more than some individualistic or even social reconciliation to God. It is the world (*kosmos*), the corrupted creation (*ktisis*), that is reconciled to God through Him who became an offering for sin. Cosmic reconciliation corresponds to cosmic creation and cosmic corruption.

The concept of cosmic reconciliation in the new creation has a corporate corollary in the idea of the new man. Christians are commanded to put off the old man with his practices and to "put on the new nature, which is being renewed in knowledge after the image of its creator" (Col. 3:9f.). This "one new man" is the "one body," not some isolated individual (Eph. 2:15f.). Corporate redemption in the "one body" of Christ is consummated in the cosmic redemption of the new creation. The new man belongs to the new creation in the new age, as the old man belongs to "the old" in "the present evil age."

The new creation is also reconciliation. The luminous liturgical poem preserved in Colossians 1:15-20 is the most comprehensive statement of the cosmic relations of Christ.[165] On the basis of Eduard Schweizer's reconstruction the relations are remarkable.[166]

The first stanza (vv. 15f.) depicts Christ as the mediator of creation, as already noted in 1 Corinthians 8:6. With comments in parentheses and the references to the Creator and Saviour of all things underlined, the following arrangement may be made:

165. A detailed formal analysis that leaves only two strophes is offered by James M. Robinson in the *Journal of Biblical Literature*, LXXV (December 1957), 270-287.
166. In *New Testament Studies*, VIII (October 1961), 6ff.

> *He is the image of the invisible God, the firstborn of all*
> *creation,*
> *for in him all things were created, in heaven and on earth*
> *(visible and invisible,*
> *whether thrones or dominions*
> *or principalities or authorities)*
> *through him and for him all things have been created.*

In Egypt Tutankhamen was called "the living image of Amen," Ptolemy "the living image of Zeus," and Pharaoh "Horus, son of Unseen Osiris"; but the firstborn recalls the Hebraic belief that the first place belonged to the first-born (Exod. 4:22; Jer. 31:9; Ps. 89:27). Christ is the visible manifestation of the invisible God, but He is also the mediator of the whole creation. He is not a creature because "all things" (*ta panta*) were created "in him," "through him," and "for him." Again he is the one "for whom and by whom all things exist" (Heb. 2:10). There is no creature Christology here. He is Creator, the "one mediator" of the "one God."

The intermediate stanza (Col. 1:17f.) speaks of cosmic cohesion of "all things" in Christ, the preserver and sustainer who is "before all things" and "head of the body." Only "the body" calls for comment in this part:

> *And it is he who is before all things,*
> *and in him all things hold together,*
> *and it is he who is the head of the body (the Church).*

Cosmic and corporate wholeness belong to Him.

The last stanza (vv. 18b, 19f.) is parallel to the first, but the mediator of creation is now declared to be the mediator of reconciliation.

> *He is the beginning, the firstborn of the dead*
> *(that in everything he might be pre-eminent).*
> *For in him all the fullness was pleased to dwell,*
> *and through him to reconcile to him all things*
> *(whether on earth or in heaven,*
> *making peace through the blood of his cross).*

At the beginning was the Eternal Son of God, and He holds first place as "the firstborn of the dead" in the realm of reconciliation as well as in the realm of creation. Over creation and over death He has supreme command. The primate (*prōtotokos*, firstborn) has primacy (*prōteuōn*, pre-eminence). All supernatural and creative powers (the *plērōma*, fullness) dwell in Him, and there is no need to worship any other (Col. 2:8–23). Again and again it should be remembered that "all things" (*ta panta*) in creation and in reconciliation are related to Christ.

Another feature of the new creation is that which has come to be called recapitulation, using the term as it has come to be associated with Irenaeus' interpretation of Ephesians 1:10. Ephesians 1:3–14 is a Trinitarian prayer, perhaps a baptismal *berakah* (benediction), blessing the Father, Son, and Holy Spirit for the benefits of redemption.[167] Words of comment explain that God plans "to unite all things in him, things in heaven and things on earth" (1:10). "All things" in Ephesians (1:10f., 20–22; 4:10), as in Colossians 1:15–20, means all that God has created, and God has this purpose because He is the "one God and Father of us all, who is above all and through all and in all" (Eph. 4:6).

The infinitive *anakephalaiōsasthai* (to unite) has reference to the restoration of the original unity of all creation, disrupted by demonic and destructive powers, now in the process by which the corporate unity of the Church is consummated in the cosmic unity of creation.[168] As personal and social estrangement are involved in a cosmic estrangement of the creation from the Creator, so the act of God in Christ, by which reconciliation is accomplished, is personal, social, and cosmic.

Irenaeus of Lyon also thought of recapitulation as a return to the original unity of creation through the activity of God in Christ, in the incarnation, in the Church, and in the final consummation when Christ the recapitulation of righteousness overcomes Antichrist as the recapitulation of evil.[169] From creation to consummation God has a purpose made manifest in Christ and made perfect in glory. If this be God's ultimate intention, all disruptive and schismatic efforts in the Church or in the whole creation are out of harmony with the will of God.

The new heaven and new earth. God's new order and new creation, described as "a new heaven and a new earth," is a consummation after cataclysm when "the first heaven and the first earth had passed away" (Rev. 21:1). Such is the vision of John the seer.

> The seer's gaze is now at last fixed on the furthest point of his vision; his eye dwells on the perfection of a new creation, wherein God's agelong purposes are consummated, in the eternal bliss of the loyal. The old order has entirely vanished away, we must emphasize that it is essentially the old *order* of things, vitiated as it was by every conceivable evil, material and spiritual, which has disappeared. It is unnecessary and misleading to wander into speculations about the cosmic processes assumed by John in the summoning into being of a new order of things after the judgment. For although a radical refashioning of the universe is undoubtedly in

---

167. A formal analysis is done by J. Coutts in *New Testament Studies*, III, 115-127.
168. Franz Mussner, *Christus das All und die Kirche* (Trier: Paulinus Verlag, 1955), p. 66.
169. Gustaf Wingren, *Man and the Incarnation*, tr. Ross Mackenzie (Edinburgh: Oliver and Boyd, 1959), pp. 187f.

the background of his thought, it is spiritual rebirth which he tried to describe.[170]

With this emphasis one can agree, but it should also be emphasized that "a radical refashioning of the universe" is essential to complete "spiritual rebirth." Even now in this present evil age the transformation has begun, "for the form of this world is passing away" (1 Cor. 7:31).

The positive consummation has as its corollary the negative picture of a cosmic cataclysm. The destruction of Noah's world by the great deluge is evidence that smooth continuity does not rule supreme in all human history and divine judgment. In answer to the scoffers, 2 Peter 3:5–7 warns:

> They deliberately ignore this fact, that by the word of God heavens existed long ago, and an earth formed out of water and by means of water, through which the world that then existed was deluged with water and perished. But by the same word the heavens and earth that now exist have been stored up for fire, being kept until the day of judgment and destruction of ungodly men.

This cosmic cataclysm is not the true *telos* (end) of creation and redemption. Patiently, and with detachment from the passing world, the righteous are recalled to God's eternal purpose and promise (3:11–13).

> Since all these things are thus to be dissolved, what sort of persons ought you to be in lives of holiness and godliness, waiting for and hastening the coming of the day of God, because of which the heavens will be kindled and dissolved, and the elements will melt with fire! But according to his promise we wait for new heavens and a new earth in which righteousness dwells.

Judgment is never the ultimate purpose in the ways of God. Beyond cataclysm there is consummation, beyond woe there is weal in the wonders of the Holy City of God.

A comprehensive theology of cosmic redemption, related in detail to modern scientific knowledge, has seldom been attempted on a satisfactory scale. Among ancient Christian writers the daring system of Origen in the third century suggests how revolutionary this type of eschatology can become, but the failure to comprehend the whole cosmic order is always an abbreviation of the biblical perspective. Despite the philosophical and scientific inadequacies of Origen's thought, he stands out as the most courageous theologian in the early Church.[171]

Cosmic fall and cosmic redemption were corollaries for Origen. An original unity of all things is posited, but from this state of blessedness

---

170. Martin Kiddle, *The Revelation of St. John* (New York: Harper, 1940), pp. 409f.
171. A good summary of his eschatology as a whole is in R. P. C. Hanson, *Allegory and Event* (London: SCM, 1959), pp. 333-356.

some angelic and all human creatures have fallen into a state of defection and loss (*De prin.* I.IV). This loss is both cosmic and human, and all must pass through a process of punishment and moral education before restoration of the primeval harmony of the whole.

Redemption as well as the fall is not confined to man. The redemptive process moves toward a consummation, described as a conflagration, but it is a fire of purification rather than a destructive cataclysm. "For the end is always like the beginning; as therefore there is one end of all things, so we must understand that there is one beginning of all things, and as there is one end of many things, so from one beginning arise many differences and varieties, which in turn are restored, through God's goodness, through their subjection to Christ and their unity with the Holy Spirit, to one end, which is like the beginning" (I.VI.2).[172]

It is unfortunate that presuppositions influenced by the Stoic ideas of immanent and impersonal reason, together with Platonic dualism and universalism, limited the thrust of Origen's cosmic eschatology, but the movement from a transcendent unity of all things which is the beginning to an ultimate harmony that is the end (*telos*) belongs to an eschatology of basic monotheism.[173] Any confinement of redemption to man alone, to the exclusion of the rest of the cosmic order, is an eclipse of biblical eschatology. Ultimate harmony, as has been pointed out, does not lead necessarily to universal salvation, but it does lead to the elimination of all disorder and disobedience in the arena of God's glory.

Among modern philosophical theologians Hegel has revived the comprehensiveness that belongs to cosmic redemption.[174] But as Origen attempted to overcome the dualism inherent in the Gnostic system, so Hegel fell heir to the antinomies of reason and the dualism of the noumenal and phenomenal that was the legacy of Kant.

In the *Phenomenology of Mind* a movement of diremption is traced from an original thesis in which subject and object are one in the Absolute Spirit, through an antithesis of self and not-self, or "this" subject and "this" object, to an ultimate synthesis in the Absolute Spirit. The unity of the Father and the Son in the Spirit is the ground of ultimate unity between the Creator and the creation, God and man.

Cosmic redemption overcomes cosmic diremption in a unity that transcends the dichotomy of subject and object, but there the idealistic principle of identity, removing as it does the personal distinction between God and man and the ontological distinction between God and the world, weakened Hegel's conclusions as much as Stoic immanence created difficulties for Origen. The process absorbs into God, in undifferentiated unity, that which

172. G. W. Butterworth, *Origen on First Principles* (London: S.P.C.K., 1936), p. 53.
173. Galloway, *op. cit.,* pp. 84-98.
174. *Ibid.*, pp. 156-185.

in biblical faith is an incorporation of the parts into a larger whole in which God is "all in all" (1 Cor. 15:28).

A third effort to formulate a theology of cosmic redemption is evident in Karl Heim's six-volume *Der evangelische Glaube und das Denken der Gegenwart* (*The Evangelical Faith and the Thought of the Present*), especially in the volume *Weltschöpfung und Weltende*. He views both the disobedience of man and the discords of the world as manifestations of a cosmic rift that has plunged creation into a condition of polarity, a situation in which one group survives by the destruction of others. Even the vegetable kingdom, devoured by omnivorous men and beasts, is involved in this destructive polarity.[175]

God alone, who has made victory manifest in the resurrection of Jesus Christ, will ultimately overcome conflict between the objective past and the subjective present by a deliverance of his creation into an eternal consummation in which all relations are personal (subject–subject) relations and only the realm of the present, the eternal now, reigns. It is one of the monumental and astonishing accomplishments of modern thought that Heim has combined a saintly piety and keen scientific perception in his appeal to a supra-polar dimension, which to him is the living God of the Christian faith.

Is it possible to harmonize the New Testament hope of a new creation with the views adopted by modern science? The answer to this question will be conditioned by one's concepts of both Scripture and science. For the present author, especially in this chapter, the tension between Scripture and science is a creative one that generates no personal pain.

This chapter presupposes that at one point in space–time the energy that has become concrete matter came into being by an act of God. At a second point life appeared, first plant and then animal, and this too was the creative act of God, who never withdraws His presence from His creation. A third unique point in the creative process saw the appearance of mind, the transcendence of the human spirit over the process of nature. The greatest point in the historical movements which followed was that unique point in which "the Word became flesh and dwelt among us" (John 1:14), when "God sent forth his Son, born of woman" (Gal. 4:4).

All of these points were unique, never to be repeated, and on the basis of these events we hope for yet a higher dimension of the Spirit, which transforms all matter, life and mind in an event that can only be described as the New Jerusalem. This is the event toward which the process of the whole creation and human history, especially salvation history, point. It is then that the contradictions of creation and the ambiguities of history will be clarified and consummated.

175. Karl Heim, *The World: Its Creation and Consummation*, tr. Robert Smith (Edinburgh and London: Oliver and Boyd, 1962).

81. The Holy City

In the midst of gathering gloom, when men tire and civilization begins to crumble, God has a way of stirring man's hope by a vision of an invisible city that will not pass away. Plato, without the lens of Holy Writ but pondering the eternal, spoke of "the city whose home is in the ideal," the pattern of which is "laid up in heaven for him who wishes to contemplate it and so beholding to constitute himself its citizen" (*Republic* IX, 592, tr. Shorey).

Augustine, drawing insight from the Scriptures as well as from Plato, sees two cities: "These two cities are made by two loves: the earthly city by the love of self unto the contempt of God, and the heavenly city by the love of God unto the contempt of self" (*The City of God*, XIV, 28). The vision seems never to vanish completely, even though as at times in Augustine, it is dimmed by the tendency to identify the heavenly city with historical institutions of church or state.

Modern history has often followed the medieval dreamers, even when some transformed the dream into the nightmare of the secular state. Sir Thomas More, modeling his *Utopia* after the external frame of Plato's *Republic*, protested against the perfidy of politics in the interest of an ideal community that would produce good citizens and men of intellectual and moral freedom, honest labor, and a society free from luxury and poverty.

Martin Butzer's *De Regno Christi* (1557) outlines a plan for the "solid restitution" of the kingdom of God in England by the reorganization of public and national life in obedience to the gospel of Christ. In the next century Valentin Andrea, German theologian from Tübingen, proposed a similar society in his *Christianopolis* (1619).

Long before Karl Marx published his secular version of a communistic society in *Das Kapital* (1867), the Italian monk Tomaso Campanella, on mystical grounds far removed from Marx's materialism, was concerned with a communistic society in his *Civitas solis* (The City of the Sun, 1623). The appeal of modified Marxism to the multitudes today should be evidence to all that the dream never dies, and the secular version will continue to demand loyalty until men find a higher loyalty in the Holy City, "the New Jerusalem which comes down from my God out of heaven" (Rev. 3:12).

God took Israel and the Church through three stages (the earthly Jerusalem, the heavenly Jerusalem, and the new Jerusalem) to teach the faithful that man's undying dream of a Holy City is not a delusion and a snare but the Omega point toward which redeemed men, salvation history, and the whole creation move.

The Earthly Jerusalem

As the abode of God's name. Jerusalem as the earthly symbol of God's abode with His people finds expression in both the "Name" theology and the "Glory" theology of the Old Testament.[176] The Name theology is associated with Shechem, the shrine for the old amphictyony of Israel long before Jerusalem became the holy city (Deut. 27:12ff.). In ancient times the presence of God was signified by an altar in the place where God caused his "name to be remembered" (Exod. 20:24). At other places the ark of the Lord was understood as a type of visible throne for the invisible God (Num. 10:35f.; 1 Sam. 4:4; 2 Kings 19:15).

Jeremiah (3:16f.) prophesied of the time when Jerusalem would displace the ark as "the throne of the Lord," and this is the theme of Deuteronomy, the central source of the Name theology.

The distinction between the ark as the throne of the Lord and the city of Jerusalem as such is verbalized in the prophetic vision of Jeremiah: "At that time Jerusalem shall be called the throne of the Lord, and all nations shall gather to it, to the presence of the Lord in Jerusalem, and they shall no more stubbornly follow their own evil heart" (3:17; cf. 14:21; 17:12). The ark, removed at some time around the fall of the city, would not figure in the future. "Jerusalem shall be called the throne of the Lord."

The pillar passage on Jerusalem, "the place" where the Lord would "put his name and make his habitation," is Deuteronomy 12. The chapter begins with an appeal for the people to "destroy all the places where the nations whom you shall dispossess served their gods, upon the high mountains and upon the hills and under every green tree" (12:2). They are to "destroy their name out of that place" (12:3). Only one central sanctuary is to be tolerated as the place of Israelite worship. In the time of the judges Shiloh had been the central sanctuary, but this was destroyed by the Philistines. David erected a new tabernacle in Jerusalem, later superseded by the temple of Solomon, but the numerous pagan sanctuaries threatened the true worship of the one God revived by Hezekiah and Josiah. The tug of theological war between the worship of the Lord and the worship of various Canaanite deities made Jerusalem the historical symbol of God's abode among his people.

Israel is commanded: "But you shall seek the place which the Lord your God will choose out of all your tribes to put his name and make his habitation there" (12:5). When the Lord chooses to "put his name" in Jerusalem He has also chosen to "make his habitation there." The noun "habitation" (*sheken*) occurs nowhere else in the Old Testament, but the idea is the same as that expressed later: "to make his name dwell there" (12:11). The name "tabernacle" is used here much in the sense of the tabernacling

176. Gerhard von Rad, *Studies in Deuteronomy*, tr. David Stalker (London: SCM, 1953), pp. 37-44. Backgrounds are discussed in detail by Roland de Vaux, *Ancient Israel*, tr. John McHugh (New York: McGraw-Hill, 1961), pp. 271-344.

presence of the *Shekinah* in later Hebrew thought.[177] Jerusalem is "the place" (12:5, 11, 14, 18, 21, 26).

A second example of Name theology that makes of the earthly Jerusalem a heavenly symbol is found in Solomon's prayer at the dedication of the temple (1 Kings 8:22–53). Solomon's prayer that the temple may always be the place to which Israel may turn for the forgiveness of sins conceives of God as beyond all the limits of heaven and earth (8:27):

> *But will God indeed dwell on the earth?*
> *Behold, heaven and the highest heaven cannot contain thee;*
> *how much less this house which I have built!*

The words recall Deuteronomy 10:14 ("Behold, to the Lord your God belong heaven and the heaven of heavens, the earth with all that is in it"), but the Lord overflows both.

The Lord God, whom "the highest heaven cannot contain," has promised: "My name shall be there" (1 Kings 8:29), i.e., in "the place" that is in the temple of Jerusalem. It is not difficult to see how this Name theology made the temple such a symbol of security, even if it was a false security. Jeremiah was one of the few who was able to see the great reality of God beyond the earthly symbol. His temple sermon (Jer. 7:1–15), one of the most crucial and courageous events in his life, blasts the belief expressed in the deceptive words: "This is the temple of the Lord, the temple of the Lord, the temple of the Lord" (7:4). The rebel prophet renounced such false security and called on the people to find security in the inward reality of a transformed heart and life. Shiloh, the ancient sanctuary eighteen miles to the north, was no security against the Philistines. Security is in the Lord who says: "Go now to my place that was in Shiloh, where I made my name dwell at first, and see what I did to it for the wickedness of my people Israel" (7:12). The earthly symbol had given the people an edifice complex that only tragedy could transform.

As the abode of God's glory. The second stage in the developing symbol of the earthly Jerusalem may be seen in the Glory theology. This "southern" theology, associated perhaps with Hebron, blossoms in Ezekiel's vision of an eschatological Jerusalem (Ezek. 40–48). The eschatological Jerusalem is to be understood against the background of the earthly Jerusalem which was viewed as the center of the nations: "This is Jerusalem; I have set her in the center of the nations, with countries round about her" (Ezek. 5:5). In one vision (43:1–5) the Lord's glory returns to the temple: "And behold, the glory of the God of Israel came from the east; and the sound of his coming was like the sound of many waters; and the earth shone with his

177. See my article "Shekinah" in *The Interpreter's Dictionary of the Bible* (New York: Abingdon, 1962).

glory" (43:2). Twenty years before, Ezekiel had a vision of the departure of God's glory from the temple (10:1–22; 11:22f.), but now as of old the temple is flooded with the glory of God. Ezekiel testifies: "As the glory of the Lord entered the temple by the gate facing east, the Spirit lifted me up, and brought me into the inner court; and behold, the glory of the Lord filled the temple" (43:4f.).

The Lord spoke to Ezekiel from the inner sanctuary to explain to him that the eschatological temple was to be His eternal abode with His people. The conception of dwelling is seen in the descent of the *kabod* (glory) from heaven so that God may never leave His people. God says to Ezekiel: "Son of man, this is the place of my throne and the place of the soles of my feet, where I will dwell in the midst of the people of Israel for ever" (43:7).

The name of the eschatological Jerusalem will be *Yahweh-shammah* (the Lord is there, 48:35), and the priestly picture does not obscure the fact that this eschatological Jerusalem is the incorporation of His people into God himself. It was not easy for the Israelites to see beyond the earthly symbol to the eschatological reality, but the vision of the heavenly hope did not die in Babylon. Haggai set out to restore the temple to its former glory, but the God who brought Israel out of Egypt will yet perform the eschatological event of which God promises: "Once again, in a little while, I will shake the heavens and the earth and the sea and the dry land; and I will shake all nations, so that the treasures of all nations shall come in, and I will fill this house with splendor, says the Lord of hosts. The silver is mine, and the gold is mine, says the Lord of hosts. The latter splendor of this house shall be greater than the former, says the Lord of hosts; and in this place I will give prosperity, says the Lord of hosts" (Hag. 2:6–9). Jerusalem is "this place" where the glory and splendor of God will be made known — the eschatological Jerusalem, the place of endless *shalom* (prosperity, peace).

To Zechariah the promise is made (Zech. 8:3): "I will return to Zion, and will dwell in the midst of Jerusalem, and Jerusalem shall be called the faithful city, and the mountain of the Lord of hosts, the holy mountain" (cf. 2:10).

God dwells in heaven, but He descends to dwell with His people. One of the most notable examples of "the paradox of grace" in the Old Testament, which expresses God's transcendence and immanence, remoteness and nearness, is the oracle on the divine dwelling place in Isaiah 57:15:

> For thus says the high and lofty One
>   who inhabits eternity, whose name is Holy:
> "I dwell in the high and holy place,
>   and also with him who is of a contrite and humble spirit,
> to revive the spirit of the humble,
>   and to revive the heart of the contrite."

No other call to worship and reverence binds God to His people more closely and brings more hope that He will ultimately dwell with His people for ever.

The Glory theology was kept alive by faith in this Holy One "in the high and holy place." The hope of an eschatological Jerusalem revives at the dawn of glory announced in the call (60:1):

> *Arise, shine; for your light has come,*
> *and the glory of the Lord has risen upon you.*

The full splendor of this dawning glory is focused on the eschatological Jerusalem, of which the earthly one is but a frail symbol. The vision is real and the voice is sure in Isaiah 65:17f.:

> *"For behold, I create new heavens*
> *and a new earth;*
> *and the former things shall not be remembered*
> *or come into mind.*
> *But be glad and rejoice for ever*
> *in that which I create;*
> *for behold, I create Jerusalem a rejoicing,*
> *and her people a joy."*

Such visions are of a glory that only God can give from His throne in heaven to His children on His footstool on earth below (66:1).

As the earthly symbol of God's abode with His people, Jerusalem stirred feelings expressed in what have been called "Songs of Zion" (Pss. 48, 84, 87, 122, 126), sung by pilgrims as they made the journey to the sacred festivals with hopes of an ideal future and final glory. Psalm 48 speaks of Jerusalem as "the city of our God" (vv. 1, 8), "the city of the great King" (v. 2) and "the city of the Lord of hosts" (v. 8). There is God's "dwelling" and "house" (Pss. 84:1, 4; 122:1, 9). In the spirit of these pilgrims' Psalms, Isaac Watts sang:

> *The hill of Zion yields*
> *A thousand sacred sweets*
> *Before we reach the heavenly fields,*
> *Or walk the golden streets.*

All this is symbolism, to be sure, but it symbolizes an ultimate reality that is awesome and sublime, a mystery before which men can only wonder and worship.

Jerusalem continued to be the symbol of God's dwelling among His people in apocalyptic thought. God promised through Joel (3:17):

> *So you shall know that I am the Lord your God,*
> *who dwell in Zion, my holy mountain.*
> *And Jerusalem shall be holy*
> *and strangers shall never again pass through it.*

An oracle at the end of Zechariah promises God's universal reign and true worship in the holy city of Jerusalem (14:16–21), and the angel Gabriel speaks of Jerusalem as the "holy city" (Dan. 9:24).

The New Testament has preserved a saying of Jesus that summarizes the Hebraic view of God's relation to heaven and earth and to the city of Jerusalem (Matt. 5:34f.):

> *Do not swear at all,*
> *either by heaven,*
> *for it is the throne of God,*
> *or by the earth,*
> *for it is his footstool,*
> *or by Jerusalem,*
> *for it is the city of the great King.*

God is the "great King," and Jerusalem is His city (cf. Ps. 48:2). It is therefore "the holy city" where our Lord, Jesus Christ, was tempted and died (Matt. 4:5; 27:53), but His death was the point of transition, in God's historical revelation, between the earthly city below and the heavenly city above.[178]

The Heavenly Jerusalem

The tension between the earthly symbol and the heavenly reality became taut after the death of Jesus in Jerusalem. Even before the fall of the city in A.D. 70, Paul put the two in strong contrast in his polemic against what he considered "another gospel" (Gal. 1:7). With the figure of God as Father of both his Son Jesus Christ, and his sons, true Christians, he describes how we are delivered from slavery to sonship by God first sending forth His Son from heaven to earth, and then sending forth His Spirit into the hearts of His sons (4:1–7). Paul is alarmed lest the process be reversed and they turn from sonship back to slavery "to the weak and beggarly elemental spirits" (4:8–11). This is his travail for their souls (4:12–20).

The allegory of the two women. The allegory of the two women, Hagar and Sarah as the two covenants, follows (Gal. 4:21–31), and the system of slavery advocated by Judaism is represented by Hagar, Sinai and the present Jerusalem. But there is a heavenly Jerusalem, the Jerusalem above, which is free: "She is our mother" (4:26). With God as our Father and the heavenly Jerusalem as our mother we are free, and we should "stand fast therefore" and "not submit to a yoke of slavery" (5:1). Sarah has become the symbol of freedom as Hagar was the symbol of slavery.

---

178. J. C. De Young, *Jerusalem in the New Testament* (Kampen: J. H. Kok, 1960), pp. 76-116. The earthly city of Jerusalem, founded by David, is a type of the heavenly Jerusalem, founded by God, according to Augustine, *De Catechizandis Rudibus*, 20, 36.

Our mother, the heavenly Jerusalem, is not the Church, as Tertullian and Cyprian, Calvin and Luther all thought. We are unable to agree with Cyprian's use of the father and mother symbols when he declares: "No longer can he have God for his father who has not the Church for his mother."[179] He pushed the mother metaphor so far that he says: "It is of her womb that we are born, by her milk that we are nourished, by her breath that we live."[180] Calvin's comment on Galatians 4:26 makes the same mistake of identifying the heavenly Jerusalem with the Church. The Church is the body of Christ on earth, not the heavenly Jerusalem from above (*anō*). The heavenly Jerusalem is no more the Church, viewed as the pilgrim people upon the earth, than it is the earthly Jerusalem. It is heaven itself, the mother of all who are within the fellowship of the body of Christ.[181]

The heavenly Jerusalem is now "above," the abode of Christ. That is why Paul points away from human tradition to this heavenly realm of reality when he says: "If then you have been raised with Christ, seek the things that are above, where Christ is, seated at the right hand of God. Set your minds on things above, not on things that are on earth" (Col. 3:1f.). The Church is on earth, but she is called to give attention to the things of heaven. She may worship *with* the angels, but she must not worship the angels and become in bondage again to "the elemental spirits of the universe" (2:20).

It is not necessary to demythologize and thus de-eschatologize the New Testament in order to make this transcendent and heavenly realm of freedom real to the so-called "modern man." F. F. Bruce has well commented on Colossians 3:1:

> The apostles knew very well that they were using figurative language when they spoke of Christ's exaltation thus: they no more thought of a location on a literal throne at a literal right hand of God than we do. The static impression made by conventional artistic representations of such a literal enthronement of Christ is quite different from the dynamic New Testament conception.[182]

The Christian does give his supreme allegiance to this heavenly realm above. Of those who mind earthly things it is said: "Their end is destruction, their god is the belly, and they glory in their shame, with minds set on earthly things" (Phil. 3:19). Of us who set our minds on heavenly things it is very different: "Our commonwealth is in heaven, and from it we await a Savior, the Lord Jesus Christ, who will change our lowly body to be like

179. *De Unitate Ecclesiae*, 6.
180. *Ibid.*, p. 5.
181. De Young, *op. cit.*, pp. 133f.
182. E. K. Simpson and F. F. Bruce, *Commentary on the Epistles to the Ephesians and Colossians* (Grand Rapids: Eerdmans, 1957), p. 258. Cf. De Young, *op. cit.*, p. 129.

his glorious body, by the power which enables him even to subject all things to himself" (3:20). Heaven is our home town, our native land.

To the Philippians as a "Roman colony" (Acts 16:12) and living in a political situation that often looked on Caesar, to whom many gave supreme allegiance, as Savior, with his capital city in Rome, it was meaningful to say that our supreme allegiance is in heaven. As citizens had their names enrolled in their native city, so Christians have their names in "the book of life" (Phil. 4:3).

The political metaphor continues in the heavenly language of the Ephesian letter. "So then you are no longer strangers and sojourners, but you are fellow citizens with the saints and members of the household of God" (Eph. 2:19). We are blessed "with every spiritual blessing in the heavenly places" (1:3). God not only raised Christ "from the dead and made him sit at his right hand in the heavenly places," but He also "raised us up with him, and made us sit with him in the heavenly places in Christ Jesus" (1:20; 2:6).

Through the Church God plans to make known His manifold wisdom "to the principalities and powers in the heavenly places" (3:10), and it is in this heavenly realm that the spiritual warfare is waged "against the principalities, against the powers, against the world rulers of this present darkness, against the spiritual hosts of wickedness in the heavenly places" (6:12). The heavenly realm from "above" can become a spiritual reality "now," and ultimately the demonic powers will be defeated.

The typology of the two worlds. The typology of the two worlds is a further illumination of the heavenly Jerusalem. Peter speaks of "an inheritance which is imperishable, undefiled, and unfading, kept in heaven" (1 Pet. 1:4) for those who are "aliens and exiles" (2:11) on the earth, but it is Hebrews that holds forth most hope for those "who share in a heavenly call" (Heb. 3:1) and look to the "heavenly sanctuary" (8:5). The higher order of the heavenly is blended into the future order of hope. "The heavenly tabernacle in Hebrews is not the product of Platonic idealism, but the eschatological temple of apocalyptic Judaism, the temple which is in heaven primarily in order that it may be manifested on earth."[183] The passion of the past and the *parousia* of the future are united by the high-priesthood of the present. "Thus it was necessary for the copies of the heavenly things to be purified with these rites, but the heavenly things themselves with better sacrifices than these. For Christ has entered, not into a sanctuary made with hands, a copy of the true one, but into heaven itself, now to appear in the presence of God on our behalf" (Heb. 9:23f.). "We have this as a sure and steadfast

---

183. C. K. Barrett, "The Eschatology of the Epistle to the Hebrews," *The Background of the New Testament and Its Eschatology*, ed. W. D. Davies and David Daube (Cambridge: Cambridge University Press, 1956), p. 389. Abundant sources are supplied in this essay.

anchor of the soul, a hope that enters into the inner shrine behind the curtain" (6:19). The old ceremonies of the earthly Jerusalem were only a shadow of the heavenly Jerusalem and the heavenly sanctuary.

God is, first of all, the founder of the heavenly Jerusalem, It is not the creation and the achievement of man's labor, but *The Saints' Everlasting Rest*, as Richard Baxter's immortal classic called it, a rest that begins in grace and is consummated in glory. On Baxter's monument at Kidderminster are words descriptive of a fearless and faithful man of God sustained by grace and waiting for glory: "In a stormy and divided age he advocated unity and comprehension, pointing the way to everlasting rest."

The classic biblical example of persevering faith is Abraham, and all his children inherit the heavenly Jerusalem. Hebrews 11:8–10 states:

> By faith Abraham obeyed when he was called to go out to a place which he was to receive as an inheritance; and he went out, not knowing where he was to go. By faith he sojourned in the land of promise, as in a foreign land, living in tents with Isaac and Jacob, heirs with him of the same promise. For he looked forward to the city which has foundations, whose builder and maker is God.

Abraham traveled from Mesopotamia toward a heavenly Jerusalem, transcending by far the earthly city of David and Solomon. The earthly city is only an immanent and visible sign of the transcendent reality that "has foundations, whose builder and maker is God."

God has prepared the city for a prepared people, a people that do not "shrink back unto perdition" but go on toward the city and "have faith unto the saving of the soul" (10:39, ASV).

> These all died in faith, not having received what was promised, but having seen it and greeted it from afar, and having acknowledged that they were strangers and exiles on the earth. For people who speak thus make it clear that they are seeking a homeland. If they had been thinking of that land from which they had gone out, they would have had opportunity to return. But as it is, they desire a better country, that is, a heavenly one. Therefore God is not ashamed to be called their God, for he has prepared for them a city (11:13–16).

Canaan is not their country (cf. 4:8). Their country is the heavenly homeland toward which faithful men journey to a destiny beyond the bounds of this transient land of shadows and shattered hopes. It belongs to the higher realm of God and to the coming age of glory.

God has, by His mercy and grace, called man forth to make this journey that makes life meaningful and destroys the dread of death. His promise is heard in faith, a faith which "is the assurance of things hoped for, a conviction of things not seen" (11:1). Assurance (*hypostasis*) is a title-deed, as the word was used in property transactions, and he who holds his title-deed inherits the heavenly city of God. The worst of all human tragedies is to see the lights of home, but die in the desert (6:4–6).

A second significant teaching has to do with the inhabitants of the heavenly Jerusalem. Although invisible now and visible only in the future, it is never far away from the faithful.

"But you have come to Mount Zion and to the city of the living God, the heavenly Jerusalem, and to innumerable angels in festal gathering, and to the assembly of the first-born who are enrolled in heaven, and to a judge who is God of all, and to the spirits of just men made perfect, and to Jesus, the mediator of a new covenant, and to the sprinkled blood that speaks more graciously than the blood of Abel" (Heb. 12:22–24). The heavenly city has never been an empty city, for it is the city of God and His angels, the heavenly abode of departed saints, and the hope of all who come to the end of life's pilgrim journey.

Heaven hovers low in Hebrews. With spiritual vision the early Christians knew that they joined the heavenly hosts of angels and the company of departed saints in worship. They did not worship angels and saints now in glory, who are ever active in the adoration of God, but they did join to worship with them when they assembled in the name of the Lord Jesus. In the celestial choir loft above, the heavenly beings lead the congregation in the adoration of God (1 Cor. 11:10). It is unfortunate that so many Protestants spend so much time protesting against what they believe to be the worship of the angels and the saints that they forget to worship *with* the angels and saints in glory. The angel forbade John to worship him, but he also said: "Worship God" (Rev. 19:10).

The final mention of the heavenly Jerusalem in Hebrews (13:14) speaks of its permanence. Here in the land of shadows below, men drop by the way in the desert sands if they lack the faith of Abraham. Time is a tent city of transient men moving across the nomadic wastelands of the world. Nothing seems to stay very long, and man gropes out into the great unknown that will not pass away. The saintly Newman spoke for many when he said:

> Lead, kindly Light, amid the encircling gloom,
> Lead thou me on!
> The night is dark, and I am far from home;
> Lead thou me on!

He spoke with the sure words of a faith that did not fail in the crucial hour.

Jesus suffered outside the gate of the earthly Jerusalem, the transient city with the earthly tabernacle and temporal sacrifices. It has now passed away and may never be rebuilt, but the heavenly Jerusalem that belongs to the eternal world will never pass away. "Therefore let us go forth to him outside the camp, bearing abuse for him. For here we have no lasting city, but we seek the city which is to come" (Heb. 13:13f.). It is the city that belongs to the world above, but it also belongs to the world to come. The whole Church of God joins Bernard of Cluny in singing:

> *Jerusalem, the golden, With milk and honey blest!*
> *Beneath thy contemplation Sink heart and voice oppressed;*
> *I know not, O I know not What joys await me there;*
> *What radiancy of glory, What bliss beyond compare.*
>
> *They stand, those halls of Zion, All jubilant with song,*
> *And bright with many an angel, And all the martyr throng;*
> *The Prince is ever in them; The daylight is serene;*
> *The pastures of the blessed Are decked in glorious sheen.*
>
> *O sweet and blessed country, Shall I e'er see thy face?*
> *O sweet and blessed country, Shall I e'er win thy grace?*
> *Exult, O dust and ashes! The Lord shall be thy part;*
> *His only, His forever Thou shalt be and thou art!*[184]

Even the sorrows of the delay are not bitter when we remember His words who said (John 14:1f., NEB):

> *Set your troubled hearts at rest.*
> *Trust in God always;*
> *trust also in me.*
> *There are many dwelling-places in my Father's house;*
> *if it were not so I should have told you;*
> *for I am going there on purpose to prepare a place for you.*

The Holy City is the Father's house and the New Jerusalem.

The New Jerusalem

The new Jerusalem is the fulfillment of the forlorn hopes of the earthly Jerusalem and the faithful promises of the heavenly Jerusalem. Its newness is a newness never seen before. It is the new Jerusalem for those who have the "new name" and sing "a new song" in "a new heaven and a new earth." The very word for new (*kainos*) means a newness that is new is a new way.

A new name is promised the conquerors in the church of Philadelphia. "He who conquers, I will make him a pillar in the temple of my God; never shall he go out of it, and I will write on him the name of my God, and the name of the city of my God, the new Jerusalem which comes down from my God out of heaven, and my own new name" (Rev. 3:12). The name is identified in Revelation 19:12 and 16. A name stands for personal identity and reality, and to write one's name on another means personal possession and relation. This threefold name establishes a personal relation between

184. "Jerusalem the Golden," *The Broadman Hymnal*, no. 219. Cf. Peter Abelard's "O Quanta Qualia."

the conquerors and God, the city of God with a temple of living souls incorporated into Christ, and Christ Himself. All relations in the new Jerusalem are personal relations to God, human beings and Christ. No "person" is a "thing" in the new Jerusalem. Personal relation to Christ protects in the hour of trial (3:10) and provides access to the Holy City through the open door of the new David's new Jerusalem (3:7f.).

A new song is sung by the martyrs "who had his name and his Father's name written on their foreheads" (14:1). These martyrs are the servants of God on whose foreheads a seal was set, just as blood was sprinkled on the doorposts at the first Passover, to protect them from the plagues of judgment soon to come upon the earth (7:3). The saints or martyrs are removed from earth before the *parousia* in 19:11–16 only by death. They are no more raptured from earth before the tribulation, than Israel was taken from Egypt before the ten plagues. A parallel may be seen in Ezekiel 9:1–8, where the righteous are sealed before the destruction of the earthly Jerusalem. The martyrs on Mount Zion (Rev. 14:3) join the multitude of 7:10 in singing a new song, perhaps "the song of Moses, the servant of God, and the song of the Lamb," saying,

> *Great and wonderful are thy deeds,*
> *O Lord God the Almighty!*
> *Just and true are thy ways,*
> *O King of the ages!*
> *Who shall not fear and glorify thy name, O Lord?*
> *For thou alone art holy.*
> *All nations shall come and worship thee,*
> *for thy judgments have been revealed (15:3f.).*

The new Jerusalem in "a new heaven and a new earth" (21:1f.) is the ultimate destiny, a redeemed environment in which those with the new name sing the new song. There the voice from God on His throne states: "Behold, I make all things new" (21:5).

A German theologian and church historian, born of Jewish parents and destined to be the father of modern church history, changed his last name from Mendel to Neander (the Greek for new man) when he received Christian baptism in 1806. This symbolizes in some way what happens to every person who takes up the cross to follow the Lamb of God wherever He may lead. He leads ultimately to the Holy City, the realm of redeemed relations where all relations are personal — the "it-less" universe in which all is "thou," where the name makes newness and the song is without discord.

All of this, as the author of Revelation knew far better than modern literalists, is religious symbolism, but it is the symbolism of a real relation in which all the redeemed are incorporated into the Holy City of God. There will be no separate suburbs, "that God may be all in all" (1 Cor. 15:28, KJV). Then as now, in the body of Christ, "Christ is all, and in all" (Col.

3:11). This is not pantheism, in which all is absorbed in God, but *pan-entheism*, in which all created "things" are so incorporated into the being of God that all relations are personal relations. Revelation 21:1–22:5 symbolizes this spiritual symphony in three ways: a tabernacle, a city, and a garden.[185]

The tabernacle of God. The tabernacle (Rev. 21:2–4) symbolizes eternal fellowship between God and His people, and is God's answer to the problem of human loneliness and estrangement. Indeed, lonely and God-forsaken feelings of human subjectivity, doubt and despair often displace the simple awareness that God is with us; and man becomes obsessed with the fear that he is all alone in an impersonal universe behind which there is no concern and compassion for the plight of man. Into this empty and futile situation the presence of God was made known in a body of flesh. It was the presence of One in whom all things were created. John 1:1–5, with a poetic arrangement and a slight revision of the *New English Bible* translation, is the early Christian proclamation of the creation:

> *When all things began, the Word already was.*
> *The Word dwelt with God,*
> *and what God was, the Word was.*
> *(The Word, then, was with God at the beginning.)*
> *Through him all things came to be:*
> *no single thing was created without him.*
> *All that came to be was alive with his life,*
> *and that life was the light of men.*
> *The light shines in the dark,*
> *and the darkness has never quenched it.*

The first stage in the fulfillment of this is the incarnation. Another stanza of this early hymn to the Word speaks of the tabernacle of flesh in which the glory of God was veiled (1:4, NEB):

> *So the Word became flesh:*
> *he came to dwell among us,*
> *and we saw his glory,*
> *such glory as befits the Father's only Son. . . .*

That which was in the bosom of the Father from before creation and was made known as a body in the incarnation will appear as a bride in the Holy City of the consummation. The bride is a most fitting symbol for this eternal relation, for the nearest parallel to the heavenly relation is the human relation of love, love that at times may be so complete that the two, as with

185. Cf. Ray Summers, *Worthy Is the Lamb* (Nashville, Tennessee: Broadman, 1951), pp. 211-215; *The Life Beyond* (1959), pp. 202-207.

husband and wife, become one. It is then that even physical relations become personal relations.

The apocalyptic voice, composed of a constellation of the Old Testament phrases, is translated by James Moffatt with these phrases underlined so that the shattered hopes of the past become the sure hope of the future (Rev. 21:3f.):

> *Lo, God's dwelling place is with men,*
> *with men will he dwell;*
> *they shall be his people,*
> *and God will himself be with them:*
> *he shall wipe every tear from their eyes,*
> *and death shall be no more —*
> *no more wailing, no more crying, no more pain,*
> *for the former things have passed away.*

Creation and incarnation have come to the Omega point of the consummation, the goal of the whole creative and redemptive process by which we are made persons to love and be loved. Love has created a fellowship that is eternal, and this fellowship of love is the ultimate purpose that gives meaning to even the painful moments in the process of making us persons.

The city of God. The city (Rev. 21:9–27), still identified with the bride, symbolizes eternal glory and is God's answer to the problem of human hostility, individual and collective. In this relation the individual becomes a person and the collective crowd becomes a community of self-communication. The very glory of this city is the radiance of personal relations. John "saw no temple in the city, for its temple is the Lord God the Almighty and the Lamb. And the city has no need of sun or moon to shine upon it, for the glory of God is its light, and its lamp is the Lamb" (21:22f.). This is the temple in which all conquerors are made pillars (3:12) as they are incorporated into the eternal glory of God's presence.

A real "united nations," the corporate relations of the Holy City, will be fully realized in this eternal relation. "By its light shall the nations walk; and the kings of the earth shall bring their glory into it, and its gates shall never be shut by day—and there shall be no night there; they shall bring into it the glory and honor of the nations" (21:24f.). This ultimate and eternal pattern by which all nations are to be related to one another in God and the Lamb is not so remote from this world of relativity that it justifies a pessimistic attitude toward world peace. It is true that eternal peace does not and cannot exist on earth, as Immanuel Kant's essay on the subject assumes and as Woodrow Wilson dreamed, but it is fatal when men dismiss the dream as a delusion and sink back into the despair of international discord and possible destruction. The earthly city is not the eternal city, but that is no reason for men to make this earth into an inferno of hell.

The twelve gates and the twelve foundations of the city represent the whole Church of God, the old covenant and the new covenant, the time when the fullness of Israel follows the fullness of the Gentiles, when the hundred and forty-four thousand sealed "out of every tribe of the sons of Israel" (7:4) have joined the "great multitude which no man can number from every nation, from all tribes and people and tongues" (7:9). This vision helps us to understand why Paul was willing to be "accursed and cut off from Christ" himself, that his Jewish brethren might be saved (Rom. 9:3). Through the gates of the city that will never be shut people who are purified by the blood of the Lamb may pass. "But nothing unclean shall enter it, nor any one who practices abomination or falsehood, but only those who are written in the Lamb's book of life" (Rev. 21:27). The "beloved city," which was only "the camp of the saints" before the deceived of the nations were "consumed" and "the devil who had deceived them was thrown into the lake of fire and brimstone where the beast and the false prophet were" (20:7–10), is now the Lamb's bride and God's eternal city.

The garden of God. The garden (Rev. 22:1–5) symbolizes eternal life and is God's answer to the problem of human mortality. The Scriptures speak of three Edens, corresponding to the three pictures of Paradise. "Before" all history was that state of dreaming innocence when the personal relation between God and man was as real as the gentle breeze that blows in the cool of the evening. The consciousness of guilt and estrangement disrupts this relation and fills mankind with fear and dread. "And they heard the sound of the Lord God walking in the garden in the cool of the day, and the man and his wife hid themselves from the presence of the Lord God among the trees of the garden" (Gen. 3:8).

A second condition of Eden is "above" all history. This Eden is "the garden of God" that symbolizes the perfection that belongs to God and all who are in harmony with God (Ezek. 28:13). There are three stages to Eden as there are three stages to Paradise and three stages to the Holy City, and the Eden "above" corresponds to the Jerusalem above. Ultimately as the city comes "down out of heaven from God" (Rev. 21:2) it is the Lamb's bride, at once a tabernacle, a city, and a garden.

In the garden of eternal life all living is knowing. Jesus came into the world to give this eternal life to all whom the Father has given Him. This eternal life is the intimate personal relation by which we come to "know" the true God and Jesus Christ whom He sent into the world (John 17:3).

The symbolism of the garden has the same personal significance. Living with the eternal life of God is symbolized by "the river of the water of life, bright as crystal, flowing from the throne of God and of the Lamb through the middle of the street of the city; also, on either side of the river, the tree of life with its twelve kinds of fruit, yielding its fruit each month" (Rev. 22:1f.). Knowing God in the eternal relation of love is the experience of His servants who worship Him as they "see his face, and his name shall be on their foreheads" (22:4). To live is to know, and to know is to live.

Thus far the eternal destiny of redeemed humanity has been expressed in "the language of Zion," the concrete symbolism that "speaks to the condition of those saturated with the words of Holy Scriptures." Unfortunately this rich symbolism may be a stumbling block, not only to those without biblical background but also to those who would reduce the symbolism to rationalistic literalism. Symbolism always points to a reality too great for ordinary language, and this is especially the case with religious symbolism. We are forced to speak of heavenly things with an earthly language.

An ancient writer like Augustine, uninhibited, and free of scientific and semantic problems, gave expression to the same longings that make modern man restless. His "I–Thou" relations were as powerful as any modern personalist could express it. Of man in praise of God he says: "Thou hast prompted him, that he should delight to praise thee, for thou hast made us for thyself, and restless is our heart until it comes to rest in thee."[186]

At the end of his book *The City of God* this personal relation is viewed as an eternal relation. "There we shall rest and we shall see; we shall see and we shall love; we shall love and we shall praise. Behold what shall be in the end and shall not end" (XXII.30).[187] The I–Thou relation in the prayer and praise of worship is but a preparation for the eternal adoration of God's grace and glory in the Holy City.

At the end of our own meditation on heavenly things, in a time of world turmoil and personal testing, the apostolic words at the end of an ancient protest against religious apostasy give expression to our deepest feeling (Jude 24f.).

> Now to him who is able to keep you from falling and to present
> you without blemish before the presence of his glory with rejoicing,
> to the only God, our Savior through Jesus Christ our Lord, be
> glory, majesty, dominion, and authority, before all time and now
> and for ever. Amen.

Any effort to translate biblical symbols into modern language is in danger of distortion, but a translation is often necessary if our witness is made to those who do not speak "the language of Canaan." Personalistic philosophy, meeting the challenge of modern secularism, often uses language that helps considerably in the evangelistic work of the church, especially among "emancipated" intellectuals.[188]

The first example is an analysis of the self, written by a prophetic

---

186. *Confessions*, I.1. Translation of *Library of Christian Classics*, VII.31.
187. The translation, from a beautiful little book with many other classic quotations, is by E. L. Mascall, *Grace and Glory* (London: Faith Press, 1961), p. 13.
188. This has been given impetus in the personalistic idealism of C. A. Campbell, *On Selfhood and Godhood* (London: Allen and Unwin, 1957).

personality who has spoken to the secular minds of modern men as few are able to do. Reinhold Niebuhr's *The Self and the Dramas of History*, written in a time of great personal crisis, elaborates the three dialogues of the self "with itself, with its neighbor, and with God" in a manner that greatly illuminates human uniqueness. Rejecting the rationalism of Aristotle as an inadequate analysis of human freedom and responsibility, he finds man's uniqueness in his capacity to transcend the flux of natural process of the present, as well as to remember the past and anticipate the future. This unique capacity includes reason, but the empirical self is far more than the rational faculties.[189]

The analysis of the self belongs to the realm of empirical investigation. Every person knows the dialogue of his internal life in which he *believes* himself to be free, and it seems impossible to speak of human responsibility and a meaningful human existence if this is a delusion. Social intercourse is necessary not only for social security but also for spiritual security, for loneliness is a muttered monologue of incipient hell. Even monks, living in monasteries, and hermits often relate themselves to animals and material objects as if they are personal. The paralyzed positivist must at least admit that it is an empirical fact, even if a delusion, that "the self imagines itself in an encounter with the divine" or "distinguishes itself by a yearning for the ultimate."[190]

The development of "the three dialogues" belongs to the deepest levels of experience, the desire for the good life, and it is difficult to conceive of human culture and civilization in which all this is dismissed as a delusive dream that ends in the night of oblivion. But when personal relations are taken seriously, mere events become acts, and the meaningless maze of things becomes a mosaic that falls into order. It is difficult to suppose that this order is an illusion.

Niebuhr's rigorous realism restrains him from flights of apocalyptic imagery, but his panoramic personalism has impressive implications for understanding the ultimate destiny of man in an it-less universe in which all relations are personal relations. "Thus the Biblical faith and hope, which gives meaning to human existence, may be proved inferentially to be true, or to be more in accord with experienced facts than alternative faith and hopes."[191] It is this hope that is symbolized by the vision of the Holy City of God.

A second approach turns more definitely to an analysis of society. In 1953-54 John Macmurray delivered the Gifford Lectures of the University of Glasgow on *The Form of the Personal*. However, the two volumes were not published until 1957-61. His impressive analysis of the personal in all

189. Reinhold Niebuhr, *The Self and the Dramas of History* (London: Faber and Faber, 1956), pp. 16f.
190. *Ibid.*, p. 17.
191. *Ibid.*, pp. 259f.

of its possible relations concludes with what we have been calling the it-less universe in which all relations are personal relations, or, as Macmurray terms it, "the personal universe."[192]

The implications of this philosophical study for religious belief, in both immanent and transcendent relations, are destructive for dualistic thinking, but the concrete realism of biblical thought becomes more relevant to our understanding of the good society on earth and in heaven. Macmurray makes a radical shift from the perspective of the spectator who says "I think" to the participant who says "I do." "I think" is not excluded, but it is included in the more fundamental form "I know." The relation is I–Thou rather than I–It. The outer becomes the Other. All existence is co-existence with other persons, even though these relations employ the means of impersonal science.

An approach of this type is neither atheism nor pantheism. God is the ultimate personal reality; the universe is His act and agent, the instrument of His intention and the arena of His glory. It is not possible on these grounds to exclude either His immanence or His transcendence. All that which is more than body, and the universe itself, is the agent of God as the human body is the instrument of man. When the personal intentions of man are in harmony with the personal intentions of God, frustration falls away and fulfillment follows; this is an immediate experience which ultimately implies that the consummation is the realization of "persons in relation," an it-less universe. "To conceive the world thus is to conceive it as an act of God, the Creator of the world, and ourselves as created agents, with limited and dependent freedom to determine the future, which can be realized only on the condition that our intentions are in harmony with His intention, and which must frustrate itself if they are not."[193] Ultimate frustration is condemnation, and ultimate realization is the community of personal relations, the Holy City of God.

A third approach concentrates on the analysis of science, especially as it has been formulated in the philosophy of logical positivism. All references to future life are related to some type of "present disclosure situation" which expresses purpose, moral retribution, or personal affection, or all of these.[194] "Disclosure-models" manifest a meaning that suggests "more than observables" beyond "observables." From the perspective of purpose, moral retribution and personal relations of love are seen with a variety of ultimate implications.

That which has been called the Holy City of God, the ultimate community, is illuminated by the disclosure-models of love. A disclosure-situation is a personal relation in which self-disclosure and sharing are seen

192. John Macmurray, *Persons in Relation* (London: Faber and Faber, 1957), pp. 206-224.
193. *Ibid.*, p. 222.
194. I. T. Ramsey, *Freedom and Immortality* (London: SCM, 1960), pp. 122-136, 146-148.

to be what is called *agapē* in the New Testament. *Agapē* abides beyond the vast enigma of vanishing vicissitudes and has a relation to the historical process that is both immanent and transcendent. *Agapē* may be experienced and expressed here and now, but the perfect fulfillment is not yet.

In the interim, personal relations of self-communication have intimations of immortality, intimations symbolized in history as the body of Christ and in ultimate destiny as the bride of Christ, "the Bride, the wife of the Lamb" (Rev. 21:9). Other symbols, less concrete and often less meaningful, may be substituted for the Biblical metaphors, but man's ultimate yearning remains the same.

The ultimate personal relation that is man's concern requires utter openness to all, to God and man, complete communication and communion, a situation stripped of sham and delivered from deception. The disclosure-situations of the present, in which souls grasped by *agapē* become a medium through which the ultimate reality appears, are evidence of an eternal relation that knows in love and loves in knowledge. "For now we see in a mirror dimly, but then face to face. Now I know in part; then I shall understand fully, even as I have been fully understood. So faith, hope, love abide, these three; but the greatest of these is love" (1 Cor. 13:12f.).

God is love, not the abyss of nothingness into which man has his final plunge. The concrete situations of life disclose the dramatic dialogues of the self with itself, with others and with God. This is the good life that now is and the eternal life that is to be. God is the ultimate mystery, hidden and revealed, the source of all life and immortality, to whom man may flee for refuge that he may not fall back into the empty void of nothingness from which he came. Life now is a decision-situation in which the choice is made between God and nothing.

This does not mean that man can ever be as if he had never been. God is a part of all He has made, even as we are a part of all we have met. Once we have become related to God in creation, and especially in redemption, this relation is in some sense eternal, being as it is the experience of the living God. That is why the biblical picture of destruction and damnation is never one of absolute annihilation. Religion is relation, and our relation to God is eternal, either without or within the Holy City.

INDEXES

SUBJECTS

AUTHORS

SCRIPTURES

Apocrypha